THE

CAMPAIGNS OF LIEUT.-GEN. FORREST,

AND OF

FORREST'S CAVALRY.

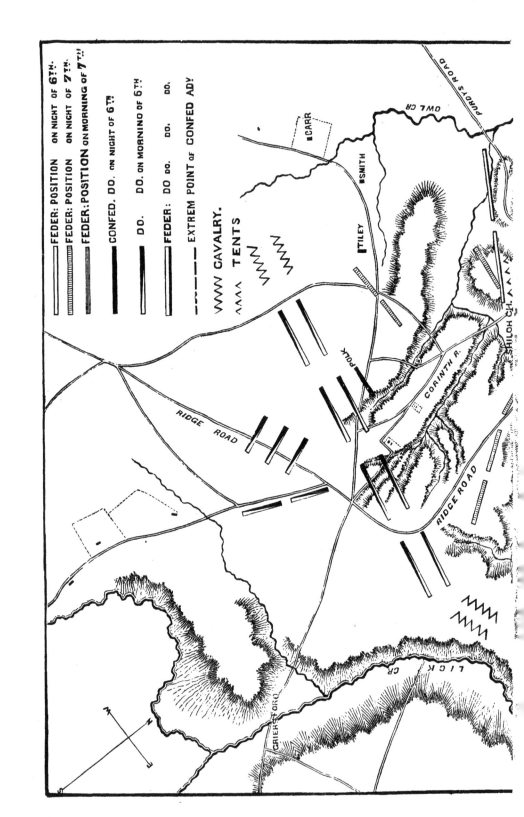

FEDER: POSITION ON NIGHT OF 6TH.
FEDER: POSITION ON NIGHT OF 7TH.
FEDER: POSITION ON MORNING OF 7TH.
CONFED. DO. ON NIGHT OF 6TH
DO. DO. ON MORNING OF 6TH
FEDER: DO DO.
EXTREM POINT OF CONFED ADV.
WWW CAVALRY.
AAAA TENTS

CARR

SMITH

TILEY

POLK

RIDGE ROAD

CORINTH R.

SHILOH CH.

RIDGE ROAD

CRIEKSFORD

LICK CR

OWL CR

PURDYS ROAD

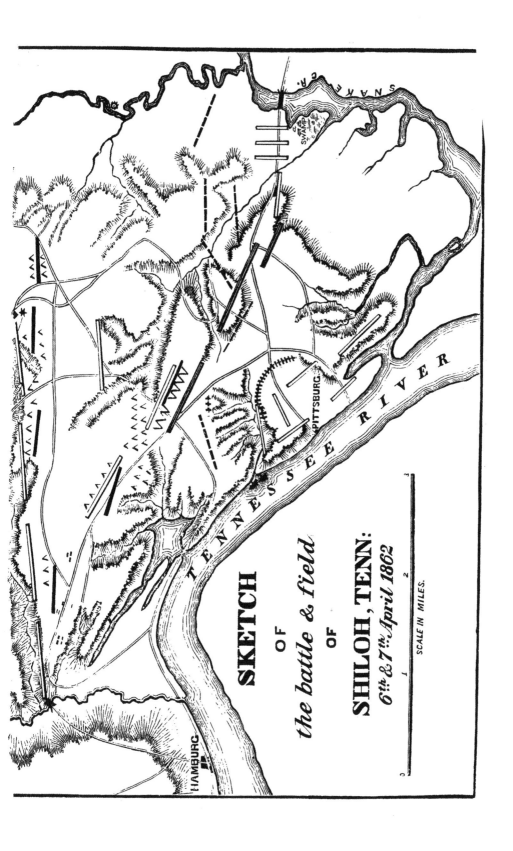

SKETCH
OF
the battle & field
OF
SHILOH, TENN.:
6th & 7th April 1862

SCALE IN MILES.

TENNESSEE RIVER

SNAKE CR.

SWAMP

PITTSBURG

HAMBURG

THE CAMPAIGNS

OF

LIEUT.-GEN. N. B. FORREST,

AND OF

FORREST'S CAVALRY,

WITH PORTRAITS, MAPS, AND ILLUSTRATIONS.

"Possunt quia posse videntur."—VIRGIL.

BY

GENERAL THOMAS JORDAN AND J. P. PRYOR.

NEW INTRODUCTION BY
Albert Castel

DA CAPO PRESS

Library of Congress Cataloging in Publication Data
Jordan, Thomas, 1819–1895.
   The campaigns of Lieut.-Gen. N. B. Forrest and of Forrest's
Cavalry / by Thomas Jordan and J. P. Pryor; new introduction by
Albert Castel.
      p.   cm.
   Previously published: Dayton, Ohio: Morningside Bookshop,
1977.
   Includes bibliographical references (p.   ).
   ISBN 0-306-80719-X (alk. paper)
   1. Forrest, Nathan Bedford, 1821–1877. 2. Confederate States of
America. Army—Cavalry. 3. Generals—Confederate States of Amer-
ica—Biography. 4. Army—Biography. [1. United States—His-
tory—Civil War, 1861-1865—Cavalry operations.] I. Pryor, J. P. II.
Title.
E547.F6J8   1996
973.7'415—dc20   96-20640
                                                                     CIP

First Da Capo Press edition 1996

This Da Capo Press paperback edition of *The Campaigns of
General Nathan Bedford Forrest and of Forrest's Cavalry* is an
unabridged republication of the edition first published in
New Orleans and New York in 1868, with the addition
of a new introduction by Albert Castel.

   5 6 7 8 9 10   02

Published by Da Capo Press, Inc.
A member of the Perseus Books Group

To the Memory

OF

THE DEAD, WHO BY THEIR ENDURANCE, HARDIHOOD, VALOR,
WHILE LIVING, AND THE SACRIFICE OF THEIR PRE-
CIOUS LIVES, LARGELY HELPED TO
BUILD UP THE FAME,
AT HOME AND
ABROAD,
OF

FORREST'S CAVALRY.

———————

" The memory of their proud deeds can not die.
They may go down to dust in bloody shrouds,
And sleep in nameless graves.   But, for all time,
Foundlings of Fame are our beloved lost."

INTRODUCTION

On June 14, 1861–two months after the Civil War began–
Nathan Bedford Forrest, slave-trader and planter, enlisted in
the Confederate army as a private. He was soon (July 13) to
be forty. This made him one year older than Ulysses S.
Grant, three years older than Thomas J. "Stonewall" Jackson,
and nearly nine years older than Philip H. Sheridan. Furthermore, unlike those three future generals, he was not a
graduate of West Point (nor, for that matter, of any school)
and had no previous military experience whatsoever. Yet by
the end of the war he was a lieutenant general whose spec-
tacular exploits caused him to be regarded as a "devil" by
his Northern opponents and as a living legend by Southerners. Today historians consider him to be one of the greatest
cavalry commanders of all time, while the Civil War public
accords him a hero's status surpassed among Southern leaders only by that of Robert E. Lee and Stonewall Jackson.[1]

Inevitably Forrest has attracted biographers. The first were
Thomas Jordan and John P. Pryor, authors of this book, published in 1868 by Bielock & Co., New Orleans and New York.
Born in 1819 in Virginia, Jordan was an 1840 graduate of
West Point, where he was a roommate of William T. Sherman.
After serving in the Seminole and Mexican wars, he resigned
his captain's commission on May 21, 1861 to enter the Confederate service with the rank of lieutenant colonel. During
the First Manassas Campaign (July 1861) he was adjutant gen-

eral to General P. G. T. Beauregard. At the Battle of Shiloh (April 6–7, 1862) he acted as *de facto* chief of staff to the Confederate commander, General Albert Sidney Johnston, and upon Johnston's death to his successor, Beauregard, receiving promotion to brigadier general for his performance. In July 1862 he became chief of staff to Braxton Bragg after that general replaced Beauregard as head of Confederate forces in Mississippi. Soon, however, he left Bragg to rejoin Beauregard, on whose staff he served during the 1863 siege of Charleston. He concluded his Civil War career as commander of a military district in South Carolina.[2]

Although trained to use the sword, Jordan's true talent was with the pen. In 1860 he had published *The South, Its Products, Commerce, and Resources*; after the war he became editor of the *Memphis Appeal* and wrote numerous articles on that conflict in addition to coauthoring *The Campaigns of Forrest*. In 1869–70 he again took up the sword to lead an abortive attempt to overthrow Spanish rule in Cuba, after which he returned to journalism as founder and editor of the *Financial and Mining Journal* in New York. He died there in 1895.[3]

Little is known about Pryor and that little is unimpressive. Born c.1824 in Alabama, he engaged in the newspaper business in Memphis before the war and during it became a Confederate captain. In 1862 he served as acting inspector general on the staff of General Dabney H. Maury, who later described him as "intelligent, well educated and habitually polite and gentlemanlike." Unfortunately, he also was too fond of the bottle: in the fall of 1862 Maury relieved him of duty for incorrigible drunkenness. Thereafter, he disappears from the historical record until 1866, when he showed up again in Memphis, listing his business address in the city directory for that year as *The Argus* and his residence a hotel. Available sources contain nothing about his subsequent career and perhaps he had none: the book's preface is signed solely by Jordan and dated October 1, 1867—not proof but an indication that Pryor no longer lived in this world or, at least, in that portion of it occupied by the city of Memphis.[4]

The origin and nature of Jordan's and Pryor's collaboration also must be a subject for surmise. As to the first, Forrest's own statement about the book in the footnote on the second page of the preface suggests that he either commissioned or authorized them to write the book with the object, so he states, of providing "a timely and lasting record of the deeds and services of those whom I have been so fortunate as to command." Concerning the second, almost surely Jordan was its chief author. Not only did he possess a much higher personal status and far greater knowledge of military affairs than Pryor, he also presumably had become acquainted with Forrest while serving in Tennessee and Mississippi in 1862. Moreover—and this would seem to clinch the matter—the literary style of the work throughout is that of Jordan. He alone saw the book through the process of publication, for which purpose he went to New York, and, as he observes in the preface, he added critiques of the Battle of Shiloh and other engagements to the text (p. ix). Therefore, Pryor's role probably was to assist in the research and possibly prepare first drafts for Jordan to use as the basis for his descriptions of Forrest's operations.

The main source of information for the book was Forrest himself. He gave Jordan and Pryor access to his official reports and correspondence; the authors conducted frequent interviews with him which are cited in the footnotes as "Notes of General Forrest." (No evidence exists that Forrest made or dictated such notes during the war). In addition, they obtained written statements, some of them very long and detailed, from officers who served under Forrest (notably Captains Charles W. Anderson and Walter A. Goodman of his staff), and they consulted Frank A. Moore's multi-volumed collection of documents, *The Rebellion Record* (New York, 1862–68), Northern and Southern newspapers, and those general histories of the war that had appeared by 1866–67. All in all, Jordan was justified when he boasted in the preface (pp. viii–ix) that "we collected a mass of original matter such as seldom or never has been available in the preparation of contemporary history."

What Jordan and Pryor wrote, Forrest read, then revised and corrected wherever he deemed it appropriate to do so. Hence, he too was, in a sense, one of the authors, declaring in his endorsement of the book that appears in the afore-mentioned footnote, "For the greater part of the statements in the narrative I am responsible." Such being the case, the book is as close to being Forrest's memoir as was possible, given the fact that owing to his skimpy formal education he was subliterate when it came to writing. "I never look at a pen," he is quoted as saying, "without thinking of a snake."[5]

Because it is Forrest's *de facto* memoir, the book contains much valuable information about his personal and military careers that otherwise would not exist. This is its greatest strength. It also constitutes its greatest weakness. Forrest was a superhuman warrior—probably no high-ranking commander since medieval times personally killed as many enemies in combat as he did (thirty)—but in other respects he was quite human—indeed, all too human. Consequently, he sometimes exaggerated his deeds and successes and either minimized or ignored his misdeeds and failures. Thus, for example, he did not single-handedly hold off a would-be lynch mob in Memphis in 1857 as described on pages 29–33; instead the mob's intended victim was saved by the tearful pleas of his mother, with Forrest's role in the affair confined to the respectable but unsensational one of being a member of an ad hoc committee that had been established for the purpose of improving law and order in Memphis.[6] Likewise, the book simply passes over his refusal to serve under Joseph Wheeler and Braxton Bragg out of contempt for them; his near-altercations with Earl Van Dorn and Benjamin F. Cheatham; and his savage slaying of a young officer who shot and, so he thought, mortally wounded him. And, as is typically the case with memoirs, especially military ones, he never is described as making a mistake, at least not a serious one. His rare setbacks invariably are the result of someone else's blundering or of circumstances beyond his control.

These, however, are not serious flaws and certainly not nearly as bad as the distortions, prevarications, and deliberate vilifications of fellow generals that fill the memoirs of Joseph E. Johnston and John Bell Hood, of George B. McClellan and William T. Sherman.[7] Furthermore, although the story of Forrest rescuing a man from lynching is a concoction, the other incidents of Forrest's courageous conduct prior to 1861 that appear in the "Introductory Sketch" are confirmed by contemporary sources. The book is free of some of the tall tales found in later biographies, notably the one about Forrest, when surrounded by enemy troops, picking up by one hand and placing on the back of his horse a Union soldier to serve as a human shield while he escaped beneath a hail of bullets. Forrest possessed enormous physical strength but doing this would be a physiological impossibility unless his arms were double-jointed or five feet long!

Taken as a whole, Forrest's quasi-memoir is generally accurate in its accounts of his military operations; perceptive in its analyses and assessments of those operations; and as fair and balanced in its treatment of his Federal opponents as could be reasonably expected, given his and Jordan's Southern bias and the time of its composition. Indeed, it reserves its harshest criticisms for other Confederate leaders, and these come from Jordan who, because of his close ties to Beauregard, shared that general's dislike of Jefferson Davis and those (such as Bragg) he deemed to have been favorites of the Confederate president. Consequently, when reading these criticisms, Jordan's animus should be kept in mind and what he says should not be regarded as necessarily reflecting Forrest's attitude (although in the case of Bragg it no doubt did).

The most controversial episode in Forrest's wartime career was, of course, what is usually referred to as the Fort Pillow Massacre (April 12, 1864). While the book goes too far in minimizing the extent to which Forrest's troops slaughtered Union soldiers, in particular black ones, after capturing the fort, it does admit (p. 439) that such murders took place, correctly asserting that "insania belli" (fury of battle) was a major cause for their occurrence. By the same token, its rebuttal of charges that the Confederates took the fort by violating a cease-fire and that they committed such atrocities as burning wounded Federals alive is valid, as is its exoneration of Forrest of personal responsibility for the massacre: he did not order it (he did not have to) and hence, he was no more to blame for what happened than Lee was for the similar mass killing of black troops in the Battle of the Crater in Virginia on July 30, 1864.[8]

Jordan and Pryor's work remained the sole full-length study of Forrest for thirty years. Then came John Allan Wyeth's *Life of General Forrest* (New York, 1899). Written by a renowned physician who as a teenager served with the Confederate cavalry in the West (but not under Forrest), Wyeth's book drew on the *Official Records of the Union and Confederate Armies* (Washington, D.C., 1880–1901) and many other sources unavailable to Jordan and Pryor to produce a fuller, deeper, and more precise historical portrait of Forrest and his campaigns than they did. Three years later it was followed by J. Harvey Mathes's *General Forrest* (New York, 1902) the main value of which was to provide additional information about Forrest's pre-1861 life. Then, apart from Andrew Lytle's *Bedford Forrest and His Critter Company* (New York, 1931), which was more a contribution to folklore than to scholarship, there was not another major biography until World War II, when Robert Selph Henry published his *"First with the Most" Forrest* (Indianapolis and New York, 1944). Better written and more sophisticated than Wyeth's work, although no less admiring of its subject, it became and, in certain respects, remains the best account of Forrest's campaigns.

Not until nearly fifty years later would two new biographies emerge: Brian Steel Wills's *A Battle from the Start: The Life of Nathan Bedford Forrest* (New York, 1992) and Jack Hurst's *Nathan Bedford Forrest: A Biography* (New York, 1993). Both authors, in particular Hurst, offer a fuller coverage of Forrest's pre- and postwar careers than Wyeth and Henry. On the other hand, neither provides as detailed a description of his wartime activities (which after all are his main claim to historical importance) as do those writers or even Jordan and Pryor. Moreover, these recent biographies also fail to do what so far no one has done, yet which badly needs doing—namely to place Forrest's operations in the broad strategic context of the Civil War by asking and attempting to answer in a thorough, systematic fashion two questions: (1) Exactly what impact did Forrest's dazzling raids and victories have upon the overall course of the war? (2) Had Forrest been given a higher command and/or greater opportunities, what would have been the potential outcome as regards the fate of the Confederacy? These are the subjects that future biographies of Forrest—and such there will be—should address, rather than, as do the two most recent ones, retelling the same old anecdotes, piling up more facts about his business dealings, or propagating fantasies about his alleged role as the putative "Grand Wizard" of the Ku Klux Klan, something that neither he nor anybody else was nor could have been.[9]

With the exception of Lytle's, these subsequent biographies, especially Wyeth's and Henry's, contain significant information not present in Jordan and Pryor's book and on certain aspects are more accurate. Even so, they by no means render Jordan and Pryor's work obsolete. As their notes demonstrate, they derive much of their material, including some of the most important, from *The Campaigns of Forrest*, which is second only to the *Official Records* as a source on him. Reading this material in its original form, rather than through the eyes of someone else, will prove worthwhile. Although the later biographies give us a more complete picture of Forrest the man, it does not differ in essence from the one painted by Jordan and Pryor—which, it should be noted, was how Forrest saw himself or at any rate wished to be seen. Finally, Jordan and Pryor's work is not only a contribution to Civil War history but also to the history of that history. When it was written, Southerners still were reeling from the emotional shock of defeat in a struggle in which they had expected to be victorious. They craved assurance that they had fought the good fight and failed only because they lacked sufficient numbers and the right leaders in the right places. Jordan and Pryor, and surely Forrest too, were aware of this craving, for they shared it. Hence, they combined to produce a book that would give the "plain folk" of the South a hero with whom, unlike the godlike Lee and the sainted Jackson, they could personally identify. He was, of course, Forrest—a rough-and-ready fighting man with a natural knack for war that made him invincible when not hamstrung by incompetent superiors or beset by overwhelming odds. Reading of his exploits, Southerners could and did think, "Had we more commanders like him, or had he been given a higher command, we would have won, not lost."

Perhaps they were right.

ALBERT CASTEI
Hillsdale, Michigan
January 1996

Albert Castel, one of the leading authorities on the Civil War, is the author of many books, including the award-winning Decision in the West: The Atlanta Campaign of 1964, General Sterling Price and the Civil War in the West, *and, most recently, his collection of essays,* Winning and Losing in the Civil War.

NOTES

1. A recent advertisement of the Civil War Store in New Orleans offered a railroad bond signed by "N. B. Forrest" for the price of $1,950.

2. Ezra J. Warner, *Generals in Gray* (Baton Rouge, 1959), pp. 167–68; Patricia L. Faust, ed., *Historical Times Illustrated Encyclopedia of the Civil War* (New York, 1986); Thomas Jordan, "Notes of a Confederate Staff-Officer at Shiloh," Underwood Johnson and Clarence C. Buel, eds., *Battles and Leaders of the Civil War* (4 vols.; New York, 1887), 1: pp. 594–603.

3. Ezra J. Warner, "Foreword," Thomas Jordan and J. P. Pryor, *The Campaigns of Lieut. Gen. N. B. Forrest and of Forrest's Cavalry* (reprint; Dayton, Ohio, 1973), no page numbers.

4. Ibid.

5. Brian Steel Wills, *The Life of Nathan Bedford Forrest* (New York, 1992), p. 12.

6. William S. Fitzgerald, "Did Nathan Bedford Forrest Really Rescue John Able?" *Tennessee Historical Quarterly*, 39 (Spring 1980): pp. 16–26.

7. The falsehoods and slanders in the memoirs of Johnston, Hood, and McClellan are well known. For Sherman's memoirs, see Albert Castel, "Prevaricating through Georgia: Sherman's *Memoirs* as a Source on the Atlanta Campaign," *Civil War History*, 40 (March 1994): pp. 48–71.

8. For a full discussion of the Fort Pillow Massacre, see Albert Castel, "The Fort Pillow Massacre: A Fresh Examination of the Evidence," *Civil War History*, 4 (March 1958): pp. 37–50. Subsequent scholarly studies of the subject concur in the basic conclusions of this article.

9. Because they supposed that Forrest headed the KKK throughout the South, Lytle's *Forrest and His Critter Company* (p. 390) credited him with being the "spiritual comforter" of the Southern people during Reconstruction, whereas Hurst's *Forrest: A Biography* (p. 4) accused him of having "overturned" the outcome of the Civil War by enabling white Southerners twelve years afterward "virtually to reenslave" blacks. Both assertions have no factual nor logical foundation.

PREFACE.

WE are aware of the belief obtaining among the Southern people that the time has not yet come for the publication of histories or memoirs of the more prominent operations of Confederate commanders and officers. Many, indeed, of our countrymen we know earnestly deprecate all such publications at this juncture, as fraught with the provocation of unfriendly controversies at the South; as sure to breed ill-feeling and strife there, among the survivors of the battles, marches, and exploits recounted. We are conscious, moreover, how impossible it were so to write the annals we here present, as to steer clear of giving pain to some, umbrage to others, dissatisfaction also, and some grounds for disputation and criticism.

However, we are of those who believe it to be essential to the truth of history, that the Confederate story of the war should be told without delay—told with all possible fullness and unreserve. Unquestionably somewhat intemperate discussions may spring up. But even this, in the end, will not be without downright profit; for in the sharp, vehement clash and collision the truth will be evolved, as the fire-spark is born of the violent encounter of flint with flint. One account of a campaign or affair will evoke another, and that, others again; and all will be found adding their important *mite*, at least, to the general store of true historical matter, and of a kind, for the most part, which would never have come to light at all, had each annalist kept his notes *in petto* during the lifetime of those who were chief actors in the war. The early multiplication of these *memoirs to serve*, (as the French term them,) of Southern origin, is

Preface.

indispensable, in fact, for any adequate summary hereafter of what was achieved by the armies and the people of the Confederate States, as well as under what circumstances of disadvantage and incommodity. Otherwise, there can never be a vivid portraiture of the splendid martial qualities of that people, their peculiar aptitude for war, their vigorous, ardent spirit, their manhood and heroism in the face of prodigious odds, and the constant mismanagement of their defensive resources. Only from manifold narratives of each and every important phase of the war will the historian be able hereafter to shape a faithful, life-like delineation of their mighty struggle for a separate nationality, just as the photo-sculptor moulds his marvelously exact image of the human features from the reflections of his camera, taken from every possible side of his subject.

Having been placed in possession of the papers and military records of General Forrest, as well as copious notes, taken down from his lips, of the principal occurrences of his remarkable career,* we were led to adventure upon a work that might be accepted as an approximate sketch of what General Forrest and his men actually accomplished, and give a somewhat just conception of what manner of man and leader he was, the nature of his tactics, the scope of his operations, and the character of his soldiery, or how he was seconded. Undertaking this, we next sought out every possible source of information likely to be of use, until we collected a mass of ori-

---

* MEMPHIS, TENN., October 3, 1867.

In the work, now in course of preparation by the Messrs. Blelock & Co., will be found an authentic account of the campaigns and operations in which I took part during the war for the independence of the Confederate States. Believing it to be proper that there should be a timely and lasting record of the deeds and services of those whom I have been so fortunate as to command, I placed all the facts and papers in my possession or available to me, in the hands of accomplished. writers, who have done their part with close and conscientious research, and have endeavored to make up a chronicle neither over-wrought nor over-colored, as I can testify. For the greater part of the statements of the narrative I am responsible, and all facts and incidents derived from other sources are properly credited in the foot-notes. It is hoped that justice will be found done in some degree to the courage, zeal, fortitude, and other soldierly qualities of the men of "Forrest's Cavalry," for that has been the main purpose of the work.

N. B. FORREST.

ginal matter such as seldom or never has been available in the preparation of cotemporaneous history. And we may claim that we have related no important event without carefully consulting many representations of it, written at widely separated points, by Federal as well as Confederate officers. At the same time, we have carefully avoided all embroidery of the narrative with florid phrases or romantic, picturesque descriptions, preferring to present the incidents of a remarkable story in the simplest phraseology. This has been our constant effort. Having to enter largely into details of daily marches, occurrences, and incidents possessed of little interest for the general reader, we have striven to do this as tersely as possible.

If we have done all we could to set in strong light the courage and other prominent military virtues of the Confederates, we do not believe we shall be found wanting in a just acknowledgment, on all proper occasions, of the good qualities of their adversaries.

General Forrest's note, affixed to the preceeding page, shows to what extent he accepts the responsibility for the statements of this work. It remains to be added, that he did not have an opportunity to revise that chapter of it which touches upon the battle of Shiloh, and therefore, is only responsible for so much as was written from his notes, in regard to the incidents of the night of the 6th of April. The responsibility for all of narrative and commentary in that chapter (IV.) belongs to the one whose initials are affixed to this paper. The same, indeed, may be said in regard to all the military criticisms found in any part of the work.

NEW-YORK, October 1, 1867.   T. J.

P. S.—We had prepared a great deal of documentary matter to present in the Appendix. Also, a series of sketches of the principal officers who served under General Forrest ; but the size to which our volume (700 pages) has extended has made their exclusion inexorable ; but we trust the actions and services of those officers will be found set forth in a satisfactory manner in the body of the work, as leading members of Forrest's Cavalry.

NEW-YORK, January 22, 1868.

ϹONTENTS.

— • • • —

INTRODUCTORY SKETCH.

CHAPTER I.

CHAPTER II.

CHAPTER III.

CHAPTER XIII.

CHAPTER XIV.

CHAPTER XV.

CHAPTER XVI.

CHAPTER XVII.

CHAPTER XVIII.

CHAPTER XIX.

Contents. xxi

INTRODUCTORY SKETCH.

INTRODUCTORY SKETCH.

July, 1821, *to June,* 1826.

IT will be expected that a work of this kind should give some insight of the origin, life, and character of the leading personage who figures in its pages, at a period anterior to the notable events which have brought him renown.   In compliance with that natural expectation, it becomes proper to state that NATHAN BEDFORD FORREST was born on the 13th day of July, A.D. 1821, near Duck river, at a small wayside hamlet known as Chapel Hill, in what was then Bedford county, Tennessee.*

His father, William Forrest, having married Mariam Beck,

---
* But is now within the borders of Marshall county.

their first-born were twins, one of whom was Nathan Bedford. A paternal ancestor, his great-grandfather, Shadrach Forrest —of English descent—it is known, emigrated from West-Virginia, about 1730, to Orange county, in the colony of North-Carolina. His second son, Nathan, was the grandfather of the General. Remaining where he had settled in North-Carolina until 1806, the great-grandfather then removed, with the larger part of a numerous family of children and grandchildren, to the wilds of Tennessee, and, after tarrying for a time in Sumner, finally established his home, surrounded by his descendants, in Bedford county. Previous to their departure from North-Carolina, Nathan Forrest had married a Miss Baugh—of Irish origin—and their eldest son, William, was born about 1800. Growing to manhood in Tennessee, he married, as we have said, Mariam Beck, whose family—of Scotch-Irish descent—emigrating from South-Carolina, were among the earliest settlers in Bedford county.

Thus it will be seen Nathan Bedford Forrest is of pure, though mixed, British stock, and springs directly from those hardy, stout-handed pioneer families who, ever far out on the border, wrested the wilderness from the savage by their ready rifles ; and, felling the thick forests, let in the vivifying sunlight upon the virgin, teeming soil—creating mighty States, filled with an energetic, intelligent, manly people, the masses of whom, American born, are the lineal offspring of the original British emigrants to the colonies.

The pecuniary affairs of William Forrest having gone to wreck, he removed, in 1834, with his now large family of young children, from Tennessee to the vicinage of Salem, in Tippah county, North-Mississippi, a region just then opened to emigration by its purchase from the Chickasaw Indians by the Federal Government. It was here the father of Bedford Forrest died, early in 1837, leaving his son, as yet not sixteen years of age, the head of a family embracing his widowed mother, six brothers, and three sisters, and to these was added, four months later, his brother Jeffrey—a posthumous child.

The impoverished condition of his father had debarred the young Bedford from almost the opportunity to receive even a rudimentary education ; for his labor was absolutely necessary from his outset from childhood for the support of the family. His education, therefore, was of the scantiest character, affording no development of the native capacities of the man, and being such only as was to be acquired at a primary school of the neighborhood, for a short time, in Middle Tennessee, and subsequently in Mississippi, during the winter months of 1836 and 1837, when the interval between the harvest and planting seasons suffered him to attend a school. The untimely death of his father, however, now made that labor even more essential than ever for the support of the near kindred left dependent upon his hands, and for the most part too young to be of the least aid in the toilsome struggle with adverse fortune which was his lot for several years following that untoward event. But though deprived of every advantage of fortune but a robust constitution and a resolute soul, he faced his duties with all that force of character, those varied resources of head and hand, and the same manful traits which twenty-five years later were displayed in so conspicuous a manner by him as a cavalry commander, whether as the colonel of a regiment or a lieutenant-general. Striving diligently in manifold ways to gain the means requisite for the comfortable maintenance of those intrusted to his charge, this youth, by his unflinching industry, clear, good sense, and thrifty management, had wrenched success from every counter force, and consequent comparative prosperity for his household, as early as 1840.

But, meanwhile, sickness had sorely harassed the family, and typhoid fever had proved fatal to two of his brothers and his three sisters, including the one twin-born with himself

He, too, had been assailed by this wasting disease, and well-nigh succumbed to its prolonged grasp upon his system. A superb constitution, however, annealed by toil and exposure, empowered him, now about twenty years old, to wage triumphant battle with this enemy, and, after a protracted convalescence, he was happily restored to sound health.

An incident that happened soon after the death of his father is so characteristic of the man into whom Bedford Forrest was developed that it should not be omitted here. A neighbor had an ox which lived at free quarters upon the Forrest farm, throwing down fences and ravaging the growing corn at will. So injurious were these habits of the troublesome brute that they became insufferable. The attention of the owner was repeatedly called to these depredations. He was urged to take measures to put an end to this annoyance, but failed to do so, and the ox continued as destructive as ever. Young Forrest then notified his neighbor that he would tolerate these trespasses no longer, and therefore should shoot the offending animal if ever again found in one of his fields. To this an angry retort was made, and a menace likewise to shoot whomsoever might shoot the ox. In a few days following, the inveterate marauder was found, as usual, feeding in a corn-field. Sending the owner information of the fact and of his consequent purpose, Forrest repaired, rifle in hand, to the scene, and, without delay, did what he had said he would in such an exigency — shot the roguish beast. Scarcely had this been done, and as he was reloading, the neighbor appeared, also armed with a rifle, hurrying toward the field and manifestly bent on violence, as he had threatened. Standing on his own ground, and having reloaded his piece, no sooner did his adversary attempt to surmount the fence that limited the field than the determined youth brought his rifle to bear, and fired with such steady aim that the ball passed through the clothes of the intruder, who, brought to his senses by the report of the gun and the whistle of the ball, tumbled from the fence to the ground exterior to the field, and, speedily recovering his feet, scampered off homeward as fast as he could run. And in this affair in his boyhood may be seen the full promise of his subsequent system of military operations—the same quick recognition of the situation, the like swift plan for meeting the exigency, and the same resolute adoption of the *active* defensive.

Engrossed with the labors of the farm and other efforts to procure the ways and means for the subsistence of his dependent mother and her young family, his only relaxations were found in the recreation of hunting and an occasional horse-race : for, in common with his whole family, as far back as they are known, an ardent taste for horses and dogs possessed him. And thus, trained to the hardest manual toil, practiced as a hunter of the game of the country, and hardened by the manly exercises of the border, Bedford Forrest grew up to the verge of manhood.

About this time the people of Texas were engaged in their contest with Mexico for independence, and the young men of the Southern States were greatly stirred by the opportunity for adventure thus offered them. In all parts of the Mississippi Valley, therefore, companies of volunteers were mustered. Having established his kindred in a comfortable home, and provided them with the essential resources of a comfortable life, young Forrest, catching the infection of the hour around him, enrolled himself as a volunteer in a company organized by Captain Wallace Wilson ; and soon after, February, 1841, started with his comrades for Texas. At New-Orleans, however, a serious mismanagement of the funds needful for the transportation of the company having resulted in the dissolution of the organization, a large number of the members returned to their homes ; but the others, including Bedford Forrest, now near twenty-one years old, adhered to their purpose, and made their way to Houston, Texas. There it was found there was no present or prospective need for the services of these ardent young "*voluntaries*," and, by this time being entirely destitute of money, the band was forced to dissolve. Some, through the aid of friends, were able to return to their homes ; others remained as settlers of the new republic. Bedford Forrest, with his wonted spirit of independence, immediately sought occupation as a laborer on a plantation, where, by his skill with the ax, he soon earned money enough making rails to enable him to return to his home in Mississippi, after an absence of about four months and a half. The seeds of disease, however, were carried back from Texas, and he was again prostrated and disabled by a lingering illness through the autumn of that year. Restored to health, in association with an uncle, he next embarked in a trading venture in horses, of which, already, he was an excellent judge. This knowledge, and a sedulous attention to the business in hand, resulted in success.

Returning in due season to his homestead, he remained occupied in a laborious, thrifty husbandry until the autumn of 1842, when circumstances led him to establish himself in business in conjunction with another uncle in the county-town of Hernando, Mississippi, about twenty-five miles south of Memphis. And there he remained for some nine years, an active, energetic man of business, turning his small means habitually to a good account, and noted for the resolution with which he undertook as well as the judgment with which he carried out his enterprises.

It was during this period, on the tenth of March, 1845, that occurred one of those tragical personal *rencoutres* so common in the settlement of the Mississippi Valley, and in which Bedford Forrest necessarily became the chief actor—the scene being the public square of Hernando, and the other actors three.planters and their overseer.

Without going into the details of the origin of the quarrel, it will be sufficient to mention that Jonathan Forrest, the aged uncle and partner of Bedford, having been the "security" on the bond of one Martin James, of the vicinage, as the guardian of some orphan children, a misundeistanding and violent controversy arose between him and another citizen of the community—one William Matlock. At length, Bedford was drawn into the dispute in behalf of his elderly uncle ; and to such a height did the discord and passions of his opponents soon rise that, on the day we have mentioned, William Matlock, accompanied by his two brothers, James and Jefferson, and their overseer, one Bean, sallied forth into the public square of the town as Bedford Forrest chanced to be passing through it, and all four joined in an immediate savage attack, with revolvers, upon their single-handed enemy.

Without word or act of provocation from Forrest, Jefferson Matlock fired upon him. Unharmed, Forrest promptly replied in the same fashion, and the whole Matlock party taking immediate part with the aggressor, a general engagement ensued, in the course of which thirteen shots were exchanged, and the dread bowie-knife of the country was freely used. Strange to say, however, the speedy issue was the discomfiture of the Matlocks, all three of whom were severely wounded, and their auxiliary, Bean, being driven from the field : but not, unfortunately, until, firing at the nephew, he had inflicted a mortal wound upon the uncle, who, having come upon the scene, had really taken no part in the affray. Forrest himself was wounded, but not severely. Unsupported throughout, except by the natural sympathy of bystanders, who limited their aid to the opportune provision of weapons, he had waged this unequal battle with the distinctive audacity, coolness, and determination which were brought to bear so brilliantly, twenty years later, on his shining military career, and with very much the same notable results.

So strongly, indeed, were the sympathies of the community excited by the courage displayed by young Forrest in this affair, that the aggressors, though seriously wounded and worsted, were at once arrested, refused bail, imprisoned, and subjected to a stringent prosecution, from which they were only relieved, finally, after heavy costs and losses, and a protracted, harsh confinement. He, too, was arrested : but after a brief examination into the circumstances before a magistrates' court, he was speedily released as having acted merely in self-defense.

By mere chance, some months later, he became the witness of another one of those fierce border scenes of malice and murder which stain the early annals of the South-West, and revived in the nineteenth century the savage temper and practices in private feuds of the fourteenth. It was only by his dauntless nerve and coolness that he was preserved, moreover, from being involved as a participant in defense of his life. Riding, one day, along the highway from Hernando to Holly Springs, in company with Mr. James K. Morse, a well-known lawyer of the former place, they were suddenly met in the road by a planter of the neighborhood in which they were, James Dyson by name, notorious for his lawless, blood-thirsty courses, and who cherished, it happened, a deadly grudge against the lawyer. Dyson carried a double-barreled gun, and, without uttering one word or making one gesture of warning, shot Morse, who fell without a groan from his saddle to the ground, with a rifle-ball in his heart. Instantly turning the other barrel—loaded, it seems, with buck-shot—upon Forrest, the murderous Dyson threatened to shoot him also, though with no other cause of animosity than that he had witnessed the affair. But Forrest was not to be thus " taken lightly by the beard "—sudden and unexpected as had been the deed ;

for he had drawn and held his revolver, cocked, with a steady aim at the ruffian who menaced him, and whom he coolly warned that ·he had " better make sure work, for it was now a game at which two could play."

Dyson then lowered his weapon and forebore his sanguinary purposes upon Forrest,* who at once became the stern, inflexible prosecutor before the law of the murderer, and did all in his power to secure his conviction and punishment. Dyson was arrested, tried, and convicted of murder in the first degree. But the power of money, so constantly potent to shield crime, was successfully applied, and he subsequently escaped the rightful penalty of this murder.

It was not long after this affair that General Forrest, on the 25th of September, 1845, in the twenty-fifth year of his age, was married to Mary Ann Montgomery, a descendant of the same stock with the gallant Irish general who fell in December, 1775, under the walls of Quebec.

Continuing to reside and prosper in his business undertakings in Hernando, in 1849 Forrest experienced his first pecuniary disaster. Having engaged in the manufacture of brick, he was led to become the contractor for the erection of a large academy there, which resulted in a severe loss through the breach of trust of an agent empowered to draw money for him from a bank in Memphis. Undepressed, however, by this mischance, he determined to adventure into a broader field for his capacities and energies. Accordingly, in the spring season of 1852, he quit Hernando and established himself in Memphis as a broker in real estate and a dealer in slaves.†

---

* He, however, said afterward that he did so because the remaining barrel of his gun only contained buck-shot, and he feared they would neither be fatal nor disable Forrest.

† An attempt has been made to cast discredit upon General Forrest because of the fact that he once dealt in slaves. Not only was this done at the North, at a juncture when all persons promi-

Successful in all his undertakings, which, if boldly planned, as his means expanded, were always carried on with a sound judgment allied with marked vigor and decision, by 1859 Forrest had achieved a large measure of success and accumulated a considerable fortune. He had previously, for several years, cultivated a cotton plantation near Memphis. Now, disposing of the larger portion of his active business in that city, he bought two extensive plantations in Cohoma county, Mississippi, and began planting on a large scale—growing a thousand bales of cotton in 1861 ; and transferring to the culture of his fields all that natural intelligence and aptitude for affairs which, displayed from youthhood, had developed in scope as he grew and with the increase of his fortunes, showing that he is clearly one of those men, who Schiller says,

" Grow with the circle wherein they move."

As we have seen, narrowly escaping death, once from a

---

nently connected with slavery had become objects of a passionate dislike ; but even to some extent with the people of his own section. Indeed, it has been one of the strangest of paradoxes that, while earnestly impressed with the belief that not only the prosperity of their section was linked with the preservation of slavery, but also the perpetuity of those traits of which they were proudest, the Southern people, nevertheless, in no small degree, looked with disfavor upon traffic in slaves. Selling their slaves at pleasure or purchasing of the dealer, they were yet prone to disparage his avocation. This probably arose, at first, from personal causes. But there were many dealers who overcame the prejudice by their individual worth and standing ; and prominent in this class stands Bedford Forrest, who, it may be justly claimed, carried on his business with admitted probity and humanity. It is notable that he never sold separately the members of a family ; and made it a rule, as far as practicable, after acquiring the heads of a family, to purchase the others, howsoever widely scattered, and this, indeed, proved profitable in the end. Habitually kind as a master, we are satisfied his slaves were strongly attached to him. That in Memphis he rose above any prejudices against his calling is fully attested by his personal influence in the community ; by the call upon him, as will be seen, by the Governor of his State, after he had enrolled as a private, to raise a regiment of cavalry ; and the ease with which he made up his regiment out of the best young men of North-Alabama and Tennessee.

deadly disease and twice from murderous violence, previous
to his removal from Hernando, just at the threshold of his
career at Memphis, he was once more brought within the
closest contact with death, and narrowly escaped falling a victim to the atrocious recklessness of human life and incapacity
of the officers of a steamboat upon which he was a passenger.
It was in the spring of 1852 ; the adjustment of some business
affairs having called him to Texas, he was about to return
homeward.   Arriving at Houston, *en route* for Galveston, it
was found his only means of transportation was the steamboat Farmer, represented as extremely dangerous from age,
long use, and the reckless, bad habits of her captain.   Anxious to reach Memphis as speedily as possible, Forrest resolved to venture the hazard, and accordingly embarked just
as the Farmer was being pushed from the landing.   No
sooner was the boat well under way than another steamer
made her appearance, and it was evident there was a race between them.   Soon after supper, being fatigued, Forrest
sought his state-room and berth, but was not suffered to sleep,
weary and drowsy as he was after his long ride across the
country.   A party of gamblers was established in the saloon
of the boat ; the vicissitudes of their game speedily brought
on a clamorous altercation, and pistols were right soon drawn
and cocked.   All this was audible to Forrest, who further
saw that, from the position of the brawlers, he was in imminent risk of being shot in his berth.   Promptly rising, and
but partially dressed, he hastened among the desperadoes,
and, by a few peremptory words, his resolute manner, and imperious will, quelled the disturbance just on the verge of a
general *mêlée.*   This effected, walking out upon the deck
and forward, he was startled to find the chimneys of the Farmer red-hot as high as the roof of the cabin, which was only
being kept from breaking into a blaze by the constant dash
of water by the bucketful upon the adjacent timbers by all

the servants of the boat. At the same time all kinds of the most combustible fuel were being lavishly thrown into the already volcanic furnaces of the steamer, to increase steam and accelerate her speed. To all but the insensate captain and the absorbed gamesters the situation of all aboard that trembling, overpressed boat was one of apparent, fearful peril. Forrest, remonstrating with the captain, sharply reprobated his criminal exposure of the lives of his passengers, some of whom were women and children, and urged an immediate cessation of the race and a timely effort to reduce the steam. But, excited by liquor as well as the race, the captain, with a coarse oath, exclaimed he was one hundred yards ahead of his rival, and would preserve that distance to Galveston, six miles distant, or he " would blow the old tub with every soul on board to h—l." Seeing that he was unable to avert the impending catastrophe, Forrest walked to the extreme after part of the vessel and there awaited the crisis. Nor did he wait long ; in a few moments a loud explosion was heard forward, and the whole forward cabin and deck, torn into numberless shreds and fragments of beams and boards, were thrown with fearful uproar high up in the air, amid the harrowing death-shrieks and loud cries of anguish and terror of more than a hundred human beings who were aboard the ill-fated craft at the time of the explosion. This took place just as the Farmer was crossing Rockfish bar, where the water fortunately was shallow ; and the competitor in the race, being near by at the juncture, came alongside immediately, and the unhurt and wounded were sought out and rescued from the water or from the wreck. Among those taken from the hulk was Forrest, half-clad as he had happily left his state-room a few moments before. His only hurt was a severe contusion of the shoulder : but the state-room abandoned so timely, with his luggage, had been destroyed. With characteristic energy, however, he assisted in removing the survivors to the other steamer, with such of the dead as could be found, and did what he could, by his presence of mind and thoughtfulness, to alleviate the suffering of the wounded on the way to Galveston, where he disembarked several hours after the disaster.*

Returning, without further incident or delay, to his newly opened field of enterprise at Memphis, Forrest set to work to extend its area each year. Temperate in his habits, cool and far-seeing in his outlook, recognizing the possible with a rapid glance, and bringing his good sense to bear on whatsoever he pursued, a large measure of success crowned his every effort, and made him noted in his community as a man of uncommon aptitude for large and happy business affairs. As a natural consequence, too, no small degree of influence among his fellow-citizens followed, and this was strikingly illustrated by an occurrence thereafter memorable in the history of Memphis.

In 1857, there lived in the city two men—Joe and John Able, father and son—who had rendered themselves generally odious as gamblers and by their acts of lawless violence, until the father, having killed a man in a public saloon, was forced to abscond to escape justice. In June of that year, the son, John Able, and a man by the name of Everson were seated together on the "sidewalk" of the Worsham House, in conversation touching or in explanation of an insult which it was alleged had been offered by the latter to the mother of Able. Suddenly the interview was brought to an end by a heavy blow in the face of Everson, given by Able with his pistol. In the blow the pistol was discharged, and the ball, passing through the brain of the stricken man, he was killed instantly. Surrendering himself to the police, young Able was at once lodged in prison ; but the intelligence of the deed was soon broad-spread through Memphis. Other recent

---

* About sixty souls were swept from mortal existence by this dreadful affair, including the wretched captain.

acts of similar character had tarnished the repute of the place by the impunity with which they had been perpetrated, and the ease with which flagrant culprits had been able to break through the feeble meshes of the law. Recollecting this, and coupling with it the past life of the Ables, the populace swiftly congregated on the streets and in public places, and in free conversation in regard to this particular homicide, as well as the prevalence and immunity of open murder in their midst, soon became so excited that, swept on by their passionate resentment, they flocked in a dense crowd to the scene of the murder. Surrounding the Worsham House, they grew more and more angry, and, as on all such occasions, ringleaders being found to begin the cry, the whole throng followed in a clamorous demand for the object of popular wrath, to the end that they might inflict summary and condign punishment. Among those attracted to the spot was Bedford Forrest : but, while the masses were inflamed by ungovernable passions, he had remained unaffected and loyal to the laws of the land. Counseling with the mayor and some other prominent citizens, he made his appearance upon a balcony of the hotel, and, attracting the attention of the vast throng there assembled, addressed the people in behalf of moderation and deliberation ; and, in order to insure heed to this counsel, announced that a mass meeting of the citizens was called at the Exchange Building, at a special hour the next evening, to consider what should be done for the public good, and for the punishment and suppression hereafter of these acts of murder. This speech had the desired effect ; the clamor for immediate punishment subsided, and ceased as the people gradually dispersed and retired to their homes.

At the time appointed, however, vast numbers reassembled, and the large hall and corridors of the Exchange Building were packed to overflowing, while the neighboring streets were thronged with groups of people, gradually growing as

excited and clamorous for swift justice upon the murderer as
on the previous night. The mayor having been called to
preside, Forrest was one of the vice-presidents ; but scarcely
had this organization been effected than some one in the
crowd shouted, " Let's go and hang the murderer !" Instantly
this was accepted as the public judgment and *fiat*, and in spite
of every effort made by the officers of the meeting and a few
other prominent citizens present to restrain and turn them
aside from their harsh purpose, the infuriated people rushed
forth and again crowded all the approaches to the city prison.
Ringleaders, seizing the control, at once demanded the keys
and access to the object of their vengeance — threatening
force if not instantly complied with. The universal echo
that resounded from the thousands around to this demand
made it apparent that resistance were useless, and the jailer
yielded up the keys to the mob-leaders, who, entering, soon
brought young Able forth, without giving time even to dress.

Throwing a rope around his neck, Able was hurried, without delay, in the direction of the navy-yard, in the relentless
hands of the master-spirits of the occasion, followed by a
boisterous multitude, heated by excitement, for the most part,
into a fierce thirst for his life. It was there, upon one of the
projecting beams under the eaves of the rope-walk, it had
been determined to hang him. Some time was occupied,
however, in the preparation for the execution, but the rope
was finally and satisfactorily adjusted, and Able was on the
eve of being hung beyond rescue. But, meanwhile, Forrest,
who had remained for a time in the court-hall in consultation
with those opposed to the courses of the mob, hearing of the
delay, resolved to extricate Able and deliver him into the
custody of the officers of the law, and hurried to the navy-
yard to make the attempt. Pressing through the turbulent
masses with much difficulty up to where Able was standing
with the rope around his neck, his mother and sister by his

side making piteous, tearful appeals to the implacable throng
around for the life of their kinsman, Forrest was still further
confirmed in his purpose by their presence, and the dauntless
bearing of young Able at that instant of supreme peril. Pallid,
and slender to effeminacy, and scarcely twenty-one years of
age, he nevertheless faced the angry crowd, intent on his
death, with the utmost cool courage, and without the least
tremor in his voice firmly protested against the impending
violence as unjust under the circumstances of extreme provocation from which he had acted, as he could fully establish if
allowed a fair trial before the law, which he demanded as his
right. "Hang him! hang him!" were still the loud and general cry of the enraged people. But Forrest, drawing his
knife, with a swift sweep severed the rope, and, taking Able
by the arm, announced aloud his intention to remand him to
the custody of the rightful authorities.

Scarcely ever was a mob more uniformly animated by a
single aim, nor one more inflexibly bent upon its execution,
than that which stood between Forrest and the city prison.
The attempt, therefore, to snatch the victim from its clutches
at such a moment was supremely dangerous, and, under all
the circumstances, naught but the influence of the resistless
magnetism of a robust, right royal manhood made success
possible, and averted a fearful tragedy, of which the lawless
hanging of Able had been the least part. Some few stout-
hearted, able-bodied friends rallied around Forrest and his
charge at the moment, and as, proceeding to carry out his
announced purpose, he moved through the press toward the
jail. At first, no resistance was encountered ; but right soon
the more tempestuous spirits of the mob gathered to a head,
rushed after, and with such violence that Forrest's little band
of supports were swept away in the torrent, and he was left
alone with his self-assumed charge, still held firmly by the
arm. Fortunately, at the instant, he was close to some small

piles of lumber, and, stooping behind one of these, the frantic throng actually passed over Able and himself, but with a narrow escape, as several attempts were made by ringleaders to strike them with bludgeons and knives, which, however, his watchful, wary habits enabled Forrest to ward. Impelled forward by the weight of the masses behind them, the leaders were forced beyond their mark, and Forrest, taking advantage of the opportunity, made directly for the jail, which he happily succeeded in reaching, and restored Able to his cell.

Meanwhile, the mob again surrounded the building and re-demanded their victim, as strongly resolved on his immolation as ever. In reply to a threat that they would break down the door if the prisoner were not delivered up, Forrest, presenting himself upon the steps of the prison, drew a revolver, and declared it to be his determination to shoot the first man who approached to the door. The collected, stern courage of the man, and his previous intrepidity in wresting Able from their hands, made it apparent that he would actually execute his declaration if forced to the exigency, and no one seemed inclined to bring on that issue. The ringleaders quailed, the spirit of violence quickly ebbed away, the people again began to disperse—and a little later naught remained of the " Able Mob," as it had been designated.

The genuine worth and potential qualities of the man who could thus spring forth, take fully three thousand excited men, as it were, by the throats, and by his own imperious will force them to recognize the plenitude of discarded authority, were now fully appreciated in Memphis. Accordingly, the year following, Bedford Forrest was put forward, wholly without his own seeking, for the important office of alderman of his ward, and easily elected. Serving out his term, in June, 1859, he was as easily reëlected ; but before the close of the official year, having been called away from the city by his affairs, he resigned. But soon returning, he was rechosen—·

his own successor — by the board of aldermen, upon whom the election had devolved.   Throughout his whole official life an active public servant, he was one extremely watchful over every public interest confided to the city government, and was ever animated by decided views upon every question touching those interests, as might be abundantly illustrated. One transaction, however, must suffice.   It was proposed to sell the stock of the city in the Memphis and Charleston Railroad to the extent of half a million of dollars at a certain rate below par.   This Alderman Forrest strenuously opposed as manifestly below the real intrinsic worth of the stock, and therefore seriously detrimental to the people's interests, especially since the stock was advancing in value.   The measure, however, was carried over his obstinate opposition and arguments, and the sale took place.   Assured of the correctness of his views, Forrest, seeing that the transaction was irrevocable, did not hesitate, as a business man, to secure as an investment some fifty thousand dollars of the bonds at the rate established by the Board, which within a year thereafter he sold at a profit of twenty thousand dollars.*

Thus, beginning life a fatherless youth at the age of sixteen, with a comparatively helpless family of twelve persons dependent for their support upon his labor on a leased farm in the rugged hill-lands of Tippah, denied the advantage of even an ordinary English education, and left to struggle without the least extrinsic aid, steady, straightforward, strong, and self-reliant, we find him climbing year by year, with scarce a

---

* In this connection it will be in place to cite the observations of R. D. Baugh, Esq., who was Mayor of Memphis while General Forrest served as an alderman : " While alderman, General Forrest never offered a resolution in the Board on any subject, or to carry out any measure, no matter how unpopular it might be at first, that he did not stick to it and work at it until he carried it triumphantly through."—*MSS. Notes.*

pause in his ascent. With him, indeed, it was as Milton
tells us :

> " The way found prosperous once
> Induces best to hope of like success,"

until, after the lapse of little more than a score of years, he
stands—in 1861—in the front rank of the prosperous business
men of the largest city of his native State, the owner of large,
well-stocked plantations, the grower of one thousand bales of
cotton per annum, and possessed of a handsome estate besides in stocks and other personal property. All this acquired by his own unassisted endeavor ; and withal, he was
now generally recognized by his fellow-citizens as a man of
growing mark, already, indeed, one of much public usefulness,
and calculated by a strenuous temper and strong will to sway
others and move them for the public weal.

It remains to be added here : In person, he is six feet one
inch and a half in height, with broad shoulders, a full chest,
and symmetrical, muscular limbs. Erect in his carriage, his
average weight is one hundred and eighty-five pounds. Dark
gray eyes, singularly bright and searching, dark hair, mus-
tache, and beard worn upon the chin, a set of regular white
teeth, and clearly cut, sun-embrowned features make him a
much handsomer man than any of his pictures, and personally noticeable before the fame of his successes as a cavalry
officer attracted general attention to General Forrest.

THE

CAMPAIGNS OF LIEUT.-GEN. FORREST,

AND OF

FORREST'S CAVALRY.

CHAPTER I.

June 1st, 1861, to February 12th, 1862.

IN the pages which follow we have undertaken to present a sketch of the military career of Nathan Bedford Forrest, and a memoir, in detail, of the campaigns, marches, and battles of those Confederate soldiers whose remarkable achievements, from an early day in the winter of 1861–2 to the 9th of May, 1865, made the name of " FORREST'S CAVALRY " redoubtable to their adversaries, a high distinction with their countrymen, and a designation proudly worn by all who bore it.

At the outburst of the war inaugurated by the evacuation

by Major Robert Anderson of his post at Fort Moultrie, in Charleston Harbor, and the hostile occupation of Fort Sumter, he who in the course of a year subsequently, as will be seen, became a renowned cavalry commander was living quietly on his plantation in Coahoma county, Mississippi. Always a strong and decided States Right Democrat in politics, he had been deeply attached, however, to the Union, and was earnestly opposed to its dissolution so long as there were reasonable hopes of an adjustment of the questions in issue between the sections consonant with the safety and rights of his immediate State and section. But that hope having been destroyed by the Proclamation of President Lincoln on the 15th of April, 1861 ; and, seeing that a great conflict was inevitable, he set to work to prepare his large private affairs for the emergency, so that he might at once and thenceforward take an earnest part in the struggle for the independence or separate political existence of the Confederate States. This arranged as far as practicable, early in June he repaired to Memphis with the intention of joining the Confederate force then engaged in fortifying the position of Randolph, Tennessee. On reaching Memphis, however, following the strong bent of his nature for cavalry, he at once attached himself, as a private trooper, to the "Tennessee Mounted Rifles," a company which he found forming at the time,* under Dr. Josiah S. White, and in less than a week afterward he became a part of the garrison at Randolph, whither his company was ordered.

About the 10th of July, Private Forrest was called to Memphis by a dispatch from the Governor of Tennessee, Isham G. Harris, at whose urgent desire, united with that of Major-General Polk, Commander-in-Chief of the Confederate Forces in all that quarter, he undertook to raise a regiment of volun-

---

* June 14th, 1861.

teer cavalry, and the necessary warrant was given to that effect.

After making this authority properly known in Memphis, Colonel Forrest, with characteristic energy and comprehension of his needs, hastened to Kentucky, for the purpose not only of procuring arms and horse-equipments in that State, but with a view, also, to recruiting there for his regiment. This, in his judgment, was desirable, inasmuch as a very large portion of the young men of West-Tennessee had already become attached to other organizations of the several arms of the service. Visiting the towns of Paris, Lexington, Mount Sterling, Frankfort, and intermediate places, he found, however, that, while the mass of the people, apparently, were in strong sympathy with the Confederate cause, comparatively few were prepared to take up arms at that moment.

Turning back at Frankfort, Colonel Forrest visited Louisville about the 20th of July, and there purchased, with his own means, five hundred Colt's navy pistols, and one hundred saddles and other horse-equipments. While thus engaged, receiving information that a company of cavalry was being organized for his regiment at Brandenburg, Meade county, Kentucky, he went to that point and mustered in the "Boone Rangers," some ninety strong, under Captain Frank Overton, which thus became the first company of a regiment subsequently so conspicuous.

Returning to Louisville, he found it a matter of no little difficulty to get his arms and equipments out of the city, as by this time the objects of his presence there had become suspected, and a strict surveillance was established over his movements. But with native address and shrewdness, assisted by only two gentlemen,* he baffled the vigilance of those

---

* Colonel Richard C. Wintersmith, a native of Kentucky, but then, as now, a resident of Memphis, and M. Garri- son, Esq., a Kentuckian, residing near Louisville.

opposed to his purposes, and eluded all the efforts made to detect and arrest him. Favored by the happy chance that his person was not known, he and his two associates were able to carry, from time to time, the pistols, concealed under their linen "dusters," to a livery stable, whence they were subsequently taken in a market-wagon to Mr. Garrison's farm in the country as so many bags of potatoes, while the saddles and other equipments were conveyed, under the guise of leather, to a tan-yard some three miles south of Louisville. Meanwhile, a detachment of Captain Overton's company had been brought to the vicinage with the necessary wagons ; at dusk, these were driven to the tan-yard in question, and, receiving the freight awaiting them, hastened southward, taking up the arms also as they passed on toward the mouth of Salt river.* These dispositions successfully made, he mounted a horse and rode leisurely in the direction opposite to that in which the tan-yard lay until he reached the suburbs, when, being now quite dark, he swiftly made the circuit of the city and took the road southward on the track of his wagons, which he soon overtook ; and, pushing rapidly on with them to Brandenburg, found the Boone Rangers ready to take the field.

Leaving Brandenburg the same day, he proceeded with the Boone Rangers, *via* Bowling Green, Ky., in the direction of Clarksville, Tenn. Fed and received on the way with great hospitality by the citizens, they encamped the second afternoon after leaving Brandenburg within fifteen miles of Munfordsville. Here intelligence was received that a Union force of two companies of "Home Guards" were in wait at the latter town to contest his march. Many gentlemen, relatives

* As before said, his presence and business in Kentucky was known to the Union leaders, who had a watch set over his movements. One day, in the train between Lexington and Frankfort, he heard the subject discussed, and the Hon. John J. Crittenden declared that "Forrest ought to be arrested."

and parents of the members of the Boone Rangers, had accompanied their beloved sons or young kinsmen thus far, as indeed for several days thereafter. These Forrest drew up in a line with his men, under the Confederate flag, forming an imposing array, as the railway train approached from Munfordsville. So strong, indeed, was the appearance thus presented, that the passengers in their report magnified this little band into a regiment. The result was, as he drew near Munfordsville, resolved to fight his way, if necessary, through any obstacles, on making a reconnoissance with a squad of five men, it was ascertained the main force of the Home Guards had retired. A small body, however, had remained, and made show of resistance, until put to flight by a prompt charge on the part of Forrest and his petty detachment.

Taking the route by Bowling Green* and Russellville, Ky., and Clarksville, Tenn., the Confederate flag flying at the head of his little column all the while, Forrest reached Memphis, without incident or delay, about the 1st day of August, thus achieving an operation seemingly insignificant, but really, at this juncture, one of much delicacy and hazard, requiring for its success no small sagacity and resolution. For, until he had crossed the Tennessee river, a superior force of Home Guards was organized or mustering in every county through which he passed.

A fine company for his regiment had been raised and organized in Memphis in his absence, under Captain Charles May, which had been named the " Forrest Rangers," and this and the Boone Rangers formed the nucleus around which, in the course of the next six or eight weeks, was formed a battalion of eight companies.†

---

* The parents and kinsmen of the Boone Rangers returned from this place.

† Namely, Overton's (A) Company, which, as mentioned *ubi supra*, from Brandenburg, was some 90 strong;

An election for field-officers, held in the second week of October, of course resulted in the choice of Forrest for the Lieutenant-Colonelcy, while Captain D. C. Kelly was made Major.*

The day following the final organization by this election of field-officers, one squadron was put in motion, under Major Kelly, for Fort Donelson, (Dover,) Middle Tennessee. In a day or two the remainder followed, and the whole battalion was assembled at that point during the last week in October. The immediate commandant there at the time was Colonel A. Heiman, Tenth Regiment Tennessee Volunteers, and the garrison, a small command of infantry, did not exceed four hundred men, who were engaged throwing up fortifications. Going into camp, some four or five days were employed in drilling and other camp duties. But a Federal gunboat, the Conestoga, having made its appearance in the Cumberland as high as Tobacco Port, Colonel Heiman ordered Colonel Forrest to proceed with his battalion in that direction to watch this movement. Under these orders, having proceeded as far as Canton, Ky., an order was received from Brigadier-General Lloyd Tilghman, commanding the defenses of the Cumberland and Tennessee rivers, to bring the command to his headquarters, at Hopkinsville. At that place orders were again given, about the middle of November, to proceed to the Ohio river, and report any movement of a hostile character observed between the Cumberland and Green rivers. Proceed

---

Logan's, (G,) 45 strong, was from Harrodsburg, Ky.; Kelly Troopers, (F,) 90 men, from Huntsville, and Trewhitt's, (E,) 80 men, from Gadsden, Ala.; Bacot's, (B,) 80 men, from South-Alabama, and Milner's, (H,) 85 men, from Marshall county, Ala.; Gould's, (D,) 90 men, from Texas; and May's, (C,) 90 men, from Memphis — in all, 650 men, rank and file.

* Captain Hambrick succeeded to the command of the Kelly Troopers, Lieutenant C. A. Schuyler was appointed Adjutant of the battalion, Dr. S. M. Van Wick, of Huntsville, Surgeon, and J. P. Strange, of Memphis, Sergeant-Major.

ing on this errand as far as Princeton, Ky., there the main body of the battalion halted, while Major Kelly was detached with a squadron, with orders to repair to the banks of the Ohio and intercept a steam transport which was to pass on the following day. Soon after the Major had reached the river and disposed his men for the execution of his orders, the expected steamer made its appearance, and was speedily brought to without resistance. It proved to be freighted with sugar, coffee, and considerable quantities of other army stores, including blankets, all most desirable supplies for the Confederates. Meanwhile, the Federal gunboat Conestoga having gone up the Cumberland river with the object of seizing some clothing in store for the Confederates at Canton, a gentleman of Smithland, made aware of it, hastened, on horseback, from that place to Princeton, to give Forrest the information, riding the distance of eighty-four miles in twelve hours with one change of horses. Major Kelly having returned, Forrest immediately set out with the whole battalion for Canton, which place, thirty-two miles distant, was reached early the next morning, after a fatiguing night-march of eight hours. Scarcely were the Confederates at the village and disposed for the then novel operation of an attack by cavalry on a gunboat, when the Conestoga came in sight. A small four-pounder piece of artillery, under Lieutenant Sullivan, which had been brought along from Princeton, was placed in position, and so masked as to be hidden from view from the approaching vessel. The greater part of the men likewise were concealed, while a few were displayed with the hope that a party of marines might thus be inveigled ashore and entrapped. The Conestoga, however, coming to anchor at the Canton Landing, remained there half an hour without landing any one ; then she dropped back some few hundred yards, anchored again, and prepared for action. Scarcely were her ports unclosed than the four-pounder was opened upon her, and the few men in sight delivered a rapid fire with their Maynard rifles through her wide-open ports.* Firing two rounds, Lieutenant Sullivan, of course, was obliged to with-draw : but, meanwhile, the whole battalion joined in a rapid fire, returned from the Conestoga by all the guns she could bring to bear upon the shore, which was swept with grape and canister from her heavy battery.† Forrest's men, taking advantage of every possible shelter, directed their fire at her ports, and the people of the country report the Federal losses in killed and wounded were some seventeen. After six or seven hours of this combat, the commander of the Conestoga closed her ports and made off, leaving his opponent in pos-session of the field.

This affair, as may be readily supposed, was the source of no small elation in this command of untried soldiers, especially since it was a decided triumph over a species of adversary that hitherto had been regarded with actual terror by the raw troops of the Confederate service, on account of the large calibres of their armament and their comparative invulnera-bility. The effect upon the spirit of the men was most salu-tary, giving them that confidence in themselves and their commander which, doubtless, was sensibly felt on many sub-sequent occasions.

Immediately after the departure of the Conestoga, Forrest set out, by way of Cadiz, to return to Hopkinsville, which, by making a night march, he reached on the 21st of November.

---

* These were good marksmen, name-ly, Sergeant Thomas B. Sheridan, after-ward a Major, Private R. H. Balch, afterward Lieutenant-Colonel, Private Aaron Burrow, and Surgeon Van Wick, killed a few days subsequently. They were stationed under partial cover, not more than thirty yards from the Cone-stoga at her second anchorage, and fir-ing in the order named. Therefore, the honor of firing the first shot in action by the Forrest Cavalry may be claimed, apparently, by Major Sheridan.

† Her armament consisted of nine heavy guns.

and remained there to the end of the month, Brigadier-General Charles Clark being in command of the whole force assembled in the vicinage. It was here his command was increased to ten companies by the accession of Captain Charles McDonald's company, " *The McDonald Dragoons*," and Captain D. C. Davis's company of cavalry, from Huntsville, Alabama.

About the 1st of December, weary of the routine of camp service, and of short tours of scouting duty through the surrounding country, Colonel Forrest applied to General Clark for authority to make a reconnoissance, in force, to the immediate presence of the enemy at or near Calhoun, on the north bank of Green river, where General T. L. Crittenden was reported to have assembled a force of some 10,000 infantry and 1200 cavalry. This having been granted, he straightway took the field, with about 450 rank and file, and scoured the region between Green river and the Cumberland, approaching close to Henderson, but first reaching the bank of the Ohio at Cayceville. Twelve days were occupied with this expedition; twelve days of rigorous December weather, in the course of which these raw troops, wholly unaccustomed to such exposure, and many of them affected by the measles, suffered greatly. However, their commander bivouacked with them, shared their hardships; and the substantial advantage of the expedition was, that it served to temper and harden the young men who mainly constituted the force, served to develop their martial qualities, and to accustom their chief to military command and the handling of men in campaign.*

---

* Lieutenant-Colonel, then Major, D. C. Kelly, and second in command, writing of this expedition, observes: "The command found that it was his (Forrest's) single will, impervious to argument, appeal, or threat, which was ever to be the governing impulse in their movements. Every thing necessary to supply their wants, to make them comfortable, he was quick to do, save to change his plans, to which every thing had to bend. New men naturally grumbled, and were dissatisfied in the execution, but, when the

Without noteworthy events, there were, nevertheless, several incidents connected with this march which, though not of military moment, must be related as characteristic of the men engaged and of the time.

Near Marion, in Crittenden county, Ky., just before Forrest's appearance there, a man, at the instance of a "Union" neighbor, had been arrested, and carried off from his family. The wife reporting these facts to the Confederate officer, it was determined to capture the informer, which he proceeded to do in person, with a small detachment. Unhappily, this attempt cost the life of Dr. Van Wick, surgeon of the regiment, who, riding abreast with Colonel Forrest as they approached the house, was shot through the heart by the object of their quest, who then made good his escape rearward, and eluded all pursuit. Dr. Van Wick was the first man of the regiment slain. "He was," says one of his comrades, "a gentleman of the highest education and refinement; his heart warm with the loftiest patriotism and purest friendship; a skillful surgeon and an humble Christian."*

A few days previously a Federal detachment had crossed the Ohio, from Illinois, and abducted some Kentuckians charged with sympathy for the Confederate cause. One of Forrest's detachments sent in pursuit of the murderer of Dr. Van Wick happened to meet ten Baptist clergymen, who had just returned from Illinois, whither they had been to attend one of the yearly "Associations" of their church. Well known for their stringent "*Unionism*," they were brought to the Confederate commander, who at once determined to use them as the means for the recovery of the gentlemen, then prisoners,

---

work was achieved, were soon reconciled by the pride they felt in the achievement."

   * We regret to be unable to append a brief sketch of Dr. Van Wick, all our efforts to obtain the requisite information having failed of results.

northward of the river. Accordingly, placing eight of the number under guard as hostages, he set two at liberty on condition that they should follow the Illinois kidnappers, effect the release of the Kentuckians, and return with them in twenty-four hours, remarking, with an emphasis of tone and language which carried assurance of seriousness, that, unless it were done, he "would hang the remainder all on one pole." At the appointed time they reappeared at Marion, entirely successful in their mission; and they and their associates were then dismissed, to return to their respective homes.*

It was about the 20th of December, when Forrest and his battalion returned to their station at Hopkinsville, which, it should here be noted, was an outpost of the main Confederate force at Bowling Green, holding in observation the approaches from the mouth of the Cumberland and from Green river, and being at the junction of the railroad from the Ohio, at Henderson, with one to Nashville. The men of the command were set to work to arrange their camp for winter, and had been several days engaged building "huts," when rumored movements of the Federals, looking to an advance upon the Confederate lines into Kentucky, led to orders from General Johnston for a cavalry reconnoissance for the definite ascertainment of the military situation. This duty was assigned to Lieutenant-Colonel Forrest and his battalion.† On the 26th

---

* After this reconnoissance, a report of it having been required, one was written by the Major of the battalion, "at the dictation" of Colonel Forrest, which General Sidney Johnston complimented very highly for the precision and value of the information furnished. The writer of that report observes: "Though he (Forrest) was indisposed to the use of the pen himself, he had clear and exact ideas of what he wanted written, and few were more exacting in requiring a precise statement of the ideas furnished."—*MS. Notes of Lieutenant-Colonel D. C. Kelly, of Huntsville, Alabama.*

† Lieutenant-Colonel James W. Starnes, subsequently distinguished as one of Forrest's colonels, and for a while as a brigade commander, and Captain W. S. McLemore, joined several days later at Greenville, with a detachment of fifty select men from his battalion, stationed then at Russellville.

of December, therefore, taking 300 of his most effective men, he was again in movement in the direction of Green river, by way of Greenville, Muhlenburg county, the quarter of apprehended hostile approach. The roads, deep with mud and rough with ice, were excessively severe on the animals; and it was the 28th when the several detachments, moving and observing on different roads, assembled at Greenville. Having learned nothing definite of the enemy in that direction, Forrest concluded to reconnoitre on the road toward and also in close proximity to Rumsey, directly opposite to Calhoun, where it was understood General Crittenden was still in force. Moving on that road, with proper military precaution, but at a good pace, some eight miles beyond Greenville, on the morning of the 28th, it was there reported that a detachment of Federal cavalry, some four or five hundred strong, had crossed from Calhoun that morning to the southern side of the river at Rumsey. This news, quickly communicated among the men, exhilarated them perceptibly, notwithstanding the fatigues of their long march; and with one impulse the whole command moved ahead, at an accelerated gait, which was soon increased to a gallop under the inspiration of the kind greetings and hearty cheers of many of the women of the country, from their houses by the roadside. Pushing on, in this spirit, several miles, before reaching the small village of Sacramento, the column was met by a beautiful girl, riding rapidly, her features glowing with excitement, her fallen tresses swayed by the air, who reported that, returning from the village ahead, she had been obliged to pass through the Federal column, which was but a very short distance in front.* The road, as before said, was very rough and heavy, a gentle

---

* This was a Miss Morehead of the neighborhood. Deeply sympathizing with the cause of her section, and excited by the scene, waving her hat in the air, she urged the Confederates to "hurry up;" and rode back at a gallop

rain having been falling for the twenty-four hours preceding; but the Confederates dashed onward so rapidly that in a little while the rear-guard of the Federal force was overtaken by the Confederate advance, one mile from Sacramento. Apparently in doubt as to the character of the latter, the former had halted for some moments. This doubt, however, was speedily solved, as Colonel Forrest, taking a Maynard rifle from the hands of one of his men, fired at their ranks as a sort of gauge or challenge to battle. At this, they retired hurriedly upon their main force, which, ascending through a lane to a wooded ridge close by, drew up in line just along its brow, at right angles to the road, evidently ready to contest the further advance of the Confederates. Their position was highly advantageous and sheltered; but, as soon as Forrest had assembled a sufficient force—about 150 men*—to satisfy him, he, too, pushed onward through the lane. The enemy opened a sharp fire, but the Confederates moved up steadily, only returning the fire when within less than seventy-five yards of their adversary, who, giving some indication of a disposition to retire, Colonel Forrest ordered his men to fall back, with the hope of drawing the Federals after him. In this he was successful, for they quickly advanced, as if aiming to turn his left flank. Just then the remainder of the Confederates reached the scene; dismounting a portion of his men, armed with Sharp's carbines and Sharp's and Maynard's rifles, Forrest also directed flank diversions, under Major Kelly and Lieutenant-Colonel Starnes, on their right and left

---

for several hundred yards by the side of Colonel Forrest, before she was induced to return. Such was the spirit which animated so many of the Southern women.

* The command had become somewhat scattered, having marched over thirty miles that day, at least ten of which had been at a canter or full gallop.

respectively, while he, with the mounted men, bore down directly upon the centre.   This was done with an animating shout, and all possible spirit and resolution, but in face of a sharp fire, under which the brave Captain Merriwether, the Confederate guide of the expedition, fell, shot with two balls through the head, by the side of the commander.   Seeing the movement upon their flanks, despite the zealous efforts of a few gallant officers, the Federals could not be made to stand the brunt of the Confederate charge, but broke in the utmost disorder at such speed through Sacramento that, though hotly pursued by Forrest and his mounted detachment for some time, only occasional discharges could be delivered from his shot-guns.   But gaining upon them, Forrest and a number of his best mounted men at last were in the thick of a stream of panic-struck fugitives, many of whom, having thrown away their arms and accoutrements, depended solely upon the speed of their horses for further safety, deaf, in their dismay, to all demands for their surrender.*   On sped the Federals, and on followed their Confederate adversaries, with the rage of a first battle fierce upon them.   And the road was soon, and for several miles, thickly dotted with the wounded and slain—a number of whom had been cut down by the sabres of the untrained but heavy-handed Confederates who followed Forrest that winter afternoon.   For three miles beyond Sacramento this bloody pursuit was continued—its course, howbeit, marked by a hand-to-hand conflict between the Confederate leader and two Federal officers and a private, whom he overtook and engaged, his excited horse having carried him somewhat in advance of any of his men.   Shooting the trooper, whose ball had passed through his collar, Forrest was assaulted

* An eye-witness relates that apparently no heed was given by the terrified fugitives to the repeated demands of surrender and offers of safety made them. They seemed only to look for security in flight.

simultaneously by the two officers with their sabres; but, eluding the full force of their thrusts by bending his body suddenly forward, their sword-points only touched his shoulder. Carried a few paces ahead by the impetus of his horse, checking and drawing which aside in time to shoot one of his opponents* as he came up, he thrust his sabre-point into the other,† who, by this time, was in his front. Ordering his wounded opponents to surrender, they still made show of battle, obliging him to run his sabre through one, (Captain Bacon,) and disable the other (Captain Davis) by a heavy blow on the sword-arm. Both these officers, now gravely wounded, fell from their horses, which, riderless, coming in sharp collision at full speed, knocked each other over at the bottom of a short, abrupt hillock, where, a moment after, Forrest, eagerly resuming the head of the pursuit, also came in contact with them, and horse and rider were thrown prone to the earth, he falling headlong some twenty feet in advance of the heap of horses that had wrought his downfall.‡ Some of the enemy who chanced to be still behind, now dashing on, in their reckless flight, likewise encountering the fallen horses, too much exhausted to rise, were also overthrown in quick succession, and added to the floundering mass of fallen horses and men, and the latter were taken prisoners. The main force of the fleeing Federals being out of sight, and their camp and other troops not being more than three or four miles distant, further pursuit was abandoned.§

---

* Captain Bacon.

† Captain Davis.

‡ These particulars are furnished by MS. notes of Lieutenant-Colonel Kelly.

§ Major Kelly, in notes written soon after the occurrence, thus depicts Colonel Forrest as he appeared in this combat and chase of Sacramento : " It was the first time I had seen the Colonel in the face of the enemy, and, when he rode up to me in the thick of the action, I could scarcely believe him to be the man I had known for several months. His face flushed till it bore a striking resemblance to a painted Indian warrior's, and his eyes, usually mild in

Colonel Starnes likewise was greatly distinguished in this affair for his personal courage; and another individual combat deserves notice as showing the spirit which animated these raw Southern soldiers in their first battle, fresh from their civil avocations, and untrained in the imminent deadly perils of war. Private W. H. Terry,* of Lieutenant-Colonel Starnes's detachment, riding with his commanding officer, after conspicuous gallantry, while engaged single-handed with a Federal trooper whom he was hammering with his exhausted rifle, was run through the heart by Captain Davis; and thus fell one of the most daring members of the command.

Nor must we omit another incident of this field, personal to Colonel Forrest. Among those whom he had felled to the earth in the pursuit, there happened to be a man from Greenville, who, being found afterward severely though not dangerously wounded, was carefully carried back with the Confederate command, and delivered to his wife on his parole.*

The fighting and pursuit being at an end, the Confederate commander set his men about collecting the wounded, including Captains Bacon and Davis, who were removed as soon as possible to the nearest farm-houses, and turned over to be nursed by the inhabitants; to whom, also, was assigned the duty of giving proper burial to the dead, which was faithfully done. The Federal loss in this encounter was comparatively very severe. Sixty-five were found dead on the ground,

---

their expression, were blazing with the intense glare of a panther's springing upon its prey. In fact, he looked as little like the Forrest of our mess-table as the storm of December resembles the quiet of June."

* Of Captain McLemore's Company, Williamson county, Tennessee.

† His name was Williams. Passing through Greenville, on a subsequent expedition, Forrest called and inquired after his prisoner, when the wife and children of Williams displayed so much genuine feeling and gratitude for his course that, as he emerged from the house, he was seen to wipe a visible tear from his eye.—*MS. Notes of Colonel Kelly and Major J. P. Strange.*

including two captains and three subalterns ; also seventeen wounded, some mortally ; and some eighteen were captured. A number of wounded must have made their escape.

The affair gave great satisfaction to the Confederates engaged, and had an admirable effect upon the *morale* as well as the physical training of the command.

Returning leisurely to Hopkinsville, and reporting his operations, Forrest and his men resumed their position in camp, with its routine duties, for several weeks, or until about the 10th of January, 1862, when General Clark again threw him forward on the road toward Calhoun *via* Greenville, to observe in that quarter the movements of the enemy, supposed to be concentrating for an early advance upon Bowling Green. Assured by the recollections of the combat at Sacramento, the Confederate cavalry commander led his now confident men very close to the Federal forces on Green river, and carefully reconnoitered their position, thus ascertaining that, not less than ten thousand strong, they were evidently on the point of an early forward movement. Reporting these facts to his superior at Hopkinsville, by a dispatch he was ordered to return, burning the bridges on Pond river, a tributary of Green river ; and this was duly executed.

The several weeks ensuing were unmarked by adventure, though detachments from the command were actively employed, from time to time, scouring the country in advance of that outpost ; and its commander improved the time in giving attention to its interior administration and organization, in which he was exacting of all subordinates, especially of his staff officers, from whom he required a ceaseless attention to the wants of both men and horses.

Under orders from headquarters, in view of threatening Federal movements, both from the direction of Cairo, up the Tennessee river, and from Louisville, General Clark evacuated Hopkinsville, on or about the 7th of February ; and in this movement the cavalry under Lieutenant-Colonel Forrest covered the rear as far as Clarksville, where he was detached, and ordered to report with his own force to Brigadier-General Pillow, from whom he received orders to repair at once to Fort Donelson, on the west bank of the Cumberland river, and for the attack of which a large Federal force was then assembling. Reaching the vicinity on Sunday, the 9th of February, the regiment was not ferried across the river, however, to the fort side until the next day. As the senior cavalry officer, he was immediately assigned to the command of all the cavalry present; that is, his own ten companies, Lieutenant-Colonel Gantt's battalion of Tennesseeans, and Captains Huey's, Wilcox's, and Williams's Kentucky companies—in all not more than eight hundred troopers.

A camp was then selected rearward of the intrenched lines; forage was drawn and the horses were feeding when orders came from General Pillow to move out at once upon and observe the road toward Fort Henry, only ten or twelve miles distant on the Tennessee river, and which, having fallen into the hands of the Federals on the 6th, had now evidently become the base of formidable impending operations hostile to Fort Donelson. Scarcely had Forrest advanced three miles, pursuant to his orders, when he encountered suddenly a squadron of Federal cavalry, evidently the escort of staff officers making a reconnoissance. This detachment, dismounted as the Confederates appeared, quickly springing to their horses, made off precipitately to the rear, eagerly pursued by Forrest to the immediate vicinity of Fort Henry, with a running discharge of fire-arms all the way, resulting in the loss to the Federals of several killed and wounded, a prisoner, some twenty stand of arms, and a lot of overcoats and cavalry equipments. In examining the intermediate country, another detachment of Federal cavalry was observed, and an ambush laid to entrap it; but the men as yet had not been

reduced to that subordination essential for the nicer stratagems of the field, and a premature discharge of fire-arms
from some over-eager men upon the advance warned the
enemy in time to withdraw by rapid flight. From all the
movements within the Federal encampments, Colonel Forrest
was satisfied that General Grant was on the eve of moving
against Fort Donelson with all his army ; and this was reported to his superior.

CHAPTER II.

Topographical Sketch of Fort Donelson—Construction of a larger System of Exterior Lines upon the Fall of Fort Henry—Concentration of Reën-forcements and Arrival of Generals B. R. Johnson, Buckner, and Floyd—March of two Federal Divisions from Fort Henry—Forrest's Skirmish on 12th February—Disposition of Confederates—Offensive Arrangement of Federal Force—Baffled Assault on Heiman's Position on the 13th February; also on Confederate Right—Obstinate Conflict between Gunboats and Water-Batteries, afternoon of 14th—Confidence inspired among Confederates by their Success—Council of Confederate Generals, and Determination to sally and attack Federals on Morning of 15th—Resolute and Successful Sortie made by Pillow's Division at Daybreak—Buckner delays his Movements until after nine A.M.—Brilliant Charge upon and Capture of Battery by Forrest's Regiment—McClernand's and Wallace's Divisions driven westward of Wynn's Ferry Road by two P.M., and Confederate Left uncovered—Pillow withdraws Confederates from the Field—Council of War, Night of 15th, and Determination to capitulate—Forrest urges possibility of Escape, and ultimately is allowed to make the Attempt with his Command—Discovered by a Personal Reconnoissance that Enemy had not reinvested the Left—Effected egress of Command without molestation—Commentaries.

THE operations embracing the attack upon and surrender of Fort Donelson, in February, 1862, are so closely connected with the military career of General Forrest that we are obliged not only to relate the part which he and his immediate command bore in that ill-fated affair, but must adventure upon a detailed sketch of the investment, the attack, and the defense of the position, together with such observations, from a military point of sight, as have seemed fit and proper in regard to one of the most import&nt events of the war.

The position immediately occupied by the Confederate troops rested on the Cumberland river on the north. Westwardly, it was limited by a deep ravine, with precipitate sides, through which meandered a considerable creek, swollen at the time by backwater from the river. A valley and backwater slough separated it on the east from the county-town of Dover; and a line of rifle-pits, with positions for field-guns, formed its exterior southward boundary, along the crest of the ridge, about twelve hundred yards distant from the river's edge. A field-work of an irregular bastioned *trace*, fronting southward, surmounted a plateau which rose about one hundred feet above the level of the water, in which direction it commanded and protected, at close musket-range, the water-batteries that were established so as to sweep the river approach, which, by an abrupt turn in the course of the stream at that point, is almost due north. Unfortunately for the Confederates, this work was commanded by a chain of ridges southward, and by an eminence between it and Dover, where the Confederate hospitals and depots were situated. It was necessary, therefore, to enlarge the intrenched area considerably, so as to encompass and hold those otherwise menacing positions. This led to the construction of a new series of intrenchments, fully three miles in scope, along the irregular ridges indicated, and including a space divided into two parts by the valley and backwater westward of Dover, the communications between which were so difficult as to add materially to the perplexities of the defense.

The ground in front or southward, and environing these lines, is a rugged, undulating upland, densely wooded, covered with undergrowth, and broken into ridges by deep, narrow ravines, with a general direction perpendicular to the river. Unfavorable for the free movement and maneuver of troops, especially artillery and cavalry, it afforded, however, excellent cover for sharp-shooters, and strong positions for field-batteries, once established there. The declivity, directly southward of the field-work, was thickly spread with *abatis*, which, being now inclosed within the new line of infantry *épaulements*, were not only useless, but an absolute hinderance to the operations of the Confederates within their exterior intrenchments.

At the time Fort Henry fell, not more than one third of these outer works had been thrown up. An experienced military engineer, Major J. F. Gilmer, was at hand, however, to lay them out and superintend their erection.* Meanwhile, on the 7th, Brigadier-General Bushrod R. Johnson, also an officer of military education and experience, had likewise reached and assumed command of the place. And, on the 9th, Brigadier-General Pillow, coming upon the scene, brought to bear upon the works under construction the natural energy of his character. Much delay, however, was inevitable, in consequence of the scanty supply of tools. Nevertheless, by the night of the 12th the water-batteries had been greatly strengthened ; and the infantry cover placed in a fair defensive condition, though somewhat vulnerable in the valley and ravines. The heavy guns available had also been mounted in the water-batteries, giving an armament of one ten-inch Columbiad, (128-pounder,) one rifled 32-pounder, (64-pound bolt,) eight 32-pounders, and three 32-pound carronades.

In the *interim* reënforcements had been gathered thither from different quarters. Brigadier-General Buckner, regarded as one of the most accomplished officers of either service, came with one division of these new troops, and was assigned

---

* Major Gilmer was Chief-Engineer on the staff of General Sidney Johnston, and subsequently became Chief-Engineer of the Confederate Army. He is a graduate of West-Point ; and at the time of the secession of his State, North-Carolina, was an officer of repute in the corps of Military Engineers U. S. A.

to the command of the right wing or flank of the defenses, while Johnson was placed in charge of the left. And, finally, at daylight, on the 13th, General Floyd arrived with two small additional brigades, making the total Confederate force of all arms assembled somewhat over fourteen thousand men*.

Two divisions of the Federal army, on the 12th, had been thrown forward, by two roads, from Fort Henry toward Fort Donelson. These were McClernand's, of eleven regiments of infantry, and one or two regiments of cavalry, and at least four field-batteries ; and C. F. Smith's, also of eleven regiments of infantry, including Birge's sharp-shooters, and four or five field-batteries—in all about fifteen thousand men.† At the same time six regiments were dispatched by water,

---

* At the time of the attack on Fort Henry, the garrison at Fort Donelson consisted of some artillery detachments and two or three regiments of infantry, under Colonel J. W. Head. This was reënforced on the night of the 6th by two thousand six hundred men, brought by Colonel Heiman from Fort Henry ; and later by Buckner and Floyd's commands, so that on the 13th the force concentrated included the following regiments, batteries, and companies, namely, the Third, Tenth, Eighteenth, Twenty-sixth, Thirtieth, Thirty-second, Forty-first, Forty-second, Forty-eighth, Forty-ninth, Fiftieth, and Fifty-third Tennessee, with an average rank and file of five hundred each ; and Colmes's battalion of five companies ; the First, Third, Fourth, Fourteenth, Twentieth, and Twenty-sixth Mississippi regiments, with an average strength of four hundred and sixty-five effectives ; the

Second and Eighth Kentucky, Seventh Texas, Fifteenth Arkansas, Twenty-seventh Alabama, and Thirty-sixth, Fiftieth, Fifty-first, and Fifty-sixth Virginia, with an average of three hundred and seventy-five effectives ; and several small battalions ; or, in all, thirteen thousand infantry ; Forrest's regiment of cavalry, Lieutenant-Colonel Gantt's battalion of five companies, three Kentucky companies, and Porter's and Maney's Tennessee, Graves's Kentucky, and Jackson's, French's and Lucas's Virginia batteries. The heavy guns were manned by details from infantry regiments.

† McClernand's division was constituted of Oglesby's brigade of the Eighth, Eighteenth, Twenty-ninth, Thirtieth, and Thirty-first Illinois volunteers, Swartz's and Dresser's batteries, and Stewart's, Dollin's, O'Harnett's, and Carmichael's (companies of) cavalry ;

while seven more, known to be *en route,** were ordered to proceed at once from Paducah, on their transports, to the scene of operations on the Cumberland. These thirteen regiments constituted a third division, nearly ten thousand strong, under command of General Lew Wallace.†

The weather being mild for the season and highly favorable, the land column reached the vicinity of the theatre of war early in the afternoon of the day of its departure from Fort Henry. Meanwhile, Forrest, who had been sent forward with his whole cavalry in observation, encountered the Federal advance-guard about two miles from the Confederate intrenchments. Promptly dismounting his men, he formed a line of battle along the crest of a ridge obliquely across the

---

W. H. L. Wallace's brigade of Eleventh, Twentieth, Forty-fifth, and Forty-eighth infantry, Fourth Illinois Cavalry, and Taylor's and McAllister's batteries ; and of McArthur's demi-brigade of the Seventeenth and Forty-ninth Illinois. C. F. Smith's division was formed of Cook's brigade of Seventh and Fiftieth Illinois, Twelfth Iowa, Fifty-second Indiana, and Thirteenth Missouri regiments, and of Lauman's brigade of Second, Seventh, and Fourteenth Iowa, and Twenty-fifth and Fifty-sixth Indiana regiments, and, as previously said, Birge's sharp-shooters, acting independently. [*See official reports of General Grant, and Colonels Wallace, Lauman, etc., etc., and correspondence of New-York Times and Missouri Democrat. Rebellion Record*, Vol. IV., *Doc.* 46, pp. 138 to 182.] The New-York *Times* correspondent estimates this column at twenty thousand, in round numbers, with fifteen to seventeen batteries, and twelve to fifteen hundred cavalry ; and the St. Louis *Democrat* places the number at eighteen thousand. General Grant, however, fixes his strength at fifteen thousand ; this would give an average to his regiments of six hundred and fifty, which they scarcely exceeded.

* Drawn, we infer, from General Buell's "Army of the Ohio." [*See his letter to General Halleck, March* 14*th,* 1862, *embodied in a paper published in New-York, April* 18*th,* 1866.

† These troops were the Eleventh, Thirty-first, and Forty-fourth Indiana, Seventeenth and Twenty-fifth Kentucky, Forty-sixth, Fifty-seventh, and Fifty-eighth Illinois, Fifty-eighth, Sixty-eighth, and Seventy-sixth Ohio, First Nebraska and Eighth Missouri regiments of infantry.

road, to command which specially he placed May's and Hambrick's companies of his own regiment, armed with Maynard rifles. In front of his centre was a narrow vale of cleared land, through which the enemy must advance ; and, accordingly, as this was attempted, he opened with a lively *fusilade*, which led to an immediate halt, and soon a retrograde movement to a neighboring ridge, along which a little later a detour and advance by another road were attempted, with an evident purpose to turn his left. Observing this, his force was quickly redisposed to confront and check that movement, while May's and Hambrick's companies, remounting, made a gallant charge down the road upon some Federal cavalry, driving them back upon the infantry. And soon after, Major Kelly, with three squadrons, making a vigorous advance from the centre, resolutely engaged a large infantry force in that quarter. For several hours was this maintained, with the effect of keeping the whole Federal column in hesitation and check, until about three o'clock P.M., when General Buckner, in command during the temporary absence of General Pillow, directed Colonel Forrest to return behind the intrenchments. The Federal column was then pushed forward without further resistance, and, deploying along the ridges, in proximity to the Confederate lines, their sharp-shooters, about dusk, drove in a working party engaged in planting *abatis* in front of Johnson's line, in the quarter of the Wynn's Ferry road, killing one, wounding one, and capturing another of his men outside of the trenches. And by the morning of the 13th they had completely invested the position, McClernand's Division occupying the extreme right — Confederate left — and C. F. Smith's holding the left—Confederate right. Batteries had also been established, without opposition, in the night upon salient eminences along the Federal lines, at points highly favorable for annoying the Confederates, and a regiment of sharp-shooters,* a picked corps, had taken up an advanced position, from which it began early, from easy range and well sheltered, to give excessive disturbance to the Confederates at work on their intrenchments. But General Pillow, calling on Colonel Forrest for May's and Hambrick's companies, with their rifles, these were led to the trenches, accompanied by their Colonel, and matched with the Federal riflemen in an animated, effective skirmish for about an hour, in which the latter suffered so sharply as to compel them to withdraw from the conflict for several hours.†

In the mean time the Confederates had not rested inactive, but labored in the trenches throughout the night of the 12th with very much their whole force, General Bushrod Johnson and Colonel Forrest, as an example and stimulant, sharing in the work with their men. Every possible disposition was made for the most efficient defense. Buckner, as before said, commanding on the right, had under him the Second Kentucky, (Hanson,) Fourteenth Mississippi, (Major Doss,) and Third, (Brown,) Eighteenth, (Palmer,) Thirty-second, (Cook,) and Forty-first (Farquharson) Tennessee regiments, some 3588 men, and Porter's and Graves's batteries, each of six pieces. Heiman, on the right of Johnson's wing, held the salient and nearly central position of the Confederate line—a hill separated by broad ravines on the right from Buckner, and on the left from Drake's Brigade of Johnson's command— with a brigade formed of the Tenth, Thirtieth, Forty-eighth, and Fifty-third Tennessee and Twenty-seventh Alabama,

---

* Birge's Regiment, which was armed with choice, long-range rifles and uniformed in *gray*.

† When in the trenches on this occasion, Colonel Forrest, observing a small portion of a sharp-shooter exposed in the top of a tree six hundred yards distant, took a rifle from one of his men, and, in another instant, firing, brought him headlong to the ground.—*Major Strange's MS. Notes.*

with Maney's Battery; and on his left were posted, in succession, the Fourth Mississippi, Fifteenth Arkansas, a small
battalion of Alabama troops, another of Tennessee infantry,
the Fifty-first Virginia, Third Mississippi, Eighth Kentucky
Regiment, Seventh Texas, Fifty-sixth Virginia, and First and
Twenty-sixth Mississippi regiments; with the Forty-second
and Twenty-sixth Tennessee, Twentieth Mississippi, and
Thirty-sixth and Fiftieth Virginia regiments held in reserve
at different points in rear of the lines, with French's, Green's,
and Grey's batteries, disposed at suitable intervals. At the
same time, two regiments, the Forty-ninth and Fiftieth Tennessee, formed the garrison of the field-work near the river.

Between eleven o'clock A.M. and twelve M. on the 13th,
during a warm artillery practice from many of the Federal
batteries along their whole line, a dashing assault on the salient of Heiman's position, occupied by the right wing companies of the Fifty-third Tennessee, was made by four regiments
of McClernand's Division.* The left of the attacking force
advanced along a ridge obstructed by *abatis*, but the right
made the assault handsomely up the hill. Repulsed in their
first effort, the Federals were rallied and brought forward
with great nerve to the charge, but to be again driven back
with much loss. Federal officers on horseback urged their
men up to within fifty yards of the breastworks, while a number of the Confederates, mounting the parapets, would take
deliberate aim, fire, and jump down, reload, and again deliver
their fire in the same manner. The brunt of this attack was
borne by the left of the Tenth Tennessee, Lieutenant-Colonel
McGavock, the Fifty-third Tennessee, Lieutenant-Colonel
Winston, and the right of the Forty-eighth Tennessee, (Voor-

---

* Namely, Seventeenth, Forty-fifth, Hayne.—*Reb. Rec.* IV. Doc. 46, *Official*
Forty-eighth, and Forty-ninth Illinois *Reports of Colonels Hayne and Wallace.*
regiments, under command of Colonel

hies,) and Captain Maney's Battery ; and during the second assault, the Forty-second Tennessee, Colonel Quarles, shared in the perils, the losses, and the glory of the repulse. An important and distinguished part is justly to be ascribed to Maney and his men, who handled their pieces, greatly exposed, with equal skill and courage, losing Lieutenants Burns and Massey, slain, and so many of their number were either killed or disabled that only enough were left to man one section of the battery after the action.* Graves's Battery, on the left of Buckner's position, also brought to bear very effectively upon the Federal storming party, contributed to the general result. While this attack was going on in the centre, another was attempted, with more spirit than judgment, by a demi-brigade of Smith's Division on the Federal left, but it was easily repelled, with some casualties to the assailants. Meanwhile, too, the only gunboat—an iron-clad, the Caron-delet—that had yet arrived, steaming up within range, had opened a fierce cannonade upon the water-batteries, throwing about one hundred and fifty shot and shells. She then drew off, discomfited and damaged by a one hundred and twenty-eight pound bolt in her engine-room.

The weather, for several days unusually mild and pleasant for the season, in the afternoon of the 13th changed suddenly and radically. It began to snow, which later turned into a sleet, and, during the night, a keen north wind made the cold so excessive that both sides suffered acutely, especially the Confederates, who continued to strengthen their incomplete intrenchments without intermission.

That night the Federal reënforcements, *en route* by water, reached the landing near their left flank, and, disembarking, were put in motion by midday on the 14th, to take position on

---

* MS. Notes furnished by General B. R. Johnson, dated November 25th, 1866.

the line of investment between Smith's and McClernand's divisions, which was accomplished by nightfall.*

In the mean time, however, about three P.M., the Federal fleet which had convoyed these reënforcements to their place of debarkation made a prolonged and truly formidable attack upon the water-batteries, testing their defensive value to the utmost. Two wooden and four iron-clad gunboats were engaged, and these last, at one phase of the action, were brought up within three hundred yards, or, as it were, into the very teeth of their antagonist batteries.† The cannonade was appalling, yet the conflict was bravely maintained on both sides. The Confederates, wholly unpracticed as artillerists, and more exposed than their adversaries, fought with ordnance very much inferior in weight of metal, with two exceptions, as in all other respects, to those employed against them, a battery of twelve of the heaviest guns at a broadside. For thirty minutes the battle raged at these close quarters, when the iron-clads succumbed, and one by one dropped out of action, badly crippled and worsted in the encounter, with a heavy loss in killed and wounded.

At this juncture, as the flag-ship, the St. Louis, disabled by a crushing shot in her wheel, began to drift back before the current, a feeling of intense anxiety filled the hearts of

---

* Official Report of General Wallace, *Reb. Rec.* IV., Doc. 46. Also correspondence, *ibid.*, of New-York *Times*, etc.

† The "iron-clads" were the St. Louis, Louisville, Pittsburg, and Carondelet, each of thirteen guns of the heaviest calibre. The wooden vessels were the Tyler and Lexington, of nine guns each, equally as heavy as those on the iron-clads. The latter had an armor of rabbeted iron plates, two and a half inches thick, upon sloping walls of thick timber, making strong casemates All were built and armed alike, with three nine or ten-inch guns in the bow, four heavy guns on each side, and two lighter pieces in the stern. The armament of the Carondelet, for example, we find included *three* nine-inch, *four* eight-inch, smooth-bores, and *two* one hundred pounder rifled guns. *Vide* Boynton's *History of the Navy during the Rebellion.*

the Confederate officers and men, and the apprehension was
fast forcing its way into and chilling their souls that the new-
fashioned armor of their redoubtable foes had indeed been
made impenetrable. Their heavy projectiles, hurtling through
the air, tore up the parapets of the water-batteries in great,
gaping fissures, almost burying the guns beneath the mass of
earth dislodged. For thirty perilous minutes it seemed inevitable that the Confederate batteries must prove altogether
overmatched by adversaries fighting from behind an impregnable shelter; and, as a consequence, the garrison, taken un-
avoidably in reverse, in a short while would be exposed to an
insupportable fire from the rear. And already numerous
shells, thrown with ease from the wooden gunboats at long
range in all directions, were falling and exploding with a continuous din in the valleys and on the ridges occupied by the
Confederates, though so far without harm to men or animals.
Nevertheless, the Confederate artillerists, standing to their
guns, worked them with astonishing intrepidity and skill
under the circumstances, coolly throwing back the unsettled
earth with their shovels as fast as it incommoded the service
of their pieces. Such, too, was the interest of the garrison in
this conflict that all whose duties did not call them to posts
in the trenches were eagerly watching its progress, heedless
of exposure to themselves. Among these was Colonel Forrest himself.* Taking a position near to the principal battery, with profound solicitude he observed the spectacle so
novel at the time in its character to him, and was the first to
dispatch tidings of the happy issue to General Floyd. Grown
deeply fearful previously of disaster, the reaction wrought by
the triumph of the batteries was broad-spread, and many who
had witnessed the scene, sinking spontaneously to their

---

* His command, meanwhile, was   ready for action, in a valley on the left,
drawn up, standing by their horses,   near the intrenchments.

knees, gave utterance to devout thanks to their Heavenly Father for the result. The heartiest cheers and shouts from the great body of the men resounded from one end of the line to the other as fast as the good news spread. The effect on the *morale* of officers and men was electrical, and all were inspired with the highest hopes of ultimate success.*

---

* In the face of his own statement of the heavy armament of these vessels— eight and nine-inch smooth-bores and one hundred pounder rifles—the *Reverend* Mr. Boynton, in his *quasi*-official history of the navy, is *careless* enough to allege that the superiority in weight of metal and number of guns was with the Confederates. He and other *Federal* chroniclers have asserted that these vessels only used their bow-guns. Assuredly this is inaccurate, for they were forced up close enough (three hundred yards) to use their broadside, and we are satisfied did so ; that is, twenty-eight guns, either eight or nine-inch smooth-bores or one hundred pounder rifled pieces. In the Confederate water-batteries there were but thirteen pieces, eight of which were thirty-two pounder smooth-bores, and three thirty-two pounder carronades, leaving really but the ten-inch columbiad (one hundred and twenty-eight pound bolt) and a rifled thirty-two effective against the armor. Hence, granting that only the bow-guns were used — that is, twelve eight or nine-inch (smooth) and one hundred pounder rifled—still the superiority was greatly with the naval ordnance ; for, while they threw at least nine hundred pounds of metal at a broadside, the Confederate batteries alto-gether could throw but four hundred and forty-eight pounds, of which, in fact, only one hundred and ninety-two pounds were effective and did the damage inflicted. That in such a conflict thirty-two pounders were valueless Mr. Boynton *knew*, for, at pages 291–2, in connection with a discussion of the proper armament for a ship, he says so virtually. He would intimate likewise that there was an advantage on the part of the Confederates in having "land-batteries." In so far as they had a somewhat plunging fire, there was an advantage, but one partially neutralized by the sloping sides of the gunboats. At sea, batteries afloat, of course, tossed and unsteadied by the waves, are at a disadvantage, but not so on a river. But the reverend historian chooses to ignore the fact that, while the Confederate batteries were open, the Federal guns were fought in casemates of a character that, (page 519,) when he is speaking of the energy with which these vessels were built by their constructor, he declared were "*a good defense against such guns as were mostly found in the rebel works of the West,*" but which dwindled down into "light armor" when (page 530) he comes to palliate their defeat. Only heavy, solid shot were of any worth against the vessels ; grape, shell,

Before this occurrence, on that morning, a council of general officers had met. In view of large Federal reënforcements for the reduction of the position, it had been determined to make a sally that afternoon upon the Federal right flank with the Confederate left wing, under General Pillow, and attempt to reopen communications with Nashville and an outlet for retreat, while to General Buckner was assigned the duty of covering that retreat with his division when attempted. Accordingly, the troops of Johnson's Division and Forrest's Cavalry had been disposed for such an operation, and were held for some time in expectation of orders to begin it. But instead, General Pillow, becoming indisposed to essay the movement that afternoon, procured a countermand of the order from General Floyd, and the several regiments were remanded to their respective positions.*

Friday night, soon after dark, another council of war was called. Generals Floyd, Pillow, and Buckner were present, and apparently all the brigade and regimental commanders. All now saw that, completely invested and cut off from reënforcements, the Confederates must either break through the

---

and canister were the most effective missiles against the Confederate batteries at certain stages in the fight at the short range reached. Other Federal historians have treated this affair in the same disingenuous manner, and it is not reputable, if not purblind, to write history in this fashion.

* Both Generals Floyd and Pillow omit all mention of this arranged plan of attack, but General Buckner is specific upon the point. Colonel Forrest, in his report, likewise states that it was ordered, and his men and the infantry moved out of the intrenchments, "but, after maneuvering a short time and some sharp-shooting between the cavalry and the enemy, were ordered back." Colonel Baldwin also states that on the 14th General Pillow directed the "left wing to be formed in the open ground to the left and rear of our position in the lines, for the purpose apparently of attacking the enemy's right;" that his brigade had been advanced about a quarter of a mile with that object, when General Pillow countermanded the movement, saying it was "too late in the day to accomplish any thing." And this is further corroborated by Major Brown, of the Twentieth Mississippi.

well-set toils of the enemy or resign themselves to the fate of ultimate surrender, as the Federals could be reënforced at pleasure from abounding resources. It was, therefore, unanimously decided to make, at the first streak of daylight on the following morning, a resolute, in sooth desperate, sortie upon the enemy's right wing, McClernand's Division, with the purpose of sweeping it aside and back behind the Wynn's Ferry road upon the other wing, so that the road to Nashville by way of Charlotte should be left open.

Pillow was to lead in the inauguration of this operation, with General B. R. Johnson as his second in command, and was to move out of the trenches with the whole force on the Confederate left flank, (including the cavalry,) except Heiman's Brigade* and the garrison of the field-work,† in all some seven regiments. Heiman's regiments were to be retained in their position, except the Thirtieth Tennessee, Colonel Head ; that was to repair to and occupy the trenches belonging to Buckner, who was then to proceed to the Confederate left, and likewise advance thence, in aid of Pillow, upon the enemy along and leftward of the Wynn's Ferry road. And this plan of operations seems to have been fully understood by all the subordinates who were to execute it. Colonel Forrest having already made himself well acquainted with the surrounding country, important parts in the drama were assigned to him and his command.

After another bitterly cold night, by which the men were greatly harassed, at four o'clock Saturday morning, 15th, the hour appointed for the formation of Pillow's attacking column, Forrest had promptly taken his designated position on the extreme Confederate left, south-eastward of Dover. Detach-

---

* Tenth, Thirtieth, Forty-second, Forty-eighth, and Fifty-third Tennessee, and Twenty-seventh Alabama volunteers.

† Forty-ninth and Fiftieth Tennessee.

ing Overton's Company to reconnoitre, the enemy were found, already formed in battle order, not more than five hundred yards distant. And, meanwhile, their sharp-shooters or skirmishers, early as it was, had opened a brisk fire along the whole front.

The column assigned to this urgent, paramount work was composed of Forrest's Cavalry, not exceeding eight hundred troopers, Baldwin's, McCausland's, Wharton's, Simonton's, and Drake's brigades of infantry, fourteen regiments, and two small battalions, with an effective total of not more than six thousand five hundred rifles and muskets.*

Some delay ensued in forming the column in consequence of the omission of a brigade commander to communicate the proper orders. Nevertheless, all were in their assigned positions by five A.M., when the operation began, Baldwin's Brigade leading the infantry, and Forrest, somewhat yet in advance, covering the left flank, with a view at the same time to a movement around the extreme Federal right. As reported by Overton, the enemy were found ready for the onset. The rugged character of the ground and abundance of tangled brushwood made the advance tardy, and greatly hindered the deployment of the Confederate regiments as they reached the scene. Especially difficult was it for the cavalry to act with celerity and cohesion, so dense being the undergrowth that the horses could scarcely be made to push their way through.

Baldwin began the action, encountering Oglesby's Brigade

---

* Baldwin's Brigade was formed of Twenty-first and Twenty-fourth Mississippi; McCausland's, of the Thirty-sixth and Fiftieth Virginia and Twentieth Mississippi; Wharton's, of the Fifty-first and Fifty-sixth Virginia; Simonton's, of the First and Third Mississippi, Eighth Kentucky, and Seventh Texas; and Drake's, of the Fourth Mississippi, Fifteenth Arkansas, and Garvin's Alabama and Browder's Tennessee battalions.—*MS. Notes of General B. R. Johnson.*

of McClernand's Division. McCausland's Brigade, coming up on the left, was followed quickly by Simonton, whose regiments were pushed into action, however, between Baldwin and Wharton. The enemy fighting stoutly, the rattle of musketry soon was swollen into a deafening uproar. The Federals gave way, but, quickly reënforced by W. H. L. Wallace's Brigade, increased to six regiments of infantry,* a resolute, prolonged resistance was made. The enemy being now in a favorable position, over seven thousand, strong and well supported by an ample artillery, the combat grew fierce and obstinate. Drake's Confederate Brigade had also become engaged. Both sides unquestionably displayed excellent martial qualities and spirit. The Confederates, though on their first field, pressed forward with the deliberate vigor of veterans, and the Federals met the shock of their onslaught with uncommon steadiness. And so splendid, in fact, was the courage of the assailants, that a Federal chronicler and an eye-witness observes : *" It was only by a bravery that equaled that of the Confederates that they were withstood."* The enemy, howbeit, had to yield the ground, and fall back from ridge to ridge toward their left flank, nearly parallel with the exterior Confederate intrenchments.

While the infantry were thus effectively engaged, Forrest had been moving steadily around the enemy's right until he found he had turned it. Thereupon, changing direction, he swept down upon the Federal flank and rear, just as the combat had become general with the whole of McClernand's Division.

This, at the moment, was a most opportune auxiliary to a charge made by the Confederate infantry. It assisted notably

---

* To wit, Eleventh, Seventeenth, Forty-seventh, Forty-eighth, and Forty-ninth Illinois infantry, with Taylor's and McAllister's batteries, or, at least, 4200 men.

to break the stubborn stand made by the enemy, and forced them again to recede still more to the left or northward. Following up eagerly, he continued the pressure upon the Federal right and rear over some very rough ground and through thickets, until an open field was reached, across which could be seen their flank greatly exposed, as they were falling back in much disorder. Attempting to charge across this field, it proved marshy and impracticable for cavalry. Meanwhile, the enemy had rallied somewhat, and formed a line at the edge of a second field to the front and right, with a flanking relation to the left of the Confederate infantry. Unable to get at their flank, as before said, because of the boggy character of the intermediate ground, Forrest so maneuvered in their front and to their right as apparently to disquiet them, while the infantry made a gallant advance ; and again they gave back, leaving the ground, as previously, thickly strewn with their dead and wounded. There was now, after much steadfast fighting on their side, a good deal of disorder in the Federal ranks, and strong indications of an impending panic, such as so often seizes and in a moment destroys brave armies. Believing that such a crisis was at hand if energetically pressed, Forrest, at the moment in the presence of a superior, General Johnson, requested permission to make a charge upon the disordered masses of the enemy in sight, many of whom, indeed, had halted and hoisted white flags, while other evidences of demoralization were numerous. But General Johnson, apprehensive of an ambush, regarding such an advance at the moment hazardous, withheld his assent,* and

---

* General Forrest is of the belief that this was the critical instant in this battle, which, if it had been vigorously improved, must have resulted in the complete rout of the enemy. And General Lew Wallace, in his official report, admits that about this time the fugitives were crowding back with unmistakable signs of disaster ; and that the cry was prevalent, " We are cut to pieces,"

the enemy retreated in haste out of sight. Shortly after this, moving somewhat westward, with orders from General Johnson to guard the left flank, Forrest came upon a battery just preparing to quit its position, after having several times repulsed the efforts of the infantry to seize it. A narrow ravine separated him from this battery, and fallen timber and thickets concealed its supports. Charging as he delivered a volley, the most of the artillerists who were not disabled fled and left the pieces, six in number, in his hands, as also many of the horses and a number of prisoners, while the ground was thickly spread with dead and wounded, the effects of his charge as also of previous attacks on the position by the infantry.

It was about this phase of the conflict that Wallace's Division was brought up to support McClernand's—that is, thirteen regiments, or about 8500 fresh rifles—thus opposing a Federal force of fully 15,500 men, only diminished by the casualties of the morning, to Pillow's force afield, including Forrest, of about 6500 men, or less than one half of those attacked. For as yet Buckner's Division had not advanced, as had been arranged in the plan of operations for the day, beyond the trenches ; and Pillow's men and Forrest's alone had thus far been engaged, though they had been substantially supported by a fierce and admirably served cannonade from Graves's, Porter's, and Maney's batteries, from three several positions within the intrenchments.

Cruft's Brigade, of four regiments, was first thrown into the vortex of the battle. This was about ten A.M., and Oglesby's Brigade, breaking through his ranks, caused some disorder ; and Cruft's too, like the rest, had to give way before

---

which had for a time a perceptible effect on his own men, so threatening that he was induced to counteract it by a forward movement, — *Reb. Rec.* IV. Doc. 46, p. 141.

the vigor of the Confederate onset, doing so, however, in creditable order to another position, whence, after a handsome
stand, he was likewise forced to retire to another and commanding ridge further leftward. Thus the current of battle
set stronger and stronger against the Federals.* Meanwhile,
Thayer's and Smith's brigades, of the same division, had also
become engaged. Meeting the men of McClernand's Division in retreat, between ten and eleven o'clock A.M., in the
vicinity of Wynn's Ferry road, and rightward of Cruft's, these
fresh brigades, embracing nine regiments, were thrown across
the path of the triumphant Confederates, and by their opportune interposition gave time to McClernand's broken battalions to rally, reform, resupply their exhausted ammunition-
boxes, and resume the struggle.†

Meanwhile, Forrest, after the capture of the battery, as
mentioned, pressing onward, ere long found himself, with his
own regiment, rearward of a Federal force, strongly posted in
a deep road-cut at right angles to the general line of battle.
Opening upon their right flank, he drove them speedily from
this covert and forced an immediate retreat. This was about
eleven A.M., and the battle at the time was raging with intense
heat. The whole Federal right wing had been driven from
its position for quite a mile : many had thrown down their
arms‡ and fled away into ravines and thickets for shelter.
But their main body, however, had receded doggedly from
ridge to ridge in the direction of their left wing and upon
their advancing supports, making repeated spirited efforts to
recover lost ground. Still pushing on, Forrest now effected

---

* These details are gathered from Cruft's Official Report.—*Reb. Rec.* IV. Doc. 46,
pp. 144–5.

† Official Reports of Colonels Thayer and Smith and their subordinates.—*Ibid.*
pp. 155–6.

‡ Nearly five thousand small-arms were picked up after the battle, Saturday
afternoon, by the Confederates.

a junction with the rest of his cavalry, which had been detached, operating conjointly with the infantry ; and, about the same time, he.was addressed by General Pillow, inquiring as to the whereabouts of General Buckner, with the remark that as yet he had heard no sound of battle from the part of the field assigned to that officer. Colonel Forrest, replying that he had been too busy himself to know of the movements of others with whom he had not been coöperating, Pillow exclaimed :

"Well, then, Colonel, what have you been doing since I saw you last ?"

"Obeying orders, General, by protecting your left flank," was the ready rejoinder. And, for witness, Forrest pointed to the captured guns and prisoners, just then happening in sight as they were being sent within the intrenchments. After a few kind words of commendation, the General then galloped away rightward and toward the trenches, saying that he would go and see in person what was going on in that quarter, leaving Forrest with orders to watch the left flank.

Very soon afterward the Fifteenth Arkansas, Colonel Gee, hotly engaged with a greatly superior force, was repulsed in a bold charge upon a Federal position. Seeing this, Forrest rushed up with one of his squadrons into the gap and checked the now advancing enemy. The infantry at once rallied, and, reforming, moved up again with such spirit and signal courage that they drove their lately successful foe from the position. Several of Forrest's best men fell in this affair, and his brother, Lieutenant Jeffrey Forrest, at the head of the squadron, having his horse shot under him, received a painful contusion by the fall, but, nevertheless, kept the field to the last, severely as he suffered.

In the mean time, delayed a little at the outset waiting for Colonel Head and the Thirtieth Tennessee to take the place of his men in the trenches on the right, General Buckner had reached the position rearward of the intrenchments on the left, where they are intersected by the Wynn's Ferry road, and immediately to its left, and which had been vacated by Pillow's men, who were already in deadly but successful grapple with McClernand's Division outside of the intrenchments further leftward. It was from this point that his division, as arranged the night before in council, was to move out and assail the enemy along and to the left of the road just mentioned, as nearly simultaneous with Pillow's attack as possible. The situation of affairs, however, appeared to General Buckner to authorize him to depart radically from the settled plan of operations for the day.* For, instead of launching his division forthwith into the *mêlée* outside, deploying one of his regiments in the rifle-pits and placing the others under cover of the neighboring ridge-crests, he brought Porter's and Graves's batteries to bear upon the enemy in his front in an animated, sustained cannonade.† Until nine o'clock A.M. did

---

* A plan that was of his own suggestion.

† General Buckner, in his Official Report, which we follow strictly in this part of the narrative, states that he had regarded it as "unadvisable to attempt the assault at this time," or until he had to some extent crippled the enemy's batteries by his artillery, "in view of the heavy duty" which he expected his division to undergo in covering the retreat of the army.

Unquestionably, it was highly desirable that this division should be kept fresh and in reserve, if possibly consonant with the assured success of the sortie in which Pillow was engaged. But incontestably, also, the course was fraught with extreme peril to the whole operation of the day, leaving, as it did, Pillow with but 6500 men, embattled with the fearful odds of full 15,000 Federal infantry and a numerous artillery. For were Pillow to be repulsed, of which, under the circumstances, there clearly was a portentous risk, of course the whole affair, the sally itself, would prove abortive; and Buckner's providence of his men, upon which he founds his delay to engage as originally contemplated and arranged, must then have been useless—at the deplorable cost of defeating the operation, upon the success of which rested the only hopes left the Confederates for escape. A graver change of the plan of operations by a subordinate can not well be conceived than this.—*See General Buckner's Official Report*, p. 164, *Official (Confederate) Reports of Battles, Richmond, Va.,* 1862.

he remain thus rearward of the intrenchments, his batteries handled with admirable coolness, vigor, and effect unquestionably upon the enemy, though provoking a furious return fire from their heavy rifled batteries and strong line of infantry skirmishers, under which the Confederate artillerists suffered severely, but endured with a courage that may not be excelled. Between nine and ten A.M., however, at the urgent instance of General Pillow, Buckner threw out the Fourteenth Mississippi, under command of Major Doss, deployed as skirmishers, to carry a battery about three hundred yards distant from the trenches ; and quickly supported the movement by the Third Tennessee, Major Cheairs, and Eighteenth Tennessee, Colonel Palmer, while Pillow personally ordered Colonel Cook, of the same division, to move forward, on the like errand, with the Thirty-second Tennessee.* The ground was broken into ravines and bristling with *abatis* and snow-clad undergrowth ; but, despite these difficulties and a scorching artillery and musketry fire, the movement was executed. Terrible as was the exposure, and though for a while thrown into critical confusion, these regiments pressed onward in emulation of their brethren of Pillow's Division, and speedily obliged their immediate opponents to yield the coveted position. But this entailed a heavy loss, and, notwithstanding the successful issue, under some misapprehension on the part of one of General Buckner's staff-officers, the brigade, Colonel J. C. Brown's, was immediately thereafter ordered back behind the intrenchments from which it had so effectively, though tardily, sallied. General Buckner, however, quickly

---

* Official Reports of Colonel Cook and others engaged. It is difficult to fix the hour satisfactorily of this affair. Cook places it at ten A.M. Harrison says that he did not advance until twelve M., and then on his own responsibility.

sent it forth again, under Colonel Brown, while Porter's, Graves's, and Maney's batteries poured from their guns a concentrated fire, sweeping the face of the ground over which the brigade was to advance. This affair, bravely led and admirably pursued by the men, resulted in the dislodgment of the Federals from two positions in succession, and the capture of a section of artillery, with small loss comparatively, but including that of the brave and accomplished soldier Lieutenant-Colonel W. P. Moore, of the Thirty-second Tennessee, and of the lamented and distinguished Captain Frank M. Rogers,* Fourteenth Mississippi.† The Confederates were now masters of this part of the field, the line of the Wynn's Ferry road, as Pillow's Division was of the remainder of that flank of the recent Federal position.

By the plan of operation for the day, it will be remembered that, in the event of the success of the sortie, Buckner was to remain exterior to the trenches with his division in position on the Wynn's Ferry road, in order to cover the retreat of the whole force, to secure a route for which had been the main object of the attack and battle. But it would seem that an unfortunate disposition to vary or ignore at will the several parts of that plan affected the two superior officers charged with its execution, without regard to the effect upon the object to be attained. And, therefore, it will be seen that General Pillow, wholly overlooking what had been thus deter-

---

* Captain Rogers was an officer in the celebrated " First Mississippi Rifles " in the Mexican War. Subsequently, while still a young man, he was a popular Circuit Judge in Mississippi for several terms. Chivalrous and cultivated, this gallant gentleman was a fair example of the class that filled even subordinate grades in the Confederate service at the outset of the war.

* Lieutenant-Colonel Gordon, of the Third Tennessee, was also severely wounded.

mined, ordered General Buckner's Division, as well as his own, back to their former positions in the trenches.*

Just as Brown's Brigade, Buckner's Division, was becoming engaged for the first time, Pillow, having dispatched an order to Forrest to leave Lieutenant-Colonel Gantt to guard the left flank, while he repaired to the right with the rest of his cavalry, the latter, proceeding to the point indicated, was met by General Pillow, who, pointing to a battery formidably planted at the head of and sweeping a ravine, inquired of Forrest whether or not he could take it, adding that it had baffled several previous attempts. Proud of the superb conduct of his men in the course of the campaign as on that morning, Forrest confidently answered, " I can try ;" and, immediately turning off, drew his men up for the work in an open space, in a column of squadrons. But, as he did so, noticing some infantry in the trenches, rearward, only about four hundred yards distant, he sent an officer to request its support in the charge. This was the regiment of that excellent officer, Colonel Hanson, Second Kentucky, and he promptly advanced to coöperate. At least two regiments supported the Federal battery. May's company being in advance, the order to charge up the ravine was given, with instructions for the first and second companies of the squadrons severally to deploy to the right and left as they advanced. Right courageously and well were these orders executed. It was almost a desperate venture ; but this thought checked the pace of none of that brave-hearted band as they pressed onward, receiving in their breasts an appalling volley from artillery and riflemen. Hanson followed with equal ardor and eagerness, but withholding the fire of his men, and determined to depend on their bayonets.

---

* *Vide* Reports of Generals Buckner and Pillow and MS. Notes of General Johnson.

Turning with his squadrons upon the battery, Forrest charged it, leaving Hanson to engage the infantry. About the battery a hand-to-hand struggle ensued for a few moments. The Federals stood their ground manfully and fought obstinately. Sabres, pistols, and carbines were lavishly used, with much cost of life and wounds on both sides. It was here that Captain May, after displaying the highest martial qualities and a cool and splendid valor, fell, shot through the heart.* As

---

* Charles May was born in Buckingham county, Virginia, in 1818, of highly respectable parentage, whose families had long resided in that vicinity. Of his early life little is known, further than that he received what is called a good English education at home, where he remained till he was seventeen, when he moved to Richmond, and became a merchant's clerk. Thus employed two or three years, or until about 1838, he removed to North-Mississippi, and established himself at the town of "Commerce," at that time the county-seat of Tunica county. There, rapidly winning the confidence of his fellow-citizens, he was successively chosen to fill the most responsible offices of the county, including that of Representative in the Legislature and Sheriff. His urbanity, integrity, and intelligence, combined with uncommon firmness and a knightly courage, gained Charles May friends and influence wheresoever he was known. For a number of years he was also an active planter, when finally he determined to remove to Memphis. Resigning the shrievalty, he took up his residence in that city about the year 1854, and at once engaged in the livery business, to which he was attached very much by his love of fine horses, and which he conducted with success and a marked regard for commercial probity and honor down to the breaking out of the war in the spring of 1861.

Soon after the fall of Fort Sumter, Mr. May entered Captain Charles McDonald's company of " Independent Dragoons," and, at its organization, was elected junior second lieutenant. He served with this company during the term of its enlistment, a period of sixty days, mainly in the vicinity of New-Madrid. At that time several gentlemen were engaged in Memphis in the effort to raise a company of cavalry for " Forrest's Regiment." After collecting volunteers sufficient to organize a company, Lieutenant May was unanimously chosen captain ; and the company, in compliment to Colonel Forrest, was named the " Forrest Rangers." Captain May immediately began to drill and prepare his command for active service. Thus engaged up to the 25th of October, 1861, he then took up the line of march, with his own and three other companies, to Fort Donelson. There he renewed his attention to the drill and discipline of his men,

many as fifty of the Federal dead lay immediately around the pieces taken. And so sanguinary was this affair, it is credibly related that, at one spot, the feet of the horses splashed in the blood of the slain and wounded, flowing along the surface of the snow until it froze. No more gallant charge than this, indeed, can be found in the annals of war; and all bore themselves worthily, officers and men alike. A section of artillery and about seventy-five men were taken, and some horses; whilst a little later and further on, another gun with hospital tents and ambulances were also captured, with about sixty Confederate prisoners recovered.

Forrest's horse, in the course of the morning, had received as many as seven wounds, but, being an animal of rare vigor and spirit, had, notwithstanding, borne up under its rider until now, when it fell exhausted from loss of blood.*

Hanson, as before said, had assailed the infantry supports of the battery, while Forrest charged the latter. His adversary being sheltered in timber and thick undergrowth, he lost some fifty of his men as advancing at quick time, and closing to within fifty yards without the discharge of a gun. He then

----

thus insuring that efficiency which they subsequently displayed in so many hard-fought battles, and in none more conspicuously than that which a few months later illustrated their last drill-ground at Fort Donelson — with the highest phases of a manly courage, the fame of which was heightened by that crowning act of gallantry just recounted, which closed Captain May's brief career, and left his companions-in-arms a memory they " would not willingly let die."

After he fell, this lamented officer's body was immediately forwarded to Nashville, and thence for burial to Memphis, whose citizens received the remains of their gallant townsman with distinguished honors, and bore them to their last resting-place in the quiet shades of Elmwood, followed by one of the largest funeral processions ever witnessed in that city. In person, Captain May was a little above the medium height, straight as an arrow, rather slender, but well knit, lithe, and agile; blue-eyed, light-haired, and of gentle features.

* Forrest's overcoat had no less than fifteen marks of bullets in it.

opened a destructive fire, when they broke and·abandoned the position in great disorder. Graves's battery was then brought up, and Hanson prepared to occupy and hold the point in accordance with the general plan of arrangements for the day ; but he also was now remanded to the trenches by General Pillow.

In the mean time, mounting a captured horse, Forrest had resumed his place with his cavalry, now some half a mile ahead of the infantry ; and, riding in advance with two troopers to reconnoitre, he discovered the Federals near by, in occupation of a ridge four hundred yards distant, across the Wynn's Ferry road. Wheeling, he dashed down a ravine, drawing the fire of a whole regiment, and his horse was wounded in the thigh. Instructing Major Kelly to repair to the right to ascertain the posture of affairs in that direction, he rode his wounded horse slowly back toward the trenches ; but, as he surmounted a ridge exposed to a Federal battery, a solid shot, passing through his horse just in rear of his legs, grazing his pantaloons, covered his feet with blood, and for a moment left his limbs benumbed. Now, once more afoot, he made his way back to where the last battery had been captured, at which place he found assembled several companies of his regiment. This was about 2 P.M., and shortly after General Pillow, coming up, instructed him to employ his men in collecting the captured artillery and small-arms, and removing the Confederate wounded from the field. Thus occupied until about dark, as many as five thousand stands of small-arms and a large quantity of blankets and knapsacks were gleaned.*

About the same time that Forrest and Hanson carried the last battery and dispersed its supports across the Wynn's Ferry road, Pillow's whole division, reaching the scene, took

---

* Two hundred prisoners also had been taken during the day.

part in the subsequent and closing operations of the day, Johnson striking the road in question with Drake's Brigade, the left of the division. At that time there were no Federals, except the dead and wounded, eastward of that road ; nor nearer westward than on a ridge some four or five hundred yards distant, where a battery in position with infantry supports could be plainly seen separated from the line of the road by a deep, cleared ravine. Riding rightward, Johnson found that there were no other Confederate troops between Drake's and the breastworks. Some had gone in for shelter under the stress of the recent severe fighting, *but the main force by, order of superior officers.* He then sent an aid-de-camp to ask for reënforcements ; but instead of these came an order to retire within the intrenchments. Johnson, however, repairing in person thither, suggested a continuation of the battle, by a general advance from the breastworks ; it was then decided, after some discussion between Generals Floyd, Pillow, and Johnson, that Drake's Brigade might remain exterior to the trenches, while the other troops should be established within the rifle-pits. But a little later, after Drake had repulsed a feeble attempt to dislodge him, his brigade also was again ordered in. And no Confederates now remained on the field except those engaged, as previously mentioned, collecting the spoils of war, and the wounded and burial-parties.

Meanwhile, about the time that Buckner's Division had begun to return to the trenches, Lauman's Brigade of C. F. Smith's Division, led by that distinguished soldier in person,*

---

* General C. F. Smith was one of the most accomplished officers of the United States Regular Army. Graduating at West-Point in 1825, he was a captain in the army and commandant of that school when General Grant entered it as a cadet. He had been the tactical instructor and disciplinarian of the greater part of the most distinguished officers on both sides during the war, and had won signal distinction also as a soldier in the war with Mexico. His subordinate position at this time was one of the strangest anomalies of the war.

and a battalion of sharp-shooters, in all some three thousand two hundred rifles, made a well-conceived diversion on the extreme Confederate right flank—a line of three quarters of a mile—which was occupied at the time, as will be recollected, by Head's Thirtieth Regiment Tennessee infantry, about four hundred and fifty strong.* The point immediately assailed was held, however, by only three companies under Major Turner, whose conduct may be fitly measured by the fact that the two regiments leading the assailing column (Second Iowa and Twenty-fifth Indiana) lost three hundred and thirteen rank and file.† Overwhelmed by the force opposed, Major Turner coolly withdrew his intrepid men across a ravine to a commanding eminence, and renewed the fight until reënforced by the Forty-ninth and a battalion of the Fiftieth Tennessee, withdrawn from the field-work by Colonel Head in the emergency. The Forty-second Tennessee, Colonel Quarles, was also detached by Colonel Heiman at a "double-quick," through freezing mud and snow, and reached the scene in time to coöperate effectively in checking the progress of the enemy beyond *the mere narrow foothold seized on the extreme right of the trenches.* This was about four P.M., or near dark ; and by that time the whole Confederate force had resumed their several positions, after a day of as signal and brilliant valor as ever illustrated or was thrown away upon any battle-field.‡

---

* Head's official report; also Lauman's.

† See Colonel Lauman's official report of casualties.—*Reb. Rec.* IV. Doc. 46.

‡ As evidence of the heavy loss inflicted on the Federals on Saturday, it may be mentioned that on Monday, the 17th, Captain L. D. Waddell, of Company E, Eleventh Regiment Illinois volunteers, wrote to his father in New-York that only one hundred and sixteen men of his regiment remained uninjured ; and of the eighty-five composing his own company only seven came out. "The most wholesale slaughter," says the Captain, "that ever was heard of."

Conspicuous among the bravest of the Confederates on this occasion were the officers and men of the several batteries of field artillery, Porter's, Maney's, and Graves's companies exciting the admiration of the whole army by their efficiency, their coolness, and their shining conduct. It was said of Porter's guns that they were always fired at the "right time and to the right place." Porter, shot through the thigh by a Minié-ball, as he was carried bleeding from the field, exclaimed to the only unwounded officer left with his battery, Lieutenant John W. Morton, a mere lad of nineteen : "Don't let them have the guns, Morton !" And we are told that that beardless youth handled them with a courage and intelligence which emulated the example of his accomplished Captain.* Nor were the batteries of Captains Guy, French, and Green less admirably and effectively handled and fought.

Forrest, having executed his orders last mentioned, led his men at dark back to their encampment, where he advised them to seek all possible repose, so that they might be ready to play their part in the operations of the next day, which he confidently anticipated would be successfully momentous for his countrymen, inasmuch as the investing force had been driven aside from the entire front of the Confederate left flank, as fully as the most sanguine had anticipated. This opinion of the results of the day was not confined to Forrest and his men. In the whole division, mainly engaged, it was thoroughly shared. And, as a corollary, Johnson, under orders from his superior, about midnight, drew that division out and massed it—now including Heiman's strong brigade—in column of regiments, in the same position as on Saturday

---

* Captain Porter was an officer of the United States Navy up to the breaking out of the war. (See Index.)

morning, to make another sortie, with a view, if opposed, to cut his way through to Nashville.

In the mean time, however, a council of war had been assembled by General Floyd, at Pillow's headquarters, to attend which Forrest had been roused from his slumbers between eleven and twelve o'clock Saturday night. Generals Pillow, Buckner, and the other superior officers, except Johnson, were present ; and, to Forrest's amazement, he found them, as he entered, discussing the subject of surrender, with the idea predominant that the Federals had already reoccupied the positions taken from them that morning. Forrest, immediately expressing his earnest disbelief of this assumption, represented that the battle-field had been widely examined as late as nine o'clock that night by reliable men, who reported that they had seen no traces of the presence of any hostile force ; and he offered to send out two other trusty scouts to obtain further and conclusive information upon this vital point.* This being assented to, the scouts were dispatched, and, returning in an hour, reported that they could find no Federals on the Randolph Foundry road, except the wounded, and possibly some few stragglers searching for the killed and wounded. The night was extremely cold ; and the smouldering fires on the battle-field had been rekindled by the freezing wounded, which, seen by previous scouts, were mistaken for the new fires of a heavy force. This information, however, was not received as conclusive against the preconceived supposition that the investment had been reëstablished, a conclusion in which those in chief command were immutably fixed, though Colonel Forrest continued to urge his conviction that the whole force could be safely withdrawn by the

---

* Namely, Adam R. Johnson, subsequently a Confederate general officer ; and S. H. Martin, who became lieutenant-colonel of a Kentucky regiment. Two gentlemen of peculiar gifts for the service in question.

road reported as unobstructed, and though he earnestly invoked full credence of the reports of his scouts.*

General Floyd, the senior, expressed himself satisfied the place was no longer tenable, and escape for the main force impracticable ; but that circumstances peculiarly personal to himself determined him not to surrender, for that he would rather die than become a prisoner. General Pillow likewise asseverated his preference individually for death rather than capture, and hence his utter unwillingness to surrender the army. General Buckner, next in rank, remarking that at such a crisis personal considerations should have no influence with an officer, expressed his own purpose to abide by the fortunes of the troops ; and, if the command devolved upon him, to take upon himself the responsibilities of the capitulation. That step he conceived to be inexorably necessary in view of the fact that any effort to cut their way out as matters stood, he insisted, would inevitably result in the sacrifice of at least *three fourths* of the troops, a sacrifice utterly unjustifiable. That his men were so worn out by exposure, by watching and fatigue, and so reduced in numbers and demoralized, he could not hold his position half an hour against the assault which he was satisfied would be made next morning at daylight. That his ammunition was nearly expended ; and the men, for several days without regular or sufficient food, were not in condition to undertake such a battle and march as would be involved by a successful sortie. And, therefore, regarding delivery as hopeless, any attempt toward that aim were sure to result in a fruitless massacre.†

General Pillow unquestionably did not regard the situation

---

* This is the positive assertion of General Forrest, confirmed, as he alleges, by his subsequent personal reconnoissance of the ground.

† General Buckner's official report, dated Richmond, August 11th, 1862. It is but fair to General Buckner to append here the views of a participant in

as nearly so desperate, and favored an effort to withdraw the garrison. But assuredly he yielded his judgment at the supreme crisis to that of his junior, to whom he passed the command when it was devolved upon him by the abdication of General Floyd, their common senior. That junior, with the soldierly decision due to his conviction and his views of the situation, made immediate preparations for opening the necessary communications with General Grant, preliminary to a surrender ; and gave the necessary notice to General Johnson, then absent with the column preparing to make the sortie.

Meanwhile, Colonel Forrest, hearing the decision with keen dissatisfaction, expressed to General Buckner his utter indisposition to surrender, since he was thoroughly convinced he could readily carry his command in safety to the headquarters

---

the operations at Fort Donelson, which appeared soon after in one of the Memphis newspapers :

" The *surrender* was admitted by all to be a military necessity. The troops had been four days and nights in the trenches, exposed to the cold, with but little fire ; their feet were frosted from standing in the cold water and mud in the bottom of the ditches ; they had received no regular rations, and had not had time, from being closely confined to the works, to prepare more than one meal a day ; they were thoroughly exhausted. I saw many sleeping while standing in place at ordered arms, just before entering the battle Saturday morning. The exhausting effects of the battle on Saturday, and another sleepless night in the cold, damp trenches, must be added to their weakened state of that morning. To

have attempted to have cut our way through the enemy's lines with but ten thousand men in this condition, having fifty thousand opposed to us—twelve thousand of whom were fresh troops— [two assumptions we have shown to be totally unfounded] would simply have resulted in the loss of three fourths of the entire command. . . . I can safely say, from having walked a part of the way myself, that no portions of the force could have marched ten miles without being completely exhausted and disabled. The question of surrender resolved itself into just this : Shall the remnant of this gallant little army, after defeating the enemy in three of the hardest fought battles in our country's history, and covering itself with glory, be sacrificed to avoid the humiliation of a surrender ?"

of General Sidney Johnston. He further declared he had promised the parents of many of his young men to protect them when in his power to do so. Growing excited, indeed, as he spoke, he asseverated he would prefer that the bones of his men should bleach on the surrounding hills rather than they should be carried to the North and cooped up in open prison-pens during midwinter.

General Pillow, at this, suggested that Forrest should be suffered to attempt to escape. This was sanctioned, on express condition, however, that he should do so before the flag of truce had communicated with the enemy, and, upon this conclusion, Forrest hastened to his encampment to execute the movement.

Sending for his field and company officers, he announced, in brief terms, the situation and his own fixed purpose. Resolved not to surrender himself, he declared that he would lead forth all who desired to accompany him, and then inquired how many would make the attempt. The answer was unanimous that they would follow him to the last. Orders were issued accordingly for an immediate movement. Major Kelly was dispatched to communicate the state of affairs to Lieutenant-Colonel Gantt, who was not present. The cavalry encampment was soon alive with drowsy troopers, roused at first with difficulty from their profound slumber after four days and nights of sleepless, fatiguing service. As soon as made fully aware, however, of the exigency, an intense eagerness to be in saddle and *en route* took the place of that sluggish mood in which they were found at the outset ; and little time was lost, notwithstanding the habitual confusion attending night movements. When the time for departure was at hand, as Colonel Gantt had not made his appearance at the place of rendezvous, Major Kelly was again sent to hasten or insure the movement of that battalion.

About four o'clock Sunday morning, Forrest was ready

with the main part of his men to begin their critical adventure, and took the road through Dover, where he ascertained
General Pillow, whom he had expected to escort, had already
crossed the river fully an hour before.

About five hundred officers and men formed the column
that now followed Forrest upon the road by way of Cumberland
City.   Sending forward a subaltern and three men to reconnoitre, after an advance of three fourths of a mile they returned with the intelligence that they had seen the enemy in
line of battle moving around and across their proposed road.
Another "scout" was ordered, but no one appeared willing to
volunteer for it.   Thereupon, turning the command over to
Major Kelly, Forrest announced his intention to make a reconnoissance himself, and, if killed, the Major would then do the
best he could, but *must, in the mean while,* advance along the
road upon which they had set out.   Calling for his brother,
Lieutenant Jeffrey Forrest, they rode to the point from which
it had been reported the enemy were seen.   There, scanning
closely and listening attentively, nothing was to be seen or
heard of any hostile presence.   Then advancing, the supposed Federal battle array was speedily resolved into a line
of fencing, formidably staked with short rails into somewhat
the resemblance of a line of infantry in the dim light and
gray atmosphere of that early hour.   And, it may be safely
asserted, it was this very fence which had been seen and mistaken for the enemy by the scouts whose reports had had
such untoward weight in producing the capitulation.*   Colonel Forrest and his brother, after this important discovery,
rode ahead up the ridge to the rightward for three fourths of a
mile, to the place where the fight had commenced the morning before, and there found the blankets which his men had
left on going into action.   Riding a little further, they came

------

* This is General Forrest's conviction.

upon fires, around which were gathered a number of wounded Federals, who, in reply to inquiries, satisfied them that none but a few scattering scouts from both sides had been among them that night. This had been the scene, near the extreme Federal right, of severe fighting early Saturday ; the Federals had occupied it Friday night, and their fires, left burning, had been kept alive by the wounded, driven to the exertion through suffering from the extreme cold.

Thus assured that the road was still open, Forrest and his brother returned to the command, that meanwhile had continued on the road to the crossing of the creek eastward of Dover. In view of what he had ascertained in regard to the falsity of the reported presence of the enemy in their old position, he would have felt it his duty to announce the facts to General Buckner ; but this he deemed now useless, inasmuch as he knew that already all the steps for a surrender had been taken, and it were therefore altogether too late to recede from it.

The creek, expanded by backwater to a breadth of about one hundred yards, looked formidable ; lined with ice, it was also supposed to be *swimming*. Calling for some one to ride in and test this question, no one came forward promptly enough, and their commander, with the characteristic self-reliant spirit of the born leader, dashed through the ice as their pioneer, just as but lately he had been their scout. Passing entirely across, the water proved not deeper than to the saddle-skirts. Elated at this happy occurrence, the whole command now moved speedily and joyously over, and took up the line of march for Cumberland City at a slow pace, with all proper precautions of advance and rear-guards, scouts and flankers ; the men, however, much of the time were forced to dismount and walk to keep from freezing.*

* Captain Gould's Company of ment, and was surrendered. Why it
Texans failed to accompany this move- did not come out was never explained

General Floyd, having turned over the command, as before said, to General Buckner, stipulated that he might take with him his three Virginia regiments, and this, it remains to relate, he effected.

When it was announced to the rest of the forces that they were to be surrendered, they evinced much surprise, especially those of the left wing, for they did not feel they had been vanquished! General B. R. Johnson, who subsequently witnessed all the prolonged trials and hardships of the illustrious "Army of Northern Virginia" in the trenches at Petersburg, says that "the fatigue, cold, and privation endured by the men" at Fort Donelson "were equal to any thing I have known; but there was no repining," except, indeed, at the hard fate of a capitulation after so splendid and successful fighting as had signalized them the day before—a capitulation to men whom they had clearly beaten, notwithstanding the odds of two to one.

For the details of that sad conclusion to these operations, we have now no space in these pages, beyond the statement that it does not appear that more than 9500 officers and men were actually surrendered into the hands of the Federal commander as prisoners of war; the remainder had either fallen in the course of the struggle or made their escape.

COMMENTARIES.

I. Whenever the critical historian shall take up and relate

---

*o its commander. Lieutenant-Colonel Gantt subsequently explained that he had misunderstood the place of rendezvous, and had promptly repaired with his battalion to the place he supposed. A portion of Forrest's Regiment, overlooked in rousing the men, followed after sunrise, *without interruption.* It will be seen from the foregoing narrative that the popular idea that Forrest and his men "cut their way out" of Fort Donelson through the Federal lines is wholly unfounded or a war myth. It is also an error in certain official reports that Captain Overton's Company of Forrest's Regiment remained. That officer did, but his company came out.

the campaign ending in the reduction of Fort Henry and capitulation of Fort Donelson, he must necessarily consider whether both might not have been easily averted and the Federal forces overwhelmed by resources which the Confederates had within easy reach by rail. A glance at the map will show any reader that the Confederates had the interior lines, so potential in war. At Columbus, Ky., there were about fifteen thousand infantry, and at Bowling Green as many more after Floyd, Pillow, and Buckner had been sent to Fort Donelson ; and there was railroad communication, with a large equipage of rolling stock, between each position and the Tennessee river, not far above Fort Henry, as also a number of steamers on that stream, so that the work of transportation had been unusually easy. Moreover, Buell being afield, the early evacuation of Bowling Green was a foregone conclusion, and the transfer of the force there to Fort Henry placed them in the most advantageous position to cover Nashville against ulterior operations. As it was, Grant, landing with a petty force of fifteen thousand in the very centre of a force of nearly forty-five thousand, having the interior lines for concentration and communication, by railway at that, was able to take two heavy fortifications in detail, and place *hors de combat* nearly fifteen thousand of his enemy. But with this matter, at present, we have nothing further to do than to indicate the questions that must arise and be solved.

II. Having permitted Fort Henry to fall, and with it suffered the loss of the Tennessee river, by an unpardonable adherence to the *defensive-passive*, the Confederate authorities committed another egregious, mortal error in persisting in that baleful policy of the *defensive-passive* subsequently on the appearance of Grant before Fort Donelson on the afternoon of the 12th of February, with only two divisions, or fifteen thousand men. By daylight next morning, 13th, all the Confederate reënforcements it had been determined to throw into that work, as was known to its commander, had reached the scene. Hence the Confederates were stronger then than they would be at any subsequent period of the defense, and in better condition to fight successfully. On the other hand, every day would assuredly increase the numbers of the enemy. That is, delay insured a daily material diminution of the strength of the Confederates by ordinary wear and tear ; a heavy increase of offensive power on the Federal side, and the inevitable loss of the whole Confederate army! The *defensive-active*, therefore, manifestly should have been adopted on the 13th. Then every man but the heavy artillery in Fort Donelson should have been thrown upon Grant *en masse*, for only one of the Federal gunboats had reached the vicinity on the night of the 13th. But instead of this, the Confederate generals waited two whole days, and until Wallace reënforced Grant with thirteen fresh regiments, and then determined upon and took the offensive. But even then, as planned in council, an unnecessary number of regiments were left inactive in the work during the sortie.

III. After it was determined that the forces at Fort Donelson should not be further reënforced from Bowling Green than by the small divisions of Buckner and Floyd, and that no troops could be drawn from Columbus, Ky., surely it was a fatal error to attempt to hold Fort Donelson and thus expose so many fighting men to be beleaguered, with the absolute certainty that an overwhelming force would be concentrated upon them. Far better lose the position than to sacrifice, at that time, fourteen thousand men. Whether considered in a moral or military point of view, scarcely á greater blunder was ever committed in war affairs.

IV. In regard to the reinvestment by the Federals on the night of the 15th, unfortunately assumed to be so by Generals Floyd, Pillow, and Buckner, aside from the evidence of Forrest's scouts and General Forrest's own personal reconnoissance on the morning of the 16th, the Federal official reports, though asserting that the reinvestment took place, contain abundant evidence that they bivouacked west or north of the Wynn's Ferry road, leaving the Confederate left almost entirely open. General Wallace says expressly that at five o'clock he was ordered by Colonel Webster, Federal Chief of Staff, to withdraw, "as a new plan of operations was in contemplation ;" but that he disobeyed the order and retained his position, which, from his description of it and his proximity next morning at the time the white flags were discovered, was evidently in the vicinity of Wynn's Ferry road and in front of the centre of the Confederate lines. (See *Reb. Rec.* IV. Doc. 46, p. 147.) This, too, is more plain by the statement of Colonel Thayer, one of Wallace's brigade commanders, that he encamped on the "road," which could only have been the Wynn's Ferry road. (*Ibid.* p. 156.) Colonel Wallace, McClernand's Division, says that his brigade was taken to the rear and encamped in position convenient for support of either wing, and that he marched thence "down valley (next morning) into centre of enemy's works." (*Ibid.* p. 151.)

V. The sources of the failure to make the attack of the Confederates thoroughly successful and decisive on Saturday are obviously these :

1. Deviation on the part of General Buckner from the plan of operations which in council he had had the sound judgment to ·advise, and 'by which it was prescribed that he should throw himself with his division upon the enemy along and leftward of the Wynn's Ferry road, as nearly simultaneous with the attack made by Pillow as practicable. Had he done so, Lew Wallace, finding employment in that quarter, would have been hindered from taking any part in the combat with Pillow's forces. And McClernand's Division, beaten back as they were before the impetuous onslaught of the Confederates, assuredly would have disordered and demoralized Wallace's men while assailed in front by Buckner. Thus a disastrous rout must have befallen the two divisions beyond the ability of Smith to counteract.

2. The deviation of Pillow subsequently from the settled order of the day was likewise mischievous ; that is, in the event of such a success as was actually achieved, Buckner was to remain exterior to the works. Pillow, however, ordered him back to his position within those works.

VI. It is true General Smith effected a lodgment within the Confederate lines on the extreme right, but the position acquired did not give an enfilading fire, as has been generally alleged. For, from the nature of the ground, a stronger ridge was now occupied in that quarter that enabled the Confederates to reëstablish a new, strong line connecting with the old one, acting as a *traverse* and defilading the leftward intrenchments.

VII. The Federals were beaten so badly by Pillow, Johnson, and Forrest's attack, that there is no doubt they had no expectation of a surrender ensuing from that day's work. So beaten, in fact, were they, that, as General Lew Wallace says, he was informed by General Grant's Chief of Staff "a new plan of operations" had been arranged.

CHAPTER III.

Alarm of People in consequence of actual Disaster and exaggerated Reports—Conduct of a State Senator—Panic in a Confederate Cavalry Regiment near Charlotte—Forrest's Regiment fed by the Munificence of a Tennesseean—Reached Nashville February 18th, with about 500 Men—General Johnston, quitting Nashville, directed Forrest to report to General Floyd, who left Colonel Forrest in Command—Found place abandoned by Staff-Officers—Warehouses full of Supplies and Ordnance Stores—Spoliation by a Mob of Men and Women—Supplies removed to the Railroad—Removal by Rail of six hundred Boxes of Clothing, quarter of a million Pounds of Bacon, and forty Wagon-Loads of Ammunition—Final Evacuation of Nashville by Confederates—Forrest repaired to Murfreesboro—Regiment reassembled—Field Officers elected—Ordered to Iuka—Confederate Army concentrated at Corinth, General Johnston in Command—Federal Army established at Pittsburg Landing—Buell's en route for same point—Confederate General resolved to take the Offensive—Inauspicious Delay of Twenty-four Hours on the March—The two Armies in presence of each other.

February 16th to April 6th, 1862.

HAVING, as related in the preceding chapter, safely and easily withdrawn the main part of his force from the Confederate lines, Colonel Forrest moved that afternoon about twenty-five miles, in the direction of Charlotte, Dixon county, Tennessee, and encamped. Reaching Charlotte next morning, he found its inhabitants in a state of wild alarm and agitation from a report spread by the State Senator of the District, just from Nashville, that that place was assuredly in possession of the Federals, who likewise had dispatched a column of some ten thousand cavalry thitherward to cut off retreating Confederates. The Senator's horse, white with sweat-foam, gave other evidences of a long, hurried ride, but the Confederate commander was too cool and circumspect to be misled by an incredible story from an evidently panic-stricken civilian. He, therefore, silenced the personage by a stern threat of summary punishment for the circulation of "false intelligence," and sought, as far as possible, to quiet the distress and anxiety of the people by exposing the improbable nature of the rumor. At the same time, he improved the occasion by having a number of his horses shod before resuming his march that afternoon to Nashville.

As a consequence of the evacuation of Bowling Green and the successive disasters at Forts Henry and Donelson, the utmost consternation pervaded the whole region traversed. The roads were alive with invalid and furloughed soldiers, many of whom, having been scattered through the country and in the hospitals north of the Cumberland, were now hurrying southward to avoid capture. This continued stream of fugitives stimulated the degree of apprehension among the country people, until many of them also fled wildly from their homes.

Nor was this disposition to panic confined to non-combatants and the disabled. A regiment of cavalry, subsequently distinguished on many a hard-fought field, happening to be in that vicinage, and having heard of the fall of Fort Donelson, had countermarched at Charlotte, and was moving back toward Nashville, not far in advance of Forrest. When one mile beyond Charlotte, the latter halted, and took the precaution to secure readiness for action by discharging and reloading his fire-arms and redistributing his ammunition. At the sound of the volley and rattling fire that ensued, the neighboring regiment, already cognizant of the Senator's story just mentioned, was suddenly seized with the belief that the musketry was of hostile origin. An instantaneous and irrepressible panic spread and enveloped the whole force. Breaking at first into a trot, a sharp gallop quickly supervened. And before long the road was thickly sprinkled with cooking utensils, provisions, tents, and baggage, thrown from the wagons to lighten and enable them to keep up with the fast-speeding horsemen, until the teamsters finally, apprehensive that even this would not avail, abandoned their wagons also, leaving them broken or hanging against trees along the roadway. Following shortly after, Forrest's men came upon these castaways, and collected almost enough provisions and other supplies to replenish those that had been necessarily left at Fort Donelson, and which, to these fatigued and battle-scorched troopers, were a great windfall.

After this, moving on, Forrest halted for the night some eighteen miles from Nashville, on the Harpeth river, at a point where food and forage were liberally supplied by a gentleman most zealous in his devotion to the Confederate cause, in whose house a sumptuous supper was set for the Colonel and his officers. That night, after their severe work at Fort Donelson, many of his officers were disposed to enjoy the comforts of a bed under this hospitable roof; but Forrest, ever watchful, soon missing them from the encampment, had all roused, and inflexibly required them to remain with their respective companies, the men of which, with horses saddled and arms by their side, slept in the open air on the ground, as a precaution against the possibility of surprise.

Having ascertained definitely by scouts sent out in advance, as he had anticipated, that there was no enemy at Nashville, early on the morning of the 18th he resumed his march toward that city, where he arrived before midday with about five hundred officers and men. Establishing his camp in the suburbs, near the penitentiary, he then repaired to headquarters and reported in person to General Sidney Johnston. The General was at the point of leaving for Murfreesboro, and therefore directed Forrest to report to General Floyd, who was left to remove to the rear all the subsistence and other public property that could be done.*

Reporting as directed without delay, orders were received to employ his command, as soon as practicable, to patrol and guard the interior of the city. So greatly fatigued and fagged were his men, however, that he did not execute this order until the next morning. But, meanwhile, all possible exertions were made to have his animals well shod. Appearing on Thursday morning, the 20th, at headquarters in the city, with his guards and patrol detachments, Forrest found General Floyd about to quit the place, *en route* for Murfreesboro, and orders were given him by that officer to remain until the next afternoon, and then to follow.

Addressing himself actively to his duty, according to his wont, first looking to the question of supplies for his men, Forrest found that all the officers of the quartermasters' and commissary departments, except one,† had left their depots, which were now scenes of spoliation by a ravenous mob of thousands of men and women, including numerous well-dressed people, evidently of the respectable classes of the population. Riding among those thus engaged, he besought

---

* In regard to the orders given General Floyd, we have had access, by the kindness of Colonel E. W. Munford, Aid-de-Camp on staff of General Johnston, of Memphis, to a memorandum in the handwriting of General Johnston, which says : " General Floyd is left in command at Nashville to forward subsistence stores and whatever else of public property he can. He is covered by a heavy battery below town. Has Bowen's Regiment, (infantry,) Mississippi, Alabama, and Tennessee cavalry.

† Patton.

them to desist, so that stores collected and essential for the army should be saved for military purposes, which he felt he would have ample time yet to accomplish before the advent of the enemy, and this he explained to the mob. But the greedy populace were as deaf to his entreaties as heedless of all mild efforts to clear the warehouses of their presence, and he was compelled to employ force. The order accordingly was given to charge with drawn sabres and expel the intruders, and right effectively was it executed. The doors were then closed and barred, and Forrest went elsewhere, to make himself acquainted with the state of affairs. But, soon learning that in his absence the depots had again been broken open and were being pillaged, he returned, and once more tried remonstrance with the marauders, whereupon one of the most active, a stout Irishman, suddenly rushing upon, seized him by the collar, swearing loudly that he and the populace had as much right to the stores as Colonel Forrest or any other person. Not the man to be thus "taken by the beard," Forrest's revolver was quickly brought down in swift contact with the ruffian's head, breaking his hold and sending him howling with pain through the door. And again the depots were cleared and placed under guard of small detachments of his men, and again Forrest left to attend to other duties.

But another and even more persistent effort than before was soon made by the mob to overmaster the guards. A happy thought suggested itself to Forrest—to use the effective but harmless weapon of a steam fire-engine in dispersing the crowd. Therefore, quickly bringing it upon the scene, a powerful stream of ice-cold water was brought to bear upon them. The suddenness and novelty of the attack had an instantaneous effect, and no further trouble was afterward encountered from these incorrigible but baffled depredators.

Trains were now asked for by telegraph. Drays, carts, and

all available wagons were impressed into the service, and set to hauling these stores and a quantity of ammunition from the arsenal to the railroad depot during Thursday, Friday, and Saturday, so that by noon of the latter day he had ready for transportation some six hundred boxes of clothing, two hundred and fifty thousand pounds of bacon, forty wagon-loads of ammunition. And the greater part of these supplies were actually sent off by rail, while more would have followed but for an untoward break on the road caused by a heavy freshet.*

Directing Major Kelly, with the main part of the command, to begin the movement on Murfreesboro Friday afternoon, Forrest remained, with a small detachment, to save, if possible, the remainder of the ammunition. Thus was he occupied through Saturday and until Sunday morning, when the advance of General Buell's column made its appearance, about eleven A.M., in Edgefield, on the opposite bank of the Cumberland. Soon thereafter they were there met by some of the citizens, followed by the mayor, and negotiations for the capitulation of the city were initiated.†

Some of the citizens now brought a request from the mayor to Colonel Forrest to retire. As the last load of ammunition was already *en route* from the arsenal to the depot, and a little later the wagon-train having taken the Columbia turnpike, he also rode away with his little party on the road to Murfrees- boro.

In this affair assuredly were displayed many of the characteristic traits which subsequently, making Forrest so valuable and distinguished, carried him to the grade of Lieutenant-General in the Confederate States service. Cool in the pre-

---

* Some five hundred barrels and tierces of wines and liquors belonging to the Confederate government were destroyed at the railroad depot.

† General Buell did not come up until Monday evening, and the formal surrender took place on Tuesday, the 25th of February, 1862.

sence of confusion, clear in his comprehension of the possible, untiring in his activity and personal energy, ready and afflu- ent in resources to remove or surmount obstacles that would paralyze most men, by the exercise of these qualities on Thursday, Friday, and Saturday he managed to rescue for the use of the army large quantities, as we have shown, of the munitions of war that had been abandoned by those whose special duty it was to remove them. And in this he rendered a service scarcely less in degree than that wrought, with such intelligence, and endurance, and courage, in front of Fort Donelson, and little short even of his escape from its ill-starred precincts with five hundred brave and now trained veteran troopers.

Moving with his accustomed celerity, Colonel Forrest reached Murfreesboro Sunday night, and there rejoined his men, now the objects of general commendation for their ex- ploits during the investment and their subsequent delivery from the hard fate of a surrender after so much admirable conduct. And, in this connection, it were unjust not to say that he had been efficiently served by the mass of his men and was happy in the assistance of many of his officers. Throughout the scenes and events we have sought to sketch, Major Kelly, his second in command, was both a willing and capable soldier, quick and studious in the acquisition of mili- tary knowledge, as also of the highest courage. Of Captain May we have already spoken. Captain Frank Overton, Lieu- tenant Jeffrey E. Forrest, and his Adjutant, Lieutenant Schuy- ler, rendered special aid, while all his officers, indeed, were as zealous as brave in the discharge of their duties.

On the morning of the 23d, reporting to General Sidney Johnston, Colonel Forrest received orders to proceed to Huntsville with his regiment and there refit for duty, with the privilege of giving his men a fortnight's furlough. This indulgence gave the greatest satisfaction. It was attended, moreover, with the best moral effect and an enhanced efficiency; for, at the expiration of their furloughs, all returned with recruited outfits, and not a few with comrades also, secured to swell their ranks and share the reputation already beginning to cluster around " FORREST'S CAVALRY."

II.

It was on the 10th of March that the regiment reassembled at Huntsville. At the same time a new company (D) was added to its line, under Captain Jesse A. Forrest.* Several days later the regiment was ordered to and reached Iuka, Miss., on the 16th, and thence seven miles westward to Burnsville, on the Memphis and Charleston Railroad   There another company (I) was added, under Captain C. N. Schuyler,† its late Adjutant, who had raised it, while on furlough, in Fayette and Hardeman counties, Tennessee.

With ten companies now present, even in the absence of Captain Gould's, which had failed to leave Fort Donelson, an election was held to complete the regimental organization, hitherto omitted in the press of active and urgent service in the presence of the enemy.   Forrest, of course, became Colonel by acclamation, Major Kelly was raised to the grade of Lieutenant-Colonel, and Private R. M. Balch was chosen Major.   Sergeant-Major Strange was then appointed Adjutant in the stead of Lieutenant Schuyler, who, as before mentioned, had become a captain in the regiment.

Nothing of stirring character or moment occurred for the next ten days, which were usefully occupied, however, with drills, and the training of the men in the several duties of a soldier's life, and that routine which, though irksome, adds so

---

* Enrolled at Memphis, with Jesse A. Forrest, Captain, and W. W. Joyce and D. C. Crook as Subalterns.

† C. N. Schuyler, Captain ; W. F. Hancock, G. W. Buckingham, and S. A. Hoague, Subalterns.

much to the efficiency of military bodies. In the mean time, also, the Confederate forces that had abandoned Kentucky and Middle Tennessee were assembled by railroad from Huntsville at Corinth, in North-Mississippi. Major-General Polk's forces, from Columbus, Ky., and West-Tennessee, had likewise been concentrated at the same place, as well as a splendid corps under General Bragg, drawn from Pensacola 'and New-Orleans, with the addition of some newly enrolled Mississippi regiments. This force, at the instance of General Beauregard, was reorganized during the last week of March into three army corps.

The *First*, commanded by Major-General Polk, with an effective aggregate of about ten thousand, was parceled into two divisions, under Major-General Cheatham and Brigadier-General Clarke respectively, of two brigades each.

The *Second*, under Major-General Bragg, was arranged also in two divisions, commanded by Brigadier-Generals Withers and Ruggles, with three brigades each, and an effective force of fifteen thousand.

The *Third*, commanded by Major-General Hardee, was formed of three brigades present at Corinth, and three, under Brigadier-General Breckinridge, holding the line of the Memphis and Charleston Railroad, and numbering about thirteen thousand five hundred effective men.

At the same time, the cavalry had a separate organization, about four thousand five hundred strong, but was indifferently armed for the most part, as well as very recently regimented.

The whole was under the chief command of General Sidney Johnston, with Beauregard, as second in command, specially charged with the preparation of the troops for an impending campaign.

III.

While the Confederates were thus occupied, their adversary had not been dilatory. General Grant, under orders from his superior, had proceeded, with the three divisions engaged in the operations ending in the fall of Fort Donelson, and established himself at a point upon the west bank of the Tennessee river, known as Pittsburg Landing.   Here, too, he had been followed soon by three other divisions of at least the same strength, namely, those commanded by W. T. Sherman, Hurlbut, and Prentiss.* That is to say, the Federal force consisted of six strong divisions, admirably armed and equipped, several regiments of cavalry, and an unusually large number of field batteries of the best description.   Moreover, Buell's Corps, of at least five heavy divisions, was known to be rapidly converging to the same theatre of operations.†

Thus matters stood on the evening of the 2d of April: Two considerable hostile armies had been brought within eighteen miles of each other, with no physical barrier such as a large river or mountain between them.   The one not a little elated by the success achieved at Fort Donelson, the other anxious and impatient to efface the painful emotions caused among their countrymen by that disaster.

That evening, satisfied the time had come to spring upon tne enemy before Buell had effected a junction with Grant, and, if possible, taking the latter by surprise, to crush him before the former had come up, General Beauregard proposed that such an operation should be attempted at once.‡

Weighing with deliberation and great ability the reasons in favor of such an adventure, as well as those that were opposed—which, indeed, were neither few nor light—General Johnston, about eleven o'clock that night, decided to put his

---

* Grant's original objective was the seizure and destruction of the railroad junctions at Corinth.   *Vide* official dispatch of Major-General Halleck to Major-General Buell, U.S.A., dated March 4th, 1862.

† One of these divisions (Mitchell's) was diverted toward Huntsville.

‡ The present writer, the Adjutant-General of the Confederate forces, bore the suggestion from General Beauregard to General Johnston.—T. J.

army in movement the following day, and trust its fortunes to the "iron dice" of battle. Accordingly, the orders to that end, issued at once by his Adjutant-General, were received by his several corps commanders by forty minutes past one on the morning of the 3d of April,* while a reserve was organized, at the same time, of the three brigades under Breckinridge,† to move directly from Burnsville and join the main body at a petty cross-road village called Monterey. And with this last force Forrest was to move.

On the following day, the plan of march and battle, as prescribed in the General Order printed in the Appendix, was discussed and arranged between Generals Johnston and Beauregard.‡

The country to be traversed was thickly wooded, and the way through it was by two or three very narrow roads, which made it a most difficult affair to move such a force and the artillery without confusion and hazardous delay. This process settled, the details were explained orally to Generals Polk, Bragg, and Hardee before midday by General Beauregard, and they were then severally directed to begin the movements at once, as provided for in regard to that day's operations. Nothing could have been more inspiriting or of better presage than the enthusiasm with which the whole army received the order and entered upon the preparation for its execution. By noon, the 3d of April, the whole Confederate army was under arms and ready to begin the march. But from untoward causes the first corps, though ready quite as early as one P.M., did not get in motion so soon as had been expected, and did not *bivouac* as far in advance as was desirable.

---

* That is, to hold their several corps in readiness to move at a moment's notice, with three days' cooked subsistence in their haversacks and two uncooked in wagons, forty rounds of ammunition in cartridge-boxes and sixty rounds in wagons.

† Hardee's Corps.

‡ See Appendix.

Moreover, the badness of the roads, caused by the fall of a very heavy rain the night of the 3d, so retarded the movement that Bragg's Corps was not able to advance the second day further than Monterey, whereas it had been confidently anticipated by the night of the 4th the whole army would have assembled in the vicinity of their antagonist.*

Meanwhile, a force of Confederate cavalry had been pushed up, and somewhat injudiciously though boldly landed in the immediate front of the Federal position. The original purpose was mainly to procure topographical information which hitherto the Confederate Generals had been unable to acquire of that region, and of which, indeed, they could learn nothing definite.† Yet such was the spirit of officers and men, that this movement was made so aggressively that it ought to have warned the Federal General of what was impending ; but, strangely enough, he remained imperturbably indifferent to the plainest signs of the looming tempest.

Instead of being able to attack Saturday morning, as anticipated, General Polk's Corps did not reach the vicinity of the designated point of concentration until quite as late as two o'clock Saturday afternoon, 5th of April. At least one division, if not the whole of Bragg's Corps, was likewise inexplicably tardy in movement on Saturday, though General Johnston, through his staff, had made every effort to get his troops in position for an attack that day. Supremely chagrined that he had been balked in his just expectations, it was evidently now

---

* Nevertheless, it is hard to comprehend or rationally explain how it really happened that Polk's and Bragg's corps were so long in marching the short distance from Corinth to Monterey.

† For the want of staff-officers (Topographical Engineers) to make reconnoissances. They had been applied for and their names designated to the Confederate War Department by General Beauregard in the first week in February, 1862, but were not sent him for sixty days. To the need for such staff-officers with their armies the Confederate War Administration was singularly blind or heedless for at least the first year of the war.

too late for a decisive engagement that afternoon, so General Johnston called his corps and reserve commanders together, and a council was held within less than two miles of Shiloh Chapel, the headquarters of the Federal General Sherman.*

It was now learned that many of the troops had improvidently thrown away or consumed their provisions, and at the end of three days were out of subsistence. General Bragg promised, however, to remedy this from his alleged well-stocked commissariat. But General Beauregard earnestly advised the idea of attacking the enemy should be abandoned, and that the whole force should return to Corinth, inasmuch as it was now scarcely possible they would be able to take the Federals unawares after such delay and the noisy demonstrations which had been made meanwhile. He urged the enemy would be now found formidably intrenched and ready for the attack. That success had depended on the power to assail them unexpectedly, for they were superior in numbers, and in large part had been under fire.† On the other hand, few comparatively of the Confederates had that advantage, while a large part were too raw and recently enrolled to make it proper to venture them in an assault upon breastworks which would now be thrown up.‡ And this unquestionably was the view of almost all present.

General Johnston, having listened with grave attention to the views and opinions advanced, then remarked in substance

---

* The Federal Commander-in-Chief, it appears, had gone that afternoon down the river to Savannah, some twelve miles distant.

† Three of Grant's divisions had been at the taking of Fort Donelson, or at least forty per cent of his whole force.

‡ In this advice, Beauregard had a precedent in the course of at least one illustrious soldier under very similar circumstances. In 1810, Wellington, moving out to attack Massena at Santarem, found the French general unexpectedly on his guard, and his position stronger than he was led to believe. He did not hesitate to withdraw without fighting.

that he recognized the weight of the objections to an attack under the circumstances involved by the unfortunate loss of time on the road. But, nevertheless, he still hoped the enemy was not looking for offensive operations, and that he would yet be able to surprise them. And that, having put his army in motion for a battle, he would venture the hazard.* This decision being announced, the officers rapidly dispersed to their respective posts in high and hopeful spirits, notwithstanding the probabilities that all previous expectations of a surprise would fail of accomplishment.†

---

* Before leaving Corinth, an address to the Confederate troops had been prepared and signed by General Johnston, which was read at the head of each regiment of the several corps on the night of the 4th or 5th of April. This order has always been so grossly misprinted that we shall reproduce a correct version :

HEADQUARTERS ARMY OF THE }
  MISSISSIPPI,   }
CORINTH, April 4, 1862. }

SOLDIERS OF THE ARMY OF THE MISSISSIPPI : I have put you in motion to offer battle to the invaders of your country. With the resolution, and discipline, and valor becoming men fighting, as you are, for all worth living or dying for, you can but march to a decisive victory over the agrarian mercenaries sent to subjugate and despoil you of your liberties, your property, your honor.

Remember the precious stake involved. Remember the dependence of your mothers, your wives, your sisters, and your children on the result. Remember the fair, broad, abounding land, the happy homes that will be desolated by your defeat. The eyes and hopes of eight millions of people rest upon you. You are expected to show yourselves worthy of your lineage, worthy of the women of the South, whose noble devotion in this war has never been exceeded in any time. With such incentives to brave deeds, and with the trust that God is with us, your generals will lead you confidently to the combat, assured of success.

(Signed)   A. S. JOHNSTON,
                        General Commanding.

About the same time another order was prepared and issued by General Beauregard, touching the conduct of the troops in the impending battle, which, republished in Europe, was characterized as a model for such occasions. It, too, was read at the heads of regiments.

† Various melodramatic, imaginary accounts of this council have been published, especially in works of Federal origin. It may, therefore, be well to mention that it actually took place, not as has been described, but about four

Meanwhile, Colonel Forrest, as we have indicated, had marched with Breckinridge as far as Monterey. There he was detached, with orders to picket along and immediately south of Lick creek, and accordingly slept Friday night within three miles of its mouth. During Saturday, having disposed his pickets, there was a good deal of unimportant but lively skirmishing with those of the enemy on the other bank. A company of Federal cavalry having also crossed by the Hamburg road to that place, it was promptly driven back. Leaving his regiment under command of Lieutenant-Colonel Kelly, Forrest, late in the afternoon, rode, with characteristic directness of purpose, to the headquarters of the Commander-in-Chief, to ascertain what was on foot for the next day, and his part in it. Meeting General Johnston, with whom he was a favorite since Fort Donelson, after some general conversation and instructions, the General took occasion to express his strong confidence both in the regiment and its Colonel, and his assurance that they would do their duty more than well in the impending battle. They then parted cordially, to meet no more alive.

P.M., and was held in the open air. All who took part met and stood on foot in the road, surrounded, at a short distance, by a number of staff-officers. They were Generals Johnston and Beauregard, Major-Generals Polk, Bragg, and Hardee, and Brigadier-General Breckinridge. The conference was of short duration, and, immediately after the announcement of the Commanding General's decision, all repaired to their several commands. There was no further conference that night. Even Generals Johnston and Beauregard did not meet again until on their horses as the movement was about to be inaugurated.

CHAPTER IV.

Confederates in Battle Order by Dawn—In Movement, Hardee's Corps in advance—Topographical Sketch of Theatre of Battle—Federal Forces and Dispositions at the moment—Sherman's and Prentiss's Divisions taken completely by surprise—First Federal Line swept away— Their Encampments and Artillery captured—General Gladden killed—All Federal Forces engaged and forced back—Obstinate Fighting, and Death of General Johnston—Federal Position carried, with Loss of Artillery and 3000 Prisoners—Immense Number of Stragglers under the River-Bank—Federals finally driven to the Ridge overhanging Pittsburg—Timely Arrival of fresh Federal Troops at Night—Cessation of Battle—Picket Service of Forrest's Cavalry—Federals take the Offensive—Obstinate Battle until two P.M. 7th of April—Confederates withdraw in admirable Order—Not pursued—Combat of Forrest on the 8th—Severely wounded—Commentaries.

April 1st to June 1st, 1862.

DESPITE the minute precautions urged in the order for the day against all courses calculated to divulge to the enemy

the approaching danger, there had really been little circumspection on the part of the Confederate soldiery, one third of
whom were fresh levies, wholly raw and undisciplined. Fires
had been kindled, drums, too, were lustily beaten in a number
of regiments, and scattering discharges of small-arms had been
kept up all night in most of the brigades, the men being apprehensive that otherwise the charges of their guns, possibly
wet, would fail them when needed. These with other noises
ought to have betrayed to the Federal Generals on the first
line the presence in front of more than a reconnoissance in
force.

By three o'clock Tuesday morning, however, the Confederate army was all astir, and, after a hasty, scanty breakfast,
the lines were formed.

The Third Corps, under Major-General Hardee, 6789, artillery and infantry, augmented by Gladden's Brigade, 2235
strong, of Withers's Division, Second Corps, constituted the
first line, of about 8500 bayonets, deployed in battle order on
the grounds upon which they had bivouacked.*

The second line, five hundred yards rearward, of some
10,000 bayonets, was formed of Ruggles's and two brigades of
Withers's Division of the Second Corps, under Major-General
Bragg.† The artillery of both corps followed their respective
lines by the Pittsburg road.

The First Corps, of not more than 8500 bayonets, under
Major-General Polk, was drawn up in a column of brigades
deployed in line about eight hundred yards to the rear of

---

* Hardee's Corps was subdivided
into Hindman's, Cleburn's, and Wood's
brigades. Effective total of artillery
and infantry of this line was 9024.

† The actual total of this line was

10,731 infantry and artillery. Ruggles's
Division consisted of Anderson's, Gibson's, and Pond's Brigades. The other
brigades, Withers's Division, were
Chalmers's and J. K. Jackson's.

Bragg.* It was subdivided into two divisions of two brigades each,† and, with the special reserve of three brigades under Brigadier-General Breckinridge, about 6000 bayonets, constituted a reserve for the support of the attacking lines as might be needed on either flank.‡

The cavalry, about 4300 strong, was distributed, for the most part, to guard the flanks. With the exception of Forrest's and Wharton's (Eighth Texas) regiments, lately regimented, insufficiently armed, and wholly without drill, the nature of the scene of operations rendered it almost valueless, and only the two regiments mentioned took any material part in the actions of either day.

About sunrise, accompanied by their respective staffs, Generals Johnston and Beauregard met, in their saddles, at the bivouac of the former, near Hardee's line, just about to move forward. It was now near six o'clock, and in a few moments later about 34,000 Confederate infantry, with some fifty guns, were in movement, with a bearing never surpassed, to fall upon their enemy—an enemy as yet undeveloped, but known to be ensconced near at hand in the fog and forest, superior in numbers and equipments, for their many drums the evening before had plainly told their formidable strength.

At first a heavy white mist hung low in the wooded valley between Hardee and the supposed quarter of the enemy, and into it plunged his sturdy men, not knowing nor caring what

---

* Actual total of infantry and artillery was 9136.

† Clark's Division formed of Russell's and A. P. Stewart's brigades, and Cheatham's (a Major-General) of B. R. Johnson's and Stevens's brigades.

‡ Breckinridge's Reserve was composed of Trabue's, Bowen's, and Statham's brigades, with a total infantry and artillery of 6439. We may here say, *en passant*, we vouch for the accuracy with which the returns were compiled from which we have taken the strength of these corps, for they were made with especial care in the office of the present writer, the Adjutant-General of the Confederate Army engaged.

hostile force and appliances lay ready within to receive their onset. To find that force as speedily as possible and overwhelm it was the errand upon which they and their emulous comrades were afield so early.

Here a topographical sketch of the theatre of war may serve to make more readily intelligible the occurrences and vicissitudes of the battle. Two streams, Lick and Owl creeks, taking their rise very near each other, just westward of Monterey, in a ridge which parts the waters that fall into the Mississippi from those which are affluents of the Tennessee, flowing sinuously with a general direction, the latter to the northeast and the former south of east, finally empty into the Tennessee about four miles asunder.* Between these watercourses is embraced an area of undulating table-land, some five miles in depth from the river-bank, from three to five miles broad, and about one hundred feet above the low-water level of the river. Intersected by a labyrinth of ravines, the drainage is into Owl creek, as the land rises highest and ridgelike near Lick creek. Adjoining the river, these ravines, deep and steep, have a water-shed in that direction. Recent heavy rains had filled them all with springs and small streams, making the soil boggy, and hence difficult for artillery for much of their extent. A primeval forest, cumbered with a great deal of undergrowth, covered the region, except a few small farms, of fifty or seventy acres, scattered occasionally here and there. Pittsburg Landing—a warehouse and a house or two by the water's side—lay three miles below the mouth of Lick creek. Two roads leading from Corinth, crossing Lick creek about a mile apart, converge together about two miles from the Landing. Other roads also approach from all directions. One passing Owl creek by a bridge, before its junction

---

* Owl creek does not empty directly into the Tennessee, but into Snake creek.

with Snake creek, branches, the one way trending westward toward Purdy, the other northward toward Crump's Landing, six miles below Pittsburg. Another, nearer the river-bank crossing Snake creek by a bridge, also connects the two points.

Though completely vailed at the moment from the sight of their approaching enemy, it appears a Federal force of five strong divisions occupied the space we have described, and were thus disposed:

Three brigades of Sherman's Division, or nine regiments, supported by eighteen guns and eight companies of cavalry, stood directly across the upper Pittsburg road, facing southward. One of these brigades rested its right at the crossing of Owl creek on the Purdy road, and the other two lay, the one with its right, and the other with its left, near a rustic, log "meeting-house," called Shiloh. There also were established the headquarters of Sherman. In front of this position were a ravine and rivulet, which gave some natural strength if merely held with soldierly circumspection. As these regiments had but lately come from the depots and cantonments of Ohio and Illinois, their ranks were doubtless full, and did not fall short of a total of 7000 infantry, with 18 guns and 450 cavalry.* A fourth brigade of the same division, by an anomalous arrangement, was posted, on the extreme Federal left, at the crossing of the road from Pittsburg to Hamburg, and only about a mile from the former landing.† The space thus left was filled by the division of Prentiss, of some eight or nine regiments, which we assume to have mustered as many

---

* These brigades were McDowell's, of Forty-sixth Ohio, Fortieth Illinois, and Sixth Iowa ; Buckland's, of Forty-eighth, Seventeenth, and Twenty-second Ohio regiments ; and Hildebrand's, of Fifty-third, Fifty-seventh, and Seventy-seventh Ohio regiments.

† This brigade consisted of Fifty-fifth Illinois and Fifty-fourth and Seventieth Ohio, and was at least 2200 strong.

as 6000 bayonets, one third of whom, however, at the moment of attack may have been detached at the landing.* Another division, that of McClernand's, of twelve regiments, ten of which were entitled to wear "Fort Donelson" on their banners, were in supporting distance of Sherman at the confluence of the two Corinth roads. It assuredly did not fall below 7300 men.†

A second line, to the rearward, was composed of Hurlbut's and W. H. L. Wallace's (C. F. Smith's) divisions, the first of which was stretched across the Corinth road, and the other extended to the leftward in the direction of Stuart's Brigade, on Lick creek. Five of Hurlbut's regiments had fought at Fort Donelson. This division, in the studious absence of official data, we may safely set down at 7500 bayonets.‡ Six of Wallace's regiments also had assisted at Fort Donelson, and not less than 7000 effectives did he command. In fine, to recapitulate :

	Regiments.	Men.	Guns
Sherman's Division, ...	12	9,200	18
Prentiss's "	8 or 9	6,000	12
McClernand's "	12	7,300	18
Hurlbut's "	12	7,500	18
Wallace's, W. H. L., Division, . .	12	7,000	18
Minimum Federal Infantry force, ...		37,000	84

---

* The regiments of which this division was formed we can not ascertain with precision.

† Thanks to the correspondent of the *Cincinnati Gazette*, we are able to fix the complete force of this division as follows : Hare's Brigade, Eighth and Eighteenth Illinois, Eleventh and Thirteenth Iowa; Marsh's Brigade, Ele-

venth, Twentieth, Forty-fifth, and Forty-eighth Illinois ; Rait's Brigade, Seventeenth, Twenty-ninth, Forty-third, and Forty-ninth Illinois regiments. The Thirteenth Iowa was 1017 strong, as stated in official report of the Colonel.

‡ It was constituted of the Fourteenth, Fifteenth, Twenty-eighth, Thir-

We find in such official reports as have reached us the names of at least sixteen light batteries present and engaged, also of four or five battalions of light cavalry, which would swell the Federal army, about to be assaulted in their very camps, to 40,000 men of all arms, with not less than 37,000 infantry, full forty per cent of whom were flushed with their recent success at Fort Donelson. Nor was this all; not more than four or five miles from Tecumseh Sherman was Lew Wallace's Division, over 7000 strong and 12 guns.

It is bruited that both Generals Grant and Sherman felt and expressed premonitions of the attack. Indeed, some feeling of that kind may have been in their minds; for the great poet says:

> " By a divine instinct men's minds mistrust
> Ensuing danger; as, by proof, we see
> The waters swell before a boist'rous storm."

But in that event it is passing strange they did not take even the ordinary precautions which habitually hedge an army in the field. Instead of that, in sooth, there was no line of infantry pickets in advance of the ordinary chain of sentinels; apparently no cavalry exterior either to Sherman or Prentiss, and that invading army lay drowsily in its cosy encampments, as if supremely confident no harm were threatening and no disaster could befall it! Many as yet were in their blankets fast asleep, many others washing and dressing, others cooking their morning meal. Some were eating leisurely at bounteous mess-chests, and the arms and accoutrements of all were spread around in the orderless fashion of holiday soldiers. Meanwhile, swiftly forward through the woods strode the

---

ty-second, Forty-first, and Forty-sixth Illinois; Twenty-fifth, Thirty-first, and Forty-fourth Indiana; Seventeenth and Twenty-fifth Kentucky, and Third Iowa. They were brigaded under Veach, Lauman, and Williams. Two battalions of cavalry also belonged to this division.

Confederates. With an elastic tread, inspired by hope and the fresh April morning air, they surged onward and foeward, until, the mist gradually lifting, the sheen of the white tents, their goal, might be seen through the trees. On poured the living current of the Confederates. By a mischance their left had not been thrown sufficiently near to Owl creek, so when thè collision came it was only with the left brigade (Hildebrand's) of Sherman's Division ; but it fell with overwhelming force upon Prentiss from flank to flank. Their sentinels, taken by surprise, were run in with barely time to discharge their pieces. Just at their heels came the Confederates, cheering heartily ; and so complete a surprise of an army has not the like in history. Officers and men were killed or wounded in their beds, and large numbers had not time to clutch up either arms or accoutrements. Nevertheless, few prisoners were taken, nor were many either killed or wounded in the first stage of the battle. Hildebrand's Brigade of Ohioans, swept by the violence of the onslaught from their encampment, scattered and was heard of no more as a belligerent organization on that field ! Prentiss's Division, rallying, was formed in good time on a neighboring ridge, but, little able to stand the torrent that streamed after it, was swept further back. Meanwhile, Sherman's rightward brigades, which escaped collision with Hardee, he had had time to form, and with them right manfully did he strive to make head against Ruggles's Divison of Bragg's Corps, that by this time had come upon the scene and bore down vehemently upon them. As we have said before, the position held by Sherman was one of natural strength ; with a small water-course in front, it afforded a converging fire upon the approaching Confederates. McClernand, apprised of the attack, was also advancing to support him. Such, however, was the vigor of the assault that Sherman, with the loss of five or six guns, was forced back just as McClernand came up. They were both then swept rearward near the line of the cross-road from Hamburg to Purdy. There Sherman, with McClernand, gained a foothold, and, with several batteries favorably posted, made another stand on a thickly wooded ridge with a ravine in front. But, speedily assailed by Ruggles and some of Polk's brigades with a fury not to be withstood, the Federal line again yielded, losing several pieces of artillery, and receding to the position of McClernand's encampment.

About forty minutes past seven A.M., hearing the uproar in front, Hurlbut also sent Veach's Brigade of his division to support Sherman, and with his other two brigades moved swiftly to the succor of Prentiss, who had called for aid. With these went forward eight companies of cavalry and three batteries. Prentiss's Division was met, however, in broken fragments, which filtered through his lines as he formed in the edge of a field, sheltered by timber and thick undergrowth, near the Hamburg road, south of the position last taken by Sherman and McClernand. There Hurlbut also was speedily assailed by the Confederates, now reënforced in that quarter by Chalmers's and Jackson's brigades of Bragg's Corps ; and such was the vehemence of the attack that he was soon swept back with the loss of some artillery. Thus the whole front line of Federal encampments was left in the hands of their adversary, filled with equipage and baggage, the most abundant and luxurious that ever encumbered any except an oriental army.*

By this time both Cheatham's and Clark's divisions, Polk's Corps, were also strenuously engaged, mainly on the left, where Sherman was making able, desperate efforts to redeem

---

* The tents were full of new, capacious trunks ; in many instances were furnished with stoves, and the ground around was thickly strewn with a spe- cies of *vest-armor*, of sheet-iron or steel, whose owners had not had time to don and test them.

the losses of the morning. Several of his positions, as the Federals drifted riverward, were quite strong, fronted by tangled ravines and affording thick cover, from which they poured a desolating fire, that more than once checked the ardent press of their adversaries. But gathering volume and resuming the onset with fresh spirit, the Confederates still drove their enemy nearer the river.

Wallace (W. H. L.) had soon become involved in the battle. Manifestly a gallant soldier, he fought his division, men who had been at Donelson, with decided stamina. Stuart's Brigade, Sherman's Division, had also been attacked, and the Federal line of battle was pushed back to within a mile of the Landing, and to the ground of their last encampments. There were massed what remained of their artillery and the fragments of Sherman's, Prentiss's, McClernand's, and Hurlbut's divisions, as well as Wallace's and Stuart's.

In the mean time, from the nature of the field—the net-work of ravines, the interlaced thickets, and wide scope of forest—the Confederate organizations had become greatly disordered. Not only divisions and brigades had been dislocated, but regiments also ; and the troops of all three corps, in fact, were intermingled. For the most part, confident of the issue and bent on pressing toward the enemy, there was yet a lack of harmonious movement. Superior officers led, with notable courage, regiments or parts of brigades, and doubtless stimulated their men, not a little by their example, but at the same time lost sight of the mass of their commands, which were thus not infrequently left at a halt without orders and uncertain what to do. And this was the case with batteries also, which, moreover, were too often employed *singly.**

---

* General Beauregard, through the present writer, had given special orders to Chiefs of Artillery to mass their batteries in action and fight them twelve guns on a point.

General Johnston, the Confederate Commander-in-Chief, was now in the very front of the battle. Assured of a great victory after the marvelous success of his planned surprise, he now stimulated the onslaught by his personal presence on the right, where the press was fiercest, the resistance the most effective. More than once brigades that faltered, under the inspiration of his leading bore back the enemy and wrested the position fought for. As far as can be ascertained, General Grant was not upon the immediate field earlier than mid-day. On Saturday afternoon he had gone to Savannah and slept there. The sound of many cannon at Shiloh was his first tiding of a hostile juncture at Pittsburg Landing ; but even that was scarcely regarded as the announcement of a serious battle, for one of Buell's divisions, Nelson's, lay at Savannah, and, as he was leaving for Pittsburg, General Grant merely ordered that division to march thither by the nearest road. However, as the Federal General steamed toward the scene, the banks of the river were soon found alive with his men, fleeing from the danger which so early that morning had routed them from their comfortable beds.* When, too, he reached Pittsburg, it was to find his whole front line surprised, overwhelmed, routed, and the ravines and river-bank adjacent packed with thousands of crouching fugitives. These were not to be rallied nor reorganized, not to be incited to return to the side of their imperiled comrades who still battled manfully, and by coöperation make an effort to recover the fortunes of the day.

Within the hollows and on the slopes and flat ridges of that circumscribed Tennessee woodland at least sixty thousand muskets and rifles were now at the dire work of carnage in the hands of sixty thousand men, in whom burned all the

------

* *Agate.—Cincinnati Gazette, Reb. Rec.* Doc. 114.

"Fierce fever of the steel,
The guilty madness warriors feel."*

The sun had dissipated the fog, and shone bright and warm through the young budding foliage. But the continuous roll, roar, and blaze of small-arms, the hurtle, shriek, and crash of rifle projectiles through the trees, the explosion of shells, the louder discharges and reverberations of more than a hundred cannon, and the hoarse cheers and shouts of the Confederates filled every nook of the forest with the varied, commingled clamors of one of the bloodiest of modern battles.

Earlier, General Gladden, at the head of his brigade, in the first line, had fallen mortally hurt. A merchant in New-Orleans when the revolution began, full of martial instincts as well as love of the section of his birth, A. H. Gladden was among the first to take up arms. With some soldierly experience as an officer of the gallant Palmetto Regiment of South-Carolina in the war with Mexico, his military worth was soon apparent, and he had risen to the command of a brigade. This he disciplined in such fashion as to show in what soldierly shape the splendid war *personnel* of his countrymen could be readily moulded by men fit to lead them. Soon after Gladden was cut down in the rich promise of his career, his brigade faltered under a desolating fire. Its new commander, Colonel Daniel W. Adams, seizing a battle-flag, placed himself in front of his staggering ranks and rode forward upon the enemy.† His men, animated by the act, grew steady, resumed the charge, and carried the disputed ground, with

---

* *Sævit amor ferri, et scelerata insania belli.*
VIRGIL.

† Each Confederate regiment had a corps battle-flag. Those of Bragg's and Polk's corps were a *blue* cross on a red field, of Hardee's a white medallion on a blue field.

seven stands of colors taken from Prentiss's Division. In another part of the field similar examples were multiplied. Brigadier-General Hindman, about ten A.M., pressing his brigade forward, with notable nerve, constantly close upon the enemy, drew down an overwhelming storm of fire, under which he was severely wounded after conspicuous conduct, and the brigade for a time wavered and recoiled. There was abundant intrepidity in leading everywhere ;* but, unfortunately for the Confederate cause, too little knowledge of the right way to handle regiments, brigades, divisions, even corps, to secure that massing of troops, those weighty blows which achieve decisive victories. Though, indeed, there were far too many stragglers who ignobly shrunk from the victorious edge of battle, many going back even to Corinth that night, yet everywhere there was the largest measure of sturdy fighting by regiments, brigades, and parts of divisions. But, notwithstanding the wreck of Sherman's, Prentiss's, and McClernand's divisions were now crowded back upon the line of Wallace's (W. H. L.) and Hurlbut's divisions — that is to say, a short line scarcely a mile from the river,—and though the corps of Hardee, Bragg, and Polk, with Breckinridge not far off, were in their immediate front, there was no concerted concentration of these triumphant corps respectively, much less of the whole mass, for a well-timed, overwhelming blow at the now sorely crippled, dispirited enemy. And, as a consequence, with Sherman among them doing all possible in the exigency, the Federals were enabled to protract their defense against the desultory onsets with which they were assailed for the next hour or two.

---

* Both the division commanders of Polk's Corps were wounded, General Clark severely, and General Cheatham had three horses shot under him. Generals B. R. Johnson and Bowen were also wounded on Sunday. General Hardee likewise was slightly wounded, and General Bragg had two horses killed.

During the occurrences which we have related, Colonel Forrest had thrown his regiment, as soon as he heard the inauguration of the battle, across Lick creek, and, pressing up, held it on the Confederate right flank, ready for orders, for which he sent at once to the Commander-in-Chief. About eleven o'clock the enemy, as we have seen, having been forced back to their second line, he received an order to move his regiment onward to the front. This he executed at a gallop. Not finding the General there, or further orders, he pushed ahead to the point where the infantry seemed most obstinately engaged. It was near the centre of the line, and, on reaching the scene, Forrest found that Cheatham's Division had just received a temporary check. With his wonted impatience of the least delay, he at once proposed to Cheatham to join in an immediate charge across an open field in their front. To this, Cheatham, whose men for several hours previously had been breasting a tempest of artillery and musketry fire, demurred for the moment, as his men required some rest. Forrest's men, being mounted, were nearly as much exposed to an annoying fire where they stood — a fair mark — as in a charge, and Forrest determined to make one. Forming in a column of fours, the order to charge was given, and on they dashed, at a splendid pace, full in the face of a withering fire of small and large arms. A number of horses fell in a few instants, and several of the men ;* but on they sped, heedless of the breaks in their column, up to within forty paces of the Federal line, when the advance became entangled in an impracticable morass across their path, from which it became impossible to extricate some of the horses. The boldness of this movement, however, appeared to produce some effect

---

* We are only able to mention the name of young John Apperson, slain at this juncture, a young gentleman greatly esteemed in society and son of one of the prominent citizens of Memphis.

upon the enemy, and, Cheatham advancing with his indomitable division about the same time, the Federals, after some resistance, were borne rearward again in a good deal of confusion. Forrest now, having made a detour around the marsh,
galloped through the infantry and threw his regiment upon
the disordered mass of Federals, with the effect to scatter
them a good deal more and hurry their pace, manifestly, toward the river.

Meanwhile, to the rightward, the Confederate General-in-
Chief, taking part at a critical juncture in the charge of a brigade, and by his intrepid presence giving a resistless momentum to the onset, received a rifle-wound in the leg,—a mortal
wound, as it proved, presently, for the want of timely surgical
aid. The Governor of Tennessee, by his side when struck,
caught the fainting soldier in his arms as he sunk from his
saddle, exhausted by an apparently painless loss of blood.*
A moment after, his aid-de-camp and brother-in-law, Colonel
William Preston, of Kentucky, came up, and Sidney Johnston, with scarce a murmur, died in his arms. The scene
of this untoward death was a wooded, secluded hollow, and the
loss of their chief was not known to the Confederate army
until that night, nor even generally then.†

---

* Governor Isham G. Harris was by
the side of General Johnston all day
up to the moment of his death. On
Monday he remained with General
Beauregard, except when carrying orders to the most critical parts of the
field. His calm, collected courage attracted general attention, as subsequently on other bloody fields of the
West.

† It is not within the scope of these
pages to attempt such a sketch of this
accomplished General and chivalrous
soldier as the subject requires. We may,
however, contribute one fact to the future biography of a lofty-natured man.

In a conversation which General
Johnston had, late Saturday night, with
the present writer, he mentioned that,
though General Sumner had been sent
by steamer by way of Panama, under
an assumed name, (as we knew and informed General Johnston,) to relieve
him in California, his former Adjutant-
General, Fitz-John Porter, had been
authorized to write a letter by the over-

About the time of this calamity the reserves under Breckinridge were thrown vigorously into action. Bragg had applied, through his Aid, Colonel Urquhart, for a diversion to

---

land mail, to hold up to him the glitter-
ing promise of the highest command
within the gift of the Federal Government. There is no question that,
though they were led to relieve him
from duty on the Pacific coast, it was
nevertheless the wish to retain his services, and, could that have been effected, he would have been Commander-
in-Chief of the United States forces in
the field. It will suffice here to state
that, born in 1803, in Kentucky, General Johnston was about fifty-nine years
of age when he fell. Graduating at
West-Point in 1826, he served in the
army until 1834, when he resigned.
Two years later, going to Texas, he
soon became Commander-in-Chief of
the Texas forces in the war with Mexico. Quitting public life, however, after
several years, Sidney Johnston became
a planter until 1846, when, Texas having been annexed to the United States,
and there being a war on that account,
he was made Colonel of a regiment of
volunteers from the State of Texas, and
served under General Taylor, with
whom he stood so high that that soldier urged upon his Government his
appointment as a Brigadier-General,
and ultimately, when President, restored him to the regular army as a
Major of the Paymaster's staff. In
1856, Mr. Davis, then Secretary of
War, made him the Colonel of the Second Cavalry, just added to the army.
Under the following administration he
was placed in command of the large

force sent to repress the insubordinate
courses of the Mormons, and acted
with so rare a discretion mingled with
firmness as to give great satisfaction to
the country. After that he was assigned
to command of the department of California. No man stood in so high esti-
mation generally in the army at that
time, after General Scott. Later, feeling
it his duty to take part with Texas in
the war for independence, he resigned,
and, by the route across through Southern California, Arizona, and Texas,
with great difficulty succeeded in reaching the seat of the Confederate Government. He was at once made the second in rank of the five Generals of the
Confederate Army, and assigned to the
command of affairs in Tennessee and
Kentucky. The official announcement
to the army of his death, expressing the
feeling excited by the event at the time,
bearing date April 10th, 1862, at Corinth, is as follows :

SOLDIERS : Your late Commander-
in-Chief, A. S. Johnston, is dead. A
fearless soldier, a sagacious captain, a
reproachless man has fallen. One who
in his devotion to our cause shrunk
from no sacrifice ; one who, animated
by a sense of duty and sustained by a
sublime courage, challenged danger
and perished gallantly for his country
while leading forward his brave columns
to victory. His signal example of heroism and patriotism, if generally imi-
tated, will make this army invincible.
A grateful country will mourn his loss,

his rightward against some batteries which were distressing his front and keeping his men at bay. Breckinridge's brigades were drawn up on the gentler part of the slope of a ridge when the order for their advance was given. Clad in a dark blouse, he sat on his horse, surrounded by his staff, more like an equestrian statue than a living man, except the fiery gleam in his dark eyes as he received the order. In front was to be seen a Federal camp in the open woods, apparently quiet and without an inmate. Indeed, the stillness seemed ominous, and just ahead was an open field bordered by a dense thicket. Through the camp pressed the Kentuckians and into the open field, and still there was silence ; but not long, for a few steps beyond a hissing stream and flame of musketry burst at their breasts, mowing their ranks fearfully and heaping the ground with the dead and wounded. There was a momentary check and they gave back to the woods, while a storm of bullets rattled through the trees far behind, reaching in profusion even a battery posted in another encampment a half of a mile to the rear. But only for a little while did the Kentuckians recede. Closing their thinned ranks and animated by their officers, they retook the advance, and their adversaries were forced back, yet with not a little stubbornness and desperate fighting, on favorable ground.

By this time, Withers's Division, of Bragg's Corps, as well as Breckinridge's reserves, mingled with portions of Hardee's men, were all massed on the Confederate right in the quarter of Lick creek. General Bragg also, as he tells us, was there in person and assumed command.* Giving, he says, "a common head and a common purpose to the whole," he launched

---

revere his name, and cherish his many virtues.

   (Signed)   G. T. BEAUREGARD,
             General Commanding.

* General Bragg's Report, p. 198, *Official Reports of Battles, Richmond, Va.,* 1862.

them with a resistless weight at the enemy, who now gave way and on all sides were forced from the line of Wallace's and Hurlbut's encampments, leaving behind more of their artillery and three thousand prisoners, chiefly of Prentiss's Division, in the hands of their assailants.* At the same time, on the centre and left, Polk's divisions, with Ruggles's divisions of Bragg, and some of Hardee's also, made no less strenuous efforts to close the battle. Those of the routed Federals who were not killed or captured dropped back in great confusion toward the Landing. Some were rallied upon the ridge immediately overhanging the Landing, but large masses were added to the already dense mob of fugitives huddled below the bank.

But, meanwhile, Colonel Webster, chief of the Federal staff, an officer of the regulars, who knew his profession, observing the mortal peril of his people, had gathered upon that ridge all the guns available, including some 32-pounders and a battery of 20-pounder Parrotts, or in all twenty-two pieces, which he manned with gunners from the least demoralized of the runaways. Soon, too, the remains of the field-batteries were added, and some fifty guns were massed upon this eminence about five P.M., with a field of fire sweeping all the approaches to the river.† The position was strong ; timber and undergrowth gave shelter for the artillery and their support, while a deep ravine separated it from the table-land over which it dominated ; tangled brushwood obstructed its steep slopes, and on or behind this position, as we have said, took final refuge the entire Federal force except the remains of one of Sherman's brigades, which appear to have drifted off with

---

* Embracing the organizations of the Eighth, Twelfth, and Fourteenth Iowa, and Fifty-eighth Illinois regiments.—P. 89 Coppee's *Grant and his Campaigns.*

† Some Federal writers place these guns as high as sixty.

their General to the vicinity of the bridge across Snake creek, on the road to Crump's Landing, and, not being followed, he established them there undisturbed,—with the rear open for retreat, in an emergency, northward.

The air now resounded with hearty shouts of natural exultation on the part of the victorious Confederates, and, having established his headquarters in advance of Shiloh, General Beauregard, through his staff, urged the forward propulsion of the whole force upon the shattered fragments of the enemy. Unfortunately, however, the Federal encampments were plethoric with food most tempting to hungry men, as well as with clothing and other alluring spoil ; the thick woods, too, had greatly disintegrated almost every regiment, so that none of the divisions confronted in an embodied form the last position that remained between them and the deep, broad waters of the Tennessee. The superior officers present, howbeit, collected the men immediately around them, of whatsoever corps. Tired, hungry, and exhausted as were the Confederates, nevertheless a number of determined separate efforts were made by them, during the remaining hour of daylight, to wrench their last foothold from their elsewhere beaten adversary. But, meanwhile, at five P.M., Ammen's Brigade, of Nelson's Division, had been thrown across the river and established by Buell as a support of Webster's powerful battery ;* and the Federals, like a rat brought to bay in a corner from which there is no escape, fought with all the desperation of that animal under similar circumstances, knowing, moreover, that night with its shield of darkness, and ample succor were close at hand.

The character of these last assaults on the part of the Confederates, and their fruitless results, with the causes which

---

* Nelson's Official Report, *Reb. Rec.* IV. Doc. 114.

wrought their failure, may be best illustrated by what befell Colonel Mouton and the Eighteenth Louisiana Infantry. After four P.M. he was ordered to charge "a battery on a hill," some six hundred yards in his front. Advancing "unsupported," the regiment soon became uncovered and exposed to a cross-fire from the battery and its supports. Nevertheless, these dauntless Louisianians, well led, pressed up to within seventy yards of the Federal guns, but were then beaten back, leaving two hundred and seven of their numbers either dead or *hors-de-combat* on the ground.*

Another characteristic essay was made on the extreme Confederate right by General Chalmers, with his own and a part of J. K. Jackson's Brigade, to press forward to the Landing. But in attempting, as Mouton had done, "to mount the last ridge," they were met by a "fire from a whole line of batteries, protected by infantry, and assisted by shells from the gunboats."† The Confederates, however, stoutly persisted in storming the steep hill-side despite the impediments with which it bristled, and "made charge after charge without success, until night closed hostilities."‡ This tells the story of the closing scene,—tells how a series of disjointed attacks at that late hour upon a battery of over fifty pieces by fragmentary bodies of men who had already been embattled for ten hours without respite, failed necessarily.§

General Beauregard, in the mean time, observing the ex-

* * *

* *Official Reports of Battles*, pp. 307–311.

† General Grant, in his official report, alleges that, in effecting the repulse on this last position, "much is due to the presence of the gunboats Tyler and Lexington."

‡ Official Report of General Chalmers.

§ *Official Reports of Battles*, pp. 211 to 312, *Richmond, Va.*, 1862 ; *vide* Reports of Chalmers, Patton Anderson, Pond, Gibson, Hodge, Moore, Joseph Wheeler Deas, Looney, Reichard, Fagan, Stanly, Mouton, Chadwick, Jones, Clack, Dubrocoa, etc.

hausted, widely-scattered condition of his army, directed it to be brought out of battle, collected and restored to order as far as practicable, and to occupy for the night the captured encampments of the enemy. This, however, had already been done in chief part by the officers in immediate command of the troops before the order was generally distributed.*

Foremost in the pursuit that followed the defeat of the Federals at their second line, it remains to be said, were Forrest and his regiment. They assisted in the capture of Prentiss's men, and, being mounted, as well as comparatively fresh, led the advance upon the ridge where the battery was established. Despite the efforts of the Federal officers, such was the confusion prevalent as Forrest began to skirmish vigorously that he sent a staff-officer to report to General Polk (from whom he had last received orders) that, by a strong, rapid forward movement, the enemy might be driven into the river. Soon, however, the battery on the ridge opened with a general salvo, and the gunboats threw their ponderous shells in the thick of the up-coming mass of Confederates with such profusion that General Polk ordered the cavalry to take shelter in the wooded ravine which, beginning at the river just above the Landing, extends around the battery-ridge and for more than a mile westwardly. Here, however, they were exposed to a raking fire from the gunboats, and the artillery of

---

* This was especially so, it is to be noted, with Bragg's Corps. Yet, oddly enough, General Bragg in his own official report ventures to state that his men, though greatly exhausted, were about to charge with great alacrity upon the last position, and most probably would have carried it, when Beauregard's order was received recalling them. It is proper to state that General Bragg's report, though bearing date of 30th of April, 1862, and ostensibly made to General Beauregard *through the* present writer, was not transmitted as addressed, but directly by General Bragg, on the 25th of July, 1862, to General Cooper, Adjutant-General C. S. A., Richmond.

both sides playing over their heads, until night brought the cessation of the conflict.*

All the encampments that had been occupied by the five Federal divisions were now in possession of their adversary. They were full of the rich, opportune spoils of war, including many thousand stands of arms, all the blankets and baggage of the whole force, their subsistence, their hospital stores, means of transportation to a great extent, and large stores of ammunition. But so great was the lassitude and fatigue of the Confederates that all which could be done was to glean food sufficient for their supper, for which, indeed, all were dependent upon what they could thus find. The prisoners, however, were collected together during the night not far from Shiloh church, where Generals Beauregard and Bragg established their headquarters. There, after a time, the former had an interview with his corps commanders, and received brief oral reports of the operations of the day.

Among the prisoners was General Prentiss himself, who had much to say touching the ultimate issue of the affair, which he asserted was by no means terminated with the disasters of that untoward day ; for Buell, he stated, would effect a junction that night, the fight would break out the next morning with renewed vigor, and all losses would be recovered. At the moment, however, this was regarded as idle talk, for an official telegraphic dispatch, addressed to General Johnston from near Florence, was forwarded to the field from Corinth, announcing that Buell was moving with his whole

---

* Willie M. Forrest, the only child of the General, a lad of fifteen years of age, was with his father during the day, but, with two other comrades of the same age, happening to get detached, made their way to the river, near which they came upon fifteen or twenty Federal soldiers. Firing upon the group with their shot-guns, these boys then charged, and captured, and led away some fifteen prisoners, whom they delivered up to the provost-marshal.

force upon Florence. Emanating from a reliable officer placed there in observation, whose scouts had doubtless mistaken the movement of Mitchell's Division for the whole of Buell's army, it was credited, and Buell's timely junction with General Grant was accordingly deemed impossible. Therefore the capture of the latter was regarded at Confederate headquarters as inevitable the next day, as soon as all the scattered Confederate reserves could be brought to bear for a concentrated effort. Meanwhile, night had shrouded the bloody field in darkness; a deep silence had settled upon the scene of so much carnage,—a silence only broken through the night by the regular discharges of the heavy naval guns, the explosions of the shells, and by the low wails and moans of the wounded, of whom more than ten thousand, of both armies, were spread over the battle-field. Such, however, of the Confederate soldiery as could find shelter from a heavy rain slept undisturbed and hopeful of the fullest fruition of a great victory on the morrow.

II.

On withdrawing from the ravine in which nightfall had left him, Colonel Forrest, finding no superior at hand from whom to seek orders, with his habitual self-reliance looked at once for forage and food, and happily found both in a Federal camp near by. Afterward he threw out a squadron as pickets, confronting, as close as possible, those of the enemy, on a stretch of a mile across to Owl creek. He also dispatched Lieutenant Sheridan, (May's old company,) with other scouts clad in Federal cavalry overcoats, to reconnoitre within the precincts of the enemy's lines. Completely successful, in an hour Sheridan returned and reported that, reaching the Landing, he had seen heavy reënforcements coming rapidly by water. Also, in his opinion, such was the disorder prevailing that, if an attack were made in full force at once, they might be readily pushed into the river ! Forrest, ever a man of prompt action, mounted his horse instantly to convey this startling intelligence to the nearest corps commander ; and, soon coming upon Generals Hardee and Breckinridge, made known what his scouts announced. He also bluntly added his opinion that either the Confederates should immediately resume the battle or quit the field to avoid a damaging conflict with overwhelming odds. Hardee directed him to communicate his information to General Beauregard, and with that object he rode forth again ; but after a diligent search through the woods and darkness, unable to find that General, he became so deeply solicitous that he hurried back to his pickets. Finding all quiet, he again dispatched his scouts within the Federal lines. It was two o'clock A.M. before they returned and reported the continued arrival of fresh troops. Again Forrest repaired and reported to General Hardee the state of affairs, but was instructed to return to his regiment, keep up a vigilant, strong picket-line, and report all hostile movements. All the while, every few minutes through the night, two gunboats had been sedulously throwing their dread "bolted-thunder" directly over Forrest's bivouac, murdering sleep, weary and drowsy as all his men were.

III.

By seven P.M., Nelson's other brigades had crossed the Tennessee, and, with the one that so materially helped—with Webster's opportunely posted battery—to save the Federal army from utter overthrow, were at once thrown forward by General Buell as a shield between General Grant's army and the Confederates.* Crittenden's Division likewise came up

---

* This division was formed of Ammen's, Bruce's, and Hazen's brigades, embracing Sixth, Ninth, Twenty-fourth, and Thirty-sixth Indiana, the First, Second, Sixth, and Twentieth Kentucky, and Forty-first Ohio regiments.

from Savannah by water not long after, and was promptly established in the same manner on Nelson's right.*   Moreover, Lew Wallace, strangely unable to find the road battleward amid the thunder peals of more than a hundred cannon within six miles of him, as soon as the dusky shadows and the quiet of night had supervened, found a way to the south bank of Snake creek and to a position there commanding the bridge, and by chance, too, in the neighborhood of Sherman, with the shreds or odds and ends of his own and other divisions that had rallied around him.†   One of McCook's brigades (Rousseau's) also reached the scene about sunrise, and the other two were near at hand.‡

Thus were marshaled there or near at hand, ready to take the offensive against the victors of the day before, 25,000 fresh Federal troops, three battalions of which were regulars. On the Confederate side, to meet such an onset, there was not a man who had not fought steadfastly for the greater part of Sunday.§   In addition to the many stragglers incident to all battles, the casualties did not fall short of 6500 officers and men, so that not more than 20,000 Confederate infantry could

---

* Apparently of two brigades, (Boyle's and W. S. Smith's,) including Ninth, Eleventh, Thirteenth, and Twenty-sixth Kentucky, and Thirteenth, Nineteenth, Fifty-ninth, and another Ohio regiment.

† Smith's, Thayer's, and Whittlesey's brigades, Eleventh, Twenty-third, and Twenty-fourth Indiana, Twentieth, Twenty-third, Fifty-sixth, Sixty-eighth, Seventy-sixth, and Seventy-eighth Ohio, Eighth Missouri, and First Nebraska regiments.

‡ McCook's Division was formed in three brigades, Rousseau's, Johnson's, and Kirk's, with the Sixth, Twenty-ninth, Thirtieth, Thirty-second, and Thirty-ninth Indiana, Fifteenth and Forty-ninth Ohio, Twenty-fourth Illinois, and Seventy-seventh Pennsylvania regiments.   We find the details of these regiments of Wallace's, Nelson's, Crittenden's, and McCook's brigades in letter of "Agate," *Reb. Rec.* IV. Doc. 114.

§ A Tennessee Confederate regiment (Hill's) reached the field Sunday, and was furnished with arms and accoutrements picked up there.   Its good conduct was conspicuous.

have been found to answer to their names that morning. Scattered widely, the regiments of the brigades of Bragg's and Hardee's Corps had slept here and there among the captured encampments, wheresoever they could find subsistence. Polk's Corps had been embodied to some degree, and led during the night by their General rearward at least a mile and a half beyond Shiloh toward Corinth.

In haste to efface the tarnish of the arrant disaster inflicted on his army on Sunday, with all the attending completeness of the surprise, General Grant did not await the advent of Buell's other divisions, but directed the offensive to be assumed at dawn. An accomplished soldier, martial by nature, acquainted with the theory of grand operations, and well practiced as a staff and line officer, General Buell had known how to make soldiers of his men, formidable soldiers to the scorched, battle-jaded Confederates whom they were about to engage.

From his line of observation, Forrest discovered the first movement of the enemy, just before day, a tentative advance of some pickets, as if to feel for an enemy. His men were now generally clothed in Federal cavalry overcoats, found in their encampment of the night. These misled the Federal pickets, some fifty of whom were presently captured. About half-past five A.M., however, a swarm of skirmishers were flung boldly forward by Nelson. These Forrest engaged as he fell back slowly upon the infantry,—then being collected somewhat rearward—and behind whom, at seven A.M., General Hardee directed him finally to retire. The sound of so much musketry at the front by this time had announced, plainly enough, the advent upon the theatre of war of Buell's army, and a desperate struggle for the fruits of yesterday's hard-earned triumph. All, as we have said, were greatly fatigued, and under the influence also of that extreme lassitude which follows every great exaltation ; nevertheless the reaction was immediate, and with the utmost alacrity the Confederates sprang once more into serried ranks, bent on a manful effort to hold what they had won.

Chalmers's Brigade, with a part of J. K. Jackson's, under Wheeler, in advance, in front of Nelson, were the first to become engaged.   Nelson came out with vigor, and the Confederates retired slowly to concentrate their strength.   By eight o'clock, Hardee, however, had massed in that quarter a number of his own corps, as well as Withers's Division of Bragg's, and the combat began in good earnest.   Nelson now found a lion in his path, but Hazen's Brigade pushed forward with decided pluck, and the Confederates were driven from their position with the loss of a battery.   A well-timed concentration, however, enabled the Confederates to hurl Hazen back from his prey, and in turn pressed Nelson so sorely that by nine A.M. he was calling lustily for aid.*   In this affair the Confederate officers led their ranks notably.   Chalmers, seizing the colors of a regiment as his brigade wavered, rode forward, the men rallied, and, resuming the offensive, carried the contested point.   At the same time, Colonel Wheeler did the like with the flag of the Nineteenth Alabama;† and Lieutenant-Colonel W. A. Rankin, of Mississippi, lost his life, giving a conspicuous example of determined courage to his regiment.

Nelson was reënforced by Terrell's Battery, (regulars,) and a portion of Crittenden's Division, and an obstinate struggle for the mastery of this part of the field raged until about one P.M.   But neither party gained any material advantage, except Terrell's Battery was so cut up that he had to assist as a gunner at one of his pieces, and the battery narrowly escaped capture.

---

* *Reb. Rec.* IV. Doc. 114, p. 397.
† Subsequently Major-General Wheeler of the Cavalry.

Crittenden by this time was likewise hotly engaged in the immediate centre, and on his right were arrayed several thousand of Grant's troops, under McClernand. The Confederates on his front, at first retiring to concentrate at his advance, finally rebounded, as upon Nelson, with as great ardor and cheering as heartily as the day before in the full tide of their brilliant success. And as Nelson was borne back, so was Crittenden by the same refluent wave.*

One of McCook's brigades, under Rousseau, *leavened* by three battalions of regulars, had been on the field as early as daylight, on the right of Crittenden, neighboring Sherman and Lew Wallace. His other brigades reached and took position about ten o'clock; and just about the same time Polk's Corps coming up from the rear, on the Confederate side, entered the battle in splendid order and spirit.

Grant's shattered forces, on Sunday night, had been reorganized into three divisions, of a decidedly composite character, under Sherman, McClernand, and Hurlbut. Four or five thousand of these men were brought up under McClernand, as we have said, between Crittenden and McCook, and about ten o'clock, several thousand more, that hitherto had been collected and held near the river, were also added under Hurlbut, who, however, fusing them with McClernand's command, repaired rearward again, at McClernand's request, to seek further support.†

Lew Wallace, it will be remembered, bivouacked near the river and Snake Creek bridge, and so did Sherman. No considerable portion of Confederates had slept in that quarter of the field, so Wallace and Sherman advancing for a while without difficulty, took up a strong position on a wooded ridge, affording shelter for Wallace's two batteries, with its right

---

* *Reb. Rec.* IV. Doc. 114, p.397. † Ibid.

protected by the swamps of Owl creek.   However, by the
time Nelson was well at work on the Federal left, the Confederates opened a light fire upon Wallace and Sherman, who,
encouraged by its feebleness, adventured the offensive.   But
their speedy greeting was a sheet of flame, lead, and canister
from the woods in their front, where portions of Ruggles's and
Breckinridge's divisions stood in wait.   The Federals reeled
and rushed rearward, followed nearly a mile by the Confederates ; but here, reënforced by McCook, Sherman attempted
to resume the advance.   Now the fight waxed obstinate, and
the firing, says Sherman, was the "severest musketry" he had
ever heard.   Rousseau's Federal Brigade here was pitted
against Trabue's Kentuckians.   Both fought with uncommon
determination to win, but the Federals were repulsed, and
Wallace was so pressed that his situation became extremely
critical.*   McCook's other brigade had joined in the action
meanwhile ; and in that part of the field, including Grant's
forces under Sherman and McClernand, there were fully twenty thousand Federals opposed by not half that number of bat-
tle-battered Confederates.†   The impetus of the Confederate
attack was, therefore, slackened in the face of such odds.   Yet
several brilliant charges were made, in one of which, to the
left of Shiloh, General Beauregard himself led in person, carrying the battle-flag of a Louisiana regiment ; and Trabue's Brigade, having carried earlier an eminence near Owl creek, repulsing every effort to dislodge him, held the position until

---

* This is his own statement. It is a
somewhat noteworthy fact, however,
that in the Federal reports, whenever a
retrograde occurs, it is always a *neighbor* who succumbs, either on the right
or left.   One is reminded of the *homely*
story of the man of the Mississippi bottoms, who declared that he was not
troubled by mosquitoes, "but really
*there's no living for them just below at
my neighbor's house!*"

† That is, Wallace's Division, seven
thousand strong ; McCook's, at least
seven thousand ; and say six thousand
under Sherman and McClernand.

the retreat was ordered. Here, as on the right, the Confederate troops were animated by the greatest intrepidity on the part of their superior officers.*

It was now after one o'clock. The battle, kindled soon after daylight, had raged furiously from right to left for more than five hours. And, notwithstanding the odds of fresh troops brought up against them, despite their long-continued engagement, the Confederates had not receded from the ground upon which they had been concentrated as soon as it was apparent that the battle was on their hands.† But they were being fearfully depleted meanwhile. Beginning the combat with not more than 20,000 men, exclusive of cavalry, less than 15,000 were now in the Confederate ranks. General Beauregard, seeing the unprofitable nature of the struggle, determined not to prolong it. Directing his Adjutant-General to select a position, and post such troops as were available to cover the retreat, he dispatched other staff-officers to the corps commanders, with the order to retire simultaneously from their several positions, ready, however, to turn and fight should it become necessary. And accordingly, about two o'clock, the retrograde movement of the Confederates was inaugurated, and carried out with a steadiness never exceeded by veterans of a hundred fields.‡

During the various stages of the conflict, General Beaure-

---

* Lieutenant Sandridge, of General Cheatham's staff, seizing the colors of a regiment, holding them aloft, spurred his horse to the front, as did also Colonel Stanley, Ninth Texas, and both at a critical moment thus incited the men to advance. These are but a few of the examples that might be cited.

† This is manifest from the official reports of Generals Nelson, Lew Wallace, and Sherman. All that Wallace claims is, that he was able to hold his ground and repulse the Confederates up to about two o'clock. That is, to the hour when they had commenced to leave the field under orders.

‡ All the Federal accounts place the moment of the retreat several hours later than it actually happened, as could be demonstrated.

gard tried to use his cavalry, but so dense and broadspread were the woods that they proved altogether fruitless of results. Colonel Forrest, with ever-useful instincts, however, was able to render effective service during the morning in repressing straggling, until, about eleven o'clock, he was ordered by General Breckinridge, in whose vicinity he happened to be, to place his regiment on the right flank, where he soon became engaged in a brisk skirmish. Three times the enemy endeavored to break that part of the Confederate line, but were repulsed, as we have related, until near one o'clock, when, under an order from General Beauregard, Forrest carried his regiment to the centre, where it was dismounted and took part there in repulsing the last onset made by the Federals in that quarter, before the retreat began.

The retreat had now commenced in earnest, but so stunned and crippled was the enemy that no effort or pretense to pursue was made.* The line established to cover the movement commanded the ground of Shiloh Church, and some open fields in the neighborhood. Thence keeping up a vigorous play of artillery on the woods beyond, there was no reply, nor did any enemy become visible. That line was then withdrawn about three fourths of a mile to another favorable position. Meanwhile, the retreat had been effected in admirable order, all stragglers falling in the ranks, and that line was abandoned with no enemy in sight. Breckinridge, assigned to the duty of covering the retreat with his division, was ordered to bivouac for the night at a point not more than four and a half miles from Pittsburg Landing. The other corps were now *en route* for Corinth, by a road which that night was made almost impracticable for wheels by a heavy rainfall. Colonel Forrest, soon after the retreat began, moved

---

* General Grant states Sherman followed a short way, but found that the Confederates had retreated in good order.

over with several squadrons of his regiment to attend personally to picketing Lick creek through the night, and to guard against any aggressive movement from that direction.

The losses of the Confederates in the two days' combats are accurately and officially stated by General Beauregard at 1728 killed, 8012 wounded, and 959 missing, or an aggregate of 10,699. The Federal commander, in his brief report of the battle, estimates his own losses at only 1500 killed and 3500 wounded, an evidently large understatement, for in the official reports of three of his division generals we find their losses foot up in killed and wounded as high as 4614, with 1832 reported missing, a number of whom must have been killed, as only 3000 were captured, and most of them were of Prentiss's Division. What the real loss of Grant's army was, those who could best do it have not been at the pains to ascertain. The divisions of Buell engaged lost 3753, much the heaviest part of which fell upon McCook's Division in the obstinate struggle against the Confederate left and left-centre.* Of trophies the Confederates carried from the field some twenty-six stands of flags and colors, and about thirty of the guns captured on the 6th. The guns which figure in Federal subordinate reports as captured from the Confederates, with few exceptions, were those lost on Sunday by the Federals, which, for want of horses to draw them from the field, had been left by the Confederates where they had been taken.

IV.

On Tuesday morning General Breckinridge fell back to a position only three miles beyond, and there remained undis-

---

* Since the foregoing was written, we observe that Swinton, who always writes in a fair spirit, estimates the Federal loss at 15,000.

turbed for some days, with the cavalry thrown forward in close proximity to the Federal lines. After Breckinridge had thus withdrawn, Colonel Forrest found himself with a squadron of about 150 men, on Tuesday morning, on the road toward Monterey, in the presence of a heavy Federal infantry force, advancing in three lines of battle. About the same time, a company of Wirt Adams's regiment, under Captain Isaac Harrison, a squadron of the Eighth Texas and some Kentuckians, under Captain John Morgan, opportunely came up, making a force of little more than 350 troopers. The position, a ridge, was advantageous, and Forrest determined to attempt to hold it until his regiment could be brought up. Formed in line of battle, the Confederates boldly stood their ground, as about two battalions of cavalry and a regiment of infantry were thrown forward to assail them. The infantry advanced handsomely at a charge, with their bayonets presented. There was some confusion, however, in the Federal ranks in crossing a small stream ; and Forrest, with his characteristic quickness of sight and plans, his wonted hardihood, resolved to charge the Federals with his force, as small as it was. His bugler sounded the charge, and forward dashed the Confederates from their covert behind the crest of the ridge in superb order and spirit, and were almost upon the enemy before the nature of the movement was perceived, or they had had time to prepare for it. At twenty paces the Confederates gave a volley with their shot-guns, a formidable weapon at that short distance, and rushed in with pistols and sabres. So sudden was the onset that, despite their numbers, the Federal cavalry broke in disorder, and fled back through the woods running over their own infantry in their panic, creating a scene of singular confusion and tumult for some moments. Many of the infantry were thus knocked down ; many horses also were transfixed by the bayonets of their own infantry. Scores of other horses fell and threw their riders sprawling and bruised upon the ground ; and all around was a medley of cavalry and infantry, scattering and running to and fro, hither and thither, officers shouting and cursing, and the hurt groaning. Before the infantry could recover from the condition into which the flight of the cavalry had thrown them, Forrest was upon them also with a swift play of sabre and revolver, and they broke as well as the cavalry. The slaughter was considerable, as the flying infantry were closely pursued for several hundred yards by their eager, excited enemy. Men are merciless on such occasions. The loss inflicted was heavy, while seventy were captured.

In the ardency and exultation of the pursuit, Forrest pressed on until he found himself alone within fifty yards of the main body of the Federal expeditionary force,—and beyond, indeed, a large part of those whom he had just surprised and routed. Halting, he saw at a glance that his men, perceiving sooner the situation, had very properly halted, and were then falling back with their prisoners,—which they were doing, however, unaware of the perilous position of their leader. Immediately observed by the enemy, now all around him, Forrest was fired at from all sides. One ball from an Austrian rifle, striking him on the left side, just above the point of the hip-bone, penetrated to the spine, and, ranging around, lodged in the left side—a severe if not, indeed, mortal wound, as his surgeon apprehended. His right leg, benumbed by the blow, was also left hanging useless in the stirrup. Turning his horse, however, he resolved to escape, surrounded as he was by hundreds bent on his death, and shouting, " Kill him !" " Shoot him !" " Stick him !" " Knock him off his horse !" all of which they literally sought to do. His horse, too, was wounded, (mortally, as it proved,) but still bore up under his daring rider, as he dashed out of the throng of assailants, using his revolver with deadly aim to clear his path. In a moment more his path to the rear, at least, was clear of foes :

but their marksmen, still within easy range, sent hundreds of balls after him as he galloped down the road and over the hill. Happily, he escaped without further hurt, and rejoined his command, halted behind the ridge. Giving orders to the officer next in rank to assume command, but to avoid further action with so large a force, Forrest now went to the nearest hospital for surgical aid. There he was advised by the surgeons, who could not discover the ball, to go to the rear as rapidly as possible. Doing this, he soon was at General Breckinridge's encampment, and that General ordered him to proceed to Corinth, for which place he set out, accompanied by his adjutant, Captain J. P. Strange. Soon the wound became so painful that he was forced to dismount, and take passage in a buggy; but on the rough roads to be traversed, that speedily proving more painful even than by horseback, he remounted his wounded horse, and finally reached Corinth that night, when the horse, who had borne him so stoutly and faithfully, dropped and died a few hours later.

On the next day, Colonel Forrest, furloughed for sixty days, repaired to Memphis. There his good habits and sound constitution enabled him to surmount what would have killed most men. However, on the 29th of April, learning from Lieutenant-Colonel Kelly that there was some discontent in the regiment, originating in deficient, defective subsistence, Forrest, still suffering acutely from his wound, at once returned to Corinth and rejoined his men, whose wants, by his energy, tact, and resources, he was soon able to supply, as well as to repress the spirit of dissatisfaction which had germinated in his absence.

A week after rejoining, being one day out reconnoitering the Federal lines that had now approached near to Corinth, leaping a log, the exertion brought such an acute pain that it became necessary at once to extract the ball which still remained in his left side. The operation was very severe, and made it absolutely necessary for him to be again absent from command for a fortnight.

COMMENTARIES.

I. The delay of the Confederate army in making the march from Corinth is a signal illustration of the truth of Napier's proposition, "*That celerity in war depends as much on the experience of the troops as upon the energy of the General.*" Nevertheless, there were grave faults in the handling of several of the corps on the march. Moreover, several of these did not quit Corinth as early in the day as they might have done. We know General Johnston was profoundly disappointed and chagrined that his just expectations of delivering battle on Saturday morning were thus baffled.

II. The precise *terrain* occupied by the Federal army was unknown to the Confederate General, who, therefore, adopted the *parallel* order of battle rather than the *oblique*, which has generally been employed by great captains since Frederick the Great restored it to the Art of War. Had General John-- ston known the actual position occupied by the Federal front line, he surely would have attacked by the *oblique* order ; massing upon the Federal right (Sherman) so as to force it back south-eastwardly into the *cul de sac* made, above Pittsburg Landing, by the junction of Lick creek with the Tennessee river. As the attack was made, the shock of the onset only affected Sherman's left brigade. Had it fallen with full force upon his entire division, it is manifest that that which happened to Hildebrand's Brigade would have befallen it. The entire division must have been swept away as that brigade was, and been driven rearward so rapidly upon McClernand's, Hurlbut's, and Wallace's (W. H. L.) as to give them little or no time to form their divisions, and make the stand which Sherman's obstinate resistance with two of his brigades, near Shiloh, enabled them to do.

III. Both sides have claimed the advantage ! The Confederates found their pretension upon the facts of the heavy captures of men, artillery, and colors which they carried from the field, the complete rout inflicted on the Federals on Sunday, and their ability on Monday to hold the ground upon which they had concentrated and made the battle until two P.M., when General Beauregard withdrew from an unprofitable combat ; withdrew in admitted good order, taking with him all the captured guns for which there was transportation. Moreover, his enemy was left so completely battered and stunned as to be unable to pursue. The Federals claim the victory upon the grounds that, on Monday evening, they had recovered their encampments and possession of the field of battle, from which the Confederates had retired, leaving behind their dead and a number of wounded. In this discussion it should be remembered that after the Confederates concentrated on Monday—or from at least as late as nine o'clock A.M. up to the time of their retreat—they uniformly took the offensive and were the assailants. All substantially claimed in reports of Federal subordinate generals is that, after having been worsted between nine A.M. and two P.M., they were then able to hold their own and check their antagonists.* After that, manifestly, there was a complete lull in the battle until about four P.M., when, and no sooner, do the Federals appear to have advanced.

IV. General Beauregard has been blamed unjustly for withdrawing his troops just as they were being launched on Sunday evening against the last Federal position with such numbers and impetus by generals *on the spot* as must have insured complete success. The reports of brigades and regimental commanders completely disprove this allegation. His order

---

* *Vide* reports of Wallace, Nelson, Crittenden, etc., and correspondence of "*Agate.*" *Reb. Rec.* IV. Doc. 114.

really was not distributed before the greater part of the Confederate troops had already given up the attempt for that day to carry the ridge at the Landing. The true reason why the battle of Sunday fell short of the most complete victory of modern war by the capture of the whole Federal army is simply this: After the combat was at its height, about meridian, those superior officers who should have been occupied with the concentration and continuous projection of their troops in heavy masses upon the shattered Federal divisions were at the very front and "perilous edge" of the battle, leading forward regiments, perchance brigades, into action, with great individual intrepidity, and doing a great deal, no doubt, by their personal example to impel small bodies forward. But, meanwhile, to their rear were left the masses of their respective commands, without direction, and thus precious time was lost. The Confederates were not kept continuously massed and employed, either corps or divisions; mere piecemeal onsets were the general method of fighting after twelve o'clock, with this consequence: Sherman was enabled to make several obstinate powerful stands, by which he protracted the battle some hours. Had the corps been held well in hand, massed and pressed continuously upon the tottering, demoralized foe; had general officers attended to the swing and direction of the great war-engine at their disposition, rather than, as it were, becoming so many heads or battering-rams of that machine,*

---

* *Vide Troilus and Cressida*, Scene III. Act I.—*Shakespeare.*

————"the still and mental parts,—
That do contrive how many hands shall strike,
When fitness calls them on; and know, by measure
Of their observant toil, the enemies' weight,—
Why, this hath not a finger's dignity:
They call this—bed-work, mappery, closet-war:
So that the ram, that batters down the wall,
For the great swing and rudeness of his poise,
They place before his hand that made the engine;
Or those, that with the fineness of their souls
By reason guide his execution."

the battle assuredly would have closed at latest by mid-day. By that hour, at most, the whole Federal force might have been urged back and penned up, utterly helpless, in the angle formed between the river and Lick creek, or dispersed along under the river bank, between the two creeks, we repeat, had Confederate corps been kept in continuity, closely pressed *en masse* upon their enemy after the front line had been broken and swept back.   In that case the Federal fragments must have been kept in downward movement, like the loose stones in the bed of a mountain torrent.

V. In a remarkable letter from that distinguished soldier, General Sherman, which we find in the *United States Service Magazine*,* he virtually asserts that, even had General Buell failed to reached the scene with his reënforcements, nevertheless the state of the battle was such at five P.M., Sunday, as "justified" General Grant in giving him orders, at that hour, to "drop the defensive and assume the offensive" at daylight on Monday morning.   This to be the order of the day, irrespective of the advent of Buell!   In other words, Grant had resolved to become, on the morrow, the assailant, forsooth, with Lew Wallace's Division—which, having found it so hard for the last *ten* hours to find the road across "four miles" of country, with the sound of a great battle (and comrades in lire peril) to "quicken" its steps, was not yet on the field —and with such of his own "*startled troops as had recovered their equilibrium.*"   That is to say, with 7000 fresh troops, not yet in hand, added to such commands as Sherman's, which he confesses in his official report was now of a "mixed character,"—without any of three of his four brigades present— and such of the mass then huddled, demoralized and abject, under the river bank since ten o'clock, as might have their

---

* For January, 1865. Leading article.

"equilibrium" reëstablished.* That this was the purpose General Sherman is sure from a story then told him by General Grant of what had happened at Fort Donelson on the 15th of February; and, furthermore, he is very positive that he did not know Buell had already arrived. Now, here the *spirit* rather than the *letter* of the renowned General's paper is to be weighed. To be relevant to the question, he steps into the arena not to discuss but settle, he must mean this : That the offensive was to be taken by the Federal forces then west of the Tennessee, if Buell did not come to their assistance ; further, when the order was given to him to that end, he did not know General Buell's forces were in such proximity as must insure their advent upon the field in large, substantial force to make the projected attack. This must be the substance, "bolted to the bran," of what he utters ; for it were not pertinent to the issue nor frank to say merely that Buell was not there, when he knew that Buell must be there in due season with the requisite troops !

---

* As a proper part of the history of this battle, we here append the vivid picture of the condition to which General Grant's army was reduced, as we find it in the official reports of Generals Buell and Nelson. See also the excellent letter of "Agate," before cited in these pages : "At the Landing," says General Buell, "the banks swarmed with a confused mass of men of various regiments ; there could not have been less than four or five thousand. Later in the day it became much greater ; . . . the throng of disorganized and demoralized troops increased continually by fresh fugitives from the battle, *which steadily closed nearer the Landing*, and these were intermingled with teams striving to get as near the river as possible. WITH FEW EXCEPTIONS, ALL EFFORTS TO FORM THE TROOPS AND MOVE THEM FORWARD TO THE FIGHT UTTERLY FAILED." (*Reb. Rec.* IV. Doc. 114, p. 410.) Says Nelson : "I found cowering under the river-bank from *seven to ten thousand* men, *frantic with fright* and utterly demoralized, who received my gallant division with cries, ' We are whipped !' ' Cut to pieces !' etc. They were insensible to shame and sarcasm, for I tried both." (*Ibid.* IV. p. 413.) This was, be it noted, at five P.M., the hour General Grant was giving the order General Sherman alleges.

We have great respect for the genius, the tenacity, and the shining courage of General Sherman ; we admit his well-won fame ; we have a long personal knowledge of the man ; but, nevertheless, we are constrained in the interest of history to point out facts, as

—"plain as way to parish church,"

that show he wrote hastily, inconsiderately. Saturday night General Grant slept at Savannah, where both General Buell and Nelson's Division had arrived. Before the General-in-Chief left for the battle-field, he ordered Nelson to march thither, which, by a forced march, was done in four hours, or which by an ordinary march might have been effected at most in six. General Sherman says he saw General Grant as early as ten A.M., at a moment of sore stress. When General Buell reached Pittsburg Landing, not later than three o'clock, General Grant was at the Landing, and the two commanders met there. By five P.M., the hour Sherman alleges the order for the offensive was given, Nelson had been long enough in sight at the Landing to throw a brigade across, and upon the last ridge ; and at that hour the last assaults of the Confederates had not taken place, nor until Nelson was in position to help to repel them ! Very well. Would General Grant, knowing that Buell must be up that night, be likely, even at ten o'clock, to omit communicating such important intelligence to his doughty, right-hand lieutenant—the very " sinew and fore-hand " of his army—not only to inspire him to still more obstinate fighting, but as a solace, a relief of inestimable value at the instant ? Or would he, at five o'clock, have failed to acquaint that lieutenant of Buell's presence at the Landing, and Nelson's on the other bank ? Finally, at a moment when the Confederates were swarming down to make their crowning assault upon the last foothold of his fighting wreck, with but a few hundred yards between it and a wide

river, and when, from what had already happened, he could
scarcely hope it would not be a concentrated, terrible onset—
could General Grant, as yet ignorant of that issue, be in condition to give orders looking to the offensive on the next
morning? We are sure not, as well as that General Sherman's memory has deceived him. The fact is, the order of
which he speaks was really given later ; that is, when Generals Grant and Buell visited him together! All who weigh
evidence must come to this conclusion. Were further proof
necessary, it is found in the fact that neither Sherman's, nor
Lew Wallace's, nor any of Hurlbut's troops became really engaged on Monday before ten A.M. ; and that after that hour
even Hurlbut, turning over to McClernand such men as he
had been able to collect, was sent back to the river to glean
and assemble the still scattered fragments of the five dismem-
bered divisions.*

General Sherman is inexact in other particulars ; as, for
example, he avers that in great part General Grant's troops
were "green as militia," and "nearly all" now heard "the
dread sound of battle for the first time." On this point we
have already shown conclusively that, with the exception possibly of four at most, all the regiments he had at Fort Donelson were at Shiloh, or with Lew Wallace. That is, assuming
his force of all arms in the five divisions engaged on Sunday to be 40,000, of that number at least 18,000 must have
been at Fort Donelson, or forty-five *per centum.*† Again, the

---

* As we have said elsewhere, *ante*,
reduced to three subdivisions, respectively under Sherman, McClernand,
and Hurlbut.

† Since this work was partially in
press we have seen the clever and, for
the *Times*, singularly fair book, Swinton's *Twelve Decisive Battles of the War*.

We have ever found Mr. Swinton the
justest as well as the ablest Federal
chronicler, one who could weave a narrative very free from the errors of bias
or carelessness. He, we observe, admits that Grant was superior in numbers on Sunday, but has been misled
into an overestimate of the number of

General, in touching upon the question of the position in which they were attacked, alleges it proved to be judicious,— one that confined the Confederates to a " direct front attack." The military student, looking at the map, will not assent to that proposition. For assuredly the Confederates, as we have said *ubi supra*, might have massed their troops on their left, and upon Sherman, with such weight as to tear his right flank loose from Owl creek, in an instant, and sweep him, and with him McClernand, back upon the river above Pittsburg Landing.

General Sherman fancies that " a combat fierce and bitter" was necessary to " test the manhood of the two armies." But will it not be inquired whether the battle of Shiloh furnished that test ? At the first day's combat the weaker force sprang upon the stronger, nearly half of which was flushed with a recent brilliant success, broke its full ranks into fragments, routed it from its luxurious encampments, stripped it naked of its cannon, its equipage, and shuffled it back for nearly three miles under a steep river-bank ; that is, as far as they could go. For does General Sherman believe that had that river not been there, with its impassable flood, the army of fugitives who betook themselves by meridian to its marge would have halted that near the field ? or would have done otherwise than on another field, whereon he likewise did stout fighting, his full share of the battle, both with nerve and skill,—need we say Bull Run ? Neither can the battle of Monday be adduced as a test of relative manhood. The odds of fresh troops thrown forward, but held completely at bay

---

untried troops in that army. He was not at his usual pains to calculate the percentage that had been at Donelson ; and so also does he overestimate the portion of Bragg's Corps that had been at Pensacola, that is, not over fifty per cent ; and where, furthermore, they had only been exposed to artillery shelling at long range.

up to two o'clock by at most 20,000 Confederates, who had already been fighting eleven hours the day before, afford no nice measurement of manhood.

VI. So much has been said, so much credited and grown to be the source of irritation and ill-feeling on the part of the triumphant section in the late war, in regard to the treatment of their prisoners and wounded enemies by the Confederate officers and soldiery, beginning with Manassas and not ending with Fort Pillow, that we deem it of use here to place on record the following from a Federal newspaper correspondent of the day, (*Cincinnati Commercial :*) "I am glad," says the writer, on the battle-field, " to be able to say something good of an army of traitors. . . . No instance came to my knowledge in which our dead or wounded were treated *in so diabolical* a manner as they were *reported* to be at Manassas and Pea Ridge. They were invariably, whenever practicable, kindly cared for." (*Reb. Rec.* IV. Doc. 114, p. 416.) "A. Heckenlooper tells me," continues this eye-witness, "that one of his corporals who was wounded received many attentions. . . An officer handed him a rubber blanket, saying that he needed it bad enough, but a wounded man needed it more ; others brought him food and water, and wrapped him in woolen blankets. *Such instances were common, and among the hundreds* of dead and wounded not one showed signs of the barbarity of which the rebels are accused."

CHAPTER V.

June 10th to September 30th, 1862.

THE arduous marches, out-post service, skirmishes, and
battles in which Forrest's Regiment had been continuously
employed during the six months just ended had sensibly
winnowed its ranks. Beginning the campaign in Kentucky
with about six hundred effectives, it could not now muster
more than three hundred rank and file. The remainder had

fallen either in battle or hospital, or were disabled by wounds and diseases contracted as a consequence of their service in the field. Colonel Forrest himself was suffering a good deal from his Shiloh wound, but nevertheless continued on duty, unwilling to be absent from his regiment at the juncture.

On the 10th of June, Colonel James E. Saunders, a prominent citizen of North-Alabama, who, though over sixty years of age, had been actively connected with the operations of the Confederate Cavalry for some time previously, on the staff of Colonel John Adams, in the vicinity of Chattanooga, had visited General Beauregard, and urged that a competent officer should be assigned to command the cavalry operations which looked to Chattanooga as a base. He designated Colonel Forrest as suitable ; but General Beauregard, who already had formed a high opinion of his value as a cavalry officer, was at first loth to spare him from his own immediate army. Recognizing, however, the importance also of the command in question in connection with his own projected operations, he assented to the request. The necessary orders were given, and an application was made at once to the War Department for the promotion of Colonel Forrest to the grade of Brigadier-General, as not only essential to the position to which he had found it necessary to assign him, but as merited by past services.* Having received his orders, Colonel Forrest made some scanty, hasty preparations for the change of sphere and journey involved, bade his old comrades farewell as their Colonel, and on the 11th of June, accompanied by Colonel Saunders, set out to repair to his new and widening field of command and of martial exploits.†

---

* Really, the troops to the command of which Colonel Forrest was assigned were serving within the limits of General Kirby Smith's department ;. and the colonels of two of the regiments were senior, by commission, to him.

† For subsequent history of Forrest's Regiment, see Appendix and Index.

The journey was made on horseback, with an escort, under command of Captain William Forrest, of some ten picked men of his old regiment, with each one of whom was connected some story of peculiar gallantry, and some eight or ten others, officers and men, who attached themselves to his suite. Pursuing the most direct route, through North-Alabama, Colonel Forrest arrived at Chattanooga on the 18th or 19th of June.   Reporting forthwith through the local commander, General Leadbetter, to General Kirby Smith, orders of assignment were duly issued a few days later.   The command assigned was a brigade of cavalry, composed of the Eighth Texas, Colonel John A. Wharton ;* the First Louisiana, Colonel John W. Scott ; the Second Georgia, Colonel J. K. Lawton ;† and Helm's Kentucky regiment, commanded by Lieutenant-Colonel Woodward ;‡ a force, in all, of about two

---

* This regiment was raised and commanded by the lamented Colonel Terry, whose brief military career, beginning as a volunteer scout at the first Manassas, was full of distinction.   He was killed at Woodsonville, Kentucky, in a cavalry affair, in the fall of 1861. Colonel John A. Wharton succeeded to the command.   The Lieutenant-Colonel was John G. Walker, a distinguished lawyer, of Houston, Texas ; and the Major, Thomas Harrison, who subsequently became a most valuable and conspicuous Brigadier-General of Cavalry.   The privates included a large number of the wealthiest and best-educated young men of Texas, who, with many others specially trained in the business of stock-raising on the vast prairies of that State, had acquired a marvelous skill in horsemanship.   The career of this regiment

has been one of the most brilliant in the annals of war.

† We have been unable to gain any details of the history or organization of this regiment.   The privates were fine-looking men, and better skilled in the sabre exercise than any other of the command.

‡ The Colonel of this regiment, Ben Hardin Helm, a graduate of West-Point, was one of the most gifted and patriotic young men of Kentucky.   He was about thirty years of age, and, being a brother-in-law of President Lincoln, had a wide field for promotion open to him in the Federal service.   Nevertheless, he chose to cast his fortune with his section, and fell brilliantly at the battle of Chickamauga.

The greater part of the officers and men of this regiment were of the most respectable families of Kentucky, volun-

thousand rank and file. The latter regiment had recently undergone a surprise and night attack in the Sequatchie Valley, under the results of which it was smarting at the time. Elements of discord were at work in other portions of the command prejudicial to their military spirit and efficiency. And that fruitful source of trouble in armies, the question of seniority of commission, was likewise added, to give their new commander difficulty and concern in the outset of his association with them. Colonel Scott's Regiment, however, some four or five days later, was detached, and the First Georgia Battalion, Colonel Morrison, assigned in its stead. Thus the question of rank was removed ; but, meanwhile, another embarrassment had arisen from the expiration of the period for which the greater part of the companies of Helm's Regiment had been enrolled, twelve months. Now disinclined to reenter the service in their then organization, in a few days there only remained of it some two companies.

Looking around for an important object for operations, and by a successful expedition to raise the tone of his force to a more healthy state, Forrest determined to throw his brigade into Middle Tennessee, and there make a descent upon a Federal force which he understood was established at Murfreesboro. By the 6th of July, therefore, his preparations,

---

tary exiles from their comfortable and beautiful homes.

It is proper here to state that the reluctance of the Kentuckians to reënroll was not caused by any desire or purpose to leave the service, but grew out of a wish to become permanently a part of a Kentucky Brigade under Colonel Morgan, who had already become distinguished as a partisan officer. Colonels Forrest and Morgan had an interview during the last week in June, at General Kirby Smith's headquarters, the result of which was an urgent recommendation to their superior that the First Kentucky should be transferred to Morgan's command, while Forrest should receive in exchange Lieutenant-Colonel Starne's Tennessee Battalion ; but this exchange was deemed inexpedient and did not take place.

and plans were matured for this expedition, and on that day he began to cross the Tennessee at Chattanooga, with about one thousand troopers.* Setting out on the 8th, he reached Altamont, near the summit of the Cumberland mountains, on the 10th. Moving thence on the road in the direction of and to a point ten miles to the north-east of Sparta, he there effected an arranged junction with Colonel Morrison and his battalion, some three hundred strong, on the evening of the 11th, that battalion having come across the mountain from Kingston, in East-Tennessee.† Forrest now organized his force, increased somewhat above thirteen hundred men, for one of those operations for which subsequently he became so well known, and which in time made him a terror to all outlying Federal detachments.

At McMinnville, late in the afternoon of the 12th, some scouts previously detached met him and reported that all was quiet along the line of railroad leading from Bridgeport through Murfreesboro to Nashville, and that apparently the enemy were as yet wholly ignorant of his hostile movements. It was here he made his regimental and battalion commanders fully acquainted with his plans and expectations, and gave specific instructions as to the conduct of the expedition, including strict orders to keep each command "well closed up." These details arranged, the march was resumed and continued to the village of Woodbury about eleven at night. Here the people were found in a state of deep excitement and distress. The ladies thronged the streets, and in moving terms soon made Colonel Forrest acquainted with the cause—that the

---

* Eighth Texas, 400 men, Second Georgia, 450, a battalion of Tennesseeans, under Major Baxter Smith, 120 strong, and the two companies of Kentuckians.

† It had seen field service in East-Tennessee, and joined the brigade with a good character for efficiency.

Federals, entering the village suddenly the evening before, had arrested and carried off to Murfreesboro nearly every man, old and young, with menaces of summary punishment. Much affected by the relation of the occurrence, Colonel Forrest assured them that they might confidently look for the restoration of their husbands and kinsmen by the next sunset, a promise which he was actually able to perform. This had a happy effect. All vied with each other in a liberal hospitality, and an abundance of food and forage were provided for the command, which was halted at this point until one o'clock on the morning of the 13th. Then the movement was rapidly resumed, Murfreesboro being still eighteen miles distant.

By five A.M., the vicinity of their point of destination was attained ; here the scouts sent ahead to reconnoitre were overtaken, and reported the Federal pickets were only half a mile distant. These Colonel Wharton, whose regiment was in advance, was directed to send forward a small detachment to capture, which was successfully accomplished, and within an hour the pickets, fifteen in number, were brought to the Confederate leader.* A few moments later some other scouts also returned, and reported that they had traversed the Federal encampments, and found all evidently unaware of the impending danger.

Dispositions were therefore made for an immediate attack. The whole force was formed in column of fours, the Eighth Texas in front. The orders were to move at a trot until in

---

* The principal scouts employed in these operations were Captains Fred James and Nichols, afterward a valuable officer under Colonel Paul Anderson. Captain James belonged to Bragg's Army, from which he was absent on furlough at the time. A native and citizen of Murfreesboro, he was a gallant, well-educated gentleman. He fell at the battle of Murfreesboro, 31st of December, 1862, in sight of his mother's house.

sight of the Federal encampment, when Colonel Wharton was to charge it, with his regiment in column of platoons. At the same time the Second Georgia was to dash into and sweep through the main streets of the town in the same order, capturing provost-guard and all Federal officers and men that might chance to be in the place, and seize and secure all supplies and any trains that might be there. Major Smith, with his battalion reënforced by the Kentuckians, was to throw himself rapidly around upon the turnpikes leading both to Nashville and Lebanon, and cut off retreat in either direction, as well as to give notice of any hostile approach from that quarter ; while Colonel Morrison would get rearward and there await the turn of events, ready to give aid wheresoever most needed.

Moving with his advance, as was ever his wont,* Forrest, on arriving in sight of the suburbs of Murfreesboro, saw gleaming in the gray, subdued light of that early hour the white tents of a large encampment out on the Liberty turnpike, about half a mile eastward of the place, manifestly unaware of the nearness of the least peril.† Led by their Colonel, the gallant Texans, without waiting for the final signal for the charge, dashed on at a splendid pace, and in a few moments were in the very heart of the Federal cantonment, the occupants of which were at the instant for the most part in their tents, but from which they speedily emerged. Many, undressed and seeking all possible means of shelter from their fierce-smiting adversaries, rushed in wild confusion

---

* Instinctively he adopted this precept of the art of war, as enforced and illustrated by Napier in his *History of the Peninsular War.*

† Occupied by five companies Ninth Michigan Volunteers and a squadron of the Fourth Kentucky Federal Cavalry. *Reb. Rec.* V. Doc. 88, p. 286, Report of Colonel Duffield. There were also in the camp a considerable number of men going to and from Buell's Army.

through the mazes of the encampment, hotly pursued by the eager Texans, shouting as in a hot chase on their broad prairies, and striking right and left or using the pistol freely.* At length some of the Federal infantry, rallied by their officers, had made a handsome stand, and by a mishap at the moment of the charge only about six of Wharton's companies or some two hundred men, had followed him, the rest having been led, with the Second Georgia, directly into the public square.

The Texans, now brought under a galling musketry fire from behind wagons and other effective cover, were too weak in numbers to carry the position. So severe, indeed, did the fire become that Colonel Wharton, painfully wounded, felt obliged to withdraw from the contest, and return on the McMinnville road with the prisoners whom he had taken, including the Federal cavalry found in a camp somewhat detached from the infantry, which had been captured just as they were about to mount their horses. Major Baxter Smith's Battalion also assisted in this part of the affair.† In the mean time, four companies of the Eighth Texas and the Second Georgia Regiment, cheering lustily, had charged into the public square,

---

* Among those wounded was Colonel Duffield, the Federal commander, who was probably shot by Colonel Wharton in person, when surrounded by many of his men, whom he was attempting to rally.

† Colonel Duffield, on the contrary, says that, apprised by the noise made by the horses on the macadamized turnpike, the Federals had been roused, and were drawn up ready to receive this charge, before which, though fierce and impetuous, they retired steadily and in good order to the centre of the encampment; and there, after a struggle of some twenty minutes, nearly hand-to-hand fighting, the Confederates were repulsed; and, breaking, fled in the wildest confusion, pursued by the Federals as skirmishers; but that the latter suffered severely.

Another account, however, says that all were asleep at the first onset, and that Duffield was then wounded; that some infantry were finally rallied and made fight, but were overwhelmed and forced to surrender.—*Reb. Rec.* V. Doc. 88, p. 288.

and surrounded the court-house, which was occupied by a company of the Ninth Michigan. The noise quickly brought the inhabitants of the town forth from their houses, greatly startled but presently delighted on finding their streets swarming with the dear, gray-clad soldiers of their cause. Regardless of their *dishabille*, men and women rushed out to greet them with incoherent phrases of satisfaction and gladness ; regardless, too, of the danger, for already scattered parties of Federals had commenced firing from fences and outhouses, while a sharp fire was going on from the court-house. So severe did the fire become from the court-house, in a little while, that it wrought a hesitation in the ranks of the assailants, who were in fact twice repulsed. But the women, meanwhile, were mingling among the men, and cheering them by their smiles and heartfelt, thankful words. Indeed, the coolest Confederate was now thoroughly roused by the scene ; and with a loud cheer of " Long live the women !" the Texans and Georgians, led by Forrest, sprang forward in the face of a withering fire in front from the court-house, while Morrison brought up his men to the rear, or west side. The doors were quickly battered down, the building was carried, and the garrison captured after their formidable defense. In the charge, a German soldier, Fred Koerper, of Memphis, of Forrest's escort, conspicuous for his bravery, and endeared to his officers and comrades by his cheerfulness and soldierly qualities, was killed, to the deep regret of all who knew him.*

---

* Frederick Koerper was born in Prussia in 1829. His father, a soldier of the First Napoleon, emigrated to the United States in 1839, with his family, and became a resident of Cleveland, Ohio. Thence, at the age of fifteen, young Koerper removed to Memphis, Tennessee ; and, a few years afterward, to New-Orleans. There he resided till 1856, when he returned to Memphis, where he continued in business — a popular, fashionable barber—until the beginning of the war in 1861. First volunteering in McDonald's company for sixty days, at the expiration of his term of service he returned, and re-

Both court-house and jail were found filled with citizens, at least one hundred and fifty in number, of the place and surrounding country, including those of Woodbury, already mentioned. Arrested and thrown into prison at the instance of infamous informers, on various pretexts, six of the number, prominent citizens, were at the moment under sentence of death ; or, as expressed by a Federal newspaper correspondent, were to "expiate their crime on the gallows."* The neighborhood was filled with the wives and families of these captives, who had followed after their seizures, and who now hastened upon the scene almost frantic with joy at the happy release of their husbands and kinsmen. Soon the spectacle became so touching that no one could witness it unmoved ; and tears might have been seen to glisten on the weather-bronzed, powder-begrimed cheeks of many of Forrest's fiercest riders.

At the same time, an animated, thorough hunt had been made in all directions through the town for Federal officers and men billeted in various houses. Suddenly aroused from their comfortable beds by the dread sounds of a night attack, many had sped and sought concealment elsewhere ; but from detected coverts they were quickly dragged forth, notably a crest-fallen, unseemly gang contrasted with the more manful

---

mained at home till a few weeks before the battle of Shiloh. Then repairing to Burnsville, Miss., he rejoined his former commander, Captain McDonald, of whose second company he continued a member until detached at Tupelo, in June, 1862, as one of the "ten picked men" to accompany Colonel Forrest to Chattanooga. Meanwhile, at Shiloh, he had shown notable courage and ad-dress in the capture of a Federal colonel within the enemy's lines.

"Always gay and cheerful," (says one of his comrades,) "Fred Koerper was a fine, stalwart specimen of German manhood. And brief as was his career, it is not too much to say of him, He was one of the best soldiers that ever followed the banner of Forrest."

* *Reb. Rec.* V. Doc. 88, p. 288.

of their comrades, who, meanwhile, were making a persistent combat from all available positions.

Among those lodging in the town was the Federal commander, Brigadier-General Crittenden, to effect whose capture Colonel Forrest had sent Colonel Saunders, with a small detachment, to the inn on the square, where it was understood he had established his headquarters. After an ineffectual search through the house, Colonel Saunders and his party, emerging and remounting their horses, were making their way across the square, when a general fire was opened upon them from the windows of the court-house, and that brave and zealous gentleman received a ball which passed through his right lung and entirely through his body ; but, nevertheless, he maintained his seat in his saddle until able to ride several squares, to the residence of a citizen, south-eastward from the square, into which he was taken, as all supposed, mortally wounded.*

The court-house having fallen into his hands, and all the Federals immediately in Murfreesboro having been taken prisoner or placed otherwise *hors de combat*, Forrest made his dispositions immediately to attack the Third Minnesota, reported to be encamped on the east bank of Stone river, about one mile and a half from the town. This he deemed it best to do before attempting to capture the smaller but more

---

* This was the same gentleman at whose instance Colonel Forrest had been assigned the command of his brigade. He was not subject to military duty, being over sixty years of age, but kept the field, rendering most valuable service up to the time of his severe wounding, as subsequently, for he recovered, and at the present writing, January, 1867, is an admirable specimen physically of cultured manhood.

On the occasion in question, it is proper to add, he was accompanied by another volunteer aid-de-camp, Franck C. Dunnington, Esq., formerly editor of the *Nashville Union*, also by a well-known citizen of Huntsville, Ala., Mr. Lawrence Watkins.

General Crittenden a little later was found concealed in a private apartment of the tavern.

strongly posted force that had been rallied in the camp of the Ninth Michigan, fearing that otherwise the detached force might effect its escape. Accordingly he made a rapid detour to the right, so as to defeat that contingency. On reaching the encampment, it was found comparatively evacuated, the Federals having just moved out in the direction of Murfreesboro to join their comrades in that quarter. Forrest's force assembled for this affair consisted of the Georgians, Major Smith's Tennesseeans, the Kentucky squadron, and some twenty men under Paul F. Anderson. Seeing the Confederates approach, the Federals, then about six hundred yards southward of their camp, halted and formed in line of battle, some nine companies of infantry and four pieces of artillery. Directing the Georgians to confront and menace the enemy and engage with skirmishers, taking Major Smith with his men, including the Kentuckians and three companies of Morrison's Georgians, under Major Harper, Forrest pushed rapidly around to the right and rear of the encampment, which proved to be still occupied by about one hundred men, posted behind a strong barricade of wagons and some large limestone ledges which afforded excellent cover, difficult to carry. He thereupon ordered a charge ; this was promptly and handsomely made, Majors Smith and Harper leading their men. They were met, however, with a stubborn, brave defense. Twice, indeed, the Confederates were repulsed. But Forrest, drawing his men up for a third effort, made a brief appeal to their manhood, and, putting himself at the head of the column, the charge was again ordered, this time with success. The encampment was penetrated, and the greater part of the Federals were either killed or captured. A few only escaped to the main body, drawn up, as before said, some six hundred yards southward.*

* It was in this charge that there occurred an incident which has been grossly misrepresented, by misjudging adversaries, to General Forrest's preju-

The Georgians, hearing the struggle in the encampment, and supposing that it proceeded from an attack made by Forrest upon the rear of the main Federal force in their front, made a dashing charge, deployed in line, breaking through the enemy's array in the face of their artillery, sweeping the open field across which they charged. Nevertheless, the casualties were very few, and, unchecked, the Georgians, riding through some infantry, passed to the rear of the position.

Finding, however, that the enemy, quickly reforming their sundered line, held their ground fimly—an elevated ridge, from which evidently they were only to be driven at much cost of precious life—Forrest promptly changed his plan of operations, with that fertility of resource in sudden emergencies which has signalized his whole career. Placing Major Harper with three companies so as to hinder a retreat toward Nashville, disposing Morrison's other four companies as skirmishers in front to prevent a movement on Murfreesboro, and sending off on the McMinnville road the prisoners just taken, with such captured munitions as could be transported by the wagons found in the encampment, Forrest led Lawton's Regiment and Smith's Battalion rapidly back to Murfreesboro, sending a staff-officer at the same time for the Eighth Texas, which he found, to his surprise, had been withdrawn some four miles on the McMinnville road.

It was now about one P.M., and as yet little of a decisive character had been accomplished, while among many of his officers there was manifest a perilous want of confidence in

---

dice. While traversing the camp, he was fired at by a negro *camp-follower*, one of whose balls cut his hat-band ; but, just as the negro was about to fire the fifth time, Forrest killed him with his pistol at the distance of thirty paces. This negro displayed no common deliberation in his purpose to slay the Confederate leader.

the ability of the command to triumph. Indeed, so far did this spirit reach, that some officers urged Colonel Forrest to rest content with what had been accomplished and quit the field without further and, as they were satisfied, fruitless yet costly efforts to carry the Federal position. But, instead of heeding the suggestions of his subordinates, Forrest, dismounting Major Smith's Battalion, including the Kentuckians, threw them forward, with directions to engage in an active skirmish with the Federal force still occupying the encampment of the Ninth Michigan. Lieutenant-Colonel Hood, of the Second Georgia, at the same time, was directed to lead that regiment to a point leftward of the Federal position and prepare for a charge dismounted, while Colonel Lawton was detained to write a demand, to be sent by a flag of truce, for the enemy's immediate surrender. All the while, Smith and his men were maintaining a brisk skirmish ; and just as the Confederate demand was presented, Wharton's Regiment, under Lieutenant-Colonel Walker, came opportunely in full view. The effect was most fortunate ; without further parley, and very much to the surprise of a large portion of the Confederate officers, the surrender was at once made. This achieved, setting a portion of his command to collect the wagon-train and fill them with supplies most necessary, and to destroy such as could not be carried off, Forrest, with little loss of time, sent Captain Strange, his Adjutant-General, to the beleaguered Minnesotians, with a demand for their surrender, to save the further effusion of blood. At this, Colonel Lester, their commander, asked for an interview with Colonel Duffield, of the Ninth Michigan, who, severely wounded, was a prisoner of war at the house of Colonel Maney, a gentleman of Murfreesboro, where an interview and consultation between the Federal Colonels soon took place. Lester, however, still asked for an hour's delay, to confer with his officers. Forrest, giving him thirty min-

utes, sent Captain Strange with him to receive his final answer, fully satisfied that it would terminate in a surrender,
to insure which he ostentatiously displayed his several commands along the path Colonel Lester was led in going to and
returning from the interview with Duffield, so as to make an
appearance of greater numbers than were really present. As
anticipated, Captain Strange soon returned with the intelligence that Colonel Lester had consented to capitulate.
Forrest, now riding forward, received the surrender of some
five hundred infantry and Hewitt's Battery, and the last of
the Federal force that had been in occupation of and a terror
to the people of Murfreesboro for some time past were now
in his hands.

The proximity of large Federal garrisons at neighboring
towns and along the line of the railroad, which might be
speedily concentrated and attack or intercept his movements
with a superior force, made it necessary for Forrest to be
now both diligent and alert, and lose no time in such a dangerous position. Orders were, therefore, given to hasten the
destruction of all Federal supplies which could not be removed, and by six P.M. the last of his command had filed out
of Murfreesboro on their way toward McMinnville. The results
of this affair, it remains to say, were some 1765* prisoners,
including about one hundred clerks, teamsters, and other
staff *employés*, as many as six hundred head of horses and
mules, forty wagons, five or six ambulances, four pieces of
artillery, and twelve hundred stands of arms, which were

---

* In addition to these prisoners, thus
turned loose on their parole, one hundred and two straggling fugitive Federal soldiers came into Murfreesboro on
the fourteenth of July, after Colonel
Forrest had left, and seeking out Colonel Saunders, who had been left, as
was supposed, mortally wounded, besought him to parole them also, which
he did in due form, desperately wounded as he was. It was soon after this
affair that General Buell issued an
order forbidding his men to accept such
paroles.

largely distributed among the troops in lieu of those in their hands of an inferior character, many valuable supplies carried off, and a very large quantity of stores, including, it was said, thirty thousand suits of clothing for Buell's Army.*

The effect upon those through whom it had been accomplished was immediately perceptible. It infused a new life and energy at once into their movements, inspired a self-confidence which had been materially shattered by previous miscarriages and disaster, gave an assurance of the judgment and capacity in their leader that had been wanting,† and made that leader more willing to trust himself in the field with his brigade hereafter in delicate and dangerous operations. Besides, it was the beginning of that reputation for daring, skillfully conceived and executed forays and sudden assaults upon isolated positions which soon made Forrest's movements a source of constant apprehension to all adversaries within his reach.

This affair, it is worthy of note, happened on his birthday, and, as may be readily supposed, no *fête* in honor of the event could have been so acceptable as this martial success not many miles distant from the place of his birth. On the eve preceding, Forrest, in a short address, having acquainted his command with the fact of the approach of his birthday, pleasantly called upon them to aid him to signalize it by a substantial victory.

It must also be related, as a part of the history of the times, that the vanquished Federals had exercised a harsh and arrogant dominion over the people of Murfreesboro and the sur-

---

* A Federal writer estimates the pecuniary loss to the government of the United States at nearly a million of dollars.—*Reb. Rec.* V. Doc. 88, p. 289.

† The present writer conversed with an officer of rank who had left Chattanooga just as Forrest was leaving for this expedition, and which that officer characterized as rash, inconsiderate, and likely to lead to disaster.

rounding country, who, non-combatants as they were, had
been made the victims of constant wrongful and oppressive
exaction and restrictions discreditable to the age or civilized
warfare. The provost-marshal, churlish when not cruel, it
would seem, delighted in harassing the women, going so far
even as to refuse them permission to attend their churches or
to allow as many as three to collect in a group on the street
or elsewhere. The proof of this rigorous tyranny, we are
assured, was too abundant to be doubted.*

Desiring to avoid the risk of making invidious distinctions
between those who served under him in this expedition with
so signal bravery and zeal in his notes touching it, their
commander has limited his remarks to the fact that the conduct of almost all—officers and men—was highly creditable ;
that there were numerous instances of conspicuous coolness
and soldierly bearing, and much ability for command displayed
by his officers.

After having sent off in the direction of McMinnville all
the supplies practicable, destroying the rest, Colonel Forrest repaired with his prisoners, late that afternoon, to Reedys-
ville, nine miles eastward of Murfreesboro, and halted for the
night, having previously detached Major Baxter Smith's Battalion to destroy the bridges as far southward as Christiana.
Upon the return of this detachment, the next morning, he
threw out other detachments in observation toward Lebanon
and Nashville, Shelbyville and Winchester, to ascertain definitely the movements of the enemy after hearing of his descent upon Murfreesboro. When this had been done, he

---

* On the other hand, a Federal writer describes this very Provost-Marshal,
Oliver C. Rounds, as entirely too lax
and indulgent, though it is admitted
at the same time the jail was full, as we
have before cited, of " rebel prisoners,"
gathered from the country, many of
whom were to " expiate their crimes on
the gallows."—*Reb. Rec.* V. Doc. 88, p.
288.

found that, with a proper guard to insure the safety of his prisoners, there were not men enough remaining to drive the captured artillery and train. Separating the Federal officers from their men, and putting the former in motion for Mc-Minnville, escorted by a company of cavalry, he drew up the other prisoners, and promised, if enough would volunteer as drivers of the wagon-train and artillery as far as McMinnville, that he would there parole the whole band and let them make their way homeward to see their families. This proposition was received with hearty cheers for "General Forrest," who now resumed his march and encamped that night at McMinn-ville. Here he overtook Colonel Wharton, with a company of his regiment and some three hundred of the men who had left the field, and having in charge General Crittenden and about two hundred and fifty prisoners, the first captured on the day before. The Colonel was suffering from a severe flesh-wound in the right arm, which had prevented him from returning with his regiment the day before, when it had been called back. by Colonel Forrest.

As promised, the prisoners, except the officers, were now paroled. This having been accomplished by eight o'clock on the morning of the 15th, the number set at liberty in that manner was 1700, including, as before said, at least one hundred staff *employés.*

Provided with two days' rations, they took the roads leading in the direction of the Ohio river, manifestly delighted with the opportunity to be thus respited, by their parole, from field service for some time to come. The Federal officers retained as prisoners, but under a qualified parole not to escape on the way thither, with most of the wagons and the captured stores and the artillery, were next dispatched under a small guard to the headquarters of General Kirby Smith, at Knoxville.

Satisfied from reports of scouts in all directions that it

might be done without hazard, Forrest remained encamped, giving his men and horses rest at McMinnville until the afternoon of the 18th, by which time all detachments except a few scouts had returned. He then put his column in motion on Lebanon, about fifty miles distant, where he understood a detachment of five hundred Federal cavalry were stationed. Proposing to surprise them, he moved, with little intermission for either rest, food, or sleep, to the immediate vicinity about dawn on the 20th. Making all necessary dispositions at once for the occasion, he dashed with his now confident command into the place, but had the keen disappointment to see that his enemy had been forewarned and was leaving at full speed by the Nashville road with such a *start* as to make pursuit fruitless. Posting pickets on all the approaches, so as to guard against the possibility of a surprise, Forrest remained with his command in observation at Lebanon until the next morning, the recipients, meanwhile, of unbounded hospitality from the open-handed people of the place and neighborhood. His men were fed not only during their stay upon poultry, choice hams, and roasted pigs, but more than three days' rations of these dainties were supplied spontaneously for the march.

After leaving Lebanon, the line of march brought the command, about one P.M., to the Hermitage—in his lifetime the favorite home, and in death the burial-place of the illustrious Jackson. The Confederate leader, halting here, gave his men an hour to visit the precincts redolent with martial memories of peculiar interest and value to the young men of his brigade, and well calculated to influence them

" To matchless valor and adventures high."

And here, too, a pleasant incident served to brighten the wearisome and perilous routine of the expedition. A party of ten or twelve young ladies, escorted by a few gentlemen, appeared upon the scene to celebrate in its groves the first anniversary of the battle of Manassas, and at the same time do honor to the tomb and fame of the great Tennesseean. With these charming daughters of the neighborhood the moments sped pleasantly and with happy effect upon their young countrymen.

Soon after leaving the Hermitage, in the direction of Nashville, information was received from scouts that the Federal General Nelson had gone, *via* Murfreesboro, in pursuit of the Confederates with a force of some 3500 men, chiefly infantry. It was now determined to move to Stone river, seven miles east of Nashville, where, coming upon the Federal pickets around the city, he charged and captured a portion, driving the remainder into the city. Moving around, now, by a left-hand road to the Murfreesboro turnpike, near the lunatic asylum, another picket force was encountered, and, capturing a few, the rest were driven in. At the same time, an independent command of Confederate guerrillas, without concert, chanced to dash in upon their pickets, on the Franklin road, making the Federals suppose that the place was surrounded and threatened with a serious assault. The long roll and other signals of alarm were therefore to be heard on all sides.

Gathering his force in hand, Forrest then swept down upon a small intrenched outpost covering the bridge over Mill creek, four miles from the heart of the city, and carried it, taking some twenty prisoners ; and pursuing the rest up the creek to another bridge, half a mile southward, forty men were there surrounded and captured. Leaving a company to destroy this bridge, he next moved with celerity still further up the creek about one mile to Antioch Station, where the enemy attempted to make a stand, but were quickly routed by Lieutenant-Colonel Walker and the Eighth Texas, thirty-five prisoners and their arms and supplies falling into his hands, while the station-house, some cars, and a bridge were burned. A squadron was then sent up the road toward Murfreesboro, burned a large quantity of railroad wood, and captured some fifteen Federals ; having thus burned four bridges, and captured some one hundred and forty-five of the enemy, with fifteen to twenty killed or left wounded on the ground, without loss of one Confederate.   Forrest now moved over to the Murfreesboro and Nashville turnpike, where he was informed by his scouts that Nelson was returning with his force in all haste toward Nashville.   His command by this time, men and animals, were so greatly jaded as to make it injudicious to attempt to harass Nelson ; therefore, turning aside by a by-way, known in the country as the " Chicken road," he encamped his command not more than a mile from the turnpike.   Here the prisoners taken that afternoon were paroled, and while this was going on Nelson's column had been distinctly heard for several hours as they passed along the turnpike.

By daylight, the Confederates were again in their saddles, and on the way back in the direction of Murfreesboro.   Soon apprised of this by his scouts, Nelson countermarched and pursued.   Forrest, however, turned off within six miles of Murfreesboro, in the direction of McMinnville, while Nelson pushed on to the former place, where, finding his adversary out of his reach and his own infantry thoroughly foot-sore and fatigued, he gave up the operation as useless, expressing his disgust in energetic terms, and denouncing the folly of attempting to catch cavalry with infantry.   Reaching McMinnville in due season, Forrest halted until the 10th of August, as the position was one well calculated for observation and menace upon the movements of the enemy, and the country abounded in supplies willingly furnished.

On the 10th, Colonel Forrest, having occasion to visit Chattanooga, turned over his command to Lieutenant-Colonel Hood, Second Georgia, and repaired thither on horseback across the Cumberland mountains.   In his absence, a Federal column of three thousand infantry and eight hundred cavalry was found to be moving on McMinnville, and Colonel Hood was obliged to fall back upon Sparta. There Forrest rejoined the brigade after an absence of only four days, in the course of which he had ridden two hundred miles over the Cumberland mountains and back. Daily skirmishes took place for the next eight or ten days with the Federal cavalry, who had followed to the neighborhood of Sparta. The Confederate leader then shifted his force over, first to Smithville, and then to Woodbury, thus gaining the Federal rear.

Meanwhile, Forrest had received his appointment as a Brigadier-General;* and General Bragg had established his headquarters at Chattanooga, where he was concentrating the "Army of Mississippi," by railroad, for his subsequent campaign into Kentucky.

From Woodbury, after halting a few hours, General Forrest led his command again in the direction of Murfreesboro, now reoccupied by the Federals, and menaced the place with another descent; but on getting within eight miles, turning directly to the left and striking the railroad near Manchester, some ten miles northward of Tullahoma, he captured a picket post of twenty men. After that, moving along the line of the railroad branch to McMinnville up to within ten miles of the latter place, he destroyed all the intermediate bridges and otherwise disabled the road. Learning definitely that the Federal cavalry at McMinnville had been strongly reënforced, and that two divisions of infantry also occupied the town, Forrest concluded to take post in the mountain pass at Altamont and await General Bragg. He accordingly took the road thither, and at dusk on the 29th of August, reached a cove at the foot of the Cumberland mountains, where he halted to send forward scouts to reconnoitre the pass ahead.

---

* Commission dated 21st of July, 1862.

These returned next morning, about daylight, from the vicinity of Altamont, which they reported to be in possession of General McCook, with all the passes in that quarter.   Other scouts soon after came in with the intelligence that heavy columns of the enemy were moving toward his position by each of the roads leading to it.*   The situation evidently was most critical—one from which the Confederate leader could only extricate himself by coolness and skill. Keeping his best scouts out on all the approaches, he rode to a commanding point on the mountain to get a personal observation of the enemy's movements, and was happily able to see for at least five miles on the three roads that entered the cove, and upon each of which he observed a Federal column approaching, as had been reported.   He learned, likewise, through another scout, that General McCook was moving down upon him directly from Altamont.   There was plainly no time for delay or deliberation ; therefore, quickly forming his men in column of fours, he moved back a short distance to a dry creek that he had noticed, the deep bed of which fortunately ran almost parallel to the McMinnville road.   With that decision, that swift calculation of resources and chances, characteristic of the man, and one of his highest qualities as a leader, he did not hesitate to throw his command into this opportune shelter. Scarcely had he done so, when the enemy came up the road, and, halting in a piece of woods, began to form line not six hundred yards from where the Confederates were quietly passing, completely hidden by the high overhanging banks of the water-course just mentioned.†   Having successfully effected

---

* Namely, from Manchester, Winchester, and McMinnville, uniting in one road in the cove, leading out over the mountain by Altamont.

† So well and confidently had these toils been set, that a telegraphic message was sent to General Buell, that Forrest and eight hundred men had been captured.—*MS. Notes of General Forrest.*

this movement, Forrest, emerging from concealment, took the road rapidly northward toward McMinnville, fifteen miles distant ; but when within six or seven miles of that place, he turned off by another road toward the McMinnville-Murfreesboro turnpike, leaving McMinnville some four or five miles to the east. Striking that highway at a point near where he found a Federal force of infantry and artillery drawn up in position, and sweeping around, westwardly, at a gallop, with a loud cheer from every trooper, the Federals appeared so much paralyzed by the suddenness of the encounter that they fired only a few scattering discharges without harm to the Confederates.*

Free, now, of the several Federal columns that for a time had almost cut off his escape, Forrest led his brigade, at a less rapid rate, to Sparta, in which direction he understood General Bragg was then moving with his army, instead of through Altamont, as originally had been arranged. Bragg's advance was already at Sparta when General Forrest reached there, on the 3d of September, but the General-in-Chief being still some twenty miles rearward, he repaired to his head-quarters in person, and, on so doing, received orders to throw his brigade upon and hold in close observation the rear of Buell's army, then in retreat by way of Nashville

---

* It appears from the Federal account, *Reb. Rec.* V. Doc. 196, p. 600, that the Federal troops here encountered were only three regiments and four guns of Wood's Division, that had been encamped near McMinnville, and which had been sent, in hot haste, to intercept Forrest. The Federal report of this affair is an amusing instance of the sheer falsehood by which petty transactions were magnified into victories. It was fortunate for the Federals their actual force, as well as isolation from near support, was not known to General Forrest at the time. The close proximity of all the divisions of Buell's army had made it his first duty to disentangle his command from all possible complication with them, and hence his purpose was to avoid collisions until that was effected.

II.

Rejoining his command at Sparta, having received an accession to his force of a section of artillery,* Forrest was speedily in motion again. Hastening backward to McMinnville, he ascertained that Buell's rear-guards had passed through that place ten hours previously. Pressing on, therefore, with all possible celerity, he came up with it at Woodbury, and at once began to harass it all the way thence to Murfreesboro, which some Federal soldiers attempted to burn, and must have accomplished had not Forrest come upon them with such timely vigor as to prevent the spread of a serious conflagration and to save the court-house.† Pressed incessantly by the Confederate cavalry, they had now no time for more than petty devastations.

General Bragg was now in full movement for Kentucky, and to Forrest's brigade‡ was assigned the duty of guarding his left flank, with special view to hindering observation of the several stages as well as line of march of the Confederate army. Crossing the Cumberland river near by the Hermitage, he soon encountered a Federal cavalry force in close proximity to their army, and back upon which, after a short brush, he drove them. Hanging constantly and tenaciously upon their rear, the next morning Forrest made another attack upon an exposed force at Tyree's Springs. Some hours later, from a favorable position, he was also able to open upon the

---

* Increased by the four Alabama companies of his old regiment, under Captain Bacot.

† It is due to that accomplished, able soldier, Major-General Buell, to say that he was in no way responsible for these excesses. He endeavored to carry on the war as became a great and civilized people, with the strictest regard for the' rights of non-combatants, while his habits of strict discipline tended to repress these outrages and violations of civilized warfare. But he was badly supported by many of his subordinate commanders, not of the regular army.

rear of the main Federal force with his section of artillery, at the same time making so strong a display of his own forces as to cause the halt of the enemy's column and wagon-train, the retrograde, at a double-quick apparently, of the advance, and the formation in line of battle of very much the whole of Buell's army, at the cost of at least four hours' delay. In the mean time, Forrest had quietly withdrawn from his position in the woods, which the Federal artillery had been shelling vigorously for several hours, and at a trot made a wide circuit, of about ten miles, with the aim of getting around to the north of and striking a blow at the Federal advance. It was in the course of this movement the Confederates had a narrow escape from one of those casualties which, despite all possible precautions, so often follow in the train of and mar military operations—an accidental collision between parts of the same army. General Wheeler, another of Bragg's cavalry commanders, having been instructed to throw his force across upon the Nashville and Bowling Green turnpike, and attempt a blow in that quarter, had struck the Federal flank while moving in column. Forrest, hearing the firing, pushed forward to mingle in the affair, but, hearing from his scouts that a hostile force was approaching through an old field to his right, he disposed his command for an immediate collision. Ordering Lieutenant-Colonel Walker to charge at once in front with the Eighth Texas, he next moved around with the rest of the command, with the purpose of surprising and falling upon the flank of the approaching force. Colonel Walker, executing his orders, had reached a ridge in his front and formed a line for the charge, when he happily discovered the troops in his front were Wheeler's command, falling back helter skelter and in much confusion. But, at the same time, the latter taking the Texans for the enemy, and seeing that they were directly across their outlet, were thrown into even greater disorder, and in their efforts to get away soon ran upon the flank, where Forrest himself was arranging a surprise for the supposed enemy. For a moment the peril of a murderous conflict between the two Confederate cavalry forces was fearfully imminent, but was fortunately averted by a timely discovery of the real state of affairs. Learning from General Wheeler that he had been engaged with the enemy at about the same point where he had aimed to strike, Forrest concluded to effect a junction at once with the main Confederate army, then moving on Glasgow, Ky., where he arrived about the 8th of September, and made a verbal report of his operations in person to General Bragg, who then directed him to report, with his command, to Lieutenant-General Polk, commanding one of the corps of the army.

It will be recollected he had been in the field since the 6th of July—that is to say, for a period of quite two months—marching on an average thirty miles every day. He had lost in killed and wounded, or by disease incident to the hardships of the service two hundred men, but in the mean while had killed or wounded fully 350, and captured over 2000 prisoners of war, including one Brigadier-General, four or five field officers, and as many as sixty regimental officers, besides four pieces of artillery, two stands of colors, six hundred draught animals, and a large wagon-train. Incessantly in the saddle for sixty days, the men and horses were a good deal fatigued. Nevertheless, the spirit of all was excellent, and an unabated desire was generally prevalent throughout the ranks to have an early opportunity to be thrown into a general and decisive engagement with the Federal army.

Under orders from General Polk, Forrest's Brigade was directed to move that night by the road to Clear Point, so as to pass Green river above Munfordsville and seize the Elizabethtown and Bardstown road. Reaching Munfordsville, however, the following night, Forrest intercepted an effort made by the Federals to effect their escape from that position, and obliged them by his movements to return to their fortifications, which were surrendered, after some hard fighting, on the 17th, to the infantry that had come up in the mean time.*

Bragg's whole army was soon after assembled at this point. Buell was still in the rear, and Munfordsville was in the direct line of his march to Louisville, the objective point of his movement.† Nevertheless, for some reason which surely must ever be hard to reconcile with sound strategy, General Bragg here turned aside from the main road to Louisville, and left it fully open to his enemy, with every possible unobstructed facility to move by it to that city and there effect a junction with the Federal forces, which, of course, the Confederate commander supposed were gathered there in view of the exigencies of the situation. Indeed, why General Bragg did not force his adversary to fight him at or about Munfordsville must ever remain a mystery in the history of the war.‡

Quitting Munfordsville, Forrest's Brigade took the field again, with orders to destroy the bridges on the Louisville and Elizabethtown Railroad, and, after that, to cover Bardstown while pushing ahead toward Louisville.§

From Elizabethtown scouts were thrown out in the proper

---

* The force capitulated consisted of the Seventeenth, Sixty-seventh, and Eighty-third Indiana regiments and a company of the provost-guard of Louisville.

† According to Diary of Events, *Reb. Rec.* V. p. 84, General McCook's Division, of Buell's Army, reached Munfordsville on the 21st of September.

‡ "He had Buell in the hollow of his hand," was the remark to the present writer of the most distinguished engi-

neer of the Confederate service, who was on the staff of the Confederate army during this campaign.

§ Continuous and prolonged hard service had greatly jaded General Forrest's horses, and the night after leaving Munfordsville he was severely hurt by the fall of the one he was riding. It fell and rolled over on him, bruised him greatly, and dislocated his right shoulder, causing much pain for several days.

direction to ascertain the movements of the enemy, and several petty cavalry skirmishes occurred.   The brigade was also
employed in advance of Bardstown, picketing the several
roads toward Louisville and Frankfort, until about the 25th
or 26th, when General Forrest was summoned in person to
General Polk's headquarters.   He there learned that it was
General Bragg's direction he should repair immediately to
Murfreesboro to take command of the troops that might be
raised in Middle Tennessee, giving special attention to new
companies and organizations, and with such troops as he
could thus assemble to harass the Federal garrison of Nashville while preventing it from drawing supplies from the surrounding country.

Turning over his brigade to Colonel Wharton, except the
four Alabama companies, which he was authorized to take with
him as well as his staff, Forrest visited General Bragg at
Bardstown about the 27th of September, and, in an interview
with that officer, was given to understand the troops he was
sent to raise and organize should be placed thereafter specially under his command.

Setting out now for his new sphere of duties, he traversed
the distance from Bardstown to Murfreesboro—one hundred
and sixty-five miles—in five days.

CHAPTER VI.

General Forrest established his Headquarters at Murfreesboro, Tenn.—
Tennessee Militia and new Levies at Lavergne surprised and dis-
persed by the Federals—Enemy returned to Nashville, closely followed
by Forrest—Confederate Pickets established close around Nashville—
Battalions and Regiments formed of new Cavalry Levies—Major-
General Breckinridge assumed Command in Middle Tennessee—For-
rest proposed to attack Nashville with Infantry and Cavalry—
Assent given, Movement inaugurated—Federals pressed within
Trenches and Assault to be made, operation countermanded—Ani-
mated Skirmish on Franklin-Nashville Road—General Bragg, hav-
ing returned from the Kentucky Campaign, established Army Head-
quarters at Murfreesboro—Major-General Wheeler appointed Chief
of Cavalry—General Forrest assigned to the Command of a Bri-
gade—Directed to prepare for Expedition into West-Tennessee—
Unsuitable Condition of Arms for such a service reported to Gene-
ral Bragg—Brigade took Post at Columbia.

October 1st to December 4th, 1862.

GENERAL FORREST found but a small force at Murfreesboro, mainly made up of the Thirty-second Alabama and
Freeman's Battery of four guns. At Lavergne, however,
Brigadier-General S. R. Anderson was in command of several
regiments of Tennessee militia and about one thousand freshly raised cavalry ;* and Forrest now sent thither the Thirty-
second Alabama. The troops there were raw, and the Federal commander at Nashville, fifteen miles distant, had planned

---

* The militia were about 1700 in number.

their surprise with the hope of their capture. This plan was well executed by a march on the night of the 6th of October, and a simultaneous attack, in front and rear, on the morning of the 7th, by a force of 400 cavalry and 2600 infantry, with a battery of four pieces, under General Palmer.

At the first alarm the new levies broke and dispersed through the country, leaving the Thirty-second Alabama to bear the weight of the Federal attack, which they did right gallantly until overwhelmed by at least six times their numbers, and when Lieutenant-Colonel Maury and a number of his men were taken prisoners.*

Some of the cavalry having reached Murfreesboro and reported the disaster, General Forrest hurried to the scene with Bacot's Battalion and Freeman's Battery. The way thither was swarming with fugitives, very few of whom had arms in their hands; many were riding barebacked, and very many were shoeless and without any other clothing than that in which they had slept. Deploying his veterans, about two hundred strong, across the road, Forrest pushed boldly into Lavergne, but to find it already evacuated by its captors. Following closely to within five miles of Nashville, the Confederate commander was unable to do any thing with his small command to retrieve this mortifying affair.

Howbeit, he replaced the demoralized force that had been occupying Lavergne with Bacot's Battalion and Freeman's Battery, imposing upon the former the duty of picketing the approaches from Nashville up to the vicinity of the Lunatic Asylum, and to guard against another surprise. Returning then to Murfreesboro for the next four weeks, General Forrest addressed himself with all possible energy to restoring the tone of the troops that had been routed at Lavergne;

---

* The Federal Official Report sets the number at 175.—*Reb. Rec.* V. Doc. 215, p. 623.

also to the formation of the widely-scattered and incomplete organizations which he found in Middle Tennessee into companies, battalions, and regiments, so that he was able to muster at least three thousand five hundred cavalry by the 1st of November. They were regimented as far as possible, and three of the most distinguished regiments of Forrest's Cavalry take their date from this period—that is, the Fourth, (Starnes's,) the Eighth, (Dibrell's,) and the Ninth, (Biffle's.)* Thirteen full companies had likewise been enrolled that were not as yet brought together into a regiment.

In the mean time, Major-General Breckinridge had arrived at Murfreesboro with a force of some three thousand infantry, and assumed chief command. Forrest's headquarters were thereupon transferred to Lavergne. Meanwhile, the Eighth Tennessee and Gunter's Alabama Battalion had been added—about the middle of October—to the force in close observation upon Nashville. And, during the fortnight following, Colonel Dibrell was sent with his regiment several times across the Cumberland to scour the country between Nashville and Gallatin, to harass or cut off Federal foraging parties, and to ascertain the truth of rumors in regard to the movements of a Federal relieving force. These expeditions were conducted with promising skill, and the conduct of the men was excellent in several skirmishes with superior Federal detachments, upon whom some loss was inflicted, as well as in repeated brushes with the Federal picket-posts immediately around Nashville.

The Confederate forces assembled at Lavergne and around Nashville about the 5th of November were 3500 cavalry and some 3000 infantry, under Brigadier-General Hanson.†

---

* See Rosters, Appendix.
† This gallant, accomplished officer, captured at Fort Donelson, had only been lately exchanged and promoted.

As will be remembered, the movement of General Bragg had completely isolated the Federal force at Nashville from all available support or relief, and, knowing that force to be weak, General Forrest now proposed to his superior to attack it in concert with Hanson's infantry. General Breckinridge giving his assent, the plan of attack was duly arranged for the 6th of November.

As the greater proportion of his men were raw and Tennesseeans, Forrest thought it expedient to explain to them beforehand what he proposed to attempt, and to invoke a sturdy, resolute effort to recover their State capital from the hands of invaders. The effect was evidently good, for an admirable spirit was clearly dominant. At the time appointed, all needful preliminaries having been arranged, the troops, distributed in columns, moving by the Franklin, Charlotte, Nolansville, and Murfreesboro turnpikes, were pushed forward in close proximity to the city, driving the Federal pickets and cavalry back behind their works. Forrest, at the head of about one thousand cavalry, moving on the Murfreesboro road, supported closely by Hanson, was at the Lunatic Asylum—six miles from the heart of Nashville—by daylight. The rifle-pits in advance in this quarter were speedily carried, and, Hanson having become eager to engage his men, the main attack was ordered. It was now about sunrise ; the utmost confidence animated both infantry and cavalry, and in a few moments the assault would have been essayed, when an order was received from General Breckinridge countermanding the operation, under express instructions from General Bragg. Hanson was therefore countermarched to Lavergne.

However, leaving a squadron to picket that approach, Forrest moved the remainder of his immediate force across to the Nolansville turnpike, where Dibrell was in position skirmishing with the Federals, who were in their works in his front. Here ascertaining that a strong Federal force was outside of the lines, on the Franklin road, in front of Starnes, taking Dibrell's Regiment and Gunter's Battalion, with Freeman's Artillery, General Forrest moved across, and was soon engaged in an animated skirmish with the main Federal force, artillery being freely used on both sides at very short range. The Eighth Tennessee was here brought to its first charge, and executed it so handsomely, in the teeth of two infantry regiments firing from behind a fence, that the Federals retired rapidly in rear of their works. In this affair Freeman's Artillery, actively employed, gave earnest of its future brilliant services. Shot and shell plowed the ground and covered his gunners, while fragments of shell were scattered among the guns and carriages, killing and crippling a number of horses. For a time, in fact, it seemed that the battery would be destroyed ; but all stood staunchly at their posts, and plied their pieces with coolness, and so skillfully as to make this battery thenceforward a favorite both with the General and his men.

In obedience to the orders of his superiors, leaving Dibrell to hold and observe the Nolansville pike, Starnes the Franklin, and Morgan the Murfreesboro highways, Forrest now retired to Lavergne, deeply chagrined that he had been forced, by orders given at such a distance from the theatre of operations, to abandon an enterprise the success of which he was satisfied was almost an absolute certainty.*

In the mean time, General Bragg, having fought the battle

---

* The recovery of Nashville at that juncture was so clearly fraught with moral, political, and military advantages that those charged with the general conduct of military affairs at Richmond surely ought to have initiated measures to insure the operation. A single division detached without possible risk from the Army in Virginia for a fortnight, and moving by rail, would have easily compassed it. It was one of those numerous omissions to seize patent opportunities which, in the study of this war hereafter, will amaze and puzzle the military student, and, indeed, all thoughtful readers.

of Perryville, had been obliged to withdraw from Kentucky, and by the latter part of November had taken up a position with his army in the vicinage of Murfreesboro. General Wheeler was then assigned to the chief command of the cavalry, with his headquarters at Lavergne, and Forrest, being relieved, was directed to report to General Bragg in person. Thereupon he was assigned to the command of a brigade constituted of the Fourth, Eighth, and Ninth Tennessee regiments and Russell's Fourth Alabama,* with Freeman's Battery, with orders to take post at Columbia and there prepare for an expedition across the Tennessee river into West-Tennessee. The arms of his regiments being shot-guns and flint-lock muskets, altogether unfit for such an expedition, General Forrest made the fact known to the Commander-in-Chief, who nevertheless adhered to his orders, but promised that proper arms should be provided for issue at Columbia.

Accordingly, on the 4th of December, Forrest took position, as directed, with his brigade, about eighteen hundred strong, at Columbia.

---

* We regret that we are unable to furnish any roster of Russell's Regiment, after every effort to procure one.

MAJ. J. P. STRANGE
ADJ GEN

CAPT. C. W. ANDERSON
AID-E-CAMP

WM M. FORREST
2D LIEUT. AID-E-CAMP

M. C. CALLOWAY
A. A. G.

MAJ. C. V. RAMBAUT
CHIEF OF SUBSISTENCE

MAJ. C. S. SEVERSON
CHIEF QUARTERMASTER

CAPT. J. W. MORTON
CHIEF OF ARTILLERY

J. W. COWAN M. D.
CHIEF SURGEON

THE STAFF OF LIEUT. GEN. N. B. FORREST.

CHAPTER VII.

ON the 10th of December, orders having been received
from army headquarters to begin the expedition indicated at
the close of the last chapter, General Forrest again called attention, in writing, to the ineffective condition of his armament, as well as to the fact that his men were supplied with

only ten rounds of caps for his shot-guns, while many of the muskets were *flintless*. The reply was a curtly couched order to march without delay. Feeling aggrieved at the manner and scope of his instructions, as well as profoundly sensible of the perils which his command was soon to encounter in the passage of the Tennessee river, in mid-winter, without any means of ferriage, and subsequent penetration into a region swarming with Federal forces thoroughly armed and supplied —ten times, perchance, his superiors in numbers—Forrest, nevertheless, prepared for the expedition as rapidly as possible. Unprepared in arms as his men were to cope with even an equal force, in its outset the operation had very much the appearance of an unavailing forlorn hope; but early on the next morning his entire force, as before said, about eighteen hundred officers and men and four guns, were in motion, with a minimum of baggage. Reaching the Tennessee river the evening of the 13th, at a place called Clifton, (below at Double Island,) he effected a passage during the following day, and on the 15th, in time to advance some eight miles in the direction of Lexington, in Henderson county. An old, sodden, leaky flat-boat had been found at Clifton, and used for the ferriage of the artillery and wagon-train, while the horses and mules had been swum across; the officers and men exposed to a cold pelting rain all the time, without tents or other shelter.

On the 16th, moving some eighteen miles in the direction of Lexington, Forrest encamped to give his men an opportunity to dry their clothing, and to inspect and arrange their arms and ammunition for active service. On inspection it was found that the greater part of the small supply of caps had become wet and unserviceable. But that night, most opportunely, a citizen reached the encampment with some fifty thousand shot-gun and pistol caps, which the General had sent agents forward to procure within the enemy's lines.

This was a great relief and an auspicious circumstance. Resuming the advance on the morning of the 17th, when about eight miles from Lexington, his scouts and advanced pickets encountered those of a Federal force moving by the same road to check the Confederate expedition.

Directing Colonel Starnes to engage and remove this obstacle with his regiment, General Forrest immediately led the remainder of his command by a road to the right at a gallop, with the purpose of cutting off the enemy's retreat. In this movement the lead was given to the four veteran Alabama companies of the General's old regiment,* under Captain Frank Gurley, with orders to charge upon the Federals as soon as he came upon them.

As soon as his artillery had crossed a bridge about six miles from Lexington, General Forrest pushed on at a gallop to the verge of the place, where the enemy were found forming, in a strong position, on an elevated ridge.

Disposing Dibrell's and Biffle's regiments, Gurley's Battalion, and his escort, for the attack, he threw himself at once with them upon the left of the Federal line and broke it; then, turning to the left, he again struck them on the flank, by which Colonel Hawkins and his regiment of Tennessee (Federal) cavalry were scattered, and fled to the rear, leaving the Eleventh Regiment, Illinois Volunteers, and a section of artillery to bear the brunt of the onslaught.

These troops Captain Gurley charged with a force of some two hundred men at most, and captured the guns,† one hundred and fifty officers and men, including Colonel Ingersoll and Major Kerr, some three hundred small-arms, mostly Sharp's carbines, and a full supply of ammunition, with about

* Now constituting part of Russell's Regiment, Alabama Cavalry.

† These were two three-inch steel rifled (Rodman) guns, fully equipped, and were used by General Forrest to the close of the war.

two hundred horses and a few wagons.   The other portion*
of this force had fled in the direction of Jackson, pursued
hotly by Colonel Starnes and the rest of the command.

The artillery of the enemy was bravely handled and fought;
the men stood stoutly to their guns ; many fell at their post ;
and the remainder only yielded when the Confederates were
directly upon them and further resistance useless.   In their
capture, Private Kelly, of Kelly's Troopers, Russell's (Alabama) Regiment, lost his life with signal heroism.   He was the
first Confederate to reach the battery, and laying his hand
upon a piece just as it was discharged he was cut in twain.

Colonel Starnes, pursuing closely in the track of the fugitives, captured some fifty of them, and gathered a large number of valuable arms with which the road was strewn by the
fleeing Federals.†

Without further resistance the Confederates reached the
vicinity of Jackson on the afternoon of the 18th.   Their commander, losing no time, at once threw out skirmishers, and
drove back the Federal picket line and outposts, to take
shelter behind their works, which consisted of a heavy line of
infantry *epaulements* connecting some five or six open-gorge
works for field-pieces, that commanded all the approaches to
the position.   Meanwhile, troop-trains were evidently coming
up rapidly from the north and south ; citizens also reported
that heavy reënforcements had recently been received.

General Forrest, therefore, at eight o'clock at night, detached Colonel Dibrell and Major J. E. Forrest, each with a

---

* The Eleventh Illinois, and Hawkins's regiment and the artillery, may
be set down 1100 men.   From the official report of Colonel Jacob Fry, *Reb.
Rec.* vol. VI, page 283, Doc. 80, it may
be. inferred that 300 men of the Fifth
Ohio Cavalry were present also.

† The Confederate loss was three
privates killed and five wounded ; that
of the Federals about twenty-five killed
and fifty wounded, who fell into General
Forrest's hands.

hundred men, the former to move out on the railroad toward Humboldt, to seize the nearest station, capture any approaching trains, and break up the intermediate sections of the road; the latter with similar instructions in regard to the Mobile and Ohio railroad, south of Jackson. At the same time, Colonel Biffle was detailed to act in the like manner on the railway leading to Bolivar. These orders, promptly executed, were so far successful that Dibrell captured the station some eight miles north of Jackson, about two o'clock in the morning, with its Federal garrison of some one hundred men, with their arms and supplies. Major Forrest seized the nearest station in his quarter, and its guard, some seventy-five men, their arms and munitions; and Biffle surprised and captured an outpost of some fifty men. Each detachment tore up sufficient of the railroad to make a substantial obstruction to the approach of trains from their respective directions, and returned to their positions about daylight with their captures. The arms and ammunition thus happily acquired were immediately distributed in lieu of those of inferior species, with which Forrest had entered the field.

The force in occupation of Jackson was estimated by the citizens of the vicinage to be fully 15,000 strong of all arms, with thirty pieces of artillery in position.*

---

* The actual Federal strength at Jackson at the time of the appearance of General Forrest before it could not have been less than 10,000 infantry. A correspondent of the Chicago *Tribune*, writing from Cairo, January 6th, as he alleges, with thorough knowledge, says the regular garrison, 5000 strong, on the evening of the 18th of December was reënforced by Brayman's (from Bolivar) and Fuller's brigades, and, on the following day, by two other brigades, or 5000 men, sent by General Grant from Oxford. This would make the force present on Forrest's approach at least 13,000 men. But the same correspondent, further on, says, General Sullivan, taking the field to pursue the Confederates, the 20th inst., with 7000 men, left at Jackson only 1000 men, General Brayman having begun the pursuit apparently the day before.—*Reb. Rec.* VI. Doc. 94, pp. 332, 333.

General Forrest, on reaching the vicinage of the Federal lines, disposed his force with a view to deceive them in regard to his numbers. Posting his main force in a line across the highway from Lexington to Jackson, and about four miles to the east of the town, he placed detachments to command and observe the roads from Jackson in the direction of Spring Creek and Trenton, and in these positions the Confederate troops rested for the night. About sunrise the enemy threw forward a strong line of skirmishers, who were promptly met by the dismounted men advanced by the Confederate General, with a display, on their right and left flanks, of cavalry, and a spirited conflict with small-arms took place. Meanwhile, the Confederate artillery—six pieces—were brought up and employed with such effect that the enemy was speedily driven to his intrenchments, with a loss of about thirty (30) killed and wounded, who fell into the hands of the Confederates. Nearly simultaneously with these operations, skirmishers on foot, flanked by cavalry, had been pushed down the Spring Creek and Trenton roads, driving back all the Federal force in that quarter. Meanwhile, also, the Confederate cavalry remaining mounted or not employed as skirmishers were brought up and ostentatiously displayed within half a mile of the intrenchments along the whole line between the Forked Deer river and the highway to Trenton, with the object of deceiving as to the actual force investing the place. This and occasional *brushes* between the skirmishers were kept up through the day.

Leaving Colonel Russell with his regiment displayed in a thin line of cavalry-pickets in front of the works, between four and five P.M. General Forrest quietly withdrew his main force back by the Lexington road as far as Cotton Plant, and thence on a road leading to Trenton as far as Spring creek. It was here the Confederate commander now resorted to a clever *ruse* to spread and keep up false notions of his strength—that is, he caused a number of drums to be beaten in such manner as to produce the belief of a heavy infantry force in that quarter.*

About eight o'clock at night, Colonel Russell's command was withdrawn from the vicinage of Jackson and followed to Spring creek. General Forrest then had his whole force assembled at that position, with some five hundred prisoners taken in the several combats and surprises around Jackson ; his train was enlarged to twenty-five excellent wagons and teams, his artillery by a section, and the main part of the men well armed and munitioned.

At five A.M., Colonel Dibrell was detached with his regiment and a part of Biffle's to burn the bridge of the Mobile and Ohio Railroad over Spring creek, which was duly executed, with the capture there of an outpost of some one hundred infantry, with their arms and supplies. At the same time, another detachment under Colonel Starnes, consisting of his regiment, a squadron of Biffle's, and Captain W. H. Forrest's Independent Company,† was dispatched to capture Humboldt, which was also effected about one P.M., (December 20th,) after a slight skirmish. Two hundred prisoners, four caissons with their horses, about 500 stand of arms, 300,000 rounds of small-arm ammunition, a large supply of artillery harness, considerable quantities of subsistence, quartermasters' stores, and soldiers' baggage fell into the hands of the Confederates. These stores and materials of war were destroyed except a portion of the best of the arms and ammunition, and the caissons.

In the mean time, General Forrest had pushed forward in the direction of Trenton with his artillery‡ and train, his

---

* These drums had been recently captured.

† Not more than 750 men in all.

‡ Four pieces under Captain Free- man and the captured Rodman guns under Captain J. W. Morton, manned by details.

usual escort, and Major N. N. Cox's Battalion, of some one hundred and sixty newly-raised volunteers from Hickman and Perry counties, of Middle Tennessee, who had joined on the 19th and 20th. As he did so, he directed Colonel Russell to remain in position at Spring creek with the Fourth Alabama cavalry,* to cover the movements then on foot. There Colonel Russell was assailed in the afternoon, as his commander had foreseen, by a brigade, at least, of some 2000 infantry. Making an intrepid defense, he repulsed, however, several attacks, and finally, charging in turn, drove the Federals back across Spring creek, capturing their ammunition and subsistence-train and some prisoners, besides the casualties usually incident to a prolonged and resolute combat. Remaining master of the ground, he held it until eight o'clock that night, when he followed in the direction of Trenton, as he had been previously directed.

At one P.M. on the 20th December, General Forrest reached the vicinity of Trenton, and without delay made his dispositions for its capture. Major Cox was ordered to move with his squadron by the right, to secure a position to the east of the town and the railroad depot, which the enemy had strongly fortified by a breastwork made of cotton-bales and hogsheads of tobacco, erected closely around it. Then charging through the town with his escort, Forrest drove the enemy before him into their breastworks. Within fifty yards he and his men approached without dismounting,—firing upon the enemy and receiving their fire, with a loss of two of his troopers killed and three wounded. Now, withdrawing to a somewhat commanding position some two hundred yards south-eastward of the depot, the Confederate commander dismounted his men and disposed them quickly as sharp-shooters in some adjacent houses, whence to fire upon the enemy,

---

* Not exceeding 400 men.

a number of whom at the moment occupied the tops of the brick buildings at the depot, favorably adapted for shelter by parapet walls. After a short skirmish the Federals were forced to quit these positions, with some loss, and seek better cover. Captain Strange, the Confederate Adjutant-General, was then directed to bring up and post the artillery, which was done with judgment on an elevation southward of the depot, about three hundred˙ yards distant. Scarcely had three rounds been discharged, when numerous *nondescript* white flags were displayed from all quarters of the Federal fortalice.

Captain Strange was next directed to arrange and receive the surrender, and, at once advancing for that purpose, was met by Colonel Jacob Fry, the superior officer present, and several others. However, while the preliminaries were being arranged by his staff-officer, General Forrest went forward to the group thus occupied. As he did so, he was directly addressed by Colonel Fry, an elderly officer, with some inquiry touching the terms which would be given.

" Unconditional," was the Confederate General's brief answer.

Then, Colonel Fry, observing that having no alternative he must yield, unswung his sword and handed it to General Forrest, remarking sadly that it had been in his family for forty years. Receiving the sword and handling it for an instant, General Forrest returned it to his opponent, saying in effect :

" Take back your sword, Colonel, as it is a family relic ; but I hope, sir, when next worn it will be in a better cause than that of attempting the subjugation of your countrymen."

While these matters were taking place, an alarm of fire was made at the depot, and smoke was observed to rise within the precincts of the works. As it was too long after the shelling to have been caused in that way, it was evidently an effort to destroy property which was now his spoil of war.

Forrest, therefore, sprang to the narrow sally-port, whence the Federal soldiers were already rapidly rushing forth, and, drawing his sword, and supported by Major Strange, pistol in hand, ordered the fugitives to return and extinguish the fire on pain of death.   Sternly enforcing this order, the fire was speedily quelled.   Turning, then, to Colonel Fry, he further declared his determination to punish in the most summary manner any such perfidy as an attempt by the Federal soldiers to set the depot on fire and destroy the property captured.

In this brilliant affair, it will be recollected that General Forrest used only his escort, Cox's untried volunteers, and his artillery, or a force of not more than 275 men.   The results—the legitimate fruit of Forrest's military judgment, quickness of plan, decision, and *dash*—were as follows : Not less than 400 prisoners of war, including Colonels Fry and Hawkins and several other field officers, 300 negroes, 1000 horses, mules, etc., 13 wagons and ambulances, 7 caissons, 20,-000 rounds of artillery and 400,000 of small-arm ammunition, 100,000 rations of subsistence, together with a large amount of cavalry equipments, clothing, and quartermaster stores, and a considerable quantity of soldiers' baggage—in value at least $500,000.   That evening the several detachments under Colonels Starnes and Dibrell came up with their prisoners, and the next morning early Colonel Russell effected a junction also, so that the whole command was once more assembled. And in lieu of flint-lock muskets and shot-guns, ineffectively supplied with ammunition, it was now well armed, equipped, and supplied, as well as somewhat stronger than when it had entered West-Tennessee, despite the casualties of battle with a superior adversary.

The paroling of prisoners had been commenced soon after the surrender of the garrison at Trenton.   They numbered now fully 1300, officers and men.   Of these, the officers and

Hawkins's Regiment were paroled and suffered to repair directly, as they chose, to their several homes ; the remainder, some 800 or 900 men, were paroled, but required to march under a suitable escort, commanded by Lieutenant-Colonel N. D. Collins, to Columbus, Ky., there to be turned over to the Federal commander.

Early on the morning of the 21st of December, General Forrest, taking his usual escort, the artillery, and the wagon-train, resumed the advance toward Union City, giving orders that the command, after some requisite rest, should follow with due celerity, while Colonel Dibrell should remain in position at Trenton with his regiment until the following day, to cover the rear.

Some seven miles northward, General Forrest came upon a stockade, which, after capturing its garrison of thirty men, he burned, with the railroad-bridge and trestle at the same point. As the troops were occupied with this, the train had been sent on with such soldiers as were in charge of crippled horses—Major G. V. Rambaut, Chief Commissary, in command—and were seven miles in advance when overtaken by the General, who found him halted, and such soldiers as were with the train drawn up in front under arms, under the belief that a considerable Federal force was just in front ; and that was the fact, for the Confederate commander, advancing with his escort and Rambaut's few men, speedily encountered a force of some 250 men, who, after a short brush, were driven into their stockade at Kenton Station. Bringing up the artillery, placing it in position, and disposing his small command present, not exceeding 125 cavalry, so as to cut off escape into the swamps, adjacent, of the Obion " bottom," General Forrest summoned the enemy to surrender, which was peremptorily declined. The salvo, however, from six pieces of artillery, which speedily followed with a startling crash through the stockade, quickly produced another conclusion, and many white flags of every possible description were to be seen fluttering in all quarters of the work.

By this juncture the main command began to come up, and were immediately set to work to destroy the trestle, tear up the roadway, and burn the stockade. These dispositions having been made, their commander was again moving forward with his escort, artillery, and train, but necessarily making a detour of four or six miles to find a crossing for the train and artillery over the Obion, just beyond which he halted and encamped for the night of the 21st. The main command moving along the Mobile and Ohio Railroad, there a continuous trestle, destroyed it effectually by the torch for seven miles that afternoon, capturing another stockade with a garrison of forty men, and encamped.

That night, Colonel Starnes, the senior officer with the troops, was specially instructed to destroy, the following day, the entire track through the bottoms of the Obion, a distance of some fifteen miles, including a good deal of trestle-work fifteen feet high, which was thoroughly accomplished.

On the following morning, scouts from the direction of Jackson reported that a force of some ten thousand men had taken the field, and were moving rapidly northward, with the purpose of intercepting the return of the Confederates across the Tennessee.

Nevertheless, the ever enterprising soldier determined to complete his movement and continue his advance as far as Union City, yet some twenty miles distant.

The battalion of Biffle's Regiment, Major Cox's Squadron, and Captain Forrest's Independent company, were ordered forward. With this force, a section of artillery, and his escort detachment, or about four hundred men, and the train, Forrest now pushed forward rapidly that afternoon upon Union City. The enemy's pickets were met four miles from the place, and at once driven in, rapidly followed by the Confederates to their fortifications, which consisted of rifle-pits commanded by a small closed earth-work. The Confederates pressed forward, taking position to assail the works, with great spirit and loud cheers.

As this happened, Lieutenant-Colonel Collins, who, it will be remembered, was *en route* from Trenton to Columbus with a large body of Federal paroled prisoners, came in view about half a mile southward, presenting, doubtless, a formidable hostile appearance to the beleaguered Federals, whose capitulation was at once demanded, and yielded with little parley. Two hundred and fifty officers and men, strongly intrenched, were here surrendered, with their arms and supplies.

Encamping now for the night, the Confederate leader set his staff to work paroling the prisoners last taken. Those in the rear, captured since his departure from Trenton, were ordered to be hastened up, and on their arrival were likewise paroled, some three hundred in number, and the whole turned over to Colonel Collins, who resumed his march the afternoon of the 23d.

That night, an officer was detached with forty men, to repair to Moscow, some twelve miles distant, in the direction of Columbus, which place he reached on the following morning. Notwithstanding it was said to be strongly occupied and defended by a stockade, such was the ardor infused by this time into the whole command, that a charge was made, with a loud shout, into the very heart of the position, the commander crying aloud for the "artillery" to be pushed "forward." The Federals thereupon fled precipitately out of their works in the direction of Columbus, leaving possession to the Confederates, who then returned to their command with little delay.

On the return of this detachment, the Confederate General, having fully attained the utmost northern limit of his expedition, turned to retrace his steps. Some twelve miles south of Union City he was met by a courier from Colonel Starnes, with the information that he had destroyed the trestle-work to the south of the Obion river, and was now burning that on the north. On the 24th and 25th, the entire command* was thus employed, especially in demolishing the solid heavy trestles between the north and south forks of the river.

This achieved, the men were allowed rest for some hours.

Meanwhile, scouts reported that a Federal force, estimated to be at least twelve thousand strong, had been concentrated at Trenton.

On the morning of the 26th of December, destroying the railroad bridge over the north fork of the Obion, on the Paducah branch, Forrest then put his whole force in motion for Dresden, about twenty-six miles distant, and encamped in that immediate vicinity that night and during the following day, to give his men and animals rest, and to receive reports from his scouts. These soon announced that the Federals were advancing by the road from Trenton to Union City ; and, on the morning of the 27th, that a movement was being made in force up the Obion in the direction of McLemoresville and Huntington, with the expectation of cutting off the Confederates from

---

* Increased near Trenton by Napier's Battalion, two hundred effectives. This battalion had been enrolled and mustered in, four hundred and eighty strong, a month previously, for special service in Middle Tennessee. It consisted of five companies, namely, "A," William E. De Moss, Captain ; N. J. Robinson, First Lieutenant ; N. P. Evans, Second Lieutenant ; and N. N. Phipp, Third Lieutenant. "B," John Minor, Captain ; —— Nesbitt, First Lieutenant ; Joseph Williams, Second Lieutenant ; Andrew Nesbitt, Third Lieutenant. "C," N. N. Hobbs, Captain ; M. M. Box, First Lieutenant ; Jesse Hobbs, Second Lieutenant ; Charles E. Somers, Third Lieutenant. "D," Thomas Easley, Captain ; J. C. McAuley, First Lieutenant ; —— Hall, Second Lieutenant ; William Frazier, Third Lieutenant. "E," M. F. Alexander, Captain ; W. Dobson, First Lieutenant ; J. Dobson, Second Lieutenant. Lieutenant-Colonel Napier commanding. Harris Wiley was his Adjutant. This battalion, under orders from General Forrest, crossed the river at Reynoldsburg on the 17th. For its subsequent history see Appendix.

the Tennessee river. Upon this, their commander, as wary at such a juncture as adventurous and daring at other times, turned the head of his column and moved rapidly in the direction of Huntington, encamping at McKenzie's Station, on the Memphis and Louisville Railroad, with his command, except Colonel Russell, who was thrown forward six or seven miles nearer Huntington, to seize and hold the crossing of the Obion. Scouts, about nine o'clock that night, reported that the enemy had destroyed all the bridges over the Obion, south of the high road leading from Jackson to Paris, Tennessee; as also that Colonel Russell had come in collision with a heavy force on attempting to cross the Obion, but, nevertheless, had effected his passage and held the position. Major Cox was, therefore, dispatched, at a gallop, to seize the road leading from Paris to Huntington, and to move down, in direction of the latter place, until he should meet any Federal force, which he was to hold in check until compelled to give way, when he would move in the direction of the Tennessee river.

On being satisfied that a greatly superior force was being disposed to frustrate his repassage of the Tennessee, Forrest now concluded to attempt the crossing of the Obion to the right of Huntington, for which end, however, there was but one road left available, with a bridge reported to be impassable, and evidently so regarded by the enemy, since it was left unoccupied. The train was put forthwith in motion for what are known in that country as the "double-bridges" on the McLemoresville road, and they were reached about eleven o'clock that night.

Men were set to work with Forrest-activity to cut timber-forks, with which to stay and strengthen the bridges and trestles, to bear the artillery and train, and in an hour this was achieved, so that some cavalry were passed safely across. All the while it was very dark and cold, and a sleety drizzle was falling. The General drove with his own hands the first of his headquarter teams over the slippery, narrow, tottering bridges, in order to give an example and confidence to his men—a feat little less perilous personally, in their minds at the time, than the passage of that other bridge made famous to all time by the valor of Napoleon. The next two teams which attempted to follow were quickly floundering in the deep stream and freezing mud, from which they were only relieved with loss of time, difficulty, and exposure of the men.

Many of the officers and men were now greatly discouraged—indeed, despaired of effecting a passage in such utter darkness. But the impossible was literally unknown to the Confederate leader, who ordered up and distributed five hundred men, with their officers, twenty men to accompany each team. Too heavily loaded for safety and the condition of the road, the mud-holes were filled with considerable quantities of flour and coffee, though so inestimable to Confederate soldiers. By these means the train was safely thrown across by three o'clock in the morning ; but, meantime, the road had become so cut up as to be almost impracticable. Fifty men, however, were then attached to each piece of artillery. The horses bogged deeply and the men waded waist-deep in the freezing mud and water ; but in three hours all the guns likewise were upon the east bank of the Obion, in condition for action. By this time Colonel Russell and Major Cox had rejoined, and, moving on without delay to McLemoresville, four miles distant, General Forrest halted his troops, and gave men and animals time to feed, of which all stood in need as well as of some rest. But in an hour or two reliable scouts announced that a Federal force—reported, by the country people, 10,000 strong—was only twelve miles distant, at Huntington. Therefore, at ten A.M. on the 29th, the Confederates were again in movement for Lexington, by a rough, miry, hilly road, over which the wagons, still heavily loaded, and the artillery, were drawn with much difficulty.

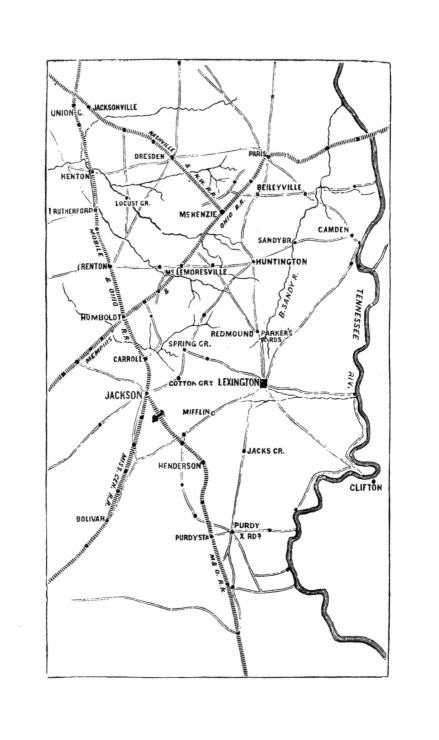

Encamping for the night some nine miles short of Lexington, the Confederate General detached his brother, Captain Forrest, with his company toward Huntington, to observe the enemy, retard his march as much as possible, and report hostile movements and appearances in that quarter. Captain Forrest encountered a column of the enemy at or near Clarksburg, within six miles of the Confederate camp and moving in that direction. A skirmish ensued, with the loss of several men to the Confederates, but with more casualties to the Federals. This was speedily reported to General Forrest,[*] who, in the jaded condition of his command, regarded it most judicious to remain in position and risk a battle on the following morning with impending odds. Accordingly, Captain Forrest was instructed through his courier to do all that he could to check the march of the Federal troops, disputing the road as obstinately as practicable, and to make frequent reports of the situation. During this time the men were left undisturbed until four o'clock A.M., when they were quickly roused, ordered to saddle up and prepare for the march.

Speedily in motion toward Parker's Cross-Roads, (or Red Mound,) about a mile and a half distant, General Forrest, informed of the near approach of his enemy, threw his command in order of battle. About the same time the Federal column made its appearance from the north-eastward and formed promptly to attack.[†]

----

[*] Through a courier, Private W. C. Hill.

[†] Colonel Biffle had been detached, about twenty-four hours previously, to capture a force understood to be moving, isolated, toward Trenton. This he overtook and captured (120 officers and men) about seven miles east of Trenton. Greatly embarrassed by his captives, he wisely determined to rid himself of them by the expedient of the *parole.* So, sending them with a flag of truce, under Captain John S. Grove, for the nearest Federal command, by hard riding he was able to effect a timely junction with General Forrest after the battle had been commenced. Colonel Starnes likewise had been detached before, and, as will be seen, returned during the combat. He had been

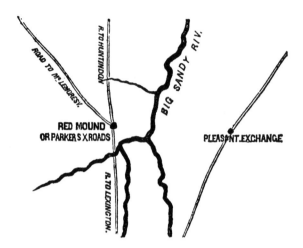

Dibrell's and Russell's regiments were at once dismounted and thrown forward as skirmishers, the artillery was brought up—six pieces—and placed in a favorable position on a ridge in an open field, within about six hundred yards of the Federal artillery and supports, which were all well posted within a skirt of woods with an open field between them and the Confederates. The Federal artillery — three or four pieces — meanwhile had been opened upon the Confederate line with spirit. As quickly as possible a vigorous reply was made, and at the first fire a Federal gun was dismounted and several of the gunners and horses killed or disabled ; the others were then withdrawn speedily to better cover, their supports falling back also toward Parker's Cross-Roads. The Confederates followed eagerly, the cavalry—300 men—disposed equally on either flank of the line of dismounted men.

At the cross-roads the Federal force was again formed, ap-

---

sent toward Huntington, and had in that quarter a severe skirmish with a Federal cavalry force, a number of whom he killed and wounded, with slight loss to his own men.

parently in two lines, in an open, undulating field, with their front to the north and at right angles to the highway, a brigade of infantry, a battery of artillery, and a detachment of cavalry, or a total not short of 1800.*

The Confederate force present on the field did not exceed 1200 officers and men, with six pieces of artillery, as before said.

Dismounting his men, except about 200, who were distributed equally on his right and left flanks, the Confederate commander disposed them in one line of battle northward of his opponent and nearly parallel to the hostile array, on ground somewhat lower, partly in a peach-orchard and partly in an open field — the two lines about six hundred yards apart—with his artillery occupying three positions, Morton's Battery in the centre, and a section of Freeman's on each flank, a few paces in advance of the dismounted men, unlimbered and ready for action. In a few moments the Confederate artillery opened the engagement in earnest, quickly driving that of the enemy under cover of a ridge in their rear.

General Forrest now pushed forward his entire line, as arranged, in battle order, and brought his musketry to bear

---

* According to the official report of Colonel C. T. Dunham, the Federal commander, it consisted of the Thirty-ninth Iowa Infantry, 405 rank and file; Fiftieth Indiana Volunteer Infantry, 525 rank and file; the One Hundred and Twenty-second Illinois Volunteer Infantry, 529 rank and file; detachments of Companies A and E, Eighteenth Illinois Infantry, mounted, 65 men, and 30 artillerists; or a total of 1554 men. (*Reb. Rec.* VI. Doc. 94, pp. 327–31.) A correspondent of the Chicago *Tribune*, however, writing at the same time, evidently with access to returns, reports the strength of the Fiftieth Indiana at 604 men and the One Hundred and Twenty-second Illinois at 600, which would make the brigade 1824 strong.

Moreover, Colonel Dunham states he had learned at Clarksburg that the Confederate force was 8000 strong, with 12 pieces of artillery, and that he had moved out to attempt "to coax or force a fight out" of that force, which he was scarcely *apt to do with as small a force as he represents present.*

with a heavy, continuous fire. The enemy fought with stubbornness and spirit, but after an hour were driven back into a skirt of woods eastward of the highway and about half a mile to the south-east of Parker's Cross-Roads. There they stood their ground stoutly, and, indeed, in turn made a resolute, well-led attempt to regain the ridge from which they had been driven, so that, as the Confederates reached the crown of that position, the Federal line was found advanced to within eighty yards of the crest also. But a withering fire was opened with all arms, and the enemy were soon obliged to fall back again under shelter of the woods, leaving two pieces on the ground, their horses killed, as well as a number of officers and men killed and wounded.

General Forrest now concentrated the fire of his artillery upon the Federals, who had retired behind a strong fence in the woods, only about two hundred yards distant, killing and disabling a number of men and horses, and silencing all their other pieces. About eleven A.M., they essayed another slight advance, but were repulsed easily. About mid-day, however, another and very resolute forward movement was made to within sixty paces of our pieces and their supports, though only to be repulsed with slaughter.*

It was at this juncture Colonel Napier gallantly, but without the orders or wish of his General, charged with his battalion upon the position of the enemy, up to the very fence behind which they were posted, there to fall mortally wounded with several of his men. Thus an intrepid and promising soldier lost his life through a spirit of martial ardor that un-

---

* The Federal commander says the Confederate batteries were so posted as to concentrate a fire upon several portions of "his" line and to enfilade a part of it; and that the "Confede- rate" fire having become terrible in its intensity, "he" determined to take "the" batteries at all hazards, the one on the right especially.

fortunately impelled him forward without due reflection or regard for the instructions and combinations of his commander.

Finding that the enemy were now weakened and doubtless discouraged by their heavy losses, the Confederate commander threw Colonel Russell around by the left to take them in flank and reverse, and meantime had several pieces of artillery so posted as to enfilade both flanks of their line. Apparently observing that the Confederate line had been diminished, the Federal force made another charge, which was met and foiled by a discharge of grape and canister from the whole Confederate artillery. At the same time, Colonel Russell dashed forward upon their flank and rear, as General Forrest moved forward in front. Under this stress the enemy's lines gave way, and, breaking, the men ran across the road westward into an open field, leaving many prisoners in our hands. In the mean time, the Confederate lines had fallen into disorder, and the several companies and regiments were intermingled ; their General, therefore, found it now necessary to pause and reorganize.

The enemy fleeing, as before said, were cut off and brought to a stand by Colonel Starnes, who at that moment opportunely came up in that quarter of the field,* and they resumed some order, but numerous white flags were displayed among them. The Confederates were now completely masters of the situation, and a staff-officer was sent to where the white flags were shown to receive the capitulation. Scarcely had this been done, however, when Colonel Charles Carroll, of the staff of General Forrest, dashed up and informed his leader that a fresh and superior force of Federals had reached the field and were forming to attack in his rear. Ordering

---

* As said, note p. 209 *ante,* he had been detached previous to the battle.

the proper disposition of his forces for this unlooked-for and untoward exigency, Forrest galloped to the indicated quarter, and there, indeed, did he find, already in battle order, about to sweep down upon him, two brigades of the enemy. They were, in fact, in possession of the peach-orchard and adjacent field, which he had occupied at the outset of the engagement, and he was within eighty yards of their line before he could discover them. Perceived then by a Federal officer, who called, "Halt and surrender!" Forrest promptly replied that he had already done so some time since, but would move up what remained of his command and surrender in form ; and with this, wheeling his horse, galloped away in the direction of his troops, notifying, as he passed, the inmates of his hospital of the emergency, that they might make their escape. Joining his command, he at once put it in motion, by the left flank, at a double-quick. Scarcely had their rapid departure been made, when the enemy, also at a *double-quick*, came in view of their discomfited comrades, who immediately resumed their arms and renewed their fire. Major Cox, being at the time with his and Napier's men on the extreme right of the Confederate line, was unable to get off the field, and was captured with about 250 men. The horses of four caissons and of two brass six-pounders were disabled as they attempted to withdraw across the open field under the fire of both bodies of the enemy, and had to be abandoned with the loss of a number of drivers and artillerists killed and wounded.

The new-comers upon the field charged onward with spirit, and, from a position on the ridge that Forrest had occupied with such effect that morning, poured into the Confederate rear a rapid fire with at least two field-guns. Wheeling, with his escort, (seventy-five men,) and a detachment, some fifty strong, of Dibrell's Regiment, under Major Forrest, the Confederate commander now made one of his characteristic dashes at their pieces, dispersed their gunners, and threw their infantry support into such confusion as served materially to aid his command at the moment to regain and mount their horses. The horses of the caissons of three pieces having taken fright and carried them in the direction of the Confederates, the General seized and carried them along with him.

Colonel Starnes, detached during the fight until now, with a mounted force of about two hundred and fifty men, observing the condition of affairs, happily and boldly fell upon the rear of Dunham's force, and brought the whole Federal army to a halt. This afforded the Confederate troops time to get beyond their immediate reach. Meanwhile, General Forrest had taken post with about two hundred men on an eminence some eight hundred yards eastward of Parker's house, whence he, too, threw himself upon the rear of Dunham's Brigade for a parting blow, capturing his wagon train, with all the baggage of that force, and which were carried safely from the field.

Gathering his whole force now well in hand, the Confederate leader moved off in the direction of Lexington without further molestation, and encamped at that place about six o'clock that evening.

In the several conflicts of the day, between the hours of six A.M. and three P.M., the Confederate losses were some twenty-five officers, including Colonel Napier, and men killed, and not to exceed seventy-five wounded, with about two hundred and fifty captured by the enemy, three pieces and four caissons, five wagons, two ambulances and their teams, with their contents—seventy-five thousand rounds of ammunition.*

The casualties on the other side were three guns put *hors de combat*, two caissons, fifteen wagons, two ambulances and

---

* By an unfortunate blunder on the part of the ordnance officer, this—the ordnance-train—had been brought back from a place where it would have been safe to the field, where it was not wanted, just as General Sullivan came up, and fell into the hands of the Federals by this mischance.

their teams, carried off the field, with some eighteen hundred knapsacks and as many blankets, and about one hundred prisoners taken, and subsequently paroled; also, at least, fifty killed, including several prominent officers, and one hundred and fifty wounded,* among whom were one of their Colonels and a Lieutenant-Colonel; and fully one hundred animals either killed or disabled. All this, be it noted, was achieved on the Confederate side by a force at no moment in the day exceeding twelve hundred men, opposed by at least eighteen hundred, whom they vanquished, and finally by two fresh brigades.†

So complete was the demoralization wrought on Dunham's Brigade that Major Strange, General Forrest's Adjutant-General, unaccompanied by even an orderly, took possession of their ordnance-train and its escort of twenty-two men, who had surrendered to him just as General Sullivan reached the scene; but soon after which that gallant and able staff-officer

---

* Colonel Dunham sets his losses down at twenty-three killed, one hundred and twenty-nine wounded, fifty-eight missing—total, two hundred and twenty—which we are bound to contradict. His own description of the fire to which his men were subjected is incompatible, we submit, with his reported loss; and being utterly wrong as to the number of prisoners, we have the right to assume equal inaccuracy as to his statement of killed and wounded; besides, we are assured by General Forrest that he saw many more dead than twenty-three on the field in the several charges which were made with much spirit by Colonel Dunham and his men.

† Colonel Dunham and the correspondent of the Chicago *Tribune*, before cited, speak of but one brigade as having come up; Dunham designates it as Fuller's Brigade, but the latter mentions the fact that General Haynie's was also on the field as well as Fuller's Brigade; and by investigation Haynie's command can be traced to include at least the 106th and 119th Illinois Volunteers, the Iowa Union Brigade, and the 7th Tennessee, or at least eighteen hundred men. [*Reb. Rec.* VI. Doc. 94, pp. 334 to 335.] Colonel Dunham claims that single-handed with his brigade he had repulsed the Confederates; but the correspondent, giving full credit for the good fighting, tells very nearly the truth, that he was thoroughly beaten. See page 335 of Doc. just cited.

was himself captured while taking the list and inventory of his own captures.*

Colonels Russell, Biffle, and Dibrell, and Major J. E. Forrest bore important parts in the brilliant combats of this field, and gave shining evidences of soldierly capacity. They handled their men with as much resolution as skill.

The lamented Napier displayed an admirable courage, and was able to lead his raw troops into the hottest part of the battle, where he fell a victim to an impetuous, brave soul, eager to do his utmost to win a victory. Captains Freeman and Morton, in command of the artillery, were conspicuous for their coolness, their intelligent, intrepid management of their guns, and their General attributes the larger part of the loss inflicted that day on the enemy to this and the bravery of their companies.

It will doubtless be asked how it happened that a commander, wary and alert, like Forrest, permitted himself to be taken unaware, as he was by General Sullivan's fresh force, and this is a question that must be duly answered. He made the proper provision to guard against such a contingency by ordering the detachment of a battalion of the Fourth Tennessee, under a good officer, to proceed to Clarksburg, on the Huntington road, with the object of holding that approach in close observation, and as a provision against the unannounced advent of any enemy from that direction. Captain McLemore was accordingly detailed with three companies, about one hundred men, for that service; but unfortunately the written instructions given him, at second-hand, proved to be vague and inexpressive of the actual purposes of the movement, and failed indeed to indicate any other object than a reconnoissance, a juncture at Clarksburg with Captain Forrest, and their

---

* He had just captured eighteen wagons with ammunition, and a guard of twenty-two men, and was taking a list of his captures when captured.

prompt return to the main body. Moving across the country on byways or through the woods, some seven miles, to Clarksburg, McLemore found that Captain Forrest had been obliged to fall back during the night before a very heavy Federal force, with infantry, cavalry, and artillery that had followed southward before daylight. The roads, too, gave evidence of the recent passage of considerable bodies of troops, and a small detachment of Federal cavalry disappeared in the same direction at a gallop as the Confederates came up. Meanwhile, hearing the sound of the artillery engaged at Parker's Cross-Roads, Captain McLemore felt that, having executed his orders, his presence was now needed as soon as possible with his regiment, evidently in conflict at the time with a superior force of the enemy. He, therefore, rapidly retraced his steps, not taking the main road, as he supposed it was occupied by the Federals, but seeking to reach the Confederates by a detour to the right. In this some time was necessarily lost, from the nature of the country, and he reached the scene only to find that Forrest was quitting the field, and that a large Federal force was interposed between him and his friends. Therefore, looking to the safety of his command, he made another detour northward and eastward, and effected a safe crossing of the Tennessee river at Perryville on the following day. But for this misunderstanding of his orders on the part of subordinates, Forrest is confident he must have vanquished, and so disposed of Dunham's Brigade, before the advent of Sullivan, as to have been in condition to encounter the new column, with strong chances of victory, flushed as the Confederates were with success and discouraged as was their enemy by defeat, while misled in regard to his numbers.

At Lexington—twelve miles from the battle-field—the Confederate force, as before said, was halted, and men and animals were fed, while proper attention was paid to the wounded. This done, that night the column was again in motion toward Clifton. Ten miles in that direction the train and prisoners, sent ahead meanwhile, were overtaken. The prisoners, some 300 in number, were then paroled between that and daybreak and turned adrift — disabled by their parole until exchanged—to find their way back to their comrades.

Early the next morning, the rear-guard and scouts having come up, the Confederate commander put his whole force in rapid march for the Tennessee river, a portion of the command having been sent in advance during the night under Major Forrest, a courier from whom met the Commanding General, when ten miles on his way, with the information that a heavy hostile force was confronting him some eight miles from Clifton. About the same time, moreover, a scout brought the intelligence of the approach of about 10,000 infantry and cavalry from the direction of Purdy, and moving on what is known in that region as the Jack's Creek-Clifton road, with the evident purpose of cutting off the Confederates from that crossing of the river. Giving the order to gallop, and keeping that pace for fifteen miles, Forrest caught up with the main body of his command about eleven miles from the river-crossing. Forming, without loss of a moment, the whole force in order of battle, with a front of one regiment deployed, the others also deployed ; and following at a distance of two hundred yards—the artillery immediately in the rear and followed by the train, with stringent orders to keep well closed up with the command — General Forrest again advanced about three miles, when the enemy (cavalry) were met drawn up, some 1200 strong, directly across his line of march. Colonel Dibrell, whose regiment was in advance, was directed to charge. This he did promptly, cutting the Federals in sunder. Next Colonel Starnes was thrown with his regiment upon the leftward fragment, and Colonel Biffle upon the one on the right hand. Dibrell continuing to push that portion retreating before him, the detachments attacked severally by Starnes and Biffle broke and scattered in all directions, with slight show of belligerency. The road thus cleared, the train and artillery now moved as rapidly as practicable toward the ferry. In this rencounter the enemy lost some twenty killed and wounded and about fifty prisoners.*

It was meridian when the river was reached. Signals were promptly made for skiffs that were on the other bank ; they were brought over, and a party was as swiftly sent back to raise the flat-boat which had been sunk to conceal it after the passage on the 15th of the month. All possible haste was used, and the flat was brought to the west bank. Meanwhile, the animals, detached from the vehicles and artillery, were being driven into the river and made to swim across to the eastern bank, as also the horses of the cavalry—a process which was hurried because of the intelligence received that the enemy was moving his whole available forces by forced marches upon the point.

It was a spectacle full of life and movement ; quite as many as 1000 animals were at one time in the river, which was about six hundred yards broad, with favorable banks. The ferriage of the artillery and wagons was very much slower. Loaded upon the old flat, it was poled up-stream a distance of nearly half a mile, close to the west bank, and, pushed out into the stream, was caught and carried by the current gradually to the other bank some distance below ; there discharged, the process was reversed on its return. In the like way did

---

* There was only one casualty on the Confederate side, and so singular in character as to deserve mention : Mr. Thornton, Forage-Master, standing not far from the General, and calling his attention to some object, was struck by a ball squarely in the forehead ; it flattened by the percussion without penetrating the bone, and Mr. Thornton fell on the ground without serious injury beyond a severe headache.

the flat ply to and fro until eight o'clock at night, when the work was completed and the men stood cheerfully once more in Middle Tennessee, with five pieces of artillery, six caissons with their horses, sixty wagons, and four ambulances with their teams, which had been successfully ferried in the short space of eight hours.

As will be remembered, it was on the 15th of December that the passage into West-Tennessee had been concluded— that is, a fortnight previously. In the interval, seldom in the annals of war had more hard, swift riding, as many sharp rencounters, affluent in results, been crowded in the same short space. That command had averaged over twenty miles a day ; it had fought three well-contested engagements, with diurnal skirmishes ; had destroyed some fifty large and small bridges on the Mobile and Ohio Railroad, and had broken up so much of the trestle-work of that road as to make it useless to the enemy for the rest of the war ; had captured and burned eighteen or twenty stockades, and captured or killed 2500 of the enemy ; had taken or disabled ten pieces of field artillery, and carried off fifty wagons and ambulances with their teams ; had captured 10,000 stands of excellent small-arms, 1,000,000 rounds of ammunition, and had returned thoroughly armed and equipped, including blankets, after having traversed with artillery and a heavy wagon-train roads which in the country were considered and pronounced impracticable at that season for horsemen, resting undisturbed scarcely one whole night during the fortnight, and all the while subjected, unsheltered, to the most inclement weather of mid-winter. Crossing the river into West-Tennessee with his command wretchedly armed and equipped, and with only ten rounds òf percussion-caps to his shot-guns, Forrest returned stronger in numbers than when he entered upon the campaign, admirably armed, as before said, with a surplus of five hundred Enfield rifles, some eighteen hundred blankets and knapsacks, and the raw, native courage of his men ripened by battle and the sharp hardships of the expedition into the perfection of cool, confident, soldierly valor, which makes men invincible except in conflict with invincible odds.

CHAPTER VIII.

Reëstablishment on Picket Service, with Headquarters at Columbia, Tenn.—Disastrous Expedition under General Wheeler against Dover—Forrest's Brigade lost one fourth its number in the Affair—Inclement Weather and Suffering of Troops—Arrival of Major-General Van Dorn at Columbia with additional Force—Confederate line advanced to Spring Hill—Battle of Thompson's Station—Capture of the greater part of the Federal Force engaged, 2200 Officers and Men—Confederates some days later retire behind Duck River before heavy Federal Force—Successful Affair at Brentwood—The entire Garrison, 759 Persons, captured—Block-House and Railroad Bridge destroyed—Confederate Reconnoissance in Force upon Franklin—Loss of the gallant Captain Freeman—Found the Federals in superior Force and prepared—Return to Spring Hill.

January 1st to April 20th, 1863.

HAVING returned to Middle Tennessee, as related at the close of the last chapter, General Forrest established his troops in cantonments around Mount Pleasant some time about the 3d of January, 1863, immediately after which he reported in person to General Bragg, at Shelbyville,* and received verbal orders to continue in position at Columbia, charged with the protection of the left flank of the Confederate army, with a line of outposts and pickets thrown for-

---

* The battle of Murfreesboro or Stone River, had been fought on the 31st of December, and Bragg had sub- sequently fallen back somewhat on the night of the 3d of January, 1863.

ward on the Harpeth river in the direction and vicinity of Triune and Franklin ; and, further, to harass the enemy as much as practicable in their use and navigation of the Cumberland.

For some eight or ten days following the reëstablishment of his brigade in position at Columbia, Forrest's attention was mainly directed to its reorganization and thorough preparation for other field operations such as were now his passion. Meanwhile, the men and animals were given time to recover from the effects of their late campaign.

About the 10th of January, however, at an interview with Major-General Wheeler, Chief of Cavalry, it was arranged to undertake an expedition to Harpeth Shoals, on the Cumberland, with the view to a blow at the Federal gunboats and transports in that quarter. Several of Forrest's regiments were employed in this operation, but took no noteworthy part in the capture, on the 13th of January, of the transports Hasting, Trio, and Parthenia, and gunboat Major Siddell, except it was a detachment under that gallant officer, Lieutenant-Colonel Holman, that crossed the river by swimming, and burned a considerable depot of subsistence and quartermasters' stores on the north side of the Cumberland. This expedition was at the cost of great suffering to the men and animals. Rain, sleet, or snow fell without cessation ; some of the men perished from the extreme cold, and many were frost-bitten.

Afterward, or for the following fortnight, the brigade was only employed on picket service ; but pushing their approaches as near as possible to Nashville, the Federal garrison of that position was kept continually on the alert and a good deal harassed. On the 26th of January, General Forrest was summoned to army headquarters at Shelbyville, and had an interview with the Commanding General, who informed him that an expedition had been directed for the capture of Fort Donelson, under the command of Major-General Wheeler, who, already *en route*, had taken a portion of the Forrest Brigade, which he must follow and command. He accordingly hastened back to Franklin, made some necessary arrangements, and hurried to overtake the expedition, which he effected by two days' hard riding, during bitterly cold weather, within fifteen miles of Dover or Fort Donelson.

Having ascertained that his own troops in his absence had been moved badly supplied with subsistence, ammunition, and cooking equipage, General Forrest at once repaired to General Wheeler, and, while reporting his own deficiencies, inquired into the state of the whole command in the same respects. Thereupon an inspection and report of the actual state of affairs of both Forrest's and Wharton's brigades were ordered. These inspections being made, it proved that the former was provided with only fifteen rounds of ammunition for small-arms and forty-five rounds for his four pieces of artillery, while the other had only twenty rounds for small-arms and fifty rounds for two field-guns, while the whole command was short in subsistence as well as lacking the means of cooking.

In view of this state of affairs, General Forrest submitted to his superior that the expedition did not promise results in any wise commensurate with inevitable losses and possible hazard of serious disaster ; that the men must suffer intensely from the constant exposure to weather so rigorous ; that at most, if successful, they could hope for the capture of only five or six hundred men, and *that* probably with the loss of two or three hundred of their choicest men ; that we could not hold the works for any time if captured, but would be speedily forced to quit them by the Federal gunboats which swarmed the waters in that quarter. Moreover, if not successful at the first onset, we would have nearly exhausted our ammunition, and be entirely out of subsistence, except such as could be gathered in the surrounding country, while we would be at least one hundred miles away from our base and depots of supplies, threatened with determined efforts on the part of the enemy to cut off the command on its way back to its position, it being reported that General Jeff C. Davis was already moving with that object from Franklin. Therefore, regarding the operation as one fraught with great exposure to miscarriage, and indeed calamity, one with scanty probable chances of success at best, he felt constrained to say so and to urge its abandonment.

These views, presented substantially as we have related, passed without heed, and arrangements were made for the work in hand. Forrest was directed to move with his force— about 800 men* and four guns—along the river road *via* the Cumberland Iron-Works to the vicinity of Dover, which was the real position fortified and held by the Federals, and not the site of Fort Donelson. He accordingly moved with his pickets well in advance, and he with them in person. Meantime, Wharton, with the remainder of the command, some 2000 strong, and two pieces, advanced by a left-hand road. As the former approached within a mile of the iron-works,† he learned from a negro, escaping under the apprehension of the Federal conscription, that the place was occupied by a company of Federal cavalry. He therefore quickened the pace and soon broke into a charge, surprising and capturing the company, except three or four men who made their escape despite precautions. Pushing on as rapidly as possible, he reached the immediate vicinity of Dover about meridian, and halted for orders, though throwing a skirmish line well forward. In a little while Major-General Wheeler came up, and

---

* Portions of Fourth Tennessee, (Starnes,) Fourth Alabama, (Russell,) Cox's, Napier's, and Holman's Tennes- see battalions, and Woodward's Kentuckians.

† Nine miles distant from Dover.

assigned the rightward position to Forrest, along the crown
of a crescent-wise ridge inclosing Dover on the south-east
and eastern side, and about eight hundred yards removed
from a rifle-pit around the village, of similar outline, which
was commanded by a redoubt thrown up in the public square
of the place, on an elevated knoll upon the same level with
the ridge occupied by the Confederates, and which ridge, be
it noted, was separated from the sight of the village and inclosing *epaulement* by a narrow valley seamed by a deep
gully.

Wharton had also reached the theatre of operations and
taken up a position to the west and south-west of the place,
between the lines of Fort Donelson and a graveyard on an
eminence, occupied by a Federal battery, immediately west
of Dover. Arrangements were at once made and watches set
to agree for a simultaneous attack by the entire Confederate
force about half-past two P.M.*

At the hour designated, Forrest charged—his men mounted
—down the slope and across the ravine upon the enemy's
intrenchments, which he carried, making some few captures,
in the face of a warm musketry fire and rapid discharges from
two brass field-pieces from behind it, and from a thirty-two-
pounder in the redoubt. The main Federal force, however,
effected their retreat with the artillery into the redoubt and
some adjacent buildings, favorably placed as auxiliary defenses;
but closely followed by their assailants. Sharp and fast was the
musketry fire from the parapets and buildings, while grape and
canister swept the line of approach. Forrest and his sturdy
horsemen breasted the storm ; his horse was now shot, and fell
with him prone to the ground, in sight of his command, who,

---

* Meanwhile, the Eighth Texas, of
Wharton's Brigade, had been detached
in the direction of Fort Henry, to observe and prevent reënforcement of the
enemy from that quarter.

supposing that he had been killed, fell back, from under fire, to the ridge, where their leader, unhurt, quickly followed, and re-formed them for another onset, this time dismounting his men. General Wheeler reappeared at this juncture, and explaining that General Wharton had been unable to get ready to attack simultaneously, another assault was ordered, as watches were again compared and arranged for conformity of movement.

At the time prescribed, Forrest once more moved his men upon the works, which the enemy had reoccupied and held with more resolution than at first. But two of the Confederate guns had been so placed on the ridge as to enfilade a part of the line, and the Federals were again driven from the position over which their enemy rushed, and moved steadily on-ward into the town, though swept by a well-sustained rifle fire and by the guns in the redoubt. On pressed Forrest and his Tennesseeans, Kentuckians, and Alabamians, forcing the Federals to quit the houses and betake themselves to the redoubt, the parapets of which flamed with rifle volleys all the while. It was at this time that Colonel Frank McNairy, of Nashville, a volunteer for the fight, on the staff of General Forrest, was killed, and several valuable officers and a number of the best fighting men of Forrest's command were killed or wounded.

The General, with his aid-de-camp, Captain C. W. Ander-son, and ten or twelve of his escort, rode up to within thirty yards, however, and fired at men behind these very parapets ; and here another horse was slain under him.

His ammunition was now exhausted, and the men were forced, of course, to cease the conflict. The enemy were quick to observe or suspect this, and sallying with spirit, cap-tured twenty-five or thirty Confederates.

Wharton's command moving, meanwhile, as arranged, drove the Federals from the strong position of the graveyard, and captured a rifled gun of the battery posted there, killed a number of the horses of the other guns,* and penetrated the town from that quarter, but in effecting this had likewise exhausted their ammunition. It was now dusk, but the moon rose and shone brightly upon the scene. The Federals, driven into a small space, poured upon the Confederates a galling fire, and the latter were obliged, from want of ammunition, to withdraw. There was no alternative.

The Confederate losses were heavy. Forrest had lost one fourth of his force, or two hundred officers and men killed, wounded, and captured ;† and Wharton's casualties did not fall short of sixty killed and wounded.‡

After the Confederates had been withdrawn from under fire, the Federal gunboats came up about eight o'clock at night, and began a noisy cannonade, expending a great many shells, but doing no harm whatsoever to the Confederates, who, an hour later, began to retire, and encamped three miles south-eastward of Dover for the night. Meanwhile, Forrest had left behind his trusty Aid, Captain Anderson, with Woodward's Battalion, to cover the withdrawal, and,

---

* See *Reb. Rec.* Vol. VI. Doc. 118. p. 419, in which is acknowledged the Federal field-battery lost forty-eight out of sixty-four horses.

† Lieutenant-Colonel D. W. Holman was also severely wounded in the hip ; Lieutenants —— Summers and A. S. Chapman, of his detachment, were killed, after the display of conspicuous gallantry ; and a private—Hill Roy— who is mentioned as having especially signalized himself on the field by his cool courage. Napier's Battalion had three officers—Captains M. F. Alexander, W. J. Hobson, and N. J. Robinson—badly wounded and captured.— *MS. Notes of Colonels Holman and*

De Moss. The Fourth Tennessee also suffered severely, some seventy-four officers and men having been killed or wounded. Its Lieutenant-Colonel, Haines, a gallant officer, was disabled for the rest of the war by a wound in the mouth.

‡ That of the enemy, as reported by the commander, were sixteen killed and sixty wounded. [See *Reb. Rec.* Vol. VI. Doc. 118, p. 417.] The defense was made with courage ; the commander was Colonel A. C. Harding, Eighty-third Volunteer Illinois Infantry, who had a force of six hundred of his regiment and a battery of artillery.

under shelter of night, to bring off the ammunition of a cais-· son, captured by Wharton, remaining just outside the works. This was handsomely done by Captain Anderson, with ten Kentuckians detailed for the purpose, notwithstanding the furious broadsides of the gunboats, one of whose shells almost covered Colonel Woodward with the coals and ashes of a camp-fire at which he was lying, wounded by a spent grape-shot in the knee, awaiting the movements of his command. At nine o'clock next morning, the entire force took up their line of march, by way of the Cumberland Iron-Works, for Charlotte. The weather continued extremely cold; the wounded suffered intensely. Marching some fourteen or fifteen miles on the 14th, the command was halted in consequence of the inclemency of the weather, and went no further that day. Intelligence having been here received by General Wheeler, in certain confirmation of the movement of a Federal column under General Jeff C. Davis upon Charlotte, it became necessary to change his route, and on the following morning the command, moving slowly along the valley of Yellow creek, marched only twelve miles, obliged by the slippery, icy condition of the road to leave it, and traverse the fields and woods, while the commissaries, with detachments, were thrown out on either flank to collect subsistence and forage, for their rations had been exhausted.

On the 16th of February, to avoid collision with Davis, the Confederate column was deflected somewhat further to the right and across the valley of Piney river some twenty miles, the cold still extremely rigorous, causing much suffering to both men and animals. Forrest with his men encamped that night at Piney Factory, Hickman county, and threw out scouts to ascertain Davis's precise position and movement; these found the Federals about fifteen miles to the eastward, on the Columbia-Charlotte road. The following morning, the command reaching Centreville, found Duck river reported "unfordable." General Forrest calling for volunteers to test the fact, Major J. M. Crews, an Acting Inspector-General on his staff, dashed at once into the surging, freezing stream. But as he reached mid-way, the water proved really as deep as was alleged, and his horse would not swim. The Major was washed from his seat, but, by a happy chance, was presently drifted across and ashore by the current, where he was rescued by some citizens ; and so intense was the cold that his clothes were frozen stiffly in a few moments after he was drawn from the water. Some miles higher up the stream, a ford was found during the afternoon, when a crossing was effected, while a portion of the command was ferried over in a small boat at Centreville. Beyond Duck river all risk of interruption by Davis was averted, and the command resumed their old quarters at Columbia on the following day, Wharton returning to the other flank of the army with General Wheeler.

II.

While Forrest was giving rest to his men for some days at Columbia, after such fearful weather-exposure, and battle-losses; Major-General Van Dorn arrived from Mississippi with three brigades of cavalry—about 4500 rank and file*—

---

* Armstrong's Brigade : First Tennessee Cavalry, Colonel James T. Wheeler, Lieutenant-Colonel Lewis ; Forrest's old regiment, Major E. B. Trezevant ; Second Mississippi, Lieutenant-Colonel James Gordon, Major J. L. Harris ; Saunders's Battalion, Major Ed. Saunders ; Third Arkansas, Colonel Earle, Lieutenant - Colonel Hobson, Major Henderson ; and King's Battery of four pieces. Whitfield's Brigade : Third Texas, Colonel Mabry ; Sixth Texas, Colonel L. S. Ross ; Ninth Texas, Colonel Jones ; and Whitfield's Legion, Colonel Brooks. Cosby's Brigade : Twenty-eighth Mississippi, Colonel P. B. Starke ; Ballyntine's Regiment, Colonel J. G. Ballyntine, Lieutenant-Colonel W. L. Maxwell ; Second Kentucky, Colonel Woodward ; and First Mississippi, Colonel Richard A. Pinson.

and thus materially strengthened the Confederate cavalry force on that flank, whose scene of operations, be it noted, embraced one of the most opulent communities, as also one of the best cultivated and productive regions of Tennessee, watered by Duck river, a very considerable stream when swollen by heavy and continuous rains, as was then the case, and by its tributaries.

In the mean time, between the 20th and 25th of February, Russell's Alabama Regiment was detached from the brigade, and Holman's and Douglass's battalions were assigned instead ; and these two battalions, being consolidated, formed the Eleventh Regiment Tennessee Cavalry, while Cox's and Napier's battalions, about the same time, were thrown together and became the Tenth Tennessee.*

It was now determined to establish outposts and picket-lines within sight of Franklin and Triune, both of which the enemy occupied in force, while the headquarters of the Confederates should be thrown forward across Duck river to Spring Hill, twelve miles nearer to the former place ; and this was done by ferrying the stream on or about the 23d of February, 1863. A series of sharp, spirited outpost skirmishes ensued for the next ten days, of which, however, we are unable to relate any notable incident, fraught as they were, we well know, with daily acts of splendid courage and hardihood.

On the night of March 4th, however, scouts returned with information that a heavy body of Federals was in motion toward Spring Hill on the Franklin-Columbia turnpike. Major-General Van Dorn, in chief command, made immediate disposition for the exigency, determining to meet the hostile movement some four miles in advance, at Thompson's Sta-

---

* See Appendix for Rosters of Tenth and Eleventh Tennessee Cavalry.

tion, on the Tennessee and Alabama Railroad. Accordingly, on the next morning early, that position was secured by the Confederates, who then awaited the enemy in very much the following array.

Forrest occupied the extreme right, his regiments—some 2000 strong—deployed in line on an eminence that bordered and overlooked a narrow valley—about half a mile wide—which meandered with a general direction across and perpendicular to the railroad and several highways converging from that quarter upon Franklin, with his artillery—a section of Freeman's Battery—posted on a knoll on his right. On

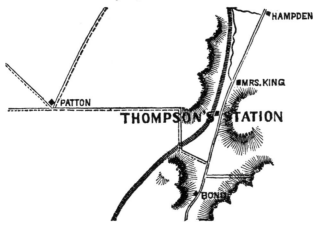

the left of these, and some paces retired, was Armstrong's Brigade, on the crest of a narrow ridge which is cut by the railroad and by the Columbia turnpike further to the east. Next on the left, in line with Armstrong, was the Texas Brigade, (Whitfield's,)* King's Battery of four pieces planted in two favorable positions on the right and left hand, respectively, of the Columbia turnpike.† Across the valley were two de-

---

* Armstrong's Brigade about 1600 and Whitfield's say 1800 strong.

† Cosby had as yet not been brought up. He had been detained at the crossing of Duck river and took no part in the combat subsequently.

cided eminences, between or in the gorge of which passed the railroad and Columbia turnpike, and the Station was also in the valley between the ground occupied by the Confederates and the uplands just mentioned.

The enemy appeared about half-past nine A.M., moving on the Columbia turnpike, with five regiments of infantry, some 600 cavalry, and a field-battery.* Posting the latter upon the right hand ridge, the Federal infantry was deployed across the pike and rightward, astraddle the railroad. King's Battery opened vigorously with shell, but the Federals pushed on handsomely, resolutely upon the Confederate position, and up to within one hundred and fifty yards. Then Armstrong's and Whitfield's brigades sprang forward and met them, and a sharp exchange of musketry fire took place for full half an hour before the Federal line faltered and fell back.

Forrest, with his apt soldier's eyes, now observing that no enemy was likely to appear in his front—with what Carlyle terms an " interior talent for war "—determined to detach Colonel Starnes with two regiments to move around by the right upon the Federal artillery and its supports, while he with the remainder of his force, present on the field, led it further to the right and rearward, in order to cut off the route of retreat upon Franklin. Meanwhile, Starnes, executing his orders with habitual energy,† opening with a deadly fire of his rifles, had driven the Federal artillery from their strong vantage ground rapidly to the rear, down the turnpike, and forced the infantry across westward of the railroad to another position upon the ridge in that quarter, where they made a most stubborn stand. In the mean while, apparently observing

----

* *Reb. Rec.* VI. Doc. 130, p. 439.

† Major McLemore, then in command of the Fourth Tennessee, had been born within a mile and a half of the battle-ground, and was thoroughly acquainted with every foot of the surrounding region.

Forrest's movement, a considerable Federal detachment fell back, and took shelter behind a strong stone fence. From this position General Forrest made two sustained attempts to dislodge these men, who maintained it with genuine courage. At the second charge, however, they were overcome, and surrendering, were sent from the field, the General having his horse shot in the affair. Moving still rearward and to the west of the railroad, he succeeded quickly in getting in a position to cut off the route of retreat of the enemy, who still fought with signal resolution and spirit. Forming his command, including his escort, in line, Forrest now dashed forward with it up the steep slope of the ridge so stoutly held by the Federal infantry, who poured a galling fire upon his men as they followed their leader. The loss was heavy, and Captain Montgomery Little, commander of his escort, fell by his side, mortally wounded.* Major E. B. Trezevant was also slain, near by, in this final charge.†

---

* This escort was organized by Captain Little, at Shelbyville, Tennessee, in October, 1862. At first some ninety strong, it reported at Lavergne, and, composed of the best young men of Middle Tennessee, became General Forrest's personal escort thenceforward. Montgomery Little was born in Rowan county, North-Carolina, on the 18th of July, 1825, whence his family emigrated to Smith county, Tennessee, in 1829. He was left an orphan in May, 1831. An elder brother secured him a good education, including at least one term at Saint Mary's College, Kentucky. Subsequently, he resided in Mississippi, superintending plantations there for several years and until he removed to Memphis and entered into business with his brother. He was a Union man up to the outset of the war. Captain Little was an admirable officer, with superior martial aptitudes, including notable resolution and decision, which made him greatly trusted and his early death deeply regretted by his chief.

† Edward Buller Trezevant, son of Dr. Lewis C. Trezevant, born in Shelby county, Tennessee, 24th of July, 1838, was educated at St. James's College, Hagerstown, Maryland. At the beginning of the war he was deputy clerk of the Circuit Court for Shelby county. In the spring of 1861, at the first call to arms, he joined Captain Logwood's Company—"The Memphis Light Dragoons"—of which he was elected Third Lieutenant. Soon

But this did not check the Confederate advance, and in a few moments Forrest stood within thirty paces of the Federal commander, Colonel Coburn, whose surrender he demanded

---

the Company marched to Randolph, where it was organized, with five others, into the battalion known as "Logwood's Battalion." Lieutenant Trezevant subsequently accompanied the battalion to New - Madrid, Missouri, and Columbus, Kentucky, with the troops under the command of General Pillow, early in September, 1861. He was present in a night attack upon the enemy's outposts in front of Paducah, in October ; and in the battle of Belmont, November 7th, where, with another company, the "Light Dragoons " made a successful charge upon the Federal infantry.

His health becoming very precarious from incipient consumption, about the 15th of December Lieutenant Trezevant resigned, and soon after repaired to Western Texas, the pure, dry air of which had been recommended by his physician as likely to restore his health. Taking up his residence near Austin, the change of climate seemed, indeed, to act like a charm, for early in the spring he felt so entirely restored, that he determined at once to rejoin the army, and attach himself to the command of Colonel Forrest. About the 1st of May, arriving at Corinth, he reported at the headquarters of "Forrest's Cavalry," and was assigned to duty as Sergeant-Major of the regiment.

About the 20th of June, when Captain Strange was transferred from the regiment—with Colonel Forrest—Mr.

Trezevant was appointed to succeed him as Adjutant. In the following month, the Alabama Companies having been permanently detached, the remnant of the regiment, with the addition of a Louisiana squadron, was reorganized at Guntown, Mississippi, as a battalion, of which Adjutant Trezevant was elected Major.

Major Trezevant served with this battalion in all its marches and battles ; in the affairs at Middleburg, Medon, Britton's Lane, Iuka, Corinth, etc., exhibiting the best traits of a soldier, until February, 1862, when, with the rest of Van Dorn's Cavalry corps, he crossed into Middle Tennessee. He was then transferred, with the rank of Lieutenant-Colonel, and placed in command of the Tenth Tennessee Cavalry. Gallantly leading this regiment, on the 5th of March, he was struck down, mortally wounded, by a rifle-ball through the abdomen. Borne to the residence of Mrs. Bond, at Spring Hill, hard by, he died there two days later. Meanwhile, " receiving at the hands of his hostess," says a near relative, " all the kindness a patriot could desire, or a Christian mother bestow."

With a strong, well-cultivated mind, were united in Colonel Trezevant a frankness and magnanimity, which made him an ornament in his social circle, and surrounded him with friends. Devoting himself to the acquirement

under the stress of a leveled revolver. Further resistance was in vain, and his brave adversary, thoroughly beaten at all points, was forced to succumb. Just at this juncture a section of King's battery having been favorably planted to enfilade the Federal position, and in the hurly-burly of battle not having observed the surrender or cessation of fire, discharged two rounds, greatly endangering Forrest and his prisoners before it could be stopped by the courier sent to notify General Van Dorn of events.

Fire having now ceased in all parts of the field, General Forrest conducted and introduced Colonel Coburn to General Van Dorn, and then returned to look after his wounded, collect and fitly care for the dead, and reorganize his command. A portion of his men—mounted—meanwhile had followed and endeavored to cut off the runaway cavalry, artillery, and some of the infantry, that had fled from the field before the last part of the conflict, but they were obliged to return without more than some seventy-five captured stragglers ; the remainder effected their retreat to Franklin, though followed hotly to within two miles of that place.

The command surrendered consisted of the Thirty-third and Eighty-fifth Indiana, Nineteenth Michigan, and Twenty-second Wisconsin Volunteer Infantry, with an aggregate of two thousand two hundred*—a fine body of men, as shown by their stout fighting.

It was the Fourth and Eleventh Tennessee Regiments of Forrest's command, as has been noted, who drove the Federal artillery from the field, and their support from their strong

---

of a knowledge of the profession of arms, he soon became fitted for the leadership of men. In person he was tall, well proportioned, and erect, he had light hair, blue eyes, and regular features, with the air and manners of a gentleman. Altogether, one of the handsomest young officers in the army.

* The 124th Ohio, in reserve with the wagon-train, was not taken : it escaped with the wagon-train.—*Reb. Rec.* VII. Doc. 130, p. 441.

position—a cedar-clad knoll on the left of the turnpike, to the other hill ; and Starnes, Edmonston, and McLemore deserve much credit for the vigor and ability with which they handled their regiments, the officers and men of which displayed the highest soldierly qualities ; as did also Colonel Biffle, and the officers and men generally engaged ; especially in the closing charge, which is represented as the "bloodiest part of the fighting" that day.*

The success was acquired at the cost to the Confederates of about thirty killed and one hundred and twenty-five wounded. The dead included several valuable officers, besides Major Trezevant and Captain Little, already mentioned. Colonel Samuel G. Earl, of the Third Arkansas Cavalry, was killed leading his men upon the enemy ; so too fell Captain Alfred Dysart, of the Fourth Tennessee, in a charge, and Captain William Watson, of General Armstrong's staff.† The Rev. Mr. Crouch, a brigade chaplain, also was slain while inspiriting the men to the discharge of their duty ; and Lieutenant John Johnson, of the Ninth Tennessee, was killed bearing the colors of his regiment. Those falling were seized by one of the color-guard—Clay Kendrick—whose right arm being severely shattered, shifted the staff, and bore it in his left hand to the close of the battle. Indeed, the conduct of all was highly satisfactory.

The results served to make material amends for the bloody Dover *fiasco*—the loss there of *prestige:* and had the effect to restore the tone of the Confederate cavalry in that army, as well as to increase the confidence in General Forrest's military capacities, and therefore enhanced his influence with his troops— his ability to lead them with even greater efficiency.

---

* See letter of Centurion, before cited.
† See Appendix for sketch.

III.

No pursuit of the force, except that already related, was made, and the troops were ordered back to their cantonments at Spring Hill. Pickets and outposts were, however, maintained within close proximity to Franklin. The usual round of daily skirmishes followed, with little profit, except that on the 7th of March, Colonel Starnes, on outpost service, captured a foraging party, with their train, very near their lines. But on the 8th, his scouts gave intelligence of the advance of a heavy Federal column from Franklin down the Columbia turnpike. The skirmishers soon became warmly engaged, and a gallant stand was made by Starnes for several hours at a point a mile northward of the battle-field of the 5th ; but the Confederate forces retired finally, though slowly and deliberately. For some days previously a heavy rain had fallen, and all the affluents of Duck river, as well as that stream, were greatly swollen. At and behind Rutherford's creek the Confederates made another stand, to secure time to cross Duck river in safety ; and all the artillery, but four pieces retained for service in that stand, and the train, were sent to the rear, to be thrown across the river.

On the 10th, the Federals, making their appearance in superior force, endeavored several times to force a passage of the creek, but were foiled. Thus baffled, they made another attempt some distance leftward, and were suffered to get well into the stream without molestation, when Captain Forrest attacked with vigor, and repulsed them with loss. It was raining meanwhile, and quite cold. That night, the artillery not engaged was conveyed across Duck river to Columbia, by means of a pontoon-bridge, which gave way immediately thereafter, obliging the Confederates to resort to White's Bridge, some twenty-five miles up Duck river, for means of passage. To Forrest was assigned the service of covering this movement by holding the line of Rutherford's creek. Moving along it accordingly, the enemy keeping pace on the other bank, a series of spirited skirmishes were kept up, with little intermission, across the stream, until apparently something seemed to cause an alarm among the Federals, for they suddenly began a rapid retrograde movement, at a *double-quick*, to Franklin, as was subsequently ascertained.* General Forrest then followed the march of the main body of the Confederates to Columbia, where he took position the 12th of March; and this retreat before a greatly superior force was safely effected without any loss, under circumstances involving great hazard, in consequence of the condition of Duck river.

IV.

The pontoon-bridge at Columbia was repaired as speedily as possible, and headquarters were again pushed forward to Spring Hill on the 15th of March. General Forrest was now assigned to the command of a division made up of his brigade and that of Armstrong's, now including the Eighth Tennessee, and occupied the right of the line, his regiments extending between Spring Hill and Ridge Meeting-House, on the Franklin-Lewisburg turnpike, with a line of outposts and pickets thrown well in advance, and stretching across as far as to the near vicinity of the Federals in position at College Grove, on Harpeth river, and connecting at Thompson's Station with a similar line furnished by the other (W. H. Jackson's) division.†

Frequent outpost affairs now took place, fruitless of consequences, as is usual in that character of petty warfare, after a campaign has well opened. The most notable of these, and,

---

* Apprehensive, apparently, of a flank movement.
† Whitfield's and Cosby's Brigades.

perchance, of some profit as a species of sharp battle-drill, and of moral tonic effect upon the men, was a dash made at the Federal outpost at College Grove by three regiments, or detachments, of Forrest's immediate brigade, their commander, Colonel Starnes, leading. The enemy giving way, fell back across the Harpeth, and there made a stout struggle for an hour, in a strong position, from which they were finally routed and forced back upon their main body at Triune, with a loss on their side of some thirty killed or captured, and on the Confederate part of ten or twelve killed or wounded.

Having learned, through reliable sources, that the troops who had escaped from the affair at Thompson's Station, on the 5th of the month, were in position at Brentwood Station, on the Franklin and Nashville Railroad, guarding the railroad bridge over the Little Harpeth, nine miles rearward of Franklin, General Forrest received permission from General Van Dorn to attempt a *coup de main*, with his division, upon them. This he proceeded to execute on or about the night of the 24th of March. Starnes with his own, under McLemore, and Edmonston's regiment, moved forward on a by-way, crossing the Harpeth some six miles rightward of Franklin, and thence through fields and woods, deftly threading and eluding the enemy's pickets without discovery, to the point of destination. General Forrest himself, with his escort—Biffle's Regiment, the Tenth Tennessee, under Major De Moss, and Armstrong, with the First Tennessee, Third Arkansas, Second Mississippi, and Saunder's battalion of his brigade, and a section of Freeman's battery, under Lieutenant Huggins—made a detour leftward, by the way of Hillsboro, crossing the Harpeth at the Granny-White-Nashville turnpike, some six miles north of Franklin, whence he moved rapidly and directly upon Brentwood. Reaching the place just at dawn, the General made his disposition at once for the attack, although Armstrong—impeded by the artillery—had not yet come up, and Starnes was not in sight.* With his force in hand, brushing some pickets aside, he moved rapidly around the position by the right or east, with his escort and Captain Forrest's company, so as to foil the effort to escape which was already being attempted.   Securing this position, he then demanded the surrender of the place, which was made without further parley. Armstrong, in the mean time, having come up in their immediate front, deployed his line, and planted his artillery so as to command the position.   The troops capitulated, as General Forrest anticipated, proved to be of those that had escaped from the field at Thompson's Station under Lieutenant-Colonel Bloodgood, who had quit the ground at the height of the conflict,† and embracing, according to Federal accounts, some five hundred and twenty-nine officers, men, and teamsters, with sixteen or seventeen wagons, and three ambulances and teams ;‡ also the arms of the men, and all the baggage of Coburn's late command, all which was secured with the loss of one man killed and two wounded.   The Federals, besides prisoners, lost about ten killed in the skirmish preceding the capitulation.

After the surrender had been arranged, Starnes came upon the ground with his command, and the prisoners and spoils of war, which were abundant, were placed in his charge. General Forrest then moved at a gallop, with the Tenth Tennessee and Freeman with one of his guns, on the road toward Franklin to the bridge, which he found defended by a stockade strongly garrisoned, the surrender of which, straightway

---

* It appears Colonel Starnes was in position and full view of the place before daylight, but finding the main force was not up, and apprehending some miscarriage as the cause, moved to the west side of the turnpike, out of view, as it happened.

† See Lieutenant Bachman's statement. *Reb. Rec.* VI. Doc. 130, p. 440.

‡ *Ibid.* Doc. 147, Chaplain Pillsbury's statement, p. 482.   The force thus surrendered included the remnant of the Twenty-second Wisconsin.

demanded through his aid-de-camp, Captain C. W. Anderson, was curtly declined. A single shot, however, from Freeman's gun, hurtling and crashing through the stockade, wrought an immediate change of purpose and brought the display of white flags. The men at this point, some 230, the remnant of the Twelfth Michigan Volunteer Infantry, another of Coburn's regiments, made the sum total of prisoners 759. The bridge and stockade being burned to the ground, the objects of the expedition were fully accomplished, making it one of the most skillfully executed of the war if the Confederates could effect their return to their lines with their prisoners and booty without serious hindérance or offset.

Detaching the First Tennessee (Colonel Wheeler) to scour the turnpike in the direction of and as near to Nashville as possible, the Confederate General now set out on his return with the rest of his force and prisoners by the Harding turnpike, passing westward of Franklin. Wheeler pushed, meanwhile, to within four miles of the outskirts of Nashville, when he encountered a small wagon-train, a gang of negro woodchoppers, and some cavalry. Charging, he captured several well-loaded sutlers' wagons and some thirty odd prisoners, whom he brought away, dispersing the rest and causing wild consternation in Nashville, as was heard afterward. This done, turning, he made a wide sweep, and passed within four miles of Triune. There, charging and capturing some picket-posts, which produced not a little alarm in that quarter, he pushed on and successfully reached headquarters at the Ridge Meeting-House with little delay.

Forrest, in the interval, after moving some seven or eight miles from Brentwood, had halted to rest and break the fast of his men and animals, as also to wait for the captured train—under escort of the Tenth Tennessee—to come up. Suddenly the alarm being given that the latter had been attacked, some three companies of the Eleventh Tennessee wcre hurriedly mounted and dispatched to its relief, General Forrest leading the succor party.   Not a little confusion was produced, however, in the Confederate command by this intelligence, and the apprehension was that a grave attempt to cut off the retreat was on foot.   General Forrest, on reaching the scene, found a considerable cavalry force in a threatening attitude, with several of his wagons and ambulances already in their hands.   As he charged boldly upon them, they cut the draught animals from their traces and fled, with little show of pugnacity.   Colonel Starnes coming up opportunely, however, on their right flank, they suffered a loss of at least fifty in killed and captured.*   The Federals engaged in this affair, we learn from Federal sources, were detachments of four volunteer cavalry regiments, 545 strong, under General Green Clay Smith,† who had been detached by General Granger from Franklin that morning to reconnoitre and ascertain the purposes of the Confederate expedition, of which intelligence had reached that officer.   Going to Brentwood, they found the bridge, camp, and stockade in ruins, and the garrison carried off as prisoners of war.   Following rapidly on Forrest's trace, they came up with the train as related, when matters, at first favorable for the Federals, were soon given an adverse turn and termination by the incisive tactics of the Confederate leader.‡

---

* The Tenth Tennessee lost in this affair three killed, including Lieutenant Andrew Nesbitt, company "E," four wounded, and twenty-five captured.— *Notes of Major De Moss.*

† *Reb. Rec.* VI. Doc. 147, p. 481.

‡ The Federal relation of this affair, just cited, is a characteristic example of the manner and matter of Federal newspaper accounts of war incidents. General Smith made no such stand, much less did he fight such odds ; he made no such persistent pursuit, as is painted by this correspondent, after coming up with the train ; and not one wagon or ambulance did he actually carry off. What we relate of the affair is taken from the lips of General Forrest, abundantly confirmed afterward by other accounts written by spectators at the

The march was now resumed homeward as far as Hillsborough without further hinderance. There the main body encamped, while the prisoners, under Captain Forrest and a proper escort, were sent forward the same night in the direction of Columbia. And, on the following morning, meeting no opposition by the way, Forrest led his command safely back to their quarters near Spring Hill. One effect of this brilliant raid was to bestir the Federals to somewhat greater watchfulness ; consequently they placed all the fords of the Harpeth under strict watch and ward, with a heavy picket-line from Davis's Mill to Franklin : but a little late, for Forrest had already gained his ends !

After returning to their quarters about Spring Hill, the usual routine of cavalry outpost service was resumed, without noteworthy incident until about the 9th of April, when General Jackson—commanding the immediate advance—having been led to suspect and express the opinion that the enemy were evacuating Franklin,* General Van Dorn ordered a reconnoissance in force of the position on the 10th.

Forrest's Division was ordered to assemble at the Ridge Meeting-House, on the Lewisburg turnpike, and move thence by that approach to Franklin, while Jackson was to advance by the Columbia-Franklin road ; and by six o'clock on that morning the movement began. By ten o'clock A.M.—Arm-

---

time. See dispatch to *Chattanooga Rebel*, dated Columbia, March 26th, 1863 ; "Centurion's" letter to Atlanta *Southern Confederacy*, April 8th, 1863 ; and, besides, there is complete evidence in the document itself of its gross exaggerations.

* The Federals had been closely observed by the Confederate scouts, and bodies of troops were known to have gone in the direction of Triune ; and it may also be inferred from General Gordon Granger's telegraphic report of the affair that he had been sending off some of his troops, though fully anticipating an attack, and having, therefore, been prepared for it with Stanley's Division of cavalry stationed on the Murfreesboro road four miles from Franklin.— See *Reb. Rec.* VI. Doc. 160, p. 518.

sion, had pressed the enemy back on the Columbia road with equal vigor and spirit, but, having become exposed to a galling fire from houses, fences, and rifle-pits, was forced to retire. We find it mentioned that in this quarter of the field the Twenty-eighth Mississippi Cavalry was engaged with conspicuous bravery.

It was now apparent the enemy had not been evacuating Franklin, as was supposed, and was prepared for this attack, and hence General Van Dorn gave the order for withdrawing at once to his lines at and in advance of Spring Hill, which were resumed that night without any molestation from the enemy.

The loss on the part of the Federals in this fruitless affair is reported by them to be "less than one hundred ;" the Confederate loss in Forrest's Division was three killed, ten wounded, and thirty prisoners, which was scarcely equaled by Jackson's Division.

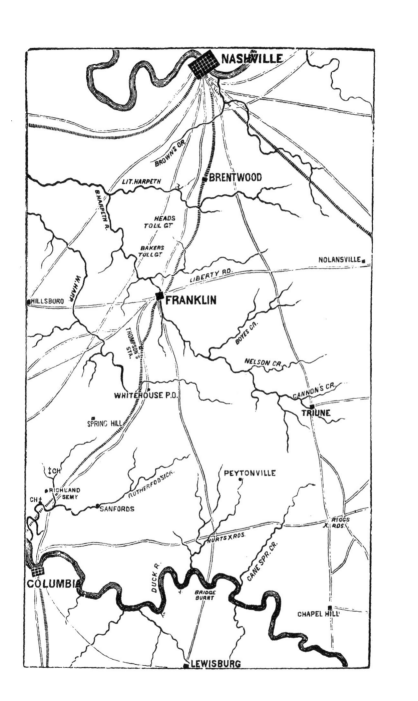

NASHVILLE

BROWN'S CR.

LIT. HARPETH

BRENTWOOD

B. HARPETH R.

HEADS
TOLL GT.

BAKERS
TOLL GT.

NOLANSVILLE

LIBERTY RD.

W. HARP.

HILLSBORO

FRANKLIN

THOMPSON'S
STA.

BOYES CR.

NELSON CR.

CANNON'S CR.

WHITEHOUSE P.O.

TRIUNE

SPRING HILL

† CH

PEYTONVILLE

RICHLAND
SEMY

RUTHERFOODS CR.

RIGGS
X RDS.

CH †

SANFORDS

NURTS X RDS.

CANE SPR. CR.

COLUMBIA

DUCK R.

BRIDGE
BURNT

CHAPEL HILL

LEWISBURG

MISS EMMA SANSON.

CHAPTER IX.

THE STREIGHT RAID.

Forrest's Brigade ordered to North-Alabama—Junction with Roddy, and Affair at Town Creek—Dibrell's Diversion—Federal Infantry retire—Desolation of the Country—Inauguration of Federal Cavalry Raid under Colonel Streight—Prompt Pursuit by Forrest—Night Combat in Sand Mountain—Series of Sharp Fights to Blountsville— Reduced Numbers of Confederates—Heroic Services of Miss Emma Sanson at Black Creek, Alabama—Federal Ambush defeated at Turkeytown—Colonel Streight overtaken and Surrender of 1365 Federals to Inferior Numbers under Forrest—Another Detachment surrendered near Rome—Rejoicing of People of Rome—Commentaries.

April 25th to May 3d, 1863.

ON the 23d of April, Forrest received orders from General Bragg to move swiftly with his own brigade, by way of Decatur, Ala., to the relief of Colonel Roddy, who, greatly overmatched, was being hard pressed by a heavy Federal column, under General Dodge, detached from Corinth, Miss., in the direction of Tuscumbia, as well as by a cavalry force that had moved up the western bank of the Tennessee river from Eastport, under the command of Colonel A. D. Streight.*

Making what preparations were needful for efficiency, For-

---

* See page 256 hereinafter. This force moved in rear of Dodge, and reached Tuscumbia on the 24th of April.—*Reb. Rec.* VI. Doc. 173, p. 556.

rest detached the Eleventh Tennessee, 600 strong, to proceed directly to the Tennessee river at Bainbridge, where, crossing it, Colonel Edmondson effected a junction with Roddy four miles eastward of Tuscumbia, and that regiment took a most creditable part in all the skirmishes which occurred westward of Town creek.

On Friday morning, 24th, the rest of the brigade * was put *en route* to make the crossing eastward of Town creek, and, moving with his habitual celerity, Forrest reached the Tennessee river at Brown's Ferry on the evening of the 27th of April, having ascertained definitely by the wayside, through trusty scouts, that the commands of Dodge and Streight, already at Tuscumbia, were estimated, the former at about 10,000, mainly infantry, with artillery, and the latter 2200 cavalry or mounted infantry.

It was also reported that they gave indications of a purpose to cross to the north bank of the Tennessee ; and to meet that emergency, Dibrell was detached with the Eighth and Tenth Tennessee and a section of artillery, with orders to repair to Florence and keep a sharp ward against any such project. Confident, however, that their real purpose would be developed southward of the Tennessee river, Forrest pushed on with the main body of his force to Brown's Ferry. There he secured immediate facilities for ferriage by two steamboats during the night, and pressed forward twelve miles to Courtland, twenty miles west of Decatur. Here he learned that the Federals were already at Town creek, a bold stream which descends from the mountains and hills of North-Alabama and empties some seven miles westward into the Tennessee, and the passage of which Roddy was then stiffly disputing.

---

* Dibrell's, (Eighth,) Starnes's, and the Tenth Tennessee, under Lieutenant-Colonel De Moss. (Fourth,) Biffle's (Ninth) regiments,

Losing no time, Forrest hastened on that night and established his headquarters on the Tuscumbia road several miles in rear of Colonel Roddy, who soon met him there, and with whom the plan of operations was arranged for the next morning. At the same time an order was sent to Dibrell to move his force westward as far as Bainbridge, and there, opening with his artillery, make a demonstration as if designing to cross the river and fall upon the Federal rear.*

The Federal force—about 8000 strong, of infantry, artillery, and cavalry—meanwhile occupied the west bank of Town creek confronted by Colonel Roddy, whose force up to the advent of Forrest consisted of scarcely 1200 men in addition to Edmondson's Eleventh Tennessee.† Their line of encampments extended from the railroad northward to the residence of Major Robert King, on the Tuscumbia road, and General Dodge's headquarters were established in the old Dearing mansion.

At dawn, on the 28th, General Forrest appeared upon the scene with and speedily disposed his forces for an obstinate contest. Posting Starnes's and Biffle's regiments out of range of the Federal artillery, with his right resting on the Tuscumbia road, he assigned Roddy's force to positions on the left, to

---

* This order was successfully carried by Captain J. J. Scanlan, a young Philadelphian, who resided in St. Louis at the outbreak of the war. The service was performed under circumstances of extremest peril. The crossing was made in a small canoe, when the river was excessively high, filled with drift, and the night dark and stormy. This gentleman first saw service at Pensacola, in the summer of 1861. Was subsequently the Adjutant of the Chief of Artillery of the Confederate army at Corinth. He served successively on the staff of several general officers until after the battle of Murfreesboro, when, resigning, he took service as a private in Colonel Roddy's Regiment, but later was restored to staff duty with the brigade commanded by Colonel Johnson, of North-Alabama.

† Namely, Roddy's (350) and Hannon's (400) Regiments, and Baxter's (200) Battalion, (all Alabama cavalry,) Julian's Battalion also, (150,) and Ferrell's (Georgia) Battery of four guns.

watch the upper crossing, known as the " Shallow Ford," and the Eleventh Tennessee was held concealed in a woods north of the railway, to command the railroad bridge, with rigid orders not to fire a gun unless the enemy attempted to seize or cross that bridge, in which eyent a stubborn contest was to be made.

Happily, much swollen by recent heavy rains, the stream was nearly unfordable. The rising sun was gilding the distant mountain-ridge to the south. All was quiet in the encampment opposite, as the Confederate commander ordered Captain Morton to throw a shell from one of his steel guns* through the Federal headquarters. The aim was skillful ; in another instant the inmates of the building in question swarmed forth, and armed men rose from the earth all along the Federal lines — literally like those of the Grecian fable, born of the dragons' teeth sown by an enemy. Their artillery, speedily placed in position, now began to play upon that with which Forrest as rapidly confronted them on a ridge seven hundred yards distant. The Federals had eighteen guns in position, Forrest not more than eight pieces, of which only two were rifled and of long. range. The cannonade soon waxed violent. Open fields intervened on both sides, unobstructed by a single tree, except the few that fringed the immediate bank of the creek, and behind which sharp-shooters kept up a warm, incessant fire on both sides. For five hours this was maintained, and for a time the artillery fire was very severe and the skirmishing excessively warm.

Meanwhile the Federal commander had sent an infantry force into an old stockade just west of the railroad bridge, when Edmondson's men opened a premature fire. The enemy, in a commanding position, were quickly supported by a battery,

---

* Captured piece, it will be remembered.

and a fierce, pelting storm of minie-balls, of grape and exploding shells was quickly poured into the woods, so that the
limbs of the trees flew and fell around in great profusion, and
caused many casualties in the Eleventh Tennessee, who stood
their ground, however, with admirable fortitude.

After the combat had begun, one of Roddy's most skillful
and daring scouts* returned, and reported the presence of a
considerable hostile cavalry force at Newberg, some distance
to the south, moving apparently eastward toward, and on the
road to Mount Hope and Moulton.

Seemingly undisturbed by this intelligence—"as if he had
no flank to be turned"—Forrest continued to battle with his
immediate adversary.† For a time the Federal artillery—
superior in weight of metal as in numbers—was gaining some
advantage over the short-range guns of their adversary, but
the well-handled rifled section of Morton's Battery, under
Lieutenant Sale, was soon brought into play at long range,
with such effect that the Federal pieces, cavalry and train,
were quickly withdrawn out of range.

In the mean time, Dibrell, by a forced march, having reached
his original destination at Florence, had sent out detachments
to raise and repair sunken boats, and by other ostentatious
demonstrations had made show of a purpose to cross the river
at Bainbridge, Garner's Ferry, and an intermediate point ;
while through a reliable citizen he had managed, moreover, to
set afloat in Tuscumbia the report of the presence of General
Van Dorn with his whole cavalry *en route* for the south bank
of the Tennessee and the rear of Dodge's position, with a
view to subsequent operations against Corinth. And about
four P.M., he opened with great din and rapidity with a section
of artillery upon the camp which the Federals had occupied

---

* Mr. James Mhoon, of Tuscumbia.
† Notes of Colonel Saunders, of Courtland, Alabama.

at South-Florence. This cannonade, and other intimations of the threatening presence of a large Confederate force in close proximity to his rear, by this time had reached General Dodge, whereupon that officer announced by a dispatch to Colonel Streight that, having now detained the Confederates long enough to secure to the latter time to get well on his way, and inasmuch as there were reasons for apprehending a serious attempt to cut off his own line of retreat to Corinth, he should presently fall back, and leave the other to push forward on his expedition. And accordingly General Dodge began a hurried retrograde movement, the impress and memory of which will be hard to efface from the beautiful valley of the Tennessee. From mountain to the river-marge, from Town creek to Tuscumbia, that night it was lurid with the flames of burning fences, granaries, meat-houses, stables, and of mansions that for years had been the scenes of a boundless hospitality and domestic comfort, but of which, the next morning, there remained little, save heaps of smouldering ashes and ruined, blackened walls.*

Several hours, however, before the Federal retreat began, another of Roddy's trusty scouts had returned with the information that the cavalry, whose movements had been previously reported, had advanced as far eastward as Mount Hope, sixteen miles directly southward, and on the Confederate left flank. General Forrest, now assured that this movement was of grave character, promptly made all his preparations to meet it, satisfied that, though he might not have the force to cope,

---

* Prominent in this and other ruthless, inexcusable works of desolation was the notorious ruffian Colonel F. N. Cornyn, who assumed for his band the designation of the "Avenging Angels." Among the edifices burned were those of Lagrange College, an old and well-founded seat of learning, with numerous buildings for many students, all of which were reduced to a mass of ruins.

ultimately, with Dodge, he would be fully able, howbeit, to baffle and beat this separate hostile operation. Roddy was ordered to take, as soon as possible, his own and Edmondson's (Eleventh Tennessee) Regiment and Julian's Battalion, and throw himself between the cavalry in question, and the force under Dodge. And before Dodge's retreat had been developed into certainty, leaving several regiments to make a show of continued resistance, he fell back that night to Courtland with Starnes's and Biffle's regiments and the artillery.* There he completed his preparations for the emergency of a prolonged pursuit as if he had fully divined the purposes of his enemy. Selecting Morton's lightest section, and Ferrell's battery of Roddy's command, he directed that double teams of the best horses should be attached, and personally superintending the provision of the best and strongest harness, was ready for the field early on the morning of the 29th, when without delay he set out for Moulton, in which direction the enemy had been reported to be moving.

II.

At Moulton, it was found the cavalry in question was certainly that which had been debarked at Eastport, commanded by Colonel Streight ; as likewise, that he had taken the road leading to the south-eastward, with the object, apparently, of a daring raid into the heart of North-Georgia, and hence a blow at the communications of Bragg's army. Therefore, Forrest divided his force into two columns, one of which, under command of Colonel Roddy, was ordered to follow directly upon the trail of the adventurous raiders ;† and the other to make a detour to the north-eastward, so as to cut off

---

* The troops left were Hannon's Regiment and Baxter's Battalion, and a section of Morton's Battery.

† Roddy's and Edmondson's Regiments, Julian's Battalion, and Ferrell's Battery.

any possible effort, under pressure from Roddy, to turn back and escape by that flank.* The pursuit—one of his most notable operations—now began in earnest, Forrest leading the last-mentioned subdivision in person.

The Federal force was of men selected for this special service, and consisted of the Fifty-first and Seventy-third Indiana, Eightieth Illinois, and Third Ohio regiments, and two companies of Alabama "Union" Cavalry. They were transported by steam, on the 11th of April, down the Cumberland,† and up the Tennessee to Eastport, North-Mississippi, where their march began, as far as Tuscumbia,‡ in rear of General Dodge, who, as has been seen, was sent in advance to vail the movement by his demonstrations. They were accompanied by guides who had lived in the regions to be traversed, and had got so well advanced as to feel secure from effective pursuit.

But the swift-riding, sharp-smiting Forrest was already sweeping down with his chosen men upon them. Quitting Moulton, and riding all Wednesday night, the Confederate General pushed after his enterprising enemy, resolved to capture or destroy him, reaching and encamping, for the last part of the night, in the vicinity of a small village known as Danville. Thursday morning, 30th, early, it was ascertained that the Federals had encamped in Day's Gap, on Sand Mountain, only four miles distant. Therefore, giving instructions to

---

* Starnes's and Biffle's Regiments and a section of Morton's Battery; the former commanded by Major McLemore, Colonel Starnes being absent, ill at Columbia.

† Probably went down the Cumberland only to Fort Donelson, and thence across by land to Fort Henry, on the Tennessee river, thence by boat to Eastport. See letter of "Centurion," in reference to note-book of C. H. Applegate, Seventy-third Indiana Regiment.

‡ Reaching Tuscumbia on the 24th of April, and left on the morning of the 27th, *via* Russellville, and thence to Moulton.

Biffle to push forward rapidly, with the best mounted of his own and Starnes's regiments, (under McLemore,) so as to cut the Federals off from any attempt to turn back and escape in that direction, Forrest transferred his headquarters to the other command, pursuing by the road. About the same time the advance-guard sent back ten prisoners, just captured, and reported that the Federals were but one mile in their front, engaged in cooking. Advancing, the Confederates were soon in full view of their camp-fires, and got within four hundred yards of the ground before the enemy were aware of their proximity. The discharge of the Confederate artillery was indeed the first intimation, apparently, of this fact, and, as may be readily understood, produced the utmost confusion, panic, and hurly-burly in their encampment. Many negroes and soldiers scattered in various mountain ravines, leaving the place where they had passed the night full of wagons, some fifty broken-down animals, cooking utensils on the fire, as also large numbers of poultry and quantities of other food newly cooked.* The Confederate soldiers, almost famished, were forced, with great difficulty, by their officers to quit the tempting stores thus broadcast around them ; and fully half an hour was lost at the spot before the pursuit was renewed. Captain William H. Forrest with his company was first dispatched, and very soon encountered the Federal rear-guard in the gorge. A rapid running skirmish then ensued, for quite two miles, when he fell, seriously wounded by a ball through his thigh, breaking the bone, and at the same time losing several

* On the approach of Dodge's column the people of the country had fled to the mountains south of Moulton, with their wagons, teams, animals, and valuable movable property, which, coming to the ears of Colonel Streight, he had *harried* the country with his cavalry in the mean time, and collected some fifty wagons and five hundred negroes, who had supplied themselves already with riding animals.

of his men under the galling fire he had affronted. The main
force of the enemy were now also in sight, strongly posted in
line of battle along a commanding ridge perpendicular to the
road.

General Forrest, pushing to the front, observed and comprehended the situation at a glance, and forthwith disposed
his men for the onset.

Edmondson's Regiment, dismounted, was deployed on a ridge
or spur parallel to that occupied by Colonel Streight, and bi-
sected by the road ; Roddy's Regiment and Julian's Battalion,
mounted, were posted to the rightward of Edmondson, on undulating, irregular ground, with orders to advance. Forrest's
escort, mounted, occupied the left flank of the line, with instructions to move around on that flank, and get a position in
the rear, while Edmondson took the offensive in front. At
the same moment, two pieces of Ferrell's Battery were pushed
forward, and opened fire at a distance of two hundred yards
from the Federal lines. This was promptly answered, but
Edmondson advanced steadily, to within less than one hundred
yards of his opponents, under a warm fire. The escort, meanwhile, had executed their orders, and vigorously attacked
Streight's right flank, losing five or six men killed or wounded.
Roddy resolutely charged on the left flank, up to within fifty
yards of the Federal line, the men of which were lying down
concealed. Rising now, they delivered a withering volley,
inflicting considerable loss. Roddy's men, comparatively raw,
gave way in much confusion, leaving forty out of three hundred and fifty either killed or wounded on the ground. Ferrell's guns by this time, however, had been bravely pushed
to within sixty yards of the Federal position, and were throwing a stream of grape and canister, though with little effect,
as the enemy were sheltered by the crest of the hill. At the
repulse of Roddy's command, Colonel Streight now charged,
and forced Edmondson back, killing the horses of the Confe-

derate guns, which were abandoned to the enemy.* But both Edmondson and Roddy's men promptly rallied, retook the position previously occupied, and were there re-formed for another struggle, Roddy having dismounted his own regiment and Julian's Battalion.† The loss of the enemy in this phase of the affair was at least seventy-five killed or wounded.

The Federal commander handled his men with decided nerve. Massing them, by a resolute charge he obliged the Confederates to fall back, quite three hundred yards, to another position, which he likewise attacked with equal spirit, but was this time repulsed, with small loss on either side. He then drew back to the position in which he had first awaited battle; and Forrest resumed possession of the ridge in his immediate front. From these opposite ridges an animated skirmish was maintained between the sharpshooters of both forces until three P.M. Starnes's and Biffle's regiments having been, meantime, ordered up, now appeared upon the scene; they were at once dismounted, and disposed to take part in an immediate grapple with the enemy. In this line of attack, Starnes's Regiment was on the extreme right and Edmondson the left; Biffle and Roddy in the centre, on the right and left of, and perpendicular to, the road along which Ferrell's Battery of four guns advanced; the escort and Captain Forrest's Company constituted a small reserve.

The enemy, however, did not await the onset; indeed, they had been gone an hour, leaving only a thin line of skirmishers,

---

* Section of Morton's Battery, under Lieutenant A. W. Gould.

† This battalion was composed of Tennesseeans and Alabamians, and was the nucleus, subsequently, of Jeffrey Forrest's Regiment. Major W. R. Julian, its commander, had seen service during the Mexican war. It lost very heavily in this affair.

which in turn gave back, without giving or receiving the fire of the assailing Confederates ; and in a field-hospital were found about seventy-five of their killed and wounded, with some thirty Confederates.

Finding his adversary now evidently disposed to push on-ward and avoid further battle, General Forrest detached Roddy to return with his own regiment and Julian's Battalion to Decatur with the prisoners and wounded men, and resume command in that quarter ; and Edmondson to make a detour with the Eleventh Tennessee through the valley in the di-rection of Summerville, on the Federal left flank, to watch and guard the passes, and to foil any effort to turn and escape in that direction. Biffle and McLemore—the latter leading—with their regiments, were directed to push on by the road taken by the enemy, while the Confederate leader, heading his escort and a company of the Fourth Tennessee, dashed ahead immediately to overtake and bring them to bay. After a sharp gallop of half an hour, the Federal rear-guard was overtaken, and a running fight took place for some miles, in the direction of Blountsville, Alabama, when Streight's main force was found formed in a highly favorable position, half a mile eastward of Long creek, with their own section of artillery, and that captured, placed at commanding points. Biffle and McLemore coming up with their regiments, were dismounted, and rapidly arranged for a charge as infantry, Biffle, with one hundred men, being held in reserve. It was now five P.M., or about dusk, as the Confederates resumed the offensive, and advanced to within one hundred yards of the enemy. For three hours the conflict was obstinate and reso-lute on both sides ; the Confederates gaining their way slow-ly, their enemy holding their ground stoutly. And at times the lines were in so close proximity, that the flashes of the fire from the small-arms illuminated the features of the com•

batants in the contesting ranks.* Always in the thickest of the *mêlée*, General Forrest had the good fortune, as in all his recent conflicts, under the hottest fire, to escape unhurt, but he had one horse killed and two wounded under him.†

At eight o'clock P.M., Biffle was ordered with his reserve force to move around by the left flank, gain the rear of the enemy, and attack their horse-holders. At the same time Forrest detached his escort on a similar service around by the right flank.

The lines of the belligerents were by this time brought to within thirty yards of each other—the Confederates deployed in single file, and scattered behind trees and other objects that greatly favored them. Soon was heard in the Federal rear the sounds which indicated that the several detachments sent by the Confederate general for that purpose had attacked the *horse-holders*. But the men, supposing it to proceed from Roddy striking the enemy from that flank, were animated with a fierce enthusiasm. An intrepid charge of the whole ine was made with one impulse, and their brave adversaries gave way utterly discomfited.

Some fifty of their number were left behind, dead and wounded, and many animals, as also the section of Confederate artillery which they had previously captured and carried off, and some thirty wagons; and some teams were found scattered through the woods.

The scene of this prolonged and desperate conflict on the barren mountain-heights of North-Alabama is remembered by participants, who have mingled in the great battles of the

---

* Letter of "G. W. A.," of May 5th, published in Atlanta *Southern Confederacy*, May 8th, 1863.

† Captain Aaron Thompson, (of Marshall county, Tennessee,) Company A, Fourth Tennessee Cavalry, was mortally wounded, at the head of his company, in this charge; and Major McLemore had his horse shot under him.

war, as one of peculiar, weird grandeur and exaltation, impossible to paint with words. With the thunder of artillery, the
continuous peal of the musketry, and their infinitely multiplied reverberations from mountain to valley, were mingled
the sharp clangor of words of command, the cheery shouts
of the men, and the uproar and cries of affrighted and wounded animals, added to which there was a splendor in the lurid
volcanic flashes of the rapidly served artillery and the fiery
blaze of the musketry, which excited admiration, attracted
notice, even in that moment of fiercest passions, when the
air was thick and perilous with deadly missives.

The Confederate loss, howbeit, was singularly light; a few
were wounded and fewer killed. Immediately the pursuit was
renewed; and for ten miles the roadway was found strewn
with saddles and bridles and boxes of crackers, from which
the pursuers drew a hasty ration, their only food for hours
of hard riding and incessant fighting. Mingled with crock-
ery and kitchen utensils, blankets and shoes and plated
ware, were to be seen scattered around embroidered skirts,
and other articles of female apparel, taken in sheer wantonness, all cast away now by the fugitives, or dropped by runaway pack-mules, or from wrecked baggage-wagons.

The Federals were evidently demoralized by this time, and
began to understand their peril. Biffle was directed to send
several men to catch up, and, in the darkness, mingle with
the enemy, so as to ascertain, if possible, their purposes as to
any other stand that night. Meanwhile, the Confederates
followed slowly, some four miles, when one of the men detached* returned with the intelligence that Streight stood
once more at bay, across the road, within a mile ahead,
which was confirmed by another scout, half a mile further

---

* Private Granville Pillow, of Grove's company, Biffle's regiment.

on. Moving up, with the least possible noise, to the supposed distance of a quarter of a mile, the Confederate commander again dismounted his men, detached the horses from his artillery, and had the pieces pushed forward quietly by hand. Biffle thrown out on the left, and McLemore on the right of the road, approached to within one hundred and fifty yards of their *quarry* before breaking the grim silence of the night with the crackle of rifle or the din of artillery ; but that now burst suddenly upon them evidently unaware, for they broke in much confusion and some loss in killed and wounded, without return of fire. Swift pursuit was made, and some captures effected, but it was so ,dark that it was difficult to distinguish friend from foe.

It was now eleven o'clock, but the darkness had been somewhat diminished by the starlight. Remounting his men, Forrest ordered the chase to be resumed. Again the way was thick sown with castaway booty, equipments, and abandoned animals, while the woods swarmed with negroes. Once again men were pushed ahead of the command to overtake and intermingle with the enemy, and, as before, returned—between midnight and one o'clock A.M.—and reported that another stand had been resolved on by the Federal leader, who surely was not wanting in courage or enterprise. The place chosen was the southern bank of a deeply-bedded, rugged mountain rivulet, and very strong, some sixteen miles from the scene of the first engagement, and six from the field of the last skirmish. The Confederate force quickly arranged for attack, McLemore was ordered to push across the stream rightward of the road ; the horses were again detached from the pieces, which were moved by hand, as before, up the road to within short range, preceded by some skirmishers who, taking position, fired suddenly in the direction of the Federals to draw a return, in order to reveal their exact locality to the artillerists, who opened at the blaze with grape and canister, while Biffle poured in sustained volleys of small-arms. McLemore, gaining his position rightward in rear, also joined in the fight. This was more than they could stand, and again they gave way, leaving some killed and wounded on the ground ; and McLemore, striking their flank, made some captures of men and horses, causing evidently a panic in their sorely pressed ranks, who now made off hurriedly, still in the direction of Blountsville.*

It was now about two o'clock in the morning ; evidently both Federals and Confederates had come upon the people of this isolated region unexpectedly, and the outburst and tumult of the battle-storm was their first warning of such fearful presence. As may be readily supposed, they were filled with wild terror ; the poor women with their little children fled frantically from their houses, and were found seeking shelter or crouching, they scarcely knew from what dire peril, in grotesque hiding-places, such as ash-hoppers, horse-troughs, and in recesses behind chimneys.

Content with the work of the past eighteen hours, and sure now of the ultimate capture of his game, Forrest halted and awaited daylight, to water and rest his fagged, foot-weary horses, overhaul his ammunition, and reassemble his command.

May day dawned brightly, the men had been without food for more than twenty-four hours, but, after two hours' rest, cheerfully renewed the pursuit. Forrest led with his escort and one squadron of the Fourth Tennessee Regiment, and about eleven o'clock A.M. reached Blountsville, where the enemy had halted to rest, and arrange their transportation henceforward exclusively by pack animals instead of wagons. Their pickets being at once driven in, setting fire to their remaining wagons

----

* Here were found twenty-five wounded Federals in charge of a surgeon.

a.id some stores, Streight made off, due eastward, in the direction of Gadsden, without offering to renew the combat. Extinguishing the fire, and replenishing his commissariat and ammunition supply from that abandoned by the Federals, with little loss of time, Forrest and his men were again in the saddle. Swift and staunch as so many sleuth-hounds, relentlessly did they now follow and overtake the Federal column before reaching the Black Warrior river, ten miles' distance from Blountsville, and a running fight occurred. The ford was rocky, rapid, and difficult, yet the Federals hazarded it rather than venture the risk of another trial of strength with their indomitable pursuer. But before all were across, the Confederates were upon the rearward, killed and wounded some, made a few captures, and caused the drowning of a number of pack-mules.* A halt was now ordered by the Confederate leader for three or four hours, to feed and rest his men and animals. After midnight the Confederates were once more in movement at their accustomed pace. The enemy, now fully aware of the urgency of their situation, were doing what they could to embarrass pursuit. To this end they destroyed a bridge over a creek on the route, the banks of which were high and sheer, and difficult to ascend. Very little time was lost, however, and by daylight the Confederates were again in

---

* Just before reaching the Warrior river, two young country girls, of seventeen or eighteen years of age, appeared, leading three accoutred horses, and driving before them as many Federal soldiers, whose guns they carried on their young shoulders. Asking for the commanding officer, they related, with much simplicity, how they had captured these men, and wished to deliver them. Their captives, in extenuation of their situation, alleged that they had no stomach for further fighting. These brave girls were poor, dressed in homespun and barefooted, though clean and neat. They said they would be willing to go on with the troops, but hardly thought their services were at all necessary. The General giving each a horse, they went off smiling and proud.

hot pursuit fifteen miles to Wills Creek in the southern part of Wills Valley—coming upon the Federal pickets, who were driven back upon their bivouac in which their main force were feeding and resting. Not making a stand, Streight retired rapidly, leaving in the hands of his ever-urgent foe fifteen or twenty-five prisoners, at least fifty negroes, including some women dressed in Federal uniforms, an abundance of forage, and some horses and pack animals.

Giving the command several hours' respite, while his weary, famished animals were feeding, Forrest, selecting his best horses for two of his most appropriate guns, prepared to move for the final struggle with not to exceed six hundred officers and men.* It was here also that he divided with his men a box of crackers, which he had picked up and carried along in his ambulance. Meanwhile, worn down by three days and nights of scarcely intermitted riding† and fighting, eating little and at long intervals, the Confederates began to show serious signs of flagging, and many, in the last stage of the pursuit, had fallen asleep on their horses. Several ladies. however, whose husbands and friends had been seized and carried off by the Federals, appeared about this time, and filled the encampment with their sad wails and appeals for the restoration of their kinsmen. This had the happy effect to rouse the men from their lethargy ; and Forrest, taking advantage of the circumstance, drew his men up and made them a brief, stirring address, full of warm words of confidence in their ability to attain speedily the objects of their mission, and the end of their hardships. Calling for all who were willing to follow or fall in the attempt, the entire com-

---

* The other two pieces, and all in-effective animals and their riders were left behind, with orders to return to Decatur.

† At no time resting more than five hours out of twenty-four, and twice only so much.

mand responded with cheers ; the women also broke out into shouts of joy and encouragement ; and in the eyes of many of that battle-stained, sun-embrowned, fierce array, we are assured, the big tear of deep emotion was seen to start, glisten, and melt. They were then moved off at a gallop, the artillery section following at the same speed. At this pace the Federal column was again overtaken by ten A.M., on the 2d ; and the Confederate General selecting fifty of the best mounted men, with whom and his escort he charged swiftly upon its rear in the face of a hot fire. For ten miles now, to Black Creek, an affluent of the Coosa, a sharp, running conflict occurred. The Federals, however, effected the passage of the stream without hinderance, by a bridge, which, being old and very dry, was in flames and impassable as the Confederates approached ; besides which it was commanded by Streight's artillery, planted on the opposite bank.

III.

Black Creek is deep and rapid, and its passage in the immediate presence of the Federal force was an impossibility before which even Forrest was forced to pause and ponder. But while reflecting upon the predicament, he was approached by a group of women, one of whom, a tall, comely girl of about eighteen years of age, stepped forward and inquired, " Whose command ?" The answer was, " The advance of General Forrest's Cavalry." She then requested that General Forrest should be pointed out, which being done, advancing, she addressed him nearly in these words :

" You are General Forrest, I am told. I know of an old ford to which I could guide you, if I had a horse—the Yankees have taken all of ours."

Her mother, stepping up, exclaimed :

" No, Emma ; people would talk about you."

"I am not afraid to trust myself with as brave a man as General Forrest, and don't care for people's talk," was the prompt rejoinder of this Southern girl, her face illuminated with emotion.

The General then remarked, as he rode beside a log near by: "Well, Miss ——, jump up behind me."

Quickly, or without an instant of hesitation, she sprang from the log behind the redoubtable cavalry leader, and sat ready to guide him—under as noble an inspiration of unalloyed, courageous patriotism as that which has rendered the Maid of Zaragoza famous for all time. Calling for a courier to follow, guided by Miss Sanson, Forrest rode rapidly, leaping over fallen timber, to a point about half a mile above the bridge, where, at the foot of a ravine, she said there was a practicable ford. There dismounting, they walked to the river-bank, opposite to which, on the other side, were found posted a Federal detachment, who opened upon both immediately with some forty small-arms, the balls of which whistled close by, and tore up the ground in their front as they approached. Inquiring *naïvely* what caused the noise—being answered that it was the sound of bullets, the intrepid girl stepped in front of her companion, saying, "General, stand behind me; they will not dare to shoot me." Gently putting her aside, Forrest observed he could not possibly suffer her to do so, or to make a breastwork of herself, and gave her his arm so as to screen her as much as possible. By this time they had reached the ravine. Placing her behind the shelter afforded by the roots of a fallen tree, he asked Miss Sanson to remain there until he could reconnoitre the ford, and proceeded at once to descend the ravine on his hands and knees. After having gone some fifty yards in this manner, looking back, to his surprise and regret, she was immediately at his back; and in reply to his remark that he had told her to remain under shelter, replied:

" Yes, General, but I was fearful that you might be wounded ; and it is my purpose to be near you."

The ford-mouth reached and examined, they then returned as they came, through the ravine, to the crown of the bank under fire, when she took his arm as before—an open mark for the Federal sharpshooters, whose fire for some instants was even heavier than at first ; and several of their balls actually passed through her skirts, exciting the observation, " They have only wounded my crinoline." At the same time, withdrawing her arm, the dauntless girl turning around, faced the enemy, and waved her *sun-bonnet* defiantly and repeatedly in the air. We are pleased to be able to record that, at this, the hostile fire was stopped ; the Federals took off their own caps and, waving them, gave three hearty cheers of approbation ! Remounting, Forrest and Miss Sanson returned to the command, who received her with unfeigned enthusiasm.*

The artillery was sent forward, and with a few shells, well thrown, quickly drove away the Federal guard at the ford, which Major McLemore was directed to seize with his regiment. The stream was boggy, with high declivitous banks on both sides, and it was necessary to take the ammunition from the caissons to keep it dry, to pull the two pieces of artillery across by hand, and to force the animals down the steep slopes, and to take the ford, but, nevertheless, the passage was successfully effected in less than two hours. Meantime, the Confederate General delivered his fair, daring

---

* The Legislature of Alabama, at the succeeding session, donated to Miss Sanson a section of the unappropriated public lands of the State, as a testimonial of the high appreciation of her services by the people of Alabama ; and directed the Governor of the State to provide and present her also with a gold medal, inscribed with suitable devices commemorative of her conduct. See Appendix and Index. We trust the people of Alabama will not permit the result of the war to hinder the discharge of this duty to a brave daughter of the State.

young guide back safely into the hands of her mother, took a knightly farewell inspired by the romantic coloring of the occurrence, and dashed after his command to resume the chase, as soon as the passage of the creek was effected.*

Gadsden—three miles distant—was soon reached, and Forrest dispatched a special courier to Rome, Ga.,† evidently one of the objective points of the Federal expedition, to apprise the people of its approach, and to urge every effort to hold Streight in check before the place until his advent upon the scene. It was Saturday afternoon as the enemy had dashed into Gadsden, to the complete surprise of its citizens, and the place was filled with people from the surrounding country, whose horses were greedily seized, the prey of all others most coveted at this moment by Streight and his men. And quite a number, consequently, of such animals were taken in exchange for their exhausted mules.

Here, selecting 300 of his best mounted men, the Confederate General again led in pursuit, his enemy having taken the road up the west side of the Coosa river in the direction of Rome. After a race of some nine or ten miles, about five o'clock P.M. Saturday, May 2d, the Federals were again overtaken at a small village known as Turkeytown, and a smart encounter followed. Finding a favorable position, they had

---

* As General Forrest reached the point of the road, on the east bank of Black Creek, opposite Miss Sanson's house, she and several ladies came to the bridge-head and hailed ; he halted, and she said she had a request to make, namely, that her brother, who had happened to be at home on furlough from the army in Virginia, had been captured by the enemy that morning, and she begged for his recapture and return to her. " It shall be done before ten o'clock to-morrow morning," responded General Forrest, a promise fulfilled to the letter.

† Mr. John H. Wisdom, of Gadsden, however, had previously hastened on the same errand, gave the people of Rome the first warning of the coming danger, for which a grateful people gave him a silver service.—See letter "Centurion," Atlanta *Southern Confederacy*, May 17th, 1863.

halted to feed, and at the same time attempt an ambuscade in
a dense thicket of second-growth pines, through which ran
the road—forty yards broad—for half a mile in a straight line,
and then narrowing and bending abruptly to the left, for perhaps about one hundred yards, turned squarely to the right
again, dividing some fields in a direction parallel to the original course. At the first bend, a barricade effectually closed
the road, and the fence was thrown down, so that the Confederates would be forced to take across the field—the fences of
which were leveled—over a small ridge, behind which were
concealed a body of some 500 Federals, while the pine thicket
through which they were to be drawn was filled with sharp-
shooters on either side of the avenue. The ambush was skillfully arranged, and might have resulted in the easy capture of
the entire command under almost any other than the tactics
of Forrest. Their skirmishers were thrown out just in advance of the thicket and throat of the avenue, as if offering
battle. The Confederates well closed up, and moving by
column of fours, Forrest ordered the bugle to sound the
charge, and, instructing his men to fire with their rifles and
pistols right and leftward, he led them forward at a brisk pace.
The Federal line gave way, as planned, but such was the speed
with which Forrest dashed ahead, that scant time was afforded
the sharp-shooters lining the road to do any damage, and the
Confederates had penetrated the field past the thicket before
the enemy supposed that they could be half-way through the
latter. Observing now the line in his front, Forrest charged
home upon it without halting, and dispersed the Federals
rearward in all directions. Some thirty were here captured,
and as many as twenty wounded or killed ; among the latter
was Colonel Hathaway, one of their best and favorite officers.*

---

* Colonel Hathaway was probably killed, at the distance of six hundred yards, by the rifle of private Joseph Martin, Colonel Biffle's Regiment, a mere youth at the time.

The Confederate loss was very light, only two privates were killed, but these were tried and gallant soldiers.*

It was now dark, the enemy were in full flight, the work of demolition almost completed, and, confident of their early capture, the Confederate General caused the recall to be sounded, and bivouacked his command for the night, so that the men who had been left at Gadsden might come up. Such, however, was the spirit of all who followed Forrest that these proved to have been not far behind, and a good night's rest was enjoyed by the men and their fatigued animals.†

By sunrise, on the 3d, the Confederates, now winnowed down to scarcely 500 officers and men, were again in motion, and on reaching Dyke's bridge, over the Coosa, found it in ashes. The men were promptly dismounted, and, stripping, carried the ammunition and pieces over, as at Black creek, by hand. In an hour this was achieved, and the chase renewed until about nine o'clock A.M., when the Federals were again overtaken, at their breakfast, which was abandoned at the sound of firing, leaving their hot coffee, mules, a number of horses, saddles, and other spoils. Their commander, however, soon rallied them on a ridge in an open field, but his men were evidently greatly disconcerted. Detaching Major McLemore, with his command, to move around on their left,

---

* Private Hunt, of Starnes's, and private Roach, of Biffle's Regiment.

† Among the casualties of the affair at Turkeytown, just related, was the capture of Sergeant William Haynes, of the Fourth Tennessee, who was taken at once before Colonel Streight, and questioned as to the strength of the Confederate force. Young Haynes was so solemn-looking and truthful a personage as to have gained among his comrades the *sobriquet* of Parson. With the utmost gravity he answered, that Forrest had his own brigade, Armstrong's, and Roddy's, with several others, the names of whose commanders he could not recall. Streight exclaimed, with a fierce oath, "Then they've got us." A little later in the night, Haynes, effecting his escape, succeeded in rejoining his regiment, and gave immediate information of the story he had imposed upon the Federal commander.

and Colonel Biffle their right flank, they were forced back somewhat on their centre, while General Forrest threatened an advance, with his escort and a detachment, in front, from a skirt of woods which he occupied.

Prone to rush in upon an adversary and crush, by the effect of swift, heavy blows, the Confederate leader was none the less an adept in the stratagems of war at fitting junctures, when he took for his example the cool, crafty Ulysses rather than the wrathful Achilles. Accordingly, he now sent forward an officer of his staff—Captain Henry Pointer—with a flag of truce and the demand of the immediate surrender of the Federal force—as he declared—"in order to stop the further and useless effusion of blood."

Meeting the flag, Colonel Streight asked to communicate directly with General Forrest. They met accordingly in the woods, and a parley ensued. Streight, howbeit, declined to capitulate unless it could be shown to his satisfaction that he was doing so to a force at least equal in number to his own. Forrest replied in effect, he could not humiliate his men by any effort to persuade the surrender of a force that they had been driving and beating in every conflict for the past three days.

Just at this moment the section of Confederate artillery came in sight at a full gallop, remarking which, Colonel Streight urged that no more troops should be brought up nearer than a ridge about three hundred yards in the rear. To this Forrest assented, and gave orders to that end, but, through an aid-de-camp, at the same time covertly instructed that the artillery should be kept in movement in a circle, so as to appear like several batteries coming up, which was so adroitly done by Captain Ferrell that Colonel Streight soon inquired of Forrest how much artillery he had. "Enough," was the prompt answer, "to destroy your command in thirty minutes." Some further discussion ensued, Colonel Streight continuing to insist that he could not surrender unless fully satisfied that he was not succumbing to an inferior force, finally asked for a delay of twenty minutes while he consulted his officers.   But in a quarter of an hour he returned and repeated his desire to be assured that he was confronted by at least an equal force.   The Confederate commander, then remarking that discussion was wholly useless, asserted that he had known of this movement almost from its inception, had been prepared for it, and therefore had his opponent completely in his toils, with a river on his right, which was not fordable, a mountain on his left, which shut him off from escape in that quarter, a force in front with which he would not be able to cope, and one at his heels all the while, that had gained strength every day.   Therefore, if he, Streight, failed to capitulate, the grave consequences must rest on himself.   Colonel Streight, greatly perplexed, still clung to the idea that he could not surrender to a force inferior to his own, and, ending the interview, turned to repair to his men.   Captain Pointer, at this, invited him take a drink before separating, observing that it might be the last that he would ever take.   This invitation, pleasantly made, was as pleasantly accepted ; the drink was taken, hands were shaken by the parting antagonists, and the Federal commander rode back in the direction of his lines, but soon to meet on the way the bearer of a white flag from his command, with whom he returned to the Confederate quarter.   He then announced that his officers desired to surrender, which he was now ready to do on condition :

1st. That all were to be held as prisoners of war.*

2d. That the officers should retain their side-arms and personal baggage.

---

* This, doubtless, was stipulated in apprehension that otherwise the Union Alabamians and guides would not be treated as " prisoners of war."

These terms were, of course, granted without discussion. It was still thought to be necessary, however, to keep the enemy deceived in regard to the actual smallness of the force that had captured them, and this Captain Pointer adroitly contrived by asking, at the moment, of his commander, what disposition should be made of some three or four imaginary bodies of troops at different near points, and specific orders were given in that connection, which he rode away as if to execute. At the same time the Confederate General explained to his prisoners that, as forage was very scarce at Rome, he would only be accompanied thither by his escort and a regiment.

These preliminaries being arranged, the two commanders repaired to the Federal headquarters. A portion of the enemy were found a mile distant, where, in a field, their whole line was finally formed, some 1466 officers and men, their arms stacked, and the capitulation was completed.*

Colonel Streight now made a short address to his men, thanking them for their gallantry and endurance, explained the reasons which caused him to surrender, and called upon them to give three cheers for the Union.†

The officers were then separated from the men and directed to be escorted to Rome, some eighteen or twenty miles distant, without delay, while the men were to bivouac under charge of Colonel Biffle, who, assisted by a staff-officer—Cap-

---

* Two Colonels, one Lieutenant-Colonel, three or four Majors, 1365 privates.

† General Forrest was present, and made no objection to this display of feeling on the part of brave men. The *fact should be remembered in his favor by those at the North who look upon him as* a harsh, relentless foe; and we do not hesitate to assert that had he, on the other hand, fallen into the hands of Colonel Streight, no such privilege would have been extended as an opportunity to harangue his men, nor would they have been suffered to cheer for the "Confederate States."

tain Pointer—was instructed to collect the arms and follow to Rome with the prisoners on the next day.*

Moving some ten miles toward Rome, the detachment sent in advance by Streight from Turkeytown to proceed direct to that place was met returning, baffled.   The commander, Captain Milton Russell, Fifty-first Regiment Indiana Volunteers, when informed of the catastrophe which had befallen the main command, was deeply moved, and, with an air of sincerity, and with tears in his eyes, declared that he had rather die than be subjected to such a disaster. He was a man of very fine, soldierly presence, and, had all his comrades been of the same martial temper, their capture would scarcely have been so easy.   But seeing that there was now no alternative, his command also laid down their arms, making the number of prisoners taken, in all, 1700.

Resuming the route to Rome, when within four miles of it, the high hills which adjoin the place were found alive with militia scouts in observation, who, evidently regarding the approaching force as hostile, it was really difficult to open communication with them.   But this was at length effected, and the people of Rome, to their profound relief, were notified of the happy results of that day.

Their emotion was great, and proved nearly fatal to the object of their warm admiration and gratitude.   Insisting on firing an artillery salute, shotted guns were discharged, with such carelessness, and in the direction of the very road of General Forrest's approach to the town, as barely to miss him.

As the Confederates entered Rome, the streets were alive with its citizens, including numerous refugees from Tennessee,

---

* The Confederates in line at the surrender were so overcome by sleep that, while standing dismounted, holding their horses by the bridle-rein, the greater part of them were nodding.

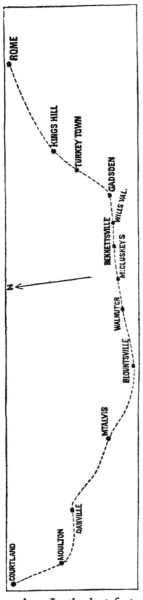

and some two thousand convalescents from the large army hospitals established there, who turned out to welcome and greet their deliverers.

" All tongues speak of him, and the bleared sights
Are spectacled to see him."

Many ladies of that joyous assemblage met with husbands or near kinsmen among Forrest's men whom they had not seen for a year or more. These meetings were inexpressibly tender and moving; indeed, the whole reception was a memorable event in the lives of all present. Every house was thrown open to officers and men with an unstinted hospitality, which embraced even the Federal officers and other prisoners to some extent, now that all danger from them was fully averted.

The surrender took place, as before said, twenty miles from Rome, in the valley between the Coosa and Chatooga rivers, some two or three miles north of the Coosa, and at a point known, curiously enough, as " Straightneck Precinct," in that country.

COMMENTARIES.

1. The merits of this operation are unquestionably very great in every aspect, and nothing handsomer, of its species, may be found in military annals. In the last forty-eight hours of the expedition, Forrest

marched his men, jaded as they and their animals were, full ninety miles ; and they had averaged forty-one miles each day, fighting for hours, several times daily and nightly, for three days previously, encumbered with artillery. The most salutary moral effect was felt throughout the country far beyond the ordinary capture of so many Federal soldiers, even by so small a force as that which General Forrest led ; and it is a fact worthy of note, that the newspapers of the South, for a month afterward, contained numerous circumstantial accounts of the expedition, its stirring incidents, and of the final stratagem by which the capitulation was brought about. The people of Georgia were enthusiastic in their sense of the services rendered by General Forrest, as evinced in various ways, among which may be mentioned the proposition to change the name of Union county to that of FORREST, as an act of " monumental significance." He had, indeed, averted the widespread destruction of the principal bridges and manufacturing and transportation resources of that State, which were of vital value to the people of the whole South, and especially to the army of Bragg. And this had prevented occurrences the injurious character of which would have been incalculable and irremediable.

2. Forrest led men to whom all honor is due ; due for qualities among the least of which we place, in sooth, their intrepidity in combat ; men whose acts of individual heroism can make no figure in battle reports ; men whose endurance of fatigue, and long abstinence from food, combined with their unbroken spirit, were indeed marvelous ; and all of them appear to have been thoroughly imbued with his own ardent, indomitable spirit.

BRIGADIER-GENERAL FRANK C. ARMSTRONG.

CHAPTER X.

May 4th to August 31st, 1863.

COLONEL BIFFLE came up on Monday, 4th, with the main body of the prisoners ; and all were now turned over to the local commander, who put them *en route* for Richmond by rail, by way of Atlanta, on the following day.

The fourth and fifth were spent in refitting the command for the field, especially in shoeing the horses. These, be it noted, were generally of the best " blooded stock" of Middle Tennessee and Kentucky ; but the hardships of the expedition had been so extreme and prolonged, that it had perceptibly affected them, leaving all greatly jaded and foot-sore. Many also were now taken with the " scours" and cramp, which proved so fatal in a few moments that, of the five hundred and fifty with which the command reached Rome, not more than two hundred and fifty remained.* Selecting the best of the captured horses, many of which proved to be excellent animals, seized by the roadside, Forrest was able, by the morning of the 6th, to remount his command, and refurnish his artillery in an effective manner.

The citizens of Rome had been, meanwhile, preparing for a formal complimentary ceremony and festival, to be given on the afternoon of the 6th, in honor of the event of their relief from the consuming visitation which had been prepared for that thriving and enterprising community. But on the night of the 5th, General Forrest was informed, at ten o'clock, by some citizens, that a heavy Federal cavalry column was penetrating the country from Tuscumbia, in the direction of Talladega, Alabama, by way of Jasper and Elyton. He was, therefore, obliged to forego the arranged entertainment and further rest for his men and animals, much as it was still needed, and undertake possibly another arduous campaign, for which all the necessary orders were at once issued. By eight o'clock A.M., on the 6th, Forrest and his men were on the road to Gadsden.†

At that place, at three P.M., on the 7th, scouts, who had been left in observation, were met, and they reported that no such movement as the one alleged was on foot, and that Dodge had unquestionably returned as far westward as Iuka. Assured of the accuracy of this information, Forrest then turned

---

* The artillery of the command had left Courtland with one hundred and twenty select horses, of which only twenty-five remained.

† The residue of the captured animals, after remounting his command, some sixteen hundred horses and mules, Forrest sent under escort, direct to Chattanooga, with the urgent request, addressed to General Bragg, that they should be sent to North-Alabama for distribution among those from whom the most of them had been taken by Colonel Streight, as he traversed the country; and this was actually done, though only four hundred and fifty survived, such had been the hardships they had undergone.

the head of his column northward, by the roads through Brookville, Peach Grove, and Summerville, as the nearest route to his base. Arriving at Decatur on the 10th, he recrossed at once to the north bank of the Tennessee.* On the 11th, the command was turned over to Colonel Biffle, with orders to take post at Athens, Alabama, whither the detachments from the brigade were likewise directed to repair.

General Forrest then proceeded by rail, by way of Huntsville, to army headquarters, still at Shelbyville, to report to General Bragg the results and details of his expedition.

At Huntsville his arrival was the occasion of an intense expression of public gratitude. The people turned out *en masse*, and emulated each other in manifestations of their sense of what Forrest had achieved by his pursuit and capture of the Federal marauders.†

Arriving at Shelbyville on the 13th, he reported immediately to General Bragg, who, receiving him with unwonted warmth, cordially testified his full recognition of the value and scope of his recent services. He said, indeed, that he should urge his promotion to the grade of major-general, with the view of intrusting to him the chief command of the cavalry with that army. To this, however, Forrest replied that he preferred the promotion to that position of another officer, whom he suggested, as having more capacity for the functions which properly belonged to the rank of major-general.

We learn, too, that the whole army, officers and men, testified in various ways, while he was among them, their satisfaction and appreciation also of what General Forrest had ac-

---

* Two companies had been meanwhile sent from Gadsden, back by the route of the pursuit, to collect and bring away all the wounded, and such captured stock and teams as had been left behind.

† One substantial and appropriate testimonial was the gift of a fine horse ; another had been given by the people of Rome, Ga.

complished.   Of these demonstrations it is fit to note a sere-
nade by the One Hundred and Fifty-fourth Tennessee Infantry, enrolled at Memphis, Tennessee.   Both Forrest and the
regiment had long been anxious that it should be converted
into cavalry, and assigned to his command ; and as they
thronged around his quarters the cry was, that the One Hundred and Fifty-fourth might now be mounted with Streight's
captured horses.   Forrest was called upon—after the American fashion, that even went with the citizens into the army—
for a speech, which he made, and while no orator, and wholly
unused to addressing crowds, he expressed himself, we are
assured, with notable felicity in his unaffected but clear narration of the stirring events which had characterized his late
operations, which all around were anxious to hear.[*]

After passing several days at army headquarters, Forrest
finally, on the 14th, received orders to return to Spring Hill,
and assume the command of the cavalry on that flank of the
army, General Van Dorn having been killed during his absence.   It was on the 16th that he arrived at Spring Hill, and
entered upon his new command, having in the mean time
directed all of his brigade to reassemble there.

As will be remembered, Forrest, just before crossing the
Tennessee river to the southward, had detached the Eighth
and Tenth Tennessee,[†] under Colonel Dibrell, with a section
of artillery, to make a diversion, by a show of passing the
river as far westward as Bainbridge or Florence, in rear of
the Federal column.   As has been noted, that service was
effectively performed, and aided materially in hastening the
retreat of Dodge in great haste, he being apprehensive that
otherwise his communications with Corinth would be cut

---

[*] MS. Notes of Colonel J. E. Saun-   [†] At the time under command of
ders.   Major Forrest.

off. The Tenth Tennessee was then ordered back as far as Decatur, to guard and hold that crossing, while Colonel Dibrell remained with his own regiment and the artillery, to watch the river in that quarter until—within a few days—an order was received from General Bragg to throw the greater part of the regiment across the river, and take position at Fulton, Miss., so as to intercept the Streight expedition, should it attempt to effect a passage back through the country in that direction to Corinth. The Tennessee was crossed at Garner's Ferry by swimming the horses; and a detachment of three hundred of the Eighth Tennessee, under Captain McGuiness,* were at Fulton—seventy-five miles from the ferry in question —early the second day after departure. Meanwhile, intelligence of the success of Forest's pursuit having been received by Dibrell, the detachment of his regiment was safely withdrawn from its greatly exposed position at Fulton, eluding a strong Federal force that had been thrown out to cut it off, by making a wide detour through Pikeville and Russellville, Alabama, at which last place a junction was effected with Colonel Roddy and the Tenth Tennessee.

The latter regiment had likewise been actively engaged in the interim; it had formed part of a force with which Colonel Roddy pursued the notorious marauder Cornyn, and had lost some eight or ten men in an affair with him at or near Hamburg, or the Tennessee river.

II.

It was the 16th of May when General Forrest assumed the

---

* Colonel Dibrell was run over by a horse at the river, and so much hurt that he was obliged to remain behind for several days; when attempting to follow, though in great pain, he had a narrow escape from capture by the Federals, who had taken the field meanwhile, to cut off the return of the Confederates from Fulton.

command to which he had now been assigned, with his headquarters at Spring Hill.   At the time, the Confederate forces
in that quarter were Brigadier-General W. H. Jackson's Division, Cosby's and Whitfield's Brigades, and Brigadier-General Armstrong's Brigade, to which, in a day or two, was
added Forrest's own brigade, now under command of Colonel
Starnes.

Rearranging his forces, Armstrong was assigned to the
command of a division constituted of his own and Starnes's
Brigades, the composition of which was severally changed in
some particulars.*   A few days later, however, Jackson's Division was detached and directed to return to their old theatre
of operations in Mississippi, and Forrest was left with the divisional command under Armstrong and Starnes's brigades.

For the rest of May, the service of the divison was exclusively that of picket duty† in the immediate proximity of the
Federals, who were in heavy force at Franklin, with a strong
outpost at Triune.   This service, while without important
events to chronicle, was occasionally varied with adventures;
among which we note one, on the Carter's creek road leading
to Franklin, on the night of the 31st of May, in which a detachment of the Eighth Tennessee figured.   The enemy in
that immediate quarter had shown enterprise and adroitness
on several recent occasions, and had surprised and captured a
considerable part of a Texas regiment on outpost service
there, through a stratagem contrived by a Federal officer, who
resided in the vicinity.   Anticipating an attempt at a similar
coup, the officer in command of the Confederate outpost exposed his picket-line to the view of Federal scouts who were

---

* The Eighth Tennessee was transferred to Armstrong's Brigade, and
Colonel Dibrell was assigned to the
command of the brigade.

† Connecting on the right with the
Fourth Georgia, Colonel Avery, Crew's
Brigade, Wheeler's Cavalry, at Be-
thesda.

noticed in observation; but after dark, the flooring of the bridge over Carter's creek was noiselessly taken up, and the pickets drawn back into a cedar thicket, from the position held when observed. Scarcely had these arrangements been made, when a Federal detachment, intelligently led through the fields and woods across the stream, some distance from the bridge, reached the turnpike in rear of the point that had been occupied at sunset by the Confederates. Here the ambuscade prepared was opened upon their party from their rear, when, of course, they broke, with a rush, for the bridge, and fell headlong into the trap there set for them. Evidently, a number of horses and men must have been crippled, from the many evidences of blood, skin, and hair that were to be seen on the bridge timbers next morning. There were no more attempts on the part of the enemy to surprise pickets for some time, and this little affair served for a while to amuse the men around their camp-fires.*

About the 3d of June, the enemy were observed, apparently transferring their main force from Franklin to Triune.† This led the Confederate General to move forward, on the next morning, to reconnoitre the former place in strong force, so as to ascertain precisely to what extent the position was still occupied. Starnes's Brigade, with Forrest at its head, advanced by the Franklin and Columbia turnpike, while Armstrong moved up by the Lewisburg road. On both routes the Federal pickets were met within three miles of Franklin. Starnes, turning their right flank, captured ten and killed several; Armstrong driving in the line in his front, the advanced-guard of Dibrell's Regiment followed to the very edge

---

* MS. Notes of General Dibrell, who thinks the Confederate officer in command was Captain Swearingen, with his company K.

† That is, the right wing of Rosecrans's army. See *Reb. Rec.* VII. Doc. 4, p. 6.

of the town. The Federals, however, rallied, and charged, in turn, with the Seventh Kentucky regiment of cavalry, forcing their bold assailants back again.

About one quarter of a mile eastward of the suburbs of Franklin, on an eminence commanding all the approaches to the place, the Federal engineers had built a strong and extensive field-work, well garnished with artillery. This opened upon Armstrong with much vigor, while their cavalry—three battalions*—were drawn up between the forks of the Lewisburg and Columbia turnpikes, close to and southward of the place. Having, meanwhile, disposed his main force behind a chain of ridges skirting the position, with his artillery posted on an elevation leftward of the Columbia road, Forrest ordered a charge to be made upon the cavalry just mentioned, by companies G and H of the Eighth Tennessee, Captains Gore and Burns—accompanied by their ever adventurous leader—gallantly leading their men, with admirable spirit, and dashed across an open field, in easy range of the Federal works, in the face of an adversary greatly superior in numbers. It was a hazardous operation, but was successful ; and the Federals, giving way before it, took refuge in the streets of Franklin.

Soon after, mistaking a signal-flag, flying on the fort, for one of truce, Forrest ceased fire with his artillery, and sent forward, under a white flag, to inquire the cause or purpose. In the mean time, also, approaching in person the quarter of the fort, with the view of meeting his own flag on its return as soon as possible ; but when within eighty yards of a garden-hedge, a Federal officer rose to his feet behind it, and, with a gesture of repulsion, exclaimed : " General Forrest, I know you, and don't want to see you hurt ; go back, sir !"†　For-

---

* See *Reb. Rec.* VII. Doc. 4, p. 5.

† General Forrest has since understood that this officer was one of those he had captured at Murfreesboro, in July, 1862.

rest, raising his hat in salute, rode rearward some fifty yards, when turning, he saw the same officer standing where he had left him, with a considerable detachment, looking after him, within short musket-range, and he again saluted in recognition of their forbearance. By this time his own flag of truce had returned, with the information that the one noticed was only a signal-flag. This ascertained, taking a detachment of two companies of the Eighth Tennessee and a section of Morton's guns, he entered the town by the street leading from Carter's creek. Formed across this street, with the artillery in the centre, unlimbered, and pushed forward by hand, they boldly entered the town, driving all opposition before them, and took and held possession of the place for some hours. Breaking open the jail, some Confederate prisoners were found, and released, while the numerous sutlers' stores, with which the town abounded, were soon found and thoroughly sacked.

Meanwhile, Armstrong moved across the Harpeth, around and rightward of the fort, with a detachment of his brigade—Woodward's Battalion and part of the First Tennessee—to reconnoitre the approach from Triune, and speedily encountered four cavalry regiments[*] coming from that direction. A vigorous skirmish ensued ; but so great was the disparity between the forces opposed, he was forced to fall back—though fighting stubbornly—across the river, losing eighteen killed or wounded out of thirty-eight of his escort. By the time he reached the river, Colonel Hobson had advanced with his regiment of Arkansians, on hearing the sound of fire-arms, and covered Armstrong's safe passage across it. Forrest, too, having heard the clangor of the engagement, leaving one regiment in observation on the Columbia turnpike, hurried toward the scene with the remainder of his force. But Armstrong

---

[*] Fourth and Sixth Kentucky, and the Second Michigan and Ninth Pennsylvania. *Reb. Rec.* VII. Doc. 4, p. 5.

having, meanwhile, returned to the west side of the Harpeth, and it being now certain that the enemy was reënforced heavily from Triune,* Forrest drew off with Starnes's Brigade and encamped in a position on disputed ground, about three miles from Franklin, where there was abundance of forage, that neither party, hitherto, had attempted to seize. At the same time, Armstrong was sent back with his brigade to resume its usual picket-line that night.

On the following day—the 8th—the Fourth Tennessee still remaining in position, about nine o'clock A.M., two Federal regiments† were observed advancing. A company of the Fourth was thrown well forward to meet it, and then to fall back rapidly, so as to draw the Federals into an ambush that had been carefully arranged. This was partially successful, and some loss was inflicted on the Federals, who withdrew, leaving the Fourth in possession of the field.‡

Some eight or ten days subsequently, General Bragg having expressed a desire that a reconnoissance should be made, to develop the Federal force at Triune, Starnes's Brigade was detached for that object, and performed the service with the nerve and thoroughness that characterized the operations of Colonel Starnes. After driving in and capturing a number of their pickets at Triune, he moved round and made a demonstration on Nashville ; returning from which, he destroyed the railroad bridge at Brentwood, which the Federals had rebuilt since its destruction in April.

Several days later—the 20th—taking his whole force, ex-

---

* The Federal force at Franklin and Triune consisted of at least three divisions, namely, those of Morgan, R. S. Grainger, and Baird. (*Reb. Rec.* VII. Diary, p. 7.) Also, Stanley's Division of Cavalry.

† Brownlow's East-Tennessee (Federal) Regiment and the Seventh Kentucky.

‡ Colonel Faulkner, Seventh Kentucky, was seriously wounded.—*Reb. Rec.* VII. Doc. 4, p. 6.

cept a strong picket-line, and Avery's and Crew's Georgia regiments of Crew's Brigade, Wheeler's Cavalry—his neighbors on the right—who volunteered to take part in the operation, Forrest again beat up the quarters of his enemy at Triune. Moving across the Harpeth to the junction of the Chapel Hill and Shelbyville roads, he there met Colonel Robert Johnson's Regiment, Federal, Tennessee cavalry, and after a sharp skirmish drove it back into their lines. Starnes's Brigade following closely, Forrest, with his escort—several companies of the Eighth Tennessee and a section of Morton's Battery—now boldly approached to within four hundred yards of the main Federal encampment, upon which he opened with his artillery. Thoroughly imposed upon by the boldness of the movement, the Federals retired precipitately to their line of rifle-pits surrounding Triune, in rear of their encampment, and began a fierce uproar with artillery from several batteries in position, which was altogether harmless to the Confederates, who were, meanwhile, greatly amused at the utter misapprehension of their strength which manifestly possessed and swayed the Federal officers and their men. The ground, howbeit, was highly favorable for the success of this brilliant act of audacity. But at length, in these daring movements, the Confederate chief stirred up the covert of an infantry brigade, and provoked a withering fire, before which he immediately drew his men out at a run rearward ; for, if impetuous and adventurous to the verge constantly of rashness, he was peculiarly quick to recognize when he had reached the extreme limit of experiment with his adversary, and prudence required a change of policy. Now, satisfied that he had ventured quite as far as was at all prudent, Forrest began to draw off his whole force, when the Federal cavalry pursued, and some sharp skirmishes took place as the Confederates leisurely retired. Assuredly, the Federal commander of the forces at Triune can not look back upon this affair without mortification ; and it is a signal

instance of what may be done in war by coolness and confidence, allied with boldness and enterprise. Among the material results of the affair, were several hundred horses and mules,
and half as many fat cattle, found at pasture. Dispersing their
infantry guard, Major Jeffrey Forrest drove them off successfully from close proximity to the Federal lines.*

III.

It was now the last week in June, and orders came from
army headquarters to break up the outposts at Spring Hill
and to repair without delay with his division to Shelbyville.
On the night of the 25th, accordingly, the march began *via*
Riggs's Cross-Roads. Detained by high water some twelve
hours on the 26th, an order from General Wheeler, Chief of
Cavalry, reached General Forrest at Bigbyville, to direct his
further movements so as to intercept the other cavalry of the
army on the turnpike from Murfreesboro to Shelbyville.
When within ten miles of Shelbyville, however, the sounds
of a considerable skirmish were audible in the direction of
the road just mentioned, and Forrest directed Armstrong to
push on rapidly for the scene. Executing this order with

---

* General Rosecrans, in his plans as in his correspondence with his government, strangely overrated the numbers of the Confederate cavalry, which he affirms to be *five to one* of his own. This estimate, we observe, is accepted as correct by Federal historians, when in fact nothing could be more inexact. The fact is, General Rosecrans does not appear to have been inferior in cavalry to General Bragg at all. Assuredly not after the 10th of May, 1863. Writing to the Federal Quartermaster-General on that day, he says he had :

Cavalry horses on hand, . .	6537
Mounted infantry, . . .	1938
	8475
Deducting 25 per cent for un-serviceable horses, . . .	2119
	6356
He had also orderlies and escorts,	2028
	8384

General Bragg could not possibly at that time have turned out more than 6000, including those on escort service.

celerity, Armstrong found the Federal cavalry engaged with and driving Wheeler's force along a dirt-road half a mile from and parallel with the turnpike before mentioned. So fast, indeed, were the Confederates falling back toward Shelbyville, that Forrest found it impossible to effect the junction indicated ; he therefore put his column at a gallop for the next eight miles, hoping to overtake Wheeler at Shelbyville, or at least in rear of the works there. But even in this expectation he was disappointed, for such was the pressure of the Federal cavalry, that Wheeler had been driven south of Duck river before Forrest could reach Shelbyville. Informed of this fact, Forrest then made a circuit rightward of that place through the mud and heavy rain, and crossing the river at a bridge about four miles to the west of it, encamped five miles beyond, on the Lafayette turnpike. On the following day, 28th, he came up with the main Confederate army, in position at Tullahoma. Here he received orders to picket and scout with his division the approaches from the northward.

A detachment from the Eighth Tennessee, 200 strong, under their gallant, able Colonel, was immediately thrown out eastward toward Hillsboro and thence southward to Deckard's. Federal pickets were met by Colonel Dibrell in the vicinity of the former place, which he ascertained was occupied* by the Federals, while a large force had gone thence to Deckard — facts which he immediately transmitted to his chief, General Forrest, by couriers. Colonel Starnes was also detached meanwhile with his brigade to develop, if possible, the movements of the enemy in the direction of Shelbyville. This brigade encountered a strong Federal force, attached to

---

* This, really, was a brigade of mounted infantry, under Colonel Wilder, sent to the rear of Bragg's army, and which, moving with uncommon celerity, in- flicted a good deal of damage to the railroad in rear of General Bragg.— *Reb. Rec.* VII. Diary, p. 21.

Crittenden's Corps, a few miles in front of Tullahoma, on the 30th, where a skirmish took place, in which the gallant Starnes was mortally wounded.*

Late in the afternoon of the same day, General Forrest was instructed to ascertain the movements of the enemy on the road from McMinnville. It was raining heavily at the time, but the General preferred to make this reconnoissance himself with his escort, some sixty strong. Setting out about three P.M., the black felt hats and oilcloth cloaks of his men gave them the appearance of Federal cavalry—a circumstance that enabled him before dark to pass the advanced-guard of a Federal column, with whom there was a short parley as they met. Coming upon the main body of the enemy about half a mile rearward, he was discovered, as, not more than one hundred yards distant, he turned to withdraw, and was fired upon by a Federal battalion. Nothing daunted, he dashed resolutely back over the road he had traveled, killing and capturing several of the detachment he had previously passed ; and, returning to headquarters, reported the presence of the Federals on that road, with an evident purpose of turning the Confederate right flank, which obliged General Bragg to resume his movement southward immediately.

While Bragg was aiming to pass Elk river near Deckard, Forrest was ordered to cover the movement from the northeast quarter, and to obstruct any endeavor from that direction to cut off the Confederates by seizing the pass in the Cumberland near Cowan. This brought the division, during the

---

* On the Tullahoma - Manchester road. At the time of his death he was with his skirmish line, encouraging the men to stand their ground against the great odds pressing down upon them. Colonel Starnes was a most valuable cavalry officer. We regret that all our efforts to procure the material for a sketch of him and his portrait have been abortive. He was a man of influence in his community, and a physician before the war.

first of July, in sharp collision with several bodies of Federal cavalry, that were severally beaten back. The Confederate army being now in possession of the pass, and Forrest's men and horses having been virtually without food for twenty-four hours, he led them to Cowan, hoping to find there both sub-sistence and forage, but, on arriving at the spot, was disap-pointed. Those who were there before him had consumed all. Gleaning the neighborhood, however, he was able to secure a meal for his men, and a feed for their horses, imme-diately after which they were again in their saddles, and the division was thrown out northward toward Pelham, to cover a pass five miles from Cowan through which Hardee's Corps was moving. Hardee having effected the passage of the moun-tain into Sequatchie Valley, followed by Forrest's Cavalry as far as University Place, on the 3d of July, Dibrell, now in command of Starnes's Brigade, was directed to hold the pass for the next twenty-four hours, while Armstrong was sent ahead to Jasper to cover the corps on that flank. On the 4th, no Federal force having appeared, Dibrell withdrew at ten A.M., and followed to the Tennessee river. During these movements, repeated short but spirited skirmishes occurred between the several regiments of both brigades and the ene-my, in which the Confederates, including the artillery, fought with their wonted spirit and efficiency ; but these we are un-able to relate in detail.

The army having been now withdrawn to the south side of the Tennessee and concentrated at Chattanooga, Forrest's Division followed, and went into cantonments near by, where, for the following fortnight, the conditions of the campaign or inaction of the enemy, gave it opportunity to rest and refit ; several changes also took place in the organization of its bri-gades.* About the 24th of July, however, the division was

---

* The Eighth Tennessee was trans-ferred from Armstrong's to Dibrell's Brigade in exchange for McDonald's Battalion — Forrest's old regiment —

ordered to Kingston, East-Tennessee, across to the north
bank of the river, General Forrest at the same time being
assigned to the chief command of the Confederate cavalry
in East-Tennessee.*   The field of service assigned, a wide
and arduous one, involved the picketing not only of all the
approaches from the Sequatchie Valley to the Tennessee
river eastward of Chattanooga and of the various crossings
of the river, but the watchful observation, also, of Burnside's
movements.   Numerous small affairs occurred, but were unimportant in results.

IV.

Meanwhile, the Eighth Tennessee had been detached on
an expedition to Sparta, beyond the Cumberland mountains,
chiefly with the object of giving the men an opportunity to
visit home and their families in that vicinity, from whom
they had been so long separated.   The Federals were in
strong force at McMinnville, twenty-six miles distant, and the
vicinage of the Confederates very soon provoked a conflict.
On the 8th of August, a Federal brigade—Minty's—attempted to surprise and capture the regiment at a time when encamped some two miles north of Sparta, and when not more
than 300 of the men were present.   This attack was made
with so much dash that the escape of any of Dibrell's pickets
was due to the fleetness of their horses, coupled with the pre-

---

which at the same time was strengthened by the addition of two surplus
companies—McDonald's and Allen's—
hitherto attached to the Eleventh Tennessee Cavalry.

　* In addition to Forrest's division
proper, consisting of Pegram's Division,
made up Pegram's brigade, commanded by Colonel J. J. Morrison, of the

First and Sixth Georgia, Sixty-sixth
North-Carolina, Second Tennessee, and
Huwald's Battery, of Scott's Brigade,
strength 1000, composition unknown,
and of Rucker's Legion of Twelfth, (six
companies,) Lieutenant-Colonel Day,
and Sixteenth battalion, (seven companies,) Lieutenant-Colonel Neal, 1100
aggregate.

sence of mind of their commanding officer, Captain Leftwich. The noise of the collision with the outpost gave time barely to the regiment to form and take up hastily a position behind a neighboring creek—an affluent of Calf-Killer river—the approach to which was through a narrow defile, made by a spur of the mountains of one side and the steep banks of a watercourse on the other, and across a bridge over Wild Cat creek, in immediate advance of which Colonel Dibrell took post himself with the men present of two companies.* The Federals, coming on Dibrell's deserted camp, fancied the whole regiment had been dispersed, and dashed on with loud yells in hot pursuit, to pick up stragglers and increase the supposed panic. The defile just mentioned, debouched into an open space just in front of the bridge, and when about 100 Federals (Fourth Michigan) had emerged into it, the Confederates poured upon them a volley that swept fifty men from their seats and laid a number of horses writhing on the ground. Those who escaped made a gallant, desperate effort to dash forward, but were shot or driven back in great confusion. Another regiment (the Fourth Regulars) now charged with spirit upon the position, and their onset was formidable ; but the consuming rifles of Dibrell's men, well posted, with a converging fire upon the bridge-head and approach thereto, swept through their ranks, and few reached the bridge ; the others strewed the ground or fell back, some quitting their horses and escaping on foot. The Federal commander, now dismounting his men, made another advance ; but no sooner did he reach the open ground, than a volley from the Eighth Tennessee sent all back under cover again. The Federals, then withdrawing, attempted to turn the position by crossing the river below the mouth of the creek, at Meredith's Mill, where, in anticipation of such a

---

* Companies G and H.—*Colonel Dibrell's Notes.*

movement, they were met by a small detachment and fired upon from a covert, with the effect of checking that movement also. Meanwhile, leaving one company to skirmish, Dibrell, knowing the country and all its fastnesses thoroughly, led the rest to another position, into which he hoped to draw his adversary. Here he was joined by many of the citizens of the surrounding country, who, with their old-fashioned hunting-rifles, and Champ Ferguson, the celebrated partisan—also a resident of the country—came up with ten or fifteen of his men. The women, too, brought supplies of cooked food, with that considerate providence for the needs of their countrymen that everywhere distinguished the women of the South during the war.

Finding, from the reports of scouts, that the enemy had disappeared, Dibrell remounted and went forth with his men to pursue, coming in sight of their rear-guard, at a fast trot, near Sparta; but, as the weather was very sultry, it was not considered expedient to pursue further than some twelve miles. So well had his command been sheltered, that Dibrell's loss did not exceed six or eight captured and as many killed and wounded; that of the Federals was heavy in both men and animals. This affair having been reported to General Forrest, he sent Colonel McLemore, with about 200 of the Fourth Tennessee and some ammunition, to strengthen Dibrell's command.

Keeping his command on the alert and actively moving near the enemy at McMinnville for the next fortnight, Dibrell kept careful watch to guard against the possibility of surprise. In this way, on the 17th, his scouts encountered a large cavalry force, several thousand, again under Colonel Minty, moving in the direction of Sparta, only three miles from the Federal encampment, and having one of Dibrell's negroes as a guide, who was thoroughly acquainted with the whole region. Dibrell was encamped at the moment at

Sperry s Mill, on the north bank of the Calf-Killer river, two miles from Sparta, as was known to his adversary, who had divided his force, one detachment taking the road through Sparta and up the south side of the river, while the main body moved up the north bank. Informed of the emergency, Dibrell had, meanwhile, made his dispositions embracing a re-occupation of his battle-ground of the 9th of August, a mile from his present encampment; but scarcely were his men mounted than the Federal advance was at the river. A small detachment of the Fourth Tennessee, posted at the ford, met and repulsed an attempt made to pass it. By this time the Fourth Tennessee had been placed in the position held by the Eighth Tennessee on the 9th, just in time to beat back a feeble attempt of the enemy, who, now more wary than previously, was indisposed to venture into the open ground, but kept up a heavy fire from long range until dark. The Eighth Tennessee, in the mean time, had taken position at the only ford for six or eight miles, at Meredith's Mills, and there held the Federals completely at bay, though many times larger in numbers. Repeated attempts were made by the enemy to force the ford, the approach to which was over an open lawn, and their check was easily effected until dusk, with considerable loss to the Federals. After dark, Colonel Di-brell deemed it expedient to take up another and even stronger position, two miles distant and safe from the possibility of be-ing turned—that is, on the summit of the Cumberland moun-tain, where Frost's turnpike crosses it. Accordingly, McLe-more withdrew from his position to join Dibrell. As he did so, the Federals, on the watch, pursued and struck Captain McGregor's company, (G,) but were immediately and hand-somely repulsed, with some loss, by the brave McGregor. Taking up now, without further interruption, the position on the mountain, Dibrell awaited quietly the movements of his opponent, who, it appears, indisposed to prolong the expedition, retired from the neighborhood the next morning, having suffered severely, and left Dibrell in undisputed possession of the district.

Soon after this affair, the 22d, General Forrest's orders were received to return to his headquarters at Kingston,* and the movement was commenced that afternoon. At the time, a number of the men and officers were absent on furlough at their homes ; others were permitted to go for their winter clothing, and some few officers and men had become disaffected and averse to returning to the army, so that the Eighth Tennessee recrossed the Cumberland 200 rank and file less than it had when it reached Sparta.†

In the interim, the other portions of the division had not been inactive. A squadron of the Eleventh Tennessee, dispatched across the mountain to Wartburg, in Morgan county, to observe the enemy reported to be moving in that neighborhood, had there encountered a heavy Federal column of all arms. In attempting to reconnoitre the position, Captain Perkins became involved with his single company with Bird's Brigade of cavalry, which he charged with characteristic daring and threw into confusion. Afterward he made good his retreat.‡ Pegram's Division had also been kept on the alert watching the various passes in the mountains.

On the 31st of August, orders having been received by General Forrest to that effect, he began the evacuation of

---

* About this time, Hamilton's Battalion of partisans had joined Dibrell, some 105 strong.

† The Lieutenant-Colonel of the regiment, who was subsequently sent to collect these men, gathered as many as 200. Instead of rejoining his regiment, he took the field, as a partisan, in Kentucky, where he was captured and re-mained a prisoner until the spring of 1865, when he was exchanged, his health permanently destroyed. Among the deserters were a captain and two subalterns. — *General Dibrell's MS. Notes.*

‡ Lieutenant-Colonel Holman's MS. Notes.

East-Tennessee with all his force except Scott's Brigade. That was left to hold the bridge at Loudon, with orders to burn it on the approach of the enemy in force, which was ultimately done after a sharp skirmish.

COMMENTARY.

General Rosecrans, as we have stated—note, *ante*, page 290—insisted that his enemy outnumbered him in horsemen *five* to *one*. Giving his own effective mounted force, exclusive of 2028 orderlies and escorts, at 6356, he provided General Bragg with no less than 31,780 cavalry. We simply notice this to show the loose manner in which even an army commander may sometimes think and write about grave, important questions.

CHAPTER XI.

BATTLE OF CHICKAMAUGA.

Topographical Sketch of Theatre of War—Federal Army thrown across southward of the Tennessee River—Bragg evacuated Chattanooga—Thomas's Corps in McLemore's Cove—Failure of projected Attack by Confederates—Isolation of Crittenden's Corps not profited by—Operations of Forrest's Cavalry—The general Offensive taken by Bragg—Battle of the 19th September—Arrival of Longstreet—Confederate Army subdivided into Wings—Battle of the 20th September—Commentaries.

ON arriving at Chattanooga, Forrest's command was soon distributed in the several quarters wheresoever the Commanding General determined that cavalry were wanted to cover the movements of the Confederates in the coming evacuation of that position ; and to observe the movements likewise of Rosecrans, who now revealed a manifest purpose to cross the Tennessee river westward of Chattanooga, with the object of striking a blow, by way of Will's Valley, at Bragg's communications.

And here a topographical sketch of the whole theatre of impending operations becomes necessary. Chattanooga, as may be seen at a glance on the map, is in the mouth of the narrow valley formed by Lookout Mountain and a lateral spur to the eastward, known as Missionary Ridge. Lookout Mountain, jutting abruptly upon the Tennessee river, a little west of Chattanooga, and stretching southwardly into Georgia, rises a broad, heavily-wooded range, 2400 feet above the level of the sea, with sides of towering rock-cliffs springing from steep, densely-wooded bases, and surmounted, in a distance of fifty miles, by only two practicable wagon-roads, the first twenty-six and the other forty-two miles from Chattanooga. Pigeon Mountain, another spur, branching from Lookout, about forty miles from Chattanooga, and extending northward, terminates in the low hills near the road from Chattanooga to Lafayette, making a larger and broader valley than Lookout, in the upper portion of which, called McLemore's Cove, the west branch of the Chickamauga has its sources. Immediately west of Lookout is Will's Valley, opening upon the Tennessee, about six miles from Chattanooga, and the other limit of which is Sand Mountain,* a chain of precipitous, barren, wooded ridges, scantily watered, with a few steep but practicable wagon-roads across it from the Tennessee river. The Georgia State Railroad, passing around the northern extremity of Mission Ridge, and down the valley of the east branch of the Chickamauga, by way of Ringgold, connects with the East-Tennessee road at Dalton, thirty-eight miles from Chattanooga. A wagon-road leads from the latter place, in a south-eastward course, across Mission Ridge, at Rossville, by way of Lafayette, to Rome, a distance of sixty-five miles. Lafayette, eastward of Pigeon Mountain, is twenty-eight miles distant from Chattanooga, and Lee and Gordon's Mills, where this road crosses West-Chickamauga, is half-way between the two points. From Caperton's Ferry, nearly opposite Stevenson, on the Tennessee, forty miles westward of Chattanooga, as well as from the intermediate ferries at Shell Mound and Bridgeport, as we have mentioned, indifferent wagon-roads cross Sand Mountain to Trenton, and other points southward

----

* The northern portion of which is known in the country as Raccoon Mountain.

in Will's Valley, and thence connect with the two roads that lead over Lookout Mountain, the northward one of which, passing through Cooper's Gap into McLemore's Cove, and onward, by way of Dug Gap, in Pigeon Mountain, to Lafayette, as well as that *via* Alpine, opened a short and easy line of march, under proper military conditions, upon the Confederate communications at Dalton, or, indeed, as far south as the bridge over the Oostenaula at Resaca.

As early as the 27th of August, some Federal cavalry, fording the river above Caperton's Ferry, repaired thither, and assisted in constructing a pontoon-bridge across the Tennessee at that point, by the 29th, upon which, in the course of the 30th and 31st, Davis's and Johnson's Divisions of McCook's and Negley's Division of Thomas's Corps made the passage to the southern bank, and began the march thence without delay upon the roads we have indicated, over Sand Mountain ; while, by the 4th September, the remaining divisions of both Thomas and McCook had been thrown across at Shell Mound and Bridgeport.* Tidings of these movements, carried to General Bragg by citizens of the country as early as the 1st September, it appears, were discredited until verified by the presence of a Federal cavalry force at Wauhatchie, in Will's Valley, within seven miles of Chattanooga ; and, as before said, Rosecrans's purposes were now apparent.†

On the night of the 3d September, Lieutenant-General D. H. Hill began the evacuation with his corps, on the road to Lafayette. Polk followed on the same road on the 7th,‡ but

---

* Thomas and McCook's Official Reports, *Reb. Rec.* VII. Doc. 42, pp. 227, 232.

† *Vide* " Historicus," *Richmond Whig*, reprinted *ibid.* Doc. 212, p. 689, a well-informed writer evidently. General D. H. Hill confirms this statement in his Official Report.

‡ Hindman's and Cheatham's Divisions.

halted at or near Lee and Gordon's Mills; and Buckner's Corps, from East-Tennessee, recently assembled at or near the mouth of the Hiawassee, was likewise drawn to the same point.*

By the 9th, Negley's Division, closely supported by Baird, of Thomas's Corps, forcing Cooper's and Stevens's Gaps, in Lookout Mountain, very strong positions, left undefended, poured down into McLemore's Cove, and on the 10th took post within a mile west of Dug Gap.† At this Hill was summoned back from Lafayette, with Cleburne's Division, to hold the passes in Pigeon Mountain, with orders ultimately to send or lead it to form a junction with Hindman's Division, Polk's Corps, in an operation against the Federals in McLemore's Cove. Circumstances, however, making the timely cooperation of Cleburne impossible, Buckner was substituted with his two divisions, on the morning of the 10th, and came up with Hindman after four o'clock that afternoon, at Morgan's Farm-house, in the Cove, four miles from Davis's Cross-Roads, where Baird's Division of Thomas's Corps was at the time. But no collision occurred; nor was an attack made, as late as daylight on the 11th, by which time Cleburne, supported by Walker's Division,‡ had taken up a position in Dug Gap, to coöperate with such movement at that hour.§ Yet no conflict ensued even then, though the Commanding General, after having ordered Polk to cover Hindman's rear, had repaired at daylight in person to the position held by Cle-

* Stewart's and Preston's Divisions.
† Two brigades of Baird's Division were in support at Davis's Cross-Roads. The position occupied by Negley was very favorable for fighting, he represented in a note at the time to Baird, if supported.
‡ A splendid command, five brigades recently arrived from Mississippi, whither it had gone from Charleston and Savannah in May, 1863, but one of the brigades, (Gist's,) of which was absent, however, at Rome, until the 20th.
§ *Vide* General Bragg's Official Report; also General Thomas's Report, *Reb. Rec.* VII. Doc. 42, p. 228.

burne, whose division and Walker's demi-corps at noon were again directed to advance and make an attack. Hill accordingly made his dispositions ; his skirmishers and those of the enemy had already come in collision ; and Cleburne's battle-scarred veterans, deployed in line, were about to spring forward with their habitual *élan*, when the movement was suspended from headquarters. Meanwhile, however, Hindman's and Buckner's proximity had become known to the enemy ; and Hindman advancing to the attack in the afternoon, Negley and Baird began to retire.* Then the order to Hill to advance was renewed, and its execution commenced with spirit ; but the Federal general, skillfully withdrawing rapidly at the first onset, refused battle, and, night being at hand, under favor of the darkness, fell back upon the hills in front of Stevens's Gap ; and was able to escape that destruction † which a skillful combination and timely, vigorous use of Confederate resources, readily available, had made the inevitable consequence of this singularly wrong-headed isolation.‡

In the mean time, McCook, after crossing the river, as we have related, moving over Sand Mountain by several routes, by the 9th had assembled his corps in the direction of Alpine, in the vicinity of Winston's Gap, in Lookout Mountain, forty-two miles from Chattanooga, and where, that afternoon, about the time Thomas's leading division had descended into Mc-

----

* Baird had " closed upon Negley's Division at the Widow Davis's house, at 8 A.M.," on the 11th.—*Reb. Rec.* VII. Doc. 42, p. 228.

† General Hill's Official Report.— *Land We Love*, Vol. I. No. 6, p. 395.

‡ The danger of the situation for the Federals becomes apparent when it is observed that at the time Thomas established his advanced divisions in the Cove, Polk's and Buckner's Corps—at least twenty thousand bayonets and fifty-six guns—were at or near Lee and Gordon's Mills, and Hill at Lafayette and Dug Gap, with over 8000 bayonets, all within easy distance for swift concentration, and such movements as might have made extrication or escape impossible. *See* Commentaries, p. 346, *forward.*

Lemore's Cove, he received orders to diverge further by pushing rapidly to Alpine, and eastward to Summerville, to intercept Bragg, then supposed by Rosecrans to be in full retreat. Reaching Alpine on the 10th, McCook, however, discovering indications that Bragg, after all, was not really retreating, and that his own isolated situation, therefore, might become dangerous, halted, and during the 11th, 12th, and 13th, awaited developments before venturing beyond to Summerville.* Previous to these events, another of Rosecrans's Corps—Crittenden's—had crossed the Tennessee at Bridgeport, Shell Mound, and the mouth of Battle Creek, eighteen or twenty miles westward of Chattanooga, and advancing on the 9th to that place found it to be evacuated. Here Crittenden received orders to push forward with the utmost vigor on the road to Dalton, by way of Ringgold, Rosecrans evidently holding his adversary of little account.

When the evacuation of Chattanooga had been commenced, Forrest was directed to leave Pegram, with his division, to cover that movement, and to hasten, with Armstrong's Division, toward Rome, to assist in repelling Mitchell's Federal cavalry, reported in movement, in that direction. Making forced marches, he found Wharton, with his division of Wheeler's Cavalry, at Summerville, and there learned that the enemy were just then ascending the mountain near Alpine.† Going forward with some twelve hundred of his

---

* McCook could now only effect a junction with Thomas, either by a march of some thirty-four miles, forcing his way to and through Lafayette, where Bragg had meantime concentrated his whole force ; or, that being out of the question, by marching back into Will's Valley, and northward about fifty miles, through most difficult mountain roads and passes. Fortunately for the Federal commander, the Confederate General was neither able to take in the true situation, nor gather its advantages.

† Three Brigades of Stanley's Cavalry, supported immediately by several Infantry Brigades of McCook's Corps.

men, in conjunction with Wharton's, the Federals were promptly encountered and checked. Here, orders were received, how ever, recalling Forrest's force to Lafayette. Putting it in movement, he hurried ahead, under special instructions, to have an interview with General Bragg, whom he found near Lee and Gordon's Mills, and orders were then given him to re- pair northward, to ascertain definitely the movements of the enemy in the direction of Chattanooga.

Late that afternoon, (the 10th,) he discovered that Critten- den's Corps—Palmer's and Van Cleves's divisions at least— whose movements we have partially indicated, had advanced just across the Chickamauga, at Red House Bridge, nine miles from Chattanooga, on the Ringgold road. This intelli- gence he at once dispatched, both to General Polk—whose force was but six miles distant from the enemy at the moment —and to the Commander-in-Chief in the same vicinity. From the well-known position of both Thomas's and McCook's corps, it was quite manifest Crittenden was dislocated from support, while within six miles of one half of the Confederate army on the field, and within easy reach of the rest. There- fore, assured in his own mind of the certainty of an immediate overpowering movement against Crittenden, Forrest at once procured guides, and made all his dispositions for a circuit, on his part, to the rear of the Federals, and the seizure of the Red House Bridge ; and this, too, he communicated through staff-officers to his superiors. Meanwhile, so transparently critical and precarious was Crittenden's position, that the Con- federate pickets in that direction, and the men around their camp-fires, were talking of his destruction as an affair fore- doomed.* Hearing nothing, however, from headquarters,

---

* That General Bragg was satisfied of the wide separation of the several corps of his enemy is apparent, not only from the letters of his staff-officers to General Hindman, during the after- noon of the 10th, but also from the fact

about midnight, Forrest rode thither to have an interview with General Bragg, but found, on reaching the point where he had expected to meet him, that he had gone to Lafayette, whither all the infantry, then in the quarter of Lee and Gordon's Mills, were also under orders to repair.

Upon this, hastening back, he immediately disposed his present command—Scott's Brigade, some nine hundred troopers, with four pieces of artillery—directly astride of Crittenden's path, just as the Federals were ready to move at daylight. With this handful of men, the advancing column was resolutely confronted. Seizing every favorable position for a skirmish, and using his artillery freely and boldly, many Federals went down as Scott's men doggedly held their ground, and only receded before the inexorable weight of the numbers opposed. For two hours, indeed, one position was stubbornly maintained in the neighborhood of Ringgold; but forced at length to give way, they fell back finally to Tunnel Hill, where Forrest made another stand. Pegram, who during this movement had hung on the Federal right flank, and between it and Lafayette with the remainder of his division, now joined, and Dibrell came up with his brigade from Dalton, where he had been sent, on reconnoissance, after the expedition to Alpine. The position was strong; and thus reënforced, dismounting his men, for the most part, and handling them as infantry, Forrest, presently bringing the column to bay,

---

that he announced in council, on the morning of the 14th, that McCook was even then as far off as Alpine, Thomas in McLemore's Cove, and Crittenden at Lee and Gordon's Mills. That is to say, Rosecrans's right and left wings were more than forty miles apart, with a difficult mountain interposed, while his centre was a day's march from support by one wing, and three days' by any available road from the other. Imagine Napoleon, Frederick, or the Duke of Wellington, with such an opportunity! *Vide* General D. H. Hill's Official Report, *Land We Love*, Vol. I. No. 6, p. 396.

was able to stay its further advance.* In this he was mate-rially aided by Pegram, who wielded his men with especial coolness and skill. Conspicuous among the incidents of this combat, was an encounter by Colonel Hart and thirty-eight or forty of the Sixth Georgia, who, at an urgent instant, charging upon a largely superior force of infantry, drove them back, and captured at least fifty prisoners. The enemy now began to retire, on the road by which he had approached, as far as Ringgold, where, as if bent on destruction, he turned the head of his column westward, toward Lee and Gordon's Mills, in the vicinity of which he was permitted to cross and take the position which Polk and Buckner had been directed to relin-quish. There, nevertheless, this corps was still isolated, and ex-posed to an overwhelming attack for several days thereafter.†

---

* General Forrest was again wounded in this affair, but so sound and vigorous was his constitution, that he kept the field, little disturbed by it.

† It will be difficult to account for General Bragg's strategy in permitting these movements of Crittenden : for no-thing could have been easier for the Con-federate General than the concentration of almost his entire force, and its in-terposition in such manner as to have effectually barred Crittenden's escape from a battle, with odds so great as to have made his perdition certain. Bragg, it seems, did indeed make some unskill-ful dispositions and inadequate fitful movements to that end ; but mainly after Crittenden had established himself on the west bank of the Chickamauga, and narrowed the break in his communica-tion with the rest of the Federal army. At six o'clock P.M. on the 12th, Bragg called Polk's attention to Crittenden, and expressed the expectation that the opportunity should be improved at day-light on the 13th ; and, in subsequent dispatches of the same evening, ordered and urged Polk to make a quick and decided attack. (*Vide* Bragg's Official Report, pp. 9 and 10.) But no attack was made, for some unexplained reason, further than that General Bragg says, on proceeding to the front, early on the 13th, he found that Crittenden had re-crossed the Chickamauga, and formed a junction—without saying when that had been effected—namely, several hours before his order to Polk had been written. (*Vide* Crittenden's Report, *Reb. Rec.* VII. Doc. 18, p. 526.) The fact is, the Confederate movements were singularly infelicitous and feeble prece-ding the battle. None of the blunders of the enemy were turned to the least profit. That "Soul of Armies," as Napier terms it, "the mind of a great

To recapitulate :* At dawn on the 13th, the Federal army was posted as follows :

20th Corps.	McCook's.	14,345.	Davis's, Johnson's, and Sheridan's Divisions of Infantry—9 brigades, 48 or 54 guns ; also, Mitchell's 3 brigades of Cavalry were at or near Alpine, Georgia.
14th Corps.	Thomas's.	24,072.	Baird's, Brannan's, Negley's, and Reynolds's Divisions—12 brigades of Infantry, and 72 guns, at Pond Spring, and on hills in front of Stevens's Gap, and rearward in the gap.
21st Corps.	Crittenden's.	13,975.	Palmer's, Van Cleves's, and Wood's Divisions—9 Brigades of Infantry, and 48 or 54 guns, at and westward of Lee and Gordon's Mills.

That is, 52,392 infantry and artillery, which, added to Minty's and Wilder's Brigades of Cavalry and the three under Mitchell with McCook, (in all at least 7500 cavalry,) made an effective Federal aggregate of all arms of 60,000, with at least 170 guns. This, exclusive of Steedman's Division—three brigades—of Gordon Granger's " Reserve Corps," at the moment about to cross the Tennessee at Bridgeport and Shell Mound, and by forced marches to attempt, by way of Chattanooga, to effect a junction with Rosecrans.†

Captain," or, indeed, one of even moderate aptitude for war, was wholly wanting ; and never in military history were *patent* opportunities so strangely squandered, as on the part of the Confederates. While, on the other hand, the strategy of Rosecrans was equally faulty—so faulty indeed, that it must have ended in complete disaster, but for the prodigious want of skill on the part of his adversary.

    * We had originally somewhat larger estimates, but have changed, as we go to press, to agree with the figures given in the table appended, p. 549 *Harper's Pictorial History of the Great Rebellion,* taken, not, however, directly from the official returns, but *second* hand from the statement of a staff-officer. Why do not Federal writers get at the returns ? The Confederate numbers are made up directly from the official statements of brigade and division commanders.

    † Granger's Official Report, *Reb. Rec.* VII. Doc. 184, p. 532.

That officer having now, howbeit, ascertained Bragg's position and movements somewhat nearly, had ordered McCook up from Alpine to the support of Thomas.*   But so difficult, indirect, and tortuous were the mountain roads to be traversed, that none of McCook's Division reached McLemore's Cove sooner than the afternoon of the 17th ; and, consequently, up to that time, the posture of affairs was still fraught with downright advantages for the Confederates, whose General, for a week previously, had had at his disposition, as we have shown, a force of 35,000 bayonets, as many as 7500 cavalry, rank and file, and some 150 guns,† with Longstreet's Corps, known to be near at hand.   And as it had been in his power, on the 10th, to have concentrated this force upon, and destroyed Crittenden, and then Thomas in detail, so after the 12th, for at least four days, it had been equally within the compass of his resources, by short movements, to have swiftly brought his army into a compact mass, and by throwing it promptly westward of the Chickamauga, about Alexander's Bridge, might have flung its whole weight, with crushing effect, upon Crittenden, whose *debris*, driven back in confusion upon Thomas, would have subjected that corps to be taken at disadvantage, in advancing to the succor of Crittenden—as doubt-

---

* Received on the night of the 13th. *Reb. Rec. VII.* Doc. 43, p. 221.

† Subdivided as follows : Polk's Corps, composed of the divisions of Cheatham and Hindman, numbering .bout 11,500 infantry and artillerists, and 84 guns ; Hill's Corps, composed of the divisions of Cleburne and Breckinridge, about 8100 infantry and artillerists, and 24 guns ; Buckner's Corps, composed of Stewart's and Preston's Divisions, say 8486 infantry and artillerists, and 40 guns ; Walker's Demi—

or " Reserve " Corps, consisting of five brigades, one of which (Gist's) was absent at Rome, present, say, 5000 infantry and artillerists, and 20 guns ; also, Bushrod Johnson's Brigade, (at Ringgold,) about 761 infantry and artillerists, and 4 guns ; Wheeler's Cavalry, constituted of Wharton's and Martin's Divisions, about 4000 rank and file, and — guns ; Forrest's Cavalry, Armstrong's and Pegram's Divisions, about 3500 rank and file, and 12 guns.

less would have been undertaken—and insured his disastrous defeat likewise, with the passes in his rear blocked up by Mc-Cook's Division coming up from Alpine. But the Confederate leader, if not wholly blind to these patent opportunities, failing to grasp them with decision, suffered them all to glide away as so many sunbeams from a child's hand. Instead of any strenuous surprise, he kept his forces moving from point to point, with little or no concert, but with some show of menace of a front attack, at Lee and Gordon's Mills, where the banks of the stream were steep and rocky, and impracticable for artillery except at one bridge and ford near by. In fact, each day opened with plans of operations, promising decisive results, that at sunset were invariably left unperformed; and in the *interim* his adversary was leisurely repairing those previous errors which we have pointed out, and massing his forces for a counter attack.

McCook, on the 17th, as we have said before, brought two of his divisions into the cove; and to make room for them, Thomas, gaining distance northward, closed in that direction upon Crittenden; and the several corps of the Federal army now stood extricated from the imminent peril, to which they had been severally exposed for a week, to be attacked and beaten in detail. By the same time, however, General Bragg had been made stronger by five small brigades which had arrived at Ringgold by railroad from Virginia and Mississippi, forming a column, that, in the absence of General Hood, was placed under command of Brigadier-General Bushrod Johnson.*

In the interval, Forrest's Cavalry had been actively employed, and had had frequent sharp, brilliant dashes with the Federal cavalry, especially Wilder's Brigade, and on several

---

* Gregg's and McNair's Brigades, from Mississippi, and Benning's, Law's, and Robertson's Brigades, of Hood's Division, Longstreet's Corps.

occasions with the infantry. One of these affairs—with Wilder—occurred on the 12th, near Leet's Tan-yard, east of the Chickamauga, and Pegram, who commanded the Confederates—Hart's Sixth Georgia and Rucker's Legion, (Twelfth and Sixteenth Tennessee Battalions)—maintained for several hours a hand-to-hand conflict of notable obstinacy and gallantry; after which, he bivouacked within a quarter of a mile of the scene. Scott's Brigade, likewise, had had several well-fought though brief encounters; and Armstrong's Division, also, was actively and usefully employed in its several positions.

Having thus carried the story of the special operations of Forrest's Cavalry down to the edge of the battle of Chickamauga, it will become necessary to embrace in the narrative of the events of the next four or five days the operations of all the forces engaged.

As we have seen, Rosecrans, by this time—the morning of the 18th—had brought together, in the valley of the Chickamauga, at and southward of Lee and Gordon's Mills, the bulk of his army. Bragg, on the other hand, had massed his corps mainly around Lafayette, with a provisional division of six brigades at Catoosa Station and Ringgold; and with his army thus disposed, resolving to take the offensive, he issued the order to that grave end.

To the troops assembled at Catoosa and Ringgold, formed into a temporary division, as before mentioned, under Bushrod Johnson, were assigned the initiative by an immediate movement across the Chickamauga, at Reed's Bridge, about four and a half miles northward of Lee and Gordon's Mills, and thence promptly southward upon the Federal position; Walker crossing at Alexander's Bridge, two miles nearer the enemy, was to support Johnson.

Buckner's Corps, the next affluent to the battle stream, was to enter it by way of Tedford's Ford, still nearer the Federal position. Polk was to swell the tide, at or near the same point, after having—during the first part of the movement —menaced an irruption upon the enemy at Lee and Gordon's Mills. At the same time, Hill was to cover the Confederate left flank from any hostile operation in that direction ; and by an advance, just south of Lee and Gordon's Mills, to ascertain whether or not the Federals were reënforcing, and, in that event, was to attack them in flank. The " utmost promptness and persistence" in the execution of all these movements were enjoined.*

II.

Johnson was early in motion on Friday morning, with four brigades,† some 4300 bayonets and 12 guns. Forrest covered this column on the front and right flank, with a small force, constituted of only Martin's Battalion of Kentuckians and his escort, and came in contact with the Federal cavalry at Keeler's Mill, on Peavine Creek. Swiftly dismounting his men, a sharp skirmish took place ; but Johnson pressing up, and throwing forward his skirmishers, the enemy were swept back without material impediment to Reed's Bridge, where another sharp affair, with severe loss, occurred, before the bridge was seized ; and the infantry began to cross about three P.M.

Here the other portion of Pegram's Division, except Scott and a part of his brigade,‡ came up, and Forrest, crossing at a ford, southward of the bridge, scoured the country westward for more than a mile ; while Johnson, after advancing westward to Jay's Saw-Mill, there turning the head of his column,

---

* Bragg's Official Report.

† Namely, Johnson's own Brigade, under Colonel John S. Fulton ; and McNair's, Gregg's, and Robertson's Brigades, with an effective aggregate of 4700 rank and file ; and Culpeper's, Bledsoe's, and Everett's Batteries.

‡ Scott had been detached in observation of the Chattanooga road.

pushed boldly southward, on the road by way of Alexander's Bridge, to a point about a mile in front of Dalton's Ford, and within half a mile of Vinyard's House on the Chattanooga-Lafayette Road, where, after a warm skirmish, it being quite dark, he bivouacked for the night, in line of battle, facing the south-west. This position was one of isolation and hazardous proximity to the bulk of the Federal army, as may be readily comprehended ; but throwing up some hasty obstructions in his front against cavalry, Johnson took the further precaution of keeping one third of his men under arms all night. Law's Brigade having come up from Ringgold, meanwhile, was formed into a division with Robertson's Brigade under General Law, and that and Johnson's were placed under the general command of Major-General Hood, who had joined at Reed's Bridge.

Forrest at the same time bivouacked in the rear of Hood's Division, at Alexander's Bridge, from which he had driven a body of Federal cavalry, capturing some thirty officers and men ; afterward he relaid the floor of the bridge that had been torn up, and lay on the west bank of the stream.

Walthall's Brigade, Liddell's Division, had, however, carried that position about three P.M., with the severe loss of one hundred and five, rank and file, killed and wounded ; but finding the flooring removed, Liddell had sought a crossing a mile and a half to the north, at Byrom's Ford, where no resistance was made, nor to his advance to a position in front of the bridge, and of Forrest's position for the night.

Buckner, as instructed, also marching that morning from the vicinage of Lafayette, had approached Tedford's and Dalton's (Hunt's) Fords late in the afternoon, and seized the high grounds commanding both, with batteries in position above and below them to cover the crossings,—Stewart's Division at the former and Preston's at the latter ; and after nightfall a brigade from each (Gracie's and Clayton's) was thrown

across to the west bank, the other brigades remaining eastward of the stream all night.

Hindman and Cheatham, Polk's Corps, meanwhile had
taken posts nearly opposite Lee and Gordon's Mills, as arranged in the plan of operations, and slept the night of the
18th on the east bank of the Chickamauga, as likewise the
divisions of Hill's Corps; that is, Breckinridge at Glass's Mill
and Cleburne in the vicinity of Anderson's farm-house,
some four miles south of Lee and Gordon's Mills, fronting the
enemy's extreme right.

Armstrong's Division of Forrest's Cavalry was still with
Polk's Corps; and Dibrell's Brigade had had several handsome skirmishes in that quarter.

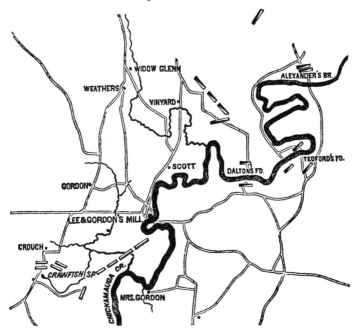

Thus it will be observed that on the night of the 18th, or
at least by dawn on the 19th, the bulk of the Confederate
army still lay eastward of the Chickamauga, and separated by

that stream from the remainder, ten small brigades with some forty guns, and about sixteen hundred cavalry under Forrest, which were in the immediate presence of three strong Federal corps and a heavy cavalry force. Clearly, this was a position fraught with extreme jeopardy for the Confederates, had their enemy been handled by a general more vigorous and with less inaptitude for war than Major-General Rosecrans. The battle, howbeit, was at hand, with forces opposed, of numbers, courage, martial qualities, and aspirations, which assured that it would be one of the most sanguinary, the most obstinate of the war. The Confederates had in the field, placed, as we have shown, not to exceed 38,000 rifles and muskets, exclusive of Forrest's Cavalry, 3500 rank and file, fighting mainly as infantry ; 4000 cavalry, Wheeler's, and 150 guns.*

The movements of the Confederates, which we have related, caused some changes that afternoon and night in the disposition of the Rosecrans army ; so that while Wood's Division remained in its position, Van Cleves's Division of the same Corps, Crittenden's, was formed on Woods's left, or northeastwardly, along Chickamauga ; and Palmer, on a prolongation of the same line, leftward of Van Cleve.† After four P.M., Thomas, with his whole corps at Crawfish Spring, was ordered forward, by a road at the foot of Mission Ridge, to take up a line on the Chattanooga-Lafayette road, leftward of Crittenden, which movement he executed in a characteristic, soldierly manner that night ; his advanced Division, Baird's, being at Kelly's Farm,‡ nearly west of Reed's Bridge, at daylight, and soon after took up a position at the forks of the road, facing Reed's and Alexander's bridges ; Brannan was

---

* Aggregate infantry and artillery,   † Crittenden's Official Report.
43,531. Cavalry, 7500. See Appen-   ‡ General Thomas's Official Report.
dix and Index.   —*Reb. Rec.* VII. Doc. 43, p. 228.

formed a little later on Baird's left, and in supporting distance ; and the other divisions were moving promptly toward the same field. McCook, at the same time, during the night, moved up, and concentrated his divisions about Crawfish Spring, until ten A.M. on the 19th, when Davis's and Johnson's Divisions were ordered northward to reënforce Thomas.*

These corps numbered 52,392 combatants, and as many as 7500 cavalry, with not less than 160 guns ;† and, meanwhile, Steedman's Division of three and a half brigades, Granger's reserved corps, had likewise been brought up from Shell Mound and Bridgeport, since the 13th, to the vicinity of Reed's Bridge.‡

III.

As previously recited, Forrest bivouacked at Alexander's Bridge, the night of the 18th. It remains to be added that he had ridden with General Hood to General Bragg's headquarters, about nine P.M., and received instructions to develop the enemy on the extreme Confederate right, as soon as possible the next morning, reporting all hostile movements to the nearest commander ; he was also assured of prompt reënforcements, in the event he brought on a general engagement,§ and General Walker was specially instructed to answer his requisitions in such contingency.‖ Promptly in the saddle, with Pegram's Division, Forrest repaired swiftly northward to Jay's Saw-Mill, about three quarters of a mile westward of Reed's

---

* McCook's Official Report.

† We give the aggregate as we find it in Federal sources. The bayonets in the *three Corps* may be estimated at not falling below 46,000, which would give 3600 officers and 2800 artillerists.

‡ *Reb. Rec.* Vol. VII. Doc. 43, p. 246.

§ General Forrest's MS. Notes.

‖ General Walker's Official Report.

Bridge, where he encountered a heavy Federal force, evidently too strong for Pegram single-handed.* Dispatching an aid, Captain Anderson, for Armstrong's Division, as yet some six or seven miles southward with Polk's Corps, and calling on Walker for the support of an infantry brigade, he nevertheless dismounted his small force, except Rucker, deployed them at once as riflemen, and, advancing boldly to the issue, brushed back for some five or six hundred yards the line of Federal skirmishers by the vigor of his onset.† But now the Federals, assuming the offensive, threatened to overlap the Confederate flanks ; and Rucker was ordered to charge, mounted, with his two battalions (Twelfth and Sixteenth Tennessee) along the crown of an open ridge, to meet the hostile movement, and right gallantly was the service performed. Breaking through the picket-line, he dashed down upon the Federal force behind, but had to give back under the fierce fusilade that he provoked, and under which many of his saddles were emptied, but, nevertheless, he did not return without some prisoners.

Forrest, now riding along in front to reconnoitre, observed two strong Federal lines in battle array, their left, in his front, nearly due west of Reed's bridge, their right stretching far to the southward, in the direction of Crawfish Spring ; and intelligence of this was immediately sent to headquarters, with an urgent request that his left should be speedily and strongly reënforced.

It was now ten o'clock A.M., when the Federals threw forward a lavish line of skirmishers, and it may be said the overture of the battle of Chickamauga began. The conflict speedi-

---

* Pegram's old Brigade was under General H. B. Davidson. Scott's Brigade was still absent.

† The Federals thus assailed appear to have been Croxton's Brigade, of Brannan's Division.

ly became warm, and was maintained with pertinacity on both sides, the advantage somewhat, however, with the Confederates. Dibrell's Brigade, of Armstrong's Division, coming up about twelve o'clock, was placed in line on the left of Pegram's troops, dismounted and acting as infantry. No sooner had this disposition been made, than a heavy body of the enemy bore down upon Dibrell with a pressure that forced him back to a rocky ridge which Forrest had previously held. Just at this moment, Huggins's and Huwald's batteries—eight guns—came up and were posted so as to be brought to bear with salutary effect, the Federals, however, advancing so closely as to require the drastic use of canister. Armstrong had now—about one P.M —brought up his other brigade, which, being dismounted like the rest of Forrest's Cavalry on the field, was posted on the extreme right. Wilson's Brigade, of Liddell's Division, likewise had arrived previously, under the guidance of one of Forrest's staff-officers sent to urge its advent ; and, thus reënforced, the offensive was resumed with renewed determination. Just then a line of Federal skirmishers was observed to extend southward of their main line, and these Armstrong turned by a sweep to the right, while Wilson threw his brigade of Georgians handsomely against the Federal lines, the fire from which was now terrific. Breasting it resolutely, however, Wilson pressed forward, and, in conjunction with Forrest's men, once more swept back the enemy in his front some four hundred yards in confusion, capturing a battery of four guns, when he was brought to a stand by a staunch, strongly-planted Federal line. The forces driven back were probably two Federal brigades, but Johnson's Division, of McCook's, and Reynolds's Division, of Thomas's Corps, just at this juncture were added to the Federal divisions already in action in that quarter, so that Thomas now had at his disposition not only three of his own divisions. but likewise one of McCook's and Palmer's divisions, of Crit-

tenden's Corps—that is to say, *five divisions.** Thus formidably strengthened, the tide was quickly turned in favor of
the Federals ; for Thomas is of the muscular school of soldiers, who strike heavy-handed, quick blows ; and the eager
Confederates were in turn driven back over the ground they
had lately gained, leaving it thickly strewn with deplorably
many brave officers and men, but the survivors carried off the
captured artillery.   Meanwhile, on his own responsibility,
Forrest had ordered up Ector's Brigade, of Walker's Corps,
and formed it in line rightward of Wilson.†   Govan's and
Walthall's—the other brigades of Walker's force—were likewise brought upon the scene by Walker, and led, with his
wonted gallantry, into action.‡   Thus far the battle had been
confined to the narrow arena, scarcely a mile and a half in
length and less than one in depth, just in front of Jay's Saw-
Mill and west of Reed's Bridge, and the whole face of which,
an undulating plateau, was clad with an oak forest interspersed
with patches of dense undergrowth.   The Federals had already thrown up cover, from behind which they poured forth
a broad, hot torrent of musketry-fire, as well as grape, shells,
and canister from a numerous artillery, before which the Confederates, as yet consisting only of Forrest's two small divisions of dismounted cavalry — less than 3000 rifles — eight
guns, and four of Walker's brigades and sixteen guns—in all,
8000 fighting men and 24 guns   first faltered and then receded, but to take breath, close their ranks, and again spring
forward, and with the furious impact of their charge were able
to burst through two Federal lines and capture many prison-

---

* *Vide* Thomas's Official Report, *Reb.*
Rec. VII. p. 229.

† Walker's Official Report.

‡ It may serve to illustrate somewhat
the character of the Confederate commander to notice the fact that Walker's
two divisions, which had been formed
and designated as a reserve corps in
the plan of battle, became the first infantry employed.

ers from as many as seven regiments of the regular service, and all the artillery in that immediate front; but there stood behind, in grim array, a third line, whose wide-stretched flanks, overlapping the Confederates, threatened to envelop them, and to escape which they were again obliged to retire hastily.*

While these events were thickening, Cheatham — Polk's Corps—crossing the Chickamauga about seven A.M. with his five brigades at Dalton's Ford,† and moving rightward and northward a short distance, formed line of battle and awaited orders, that only reached him as late as twelve o'clock M., through an aid-de-camp of the Commanding General. Directed to reënforce Walker, he hastened to the Confederate right, and at one P.M. had taken his position astraddle the road from Alexander's Bridge, just in rear of Liddell, with a frontage of three brigades,‡ with the other two in reserve.§ Making these dispositions with celerity, Cheatham at once advanced his Tennesseeans with their habitual *dash*, and they were soon in conflict, with a formidable counter-movement, pressing Walker and Forrest back. Three of Thomas's divisions,‖ two of Crittenden's, ‖ and Johnson's Division of McCook's Corps were now in this quarter of the field, and a fiery, sanguinary, fluctuating conflict followed and raged for several hours, in which Walker's and Forrest's men bore their share, as previously related. At one time the Federals were forced back fully three fourths of a mile, only gaining a foothold again when strongly reënforced and sheltered by breastworks.

---

* Aggregate of Forrest, 3500; of Walker, 5575; total, 9075.

† Jackson's, Maney's, Strahl's, Preston Smith's, and Wright's.

‡ Jackson's, Preston Smith's, and Wright's.

§ Maney's and Strahl's.

‖ Baird's, Brannan's, and Reynolds's.

¶ Palmer's and Van Cleve's. Thomas does not mention the presence of Van Cleve, but Crittenden does, and that he took part early in the fight on the Federal extreme left.

Then the tide turned once more, and the Confederates, rolled back, were followed vehemently by great odds. The brunt of this was borne for a time upon front and flank by Maney's and Strahl's brigades, disposed on a commanding ridge, and Turner's Battery,* the immediate support of which was a picked battalion under Major Dawson, of the One Hundred and Fifty-fourth Tennessee. From this admirably fought battery, at short range, a rapid, withering discharge of grape and canister mowed wide swarths through the Federal masses. Forrest, however, observing the extreme exigency, had also brought up two of his own batteries, Huggins's and Huwald's— eight guns—with the Fourth and Eighth Regiments and Shaw's Battalion Tennesseeans of Dibrell's Brigade on the Federal left flank at close quarters—eighty yards—and with them effectually stayed and turned back the wave that hitherto had swept all before it ; and nothing could exceed the cool, splendid courage of these stout-hearted officers and men, as likewise of Dawson and his battalion, and of Turner and his battery—all Tennesseeans save Turner and his men.

Meanwhile, Cleburne's Division, Hill's Corps, after having been held eastward of the Chickamauga until late in the afternoon, was then ordered to pass the stream at Tedford's Ford and report to General Polk, who, about four P.M., gave orders that the division should be formed at once in line rearward of the Confederate right, which was promptly done about dark, the line, a mile in extent, facing the west and its right resting just in advance of Jay's Saw-Mill.† The ground immediately

---

* The commander of this battery was Lieutenant W. B. Turner, of Salisbury, N. C., distinguished for his coolness, courage, and skill on that day. The commander of the support, the gallant Major J. W. Dawson, of Memphis, was severely wounded.

† Cleburne's Official Report. Polk's Brigade with Keys's Battery on the right, Wood's Brigade and Semple's Battery the centre, and Dibrell's Brigade with Douglass's Battery the left.

in front was a gentle acclivity, covered with open woods except in the centre which was an inclosed field. In front, some three hundred yards, Cheatham's Division intervened between Cleburne and the enemy in that quarter, posted in strong force behind breastworks. Notwithstanding the lateness of the hour—six P.M.—Cleburne was now ordered to advance to the attack over the ground that had been so frequently and obstinately contested, and Cheatham's Division moved forward in concert.* A furious tempest of missiles rained down upon the advancing Confederates, and for half an hour the firing was the heaviest, says Cleburne, that he had ever heard. In sooth,

> " Such a din was there,
> As if men fought on earth below
> And fiends in upper air."

It was very dark the while, and each adversary was directed in his aim by the flashing line of flame of his opponent, and hence the affair was less sanguinary than noisy and resplendent. Keys's and Semple's Batteries were run up to within sixty yards of the Federal line and fired with rapidity. Polk's Brigades of Cleburne's, and Jackson's and Smith's, of Cheatham's divisions, were likewise pushed up, when the enemy, Johnson's and Baird's Divisions, gave way, leaving in the hands of the Confederates several pieces of artillery, as many caissons, some 300 prisoners, and the colors of the Seventy-seventh Indiana and Seventy-ninth Pennsylvania ; but, unfor-·tunately, at the cost of the life of Brigadier-General Preston Smith, an officer who had no superior in that army for a shining courage, while none of his grade excelled him in the qualities of a commander; and by his side fell two gallant, excellent

---

* Some Federal writers make Cleburne take part in the battle much earlier. They have no warrant for it whatsoever.

officers, Captain John Donelson, his Adjutant-General, and an Aid, Captain Thomas H. King. For more than a mile the Federals receded before Cleburne halted, readjusted his disordered lines, and bivouacked his division upon their arms, as did Cheatham likewise.*

Meanwhile, though the main conflict had been in the quarter of the field we have sketched, there had been handsome fighting elsewhere. Preston's and Stewart's Divisions, Buckner's Corps, after crossing at Tedford's and Dalton's Fords at daylight on the 19th, remained inactive in line of battle in that vicinity until in the afternoon, when the latter was directed to repair in the direction of the firing, rightward. Applying for more specific orders from General Bragg, just at hand, Stewart was answered that Walker, much cut up and menaced with being outflanked, needed aid ; that General Polk was in chief command on the immediate field of battle, and circumstances there must govern. Moving up to the scene, unable to find Polk, Stewart, without delay, threw Clayton's Brigade into action. It was their first engagement, and their movements from the outset were worthy of the veteran brigades assembled on that field. It was Wright's Brigade, the left of Cheatham's Division, that Clayton chanced to succor by his advance. Wright's Brigade, the left of which having just been turned, had been driven back by great odds, with the loss of its battery. For an hour Clayton's Alabamians were in action with steadfast courage, as may best be measured by the fact that, in that hour, nearly four hundred of their officers and men had been killed or wounded. In the mean time, Brown's Brigade was also thrown forward to relieve Clayton, whose brigade was withdrawn to replenish its ammunition. Brown's Tennesseeans were veterans, and, despite an intense

---

* Cleburne's and Cheatham's Official Reports.

fire and an intervening jungle of undergrowth, they drove the first line of Federals, for several hundred yards, back upon the second line, which, sustained by artillery, was holding a gentle ridge. Pressing still onward, this position, also, was carried, but was not held, as a largely superior force threatened on the right ; five Federal rifled guns, however, were carried off, and three others, the horses of which had been shot, were left behind. This, it is to be added, was achieved with no slight loss, and Bates's fresh brigade was now substituted in its stead, in an impetuous attack, before the shock of which the Federals soon gave up one position after another.* Clayton's Brigade also was soon led forward again, and, in conjunction with Bates, followed the enemy for half a mile westward of the Chattanooga road, when, threatened by a heavy accumulation of the enemy's masses on both flanks, the Confederate line fell leisurely back, just about sunset, reformed eastward, and, facing the road just mentioned, and disposing his lines for emergencies, Stewart bivouacked for the night.† Twelve pieces of artillery were abandoned to Stewart's Division, and at least four of these were secured as well as several hundred prisoners, including a Lieutenant-Colonel of the staff of Major-General Thomas ; but, at the same time, the loss incurred was severe in all three brigades.

Meanwhile, the battle had extended further leftward also ; the other division—Preston's—of Buckner's Corps, and Hood's two divisions—Johnson's and Law's—after having been held, drawn up in line around the curved crest of a ridge about one thousand yards eastward from Vinyard's house, from seven A.M. to two P.M., then had their skirmish line driven in on

---

* It would seem that the tactical management of this division in this affair is open to criticism. This way of sending it in, brigade by brigade, we apprehend prolonged the fight and increased the losses. Nothing is gained by driblet fighting.

† Stewart's Official Report.

Johnson's front, and a sustained attack followed, which was repulsed with the material aid of Bledsoe's and Everett's Batteries. Hood then ordered Johnson to attack in turn, which was done promptly. Trigg's Brigade, much impeded by a thicket and dense woods, and dislocated in its brigade organization, soon became hotly engaged ; while Johnson's own brigade, under Colonel Fulton, had gone forward six hundred yards before it was fired upon. McNair's Brigade became intermingled with Gregg's, but all pressed gallantly and persistently forward, with a well-maintained battle line, to the Chattanooga road at a point north of Vinyard's house. Robertson's Brigade of Texans, of Law's Division, was also advanced in a spirited charge, and poured a galling fire into the enemy, who by this time had been driven westward of the road conjointly by Gregg and McNair. In the mean time, too, Fulton's ranks were swept by a heavy fire of musketry and artillery from an elevated position, but, after an hour's stubborn conflict, the Federals in his front were forced westward of the road into an open woods ; but they were not permitted to tarry, for Fulton's Regiment, still advancing, gaining the cover of a wood leftward of a Federal battery, presently carried it by a handsome movement, gallantly conducted by Lieutenant-Colonel R. B. Snowden, of the Twenty-fifth Tennessee. The Federals, however, received reënforcements, and, moving suddenly northward on the Chattanooga road, the left and rear of Fulton's Brigade, poured a volley into it, causing the whole brigade to fall back swiftly eastward of the road again, leaving some seventy prisoners and the captured guns in the enemy s hands. The Thirtieth and Forty-first Tennessee regiments, however, were readily halted by Captain W. T. Blakemore, of Johnson's staff, and, under Colonel Walker, bravely resuming the offensive, before long drove the intrusive column back. While Hood's command was thus engaged, about three P.M., Trigg's Brigade, of Preston's Division, was sent by Buckner to the support of Robertson, Law's Division, then sorely pressed by heavy infantry masses and the blighting fire of a battery from behind an earthwork. Moving up to where Robertson's Texans were thus holding an unequal contest, at Trigg's first volley at short range the Federals broke and were driven to cover, gallantly pressed and followed by the Sixth Florida. Here some misunderstanding led to the diversion and separation of the other regiments of the brigade, so that the Sixth Florida, left without support, was necessarily withdrawn to escape annihilation under the pitiless fire to which it was now exposed in front and on both flanks. But it was now twilight, and darkness coming on rapidly, further conflict was staid in that quarter of the field, and the Confederates rested on their arms.

The Federals encountered by Stewart, Bushrod Johnson, and Law, and finally by Trigg's Brigade, were Negley's Division, Thomas's, Davis's Division, McCook's, and Wood's Divisions, of Crittenden's Corps, with a brigade of Sheridan's Division, that came up last and opportunely saved Wood from disaster, as General Rosecrans affirms. Brannan, also, late in the afternoon was transferred from the left to this part of the field. Thus it will be seen, as General Rosecrans, in fact, observes, that the whole Federal army of three corps was brought "opportunely and squarely into action"* on the 19th, save two brigades of Sheridan's Division and Mitchell's Cavalry. But not so with the Confederates. Their General, it would seem, did not make amends for the defective operations of the previous week, and his deplorable failure to avail himself of transparent opportunities, by diligence or the rapid movement of his forces, once the battle had been delivered and accepted. For, after having been kept nearly all day

------

* *Vide* Rosecrans's Official Report.—*Reb. Rec.* VII. p. 223.

southward of Lee's and Gordon's Mills, its artillery engaged in the exchange of a noisy artillery practice with some heavy guns, doubtless left by the enemy in that quarter for that object, while all the Federal army but two brigades had gone northward, Breckinridge's Division (3395 bayonets*) was only ordered across the Chickamauga so late as to enable it to reach a position just on the right, in rear of Cleburne, the other division of his corps, at eleven o'clock at night ; and Hindman's (5621 bayonets†) was likewise suffered to remain eastward of the Chickamauga until the middle of the afternoon before it was ordered across and to a position in the quarter where Bushrod Johnson had been engaged, which was not reached until after sunset, when the conflict had ceased, though one brigade (Manigault's) had a brief skirmish with some Federals in its front.   Moreover, two of Preston's brigades, fully 3000 effective men, had likewise been kept unemployed. That is to say, while Rosecrans promptly and energetically engaged with all his infantry save a brace of brigades, Bragg, numerically his inferior, at best, by 8000 fighting men and 20 guns, had so tardily and unskillfully handled his resources as to lose the services of more than 12,000 veteran infantry, or more than thirty per cent of that arm of his army.

III.

BATTLE OF SEPTEMBER 20TH.

Lieutenant-General Longstreet, arriving at Catoosa Station in the middle of the afternoon of the 19th, repaired as soon as practicable, eleven P.M., to army headquarters.   There, General Bragg acquainted him with his purpose to give battle the next morning, by an initial movement on his right, " to be followed

---

* Aggregate, 3769.   † Aggregate, 6102.

in succession toward the left," so that the whole line should be wheeled upon the extreme left as a pivot.* Moreover, that, for the occasion, he had arranged his forces into two grand divisions, or " wings," the command of the right one of which was assigned to Lieutenant-General Polk, and of the left to Lieutenant-General Longstreet. General Polk was likewise informed of this disposition of the forces and plan of battle. His command embraced Hill's Corps, Walker's Reserve Corps, and Cheatham's Division of his own corps, while his right flank was supported and covered by Forrest's two cavalry divisions. Longstreet's wing was composed of Buckner's Corps, Hindman's Division of Polk's Corps, Johnson's Provisional Division, and Hood's† and McLaw's‡ Divisions of Longstreet's own corps.

In consequence of a radically defective staff organization, that bane throughout the war of all Confederate operations, and other causes, the orders in regard to the rearrangement of the Confederate army, and the inauguration of the battle at daylight, were not communicated to several of the officers of highest rank on the field in time to secure prompt intelligent action with their troops under these orders. Hill, whose corps was to begin the combat, after an ineffectual search for General Bragg, learned only about midnight, from his Adjutant-General, on returning to his own headquarters, of the subdivision of the army into wings, and that his own corps fell under the command of General Polk, who wished to see him. Making a fruitless effort to find that officer, he returned to his troops, and remained unaware of the orders to

---

* Doubtless with the expectation of cutting off Rosecrans's retreat to Chattanooga.

† Under command of General Law.

‡ McLaw's Division was made up of Kershaw's and Humphrey's brigades, (without artillery,) which did not reach the field until late in the afternoon of the 20th.

begin the conflict at dawn, until apprised of the fact at eight A.M., by General Bragg in person, who visited his lines at that hour. Buckner, likewise, was left equally ignorant of the plan of operations until informed of it by General Longstreet on the morning of the 20th.* Walker and Cheatham, however, receiving their orders direct from General Polk's headquarters, were both under arms at the hour prescribed for the attack, ready to advance ; but neither received orders to that effect for several hours later.† Forrest, moreover, who was not embraced in the wing organization, did not receive any orders or instructions until after sunrise.‡

Meanwhile, the Confederates were occupying very much the same positions in which the cessation of hostilities the night before had left them ; and hence little order or regularity in line of battle had been attained at or for an hour after daylight. At that hour, indeed, while the right wing was in line facing nearly westward, Buckner's Corps, the right of Longstreet's, lay almost at right angles to it, fronting nearly northward, with a part of Stewart's Division overlapping the left of Cheatham, so that the latter could not move forward. Breckinridge, not brought up before the morning of the 20th, just before daylight, as will be remembered, was placed on the right of Cleburne, of the same corps, and on the right of Polk's wing, with his right brigade (Adams's) stretching across the road leading from Reed's Bridge to the highway tò Chattanooga, at Glenn's. Walker furnished the reserve for the right wing, and Forrest was drawn up on the right of Breckinridge, with his two small divisions stretching northward, some two miles, to the Chickamauga, with Dibrell's Brigade, Armstrong's Division, immediately on the right of

---

* Buckner's Official Report.   † *Vide* their Official Reports.
          ‡ Forrest's Official Report and MS. Notes.

Adams's Infantry brigade.* Hindman's Division formed the extreme Confederate left, with his left resting within half a mile of Vinyard's house. On his right lay Bushrod Johnson drawn up in several lines ; and Wheeler covered that flank with a portion of his cavalry, at the same time having the rest holding watch and ward, southward, over hostile movements through the passes and fords in that quarter.

On the part of the Federals, Rosecrans had assembled his corps commanders at his headquarters—Mrs. Glenns's, on his right—the night of the 19th. Hearing their report, he then made known his dispositions for the next morning ; and at or soon after daylight, it would seem that his forces presented a continuous, well furnished front, extending northeastwardly, from Rosecrans's headquarters to the Reed's Bridge road, and to a point within a quarter of a mile eastward of the junction of that road with the Chattanooga highway, with a strong line of reserves. Since sunset, moreover, they had not remained idle, but were actively at work in the construction of breastworks of logs and rails, and the sound of the labor had been plainly heard by the Confederates all night. Of their line, Baird's Division formed the extreme left, while Sheridan's of McCook's Corps occupied the right, flanked by Wilder's Cavalry.† The sun had risen bright and clear, but a dense mist lay low in the valley between the two armies, concealing them from each other.

As has been mentioned, it was General Bragg's purpose to begin the combat at daylight. Circumstances, in part as yet not satisfactorily explained, as we have seen, led to a delay of some hours after that time.

---

* Scott was still absent, watching the movements of Granger, and Rucker's Legion and Martin's Kentuckians had been sent to the rear, across Chickamauga, for subsistence and forage during the night, but rejoined before the combat began.

† *Vide* a well-written newspaper arti-

In the mean time, Forrest had ordered Scott to keep the approach from Rossville closely reconnoitered. Pegram, directed to hold the rest of his division mounted, was also instructed to seize the road leading southward from Rossville to Lee and Gordon's Mills, by a strong detachment, and doing so, reported before the conflict began that there was no enemy in that quarter. Armstrong's Division was dismounted as riflemen, except the First Tennessee (Colonel Wheeler) and one battalion,* which were reserved to act as cavalry.

At length, between nine and ten, the final orders to begin the battle were received on the right. Forrest being directed to move and keep in line with Breckinridge's Division, he advanced, with Pegram's Division in reserve. Within half a mile, a brigade of Baird's Division was struck, and a warm skirmish ensued. Breckinridge, about the same time, came in contact with the enemy in his front, his left—Helm's Brigade—becoming furiously engaged with a force behind strong breastworks. The Second and Ninth Kentucky, and three companies of Forty-first Alabama, having no troops on their left by an accident, and from the form of the Federal works, were brought under an enfilading as well as front fire, that shattered their ranks, and, despite the admirable courage that twice incited these brave men to storm the position, they were forced to retire, but not until Robert C. Anderson, color-bearer of the Second Kentucky, was slain, as he planted his flag on the enemy's works. The loss, however, was fearful, including that of their accomplished commander, Brigadier-General Ben Hardin Helm, mortally wounded.† During

---

cle, reprinted *Reb. Rec.* VII. Doc. 42, p. 243, the critical portion of which we note *en passant* as very sound.

* A battalion of Forrest's old regiment.

† Lieutenant-Colonel James W.

Hewitt, Captains Madeira, Rogers, and Leedman, Second Kentucky, and Captain Daniels, Ninth Kentucky, and many other officers were also killed outright.

this bloody affair the remainder of the brigade, more fortunate, had advanced across the Chattanooga road, and captured a section of Napoleon guns in position. It was then withdrawn, and the brigade reassembled rearward, under Colonel Lewis, Sixth Kentucky.* Adams and Stoval, meanwhile, pressing steadily to the front, in their part of the field, with little impediment from skirmish lines, which they brushed aside, had reached the road just mentioned, Adams capturing a battery, the supports of which he had dispersed. Satisfied that the Federal line was substantially turned by these brigades, Breckinridge now changed their front to one at a right angle to, and astride the Chattanooga road, facing southward, Slocomb's Battery coöperating. Advancing along, and to the eastward of this road, Stoval in a short distance developed the extreme Federal left—Baird's Division, strongly intrenched—and under an enfilading as well as terrible direct fire, stubbornly withstood, was repulsed, and fell back in good order only a few hundred yards. Adams, rightward of the road, soon encountered a Federal line—Beatty's Brigade, Negley's Division—drawn up, fronting northward, and in rear of the intrenchments developed by Stoval, which he broke through by the impetuosity of his attack; but a second and stronger line—at least three brigades†—stood behind, supported by artillery, that was an overmatch for Adams's single brigade. The meeting was bloody; and the Confederates being foiled, were thrown back in confusion, leaving the intrepid Adams severely wounded in the hands of the enemy.‡ Slocomb, meanwhile, fighting his guns from a favorable position, with his wonted resolution and courage, the brigade was

---

* Fourth and Sixth Kentucky and seven companies Forty-first Alabama.

† See General Thomas's Official Report, *Reb. Rec.* VII, Doc. 43, p. 230.

‡ The gallant Major Loudon Butler, Nineteenth Louisiana, was also left dead on the field.

rallied in his rear, when, being severely cut up, he was forced to withdraw and refit.

Soon after Breckinridge had set his division in motion, Cleburne received orders to advance, keeping aligned with Breckinridge ; this caused some confusion.   Polk's and the right of Wood's brigades, already within short canister range of a line of breastworks along the crest of a ridge in their immediate front, were mowed down for some moments by a fire that they could not withstand, and they gave way.   Polk's men, however, finding partial shelter behind the crest of a neighboring ridge, renewed and protracted the fight for an hour and a half, until their ammunition was exhausted, with a loss of three hundred and fifty killed and wounded.*   Meanwhile, the left of the division had become entangled with Stewart's Division, so that Deshler's Brigade for a while was retarded from advancing.   Wood's regiments, however, were able to push forward upon the southern angle of the breastworks in their front, but having to cross an open field swept by an oblique fire from small-arms and artillery, they were repulsed, with the loss of six hundred officers and men killed and wounded.†   About the same time, Deshler, having made an ineffectual effort to form a connection with Polk's line, was thrown forward, to fill up the gap left by the repulse of Wood, when he was shot through the chest by a shell.   Overmatched, evidently, by the enemy thus encountered in their fortifications—comprising, apparently, the divisions of Johnson, Palmer, and Reynolds—Cleburne retired to

* The gallant Captain Hugh S. Otey, of Brigadier-General Polk's staff, Captains W. J. Morris, McKnight, Second Tennessee, Adjutant Greenwood, First Arkansas, and Captains Beard and George Moore were slain here.

† Four field-officers fell on this occasion, Major McGaughey, Sixteenth Alabama Cavalry, Major Carr, Thirty-second Mississippi, Major Hawkins, Hawkins's Sharp-Shooters, Major Gibson, Gibson's Battalion, all officers distinguished by former service.

a strong position rearward, some three hundred yards from the point at which his brigades had been baffled in their onset, and reorganized.

Walker's demi-corps, as will be remembered, had been constituted the reserve of the right wing, and, as soon as Breckinridge was repulsed, Hill had recourse to it for a brigade "to fill up the gap made by Helm's withdrawal." The whole command, however, was led up in line of battle by Walker, for some of the distance at a double-quick ; nevertheless, an hour elapsed between the discomfiture of Helm's Brigade and Walker's arrival on the scene, such was the general mal-disposition of the Confederate forces of that wing for battle-emergencies.* These troops were now distributed by brigades to relieve different portions of the right wing. Colquitt, thrown forward by General Hill, sought to relieve the pressure on Breckinridge's right, and was quickly under a destructive enfilading and front fire, that brought to the ground in less than half an hour fully a third of his martial brigade, and fell himself mortally wounded, while all his field-officers save two were wounded.† With shining valor did the officers an l men of this brigade make hopeless head against the fury of the battle in their front and flank, but finally had to yield and retire—but fighting manfully—to the position from which their advance had been made. Ector and Wilson, moved forward at the same time in support of Colquitt, unable to render any substantial relief, were likewise obliged to retire.‡ Walt-

---

* Gist's Brigade joined that morning from Rome, Ga., and Walker's troops were now divided into two divisions, Liddell's and Gist's, the latter composed of Ector's, Gist's, (under Colonel P. H. Colquitt, Fourth Georgia,) and Wilson's brigades.

† No more excellent soldier than Colquitt fell at Chickamauga. As a colonel, he had shown what could be achieved with proper care, military instincts, and views of discipline in bringing volunteer troops up to the highest soldierly standard of regulars.

‡ See Wilson's Report, Battle of Chickamauga, p. 181.

hall's Brigade, Liddell's Division, sent leftward in support of Brigadier-General Polk, encountered speedily an overpowering flank and front fire, before which it too had to give way with heavy loss.* Nor did the remaining brigade—Govan's—meet with more success. Detached, like the others, without support or apparent coöperation, to try to get rearward, on the right of the Federals, beyond the highway, it likewise, after penetrating some distance, was presently obliged to recede rapidly to escape destruction.† And thus, after an hour of gallant, costly, bootless fighting, Walker's troops, like their comrades of the right wing, stood repulsed or baffled despite the utmost degree of courage.‡

During these operations of the right wing, Stewart received orders from General Bragg, about eleven A.M., to attack with his division, one brigade of which—Brown's—he immediately threw forward, as it chanced at the same time and in line with Wood's Brigade, of Cleburne's Division. Clayton's and Bates's brigades, drawn up as a second line, soon followed, facing toward the south-west, as a support, and both lines sturdily rushed onward at a double-quick, in the face of an appalling fusilade, blended with grape and canister. But the troops rightward of Brown did not keep up long, and, breaking, left his right flank bare to so blighting a cross-fire from small-arms and artillery, from behind breastworks within fifty yards, that the two regiments on the right of this gallant brigade,

---

* Here the brave and accomplished Lieutenant-Colonel Reynolds, Thirtieth Mississippi, was killed.

† See Liddell's Report.

‡ Surely, it was not sound tactics thus to disintegrate Walker and throw his brigades separately into action, and no other result could reasonably have been anticipated than what happened. Really, they were not engaged as "supports," but *substitutes* for brigades equally strong, that had just been beaten by the same enemy in the same formidable positions. General Walker seems to have had the correct view as to the proper conduct of affairs on the occasion. See his Official Report, Battle of Chickamauga, p. 57.

grievously shattered, could only be rallied on the position from which it had advanced,* whither the other regiments were necessarily withdrawn, though they had penetrated beyond the road and turned the battery which had been played so fearfully upon their comrades. Bates's and Clayton s Brigades, encountering the same formidable fire, were soon so cut down that the whole division was checked and withdrawn a short distance rearward, under cover, to escape destruction. Here, however, in a little while, it was reorganized and reformed, with Bates on the right, Clayton in the centre, and Brown's Brigade, under Colonel Cook, Thirty-second Tennessee, on the left.

Preston's Division, of the same corps, had likewise moved against the enemy at the same time with Stewart, Trigg's Brigade in advance, followed by Gracie and Kelly somewhat later. Their first field of conflict that day was on the Brotherton farm, with a strong Federal force in position in some fields northward of the house, whence the enemy opened with so vigorous and sustained a fire of shot and shell that the further advance of Preston in that direction was not attempted for several hours.

Johnson's Division, which lay leftward of Stewart, supported by Law's two brigades, had thrown up cover during the night. About the time Breckinridge and Forrest began the attack on the right, Johnson's skirmishers were driven in, and then followed a spirited attack upon his lines, but which he easily repelled by a prompt, combined use of small-arms and artillery. And when Stewart was ordered to attack, Johnson received similar orders from General Hood. His immediate adversary was found posted behind several lines of breastworks along the highway in the vicinity of Brotherton's house, with other

----

* General Brown was here disabled by a severe wound.

lines in front and to the left of it, with a battery in an open field southward of the house. Traversing a wood swept by a scathing fire of musketry and artillery for some six hundred yards, the left of the division drove the Federals from around the house, killing and capturing a large number. Posting a battery in a favorable position, which opened frontward and rightward, Johnson again moved forward with his infantry upon a line of works still ahead. His advance was greeted with a fire so sustained and galling that McNair's Brigade wavered for a moment and began to fall back, but was quickly rallied and led forward again by its officers. The whole division, closely supported by Law, now pressed on with such vigor that the enemy broke and left their works precipitately, severely punished, however, especially by a fire from Johnson's left—several Texan and Tennessee battalions, under Majors Robertson and Vanzant. Pushing steadily the advantage gained, Johnson, keeping his division well in hand, had now carried it some distance through the forest westward of the road, and emerged upon some open ground and fields, over which the Federals were falling back under cover of several batteries planted around the crest of a ridge in front and on the right, while leftward another battery, on an eminence southwest of Dyer's House, bore upon and harassed Johnson's left and front. The scene at this moment is described as having been one of peculiar exciting interest. In the language of a prominent participant : " The resolute and impetuous charge, the rush of our heavy columns, sweeping out from the shadow and gloom of the forest into the open fields, the onward dash of artillery and mounted men, the retreat of the foe, the shouts of the hosts of our army, the dust, the smoke, the noise of firearms, the whistling balls and grape-shot and of bursting shell, made up a battle scene of unsurpassed grandeur."

In three lines Johnson passed on with an impetus that was

irresistible, and the enemy's centre was shattered into many fragments.

Simultaneously with Johnson, Hindman's Division* likewise advanced at a double-quick, and became hotly engaged within four hundred yards with some five or six Federal brigades posted on very strong ground; but just at a juncture, it would seem, when McCook, commanding Federals in that quarter, had been ordered to deplete that wing by sending two brigades at once, and a third soon thereafter, to reënforce the left, even at the expense of withdrawing their whole right.† Deas and Manigault led in Hindman's onset, with Anderson supporting. Dashing with a splendid impetuosity at the breastworks confronting them, these were carried. Behind was a gently rising ridge, upon which were twelve guns in battery, and another line of infantry cover on the slope of the hill in their front. Resuming the offensive, the Confederates carried this obstacle also after a short struggle, in the course of which Manigault's Brigade, brought under a severe enfilading fire of artillery and small-arms, suffered greatly, and was staggered for a time, but, rallying, as became their accomplished Brigadier, and their own martial virtues and repute, resumed the onslaught and seized the breastworks in their front and the Federal artillery in that part of the line. Deas too, in pressing onward to the summit of the hill, was brought to bay before a battery, when the weight of Anderson's Brigade was thrown into the balance, and the position was carried, the artillery all captured, and the Federals either killed, captured, or dispersed, not to reorganize on the field.

---

* Anderson's, Dea's, Manigault's brigades, 501 officers, 5621 bayonets and artillerists, and 12 guns.

† Two brigades, Davis's Division, Sheridan's Division, and Wilder's Brigade repeating rifles, or some six brigades at least, with say 9000 effective men and 36 guns.—*Vide Reb. Rec.* VIL Doc. 43, p. 234.

Longstreet's entire wing was now engaged. Handled for the most part with more concert and concentration than the right, its assaults fell with greater weight and effect upon the enemy in its front, embracing two of McCook's and two of Crittenden's divisions, with Wilder's picked brigade and a numerous artillery.

On the Confederate right, the attack beginning by divisions "in succession," as ordered, and made in single lines, was subsequently maintained with little unity of aim and offensive means, while Rosecrans accumulated his masses there to resist and foil, "at all hazards," his adversary's obvious but meagrely sustained purpose — to cut off his retreat upon Chattanooga.

Resuming the narrative of operations on that part of the field, at the time that Breckinridge and Forrest had been balked in their unsupported effort to turn the Federal left, we have first to relate that, about eleven A.M., Pegram, in observation toward Rossville, reported to Forrest the near approach of Granger from that direction. Fronting this movement promptly with Armstrong's men dismounted and sixteen guns, (two borrowed from Breckinridge,) while Pegram harassed the left flank, Forrest became quickly and warmly engaged with this new enemy, and forced Granger to deflect some distance westward from the road, but was too weak to prevent his final junction with Thomas, to whom were thus carried 4500 fresh bayonets and twelve guns.

After this there was a lull in the operations of the Confederates throughout their entire right wing for more than two hours, or as late as half-past three P.M.—two hours of as precious time as were ever squandered on a battle-field, while Longstreet was driving the Federals from every position within his reach on the left.

We are definitely told by Generals Hill and Cleburne it was half-past three P.M. when General Polk ordered a general advance ; but again there was delay, delay caused by the failure of General Jackson (Cheatham's Division) to place his brigade in a gap in the line to which it had been repeatedly ordered, and as early as midday.*

In this advance, so inexplicably postponed as late as about four P.M., Forrest's command, operating, dismounted, as rifle-men, was on the right. Breckinridge came next, on the left, with two of Cheatham's brigades filling the gap between his left and Cleburne. Very soon, from Forrest on the right to Cleburne's left, the right wing of the Confederates was again fiercely engaged with Thomas, who had now accumulated under his command, be it noted, his own four divisions, two divisions and at least two brigades of Crittenden's, and John-son's Division of McCook's, with Granger's 4500 bayonets, or more than eight divisions, mustering quite 35,000 combat-tants, notwithstanding the heavy casualties of preceding con-flicts.†

Forrest, pressing forward westwardly toward the highway to Chattanooga, found a strong Federal force drawn up be-hind a fence that skirted it on the eastward, supporting a bat-tery of six guns, which swept the field between his men and the Federals. Halting only long enough to reconnoitre, he deployed a skirmish line in front in the field in question and established the rifled section of Huggins's Battery in the same position, from which they were brought to bear upon the Federal battery as Armstrong's Division charged with im-petuosity, and the enemy gave back to another line some two hundred yards westward, but not until they had inflicted a sensible loss upon the assailants. Establishing his line in

---

* General Hill's Official Report.— *Land We Love*, Vol. I. No. 6, p. 401.

† *Vide* Reports of Generals McCook, Crittenden, Granger, and Hazen.—*Reb.*

Rec. Docs. 43 and 184, pp. 233-4-8, 529-534. These divisions before the battle numbered an effective aggregate of 45,190, infantry and artillery.

the road just abandoned by his adversary, Forrest formed his men under an angry fire from Federal musketry and field-pieces, that thinned his ranks to a fearful extent. But, nevertheless, there was no faltering with these doughty Tennesseeans, the men of Forrest's old brigade and of his old regiment, nor on the part of their brave compeers of Armstrong's own brigade. They retorted the fire which they had provoked with surpassing spirit, and pressed upon the foe slowly but steadily. Dibrell, adjoining the infantry on his left, had gained a position within seventy-five yards of the Federal battery, and Huggins was westward of the road, when the former noticed and reported to Forrest that the Confederates on his left had been repulsed and were falling back, uncovering his flank.* Withdrawing his own battery rearward to a ridge, Dibrell was now ordered to hold his ground, but was soon enfiladed by the Federals, who had pressed the infantry back ; and Forrest, too, had now to recede to shelter from the tempest behind the embankment that bordered a ditch in the centre of the field just west of the highway. But, happily, at the same time his artillery opened with such salutary effect that the further advance of the enemy was stayed. In this phase of the combat the Fourth and the Ninth (Biffle's) Tennessee suffered more than the other regiments ; but all were alike conspicuous for the most admirable courage, while the Fourth Tennessee, under McLemore, and the Eighth, under Captain McGuinis, maintained their stand after the infantry on the left gave way until they were almost enveloped by the enemy, and were ordered back by Generals Forrest and Dibrell, and but for the mishap to the infantry at that juncture,

---

* Biffle rejoined with his regiment (Ninth Tennessee) during the battle from arduous, stirring detached service of several months in West-Tennessee, and took part in the combat.

in a few moments Dibrell assuredly would have carried the battery almost within his grasp.

In the mean time, as we have said, there had been a general advance of the Confederate right wing. Breckinridge's Division, as in the morning, taking the right of the infantry conjoined with Liddell's Division, made a superb assault upon the Federal left, while Cleburne pressed strenuously forward in the centre, with Cheatham's Division moving close behind as a reserve. At first the resistance was obstinate, and at points favorable for the enemy. Thomas, strongly posted, well sheltered by breastworks, and superior in numbers to his assailants,* made a stout, bloody fight to the last tenable moment; and on his left, where he had massed his forces in heavy lines, the Confederates, as we have seen, faltered, and, giving way, uncovered Dibrell's Brigade, (Forrest's dismounted cavalry,) and forced them to fall back to the embankment we have mentioned. Seeing this misadventure, Forrest, leaving his own men thus well intrenched, hurried leftward, and, throwing himself among the infantry, aided their officers to rally them. This, indeed, was speedily attained, the offensive was finally and handsomely renewed at all points, and the Federal lines *were surmounted in all their formidable extent by the onrushing Confederates.* Just before this, however, it is proper to mention that it was known to the Federals under Thomas that a disastrous rout had befallen their right, and this doubtless aided somewhat to shorten the struggle and added to the disorder that now supervened for the most part in their ranks.

In this last and crowning attack, Brigadier-General Lucius Polk fought his brigade, of Cleburne's Division, with brilliant

---

* Thomas, we repeat, had still intact behind his lines, except from battle casualties, eight divisions. See his own report and that of Hazen as cited before, p. 341.

efficiency, and, aided by Keys's and in part by Douglass's batteries, run into position by hand, carried three lines of breastworks in succession ;* while at the same time, far and wide, the field was the theatre of acts of heroism in officers of all grades and of the private soldiery that were never surpassed.

The entire Federal army was now to be seen by the last rays of daylight rapidly escaping in swarms up the ravines and slopes of Missionary Ridge. But no pursuit was organized or ordered, and, darkness being at hand, the Confederates of that wing, including Forrest's command, bivouacked on the ground, very much where the close of the battle had carried them.

Returning to the Confederate left wing, it remains to relate of events in that quarter that, after McCook had been routed from his early positions, as we have previously narrated, an impetuous, concerted pressure was maintained by all of Longstreet's Divisions, so that little time or opportunity was given to the Federals to rally and mass for a combined resistance, that might otherwise have resulted. Howbeit, some five brigades, at least, of the Twentieth Corps, McCook's, gained a footing on a wooded height—a spur of Missionary Ridge—between the farms of Villetoe and Snodgrass. Johnson's Division was brought up to assail this position, supported by Hindman on the south, while Kershaw, Preston, and Stewart attacked from the northward. Buckner also carried up and brought to bear with his troops twelve guns, and Johnson was effectively aided by Dent's and Everett's batteries. The struggle was stubborn and the results varying, with fluctuations of success and check for the Confederates for several

---

* *Vide* General Cleburne's Official Report. Captains Beard and George Moore, Third and Fifth Confederate, fell at this time.

hours, or until about five P.M., when, completely flanking the enemy, the Confederates, with a simultaneous onset and loud shouts, sweeping all before them, were complete masters of the field, and their adversaries finally and completely routed. Many prisoners were captured on the spot and a number of guns. It was now sunset, and Longstreet ordered his forces to bivouac where they were, so that stragglers might be collected, ammunition-boxes refilled, and all be held ready for a vigorous pursuit on the following morning. Among the results accomplished by that wing on the 20th were the capture of 40 cannon, some 3000 prisoners, and 10 regimental colors. Its losses were commensurate with these satisfactory achievements, being 1089 officers and men killed, 6406 wounded, and 272 missing, or an aggregate of 7867 casualties out of 22,882 officers and men engaged.*

Of the operations of this day little else remains to be told than that, during the action, the main body of Wheeler's Cavalry was assembled on the east bank of the Chickamauga, at Glass's Mills, far to the southward of the field, and was there confronted for a time by a Federal cavalry force with artillery, which Wheeler assailed, by crossing the stream dismounted, and drove off with some few captures. At three P.M., moving up to Lee and Gordon's Mills, there too he had a brush, and, following up with spirit, overtook and captured about 1000 prisoners from the enemy, now flying from Longstreet's troops over the mountain.†

COMMENTARIES.

Reserving for a future occasion and another work an elaborate examination of the strategy of this campaign and the tactics of the battle of Chickamauga, we shall restrict present

---

* Longstreet's Official Report.   † Wheeler's Official Report.

commentary to a few observations that appear to be essential here.

1. General Bragg's correspondence with his subordinates in regard to the operation projected against the part of Thomas's Corps, isolated and imperiled in McLemore's Cove, as given in his official report of the battle of Chickamauga, suppressed the more important parts of that correspondence, and is therefore calculated to mislead. General Bragg's information at first, when he ordered the movement, was correct—that is, that the force exposed was about four or five thousand. Unfortunately, he permitted that estimate to be unsettled in his mind, and displaced by apprehensions that possibly a much stronger force might be there—in fact, one that jeopardized the force he had detached to crush it. Hence, through his Chief of Staff, General Mackall, he wrote two dispatches (not given in his report) to General Hindman, evincing that apprehension in clear terms. One, written after his arrival at Dug Gap, as late at eleven A.M. on the 11th, is in these words : " If " you find the enemy in such force as to make an attack im- " prudent, *fall back at once on Lafayette* by Catlett's Gap, from "which obstructions have been removed. Send your deter- " mination at once, and act as promptly." In the other note, Hindman was thus addressed : " The enemy, estimated at " twelve or fifteen thousand, is forming line in front of this " place,* (Dug Gap.) Nothing heard of you since Captain " Pressman, engineer, was with you. The General is most " anxious, and wishes to hear from you by couriers once an " hour. . . . The enemy are advancing from Graysville " to Lafayette. Dispatch is necessary to us."

Unfortunately, General Hindman was misled by the very boldness of Negley's movement, and regarded it as a blind to

---

* That is, Negley's and Baird's Divisions, 11,000 strong.

mask the movements of the main body of the enemy meanwhile, and so suggested to his chief, who, however, from specific information ought to have comprehended it was not so,
and that the force in McLemore's Cove, at most, could not be
greater than Thomas's Corps—(it was actually less than half
of it)—FOR HE KNEW THAT MCCOOK WAS AT ALPINE, AND
CRITTENDEN QUITE AS FAR OFF NORTHWARD. At half-past
seven P.M., on the 10th, he had the right appreciation of the
situation; for an Adjutant-General of his staff wrote to Hindman as follows: "*The enemy is now divided. Our force at
or near Lafayette is superior to that of the enemy. It is important now to move vigorously and crush him.*" (Signed,
Kinloch Falconer.)

But unhappily, he could neither keep this state of affairs
in his view nor square his operations by it. He vacillated
and left a subordinate to decide, who did not—could not—
have the same knowledge of the actual situation that he had
as General in Chief.

2. Unquestionably, General Bragg is not alone responsible
for the failure to strike and crush Crittenden's Corps on the
occasion we have described. But it would appear that he did
not give General Polk the order to move against that corps
until six P.M. on the 12th, whereas he knew of its movements
at midnight (if not earlier) on the 10th.* He, therefore,
wasted *forty-two* precious hours before he decided upon doing
what was surely apparent to the veriest tyro in war operations.
Crittenden, in fact, had already taken position at Lee and
Gordon's Mills. Bragg had now, however, subordinated
operations against the enemy in McLemore's Cove to the
attack upon Crittenden; for, in his orders to General Polk, he
expressly urged that, Crittenden being crushed, "we can turn

---

* *Vide* letter of Colonel Brent, A. A. G., to General Hindman, in General
Bragg's Official Report, p. 9.

on the force in the cove." That he knew the enemy was still divided is apparent ; for, in a subsequent note, Colonel Brent observes to General Polk : "The enemy is approaching from the south, and it is highly important that your attack in the morning should be quick and decided." General Bragg expresses in his report his disappointment that his orders for the attack were not executed on the morning of the 13th, but does not communicate his reasons for not concentrating his whole force, as he might have done, either that afternoon or, in fact, for at least the next three days, upon the same corps (Crittenden's) at Lee and Gordon's Mills. Nor does he mention why he preferred to wait until Rosecrans had brought up his three widely-separated corps and united them (not sooner than the 17th) at and south of Lee and Gordon's Mills ! Bragg, assuredly, was not waiting for reën-forcements.

3. Granger's movement should have been intercepted. Nothing had been easier than the capture of that entire force. Forrest kept his superiors promptly advised of its approach from Rossville, and Thomas was too busily engaged to spare any succor had Granger been attacked in proper force. To hold his own ground was all that Thomas could do.

4. An examination of the returns of Confederate killed and wounded, of the troops engaged on the right, will show one of the bloodiest engagements in the annals of war. Wilson's Brigade lost fifty per cent, and the average was fully thirty-six per cent. This was because divisions were thrown into action and fought by driblets. Nor was that all : largely superior in that quarter of the field, as we have shown—Thomas having eight divisions at his command, the Federals also were intrenched, and against these intrenchments the Confederates were hurled in charge after charge, when, if properly handled, they might in full force have turned

these works as was done at one time by Generals Breckinridge and Forrest.

5. It will scarcely escape the general reader that General Bragg was singularly inert on the morning of the 21st of September, not to speak of the evening of the battle, in following up and pressing his adversary, of whose utterly demoralized condition, as has been seen, he had explicit information. In the conclusion of his report of the operations of his own corps at the battle of Shiloh, he uses this significant language : "In "this result we have a valuable lesson by which we should "profit—never on a battle-field to lose a moment's time, but, "leaving the killed, wounded, and spoils to those whose spe- "cial business it is to care for them, TO PRESS ON WITH EVERY "AVAILABLE MAN, GIVING A PANIC-STRICKEN AND RETREATING "FOE NO TIME TO RALLY, AND REAPING ALL THE BENEFITS OF "A SUCCESS NEVER COMPLETE UNTIL EVERY ENEMY IS KILLED, "WOUNDED, OR CAPTURED." It is unfortunate that he could not remember his own fluent precept when he had so signal and early an opportunity to illustrate its justness ; and by his course has rather illustrated once more, in a notable manner, how much easier it is to preach than practice.

CHAPTER XII.

General Forrest pursued Enemy upon Missionary Ridge—Observes and reports state of Tumult and Disorder in Chattanooga—Urges immediate Advance upon Enemy—Obtained View of inaction on Field of late Battle of Confederates—Reports by Dispatches the Confusion among Federals—Major McLemore penetrated to within three miles of Chattanooga, and captures Prisoners—Pegram threatened Rossville, but too weak to attack Enemy in strong Position—Enemy work vigorously in trenches around Chattanooga—Forrest recalled to Red House Bridge—Army in motion—Forrest again threw his Force in Chattanooga Valley—Drove in Pickets and occupied Approaches— Dibrell seized Point of Lookout Mountain—Obliged to maintain Position by severe Fighting—Forrest's Command withdrawn to Tyner's Station—Ordered to meet Enemy crossing Hiawassee—Combat at Crossing of Hiawassee—Pursuit, with Skirmish, through Athens and Philadelphia to Loudon, Tennessee—Captured Federal Camp at Philadelphia—Received Orders to return to Cleveland —Ordered to transfer all Troops, save Dibrell's Brigade, to General Wheeler, for Expedition—Regarding Order in derogation of his Position, Forrest presents his views in writing to General Bragg—On Leave of Absence—Interview with President Davis—Assigned to a Command of Cavalry in North-Mississippi and West-Tennessee.

September 21st—November 15th, 1863.

GENERAL Forrest had his command in the saddle at four A.M. on the 21st, and taking Dibrell's Brigade, at once ascended Missionary Ridge. Throwing the Fourth Tennessee—under McLemore—across into the valley, westward, with the other regiments he moved through the woods, along the crest, northward, in close pursuit, while Armstrong swept along the slopes, eastward, toward Rossville, with Pegram still on his right in the same direction, and north-eastward also. Dibrell coming upon the Federal rear, captured several hundred, and drove the rest into Rossville.

Climbing a tree, about seven P.M., Forrest sought to satisfy himself of the situation, and discovered the enemy in a disordered retreat into Chattanooga, which lay in full view beneath him, a scene of wild chaos and tumult. This state of affairs was immediately communicated, in written dispatches, both to Generals Bragg·and Polk, upon whom it was urged that an immediate advance must be successful, while every moment was precious, or, to use his own language in one of these notes, "every hour lost was the loss of one thousand men." Meanwhile, similar information had been communicated by Lieutenant-Colonel Paul Anderson, of Wheeler's Cavalry, who had also been thrown out on Missionary Ridge by General Longstreet to McFarland's Gap, whence he reported by an officer, and several couriers subsequently, that the enemy were rushing toward, and into, Chattanooga, a disorganized multitude.

After some time spent in these observations and reports, Forrest again moved forward over very rough ground, still capturing numerous stragglers, and finding the woods thickly strewn with arms and accoutrements, ambulances and caissons, wagons and their teams. Among the captured was a vidette, who pointed out a Federal officer in a tall tree, which had been conveniently fitted up as an observatory, commanding a complete view for miles in all directions. Displacing this observer from his lofty perch, Forrest, taking his position and his glasses, had immediately under his eyes the whole situation. Rearward, on the field of the recent conflicts, the whole Confederate, army still lay torpid at the Federal breastworks, as if gorged with carnage, and languid from the ardent battle-fever of the day before ; while frontward he saw that the pontoon-bridge across the Tennessee was broken, and the streets of Chattanooga were blocked up with Federal troops, impacted with artillery and caissons, ambulances, baggage-wagons, and beef-cattle, a floundering, tumultuary mass. This state of affairs he likewise communicated to Generals Bragg and Polk, in repeated dispatches, dictated to his staff from his outlook.   After which, descending, he again moved north-ward, to a point about five miles in a line from Chattanooga, and overlooking the town. Here he found in position a strong Federal force, one too strong to be assaulted by his men.

In the mean time, McLemore had led the Fourth Tennessee so eagerly forward, that he had penetrated within three miles of Chattanooga, in the midst of large bodies of Federals, who, however, were so panic-stricken as not to recognize his expo-sure, and were only anxious to get to the river-bank.   Seeing the danger, however, Forrest recalled his Lieutenant, who came slowly back, full-handed with prisoners.

During these events, Armstrong and Pegram had become sharply engaged in front of the gap at Rossville, where Tho-mas had concentrated the wreck of Rosecrans's forces that had preserved a semblance of organization, but were able to effect nothing substantial up to four P.M., when Forrest was informed by General Bragg that he had put his infantry in movement toward Chattanooga, by the Red House Bridge road, at which point he would be found that night, and all the approaches to which were to be picketed by his cavalry.

In the mean time, the sounds were audible from Chatta-nooga of vigorous labor on the fortifications, and large work-ing parties were already to be plainly seen engaged in their trenches, as Forrest quit his position of observation on the ridge, and descended toward the Chickamauga, in the quarter designated. He was deeply chargrined and depressed in view of the strange delay and inaction, since the battle, in following up a great victory ; for he could but apprehend that all chances for substantial profit were gradually fading away.

BRIG. GEN. JAS. R. CHALMERS
Com^{ng} Division

His men and horses had now been for nearly three days almost without food or forage ; so, establishing his picket-lines as directed, he fell back several miles in pursuit of sub-sistence ; and at ten o'clock P.M., rode to General Bragg's headquarters. The Commander-in-Chief, receiving him gra-ciously, had much to say in commendation of his action during the battle ; after which, Forrest was directed to hold his com-mand in readiness, next morning, for a general advance on Chattanooga.

At eight o'clock A.M., 22d, Forrest again assembled his whole force on Missionary Ridge ; but after some delay, he could discover no traces of a material advance by the main body of the army. Yet, with characteristic disposition for action, he did not hesitate to descend into the valley of the Chattanooga, where he soon came in collision both with Federal cavalry and infantry pickets, all of whom were driven promptly back to within half a mile of Chattanooga itself ; this was done with his men dismounted, and extending in a line with a scope of nearly two miles, sweeping all before it. Having achieved this, he took up positions covering and across the roads from Chattanooga, in the direction of Rossville and Cleveland, and detached Dibrell with his brigade, to seize and hold the road around the northern end of Lookout Mountain, for which Dibrell had a stout fight, losing several officers, and some fifty or more of his men killed and wounded.

These movements having been effected and positions taken, at one P.M. McLaws came up with a division of Longstreet's Corps. Forrest, calling at once on General McLaws, pro-posed they should adventure an attack in the still demoralized condition of the enemy.* This the latter did not feel author-

---

* In illustration of the condition in which the Federals were left, we may instance the fact that Forrest, on the 22d, rode, with a score of his brave ri-ders, to within seventy-five yards of a work commanding the Rossville road,

ized to attempt under his orders, which prescribed picket service simply.

Meanwhile, several serious attempts had been made to dislodge Dibrell, which had only been defeated by hard, brave blows, Dibrell keeping his regiments dismounted.*

It was now apparent that no general operations against the place were to be undertaken that day—the second after the battle ; and as Dibrell was short of ammunition, and his men and horses almost famished, Forrest asked that the brigade might be relieved by one of infantry. With that, too, General McLaws felt unable to comply under his orders. The position was too important and valuable to be given up, so Dibrell was left to maintain it until twelve M. on the 23d, by which time it was recognized by his superiors that Forrest's Cavalry required some relief from outpost service, and an opporunity to find food and forage. For that purpose, therefore, the command was withdrawn to Tyner's Station, on the East-Chickamauga, nine or ten miles from Chattanooga.

Here, however, after twenty-four hours' rest and relaxation from actual contact with the enemy, orders were received to detach Pegram, with Rucker's Legion and Scott's Brigade of his division, to picket the Tennessee river, eastward from Chattanooga, on that flank, to the mouth of the Hiawassee, some thirty miles or more ; and Forrest, taking Armstrong's and Davidson's Brigades, was to move beyond Cleveland to meet and check a movement on the part of Burnside, as was supposed, looking to a junction with Rosecrans. At Cleveland he was also reënforced by Hodge's Brigade, some eight hundred strong, stationed in that quarter. The enemy were reported to be at Charleston, twelve miles distant, throwing

---

and so uncertain was the aim of the volley provoked, that not a man was hurt, though Forrest's horse was shot.

* Fourth, Eighth, Tenth, and Eleventh Tennessee regiments, and Shaw's Battalion.

up a work on the east bank of the Hiawassee. Detaching Davidson, rightward, to cross that stream above the place, and Armstrong to pass it at Kincannon's Ferry, some six miles below, and thence to get in rear on a road between Charleston and Athens, Forrest, after giving his lieutenants time to make the necessary circuits, as he supposed, moved by the direct road with Dibrell and Hodge, and Morton's and Huggins's Batteries. Federal pickets, met four miles in advance of the river, were brushed back to their main force, drawn up on the west bank of the Hiawassee. An attack was immediately ordered, for Forrest wastes little time in his operations, and, after a short but sturdy resistance, the Federals were forced to retire to their fortifications, eastward of the stream, which is some two hundred and fifty yards broad at this point, but shallow, and with an excellent ford, across which, under cover, secured by eight pieces of artillery that had been previously placed in a favorable position, the Confederates dashed boldly in face of the Federals. Dismounting his men as soon as they reached the other bank, they were formed as infantry, and pushed up, with the loss of eight or ten men killed and wounded before the Federals abandoned the position in rapid retreat toward Athens, along the railroad, closely pursued.

Armstrong, failing to get in their rear, was able, however, to strike their left flank at or about Breville, and gave them an exciting chase for the next five or six miles, his own men constantly intermixed with the enemy in the ardor of the pursuit, and some sixty of the Federals were killed or captured. Dibrell and Hodge, likewise, caught up with the Federal rear at Athens, where the provost-guard was captured by Armstrong. The enemy were now reënforced by Woolford's Brigade, but they, nevertheless, made little or no stand, and the pursuit was continued beyond Sweetwater, between which and Philadelphia, Dibrell's Brigade, just as it was taking the advance for the day, became engaged in an animated combat

with a strong cavalry force that suddenly made battle. Mc-
Lemore at this was deployed forward into line at a gallop,
under a heavy fire, in an open field, with a section of Huggin's
Battery, while the other regiments were promptly disposed
for the emergency of a serious affair ; but the Federals declined to accept battle, and quickly made rearward again, as
rapidly as before, and as rapidly followed, to Philadelphia, and
thence on to Loudon, where the Eighth, Ninth, and Eleventh
Tennessee came, to some extent, in a conflict with the enemy,
having several men wounded, respectively, but none killed.
At Philadelphia, the Federal camp was captured, with all their
cooking utensils on the fire. Among the incidents of this
pursuit, one can not be left unrecorded, for it is a signal, yet
not extreme, illustration of the spirit that animated the youth
of the South throughout the war—a spirit that, but for
astounding, perverse mismanagement, must have insured the
success of the struggle of the Southern people for independence. As McLemore charged up, under fire, with the Fourth
Tennessee, as we have related, at a gallop, the pony of young
Neil S. Brown,* a lad of seventeen years, was shot in the
front ranks of the regiment. Horse and rider fell together to
the ground, but the gallant youth, springing to his feet, rifle
in hand, and not halting a moment, ran forward in even line
with his older, mounted comrades, and took an active, conspicuous part in the brief fight that happened.

The pursuit was not extended beyond Loudon, orders having been received by Forrest to withdraw his command to
Cleveland, and transfer all but one brigade to General Wheeler, for an expedition to the rear of, and upon, Rosecrans's communications. Giving the necessary orders, on arriving at
Cleveland, for proper compliance with the instructions of the

---

* Son of Governor Neil S. Brown, of Tennessee.

Commanding General,* Forrest then addressed himself immediately to the task of reorganizing the brigade left him, which
had become essential after so long a period of hard marches,
frequent combats, severe, prolonged outpost service in face of
the enemy, and a great battle. To that end, he issued comprehensive orders, prescribing duties and preparations for future service, while stringently proscribing straggling, depredations, and all irregularities.

Circumstances connected with this reduction of his command gave it so much the bearing of injustice and disparage-
ment, that General Forrest felt it best to frankly present this
aspect of it to his superior ; both in writing, and likewise in a
personal interview did he do this, going to army headquarters
a day or two subsequently for that purpose. He had a conversation with General Bragg, who assured him that his old
command should be recomposed at the conclusion of Wheeler's
expedition. With this understanding, and there being no
service impending of importance on the immediate flank
where his present force was posted, Forrest now applied for
a leave of absence for ten days, to go to Lagrange, Georgia,
on the railroad, southward, to see his wife, for the first time
for eighteen months.

On the 5th of October, however, when at Lagrange, he received an order dated the 3d, placing him hereafter under the
command of General Wheeler. In view of assurances, so recent, of a different arrangement, made upon a statement of
circumstances and occurrences connected with their previous
service together, in the ill-fated expedition against Dover, in
February, 1863, General Forrest was extremely dissatisfied ;
for he felt that his usefulness as a cavalry soldier, if again

---

* Dibrell's Brigade and Huggins's gades were directed to report to Gene-
Battery were selected to remain. Arm- ral Wheeler at Cottonport.
strong's, Davidson's, and Hodge's Bri-

placed under Wheeler, must be destroyed.   He therefore determined to resign his commission as a brigadier-general,
and seek to serve his country in some other sphere, in which
he might be more efficient than he could possibly hope to be
under conditions, as arranged—so unexpectedly to him—by
General Bragg.

A month before, many of the prominent people of West-
Tennessee and North-Mississippi had made appeals to him of
such urgency to come to their section, and attempt to assemble their scattered resources for defense and offense, that he
made, at the time, an application for assignment to that field
of duty ; and in resigning, it was his purpose to go thither, confident that he could soon be at the head there of a fine command, the main elements of which were, as yet, substantially
lost to the service.

The President of the Confederate States was at the headquarters of the army when Forrest's resignation reached it,
and wrote him an autograph letter, in gracious and grace-
ful language, announcing that he could not accept his resignation, nor dispense with his services, and appointed an interview at Montgomery, Alabama, some days later, on his return
from Mississippi, whither he was about to go.

At the time designated, General Forrest repaired to Montgomery, and met the President, with whom he had a prolonged,
characteristic, and satisfactory conversation, resulting in an
assurance that he should be transferred to North-Mississippi,
with such forces as General Bragg could possibly spare ; and
Mr. Davis wrote to that effect to that officer.   The President
also gave expression to some general views as to the conduct
of operations in that quarter ; after which, Forrest returned at
once to army headquarters, going in the *suite* of Mr. Davis as
far as Atlanta.

Promptly seeking audience with General Bragg, Forrest
was promised that he should take to his new field of com-

mand and action, in addition to his escort company, McDonald's and Woodward's Battalion and Morton's Battery ; but on the following morning, on receiving the written order in the premises, it proved that Woodward's Battalion was withheld. This force, all told, embraced three hundred and ten rank and file,* and four guns, with which he repaired immediately to Rome, where two days were spent in fitting it up for the march across the country, *via* Talladega, Tuscaloosa, and Columbus, Mississippi, to Okolona, where it arrived on or about the 18th of November, 1863.

Taking the railway, *via* Selma, Forrest proceeded as soon as possible to the same point, so that he might at once begin the assemblage of the means for such operations as he hoped, before long, to set on foot in that region.

His command, remaining with the army, parted with their leader with profound regret, especially the brigade composed of the Fourth, Eighth, Ninth, Tenth, and Eleventh Tennessee Cavalry. These regiments he had organized, and commanded through his West-Tennessee campaign in December, 1862, at the combat at Thompson's Station, and in the pursuit and capture of Streight. Always successful under his lead, they had acquired so supreme a confidence in their General, and his genius for cavalry operations, that they had come to regard him as without an equal in their arm of the service ; and with this were blended feelings of strong personal attachment, though he had ever been rigid and stringent—nay, exacting with them, in all substantial matters of soldierly duty and conduct, to the verge even, at times, of transient discontent. He had led them in their charges, had exposed his life in their

---

* Escort company—2 officers, 5 non-commissioned officers, 60 privates, present. McDonald's Battalion, 16 officers, 148 privates, present ; absent, 5 officers, 91 enlisted men. Morton's Battery, 4 officers, 67 enlisted men, present ; or effective total, 280 ; aggregate, 310 present.

sight, repeatedly, to secure knowledge essential for the success of operations in which they were to be employed. They were, therefore, unwilling to serve under another commander in his stead if it could be averted ; and to that end a respectful petition was addressed to the Commanding General, praying they might be transferred with him, if possibly consistent with the necessities of the service. This transfer, however, General Bragg doubtless was not able to make, in view of the need for good cavalry with his own army.

CHAPTER XIII.

Beginning of a New Epoch in General Forrest's Career—Welcomed to New Field by General J. E. Johnston—Undertook an Expedition to glean the Military Resources of West-Tennessee—Smallness of his Available Command—Celerity and Boldness of Movement to Jackson—Joined by 3000 Unarmed Men—Formidable Plans of the Enemy for his Interception—Combat at Estenaula—Large Quantities of Subsistence and other Supplies Collected—Fight at Jack's Creek—Brilliant Affair of Forrest's Escort with Federal Regiment—Near Approach of Numerous Hostile Bodies of Troops—Sharp Conflict near Summerville—Handsome Coup de Main and Passage of Wolf River at Lafayette—Demonstration upon Collierville—Established Force around Como, Miss.—Commentaries.

From November 15th to December 31st, 1863.

W E now enter upon a new epoch in the military career of General Forrest, and upon the chronicle, too, of operations made, in the main, with troops other than those with whom he had laid the broad, deep, stable foundation of the reputation built up in the course of the war by " Forrest's Cavalry," among enemies as well as friends.

As related in the preceding chapter, Forrest reached Okolona on or about the 15th of November, and his small body of veterans a few days earlier. Meanwhile, on his way thither, he had met the Department Commander, General Joe Johnston, at Meridian, and explained, in full, his views and the scope of projected operations. That officer, giving him a cordial welcome within his department, expressed his approbation of his projects, and at once caused the proper orders to be issued, including instructions to General Stephen D. Lee, at the time Chief of Cavalry, to second his undertakings in all possible ways.

At the time three small cavalry brigades constituted the Confederate force in all North-Mississippi. These were extended in a line of outposts across from Panola along the south bank of the Tallahatchie river *via* Rocky Ford, and thence eastward to the Mobile and Ohio Railroad, about Saltills, or mayhap Baldwin, and active scouts well in advance in watchful observation of all the approaches from the northward, or hostile quarter.* At the same time, the Federals were in strong force at Memphis and Corinth, with a *cordon* of posts along the line of the Memphis and Charleston Railroad, between the two points, with rapid means of inter-communication and mutual succor.†

Preliminary to the extended operations which he hoped to be able to undertake, General Forrest's first design was to throw himself, through the Federal line, into West-Tennessee, and bring to bear his personal influence and *prestige* upon the scattered fighting elements abounding there, and thus bring them together in numbers sufficient to make an effective offensive force.

To cover his passage across the formidable barrier of the fortified line of the Memphis and Charleston Railroad, it was arranged with General S. D. Lee that two of the three brigades previously mentioned should be assembled at New-Albany, whither Forrest and Lee repaired on the 28th or 29th of November, and where, also, Brigadier-General R. V. Rich-

---

* One brigade, subdivided for convenience into two demi-brigades, (McCulloch's and Slemmons,) under General James R. Chalmers, was on the left ; Brigadier-General Ferguson and Colonel Ross, with their brigades, were on the right of Rocky Ford.

† At least 10,000 men available.

ardson was directed to be at the same time, with his brigade of West-Tennessee Partisans, to form part of the expedition as auxiliary to the veteran troops brought from Chickamauga. This brigade was reported to be 2000 strong, but on inspection and muster, on the 30th, only two hundred and forty, officers and men, appeared in the ranks ; the rest had gone to their homes on various pretexts, chiefly, as they represented, for clothing and remounts. Moreover, the long march from North-Georgia to Okolona had so materially affected his veteran command that there were only effective horses left for a section of Morton's Battery ; and some fifty of his troopers had to be left behind for want of mounts, thus reducing his force of trained soldiers to 250, rank and file, and forming, with Richardson's Partisans, a force in all of barely 500 officers and men, for the expedition.

For more than forty days the weather had been very rainy, so that the whole country was saturated with water, and all the water-courses overflown. The Tallahatchie was so swollen that a bridge had to be built ; this consumed three days, and its passage was not effected until the 3d of December, when Ferguson led the advance northward, by way of Ripley, with his own and Ross's Brigades. Meanwhile, Chalmers, with a demi-brigade under McCulloch, had crossed at Rocky Ford, to unite with Ferguson ; and the other, under Slemmons, crossing at Panola, was advancing to threaten the railroad westward of Lagrange, and occupy the enemy in that quarter. Ferguson, approaching Saulsbury on the railroad seven miles eastward of Grand Junction, encountered a Federal picket-post some six miles southward of the place, which he pressed vehemently back upon their main body. Bringing up the artillery, including Morton's section, he then opened with such spirit that that, too, speedily abandoned the position, and left it open for the passage of Forrest, who here parting with General Lee and the convoy, boldly launched his little force into West-Tennessee without loss of time, his only *impedimenta* being five ordnance wagons. Throwing out scouts along the railroad on the right and left to ascertain and follow after him with all possible reliable information of the movement of the enemy on his rear, he pushed on that evening to Van Buren, some ten miles on the road to Bolivar, and encamped there for the night. At four o'clock, scouts returning, reported that there were no troops in pursuit, and Forrest resumed his movement, reaching Bolivar at eight A.M., on the 5th. Here Forrest and his men were received by the people with profound pleasure, and a sumptuous provision was made for the entertainment of men and horses.*

After a halt at Bolivar of only two hours, during which an old raft pontoon-bridge was repaired so as to afford a practicable means of crossing the Hatchie, and detaching scouts in the direction of Memphis, Corinth, and intermediate points, to keep him advised of any hostile movement contrived to intercept his exit from the State, Forrest was again in motion.

It was late in the afternoon of the next day, 6th, that he entered Jackson, where he was welcomed by the whole population with deep feeling, and where, as at Bolivar, an abundance of forage and subsistence had been provided.

Previous to leaving Okolona, knowing that Colonel Tyree H. Bell, under orders from Generals Bragg and Pillow, was then in West-Tennessee, for the purpose of collecting absentees from the several regiments with Bragg's army from that region, Forrest had dispatched a courier to him with instructions to meet him at Jackson, and he was there accordingly with a small force already collected. At the same time, quite

---

* The General and his staff being entertained at the hospitable mansion of Colonel J. J. Neely, where he re- ceived the hearty gratulations of many friends.

a number of persons had been engaged throughout West-Tennessee in seeking to raise commands for themselves, and more than a half-score of them had enrolled detachments varying from twenty-five to two hundred in number. These detachments Colonel Bell was directed to bring together at once, while General Richardson, with his headquarters at Brownsville, twenty-eight miles west of Jackson, was required to take steps to assemble the numerous absentees from his organization, and every practicable measure for gleaning the fighting resources of the section was put on foot without delay.

Meanwhile the Federals were not idle. News of Forrest's irruption had been dispatched in all directions, and the Federal commandant of the district, Major-General Hurlbut, had set to work to organize a large force, which he hoped so to dispose as to hem in the Confederate leader, and cut off his escape or return to his base. And to this end, Forrest soon learned—about the 15th—that Federal cavalry in large numbers from Memphis had been thrown out along the Memphis and Charleston road, while a strong column was about to move down upon him from Columbus, Kentucky, another from the direction of Fort Pillow, and yet another was approaching from the quarter of Corinth. In all these directions trusty scouts were pushed in close observation, to acquire early information of all serious hostile combinations and movements ; and meanwhile all possible efforts were made to advance the objects for which the expedition had been undertaken, with such success that Colonel Bell, by the night of the 23d, had collected some 1600 or 1700 officers and men.*

---

* It may serve to illustrate the character of the times, somewhat, to relate here, that Colonel Bell's men were assembled in the dense forests of that region in small detachments of twenty-five or thirty men, and bivouacked for weeks in the woods under the rude primitive shelter known among the sol-

Richardson had brought his brigade up to about 1000 men, and Lieutenant-Colonel D. M. Wisdom had reported at Jackson with about 150 of Colonel J. E. Forrest's old regiment.

By this time scouts reported the presence of a cavalry force both at Sommerville and Bolivar, together some 2000 strong, with infantry still numerously posted on the line of the Memphis and Charleston road ; that the column from Corinth had reached and encamped at Purdy, the night of the 22d, moving on the road to Jack's creek, while those coming from the northward were as far southward as Trenton and McLemoresville.*

Meanwhile, Richardson, on the 22d, had been ordered to put his brigade in motion southward, and throw it across the Hatchie at Estenaula, and accordingly had marched early on the 23d. After passing the river in question on the 24th, scouts, about one P.M., reported, at Miller's Farm-house, the proximity of a hostile force from the direction of Bolivar. Richardson's men, with few exceptions, were raw ; scarcely any of them had ever been under fire, and less than 300 were armed. But, nevertheless, he promptly determined on a collision. Neely's Regiment, Fourteenth Tennessee Cavalry, in advance, was at once formed in line in a field eastward of the road, with Hall's Company deployed as skirmishers ; and the first skirmish of the expedition began. The Federals opposed were the Seventh Illinois Cavalry, Colonel Prince, some 600 strong ; and Hall being quickly driven in, a charge with the whole Federal force was evidently about to be made. Richardson attempted a futile effort to meet this with a counter-charge with his armed troopers ; but in face of the disparity engaged, his men wavered, and then breaking, scattered in

---

diers by the name of Shebang, that is, a pole resting on two forks, over which a blanket or captured oilcloth was stretched as a roof.—*MS. Notes of Colonel Thomas J. Freeman.*

* 8000 infantry and cavalry.

confusion, to the deep chagrin of their commander. Meanwhile, Neely, who at the time was detached from his immediate regiment, rearward, at the river crossing, hearing of the disaster, took up a position covering it, and was there re-enforced by some of the brigade under Lieutenant-Colonel H. C. Greer; and there, too, General Richardson repaired. Very soon the Federals made their appearance, and a skirmish began immediately, which lasted for an hour, howbeit, without much loss to either side. It was now after sunset, and a full moon had risen bright and clear, that Christmas eve, shedding almost the light of day on the scene. But the Federals, apparently satisfied that the Confederate position was not to be forced, withdrew, quickly followed by a detachment led by Colonel Neely, to reconnoitre their movements.*

About meridian the day before, scouts having announced that the Corinth column, unable to approach by the direct road in consequence of the overflow of the Forked Deer river, was moving up by the Jack's creek way, Forrest thought it prudent to throw out a counter-movement to hamper that of the enemy until he could remove his wagon-train and cattle south of the Hatchie; and besides, the isolation of this force was a provocation to a blow that it was not in his nature to resist. Therefore, Lieutenant-Colonel D. M. Wisdom was detached the afternoon of the 23d, with his own and McDonald's battalions, and a detachment of Kentuckians, under Lieutenant-Colonel Lannum, in all not exceeding 500, rank and file, to move forward to Jack's creek, and oppose all practicable resistance sufficiently long to cover the passage of the Hatchie; and then to draw off and swiftly follow after the main body.

Early on the morning of the 24th, Colonel Bell was like-

---

* MS. Notes of Captain V. B. Waddell.

wise directed to take up the line of march southward, with the fresh levies and Morton's artillery, the train of forty wagons and teams that had been collected in the country, a large band of beef cattle and hogs, and make every effort to get them safely boyond the Hatchie as rapidly as possible, which he proceeded to execute with characteristic energy and intelligence. These dispositions having been made, Forrest himself turned his horse's head southward again at six P.M., and brought up the rear of his command with his staff and escort.

Meanwhile, Colonel Wisdom, having encamped south of Mifflin, about fifteen miles from Jackson, the night of the 23d, in immediate proximity to several regiments of the enemy's cavalry, attacked them before daylight—the Federals being also in motion at the moment—and a spirited skirmish occurred. The attack was so sudden that the Federals at first had recoiled, scattering oilcloths, uniform caps, blankets, and even their arms by the roadside, as the sharp crackle of the Confederate rifles burst unexpectedly upon the silence of the sombre forest at that early hour. But soon rallying, and day having dawned, an animated, noisy conflict was kept up for several hours. The Federals were of at least double the force of the Confederates, and at last made an effort to turn their adversary's left flank, which Colonel Wisdom promptly met and baffled with a counter-movement, with 80 picked men, handled by Lieutenant John O. Morris, Adjutant of Colonel Lannum's detachment, who was mortally wounded ; but not until he had made his splendid courage and martial aptitudes notable to all his comrades.* Foiled in this attempt, the Federals extended their whole force, and sought to envelop the much shorter Confederate line, with so much per-sistence that it became but an act of prudence to draw out,

---

* The gallant and soldierly conduct of this young Kentuckian excited general admiration and remark.

which was accordingly done in the direction of the northwestern corner of McNairy county. McDonald's Battalion, under Major Allin, covered the movement, and a junction was effected with the main body of Forrest's command beyond the Hatchie early the next morning, traversing the distance of thirty miles in eight hours, during a dark, rainy night.*

As will be recollected, Forrest caught up with his forces at the Hatchie, while Colonel Neely was in advance reconnoitering the position of the Federals. That officer, not long absent, returning, reported that the enemy were encamped some two miles southward of Miller's house, or four or five miles distant. Thereupon Forrest directed Richardson to move forward that night, and establish himself just beyond Miller's, to which point he also transferred his own headquarters immediately, while sending forward his escort company, under Lieutenant Nathan Boon, to make a close aggressive reconnoissance. This was done with the characteristic daring and thoroughness which distinguished that gallant band, of whom we have heard more than one prominent officer remark, *" They are ever ready to undertake what their chief so often*

---

* The Federal Cavalry, it appears, consisted of the Seventh Kansas, (Jay Hawkers,) Third Michigan, and a regiment of Alabamians, commanded by a Colonel Meisner, who, shortly afterward, returning through Purdy, quartered himself in the comfortable house of Colonel Wisdom's father, an elderly gentleman residing there, making the whole family the victims of his ruffian insolence and brutality, as well as plundering them of absolutely all their corn. Evidently he was the peer of Turchin, Cornyn, and, in his smaller sphere, of Butler.—*MS. Notes of Colonel D. M. Wisdom.*

The following incident will illustrate the spirit of Forrest's men : Major Phil Allin, of McDonald's Battalion, having had his horse shot under him, was left horseless in the charge that was being made. Private Argyle Powell of the battalion, near him at the moment, exclaimed, " Wait a moment, Major ; I'll bring one from the Yankees yonder !" and dashed on ; but returning in a little while, led up to the Major a fine horse and a Federal prisoner, with the remark, " Here's the horse I promised you, Major, and a Yankee to boot."

looked to them to do—the fighting of a full regiment." Indeed, every member of that choice body of the youth of the country manifestly acted on all occasions with the fullest appreciation of the fact that, though

> " There may be danger in the deed,
> 'Twas fraught with honor too."

In this instance, not satisfied with a mere reconnoissance, Lieutenant Boon charged down upon the Federal pickets and drove them so vigorously back that the Federal commander, fancying doubtless there was a formidable movement behind, broke up his encampment immediately, and retreated hurriedly that night to Sommerville, leaving cooking utensils on the fire, considerable quantities of forage, and the vicinity strewn with dead hogs, poultry, and other plundered subsistence supplies.

Christmas came, an unusually fair and sun-bright day for the season, a delightful relief from the gloomy, soaking weather for some time preceding, and the main part of the command was suffered to remain inactive until late in the afternoon.

In the mean time, Colonel Bell had been occupied all the night before, and until mid-day the 25th, in crossing the river with his large, heavily-laden trains and cattle, having the use of only one small ferry-boat, so frail and unsteady that it was once capsized, with the loss of one man and two horses drowned, and a load of bacon. The weather was intensely cold, and the freezing mud and water almost unbearable ; but, inspired by the energy and conduct of Colonel Bell, his men labored cheerfully to the last, or until their task was faithfully accomplished.*

-----

* Some 200 head of beef cattle, 300 hogs, and over 3000 troops, it will be remembered, were ferried by this means.

In the interval, Forrest's scouts had been actively scouring the country in all hostile quarters, and had reported that Colonel Prince was now at Sommerville with his own regiment, Seventh Illinois, and a squadron of the Ninth, or some 750 troopers ; that as many as 1000 more were in the vicinity of Bolivar, and an equal force near Middleburg, on the Mississippi Central Railroad, with numerous large infantry detachments still spread along the whole line of the Mississippi Central Railroad eastward of Moscow, with three large trains held at Lagrange full of infantry, ready to be dispatched whithersoever needed to bar Forrest's way back to the Confederate lines. It was apparent from the disposition of these forces, however, that they expected him to attempt to force his way southward in the same direction from which he had penetrated northward. He therefore resolved to move by way of Sommerville, and seek egress from these strongly set toils westward of Moscow, or in the unexpected quarter of Memphis.

This involved a conflict with the Federals at Sommerville ; and Richardson's Brigade, already somewhat increased by accessions of men since crossing to the south bank of the Hatchie, was put in motion that afternoon, by way of Whiteville and a cross-road further southward, to come upon the Federal rear, while, at a concerted time, Forrest would fall upon them by the Jackson-Sommerville road. Halting for the night at Whiteville, Richardson's men were entertained in the houses of that village with a hospitality so considerate and large that it may not be passed unnoticed in these pages, and the memory of which will be ever cherished by the survivors of those weather-beaten soldiers who were made so welcome at the bright, glowing firesides and well-spread tables of the people of Whiteville. Resuming his march before day on the 26th, and turning off rightward at Boyle's house toward Sommerville from Bolivar, Richardson, soon after sunrise, learned from scouts that the country was swarming with Federals on all sides ; but, moving on as directed, his advance-guard developed a Federal cavalry force in the head of a lane near Armors, five miles from Sommerville. His orders for such an exigency were to occupy the enemy as long as practicable in a skirmish with his armed men, embracing, it will be recollected, not more than 300 rifles, to give Forrest time to come upon their rear ; and this was promptly undertaken, his unarmed men being held in a ravine rearward. Richardson's men were posted with fields on their right and left and a wood in front, in which the Federals took cover and opened thence with their carbines at easy range. Nevertheless, the affair was apparently without profit to either side, save that it brought the delay for which the Confederates fought, and they were able, more by noise than accuracy of range, to keep the Federals harmless at arm's length, though several times more numerous and thoroughly armed. However, the situation was somewhat dangerous, and Richardson detached Captain Wise A. Cooper, of one of his battalions, with thirty men, to move by way of a ravine rightward and get into position to open upon the Federal rear.

Forrest, meanwhile moving on the direct road from Estenaula to Sommerville, on reaching a point five miles from the latter place heard, through scouts, of this movement toward Bolivar, and hearing also the firing in that direction, pressed rapidly forward with some 300 men, and, taking a by-road branching to the south-eastward two miles from Sommerville, was speedily on the scene, but with only 150 of his men—his escort and a detachment of McDonald's Battalion—who had kept up, so jaded were many of the horses now from long continuous exposure to bad weather.

As before observed, the position of the Federals was sheltered, and thus far they had the advantage. But Richardson ostentatiously brought out his unarmed men, under Lieutenant-Colonel Hugh D. Greer. These were handsomely led over the crest of a hill with a loud shout as a vigorous, sustained fusilade was delivered by the riflemen in front. The effect was happy, for the Federals, deceived by the numbers thus appearing upon the flank, gave way. Forrest's men struck heavily and fast at the same time, and the rout was complete. Still there was some loss to the Confederates ; three of Forrest's escort were killed and several severely wounded, and among the slain was First Sergeant A. H. Boon, who was stricken by the side of his brother—Lieutenant Boon — while fighting with signal gallantry in the *mêlée*, when, carried together by the ardor of the combat, into a group of fifteen or more Federals.*

The pursuit was kept up for several miles, but without material results, as the enemy had broken and dispersed in so many different directions.† They left on the ground, however, some seven or eight dead, as many as thirty wounded, and eighty prisoners were captured, while their whole train of six wagons, loaded with subsistence and ammunition, and

---

* Lieutenant Boon was wounded at the same time. Not less noteworthy was the conduct of private Harry Rhodes, at the time only seventeen years old, who, boldly attempting to capture three Federal troopers, was shot painfully in the under-jaw, and, in the struggle, thrown to the ground, was savagely beaten over the head with their pistols until seemingly insensible or dead. Yet, in that condition, watching his opportunity, he sprang to his feet, and, severely hurt as he was, shot two of his assailants dead and captured the other.

† In the pursuit after a party of these fugitives, a Confederate officer, as he was about to turn back, shouted after them, "Get out of our country, you worthless rascals !" In the rear of the Federals, on a horse rather the slowest of the lot, was a trooper, who, turning his head to the rear, exclaimed, in the unmistakable brogue and with the ready wit of his countrymen : "Faith, and by Jasus, an't it that same we're trying to do *jist* as fast as we can ?"

one ambulance, and about one hundred horses and mules fell into the hands of the Confederates.

Passing through Sommerville, where Colonel Bell joined with the train and its precious supplies, the march was resumed in the direction of Whitehall, on the Memphis road, six miles westward, which was reached that night about eight o'clock. Here a detachment of some 700 men, including 50 with firearms, under Colonel Faulkner, was organized to proceed, under the special conduct of Major Strange, Forrest's trusty Adjutant-General, by the highway to Memphis, crossing Wolf river at Raleigh Ferry, and making a demonstration in the immediate vicinity of Memphis, as if designing to attack that city, sweep by to Hernando, and on to Como, Mississippi, sixty miles southward of the former place. And we may add, this operation was successfully carried out, to the great consternation of the Federals and their following in Memphis, as the Confederates passed within four miles of it ; moreover, it served to divert attention, as General Forrest calculated, from the points toward which his valuable trains were being rapidly convoyed.

It appears there was but one bridge remaining over Wolf river between Lagrange and Memphis — that at Lafayette Station — which, however, was not in practicable condition until the day before, when it was made so by the Federals for convenience in throwing troops across, and their rapid communications with reference to the envelopment of Forrest ; and this, fortunately, had been ascertained by Colonel Thomas H. Logwood, of Memphis, who happened to be in the region just northward of the river recruiting a cavalry regiment. Satisfied of this important fact by a personal reconnoissance, Logwood sent an officer to intercept and acquaint Forrest with the fact at Oakland. This opportune information determined the daring Confederate leader to attempt to seize the bridge by a *coup de main*, and use it for the passage of his trains and main force.*

After giving his men and horses some little rest, of which they now stood in great need, Colonel Bell was ordered to advance hurriedly, with some 200 hundred armed men, on the bridge in question at Lafayette Station, and if possible surprise and seize it. About the same time some 200 more of Forrest's armed force had been thrown out well leftward, as if aiming to effect a passage of Wolf river somewhere between Moscow and Lagrange, and thus cover his real line of march. A detachment of 100 good men constituted the rear-guard, and Forrest with his escort took charge of the train and stock, which were now boldly pushed forward close after Bell.

It was eleven o'clock A.M. on the 27th as Bell, well advised by the reconnoissance of Colonel Logwood and Lieutenant Williamson of the situation, approached, under the happy cover of a dense wood on the north bank of the stream, to the immediate vicinity of the bridge to be secured. It was commanded by a closed work within thirty feet of it, on the south bank, and manned by several hundred riflemen. Nevertheless, without parley or hesitancy, the vigorous, determined Bell threw his men upon it, and they splendidly charged rcaoss, on the timbers of the bridge, under a volley from the fortlet. Only a single volley was fired ; the Federals, observ-

---

* Meanwhile, also, Logwood detached Lieutenant John A. Williamson, with a small party, to make a closer reconnoissance under cover of the night. That officer, with consummate adroitness, crept between the Federal pickets and the bridge, and found that the flooring had been removed and was piled up on the southern bank, under fire from a work commanding the bridge. While thus employed, a body of Federal horse came up on the south bank, which, on being challenged, replied, " Reënforcements for Colonel Prince." The guard was then turned out, light struck, the bridge-floor relaid, troops passed over and went their way as the flooring was again removed.—*MS. Notes of Colonel Logwood.*

ing the swarming numbers in the onset, and not the unarmed condition of the main force, did not stand for another, but, breaking, took to flight down the road eastward toward Moscow, leaving their strongly fortified position, commanding the bridge, in Colonel Bell's possession, and leaving four of their number dead on the ground. The flooring was quickly re-laid, while Colonel John Newsom was sent in pursuit, with some fifty troopers, to keep up the appearance of vigorous aggressive purposes, and was so fortunate, besides, as to encounter a troop-train within two miles, which he attacked with such effect as to drive it back with the loss, it is said, of some fifty killed and wounded ; and, pursuing to Grisham's creek, he burned the railroad bridge over that stream.

By four P.M., 27th, Forrest had succeeded in bringing up his train and stock, relaid the bridge, and effected the crossing to the south bank of Wolf river without the least mishap. This accomplished, he threw out an armed detachment ostentatiously upon Moscow, with orders, if pressed, to fall back toward Memphis, and thus attract the Federals from his trains and cattle, which, with the main body of unarmed men, took the road toward Holly Springs, *via* Mount Pleasant, without delay, with orders to make a night march. At the same time, leading his escort, some 300 other armed men, and Morton's artillery, down the road westward to Collierville, whence a heavy force was reported to be advancing. Within two miles of Lafayette he met, engaged, and drove back a detachment of some 300 cavalry. These he charged, after his usual prompt fashion, and brushed back, just as scouts returned from Moscow and Lagrange, and reported the movement of heavy bodies of infantry and cavalry from that quarter. The fair Christmas weather had not continued, and, for more than twelve hours, a torrential rain had been falling. But every possible device was to be put in play to prevent these forces from pursuing his heavily laden teams. So, throwing out the scouts embodied, to open a vehement skirmish, and to fall back, when hotly pressed, westward along the road, and leaving some of his older men at Lafayette to simulate country people, and give false information of the concentration of his whole force and its movement toward Collierville to attack Memphis, Forrest moved by the "State line" road to that place, closely pressed, through mud and rain, by the enemy, until about ten o'clock at night. Then the enemy came up with him near to that place, and a sharp, noisy skirmish ensued for an hour or more, in the uproar of which the artillery in the Federal work there took a boisterous part.

Several prisoners were taken on both sides about this time, among others, Captain John Mann, Forrest's Chief Engineer, who, by a mistake, fell into the Federal hands, and, in reply to some inquiries, managed cleverly to leave the impression that General Stephen D. Lee was in the vicinity with his entire cavalry force, and with that apprehension the Federal commander retreated immediately to Lafayette, and there halted for the night, leaving Forrest in possession of the vicinity of Collierville at midnight, after having driven the Federals to their interior fortifications.

In the mean time it had ceased to rain, and, the wind changing to the north, it had become very cold. Having now gained sufficient time for the movement southward of his train, he turned the head of his column toward Holly Springs, and was at Mount Pleasant by daylight on the 28th, after a continuous night work of marches and battle. He stood now on safe ground, having accomplished in full measure what to most men would have seemed fatally rash, perilously vain to attempt.

The enemy made no further attempt to pursue, as Forrest now proceeded by short, slow marches across the country to Como, Panola county, Miss., having been met on the way, on the 29th, by Brigadier-General Chalmers, advancing with his command to assist in covering his return. It was the first day of the year 1864 when the last of the command arrived at Como, and Major Strange and Colonel Faulkner reached there about the same time, without the loss, during their wide circuit, of one man. The weather being intensely cold, and the troops without tents, the several regiments were scattered about so as to secure quarters for their men, as far as possible, in the vacant houses and cabins on the abandoned plantations in the neighborhood, of which the course of the war had left a large number.

COMMENTARIES.

1. It should be recollected that General Forrest effected his withdrawal from Jackson, and this march of one hundred and forty miles with 3000 unarmed, raw men, a large wagon-train, his artillery, and all their cattle under convoy of, at most, 600 armed men. When he began the movement, he was thoroughly encompassed with foes, some 20,000 strong, according to General Hurlbut's official admission. Under these circumstances, his troops fought successfully five combats—at Jack's creek, Estenaula, Sommerville, Lafayette, and Collierville—losing during the expedition not more than 30 killed, wounded, and captured, and inflicting a loss upon the enemy of fully 50 killed and 150 wounded and captured, or, in all, 200 at least.

2. While the mass of even the armed force at General Forrest's disposition were raw and untried, there were with him a number of officers who had seen a good deal of service, and a great deal of credit for the success of the expedition is attributed to them by their General. Both his staff and his officers behaved with distinguished courage and notable efficiency, and all his plans were ably seconded by his immediate staff, namely, Major J. P. Strange, his Adjutant-General, Captain Charles W. Anderson, A. D. C., and Major G. V. Rambaut,

A. C. S., while, as on all previous occasions, his young son Willie, now his Aid, also was a devoted, effective servitor. At the same time, nothing could be more admirable than the conduct of the men. There was no drooping on their part under the extreme fatigue and exposure to the unusually inclement weather of the season which they had been suddenly called out from their homes to undergo before they could be properly supplied with either clothing or blankets. All these privations and severe hardships these young men endured with a fortitude which we are told is that formidable and shining quality which most distinguishes veterans from raw troops.

3. Forrest, entering West-Tennessee at Saulsbury on the 4th of December with only some 500 men, two guns, and five ordnance wagons, quit it at Lafayette Station on the 27th with 3500 men, well mounted, 40 wagons and teams loaded with subsistence, 200 head of beef cattle, 300 hogs, and his artillery intact.

4. It is proper to add, that the success of this handsome operation was assisted unquestionably by General Lee's attack upon Moscow, on the afternoon of the 4th of December, with McCulloch's and Ross's Brigades. This affair, though it failed to accomplish the main purposes for which it was ordered—the destruction of the railroad bridge at that point over Wolf river and the capture of the garrison—served to inflict a heavy loss upon a strong column of the Federals, taken by surprise, and doubtless kept at a stand subsequently in that quarter a force that was destined to pursue Forrest, a force which otherwise might have brought his expedition to a premature close, far short of the satisfactory results which we have just enumerated.

5. A Federal writer sums up the results of the Confederate General's operations on this occasion in these terms : " Forrest, with less than 4000 men, has moved *right through the Sixteenth Army Corps,* has passed within *nine* miles of Mem-

phis, carried off over 100 wagons, 200 beef cattle, 3000 conscripts, and innumerable stores, torn up railroad track, cut
telegraph wire, burned and sacked towns, (?) run over pickets
with a single Derringer pistol, . . . and all too in the
face of 10,000 men." (*Correspondent Cincinnati Commercial,*
Memphis, January 12, 1864.)   We find the Federal forces
sent into West-Tennessee were General Smith, from Columbus, Ky., with 2500 cavalry and 5000 infantry, and two brigades from Memphis, respectively under Mower and Mizner.

COLONEL JEFFREY E. FORREST.

CHAPTER XIV.

*Forrest made a Major-General—Assignment to " Forrest's Cavalry De-
partment "—Headquarters at Oxford, Mississippi—Affair of the
Deserters there—The Federal Cavalry Raid into Mississippi, under
General W. S. Smith—Skirmishing—Savage Waste of the Country
by the Enemy—Federals begin to retire—Series of Sharp Skirmishes
—Engagement at Okolona—Federal Defeat in a succession of Combats—Death of Colonel Jeffrey Forrest; also, of Lieutenant-Colonel Barksdale—Running Fight, and complete Federal Rout.*

January 1st to February 28th, 1864.

DURING the absence of Forrest in West-Tennessee, there
had been a change of department commanders.   General
Joseph E. Johnston had been relieved from duty by the President, and Lieutenant-General Polk placed in his stead, and
to that officer the telegraphic report of the aggregate results
of the expedition was made, in brief but expressive terms.
General Polk in reply, acquainted him with the fact he had
been promoted to the grade of Major-General in the Confederate provisional army,* and that he would be assigned to a
proper district, embracing all the Confederate forces in North-
Mississippi and West-Tennessee.

The next ten days were devoted assiduously to the work of

---

* It is a noteworthy coincidence that   1863, the very day he entered West-
his commission for this rank was actu-   Tennessee.
ally issued the 4th day of December,

organization of the valuable war *personnel* gathered in the re-cesses of West-Tennessee ; and on the 13th of January, For-rest repaired to General Polk's headquarters, at Jackson, Mis-sissippi, leaving Brigadier-General Chalmers in command in his absence.

It was then the command of a district was formally assigned him, that is, " FORREST'S CAVALRY DEPARTMENT," embracing all cavalry commands in West-Tennessee and North-Missis-sippi, to the southern boundaries of the counties of Monroe, Calhoun, Chickasaw, Yallabusha, Tallahatchie, and that part of Sunflower and Bolivar lying north of a line drawn from the south-east corner of Tallahatchie county to the town of Pren-tiss, on the Mississippi river.   At the same time, he secured arms and ammunition for his troops, and returned to prepare his command, as soon as possible, not only for an effective de-fense of the territorial limits assigned him, but for active and extended offensive operations.

But many and grave or delicate difficulties and hinderances had to be met and overborne in this work.   The regiments and companies brought out from West-Tennessee were chiefly skeleton organizations ; these had to be consolidated and moulded into more compact and efficient forms, somewhat at the expense of the military aspirations and cherished ambi-tion of some valuable officers.   There were great contention and competition for the commissions at stake under the reor-ganization, and this bred a state of discontent and disorgani-zation among the men.   Hitherto in the habit of staying in the field very much at their own will and pleasure, the sol-diery, moreover, became very restless under the restraints imposed in this respect by their new commander, and until his firm hand and strenuous will were made apparent, they straggled numerously from their colors, and returned even by large squads to their homes.   But detachments of his veteran troops were promptly sent out to gather and bring back these

men to their duty, as well as all absentees that were encountered. By the 25th, however, the more serious obstacles having been overcome, on that day Forrest issued an order announcing the limits and scope of his command;* another,
giving the names and functions of his staff;† and a third, pro-
mulgating the provisional organizations determined upon, both
as to regiments, battalions, batteries, and brigades.

Four brigades were formed respectively under Brigadier-
General Richardson and Colonels McCulloch, Bell, and Jeffrey
Forrest, while McCulloch's and Forrest's Brigades were organized into a division, commanded by Brigadier-General J.
R. Chalmers.‡ These details having been adjusted, Major-
General Forrest removed his headquarters to Oxford, Mississippi, as a more central and favorable point, in view of a possible necessity for coöperation with other Confederate forces
against a rumored movement from Vicksburg, northward.

---

* See Appendix.

† *Ibid.*

‡ The first brigade was constituted of the Twelfth, (Lieutenant-Colonel J. U. Green,) Fourteenth, (Colonel J. J. Neely,) Fifteenth, (Colonel F. M. Stewart,) Sixteenth, (Colonel Thomas H. Logwood,) and Seventeenth, (Major Marshall,) regiments, and Street's and Bennett's battalions, all West-Tennessee troops, under the command of Brigadier-General R. V. Richardson—1500 rank and file.

The second brigade, Colonel Robert McCulloch (Second Missouri) commanding, was composed of the Second Missouri Regiment,(Lieutenant-Colonel R. A. McCulloch,) Willis's Texan Battalion, (Lieutenant-Colonel Leo Willis,) Colonel W. W. Faulkner's Kentucky Regiment, Keizer's—Franklin's—Tennessee Battalions, Lieutenant-Colonel Alexander H. Chalmers's Battalion Mississippi Cavalry, and the fragment of the Second Arkansas Cavalry, (Captain F. M. Cochran.)

The third brigade, Colonel T. H. Bell in command, formed of Colonels Russell's, Greer's, Newsom's, Wilson's, and Barteau's (Second) Tennessee regiments—2000 rank and file.

And a fourth brigade was made up of McDonald's Battalion and the Seventh Tennessee, (Veterans,) McGuirk's Regiment, Third Mississippi State troops, Fifth Mississippi, (Lieutenant-Colonel Barksdale,) and Duff's (Nineteenth) Mississippi Battalion, with Colonel J. E. Forrest as Brigade Commander.

The rest of the forces were withdrawn to the south bank of the Tallahatchie, and concentrated for the most part at Panola, under the command of Brigadier-General Chalmers.

Among other disturbing elements, fomenting and keeping up discontent, was the extreme want of clothing among the new troops, who had, as will be remembered, been brought away so hurriedly from their homes beyond the border ; and the disposition to leave camp without permission, checked for a time, breaking out again with renewed violence, prevailed presently to such a degree as to render severe measures imperative. Among those who thus abandoned their colors, were nineteen, who went off together in a body. Promptly pursued, captured, and brought back in ignominy, their commander, giving orders that in consequence of their flagrant, defiant desertion, the whole detachment should be shot, issued the necessary instructions regulating the ceremonies of an early execution. Their coffins were made, their graves dug, and the culprits advised to make their peace with their Maker and the world. News of the affair having become bruited abroad, the clergy, prominent citizens, and ladies of Oxford waiting on the General, made urgent appeals to him to spare the lives of their misguided countrymen. Some of the officers of high rank also felt it their duty to inform the General of their serious apprehension of a mutinous resistance on the part of the soldiery, to the attempt to execute so many of their comrades. But Forrest, apparently unmoved by intercessions, was unswerved by the suggestion of a mutiny, and inexorably adhered to his orders ; the preparations for the execution being proceeded with, even to the presence before the troops of the prisoners, blindfolded, seated on their coffins, and the firing party drawn up before them waiting for the command, " Fire !" before he granted a reprieve, and remanded them to prison, through one of his staff-officers. The lesson was not lost on any one who beheld the spectacle. It is

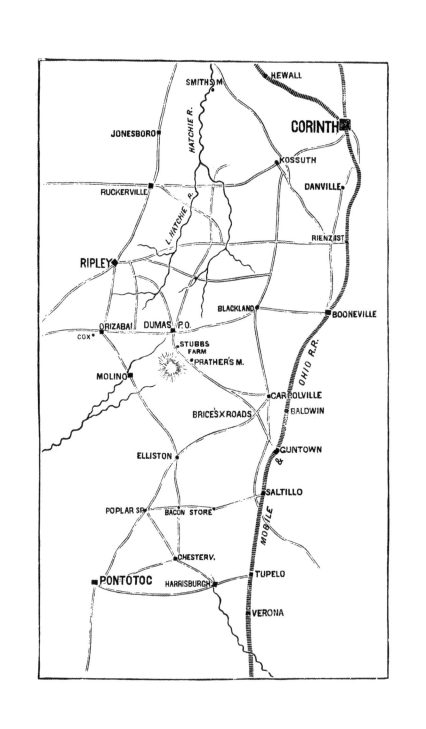

true, the lives of these men had been spared after all this display of an inflexible purpose not to do so ; but it was seen and felt, at the same time, that, on another occasion, should the spirit of desertion continue unstayed, Forrest would prove absolutely inexorable, howsoever disagreeable might be the duty to him.

Several days later, or about the 7th, General Polk notified Forrest that a Federal column, under Sherman, had taken the field from Vicksburg, in the direction of Jackson, while another had been put on foot up the Yazoo, which Forrest was to look after by establishing a part of his force in observation at Grenada. Accordingly, Colonel Jeffrey Forrest was immediately dispatched thither with the Fourth Brigade, about 1000 strong.

At the same time, through scouts and private correspondents in Memphis, the General ascertained that extensive preparations were being made in that city for a large cavalry movement, of which he gave immediate intelligence to his superior.

This was quickly followed, about the 8th, by the information than an infantry column, (brigade, or 1600 men,) with perhaps 200 cavalry, a battery and supply-train, had moved southward from Memphis, by way of Hernando, toward Panola, and another from Collierville, on the Memphis and Charleston Railroad, toward Holly Springs. To meet these hostile movements, Chalmers promptly disposed his troops to guard the crossings of the Tallahatchie ; McCulloch at Panola, Bell at Belmont, Richardson at Wyatt and Toby-Tubby Ferry, with McGuirk at Abbeville.

It at once occurred to Forrest that the cavalry preparations at Memphis were designed for a coöperative movement with that of Sherman, whose common objective would be about Meridian, and that the force, already afield from Memphis, was a mere feint to occupy attention. Nevertheless, Chalmers was directed to detach a brigade to meet it, and McCulloch was dispatched accordingly.*

Thus stood affairs on the evening of the 11th, when Captain Thomas Henderson, Chief of Scouts, reported the march of a large cavalry force from Memphis toward Holly Springs, both by the Germantown and Byhalia roads. At this Chalmers was instantly instructed to concentrate his entire force at Oxford, as soon as possible; and this movement was made, but not finally, until several skirmishes occurred in front of Wyatt and Abbeville, in which the Federals were foiled in apparent efforts to pass the river at those points, the most persistent of which (at Wyatt) was by Faulkner's Kentuckians during the night of the 13th. But, meanwhile, as was soon reported by scouts, the main Federal column had been moving around northward of the river, across the country toward Pontotoc, fully confirming Forrest's forecast as to its ultimate objective—the rich prairie region at and southward of Okolona. Therefore, Chalmers was further directed to move at once, so as to keep on their right flank, to which end his command was in movement for Houston, forty-five miles south-west of Oxford, late in the afternoon of the 14th.

Forrest also set out with Bell's Brigade, his escort, and the artillery, that morning, for Grenada, whence he had previously directed Colonel Forrest to move swiftly eastward, with his brigade, upon West-Point, on the Mobile and Ohio Railroad, in the menaced region, and from that place to establish a line of couriers to Houston, so as to open communication with Chalmers.

---

* General Forrest, as early as the 9th, expressed the opinion, in a telegraphic dispatch to General Chalmers, that it was the purpose of the enemy to move in the direction of Okolona and Meridian, and gave orders to keep his force in hand to grapple with such a movement.

Chalmers encountered heavy roads, and the rains continuing, the ways grew so difficult that it became prudent to leave the artillery and train to be brought up by details, and to press on with the troops, by which means he arrived at Houston the 16th, and at Palo Alto on the 17th, and there entered upon the fertile prairie region of Mississippi, abounding in forage and subsistence. The salutary effect upon the command was soon apparent. To quote the graphic language of a staff-officer with it : " The bountiful supplies of forage which the prairies furnished gladdened the hearts of our hungry horses, whose rations had been of the scantiest. . . . When we came in sight of the first stack-yard, with its goodly array of huge fodder-ricks, and saw a little way off the teeming cribs, a shout of joy went up from the head of the column, which was continued down the whole line, as if we had indeed reached the promised land."*

In the mean while the Federal column had been traversing the country in a line through Pontotoc, but there trending toward Okolona. And Forrest, after having gone to Grenada, had pushed across rapidly on the 18th to Starkville, a village some twenty-five miles west of Columbus, and opened communication likewise with Chalmers. He also, on the 18th, had thrown Colonel Forrest forward toward Aberdeen, to harass and delay the enemy as much as practicable.

Chalmers, on the 18th, moving but a short distance, halted at Tampico, where large supplies of public forage had been accumulated, and on the following day joined Forrest, still at Starkville. In the mean time, Colonel Jeffrey Forrest, striking the path of the Federals at Aberdeen, had become involved in a series of light skirmishes, as they pressed his brigade back toward West-Point. In view, therefore, of the pos-

---

* MS. Notes of Captain Walter A. Goodman, A. A. G., which have been of exceeding value to the present writer.

sible purpose on the part of the Federal General to throw his force across at Aberdeen, and move down the east bank of the Tombigbee, Forrest detached Bell's Brigade, under Colonel Barteau,* early on the morning of the 20th, to cross that stream at Columbus, and, moving up toward Aberdeen, oppose any such an enterprise. This movement Colonel Barteau conducted with much judgment ; and finding that the Federals had been massed as far southward as West-Point, he took up a position at Waverly, and prepared to throw himself back to the west bank, during the night of the 20th, and strike the Federal left flank.

These dispositions being made of a part of his force, Forrest marched from Starkville at sunrise on the 20th, with the rest—McCulloch's Brigade and six hundred of Richardson's, (under Neely,) and the artillery, to the support of Colonel Forrest, who was receding toward West-Point as slowly as was practicable, without becoming involved in a serious action with the largely superior force pressing him back.

The theatre of approaching operations was one that called for prudence and judgment on both sides. To the eastward was the Tombigbee, a navigable river, swollen with rains at the time ; to the west, and for miles running nearly parallel with it, from twelve to fifteen miles distant, was the Sook-a-toncha, a branch of the Oka-tibby-ha, a considerable stream, which, after receiving the waters of a number of prairie creeks, was crossed by the Mobile and Ohio Railroad, five miles south of West-Point, as it flowed nearly due east to empty into the Tombigbee, not far above Columbus. As will be seen by reference to a map of the country, these streams form a complete *cul-de-sac*, into which Forrest hoped to draw and hold the Federals until General Lee should come upon the scene,

---

* Colonel Bell being sick.

and enable the Confederates, by taking the offensive vigorously, to cut off their retreat or escape. By the road upon which
Forrest moved, the Sook-a-toncha was only to be crossed at
a bridge about thirty yards in length, some four miles west of
West-Point, the only approach to which was over a long, narrow, thrown-up, dilapidated causeway, while the banks of the
stream, on either hand, were steep and miry. These conditions made it hazardous for the Confederates to advance beyond it in much force. Nevertheless, on reaching the position, about two P.M., Forrest pushed adventurously forward
through and several miles beyond West-Point, until he met
Colonel Jeffrey Forrest holding the Federals at bay in the
prairie. Their lines extended in formidable proportions across
the highway. It was not Forrest's policy to fight as yet, but
merely to maneuver for delay until S. D. Lee came up with
reënforcements that must be near at hand; therefore, after
some very light skirmishing, he withdrew through West-
Point and behind the creek again; not a little annoyed, however, at the necessity for doing so, and thus delivering up so
much more of that opulent region to the ruthless ravages of
the enemy, whose track to the northward was marked far and
wide by a heavy, dark pall of smoke in the air, from the
buildings which had been burned or were burning.

Disposing his forces to hold the bridge we have mentioned,
Forrest at once led a portion of McCulloch's Brigade to a
point called Siloam, some four miles higher up the creek,
where it was reported that the Federals were making an effort
to cross, and thus turn his position. It was not, however, a
serious movement; but a small party had already crossed the
stream, and, taken by surprise, some were killed, and the rest,
twenty-three in number, were captured. That night the
whole country northward was illuminated by burning home-
steads, cotton-gins, granaries, and stack-yards, inspiring the
Confederates with a passionate resolution to do all in the

power of men to punish such an unmanly method of warfare.*

On the morning of the 21st, a force was again thrown to the north side of the bridge, where it was quickly attacked, but with light loss to either side, though there was a prolonged, incessant noise and rattle of firearms until about noon, when the enemy, after several attempts to force the position, drew off. Forrest followed at once, with his ever-staunch escort, to satisfy himself of the actual situation ; then calling up one hundred of Faulkner's Kentuckians, he discovered to his chagrin that the Federals were apparently in retreat. McCulloch's and Colonel Forrest's brigades were now ordered to advance ; and with this force he pressed closely at their haunches, leaving orders for General Chalmers to collect all remaining troops, and with them guard the bridge and the crossings northward of it against any possible hostile flank movement from the northward.

The Federals were soon found in position in some post-oak timber, at the edge of the prairie, four miles northward of West-Point ; but dismounting and deploying as skirmishers, the Confederates quickly drove them rearward some five miles, with a loss of some fifteen killed and wounded, when they again halted, and formed in battle array across the mouth of a lane, in which there was a narrow, slippery bridge and causeway, over a narrow *slash*, that could not be turned. About 150 Confederates had been thrown across it when the Federals charged with vigor ; but Forrest, seeing the peril, with characteristic audacity led a counter-charge, while Mc-Culloch, alive to the exigency, threw forward, on foot, at double-quick, a number of men, who rushed across with a

---

* MS. Notes of Captains Goodman and F. F. Aden. Even Federal writers have been unable to find excuses for the extent to which these ravages were carried. They were a disgrace to the age.

loud shout. The Federals, however, again gave way to their main line in a wood, a short distance northward. For a few moments the situation was dangerous, the fighting sharp ; and, as was his way, General Forrest was in the *heart* of it, killing with his ready pistol a Federal trooper who was in the act of shooting him.

The main force of the Federals now confronted did not number less than 4000 men. Forrest, dismounting the Confederates, not more than 1000 troopers, immediately threw them forward as riflemen to give battle, and a warm engagement began. The Federals, however, fell back slowly through the woods, for a mile, into the prairies to a strong position behind a stout picket-fence, quite half a mile long. Promptly detaching a regiment to move round by the right and turn this formidable barrier, he moved upon it with his men in two lines, as soon as the regiment in question became well engaged. The Federals giving way, Forrest's men rushed up to the fence, and from behind it delivered a galling fire upon their rear. Up to this time Forrest's losses that day had been about 80 killed and wounded, while that of the enemy may be set down at 200, including 75 prisoners taken.

Remounting his men, Forrest now pursued with such celerity as might be. The roads and whole face of the country, thoroughly soaked by long-continued rains, were so fearfully cut up by the feet of the Federal cavalry-horses and their swarming train of loose and pack-animals, accumulated in the course of the movement, as to make pursuit barely possible. The enemy, however, were so encumbered with plunder and negroes that they too were greatly impeded, and their retreat so slow that Forrest, with the impetuous force of his nature, was able to bring his advance into more than one sharp collision that afternoon with the Federal rear-guard, which had been made heavy, and evidently now of their best men.

Meanwhile, Bell's Brigade (Barteau) had crossed by seven o'clock that morning to the west bank of the Tombigbee, near Waverly. Coming in presence of the enemy, and moving boldly northward, it was kept between them and the river as far that day as the vicinity of Egypt Station, on the Memphis and Ohio Railroad, where Barteau encamped, after foiling a dangerous effort by the Federals to envelop his command in its isolated position, happily discovered in time to be met with decision.

Forrest kept up the pursuit until after the darkness was so great as to make it judicious to halt ; and, besides, both men and animals needed rest and food ; moreover, there was danger of a collision between detachments of his forces, as indeed did happen. In an attempt made by Forrest to traverse a field with his escort, so as to intercept a body of the enemy, he became entangled in some ditches, so that a number of the Confederates getting ahead by the road, as he came up in the darkness, they mistook each other for the enemy they pursued, and both parties fired, killing one man, and a ball passed through the General's clothes. Under these circumstances, the command was ordered into bivouac on the ground from which the Federals had just retired, leaving around a good deal of subsistence and forage,—and camp-fires, that were greatly enjoyed by the weather-beaten, jaded, hungry Confederates. During the night the whole country northward was lurid with the flames of burning mansions, outhouses, and forage.

By four o'clock on the morning of the 22d, McCulloch's and Jeffrey Forrest's Brigades were once more in pursuit toward Okalona, about fourteen miles distant. Instructing his brother, Colonel Forrest, to take a left-hand road when within nine miles of Okolona, and throw his brigade over on the Pontotoc road, so as to cut off, if possible, the enemy's retreat in that direction, the General dashed ahead with his staff and indomitable escort, to acquaint himself as soon as possible with the state of affairs in front.

Barteau, as we have mentioned, encamping somewhat further northward, was also in motion with Bell's Brigade at an early hour, and moved parallel, as before, with and in dangerous proximity to the Federals had they been handled with a resolution or skill commensurate with their great numerical advantage, for the Confederate brigade did not now muster over 1200 men. The Federals thronged into and through Okalona, while Barteau took up a position about three fourths of a mile eastward of the railroad, toward which he gradually advanced his line until within some six hundred yards of the eastern edge of the place to a position in the praitie.

Meanwhile, Forrest had overtaken and harassed the Federal rear-guard for several miles southward of Okalona, and pressed them into the place, on the western suburbs of which the Federals were seen drawn up in strong force in several lines, as if for battle, their right on an elevation across the Pontotoc road, and their left resting in an open woods. Discovering Bell's Brigade, at the same time, in the position we have indicated, he hastened thither, and as he made his appearance on the front, the effect, we are told, was profound. Every countenance was irradiated with confidence, courage, and enthusiasm, which found immediate expression in loud cheers and prolonged shouts of mingled joy and defiance, and Forrest gave immediate orders for the brigade to advance to meet an offensive movement on the part of the Federals, as was his habitual tactics. The Confederates, advancing with spirit through and north of the town, mounted, began to fire, with their long rifles, as they came within one hundred yards of the enemy ; but the short, breech-loading firearms of the Federals gave the latter one *more* advantage, that told perceptibly, and the Confederates, the most of whom young men in their first action, were staggered for some moments, which

Forrest observing, ordered to be cured by an immediate charge of Russell's, Wilson's, and Newsom's regiments on foot, while he, with Barteau's, (Second Tennessee,) mounted, swept around to attack the Federal right flank, an attack which was made with excellent spirit, and followed up by the dismounted men with equal fire. Happily, about this moment also, McCulloch's Brigade was seen by friend and foe coming up from the southward at a rapid pace, and this doubtless aided to throw the Federals into the confusion that ensued, and their rapid retreat along the Pontotoc road. The Federal loss in this affair was light, only about thirty killed, wounded, and captured ; that of the Confederates trivial, notwithstanding the superior character of arms used by the enemy.

The chase now became general and eager, Forrest leading with his escort and the Second Tennessee, but swiftly followed by the other regiments as fast as they could mount. For the next four miles Forrest's best mounted men were constantly up and in conflict with the worst mounted fugitives, and many of the latter in that distance were either killed or captured ; seven pieces of their artillery and their caissons were abandoned, with their horses dead and cumbering the road or fallen in the ditches. Meanwhile, in the keenness of the pursuit, the Confederates became greatly scattered, and the men of the several regiments were necessarily so intermingled that, for the time, there was no distinct regimental organization.

The Federals having now gained a position, six or seven miles from Okolona, the natural features of which were highly favorable for defense, rallied and made a stubborn stand. They occupied a high ridge, thickly covered with small post-oaks and a dense undergrowth, which sloped down steeply into marshy valleys on either hand, that covered both flanks, and they had besides thrown up obstructions across the road which ran along the crown of the ridge. Jeffrey Forrest's Brigade, unable to strike the road in the Federal rear, as had been hoped had meantime come up, and McCulloch's also, and these two brigades were ordered, the first to move to the right, the second to the left of the highway, and assail the enemy's position. Colonel Forrest, placing himself at the head of his brigade, deploying Duff's Mississippians and his own regiment of Tennesseeans and Alabamians, under Lieutenant-Colonel Wisdom, made the onset with splendid spirit. Both brigades swept forward at an equal pace, and quickly carried the first line of cover in the face of a withering fire ; but behind was a second position, strongly furnished, from which streamed a hissing torrent from the Federal breech-loaders, that cut down many of the dauntless men who breasted it. Among others, Colonel Forrest fell mortally wounded, shot through the neck, within fifty yards of the Federal stronghold. His men, for the most part as brave and staunch as ever rode in battle, faltered for some instants as they saw their beloved leader fall. Moreover, the Federal fire at the juncture concentrated upon a narrow front, at that short range, was warm and wasting. Meanwhile, General Forrest, informed of his great bereavement, rushed to the spot and dismounted. Jeffrey Forrest was the youngest of the family, and was its pride, its Benjamin.* The now distinguished brother had been lavish with his means for his education, so that the younger brother's many natural gifts had had liberal opportunities for culture, opportunities which had been happily improved. His premature death, with so much promise, valor, and soldierly capacity blighted in the flower, was an almost madden-

---

* We may add here that General Forrest was materially assisted to his success by the fraternal devotion with which he was served on all occasions by his brothers, some four in number, who were always near him, ready to give the most implicit obedience to his orders, and to execute any of his wishes at any exposure, risk, or hardship, with a courage and will equal to his own.

ing, almost mortal blow to the elder brother, and the scene of passionate tenderness and grief that took place made a profound impression upon all spectators. Colonel Forrest was not yet dead, and his mortal existence terminated in the arms of General Forrest, whose soul, at that supreme instant, was moved by such an access of sorrow that it served even to hush, for some ten minutes, the storm of the battle ; for, says Colonel Russell, who commanded a regiment present : "The moment was too sacred for angry passions to have sway, and, catching its inspiration, I ordered the men to cease firing, that all might join in sympathy with our suffering General."

"After nature had triumphed for a while," continues Colonel Russell, "he rose up, and, casting aside those reflections which had unmanned him for a few moments, by a strong mental effort, Forrest was himself again."

Remounting in stern silence, Forrest, taking in the situation at a glance, ordered his staff and escort to follow, and, shouting in a loud, passionate voice, " Gaus, sound the charge !"* dashed with them, (some eighty strong,) with the fury of a Scandinavian Berserk, upon the enemy in front, just as they were remounting to retreat. His spirit speedily animated all who followed—especially the brigade of his dead brother—with the same emotion, and for some moments there was sore havoc in the Federal mass, as it flowed rearward, heavily packed in the narrow road, for a mile to another position, even stronger and better prepared for defense, where they drew up and again offered battle, with the evidences of a more determined purpose to make a sturdy defense, from behind rail and log breastworks, which had been arranged, of no slight defensive character. The greater part of Forrest's Bri-

---

* Jacob Gaus was the name of his favorite orderly bugler.

gade, now under Colonel Duckworth, was dismounted on the right of the road and thrown forward to storm the cover. General Forrest took part with and led the Forrest Brigade, augmenting their ardor by his presence. The Fifth Mississippi, led by Lieutenant-Colonel James A. Barksdale, rising the crest of the hill, just rightward of the road, were met by a scathing volley that fearfully thinned their ranks, and their intrepid commander fell mortally smitten while animating them, as well by his shining conduct as by words, to be steadfast and press on. Even as his life ebbed away, he repeated the word "Charge!" and almost to the last moment urged them forward. Elsewhere on the line the defense was equally stubborn and bloody, and the assault equally strenuous, detachments of all the regiments of the brigade, led by their field-officers, taking part with emulous courage.

The Federals, however, were forced back, but only for half a mile, where the ground afforded another favorable position, with abundance of rails available for another temporary breastwork; here again they turned angrily and once more confronted their indomitable pursuers. McCulloch was now up with his Texans and Missourians, who charged forward, shouting that their colors should not lag behind any on that field; Forrest's Brigade also, though deprived of so many of their favorite officers either killed or wounded. Therefore the conflict for the position was short but very sanguinary. The Federals, evidently in stronger force than previously, fought well; but such was the fierceness, the weight of the attack that they yielded the ground, suffering a good deal as they retired, especially the Fourth Regulars and the Sixth and Ninth Illinois Cavalry. The Confederate losses also were severe before the position was carried.

A mile beyond, a cluster of log cabins and out-buildings, and some strong fencing, afforded another rallying point for the hard-pressed Federals, who promptly seized the opportunity, and again stood at bay. Forrest and his escort were with the advance, and active in the onslaught. Disposing the Second and Seventh Tennessee on the right, and McCulloch's Brigade on the left, an attack followed with little delay. The musketry was again deadly to both sides, and Forrest's horse fell under him, pierced with five balls, besides which his saddle, struck three times, was shattered under him.* Pressing on, however, on foot, with the men, so many of whose best officers were now disabled, a trooper,† observing the situation of their leader, dismounted and gave up his own horse, which was taken as promptly as it was offered, but was likewise killed before Forrest had ridden it one hundred and fifty yards, fortunately, just as one of his own horses, a favorite and conspicuous iron gray gelding, was brought to him from the rear.‡ It was about this juncture, too, that the gallant Col. McCulloch was painfully wounded in the hand, and had to quit the field—an untoward occurrence, for at the mishap, his brigade, for a while, was brought to a stand, and Forrest found himself in advance, with scarcely 300 officers and men from all the different regiments engaged, and including some of his escort ; but with this small force he nevertheless hung close upon the

---

* We may here relate an authentic occurrence which must show how unfounded are the allegations that Forrest was a ruthless enemy in battle. After this position was carried, as he was passing a hut, on which a hospital flag was flying, his attention was attracted by a cry of agony, and he entered. The cry proceeded from a Federal soldier, deserted by his surgeon, who had left the amputating saw fast in the marrow of the bone of his leg. With his habitual presence of mind, the Confederate General saturated a cloth with chloroform and applied it to the nostrils of the sufferer, and leaving, sent his surgeon, Dr. Cowan, to complete the amputation, and the man got well.

† Private J. B. Long, Jackson, Tenn.

‡ This horse, twelve years old, and sluggish on ordinary occasions, became superbly excited in battle, and was as quick to detect the presence of a blue coat as any Confederate soldier, and then as ready to make battle, which he did by laying back his ears, and rushing at the offending object with open mouth.

enemy's rear, and just at sunset came upon them, drawn up in four strong lines* upon an elevated ridge, in the western skirt of a field of the area of about one hundred acres, ready to descend upon the Confederates, who, in the eagerness of their pursuit, debouched well into the field. The Federals stood in fine soldierly array, and the spectacle was imposing though inauspicious for the petty band of Confederates that had been so defiantly thrust into the centre of the field. In a moment Forrest appreciated the jeopardy of the juncture, exposed as his men were in that open field, to be ridden over and cut to pieces, if overtaken by disaster, for they were all dismounted, except himself and several field officers, not having halted to remount in the heat of the chase. He therefore hastily drew them back across and immediately behind a gully which furrowed the field. There he formed them in line as quickly as possible, to meet the approaching onset. At the same time he appealed to these stout-hearted men, who had shared so fully with him in the fierce ardor of that afternoon's work, to stand their ground steadily. They shouted cheerily in answer: the Federal bugles sounded the charge, and at this prompting, the first line we have mentioned, dashed down the slope in excellent order, to within sixty yards of the Confederates, who, at that distance, poured into it a scorching volley, which sent it reeling rearward, and strewed the ground in front with a number of dead and wounded horses and men. Again the bugle gave the shrill charge signal, and the second line descended handsomely at full gallop, the impetus of which was only broken at forty yards, by a volley from the steadfast Confederates ; the third line, now thrown forward, was buffeted back in the same manner, but not until it had been permitted to approach within twenty yards, when a deadly

---

* Doubtless a regiment in each.

fire shattered its firm array, and cumbered the ground with horses and men. The remaining line, the largest and most menacing, was now put in action, with such persistence that, notwithstanding it was promptly met by a warm fusilade, the mass of it pressed up to the gully we have mentioned, and many even sprang across and broke through the Confederate ranks. By this time the Confederate rifle ammunition was exhausted, and the men, throwing down their guns, betook themselves to their revolvers, in the desperate hand-to-hand struggle that now came to pass, no fiercer than which occurred during the war, and whose stirring incidents have left an indelible impression in the memory of all surviving partici-pants.*

Just at this juncture, Lieutenant-Colonel McCulloch oppor-tunely brought up McCulloch's brigade, and meeting the portion of the enemy that had broken through, and passed to the rear of Forrest's position, killed and wounded a number, among others, an aid-de-camp of General Grierson, whose conspicuous bravery during the action so attracted the ad-miration of the Confederates, that Forrest directed special attention to be paid to his remains. The enemy were now broken and dispersed; many captures were made, though night and darkness rapidly supervened.

---

* And here again, we may relate one of those battle scenes which are char-acteristic of Forrest and the young men he trained and led. Major Thomas S. Tate, of Memphis, casually on his staff, became involved in a personal combat with a Federal officer, when, without any weapon, save an empty carbine, and in another moment, doubtless, would have been shot by his opponent with a revolver, though he was in the act of hurling his otherwise useless gun at that opponent's head. Happily for his staff-officer, Forrest saw his dilem-ma in time to ride up, and with a sweep of his sabre, nearly severed the Federal officer's head from his shoulders. The man toppled to the ground, and as he did so, Tate, taking the revolver from his hand, swung himself into the va-cated saddle, and with the weapon thus appropriated took an active part in the *mêlée.*

Gradually Forrest's men came up, and at eight P.M. General Gholson arrived upon the field with a brigade — only 700 strong—of State troops.

The Federal losses were not less than 600 killed and wounded, and 300 prisoners. Forrest's casualties were proportionately severe, some fifty killed, and one hundred and fifty wounded ; they were enhanced, however, by embracing his brother and others of his choicest officers.

On the morning of the 23d, early, General Gholson was directed to take up the pursuit with his troops, which he did as far as Cherry Creek, capturing some fifty stragglers. Here, too, some scouts, who happened to be in the country, fired into the Federal flank, making the impression that Forrest was upon them in that quarter ; the immediate result was a panic and scurry along the several roads towards Memphis, as fast as their jaded animals could be driven. At Tippah River, where the boat was destroyed, and a halt became necessary for the construction of a temporary bridge, some scouts having again fired upon the demoralized enemy from the surrounding bushes, a rush was made into the stream, in so frantic a manner, that many horses and some men were drowned, and thence forward to Memphis, there was little organization left in this command, which, scarcely a fortnight before, had left Memphis 7000 strong, and as splendidly equipped a corps of cavalry as ever took the field.

Meanwhile, having set parties to bury the dead, both Confederate and Federal, and pressed wagons to remove the wounded, of both sides alike, to the hospitals at Okolona, Forrest left the field with his staff and escort, and reëstablished his headquarters at Starkville, on the 24th.

Meanwhile, Major-General Lee, on the morning of the 22d, had arrived, with Brigadier-General W. H. Jackson's divison at Chalmer's headquarters, behind the Sook-a-toncha, and hearing of the retrograde movement of the Federals northward, had concluded rightly that they were effectually baffled for the present, and therefore he fell back as far as Starkville, where he waited Forrest's arrival. They had an immediate interview and consultation in regard to operations for the future, and touching their several resources for mutual support. On the 26th, Chalmers's Division had reassembled at Starkville, and on the following day, General Forrest transferred his headquarters to Columbus, Mississippi.

COMMENTARIES.

It must be recollected that the splendid success which attended Forrest's encounter and discomfiture of this large, splendidly appointed veteran Federal force was achieved by not more than half the numbers thus beaten ; achieved, too, with troops, the greater part of whom were the raw, undisciplined young men, whom, less than sixty days before, he had gathered to his standard in West-Tennessee. In that short time he had been able to impregnate them with his ardent, indomitable spirit, and mould them into the most formidable instruments, in his hands, for his manner of making war.

CHAPTER XV.

Small Brigade of Kentuckians added to Command—Another Division organized and assigned to Brigadier-General A. Buford—Affair at Yazoo City—Another Expedition into West-Tennessee—Ruse and Capture of Union City—Forrest made successful Descent upon Paducah—Death of Colonel A. P. Thompson in abortive Assault upon Federal Earthworks—Large Quantity of Supplies secured and carried off—Fruitless Demonstration upon Columbus, Ky.—Second Descent (Buford) upon Paducah—Handsome Affair of Colonel Neely's at Bolivar—Splendid Conduct of McDonald's (Crews's) Battalion near Sommerville—Measures taken for the Capture of Fort Pillow.

March 1st to April 10th, 1864.

IN the first week of March, Forrest's command was augmented by three regiments of Kentuckians, who, having served hitherto as infantry, were now sent into his department to be mounted and transferred to the cavalry arm. They were so greatly reduced, however, all three together did not number more than 700 effectives, about one third of whom had received horses already—the remainder were, as yet, to be horsed. Brigadier-General A. Buford came with them, and was assigned to the command of the Second Division of Forrest's Cavalry, which was assembled at Tibbee Station, on the Mobile and Ohio Railroad. Buford assumed. command on the 8th of March, when the division consisted of the Third (Colonel A. P. Thompson) and the Fourth (Colonel T. H. Bell) brigades, together not exceeding 2800 effectives.*

Chalmers commanded the other, or First Division, with headquarters at Mayhew Station, (four miles south of Tibbee,) where the Second Brigade, McCulloch commanding, was established on the 6th ; also the Seventh Tennessee Cavalry, of the First, or Richardson's Brigade, the other three regiments of which had been previously detached in the direction of Grenada.†

Meanwhile Richardson, after having taken post at Grenada, was called to Yazoo City—75 miles southward—to coöperate with a force attached to Major-General Lee's command, against a Federal expedition which had made a lodgment there, and established water communication with its base ; and on the 4th, he had effected a junction in that vicinity with Brigadier-General Ross, and his brigade of Texan cavalry. The position, strongly fortified by the Federals, was garrisoned by one regiment of white, and two of negro troops,‡ and these were supported by two gunboats, which could throw shells over and

---

* Third Brigade was constituted of: Third, (Lieutenant-Colonel G. A. C. Holt ;) Seventh, (Colonel Ed. Crossland ;) Eighth, (Colonel H. B. Lyon ;) Faulkner's Kentucky regiments, and Jeffrey Forrest's Regiment, (Lieutenant-Colonel Wisdom,) about 1200 rank and file, or 1004 effective enlisted men. The Fourth Brigade of: Second, (Colonel B. R. Barteau,) and Sixteenth, (Colonel A. N. Wilson,) and Russell's Tennessee regiments—1254 effective enlisted men, or about 1600 rank and file.

† The First Brigade was formed of : Seventh, (Colonel W. T. Duckworth, at Mayhew ;) Twelfth, (Lieutenant-Colonel J. U. Green ;) Fourteenth, (Colonel J. J. Neely ;) and Fifteenth, (Colonel F. M. Stewart,) Tennessee regiments, (detached at Grenada.) Second Brigade of: Second Missouri, (Lieutenant-Colonel R. A. McCulloch ;) Willis's Texan Battalion, (Lieutenant-Colonel Leo Willis ;) First Mississippi Partisans, (Major J. M. Parks ;) Fifth Mississippi Cavalry, (Major W. B. Peery ;) Nineteenth Mississippi Battalion, (Lieutenant-Colonel W. L. Duff ;) Eighteenth Mississippi Battalion, (Lieutenant-Colonel A. H. Chalmers ;) and McDonald's Battalion—(General Forrest's old regiment—(Lieutenant-Colonel J. M. Crews.)

‡ *Reb. Rec.* VIII. Doc. 109, pp. 455-458.

into the town with ease. Nevertheless, the attack was arranged between Generals Richardson and Ross, that evening,
and made on the next morning, apparently with far more of
courage and spirit than of method and judgment. The Federals were speedily driven from one of their exterior works,
through the town, which became the scene of a sharp combat
with the Federals, who, from behind houses, cotton-bales, and
fences, inflicted considerable loss upon their uncovered assailants—chiefly the Tennesseeans—including the gallant Major Gwinn Thurman, commander of the Fourteenth, who was
killed, and Captain Thrall, of the artillery, and Captain ——
Adams, of Richardson's staff, who were wounded. But several fortified positions, exterior to and commanding the place,
were still in possession of the Federals, who could not be expelled without a loss incommensurate with their value, and
which they declined to surrender when demanded by General
Ross; hence it was determined to withdraw the whole Confederate force from under fire. There was no lack of courage,
but clearly an absence of concert and of sustained movement,
in this operation ; and, worst of all, a divided command,
for though General Richardson claimed to be the senior, he
waived the chief command in deference to the fact that General Ross had a superior knowledge of the theatre of operations, and commanded a brigade of veterans acquainted with
the ground. It would appear, therefore, that each brigade
was handled in the attack as a separate force, with little regard
to the movements or purposes of the other—an incongruity in
war utterly hostile to success. Howbeit, by ten o'clock A.M.
the next day, the Federals had evacuated the position, and
withdrawn down the river—a proceeding unquestionably
brought about by the attack of the day before, even though
it had miscarried.* The Confederate forces were then sun-

---

* We ascertain the object of this ex-   least a brigade of cavalry, and thus di-
pedition was to draw to that point at   minish the force that else might have

dered, and Richardson marched back to Grenada, in which vicinity his brigade remained until the 15th, when it joined its proper division, then *en route* for Panola.*

For a week after Forrest established his headquarters at Columbus, he occupied himself actively with the duties of administration, and his order-books of the period show a wide range of judicious measures, embracing the detachment of small commands under discreet and zealous officers, to collect absentees, or persons owing military duty in different sections of Mississippi, and for the suppression of Tory marauders in Alabama, and of the illicit distillation of grain within the limits of his command, the provision of ammunition for all arms, and all that could possibly tend to the enhancement of the efficiency of his force, either in relation to organization or equipment.   At the same time he had determined to make another inroad across the line of the Memphis and Charleston Railroad into West-Tennessee, and, if possible, into Western Kentucky, to which he was incited by several motives :

1st. Buford's Kentuckians were in pressing need of clothing and equipments, and one third were on foot, while the horses of many of the rest were indifferent ; he therefore desired to give that command an opportunity to refit in their own State.

2d. The Tennesseeans brought out in December were, also, for the most part, in great need of clothing, and had left their homes so suddenly as to make it important they, likewise, should be indulged in a brief visit to that region.

Meanwhile, on the 13th, Chalmers's Division, at the time commanded by Colonel McCulloch, was ordered by General

---

been employed to prevent a junction of General Smith's cavalry force with Sherman, about Meridian, a junction which, as we learn, was very effectually baffled, nevertheless.

* General Richardson, however, had been relieved from duty with it on the 12th, and the command devolved on Colonel J. J. Neely.

Forrest to return to Panola, each regiment taking in its route thither a different road, to sweep the country as far southward as Grenada, and gather up all persons irregularly or improperly absent from the army.

All needful preparations for the contemplated expedition northward having been completed by the 15th, Buford's Division—Thompson's and Bell's Brigades—the Seventh Tennessee, and McDonald's Battalion, under Lieutenant-Colonel Crews, were in motion on that day. The route was widely different from that taken in December previously, due, doubtless, to the point of departure. It was near Corinth that West-Tennessee was now entered, Faulkner's Regiment having been thrown out, however, on the left flank, to cross the line at Pocahontas, and thence, through Bolivar, on to Denmark, westward of Jackson, which, as in December, was the point of direction for the main force, and Forrest was there as early as the 20th, five days after leaving Columbus, one hundred and fifty miles distant.

Here one of his battalions was detached in the direction of Memphis, to hold vigilant watch over and report all Federal movements or approaches from that direction, while Buford (not yet up) was directed on the 22d to send thither all his dismounted men (under a competent officer) who were unable to make the march northward, as also Colonel Wilson, with five companies of his regiment, to occupy the place during the expedition. This arranged, on the afternoon of the 22d, Forrest repaired to Trenton with his staff, escort, the Seventh Tennessee and Faulkner's Regiments, Buford encamping the same evening at Spring Creek, twelve miles north-east of Jackson.

On the 23d, the Seventh Tennessee, McDonald's Battalion, and Faulkner's Regiment—less than 500 men—were detached under Colonel Duckworth, to move upon Union City and capture any Federal force there. Approaching the place before

daylight, on the morning of the 24th, the Confederate commander discovered by the light of some burning buildings, exterior to the position occupied by the Federals, that they were
strongly intrenched in a square redoubt. A close and vigorous investment ensued, however, and for several hours there
was a good deal of sharp-shooting, while Faulkner's Kentuckians made a charge to within twenty or thirty yards of the
work, the gallant Lieutenant-Colonel Lannum receiving a
very severe wound on the occasion. Without artillery, and
the force within the works being fully equal in numbers to his
own, Colonel Duckworth now resorted to the *ruse* of presenting
a peremptory demand for the surrender of the position, in the
name of General Forrest, as if that redoubtable Confederate
were present, conducting the operations. The Federal commander — Colonel Hawkins — who once before (December,
1862) had fallen into Forrest's hands, asking delay, and time
to consider " so grave a matter as the surrender " of his post,
besought, moreover, a personal interview with Forrest, which,
of course, was impracticable, while there was danger, also, of
reënforcement.* Duckworth, therefore, cleverly answered in
the name of his chief, as before, that other important military
movements would not allow a moment for deliberation ; that
the answer, therefore, must be immediate and conclusive ;
that he (Forrest) was not in the habit of meeting officers inferior in rank to himself, under flag of truce, but would send
Colonel W. L. Duckworth, an officer of equal rank, clothed
with power to arrange terms, and any arrangement made by
him would be strictly observed. The interview took place.
Hawkins plead for delay, but Duckworth was obdurate ; the

---

* General Brayman, with a reënforcement of 2000 men, actually came to
within six miles of Union City that afternoon, after the surrender, but there
hearing of the disaster, returned to Columbus, Ky., and Cairo.—*See Reb. Rec.*
VIII. Doc. 1, pp. 6 and 49.

capitulation was therefore made at eleven A.M., and 475 men, with their arms and ammunition, camp and garrison equipage, and 300 horses, were the results of this adroitlp-managed stratagem.*

Meanwhile, Forrest, with his escort and Buford's Division, was pressing, by rapid marches, toward Paducah, before which he arrived about two P.M. on the 25th. Federal scouts had been thrown out that morning, it is stated, but finding no enemy approaching, had returned and reported the roads clear. Presently Forrest presented himself, however, and dashed into the town with his advance-guard, forcing the Federals to betake themselves, in hot haste, to their stronghold, Fort Anderson, a large inclosed earthwork, constructed for such an emergency, in the western suburbs of the town, about one hundred yards removed from the river bank, and surrounded by a broad, deep ditch, fringed with a strong *abatis*.

In this movement, Buford had been directed to dismount one hundred of his men, and throw them forward leftward, in the direction of the fort, to reconnoitre and feel the defensive means of the enemy in that quarter, while, as before recited, Forrest charged with his escort rightward upon the pickets and drove them back, down the main street, into the town. It was not his purpose to attack the fort, and he gave no orders looking to such a step. But speedily was heard the sound of rapid, heavy firing of small-arms and artillery in that direction, and, on sending Captain Anderson, his aid, to ascertain the cause, that officer, returning in a few moments, reported that an attack had been made by Colonel Thomp-

---

* It is but justice to say that Lieutenant W. S. Pope, Adjutant of the Seventh Tennessee, and Lieutenant W. M. McConnell, of Henderson's Scouts, by their presence of mind and intelligent conduct of the flag of truce, contributed largely to the success of the Confederates on this occasion. Lieutenant Pope subsequently fell at Tishemingo Creek.

son, with about four hundred men of the Third and Seventh Kentucky, which, though gallantly led and made, had been repulsed with the loss of that distinguished officer.

The work, as before said, was of a formidable class, garnished with at least six pieces of artillery, and at this time all the Federal troops at Paducah had taken refuge in it—from 700 to 1000 in number, embracing detachments from the Sixteenth Kentucky Cavalry, the One Hundred and Twenty-second Illinois Infantry, and the First Kentucky Negro Artillery, with the provost-guard of the place.* The attack was made by Colonel Thompson and his Kentuckians, with all the lustrous valor with which men are inspired to fight for the recovery of homes and firesides ; but it was deplorably thrown away ; their ranks were speedily thinned by the hot tide of musketry and grape that seethed over the stout parapets, which they had vainly aspired to scale, and the life-blood of Albert P. Thompson was poured out within sight of the place of his birth, the house of his father, the home of his proud, useful manhood, the field of his professional distinction. The fire concentrated upon this band of Kentuckians was too consuming to be endured ; and Colonel Crossland, who succeeded to the command, distributed his men promptly among the numerous houses, from the upper stories and roofs of which they poured a deadly fire over the parapets of the works.

Made aware of the situation, Forrest sent a positive order to Buford not to attempt to storm the Federal position, and at the same time causing a bugle to be sounded in indication of his wish for a parley, presented a formal demand for the surrender of the place, in order, as he stated in his note, to avoid the unnecessary effusion of blood, inasmuch as he had

---

* The lowest Federal estimate is 646, while one places the force at 1000. *Vide Reb. Rec.* VIII. Doc. 127, p. 502.

an overwhelming force at his command, a device that more than once he had found very efficacious in previous operations.* At the time of his attack upon the fort, two Federal gunboats, the Peosta and the Paw Paw, had taken an active, efficient part, from positions highly favorable, in repelling it, and probably, indeed, it was by a shell from one of these that Colonel Thompson was slain. They greatly added, it was evident, to the strength of the work;† and Colonel Hicks, the Federal Commander, flushed with his recent advantage,

---

* We find this note embodied in the report of Colonel Hicks, *Reb. Rec.* VIII. Doc. 1, p. 73, as follows :

"HEADQUARTERS FORREST'S CAVALRY CORPS, PADUCAH, KY., March 25, 1864.

COLONEL HICKS, Commanding Federal Forces at Paducah :

COLONEL : Having a force amply sufficient to carry your works and reduce the place, and in order to avoid the unnecessary effusion of blood, I demand the surrender of the fort and troops, with all public property. If you surrender, you shall be treated as prisoners of war ; but if I have to storm your works, you may expect no quarter. (Signed)

N. B. FORREST,
Maj.-Gen. Com. Con. Troops."

The menace with which the foregoing summons is concluded has been violently denounced at the North, as something infamously unusual in war ; and some of the witnesses examined by the Congressional Committee, though affecting to be as learned as a "Cathedral Doctor," in regard to the

law and customs of war in such cases, were very harsh in their condemnation, ignoring the fact that the laws of war really subject those who prolong a vain defense of a fortified place to be put to the sword, when it shall be carried by storm ; and, further, that on several occasions, as late as the Napoleonic wars in Spain, this stern right of war was exercised. Forrest having no intention whatsoever of attempting to assault the fort, (without artillery as he was, except four small, useless mountain howitzers,) simply resorted to this demand, including the threat, as a simple, legitimate *brutum fulmen.* Unquestionably, it was proper for him to seek to impress the Federal Commander with the idea that he had such a force at his back as made further defense unjustifiable, because hopeless ; and hence, one that would lay them liable to severe treatment in the event he were forced to do that (storm the place) which he had no idea of doing, as was shown by the fact that he made no attempt to storm it afterward.

† *Vide Reb. Rec.* VIII. Doc. 127, p. 504.

promptly answered the demand of his capitulation with a defiant refusal.

Meanwhile, the Confederates had complete possession of the town itself; the streets of which the guns of the fort and gunboats were sweeping with incessant discharges of solid shot, shell, and grape, doing a great deal of damage to the buildings. Scattered in detachments, Buford's men nevertheless began to collect in the various stores, warehouses, and stables, the clothing, supplies, and horses, for which the operations had been chiefly undertaken ; and other parties were set to destroy such public property and war material as could not be removed, including the quartermaster's depot and offices, railroad depot with all the rolling stock, and the Marine Way with the steamer Dacotah, on the stocks for repairs.* Immediately fronting and contiguous to the river, there was a row of buildings, mainly used for army purposes, and into these Forrest promptly threw detachments of Russell's Tennesseeans and his own escort, with long-range rifles, which were brought to bear upon the apertures of the gunboats with an accuracy so deadly, that they were driven to seek shelter under the fort. Other parties of riflemen, occupying a number of buildings in proximity to the fort itself, annoyed the garrison with such effect that, while there was considerable destruction of buildings and property, chiefly occupied or owned by the Federal government and its friends, by the virulent cannonade now turned upon the town, the Confederates, nevertheless, had ample opportunity to glean the place thoroughly for such military supplies as were wanting.†

---

* *Reb. Rec.* VIII. Doc. 127, p. 508.

† The allegation that these sharpshooters were advanced, while the flag of truce was up, is unfounded, though, we doubt not, some of them exercised their skill on the gunboats at that time, unaware that there was any truce, just, doubtless, as the commanders of the gunboats were ignorant of it, and, therefore, *did not cease their cannonade.* The truce did not last more than three quarters of an hour.

Forrest having closely reconnoitered the work, in the interval while his sharp-shooters were actively harassing its garrison from the tops and upper stories of the adjoining houses, became fully satisfied that to storm it would involve a greater sacrifice of valuable life than would be justified by the capture of the force that defended it, withdrew all his troops without making any other effort to assault the work than that which had so unfortunately resulted in the loss of Colonel Thompson. Therefore, the highly wrought narratives with which the Northern newspapers of the day abound, of successive charges—four or five in number—upon the fort, by serried masses of Confederates, up even to the very "mouths of the guns," and upon "the walls of the fort" to be ignominiously beaten back by negro soldiers with clubbed muskets,* and at the cost of hecatombs of their dead and wounded, are mean, extravagant fictions, as groundless as the infamous stories of Confederate atrocities, set afloat in the like channels, at the same period, to infuriate the Northern people.

Such were the salient events and incidents which characterized the affair at Paducah, on the afternoon of the 25th of March, when that place was in possession of the Confederates, from a little after two until eleven P.M. Then Forrest withdrew his main force some four miles southward, and encamped, taking with him some fifty prisoners, about four hundred horses and mules, and a very large supply of clothing and quartermaster's subsistence and military supplies, including saddles and other horse equipments, for the procurement of which, as we have said, the expedition had been mainly made.

---

* It would seem that negro courage and prowess were chiefly worthy of notice by these veracious chroniclers. Therefore, Colonel Thompson, after having been torn to pieces by a shell, must needs be dramatically and "simultaneously struck in the forehead by a musket-ball, fired by an ardent young African," while "colored soldiers" are those specially noticed as resorting to clubbed muskets.

Another object, however, was to confuse, distract, and defensively occupy the Federal forces that, for some time previously, had been used to harass and despoil the people of West-Tennessee and North-Mississippi ; and this, too, was accomplished in a high degree, for the most exaggerated notions prevailed among Federal officers of rank in regard both to the strength of Forrest's forces and his purposes.*

The morning of the 26th, though largely reënforced during the night, and his ammunition replenished, the Federal commander, apprehensive of another attack, threw out detachments from his fortress, and set fire to a large number of buildings, including some of the best dwelling and business houses of the place, which, in that event, might be occupied by hostile sharp-shooters, to his annoyance.† But it will be remembered that Forrest had already begun to retire, having really accomplished the purposes for which the expedition had been undertaken, and hence this waste of property was the fruit of an idle apprehension. At nine A.M., however, on the 26th, Forrest sent, under a flag of truce, a proposition for an exchange of prisoners, to the extent of those who had been captured by Faulkner at Union City, and those taken in his own operations of the day before ; but this was declined, for alleged want of authority.†

----

* *Vide* evidence of Major-General Hurlbut before Congressional Committee, *Reb. Rec.* VIII. Doc. 1, pp. 40, 41. General Sherman says, however, in one of his characteristic dispatches at the time, that it was in just such operations he wanted to see Forrest kept employed, to divert the Confederate cavalry from other operations, the results of which he dreaded more, namely, a concentrated attack on his communications as he pressed Johnston back upon Atlanta. There is no doubt the proper quarter for Forrest's operations had been upon Sherman's long, exposed, vulnerable line of communications. General Johnston had urged upon the Confederate authorities such a use of his force, but they had other views ; and not having been thus employed, Forrest did that in his sphere which could most distract, harass, and hurt his immediate enemy.

† *Reb. Rec.* VIII. Doc. 127, p. 509.
‡ *Ibid.*

Meanwhile, the main Confederate force was already in motion southward, *via* Mayfield. There the Third and Seventh Kentucky regiments were detached by squads to repair to the several neighborhoods in South-West Kentucky, in which they had been enrolled, to visit their kindred, from whom they had been long separated, and at the same time to beat up recruits—with orders, however, to reassemble by the end of the month at that place, where General Buford remained, with some three or four hundred of the Second Tennessee and Eighth Kentucky, to await their return. Forrest then moved southward with the other regiments of the force—taking separate roads severally—and sweeping the country between the Obion and Tennessee rivers, for absentees and other persons subject to military service, horses suitable for cavalry and artillery, and for government arms in the hands of citizens. Bell's Brigade, however, was left at Trenton, in which vicinity it belonged, to give the officers and men not only an opportunity to see their families and friends, and to procure summer clothing, but also to recruit.

Buford's Kentuckians having returned promptly to their colors, he reached Trenton on the 3d of April, and established the headquarters of his division there, under orders to avail himself diligently of the resources of the surrounding country, to mount, equip, and recruit both the brigades, as far as possible. To that point, likewise, were dispatched the detachment of dismounted Kentuckians, unable to accompany the expedition that had been left meanwhile at Jackson. Faulkner's Regiment also rejoined, and he was further instructed to hold his command "in readiness to move at the shortest notice," with ten days' subsistence constantly on hand.*

---

* MS. letter of Major Strange, A. A. G., to General Buford, March 31st and April 5th, 1864.

While at Trenton, Buford having noticed, in a Northern newspaper, the statement that the horses which had been recently carried off from Paducah belonged exclusively to the citizens, while those of the United States had escaped by their adroit concealment in the old foundry or rolling-mill, in the outskirts of the town, acquainted Forrest with the circumstances, and requested and obtained authority to return at once with the Kentucky Brigade, or some 800 men, and complete his remounts.

Setting out on the 8th, Buford was in the vicinity of Columbus on the 12th, when he detached his escort, (Captain Tyler,) Seay's Company of the Seventh, and Horne's, of the Third Kentucky, under Captain J. C. Horne, to make a vigorous demonstration on the position. One of his staff-officers (Lieutenant D. E. Myers) also accompanied the detachment, to carry a flag of truce, to demand the surrender, as if his superior were present with his whole force, with the hope of thus drawing thither reënforcements, and distracting the movements of the Federal forces.* Other detachments

---

* The demand was couched in the following language :

HEADQUARTERS C. S. FORCES,
BEFORE COLUMBUS, KY.,
April 13, 1864.

To the Commanding Officer U. S. Forces, Columbus, Ky. :

Fully capable of taking Columbus and its garrison by force, I desire to avoid the shedding of blood, and therefore demand the unconditional surrender of the forces under your command. Should you surrender, the negroes now in arms will be returned to their masters. Should I, however, be compelled to take the place, no quarter will be shown to the negro troops whatever; the white troops will be treated as prisoners of war.

I am, sir, yours,

(Signed)   A. BUFORD,
                  Brigadier-General.

As is seen above, only three small companies were engaged in the expedition, and it must be apparent the language of the foregoing note was resorted to as a legitimate stratagem to alarm the Federals to the utmost for the safety of the troops thus menaced, and thus attract reënforcements there, and divert them from Buford's real objective, Paducah, whither he was moving at the time with his main force.

were also thrown out, to make ostentatious display of force in the country, especially at points on the Tennessee River. And on the 14th, Buford suddenly appeared at Paducah, about one o'clock P.M., by the Paducah road, with his advance-guard, while his main body entered on the Mayfield way. The Federal force now at Paducah had been increased to quite three times that of Buford, and at least four gunboats were likewise present, with several near by. Nevertheless, the Confederates boldly entered and occupied the town, the Federals, in part, taking shelter in the fort, and the remainder occupying a position covered by the river bank — supported by several of the gunboats. Thus stood matters, when Buford proceeding to execute his plan of operations, accordingly sent a squadron of cavalry to the rolling-mill, to search for horses, and set Lieutenant-Colonel Shacklett, of the Eighth Kentucky, to investigate the quartermaster and subsistence store-houses. The horses, some 140 excellent stock, were soon found concealed, as had been anticipated, but, for the most part, the subsistence and other supplies had been removed across the river that day, in anticipation of an attack. Meanwhile, a furious bombardment had been opened on the town, from fort and gunboat, but no movement was made on the part of the Federal commander to throw his troops from their cover. Buford's next measure was now to beguile his adversary with the apprehension of a serious attack, so he formally notified the Federal commander of his intention to attack him, and granted a truce of one hour, for the purpose of moving the women and children. This was accepted, and the navy officers began to remove the women and children to the Illinois shore. Meanwhile, Buford began to withdraw, with his main force and spoils, leaving Faulkner to threaten the place for some hours longer, and then retire westward, on the road to Blandville, to continue the deception as to the objects and the strength of these Confederate movements. Buford himself fell back slowly to Dresden, on the 18th, and established his headquarters there until the 30th, under orders from General Forrest, for the purpose of recruiting and procuring additional artillery and cavalry horses.*

III.

While the events we have related in the preceding sections of this chapter were passing, other portions of Forrest's command elsewhere had not been inactive, nor without incidents that properly belong to this memoir.

It will be recollected that, as Forrest led Buford's Division and several of Chalmers's regiments and battalions toward the Ohio river, Chalmers was sent to establish himself with the main part of his division about Panola, Mississippi. But about the time Forrest was leaving Jackson, he ordered that Neely's Brigade† should likewise enter West-Tennessee, and take post at or about Brownsville, and that McCulloch's Brigade should be thrown forward across the Tallahatchie to Waterford, some eight miles south of Holly Spring. Accordingly, Neely, getting in motion on the 25th of March, was at Bolivar on the 29th, and there encountered and completely routed a Federal force under the notorious Hurst, that— leader and men—had become as conspicuous for their craven conduct in the presence of armed enemies, as for rapacity and brutal, cruel outrages toward the defenseless citizens of the country which they desolated. This band of merciless marauders, trusting to their supposed superior numbers, boldly approached Bolivar, with a confidence that was speedily dissipated when it became apparent that the Confederates intended to fight, and Hurst attempted to withdraw ; but

---

* Buford's Official Report, with other MS. accounts of the transactions.
† Recently Richardson's Brigade.

Neely, pursuing promptly and hotly, killed about twenty and captured some thirty, and their wagon-train, (five wagons and teams,) and two ambulances, with their contents, including 50,000 rounds of ammunition, much needed, as it happened, by the Confederates, at the moment. The main part of these miscreants,, however, effected their escape by way of Sommerville, to Memphis, from the lines of which, we are told, they did not emerge for the rest of the war as a band. Previously—27th—Chalmers, having learned that Grierson had been detached with a heavy cavalry force from Memphis, to operate upon Forrest's rear, ordered McCulloch to leave two battalions* to guard the crossing of the Tallahatchie, and advance with the remainder of the brigade toward the Tennessee border. With this command, General Chalmers crossed into West-Tennessee, at or near Lagrange, on the 29th, and was at Bolivar early on the next day. Meanwhile, the prisoners accumulated in the course of the expedition, at Jackson, some 600 in number, were detached, *en route* for Demopolis, Alabama, under a strong escort, in the direction of Corinth. But rumors being rife of the movement of large bodies of Federal troops in that quarter, with the purpose of intercepting and recapturing the prisoners, the officer in command returned rightward, toward Pocahontas, and Chalmers's Division likewise was detached, to insure their safe conduct beyond the dangerous ground of the line of the Memphis and Charleston Railroad. But so thick and specific were the rumors of the presence in that direction of considerable hostile forces, that Forrest could not keep aloof, and made one of his characteristic expeditions. It had been reported that a force of some 6000 Federals were at Purdy. making his escort, he rode swiftly to that vicinity, with the

---

* Nineteenth Mississippi (Duff's) and First Mississippi Partisans.

purpose of engaging them in such a series of skirmishes as should check their movements.* The information, however, was untrue. Meantime, the prisoners were safely convoyed across the border, and Chalmers's Division returned northward,—McCulloch's Brigade to Jackson, and Neely's to Brownsville and Sommerville.

As will be recollected, as Forrest moved northward, McDonald's Battalion, after the affair of Union City, was sent to reconoitre, and report all hostile movements from the direction of Memphis. Having performed this service without notable incident, and returned to Bolivar, Forrest detached Lieutenant-Colonel Crews, its commander, to repair to the western part of Fayette county, and, while keeping twenty men of each company in the ranks, to furlough the rest for a few days to visit their friends and refit, especially clothing. Accordingly, being in camp several miles west of Sommerville on the night of the 2d of April, with only sixty men present, Colonel Crews received intimation that a strong Federal cavalry force was *en route* eastward from Raleigh, on the Sommerville road. He therefore moved out early next morning to observe this movement, and at one P.M., within twelve or fifteen miles of Raleigh, encountered and was fired upon by the enemy's advance-guard, at Royster's farm. Exposing his colors and a few men upon the crest of a hill, as ostentatiously as possible, Colonel Crews kept concealed the smallness of his real force, while he reconoitered from some high ground in advance. The enemy, as he discovered, evidently apprehensive of the situation, had also halted, and were drawn up in a long line of battle, along the crown of a high ridge just in advance, behind a fence, with a company detached on each flank to cover it from any movement. Taking advantage of adjoining woods, Colonel Crews detached Lieutenant Christopher D.

---

* Dispatch of Major Strange, A. A. G., to General Chalmers, March 31st, 1864.

Steinkuhl, of Memphis, with twelve men to the right, and Lieutenant T. H. Mayer with ten men to the left, with orders to approach under cover, and attack and dislodge the Federal flank detachments at all hazards. Dismounting a small squad at the same time to engage the Federal sharp-shooters, who were annoying those of the Confederates exposed to view, and as Lieutenants Steinkuhl and Mayer and their little detachments intrepidly attacked as directed, Crews charged down the main road with less than forty men mounted. It was a rash, desperate venture, but the splendid daring and confidence with which it was undertaken and conducted so misled the enemy, that two Federal regiments gave way for several hundred yards, and took a defensive position, reënforced by two more regiments, among some houses and in a wood. Crews now moved boldly around to his right, as if seeking to take his adversaries in reverse, in that quarter where Lieutenant Steinkuhl was already creating some disturbance by his presence. But as soon as he was out of view, Colonel Crews turning, returned to, and reappeared in front of, the last position taken up by the Federals. Thoroughly deceived by these displays of force, incredible as it may seem, and evidently mistrustful of the situation, the whole Federal force immediately fell back in haste to Raleigh. It is said, also, that General Grierson, moving on another road, with another force equally large, was inoculated with the same apprehension, and a rapid retreat into Memphis was the result, with the destruction of all the bridges behind them, leaving Crews in possession of the field. The Confederate loss was merely two men and one horse wounded, while that of the enemy was five killed, six wounded, a captain, a non-commissioned officer, and one private captured.*

---

* MS. Notes of Lieutenant-Colonel Crews. That we have not given a grossly exaggerated narration of this affair is fully shown by the statement

Bell's Brigade of Buford's Division, now about 1700 strong, and McCulloch'sof Chalmer's Division, had meanwhile assembled at Jackson.   Ever since his advent into West-Tennessee, Forrest had been distressed by well-authenticated instances, repeatedly brought to his notice, of rapine and atrocious outrage upon non-combatants of the country, by the garrison at Fort Pillow.   And a delegation of the people of the town of Jackson and surrounding region now waited upon and earnestly besought him to leave a brigade for their protection against this nest of outlaws.   According to the information received, the garrison in question consisted of a battalion of whites, commanded by Major Bradford, (a Tennesseean,) and a negro battalion under Major Booth, who likewise commanded the post.   Many of Bradford's men were known to be deserters from the Confederate army, and the rest were men of the country who entertained a malignant hatred toward Confederate soldiers, their families and friends.   Under the pretense of scouring the country for arms and "rebel soldiers," Bradford and his subalterns had traversed the surrounding country with detachments, robbing the people of their horses, mules, beef cattle, beds, plate, wearing apparel, money, and every possible movable article of value, besides venting upon the wives and daughters of Southern soldiers the most oppro-

---

of Major-General Stephen A. Hurlbut, before the Congressional Committee as follows : " Forrest moved up and crossed the line of the Charleston and Memphis Railroad toward Jackson, Tennessee, and occupied it. General Grierson was directed to go out with his cavalry, feel him, attack him, and cripple him as much as possible. He went out, and reported that he was a little too strong for him, and he could not touch him. My effective force at Memphis consisted of 2200 cavalry, 2100 white infantry, and 2400 colored infantry." (*Reb. Rec.* VIII. Doc. 1, p. 40.) Thus it is admitted that Grierson went forth into the country 2200 strong, and returned after finding that the Confederates were "a little too strong for him." But we have shown he came in conflict with no part of Forrest's command but Crews and his sixty men. This may appear incredible, but nevertheless may be relied on.

brious and obscene epithets, with more than one extreme outrage upon the persons of these victims of their hate and lust.

The families of many of Forrest's men had been thus grievously wronged, despoiled, and insulted, and in one or two cases fearfully outraged, and many of his officers, uniting with the citizens of the country in the petition, begged to be permitted to remain, to shield their families from further molestation. Of course this was impossible; but Forrest determined to employ his present resources for the summary suppression of the evil and grievances complained of, by the surprise, if possible, and capture, at all hazards, of Fort Pillow; and the orders necessary to that end were issued on the 10th of April; Bell's and McCulloch's Brigades, with Walton's Battery—four mountain howitzers—being selected for the operation.

CHAPTER XVI.

FORT PILLOW.

Forrest in Movement upon Fort Pillow—Description of the Position—First Stage of the Attack, resulting in the Death of Federal Commander, Major Booth—Forrest, making close Reconnoissance, had two Horses killed under him—Confederate Sharp-Shooters envelop and command Position—Outworks and Position seized close to Parapets—Surrender demanded—Approach of Federal Transports with Troops—Forrest took Means to drive off Succor—Capitulation refused—Assault made—Parapets stormed—Garrison fled to River-Bank for Relief under Guns of Naval Vessel—Gunboat failed to render Aid—Results—Commentaries.

April 11th and 12th, 1864.

As we have stated in the last chapter, a long course of brutal, infamous conduct on the part of Bradford's Battalion toward the non-combatant people of West-Tennessee had determined General Forrest to break up their lair, and capture or destroy them before leaving that section of the country for other operations. To Bell's and McCulloch's Brigades and Walton's Battery of mountain-howitzers, as we have said, had this service been assigned, and they were immediately put in motion by way of Brownsville. Leaving Jackson on the morning of the 11th, Forrest overtook General Chalmers at Brownsville at two P.M., and, to add another to the chances of success, ordered that officer to push ahead with the troops by a forced march, so that they might be in close proximity to Fort Pillow by daylight the next morning. The distance was thirty-eight miles ; it was raining, and so dense the darkness after midnight, that it was difficult to distinguish the road or " to see a file-leader." Nevertheless, such was the eager spirit of the hardy riders who followed Chalmers, that they — McCulloch's Brigade in advance — pushed on that murky, wet night " without halting, except now and then to examine a shaky bridge."* Hence, just before dawn, the advance-guard, Captain Frank J. Smith's company of the Second Missouri Cavalry, surprised the Federal pickets and captured all except one or two, who, escaping to the Fort just·at sunrise, gave the first warning of the danger impending.†

Fort Pillow, first established in 1861, by the State of Tennessee, on the east bank of the Mississippi river, about three and a half miles above or north of Fulton, was so fortified by the Confederate States engineers, under the orders of General Beauregard, in March and April, 1862, that it effectually baffled the formidable efforts of the Federal navy to pass it. But about the last of May, 1862, the Confederates having been forced to evacuate Corinth, the line of the Memphis and Charleston Railroad, and hence Memphis, Fort Pillow was also abandoned. The Federals at once occupied it, but apparently never with any considerable force. And they never refurnished the water-batteries, which the Confederates had dismantled on retiring from the position, limiting their measures apparently to holding the position against the contin-

---

* MS. Notes of Captain Walter A. Goodman.

† Guided by a citizen of the neighborhood, Captain Smith was able to lead his company to the rear of their picket-post ; nevertheless, at least one man escaped. See also statement of Lieutenant Leming, *Reb. Rec.* VIII. Doc. I, p. 23.

gency of its becoming, otherwise, a point from which small Confederate expeditions or partisans might constantly distress if not interrupt the navigation of the Mississippi river. For of this there was peculiar danger, from the fact that the steamboat channel at that point runs within short musket-range of the eastern bank of the river, while that bank affords admira-- ble shelter and a plunging fire.* But, evidently feeling safe against any serious enterprise of any sort, the Federals neglected ordinary military precautions for the defense of the place against just such an assault as the one we have now to narrate. The lines of works erected by the Confederate engineers in 1861–2 to defend the land approaches were upon a very extended scale, with a strong profile calculated to resist siege artillery. That is, far too large to be of the least use or value to a garrison so small as that which the Federals habitually kept there, and, besides, several points upon it completely commanded, at a distance not exceeding six hundred yards, the immediate position upon which the Federals had freshly thrown up breastworks that were relied on with so much ill-judged confidence as an impregnable fastness against any hostile operation which could possibly be undertaken by the Confederates.† The Federal works were constructed with

---

* Major-General Hurlbut, in his evidence before the Congressional Committee at Cairo, Illinois, April 24th, 1864, thus precisely discusses the war value of the position to both sides : "The steamboat channel at Fort Pillow runs right under the bluff, and brings every boat as it passes within musket-shot of the shore, and a couple of guns mounted up above them would stop most effectually the navigation of the river and drive away any of the tin-clad gunboats we have, for a plunging fire

would go right through them and they could not get elevation enough to strike. The whole life of the army below, especially while these large movements were going on, depended upon an uninterrupted communication by the river, and the stopping of that communication for two or three days might deprive us of the necessary supplies just at the momen they were required."—*Reb. Rec.* VIII. Doc. 1, p. 41.

† "I received a report from him, (Major Booth,) that he could hold that

the *trace* and in the position exhibited in the map opposite—
that is, upon the highest part of the bluff chosen for occupation, and inclosing the north-west angle, formed by the river
and Coal creek, upon the last of which it jutted abruptly,
while a bench of some forty feet lay between it and the immediate river-bank at that stage of the water. Eastward there
was a gradual slope from the crown next the river for from
twenty to sixty yards, when the descent became sudden into a
narrow gorge that separated it from a labyrinth of hills and
ridges, divided from each other by a network of interlacing,
narrow ravines, and this slope was broken by several crooked
and deep gullies, affording well-covered approaches for an
enemy to within thirty to one hundred yards of the interior
intrenchments. Southward, this eminence also fell off gently
for about two hundred yards and then rapidly into a narrow
valley, the course of which was perpendicular to the river,
and in which were a number of trading-houses and other
buildings, known as the "town." This slope, as will be seen
in the diagram annexed, was seamed by a ravine which gave
hostile access to within one hundred and fifty yards of the
southern face of the works. Immediately exterior and parallel with the face of the works commanding this part of the
ground were four rows of cabins and tents, the outer line of
which (cabins) was not more than sixty yards distant from
the ditch, and rightward from these, stretched around to the
north for some two hundred yards, a rifle-pit along the eastern
verge of the acclivity. The parapets of the inner works were
about eight feet high, with a ditch six feet deep and twelve
broad. The armament consisted of two ten-pounder Parrott
rifled guns, two twelve-pounder howitzers, and two six-pound-

---

post against any force for forty-eight *Hurlbut, Reb. Rec.* VIII. Doc. 1, p.
hours." — *Evidence of Major-General* 41.

er rifled-bore field-pieces, and the whole garrison did not exceed 580 men.*

Upon the capture of the pickets, McCulloch's Brigade was pressed rapidly on, with instructions to take up a position southward of the Fort, and as near as possible to the river-bank and the work. Bell's Brigade, as prearranged, was likewise ordered up; Wilson's Regiment to deploy directly in front and occupy the close attention of the garrison by an immediate, vigorous skirmish, while the rest of the brigade should seek to penetrate to the river northward, along Coal creek, and invest and attack from that side, understood to be very weak and vulnerable. These movements were executed with care, and the many advantages of the ground were aptly used by the Confederates to avoid unnecessary exposure as they gradually brushed the small force of Federal sharp-shooters back from their advanced positions. McCulloch, on his side, soon seized a position with his left flank on the river-bank, about half a mile southward of the Fort, the remainder of his line disposed in the ravines extending around and toward the north-east, in close proximity to a high ridge upon which were the old lines of the Confederate works, the most elevated point upon which was occupied at the time by a Federal detachment. And thus, as had been predetermined, he awaited to hear the sound of Bell's musketry on the north as his signal for an attack from the south.

But Bell's movement had been barren of results : for it was

---

* Made up as follows : First Battalion, Thirteenth Tennessee Cavalry, Major William F. Bradford commanding, 10 officers and 285 enlisted men ; First Battalion, Sixth U. S. Heavy Artillery, (colored,) 8 commissioned officers and 213 enlisted men ; and one section Company D, Second U. S. Light Artillery, (colored,) 1 commissioned officer and 40 men—that is, aggregate white troops, 295 ; colored, 262 ; or, in all, 557.—*Reb. Rec.* VIII. Doc. 1, p. 62.

found impracticable to reach the river along Coal creek, and a new plan of attack had to be arranged. This brought delay, and meantime, after a ride of seventy-two miles since six o'clock the day before, Forrest came upon the field with his staff, escort, and a detachment under Lieutenant-Colonel Wisdom.

It was about nine o'clock as General Forrest reached the ground; and about the same hour Major Booth, the Federal commander, and his adjutant by his side, were killed.* Losing no time, Forrest pressed immediately to the front to reconnoitre, as was his wont, trusting that important duty to no other eyes than his own. And so thoroughly was this duty accomplished, that he had two horses killed and another wounded under him before he was satisfied, or saw enough of the ground to warrant him in forming a final plan of operations. It was thus he discovered the ravine, previously mentioned, leading up in near vicinity to the southern face of the Fort, which, if seized, would afford complete immunity from the fire of the Federals, as they could not depress their small-arms or artillery so as to command it; while two ridges, from four to five hundred yards distant, eastward and north-eastward from the enemy's position, gave the Confederate sharp-shooters excellent cover, from which they completely commanded the interior of the Federal works, and might effectually silence their fire.

Orders were therefore given immediately to "move up."† Bell threw his brigade forward until he gained a position in which his men were well sheltered by the conformation of the ground. And at the same time McCulloch advanced and gallantly carried the intrenchments on the highest part of the

---

* *Reb. Rec.* VIII. Doc. 1, p. 23.
† Forrest's favorite phrase. in such affairs.

ridge immediately in front of the south-eastern face of the work. The Federals fell back without further stand to their main work and the rifle-pit in its front, closely pressed by McCulloch, who seized and occupied the cluster of cabins on the southern face of the work, which, as we have said before, were about sixty yards from it, foiling an attempt on the part of the enemy to burn the buildings.* He also carried and occupied the rifle-pits. The positions thus secured were fatal to the defense, for the Confederates were now so placed that artillery could not be brought to bear upon them with much effect, except at a mortal exposure of the gunners. Moreover, the line of investment was now short and complete, extending from the river-bank south of the fort, to Coal creek on the north, so swollen at the moment by backwater as to be impassable, while rearward of the advanced line were numerous sharp-shooters favorably posted on several commanding ridges ready to pick off any of the garrison showing their heads above, or indeed, any men moving about within the circuit of, the parapets. Fully satisfied of his ability to carry the position without difficulty or delay, but desiring to avoid the loss of life that must occur in storming the works, Forrest determined to demand the surrender of the place. Accordingly,

---

* " They (the Confederates) kept up a steady fire by sharp-shooters behind trees, and logs, and high knolls. . . . They began to draw nearer and nearer up to the time our (Federal) men were all drawn into the fort. Two companies of the Thirteenth Tennessee Cavalry were ordered out as sharp-shooters, but were finally ordered in. We were pressed on all sides. I think Major Booth fell not later than nine o'clock. His adjutant, who was then acting post-adjutant, fell near the same time. Major Bradford then took the command. . . . Previous to this, Major Booth had ordered some buildings in front of the fort to be destroyed, as the enemy's sharp-shooters were endeavoring to get possession of them. There were four rows of buildings, but only the row nearest the fort was destroyed; the sharp-shooters gained possession of the others before they could be destroyed." Evidence of Lieutenant McJ. Leming, Adjutant Bradford's Battalion, *Reb. Rec.* VIII. Doc. 1, pp. 23, 24.

causing the signal for a cessation of hostilities to be given, he deputed Captain Walter A. Goodman, Adjutant-General on the staff of General Chalmers,* to bear a flag of truce with a formal demand in writing, couched substantially in these terms:

That, having the fort surrounded by a force sufficiently strong to take it by assault, wishing to avoid the unnecessary destruction of human life, he was prompted to make a demand for its surrender. That if this demand was acceded to, the gallantry of the defense which had already been made would entitle *all its* garrison to be treated as prisoners of war.†

This was written and dispatched from a point on an eminence included in the old Confederate lines, from which For-

---

* Captain Thomas Henderson, commanding scouts, and Lieutenant Frank Rodgers likewise accompanied the flag.

† In his MS. Recollections of Fort Pillow, Captain Goodman says: "I have no copy of this or of any of the correspondence that ensued, before me, but I am satisfied that my recollection of the substance of the different notes is correct; and I remember the proposition in the first to treat the garrison as prisoners of war, provided they were surrendered, the more clearly because, when the note was handed to me, there was some discussion about it among the officers present, and it was asked whether it was intended to include the negro soldiers as well as the white; to which both General Forrest and General Chalmers replied, that it was so intended; and that if the fort was surrendered, the whole garrison, white and black, should be treated as prisoners of war. No doubt as to the meaning

and scope of this proposition was ever expressed or intimated in any of the notes and conversations which followed it under the flag of truce." The communication in question, as printed in the *Reb. Rec.* VIII. Doc. 1, p. 24, does not differ in substance from that which we give:

"HEADQUARTERS CONFEDERATE CAVALRY, NEAR FORT PILLOW, April 12, 1864.

As your gallant defense of the fort has entitled you to the treatment of brave men, (or something to that effect,) I now demand an unconditional surrender of your force, at the same time assuring you that they will be treated as prisoners of war. I have received a fresh supply of ammunition, and can easily take your position.

(Signed)   N. B. FORREST.

To Major L. F. BOOTH, Commanding U. S. Forces."

rest commanded a full view of the interior of the Federal
works, and of their whole defensive resources ; but so close
already were the Confederates, that their flag of truce was
brought to a halt from the Fort before it had advanced beyond
the line held by the left of McCulloch's Brigade, and the conference that followed actually took place just at the left of
that line.

Booth, as we have seen, had been dead for several hours,
and the command had fallen into the feeble hands of Major
William F. Bradford, a West-Tennesseean, and commander of
the odious Thirteenth Tennessee Battalion. Nevertheless,
the answer received, after some delay, bore the name of Major
L. F. Booth, and, in effect, required an hour for consultation
with his officers and those of the gunboat, in regard to the
demand for the surrender of his post and the vessel. This
communication having been delivered to General Forrest, who
had meantime established himself at a point in the valley
about four hundred yards southward from the flag, he immediately replied, in writing, that he had not asked for, and did
not expect the surrender of, the gunboat ; but for that of the
fort and garrison, and that he would give twenty minutes for
a decision. Moreover, so great was the animosity existing
between the Tennesseeans of the two commands, he added,
that *he could not be responsible for the consequences if obliged to
storm the place.*

Pending the delivery and consideration of this communication, and during the period of the truce, the smoke of several
steamers was discovered ascending the river ; and speedily one,
crowded with troops, and her lower guards filled with artillery,
was distinctly seen approaching, near at hand, and manifestly
bearing directly for the beleaguered fortress.* Apprehensive

* These were the Olive Branch, with   the Hope and the M. R. Cheek.—*Reb.*
General Shepley and troops on board ;   *Rec.* VIII. Doc. 1, pp. 177, 8–9.

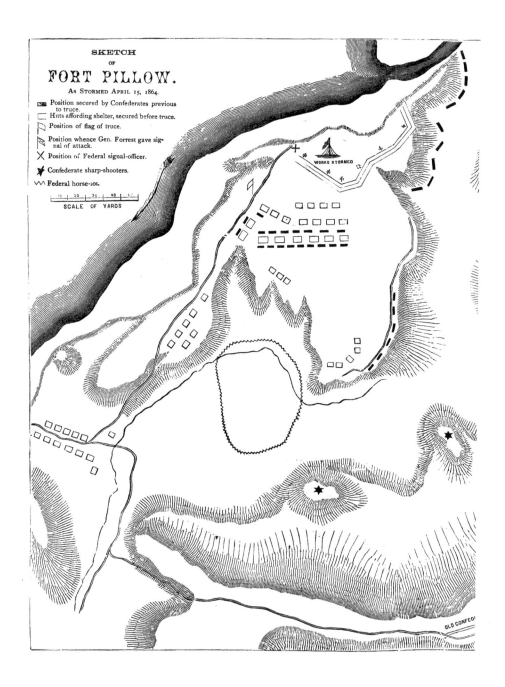

SKETCH
OF
FORT PILLOW.
As Stormed April 15, 1864.

Position secured by Confederates previous to truce.
Huts affording shelter, secured before truce.
Position of flag of truce.
Position whence Gen. Forrest gave signal of attack.
X Position of Federal signal-officer.
Confederate sharp-shooters.
Federal horse-lot.

SCALE OF YARDS

WORKS STORMED

OLD CONFED

that an attempt would be made to land reënforcements from these steamers, Forrest promptly dispatched his aid-de-camp, Captain Charles W. Anderson, with a squadron of McCulloch's Brigade, down the ravine, through the " town," to occupy the old trenches constructed by the Confederates in 1862, under the bluff at the river, above the mouth of that ravine, and just below the southern face of the invested work. That able, zealous staff-officer, promptly moving his detachment in full view of the Fort, swiftly took up the designated position, directly in sight also of the gunboat New Era. And the Olive Branch in her course soon came so near that by opening with a volley on the mass of men with whom she was laden, a heavy loss of life must have been inflicted ; but Captain Anderson, limiting himself strictly to preventing the landing of any reënforcements during the truce, caused two or three admonitory shots to be fired at the pilot-house, with the immediate effects of making her sheer off to the opposite shore, and pass on up the river.*

---

* This clearly legitimate movement constitutes in large part the *gravamen* of the charge made with so many weighty epithets, and so widely believed at the North, that Forrest acted in bad faith and violated the flag of truce. Assuredly, no allegation could be more unfounded in this connection, The movement was made under the eyes both of Major Bradford and Captain Marshall, who expressed no objections, and took no steps to resist or check it. It was the necessary consequence of the menacing approach, while the truce existed, of these steamers at a time when the river was full of transports bearing troops, and when the commander of the Fort was manifestly seeking to gain time by negotiations with the hope of receiving succor. The Federal commanders made no signal, says General Shepley, (*Reb. Rec.* VIII. Doc. 1, p. 78,) of any kind to the Olive Branch, but permitted it to approach to the immediate vicinity of the New Era—that is, past the Fort, it may be noted—before it was boarded from that gunboat, and told to " proceed immediately to Cairo, and send four or five hundred rounds of ammunition, and stop all boats coming down." (*Vide Evidence of General Shepley and Captain Thornton.—Rec. Reb.* VIII. Doc. 1, pp. 78, 79.) It is to be noted as somewhat singular that while these Federal Commissioners are lavish with their harsh

Meanwhile, Forrest's second communication having been carried into the Fort by one of the Federal officers, several of his comrades remaining with the flag, in conversation with the Confederates, expressed their belief that Forrest really was not present, and that his name was used as a mere ruse, such as had been practiced so successfully several weeks before at Union City. One of these officers having also professed to be acquainted with the Confederate General by sight, Captain Henderson immediately rode to where Forrest was—in the ravine southward of the Fort—and informing him of this suspicion, suggested that the enemy might surrender the sooner if he were to go forward and satisfy them of his actual presence. He therefore rode to the spot where the flag stood, and was formally presented to Captain Young, Twenty-fourth Missouri Infantry, and the associate claiming to know the Confederate General, who quickly remarked that he had no longer any doubt. At the same time, too, the parapets of the Fort were thronging with negro soldiers, intently watching the course of events, and some of whom were heard also to say, it was useless to deny that General Forrest was before them, for they knew him " too well for that." And so close meanwhile were the Confederate lines, that the white men of both sides were bantering each other from their respective positions, while some of the negroes indulged in provoking, impudent jeers. About the same time, likewise, the steamer Olive Branch reaching a point opposite the Fort, appeared to be turning her bow toward the landing, a fact to which Captain Good-

---

comments upon this movement as a violation of the flag of truce, their official reports exhibits clearly the fact that they examined closely into the conduct of General Shepley in not carrying succor, at that very juncture, to the Fort. Or, in other words, for not attempting to do precisely what General Forrest justly apprehended would be undertaken, and therefore took the warranted precaution to foil. They accepted as his excuse only his inability, *not that there was a truce !*

man called the attention of General Forrest, who quietly replied, "She won't land," and in a moment, in fact, she was seen to resume her course up the river.* Some instants later the answer to the last demand was brought out from the Fort and handed to Forrest by Captain Goodman. Almost illegibly written with a pencil, on a soiled scrap of paper, transmitted without envelope, it ran as follows, "Your demand does not produce the desired effect."† Reading it hastily, the Confederate General exclaimed, "This will not do. Send it back, and say to Major Booth"—whose name was attached—"that I must have an answer in plain English—Yes or No !"‡

This answer, having been dispatched, by the advice of some of his officers, in view of the now menacing deportment of many of the negroes behind the parapets, Forrest returned to the position in the valley, some three hundred yards southward, though satisfied in his own mind that the Fort would be surrendered. It was not long, however, before Captain Goodman came to him with the Federal answer—a brief but positive refusal to capitulate. As soon as he had read this communication, turning to his staff and some officers around him, Forrest ordered that his whole force should be put in readiness for an immediate and simultaneous assault. With a few energetic words, he also stimulated the State pride of the Missourians and Mississippians, Tennesseeans and Texans of McCulloch's and Bell's Brigades to an emulous struggle for

---

* MS. Notes of Captain Goodman. The time of the passage of this steamer is settled in the evidence of General Shepley and Captain Thornton, cited *ante*, note p. 433, by these facts : There was no firing as they approached and passed the Fort; the Federal flag was still flying ; a flag of truce was observed outside, immediately on passing the Fort ; and a few moments later the Federal flag, it was noticed, had fallen.

† This flippant, discourteous phraseology was doubtless the fruit of continued incredulity in regard to Forrest's actual presence, and of a stupid misapprehension of a stratagem.

‡ MS. Notes of General Forrest and Captain Goodman.

precedency in planting their battle-flags upon the parapets before them. These affairs arranged, the Confederate General, with a single bugler, rode to the commanding eminence, on the old Confederate lines—which we have previously described as giving him a complete view of the field of operations— from that point to give the signal for the assault.

At this time the main part of Bell's Brigade present, with the Second Tennessee on the right, were in position within from thirty to one hundred feet of the ditch, on the eastern face of the work, and McCulloch's men occupied the cabins, as will be remembered, within sixty yards of the southern face, and the rifle-pits on their right.   At the same time, the commanding ridges eastward and north-eastward of the work were studded with sharp-shooters, and from one of which, as may be seen from the diagram prefixed, they completely enfiladed the southern face of the Federal works ; that is, the face most strongly garnished with artillery.*

On reaching the position we have mentioned, Forrest, scanning the field, and observing that all was ready, caused the signal to be given for the resumption of hostilities ; and at the first blare of the bugle, the Confederate sharpshooters, at all points, opened a galling fire upon the hostile parapet, to which the garrison replied, for a few moments, with great spirit.   But so deadly was the aim of the

---

* It is injuriously charged against General Forrest that these positions were mainly secured by a perfidious breach of the flag of truce. That this allegation, however, is utterly unfounded, ought to be apparent even from the evidence cited, note, *ante*, p. 430 of Lieutenant Leming, the witness chiefly relied on to establish it. The fact is, the position selected by the Federals was so unfavorable that, while commanded from several surrounding points within easy range of musketry, it could also be approached with impunity by an investing force, properly handled, to within a few yards of its ditch, as was done by the Confederates before the flag of truce, which, be it remembered, did not actually advance beyond McCulloch's line.

Confederates, from their enfilading positions, that their enemies could not rise high enough from their scanty cover to fire over at their foes, nor use their artillery on the southern face without being shot down. Consequently, there was practically little resistance, when, a few moments later, the bugle still sounding the charge, the main Confederate force, as with a single impulse, surged onward, like a tawny wave, and crowning the parapet, poured over, on all sides, into the work. Leaping headlong into the ditch, these agile, hardy young men found it a feeble barrier, and helping each other, they clambered nimbly, and swiftly, and simultaneously over the breastworks beyond, opening from its crest a fearful, converging fire, from all its faces, upon the garrison within.

In anticipation of this contingency, Major Bradford, it appears, had arranged with the captain of the gunboat that, if beaten at the breastworks, the garrison would drop down under the bank, and the gunboat would come to their succor, and shelter them with its canister.* The pre-arranged signal was now given, and the garrison, *en masse*, white and black, for the most part with arms in their hands, broke for the place of refuge and naval aid there expected, leaving the Federal flag still aloft, on its staff, and turning repeatedly, as they sped down the precipitous bank, to return the fire opened upon them.† The gunboat, however, was

---

* The evidence of Captain Marshall, conclusive upon this point, is as follows : " Major Bradford signaled to me that we were whipped. . *We had agreed on a signal that, if they had to leave the fort, they would drop down under the bank, and I was to give the Rebels canister.*"—*Reb. Rec.* VIII. Doc. I, p. 55.

† Besides the positive averments of gentlemen of unquestionable veracity in this connection, we have the conclusive proof in the fact that 269 serviceable muskets were picked up and carried off by the Confederates from below the bluff, on and near the river-bank, where they had been undoubtedly carried and finally thrown by the garrison.—*MS. Notes of Captain C. W. Anderson.*

recreant at this critical moment, and failed to give the least assistance. And no timely shower of canister came from its ports to drive back the Confederates, who swiftly and hotly followed after the escaping negroes and Tennesseeans. The naval commander, evidently, was more anxious for the safety of his craft and its crew, than willing to endanger either by endeavoring to do what it had been distinctly preconcerted that he should, in the emergency ; and so he kept his vessel aloof, at a safe distance both from the captured guns of the Fort and from any effort to capture it.*

While these events were passing, the troops stationed to watch the steamers poured a volley into the left flank of the retreating Federals, killing and wounding a good many. Finding that the succor which they had been promised from the gunboat was not rendered, nor at hand, they were greatly

---

* Captain Marshall gives, as an excuse for his course, that he was fearful the Confederates "might hail in a steamboat from below, capture her, put on four or five hundred men, and come after (him) me." Also, that he was apprehensive, if he attempted to go down to the Fort from his position above, and engage in the fight, as the channel would force him " to go around the point," the Confederates in the Fort, with its guns, would sink him. "Had I been below here at the time," he continues, " I think I could have routed them out." If so, it may be asked, why, at such a time, did he take a position above the Fort, rather than the favorable one below, and thus put it out of his power to render assistance promised, and fatally relied on by the Federal garrison, when " whipped," as he terms it. It was surely in his power, previous to the onset, to have taken the favorable position. Further, he states that, during the truce, being at the bar, and observing movements on the part of the Confederates, which he regarded as in violation of that truce, he stood off for the Fort again, intending to stop it; but he does not choose to explain why he changed his mind, went above, and failed to make the least endeavor to assist his people. No one who reads his testimony carefully can acquit him of a criminal prudence, at the cost of the lives of the Federal soldiers, who, on the faith of his engagement to aid them with his guns and canister, instead of laying down their arms and capitulating when the trenches were carried, retreated, as they supposed, to be succored by him. See *Reb. Rec.* VIII. Doc. I, p. 55.

bewildered. Many threw themselves into the river and were drowned in their mad attempt to swim away from the direful danger they apprehended ; a number turning in the direction of Coal creek, dashed as wildly into that stream and perished ; others sought to escape along the river-bank southward, and, persisting in their efforts to get away, were shot or driven back.

It should be remembered that the entrance of the Confederates into the work had been achieved by an impetuous rush over the parapet by each individual, and therefore, for for some moments afterward, there was necessarily a general confusion and tumult, in fact, a dissolution of all organizations. Accordingly, as always happens in places taken by storm, unquestionably some whites, as well as negroes, who had thrown down their arms, and besought quarter, were shot under that *insania belli* which invariably rages on such occasions. Nor must it be forgotten that there was no surrender of the place at all. When the Confederates swarmed over the trenches that had been held defiantly for some eight hours in the face of numbers so manifestly superior, the garrison did not yield ; did not lay down their arms, nor draw down their flag ; but with a lamentable fatuity, the mass of them, with arms still in their hands, fled toward another position in which they were promised relief, and while on the way thither, returned the fire of their pursuers, it is true, not as a mass, but in instances so numerous as to render inevitable a fire upon their whole body, even had it not been the necessary consequence of their efforts to escape capture, whether with arms in their hands or not.*

---

* Many of the prisoners were intoxicated, and few were not, to some degree, under the influence of liquor, with which they had been lavishly stimulated previous to the final onset, as was manifest from the fact that a number of barrels of whisky and beer were found disposed at convenient

In the mean time, or as soon as he could reach the scene, Forrest, riding into the work, assisted by Captain John Overton, lowered the flag ; and immediately both he, General Chalmers, and other officers interfered so energetically to stop the firing that it ceased speedily ; ceased within fifteen minutes from the time that the signal for the termination of the truce was given, and all allegations to the contrary are mere malicious inventions, started, nurtured, and accredited at a time, and through a sentiment of strong sectional animosity. The first order, indeed, now issued by General Forrest, was to collect and secure the prisoners from possible injury, while details were made from them for the burial of the Federal dead.* Among the prisoners taken unhurt, was Major Bradford, the commanding officer of the post since nine in the morning, and at his special request, General Forrest ordered the Federal dead to be buried in the trenches of the work, the officers to be interred separately from their men. Bradford was then temporarily paroled, to supervise the burial of his brother, Captain Bradford, after which, under a pledge not to attempt to escape, he was placed for the night in the custody of Colonel McCulloch, who gave him a bed in his own quarters, and shared with him his supper. This pledge Major Bradford violated ; taking advantage of the darkness and his knowledge of the locality, when his host

---

points in the works, with tin dippers attached, for the use, evidently, of the Federal soldiers.—*MS. Notes of Colonel C. R. Barteau.*

* It is somewhat suggestive that the first eye-witness of the affair at Fort Pillow, examined by the Congressional Committee, *Elias Falls*, a negro soldier, testified expressly that Forrest gave orders to stop the shooting, and that, "after peace was made," an officer told a "Secesh soldier," if he did that again, (shoot,) he would arrest him. Subsequent witnesses, for some reason or other, appear to have been somewhat better instructed as to the character of testimony which was wanting, and supplied it " to order."

was asleep, he effected his escape through the careless line of sentinels, and, in disguise, sought to reach Memphis.*

This brilliant success, howbeit, was not achieved without severe loss on the part of the Confederates, the loss of some of their best soldiers. Fourteen officers and men were killed, and eighty-six wounded. Among these casualties were Lieutenant-Colonel Wiley M. Reid, conspicuous among his comrades for martial aptitude, courage, and ardor, who was mortally wounded within eighty yards of the Federal trenches, while leading and inspiriting the Fifth Mississippi to the onset; the intrepid Lieutenant N. B. Burton of the same regiment was slain by his side. Captain W. R. Sullivan was mortally stricken at the head of Willis's Texas Battalion, which he gallantly commanded at the time, and Lieutenant Ryan of that battalion was killed by a shell at an earlier stage of the action. Lieutenant Hubbard, of the Eighteenth Mississippi Battalion, a promising young officer, fell in the final onset; these are some of the losses among McCulloch's veterans. Lieutenant George Love, of the Second Tennessee,† and Captain J. C. Wilson, of Russell's Regiment of Bell's

---

* We have this from the lips of Col. McCulloch. For the subsequent recapture and fate of this officer, see page 455.

† "A singular instance of a premonition of death occurred in the case of Lieutenant Love. As an officer, he was popular with his men, and always calm and fearless at the post of duty. In the morning he called several of his company around him, and told them, in a quiet manner, that he should be killed that day. He gave directions for the disposal, among the command, of his horse and little possessions, arranged for the payment of his small debts, and wrote a farewell letter to his orphan sister, living at Gallatin, Tenn. He led his company on, and at eleven o'clock was laid low by a canister-shot from one of the enemy's guns. We buried him the next morning. His memory lives in the hearts of all his surviving comrades, and the regiment could boast f n l raver soldier or better man."—*MS. Notes of Colonel C. R. Barteau, Second Tennessee Cavalry.*

Brigade—two valuable officers—were slain while acting with signal bravery.

Among the prisoners taken was Captain Young, the bearer of the flag of truce, who, with Captain Anderson, was sent up the river-side with a white flag, to endeavor to open communication with the gunboat New Era, which was seen making off to the northward, under the apprehension, it appears,' of its ever-prudent master, that an effort might be made for his capture.* The object was to deliver into his hands as soon as possible all the Federal wounded ; but every signal was obdurately ignored or disregarded, and, keeping on its course, the New Era disappeared up the river.†

As fast as possible, meanwhile, the wounded of both sides were gleaned from the bloody field, and placed under shelter and the professional care of Confederate surgeons of the several regiments present, who at once set to work with that assiduity and humanity which we believe have characterized, with rare exceptions, the medical officers of both services toward wounded prisoners of war.‡

Affairs thus provided for, Forrest next turned over the command of the troops on the ground to General Chalmers, with instructions to complete the burial of the dead, the collection of the arms and other portable property, and, if possible, to transfer the Federal wounded to the first steamer that might be passing ; and, finally, to follow with the division and the unwounded prisoners, as soon as practicable, to Brownsville. These orders given, he set out about sunset to return with his

---

* *Vide* Captain Marshall's Evidence, *Reb. Rec.* VIII. Doc. 1, p. 56.

† MS. Notes of Captain C. W. Anderson.

‡ That the Federal wounded, black and white, received prompt surgical attendance is made apparent by gleams of the truth that escape here and there in the mass of suggested falsehoods, which appear as evidence taken before the Congressional Committee.—*Reb. Rec.* VIII. Doc. 1, pp. 1 to 80.

escort and staff to Jackson, Tennessee, encamping that night at a farm-house, some six or seven miles eastward.

"Before nightfall," says Captain Goodman, "the prisoners and artillery had been removed, and the troops were moved back from the river and put into camp.

"On the following morning, (the 13th,) a detail was sent to the Fort to collect and remove the remaining arms, and to bury such of the dead as might have been overlooked on the day before. They had been at work but a short time when a gun-boat (the Silver Cloud) came up and began to shell them. As this became annoying, the officer commanding the detail ordered the tents which were still standing in the Fort to be burned, intending to abandon the place. In doing this, the bodies of some negroes who had been killed in the tents, on the day before, were somewhat burned ; and this probably gave rise to the horrible stories about burning wounded prisoners which were afterward invented and circulated."*

In the mean time—the morning of the 13th—after Forrest and his staff had mounted their horses, and were about to resume their way toward Jackson, the sound of heavy artillery was heard at the Fort, and he detached Captain Anderson to return thither with Captain Young—the Federal Provost-Marshal—to make another effort for the immediate delivery of the Federal wounded to their friends. Proceeding to execute this order, Captain Anderson reached the Fort, caused the details at which the firing had been directed to be at once withdrawn, and hoisted a flag of truce and parley, which being accepted by the master of the Silver Cloud, Captain Ferguson, an arrangement soon resulted for a truce until five P.M. It was agreed that during that time the Federals might send parties

---

* We give this part of the narrative in the language of that intelligent, accurate staff-officer, Captain Goodman.

ashore to visit all parts of the scene, and look after their dead and wounded, bury any of the former that might have been overlooked by the Confederates, and to assist in removing the wounded on board the transport, receipts to be taken for all thus delivered. During the day several transports came to the landing, and before the hour when the truce was to expire, the prisoners had all been transferred to the cabin of the steamer Platte Valley, numbering at least 70, officers and men.* It remains to be added that 7 officers and 219 enlisted men, (56 negroes, 163 whites,) unwounded,.were carried off, as prisoners of war, which, with the wounded, make an aggregate of those who survived, exclusive of all who may have escaped, quite 300 souls, or fully 55 per cent of the garrison, while those who survived unhurt constituted 40 per cent.†

Several hours previously, having put his main force in motion toward Brownsville, about four P.M., General Chalmers withdrew with his staff and escort in the same direction, and there remained at Fort Pillow none save the dead who had fallen in storming it, and the dead of the late garrison, victims, not of unlawful acts of war, as has been so virulently alleged and generally believed at the North, but of an insensate endeavor, as foolishly resolved as feebly executed, to hold a position naturally untenable and badly fortified,—the victims, we may add, in all sincerity, not of a savage ferocity on the part of their late adversaries, but of the imbecility and grievous mismanagement of those weak, incapable officers, whom the fortunes of war unhappily had placed over them.

---

* The Federal surgeon of the hospital at Mound City, Ill., testified that he received 34 whites and 27 colored men. Some died on the way.

† Some of the Confederate regiments lost nearly as heavily at Chickamauga. For a place taken by storm the loss was by no means heavy.

COMMENTARIES.

1. "Valor as well as other virtues has its bounds, which, once transgressed, the next step is into the territories of vice; so that, by having too large a proportion of this heroic virtue, unless a man be very perfect in its limits, which upon the confines are very hard to discover, he may very easily unawares run into temerity, obstinacy, and folly. From this consideration it is, that we have derived the custom in time of war *to punish even with death* those who are obstinate to defend a place that is not tenable by the rules of war. Otherwise, if there were not some examples made, men would be so confident upon the hopes of impunity that not a hen-roost but would resist and stop a royal army." So wrote old *Michael Montaigne*, who then proceeded to illustrate the practice in civilized warfare by these historical examples:

"Monsieur, the Constable de Montmorency, having, at the siege of Pavia, been ordered to pass the Tesino and to take up his quarters in the Faubourg St. Antonio, being hindered from doing so by a tower that was at the end of the bridge, which was so independent as to stand a battering, *hanged every man he found within it for their labor.* And again, since, accompanying the Dauphin in his expedition beyond the Alps, and taking the castle of Villane by *assault*, and all within having been put to the sword, the governor and his ensign only excepted, he caused them to be trussed up for the same reason; as also did Captain Martin du Bellay, then Governor of Turin, the Governor of St. Bony, in the same country, all his people being cut in pieces at the taking of the place."*

Any one who has read our narrative attentively must be satisfied that Fort Pillow, at least after the Confederates secured possession of the rifle-pits and huts near the parapet,

---

* *Works of Montaigne,* (English,) Chapter **XIV**.

was untenable, and consequently its defense unjustifiable. In-deed, we know of no instance of such manifest indefensibility. It was not so, however, be it noted, merely because of the nu-merical superiority of the Confederates, but for the reason of the situation of the Federal work at the moment, even had the Confederates not been able to get so close as they did to its parapets. Every foot of it was completely enfiladed and swept, as may be seen from the map, by Confederate sharp-shooters. Furthermore, so small was the scope of the place that, when the whole garrison was driven back within it, the work was so densely crowded that a sharp-shooter's bullet could scarcely miss an object, and the jeopardy of the men was the more fearfully augmented. In fact, Forrest could have established his men under cover at good rifle-range and made the work untenable without attempting to storm it.

2. Compare what actually happened at Fort Pillow with the hideous scenes of slaughter, lust, and rapine that followed the storming of places in Spain and Portugal either by the French or English, as Oporto, for example. How trivial and insignificant in comparison were even the worst alleged at Fort Pillow to what it is not denied actually happened at Oporto, as related by Napier. Yet Marshal Soult was never overwhelmed with obloquy in prose and verse, nor besmirched with foul epithets for what occurred there. At the storming of Palamos, after the *third demand* for the capitulation of the place, the Spaniards, flying to the *sea-shore* with the purpose of finding refuge aboard some vessels—just as the garrison at Fort Pillow expected to be rescued by the gunboat—were in-tercepted by the French troops and put to the sword. We might readily fill as large a volume as this with like instances. The fact is, as was said by a recent writer in *Blackwood's Ma-gazine*, in connection with a late affair in China: " Every military man knows that whenever a place is taken by assault under the flag of any nation, many of the defenders *are put to*

death though they throw down their arms and cry for quarters."*

3. The Congressional Committee have reported that the Confederates took advantage of the truce to advance to and secure positions from which they had been beaten off by the Federal garrison up to the time that the flag of truce was first sent by General Forrest. This falsehood is asserted in the face of abundant conclusive evidence taken before them. For example, Lieutenant McJ. Leming, Bradford's Adjutant, as we have cited in note *ante*, page 430, in the body of his testimony expressly admits that the Confederates, previous to the flag of truce, had "kept up a steady fire by sharp-shooters behind trees, and logs, and high knolls ; they began to draw nearer and nearer up to the time our men were all drawn into the Fort. Two companies of the Thirteenth Tennessee Cavalry were ordered out as sharp-shooters, but were finally ordered in. *We were pressed on all sides.*" The same witness, after stating that Major Booth and his Adjutant were killed about nine o'clock A.M., adds that the Major had previously " ordered some buildings in front of the Fort to be destroyed, as the enemy's sharp-shooters were endeavoring to get possession of them. There were four rows of buildings, *but only the row nearest the Fort was destroyed; the sharp-shooters gained possession of the others before they could be destroyed.*" (*Reb. Rec.* VIII. Doc. I, pp. 23–4.) Another chief witness, Captain Marshall, commander of the Federal gunboat New Era, deposes that *previous to truce*, and when, at a signal from the Fort, he was firing up the ravine immediately to the south of it, the "rebel sharp-shooters" returned his fire "rapidly." Further, that on the north side of the Fort the Confederates were *so near as to be* able to fire at and harass some non-com-

---

* Number for February, 1867, page 187.

batants who had been removed in a barge from the Fort to the river-bank north of the mouth of Coal creek. (*Ibid.* p. 55.) One Elvis Bevel, a refugee, who was present, likewise testifies that in an hour after sunrise bullets from "rebel infantry" drove him to take position behind a large stump near (in front of) the Fort, and that, about *nine* A.M., he moved to the rear, where he "could better see *the rebels who swarmed the bluff,*" while at the same time the Confederates were so near to the gunboat that the crew "*had to close their ports and use their small-arms.*" (*Ibid.* p. 69.) Moreover, private Daniel H. Rankin, Company C, Thirteenth Tennessee, though alleging that the worst thing he saw was the rebels moving upon us while the flag of truce was up at the Fort, nevertheless defines the point attained by the Confederates by saying that they did not get nearer to the Fort than "*within twenty or thirty steps.*" (*Ibid.* p. 32.)

4. Under manifest prompting, the witnesses in hospital all claim to have been wounded after their surrender, and that the killing and wounding were chiefly done after the position was surrendered. There was no surrender at all, and all statements to that effect are untrue. When the Confederates surmounted the parapets, the garrison, as we have seen, by a preconcerted plan, leaving their flag flying, retreated *en masse* to the cover of the river bank, expecting to be sheltered there under the guns of the New Era. It was, therefore, unquestionably *a legitimate act of war to fire upon them when thus attempting to escape, whether they had arms in their hands or not!* For those who threw their arms away and ran below the bluff, simply did so, the more readily to make their escape from the Confederates. Soldiers in a place taken by storm, no more than on the field of battle, can claim to have surrendered or called for quarter, who fly as fast as they can in the direction of expected or prearranged succor. The value of the whole mass of testimony, reported

and relied on as warranting these unfounded calumnies against General Forrest and his men, may well be measured in this connection. The witness Leming states in the body of his testimony: " We kept them (the Confederates) back for several minutes. What was called —— brigade or battalion* attacked the centre of the fort, where several companies of colored troops were stationed. They finally gave way, and before we could fill up the breach, the enemy got inside the fort, and then they came in on the other two sides, and had complete possession of the Fort. *In the mean time, nearly all the officers had been killed*, especially of the colored troops, *and there was no one hardly to guide the men.* They fought bravely, indeed, until that time. *I do not* think *the men who broke had* a commissioned officer over them." And yet this same " willing witness," under manifest manipulation, in answer to the question, " Were those (officers) who were killed, killed before or after the Fort was captured ?" answered, " I don't know of but one who was killed before we were driven from the Fort." (*Reb. Rec.* VIII. Doc. 1, p. 26.) In the same connection, also, is filed an affidavit, signed by Lieutenants F. A. Smith and William Cleary, the two absent officers of the Thirteenth Tennessee Battalion, in which it is stated, on hearsay, confessedly, that Lieutenant Wilson, of their regiment, was killed, and Lieutenant J. C. Akerstrom was severely wounded after the surrender ; yet, in conclusion, they refer to an accompanying affidavit of one Hardy N. Revelle — an eye-witness — in which it is especially sworn *that the said Lieutenant Wilson was killed outside of*

---

* A man who draws no broader distinction between a brigade and batta
lion than Lieutenant Leming appears
to do, is not a very reliable witness.

*the Fort, in the morning, before the Federal troops were with-
drawn.**

5. It is the gravest of the charges against General Forrest and his men, that Lieutenant Akerstrom, Quartermaster of the Thirteenth Tennessee Battalion, was nailed, when
wounded, to the side of a house, by his clothes, and thus
burned alive. The Committee accept as conclusive a mass
of sheer vague hearsay testimony on this point, in the
face of the positive statement of private John F. Ray, Company B, Thirteenth Tennessee Battalion, that Akerstrom
was shot *at his side*, during the action, and in the forehead, falling on his face dead, as he believed.† One witness,
Carlton, a negro, who professed to have seen the Confederates have the Quartermaster, (Akerstrom,) after the conflict

---

* This man had previously said
there were ten officers belonging, only
eight of whom, however, were present at the time. Now, by reference
to the list of the prisoners in the
Appendix, it will be seen that Captain J. L. Posten and Lieutenant N.
D. Logan were taken prisoners, uninjured, leaving six to be accounted for.
One of those, Captain Potter—at the
time in hospital, wounded too badly to
testify—Leming admits "was shot in
the early part of the engagement."
(*Reb. Rec.* VIII. Doc. 1, p. 26.) Another, Lieutenant Wilson, says Revelle,
(*Ibid.* p. 67) was killed in the morning,
outside of the Fort, and yet another,
Akerstrom, as we show, is positively
stated by the witness Ray, (a white
man,) to have been shot dead in the
forehead during the conflict, and therefore only three remain to be accounted
for. These are Major Bradford, Captain Bradford, and Lieutenant Leming
himself. Major Bradford, as we know,
was not shot, but, offensive as he was
to the men who took the work by
storm, was taken prisoner. Leming
says he was shot after the place had
fallen, but he likewise says he only
knows of one officer who was not shot
in the same way, which must be Captain Potter, as also just before (p. 24)
that "nearly all the officers had been
killed" before the Confederates entered the work. Captain Bradford was
the signal officer ; it is plain he lived
long enough to give the signal spoken
of by Captain Marshall, and was found
dead at the spot where the signal was
made ; he was doubtless shot by some
one as the parapets were surmounted.
And thus we dispose of Mr. Leming's
loosely constructed tissue. Out of his
lips must the Confederates be acquitted.
† *Reb. Rec.* VIII. Doc. 1, p. 31.

was over, describes him as having three stripes on his arm, which assuredly the Congressional Committee must have known were the insignia of a non-commissioned officer, and not of an officer of the grade of quartermaster.*   Another witness—one McCoy—who was on the gunboat, swears that he saw Akerstrom in his office, under the hill, after the flag of truce was in, making signals ·for the boat to come to him; an improbable story in sooth, that he could distinguish any man at that distance — fully half a mile.†   The story in regard to this burning of houses, with persons in them, white or black, while alive, evidently originated at some distance from the scene.   Only one of the witnesses examined testifies that he was present and saw the burning. Fortunately, the published evidence affords a clue to the place where this wicked calumny was forged.   Two witnesses —McCoy and Shelton — state positively they first heard the story after they had reached the hospital at Mound City, Illinois.‡ Yet, another alleges that he heard it from the hands on the gunboat.   The witness, a negro, Haskins, who says that he saw Akerstrom's house on fire, had just sworn that immediately after the place was carried he was shot in the left arm, then ran down to the river, jumped in the water, and that at night he got into a coal-boat, and went down the river, which would make it out of his power to see the buildings burn,§ as he was made to say, falsely, by the leading questions propounded by the Committee. The burning was not done until the morning of the 13th. Private Alexander, of Company C, Thirteenth Tennessee, testifies that he heard Rebels say they would not burn the hospital, while "we wounded ones were in there," and that

---

* *Reb. Rec.* VIII. Doc. I, p. 18.
† *Ibid.* p. 30.
‡ *Ibid.* VIII. Doc. I, p. 31.
§ *Ibid.* p. 12, 13.

the hospital he was in was standing when he went down the hill to the boat, on the 13th ;* and the witness, Shelton, states that the building he was in was not set on fire.†

6. The nature and reliability of the testimony adduced by the Congressional Committee, in support of their report, may be best measured by some characteristic extracts. As for example : Thomas Addison, (negro,) having sworn that he was shot down after " surrender," as were a great many of his comrades, in reply to a question, goes on to say, " *I heard them shoot little children* not more than that high," (holding his hand off about four feet from the floor,) " that the officers had waiting on them."

Question. " Did you see them shoot them ?"

Answer. " *I did not hold up my head.*"

Question. " How, then, did you know that they shot them ?"

Answer. " I heard them say, 'Turn around, so I can shoot you good.' "

Question. " Did you see them after they were shot ?"

This was a clear prompt, but the negro, however willing, was stupid, and only replied, " *No, sir, they toted them up the hill before me, because they were small.*" To prove that men were shot to a great extent, after they had surrendered, such leading questions as the following were adventured, " The Rebels must have killed a great many of the white men after they had surrendered ?" and such evidence as this was relied on as a true reply. " Yes, two thirds of them must have been killed after the place was taken." Let any lawyer glance over the examinations of the several witnesses, and say whether questions so glaringly leading were ever at-

---

* *Reb. Rec.* VIII. Doc. 1, p. 27.

† *Ibid.* p. 31. It is a noticeable fact that while the inquiry about the burning was general of the negroes, only two or three white soldiers were interrogated upon the matter, and these said they did not see it. The whole inquiry is a marvel of unfairness.

tempted, much less permitted, in any judicial or other inquiry, in which the object was to get at the truth. Especially objectionable is it, we may add, to use leading questions with witnesses so ignorant and stupid as these negroes, the inevitable effect being to prompt the answer.

7. It is charged that among those shot below the "bluff" were some hospital patients. We doubt not that was the case : but simply because they left their hospital and took refuge *among* the soldiers who were there seeking succor by the gunboat. In the turmoil and hurly burly of the moment they could not be discriminated nor separated.

8. In the Appendix will be found a list of the prisoners taken on this occasion, and other documentary evidence concerning the transaction, to which we refer all readers who wish to know more of its details.

9. In fine : We submit to the candid and those who are capable of accepting the truth that, in what occurred after the Confederates stormed the trenches, there was neither cruel purpose nor cruel negligence of duty, neither intention nor inadvertence, on the part of General Forrest, whose course, therefore, stands utterly devoid of the essence of outrage or wrong.

CHAPTER XVII.

Chalmers detached with Command to Okolona, to meet menaced Opera-
tions—Public Reception of Forrest, Staff, and Escort, by Citizens of
Brownsville—Reëstablished Headquarters at Jackson—Occupied with
Collection of War Resources of West-Tennessee—Chalmers ordered
to Oxford—Buford reached Jackson with Division—Sharp Affair at
Bolivar—Established Headquarters at Tupelo the 5th of May—Com-
mand increased by Brigade of State Troops—Chalmers detached on
the 26th of May, with McCulloch's and Neely's Brigades and Wal-
ton's Battery—Forrest marched with Buford's Division to the Relief
of Roddy—Return to meet heavy Federal Column advancing from
Memphis—Concentration of Forces at Baldwin—Rucker's Brigade
engaged Federal Cavalry near New-Albany—General S. D. Lee at
Baldwin—Confederate Troops ordered Southward, to concentrate with
Reënforcements—Federals intercept Forrest's line of March to Tu-
pelo—Lyon's Brigade pushed up to feel Enemy.

April 13th to June 10th, 1864.

WHILE on the way from Fort Pillow to Jackson, having
received instructions to detach a portion of his command to
repel a raid understood to be immediately impending from the
direction of Decatur, through the interior of North-Western
Alabama, Forrest ordered Chalmers to repair at once, by way
of Okolona, to the menaced border, with the forces which had
been engaged in the operations against Fort Pillow. At the
same time, Brigadier-General Buford was instructed to collect
the men of his command, including all detachments and absentees from Bell's Brigade, and repair with them, by the 30th
of April, to Jackson.

At Brownsville, the citizens of all classes—men, women, and children—received the Confederate General with tokens of deep-felt gratitude. The ladies of the vicinage, assembling at the court-house, received him publicly, and testified their profound personal appreciation of his recent operations, by which they had been delivered from the apprehension of further outrages, insults, and distressing annoyances, from that pestilent band of ruffians and marauders which had been so thoroughly uprooted. And every resource of a heartfelt, teeming hospitality was extended to their cherished guests—the General, his staff, and escort—during the afternoon and night of the 13th and morning of the 14th of April.

On the 14th, headquarters were reëstablished at Jackson, where Forrest remained until the 2d of May, actively occupied with measures looking to the collection of all military resources in men, draught-animals, horses, and subsistence, to be gleaned in the region northward of that point. And to these ends the proper instructions were framed and intrusted to Buford for execution by detachments from his command while *en route* to Jackson.*

Meanwhile, on the morning of the 15th, Chalmers, turning off at Brownsville, passed through Sommerville, where, early

---

* Major Bradford, the Federal commander of Pillow, whose violation of his parole and escape is mentioned *ante*, p. 441, was, several days afterward, recaptured in disguise. At first he affected to be a conscript, but, being recognized, was remanded to custody as a prisoner of war. He was then sent in charge of a party—a subaltern and some five or six men—to Brownsville. On the way, he again attempted to escape, soon after which one of the men shot him. It was an act in which no officer was concerned; mainly due, we are satisfied, after the most rigid inquiry, to private vengeance for well-authenticated outrages committed by Bradford and his band upon the defenseless families of the men of Forrest's Cavalry. He was shot, not hung; and no superior officer had any hand in his "taking off." Had there been a wish to slay the man particularly, there was ample opportunity in the *mêlée* at Fort Pillow. He was treated with the utmost consideration and civility.

on the 16th, he divided his command ; Bell, with the prisoners
and artillery, taking the road through Lagrange, while he,
with McCulloch's and Neely's Brigades, pushed on toward
Holly Springs.   Here, on the 18th, information was received
from General Polk, by telegraph, that the presence of Forrest's
troops under his previous requisition was not needed, and accordingly the movement of Chalmers was halted, and Barteau,
with the Second Tennessee, being detached to convoy the
prisoners to Demopolis, the rest of Bell's Brigade, and Neely's
also, were ordered to return to West-Tennessee, while McCulloch resumed his old post behind the Tallahatchie river, about
Panola, and General Chalmers took up his headquarters at
Oxford until the 2d of May.   Then, pursuant to special instructions from his superior, he set out for Tupelo, with Mc-
Culloch's Brigade, except the Eighteenth Mississippi Battalion,
and, moving by regiments, swept the region, eastward to the
Mobile and Ohio Railroad, for conscripts, absentees, and deserters.*

In the interval, Bell's and Neely's Brigades had reëntered
West-Tennessee, and their several regiments were distributed
at points favorable for recruitment, and for granting furloughs
to officers and men to visit their families, renovate their clothing, and obtain remounts, as far as needful, by the end of
the month.

By the 28th, Buford had assembled his whole division, including Bell's Brigade, at Jackson, and on the 30th received
orders to move on the 2d of May with it and Neely's Brigade
to Tupelo, convoying a large and heavy ox-train, freighted
with subsistence and a large amount of liquor (for hospital

---

* The Eighteenth Mississippi Battalion—Lieutenant-Colonel Alexander H.
Chalmers—was left to hold the approaches of the Tallahatchie, scouting
as far northward, on Memphis road, as
Waterford.

purposes) and leather, and some three hundred prisoners. The Kentucky Brigade of this division, which had entered on the campaign with an effective total of 1004 men, now numbered 1717 fighting men ; and Bell's Tennesseeans, who took the field 1254 strong, now mustered over 1700 well-mounted horsemen.

Moving, as ordered, by way of Purdy and Corinth, notwithstanding his *impedimenta*, Buford accomplished the distance—seventy-eight miles—to Rienzi by the 4th of May, and there having transferred the supplies and prisoners for further transportation southward, to the Mobile and Ohio Railroad, was able to reach Tupelo on the 6th.

Meanwhile, on the 2d of May, General Forrest, breaking up his headquarters at Jackson, set out also for Tupelo with his staff and escort, taking the road through Bolivar, Tennessee, and Ripley, Mississippi. In the vicinity of Bolivar, on that afternoon, he was met by scouts with information that a Federal cavalry force, quite two thousand strong, under General Sturgis, was then engaged in a sharp skirmish with McDonald's Battalion, under Lieutenant-Colonel Crews—not more than two hundred troopers—on the Sommerville road, about two miles westward of Bolivar. Pressing on at once with his accustomed decision, Forrest found several hundred unarmed men collected in the place. These he directed to move out with his headquarter baggage-train and ambulances, some five miles southward, on the road to Ripley, and encamp, while he repaired to the point where Crews still held the enemy at bay. Placing himself at the head of the Confederates, reënforced by his escort, or now with about three hundred fighting men, boldly charging the foe in front, he presently drove back their skirmish line for three fourths of a mile upon their main force, inflicting a loss of some forty killed and wounded. Unable, however, to pursue this advantage further against such odds, Forrest now withdrew a short distance, and took post, with

Crews's men dismounted, in the outer line of fortifications, which had been thrown up some time previously by the Federals in the western suburbs of the place. His enemy, seeing in this evidences of weakness, taking heart, advanced vigorously upon his position, but were swiftly beaten back by a hot fire, at short range, from the steady, deadly rifles of the dismounted Confederates. In this affair, Major Strange, Forrest's gallant and ever efficient Adjutant-General, had his right arm broken by a minie ball. The Federals, breaking in disorder, immediately quit the field and disappeared. The Confederate General then resumed his march, and caught up with his train, encamped, as before said, on the Ripley road, five miles beyond Bolivar.*

Hurrying on without further incident, and crossing the line of the Memphis and Charleston Railroad, and thence through Ripley, the Confederate General arrived at Tupelo early on the 5th, a day in advance of Buford's Division. Here he found Gholson's Brigade of Mississippi State Cavalry, and Chalmers, with several regiments of McCulloch's Brigade. The former, some days later, having been transferred to the Confederate States Service, was attached temporarily to Buford's Division, while Neely's Brigade was returned to Chalmers.

For the remainder of the month, Forrest was closely occupied with means and measures for increasing the efficiency of his force. Now well mounted, and materially recruited by his recent campaign, he sought by every means in his power to consolidate his organizations and perfect their equipments.†

---

* Here, that night, occurred the death of the somewhat conspicuous partisan, Major Solomon Street, Fifteenth Tennessee, by the hand of a personal enemy in the Confederate ranks.

† Newsom's Regiment re-formed on 12th May; certain Alabama companies being transferred to Roddy's command, their places were filled by independent companies from Tennessee, and the regiment reorganized as in the roster. See Appendix.

His artillery was formed into a battalion of four.batteries, of four guns each, under Captain J. W. Morton, as Chief of Artillery.* The men left dismounted were formed into a pioneer detachment ; and all supernumerary officers were directed to report at department headquarters. Special reports on various subjects touching the *materiel* as well as *personnel* of his command were required from divisional, brigade, and regimental commanders ; and his order and letter-books of the period show that the mind so alert and vigorous in the field was scarcely less active or effective in connection with the interior administration of his force, which as now constituted, was as follows :

> Four field-batteries—Morton's, Thrall's, Rice's, and Walton's—16 guns.
> Chalmers's Division—McCulloch's, Neely's, and Rucker's Brigades.†
> Buford's Division—Bell's and Lyon's Brigades.‡
>
> In all, 20 regiments, 4 battalions, 5 independent companies, and 16 guns.

This command, for convenience in regard to forage and subsistence, and, in part, for observation, was distributed at several points. Chalmers's Division for a time was quartered around Verona, except a demi-brigade—Seventh Tennessee and Nineteenth Mississippi—detached under Colonel Duckworth, for temporary service at Grenada, under the special instructions of Major-General Lee ; and the Eighteenth Mississippi (battalion) still posted near Panola. The brigade of Mississippi State troops was at Tupelo until about the 26th, when it was detached and placed under command of General Wirt Adams, at Canton, Miss.,§ pursuant to orders from Ma-

---

* These were the companies of Morton, Rice, Thrall, and Walton.

† Rucker's Brigade was organized on the 24th of May, 1864, of the Seventh Tennessee and Eighteenth and Nineteenth Mississippi.

‡ Lyon's Brigade was formerly com- manded by Colonel Thompson, (killed at Paducah,) and latterly by Colonel Crossland, of the Seventh Kentucky. Colonel Lyon was assigned to the command about the 24th of May.

§ With Brigadier-General Samuel J. Gholson immediately in command.

jor-General Lee. Buford's Division, for the most of the time at Tupelo, was engaged from the 16th to the 24th in a reconnoissance as far as Corinth.* And later, about the 26th, Chalmers was detached with McCulloch's and Neely's Brigades and Walton's Battery, on an expedition into the interior of Alabama, penetrating that State as far as Monte Vallo, about fifty miles north of Selma, and forty eastward of Tuscaloosa, for the purpose of meeting a hostile raid against the iron-works of that region, anticipated from the direction of Decatur and Huntsville,† Alabama.

Among the several West-Tennessee regiments, both of Chalmers's and Buford's Divisions, was a considerable element which Forrest had been able to attract to his standard, and utilize in a substantial degree, namely, numerous runaways from the infantry regiments of Johnston's army from that district. At the time of his expedition into West-Tennessee, in December, 1863, that region was full of them. His repute

---

* Newsom's Regiment, Nineteenth Tennessee, (Bell's Brigade,) and Keizer's scouts having been left to occupy Corinth and the line of the Memphis and Charleston Railroad.

† This division reached Monte Vallo on the 31st May, and on the following day Neely's Brigade was detached to Blue Mountain, to report to Brigadier-General Pillow, for the defense of the coal and iron-works in that quarter. McCulloch's Brigade remained at Monte Vallo until the 10th of June, when it was ordered by Major-General Lee to return by forced marches to Columbus, Miss. A glance at the map will show, the great extent of country over which Chalmers's Division operated during this period. Its right wing—

Neely's Brigade—was at Blue Mountain, in the north-eastern part of Alabama, near the Georgia line ; McCulloch's Brigade — the centre — was at Monte Vallo ; and Rucker's Brigade— the left wing—was quartered at Oxford, Miss. : and from these widely distant points were these troops subsequently concentrated for the combats at Tishomingo creek and Harrisburg. Neely's Brigade, while detached under General Pillow's command, participated in an unsuccessful assault on the town of Oxford, Ga., garrisoned by the enemy, and did not return under Forrest's command until just before the battle of Harrisburg.—*MS. Notes of Captain Walter A. Goodman.*

as a successful cavalry leader, however, drew them forth from their fastnesses to the number of more than seven hundred, who attached themselves to the different regiments brought into effective existence by that expedition. Measures, however, were now instituted by the War Department for their restoration to their old commands, which, carried out by Forrest with his habitual earnestness, resulted in the untoward depletion of his own force, with little advantage to the general service ; for the greater part of these men, while willing to serve as cavalry under Forrest, though excellent fighting material, did not hesitate to desert their colors at the prospect of being remanded to the infantry.*

Information having been received that the Federals were pressing General Roddy in the vicinity of Decatur, North-Alabama, Buford's Division, on the 29th, was placed in readiness to go to that officer's succor. At the same time, Colonel Rucker's Brigade was likewise directed to be concentrated, and held in hand at Oxford for any emergency. Giving Roddy due notice of his purpose to push to his assistance, Forrest, in a dispatch, written on that day, advised that officer to keep scouts well in front of the enemy, to watch and ascertain his movements, force, etc., and to collect together and concentrate his force on the enemy's right flank.

---

* These men unquestionably were guilty of the gravest military crime, especially in the soldiers of a war for independence ; nevertheless, there were individuals among them of the greatest gallantry and devotion to the Confederate cause—men whose conduct was the result of misconception rather than purpose. Of such, private W. M. Strickland is the type. He had belonged to the Twenty-seventh Tennessee infantry ; and when on furlough attached himself to Forrest's escort. Subsequently claimed by his commander, when he had shown himself an invaluable soldier, Forrest sent him to his regiment with seven conscripts, to give in exchange for himself, so that he might be regularly and permanently attached to the cavalry. This man, after many acts of consummate courage, gave up his life on Christmas day, 1864, on the retreat of Hood out of Middle Tennessee.

Forage meanwhile had been collected or thrown forward to proper points on the line of march, and the shoeing of the cavalry horses was going on vigorously, night and day. On the 30th, however, before he had put Buford's Division in motion, a dispatch was received from Brigadier-General Roddy, to the effect, that the Federal force had fallen back to Decatur, and apparently was projecting an expedition in the direction of Kingston, Georgia. Forrest, therefore, decided to await further developments of the enemy's purposes before moving, and notified General Roddy of his conclusions. He also gave specific instructions to that commander, for the present under his orders, to draw in all detached forces, and hold his whole command well together, to get boats ready for the passage of the Tennessee, and to keep him thoroughly acquainted with the situation.*

On the 31st, Forrest, having determined that the time had

---

* The letter-book about this date furnishes a communication which, characteristic of General Forrest, at the same time illustrates a fatal vice of Confederate staff organization. We refer to the Subsistence Department, the chief officers of which — those charged with the supply of subsistence — were made independent of the control of military commanders, even of the armies of the Confederate States. This anomaly in military administration saddled upon the Confederate army at an early day, with an impracticable, pragmatical recluse as chief of the Bureau, was persistently adhered to until the cause was in its death-throes, with consequences which can not be over-estimated in their mischievous effect upon all Confederate operations. No army, no campaign, no operation was free from the malific blight of this system. Accordingly, we find one of these petty sovereignties erected in General Forrest's department; and, as a matter of course, in speedy collision with him, drawing forth a letter, from which we extract the following :

"I am directed by the General Commanding to say, that he understands you are at Okolona, and several of your men loitering around here, instead of being up at the front attending to getting out cattle. He further directs me to say that, if the matter is not given your attention, he will withdraw his cavalry, who are to aid you, and report the fact to the proper department. If

come to effect a junction with Roddy, transmitted a notification of his purpose in these terms :

" Your dispatch of the 29th just received. I will start from this place to-morrow morning, with 2400 men and six pieces of artillery, to join you. I wish you to ascertain which direction the enemy has taken, and keep me posted. I will move by Fulton, and on the road to Russellville, unless you should advise differently. If the enemy goes in the direction of Rome, I think they will join the main army. If they turn South, you will let me know at once ; if they go to Rome, I will move in another direction, and will meet you. Be certain to have with you 1000 of your best men and horses. I have sent my aid-de-camp—Captain Charles W. Anderson —to see and confer with you as regards our future movements. You will send couriers and scouts on the enemy's right flank, and keep General Chalmers posted. You will find him at Monte Vallo, Alabama, whence he was sent to find which road the enemy took from Sommerville. Send courier, also, to General Johnston, at Marietta, Georgia, giving him the facts."

Buford's Division—except Newsom's and Russell's Regiments, left, one at Tupelo, and the other at Corinth—was in motion, accordingly, for North-Alabama, with ten days' rations, by way of Fulton and Russellville, on the morning of the 1st of June. Morton's and Rice's Batteries accompanied the expedition, and Forrest followed, somewhat later in the day, with his escort. The whole force numbered some 2600 rank and file, and on the night of the second of June it en-

---

there is any thing hindering you from giving this matter your immediate attention he desires to know it at once, and expects that you and all your men will be at work while you have the op-portunity. No enemy in the country, and force sufficient to protect you.
(Signed)
CHAS. W. ANDERSON, A. D. C."

camped, eight miles westward of Russellville, to which place Forrest rode, with his staff and escort, ahead of his command, on the following morning. Several days previously, Captain John G. Mann, Chief Engineer, had been sent ahead with his engineer company, to the Tennessee river, about the mouth of Town creek, to build or repair a sufficient number of boats for the prompt ferriage of that stream. At Russellville, Forrest was met by a dispatch from his aid-de-camp, Captain Anderson, acquainting him that Roddy's command had been concentrated about Moulton, twenty-five or thirty miles distant, and the requisite number of boats would be ready to begin the passage of the Tennessee river at four o'clock that afternoon.

Thus affairs stood about mid-day, when a dispatch was received from Major-General Lee, recalling the force to Tupelo, to meet a heavy column of mixed arms, penetrating the country in that direction from Memphis. Moving with his accustomed celerity, Forrest reëstablished his headquarters at Tupelo early on the 5th June, and Buford came up with his division late in the afternoon.

On leaving Russellville, Forrest had ordered Roddy to send Johnson's Brigade from Cherokee, on the Memphis and Charleston, across to Rienzi, on the Mobile and Ohio Railroad.* And Rucker, who, under orders from General Lee, was moving with his brigade from Oxford, in the direction of New-Albany, was instructed, on the 5th, by a reliable courier, and through the telegraph, to throw a portion of his brigade between the enemy and Memphis, and capture his couriers and train, while hanging with his main force upon the Federal right flank.

----

* Was about 1000 strong. Roddy was to follow with his other brigade (Patterson's) so soon as it could be concentrated from its several stations.

GEN. A. BUFORD

Dispatches from trusty scouts were now received, reporting the main body of the enemy, some 13,000 strong, infantry and cavalry, at or near Salem, at mid-day on the 4th.* A re-disposition was now made of the scouts, with the view to the thorough investigation of the numbers, arms, and objective of the enemy in their present movement. And for the next twenty-four hours, Forrest was engrossed with all possible preparations for an effective rencounter with the Federals. General Lee, coming up in the afternoon of the 6th, the two Generals had an immediate conference touching the situation, and their means for meeting the emergency. Meanwhile, the enemy were reported by scouts to be at Ruckerville—ten miles north-east of Ripley, on the road to Pocahontas, while a body of Federal cavalry, after striking the Mobile and Ohio Railroad northward of Boonville, was already moving toward Corinth. It was supposed, from this state of affairs, that the ultimate purpose of the enemy was a junction with Sherman, then pressing Johnston back toward Atlanta. It was, there-fore, determined to concentrate all disposable forces to follow and harass the movement to the utmost, and to that end, comprehensive orders to the several officers affected were promptly distributed. Johnson's Brigade was directed to repair to Baldwin from the north ; Buford's Division, with Rice's and Morton's Batteries, was ordered to the same point ; and Rucker was instructed to hasten to New-Albany, observe the roads in that quarter, and later, pressing on to Baldwin, thence effect a junction with the main Confederate force, should it not be found at that place. The enemy, meanwhile, was reported as still moving eastward, in the general direction of the Memphis and Charleston road ; and on the 7th, Gene-rals Lee and Forrest, with the escort of the latter, setting out for Baldwin also, established their headquarters there on the

---

* 8000 infantry, 5000 cavalry, and six batteries.

morning of the 8th. Rucker, meanwhile, soon after crossing the Tallahatchie at New-Albany, late in the afternoon of the 7th, had struck a brigade of Federal cavalry, under Colonel Winslow.* Attacking vigorously with the Seventh Tennessee and a squadron of the Eighteenth Mississippi, with characteristic vigor and judgment, he drove the enemy for two miles, when darkness put an end to the conflict.

At Baldwin, the Confederate Generals learned that the main Federal force was still at Ruckerville, arranging, apparently, to cross to the south side of the Hatchie river, much swollen at the time from recent heavy rains. Fresh instructions were, therefore, transmitted to Rucker to press rapidly through Ripley and gain the Federal right flank, maintaining constant communication with the Confederate headquarters, which, with Buford's Division, were thrown forward to Boonville early on the morning of the 9th, and here Rucker effected a junction with Buford early the same day. It had been raining four or five days incessantly, and consequently the streams, brim full, were unfordable, the bridges generally swept away, and the roads scarcely practicable.

The information was now brought to the Confederate Generals, that the Federals, having broken up their encampment at Ruckerville, were moving toward Ripley, and later, that having passed that place, they were marching toward Guntown. Meanwhile, the roads from the west, from the direction of the enemy, were thronged with citizens, seeking refuge, with their portable property, from spoliation and those merciless outrages which seem to have marked the path of the Federal column, with every species of calamity for the helpless non-combatants of the region traversed. General Lee now

---

* The passage of this stream was effected with difficulty, from high water.   The ammunition was carried across by the men on their horses, to keep it dry.

determined to fall back with the whole force toward Okolona, so as to effect a junction with Chalmers, and such other forces as he hoped to be able to glean from Mobile, before grappling with the enemy. All supplies and public property were accordingly dispatched southward by rail, and General Lee proceeded in the like direction and manner the night of the 9th, while Forrest was ordered to move with Buford's Division and Rucker, and get between the Federal column and Tupelo. In motion before dawn on the 10th, with Lyon's Brigade in advance, Forrest was at Old Carrollville, four miles north-eastward of Brice's Cross-Roads.* Here scouts reported that the main force of the enemy having encamped the past night on Stubbs's farm—twelve miles east of Ripley, and eight from the cross-roads just mentioned—their cavalry, or advance, had already been met within a mile of the latter position, and hence were about to intercept the line of his march. Seeing no way of avoiding this contingency, and Johnson's Brigade having come up meanwhile, Forrest promptly resolved upon the offensive, and an immediate encounter. Lyon was therefore ordered to move rapidly forward with his brigade and feel the enemy, while Rucker's and Johnson's men were replenishing their exhausted cartridge-boxes. The night had been rainy, but the sun rose brightly, and dispelling the morning mists, became warm and somewhat oppressive to the men and jaded horses ; and the roads, saturated with water, from recent continuous heavy rains, were so much cut up as to retard the progress of the artillery. Strict orders were given, however, to keep the men well closed up, prevent straggling, and lagging, and to urge forward the artillery and ordnance trains as fast as possible.

---

* Lyon's Brigade had bivouacked the preceding night at Boonville, and Bell's Brigade at Rienzi, some eight miles northward, and General Buford had remained at Boonville to await its arrival there, so as to bring up the rear of the command.

COLONEL E. W. RUCKER.

CHAPTER XVIII.

BATTLE OF TISHOMINGO CREEK.

Sketch of Theatre of War—Confederates first engaged—Forrest takes the Offensive—Threw small Force to harass Federal Rear—Desperate Fighting—Transient Checks—Federals defeated and driven from the Field—Pursuit and Incidents—Commentaries.

June 10th to 13th, 1864.

BRICE'S CROSS-ROADS, four miles due west from the Mobile and Ohio Railroad at Baldwin, is at the intersection of thé road from Ripley through Guntown to Fulton with that leading from Carrollville through Ellistown to Pontotoc.

Forrest's force immediately in hand at the moment consisted of—

Lyon's Brigade,*	.	. .	800 rank and file.
Rucker's Brigade,†	.	.	700 " " "
Johnson's Brigade,‡	.	. .	500 " " "

---

* Composed of Third Kentucky, Lieutenant-Colonel G. A. C. Holt commanding; Seventh Kentucky, Major H. S. Hale commanding; Eighth Kentucky, Captain R. H. Fristoe commanding; and Faulkner's Kentucky Regiment, Major Thomas S. Tate commanding.

† Composed of Eighteenth Mississippi, Lieutenant-Colonel Alexander H. Chalmers; Nineteenth Mississippi, Colonel W. L. Duff; and Seventh Tennessee, Colonel W. L. Duckworth.

‡ Composed of Fourth Alabama, Lieutenant-Colonel Windes commanding; Moreland's Battalion, Major

Lyon, as we have related, had been ordered to press forward with his brigade, and, coming in contact, to feel the strength of the enemy without being drawn inextricably into battle. Therefore, his advance, Randle's Company of the Seventh Kentucky, soon coming in conflict with a greatly superior cavalry force on the road leading toward Tupelo, through Brice's Cross-Roads, west of the railroad, was forced to fall back on the brigade. Lyon then ordered Captain Randle to dismount his men and advance on foot, to develop the Federal position. This done with spirit, speedily the enemy's cavalry were found strongly posted in heavy force in front. The Third Kentucky, Colonel Holt, meanwhile dismounted, was thrown forward at a double-quick, deployed in line of battle, in support of Randle, and brought at once into action. The Federal position was strong ; Lyon, therefore, dismounting the Seventh Kentucky and Faulkner's Regiment—except two companies, held as cavalry to guard his flanks—immediately advanced, the former on the right and the latter on the left, in line with the Third Kentucky, while the Eighth Kentucky was held as a reserve, in rear of the centre, within supporting distance. Thus disposed, Lyon pressed steadily up through a skirt of timber, brushing the enemy back as he advanced. But discovering that the Federals were being heavily massed in his front, as if for an attack, Lyon halted his line, reconnoitered the position, and directed his men to throw up such cover as could be quickly made of rails and fallen timber at hand. The enemy, already having several pieces of artillery in position,

George commanding ; Williams's Battalion, Captain Doane commanding ; Warren's Battalion, Captain W. H. Warren commanding ; and Ferrel's Battery, four guns, under Captain Ferrel. This brigade had then been constantly in the saddle for a week, on a forced march from North-Alabama. Not only was this march made through an incessant torrential rain, but the streams, bridgeless and swollen, were only to be passed at a good deal of hazard, and the march effected by much energy.

opened a hot fire with shell and canister, while a large force menaced an onset upon Lyon's left.

Meanwhile, a courier had been dispatched with instructions to Buford to detach a regiment (Barteau's Second Tennessee) at Old Carrollville, to gain the Federal rear, and, if possible, destroy their train ; and to hurry forward the artillery at a gallop, as well as the other regiments of Bell's Brigade.

Informed of the state of affairs on the field, Forrest ordered Colonel Lyon to take the offensive with the Third Kentucky and Faulkner's Regiment. This gallantly performed, the ene-my was presently driven back for three hundred yards to the edge of an old field. Forrest had moved up meanwhile the Seventh and Eighth Kentucky to a position somewhat in ad-vance and rightward of the road. Lyon then brought up the Third Kentucky and Faulkner's Regiment to the same line. The ground was favorable and he awaited the onset. Rucker, at the same time, was dismounted and ordered also to form in line of battle on the left, which being done with alacrity and characteristic *dash,* he soon became warmly engaged with the enemy, who opened upon him with a sharp musketry-fire from the shelter of a fence and dense thicket of dwarf-oaks. Hear-ing the sounds of this brisk engagement, the Confederate General next dispatched Johnson's Brigade, mounted, at a rapid pace, to gain and guard Lyon's right. Meanwhile, Rice's and Morton's Batteries of the artillery having been brought up at a gallop for some eight miles, they were imme-diately thrown forward into position, in an open field·on a hill, in rear of Lyon, and opened with spirit and execution, espe-cially upon the Federal infantry confronting Rucker. Duff's Mississippians being detached leftward half a mile, to guard tha⸱ flank from being turned, Rucker now charged with the Seventh Tennessee and the Eighteenth Mississippi Battalion (Lieutenant-Colonel Chalmers) across an open field in the face of a heavy hostile force of infantry. Chalmers's Battalion, unsupported on his left at the time, being overlapped by the enemy on that flank, was thrown into confusion by a terrific enfilading fire, and receded to the shelter of the woods in its rear ; but, though warmly pressed back to that position, it was speedily rallied, and handsomely resumed the onset.* The loss was serious among these brave Mississippians and Tennesseeans.   Led, however, with noteworthy courage and vigor by Colonel Rucker, and Lieutenant-Colonels William F. Taylor (Seventh Tennessee) and Chalmers, (Eighteenth Mississippi,) they intrepidly breasted the fire of rifles and artillery that swept the ground over which they advanced, and carried the position.†

At the same time. Lyon, advancing with his brigade in the face of an actively plied artillery and warm fusilade of small-arms, drove back the force opposed in his front, after some obstinate fighting and several efforts to charge him with a superior force.   And Buford having come up at half-past eleven A.M., with Bell's Brigade, or rather Russell's and Wilson's Regiments, Forrest had placed them, dismounted, immediately in line and on the left of Rucker, about the time that brigade had faltered, as we have mentioned.

The enemy now occupied the arc of a circle three fourths of a mile, at least, in extent, and about half a mile from Brice's house, the right of which lay across the Ripley-Guntown road. They were also in heavy force of infantry, as well as cavalry ; but a large portion of the infantry had been brought up at a double-quick for some six or eight miles, and, of course, were much blown and flurried, and not in good fighting condition. Lyon's Brigade, confronting them on both sides of the Bald-

---

* Its effective strength in this battle was only 225.

† Here Lieutenant William S. Pope, the accomplished young Adjutant of the Seventh Tennessee, was killed, and nearly a third of his regiment were placed *hors de combat*. See Appendix.

win road, was formed in line in the edge of a thick wood ; Rucker, as we have stated, was next on the left ; and Russell's and Wilson's Regiments (Bell's Brigade) had taken position on his left, with Duff's Mississippians on his and the extreme Confederate left. Meanwhile, Buford had been assigned to the command of the right and centre, embracing Lyon's and Johnson's Brigades, and the artillery, (eight guns,) with instructions to attack strenuously as soon as Bell was heard in action ; and this was the posture of the combat about midday.

The ground held by the enemy, somewhat more elevated than that occupied by the Confederates, was undulating, and thickly clad with stunted trees and tangled undergrowth, which, vailing their presence, furnished excellent cover, in addition to the breastwork of rails and logs that they had erected. Nevertheless, Bell advanced to the onset about half-past one P.M., and speedily a prolonged musketry fire blazed and gushed in the face of his line, and many of his bravest officers and men went down before it.* Right gallantly and staunchly did these regiments endeavor to stem the adverse tide, but finally they wavered. Wilson's Regiment, flanked and enfiladed, gave back, and the issue seemed inevitably unfavorable for a time. But animated by their officers, the men regained a footing, and, happily, Lieutenant-Colonel Wisdom reached the ground at the same juncture, with about two hundred and fifty men of Newsom's Regiment. These were quickly dismounted, and advanced to a position on Wilson's left. The offensive was now vehemently resumed by the Confederates in all parts

---

* Here, Captain J. L. Bell, Assistant Inspector-General, was mortally, and Lieutenant Isaac Bell, aid-de-camp of Bell's staff, severely wounded, as also Major ———— Webb, of Russell's Regiment. Many others were slain or wounded, whose names will be found in the long list of casualties of this battle given in the Appendix. We may say here, the loss in officers was peculiarly heavy, for sixteen were killed and sixty-one wounded. The Sixteenth (Wilson's) Tennessee had eleven of its officers wounded.

of their line. The Federals fought well, and made several persistent charges, in heavy force, upon Johnson's, Lyon's, and Rucker's, as well as Bell's and Duff's positions, and more than once defeat seemed unavoidable. Two strong lines of Federal infantry pressing upon Rucker and Bell and Duff, through an open field, their front line came within thirty paces of the Confederates, who then drew their revolvers and drove the enemy back with great slaughter. At the same time, Lyon and Johnson repulsed those who had assailed them ;* while the escort, under Captain Jackson, with characteristic daring, had dashed down upon some negro infantry, on the Federal right, and thrown them into great confusion.† Urged forward by their officers, the Confederates pressed the enemy back by the sheer valor and tenacity with which they were handled. Nevertheless, the Federals, constantly reënforced by fresh regiments, brought up one after another, were so greatly superior in numbers, that the result was still extremely doubtful. Forrest thereupon repaired, in person, to where his artillery was in position in front of Lyon. Ordering the pieces to be double-shotted with canister—a favorite practice—and limbered up, he moved with them down a gentle wooded slope, to within sixty yards of the Federal lines, to the edge of a field about a quarter of a mile north-east of Brice's house, just at the moment a strong Federal line, resuming the offensive, was emerging from the woods into the open ground. In this position, the Confederate artillery (eight pieces) were opened with signal execution ; and, after two or three dis-

---

* Previously, Johnson's Brigade, on the extreme Confederate right, had forced the enemy back until within sight of their wagon-train, when it was ordered to oblique to the left and rear, and connect with Lyon, to defeat an attempt on the part of the enemy to penetrate the interval which had been left between its left and Lyon's right.

† So sharp was the combat in this part of the field, that the Seventh Kentucky lost thirty officers and men killed and wounded.

charges, Lyon and Johnson charged upon the Federal left.
Hotly engaged at all points—about two P.M.—the conflict had
now become general and desperate.   There was no faltering
at the juncture anywhere in the Confederate ranks.   Buford
was steadily pressing the Federals back upon Brice's house,
with Lyon's and Johnson's Brigades ; Bell's and Rucker's
Brigades, moving across the fields and over the fences, in their
front, using their revolvers freely, bore backward all before them
in the same direction. The Confederate fire of small-arms and
artillery was rapid, incessant, desolating.*   Forrest's line was
now shortened, and hence strengthened, as it converged upon
the cross-roads, and the Federals were driven back at all
points, into a broad ravine, westward of Brice's house, leading
to Tishomingo Creek, infantry, cavalry, artillery, their wagon-
train and ambulances huddled together in an almost inextrica-
ble coil, and upon this mass Morton's and Rice's Batteries
were brought to bear with fearful carnage.

By this time, six guns had been captured at Brice's house,
and several of these, manned by the Confederate artillerists,
were turned upon the Federals, disabling the horses of another
Federal battery some three hundred yards westward of the
Ripley road.†   Seeing this, Captains Morton and Rice moved
their batteries forward at a gallop up to the obstructed mass
of the enemy, and poured upon it a deadly tide of canister.
The havoc was ghastly, and the second battery was abandoned,
as the enemy crowded back along the Ripley road, toward
Tishomingo Creek, the bridge over which, still standing, was
blocked up with wagons, some of whose teams had been killed,

---

* Full eight hundred Federal officers
and men lay dead around Brice's house,
and on the field to the east and south
of it.

† The color-bearer of the Eighth

Kentucky, having been disabled in the
charge upon this battery, Sergeant ——
Brown, Company A, of the regiment,
seizing the flag, rushed forward and
planted it upon a caisson.

and more than one hundred of the Federals were killed or wounded in attempting to press across the bridge thus obstructed. Finding their way thus barred, the enemy rushed into the creek on both sides of the bridge ; but as they emerged from the water on the west bank, in an open field, the Confederates' artillery played upon them, for half a mile, killing or disabling large numbers.

In the interim, the wagons left on the bridge had to be thrown into the stream before the Confederates, in any effective numbers, could pass over ; otherwise, the captures must have been much more numerous. A section of Rice's Battery, however, was worked across, and, supported by the escort, overtook, and was opened upon the negro brigade, with double-shotted canister, with appalling effect.

Meanwhile, the obstructions having been removed from the bridge, by throwing the wagons into the water, the rest of the artillery followed swiftly the advance section, ahead, for the moment, of any support, and securing favorable positions, joined in the havoc.

The order was now given for the cavalry to halt, reorganize, remount as fast as possible, and pursue. The road was narrow, with dense woods on either side, so that it was impossible to use more than four pieces at a time ; but that number were kept close upon the heels of the retreating enemy, and in murderous play, preventing them from making a stand. Nothing could exceed the daring spirit, energy, and execution with which the Confederate artillery was handled by its officers.*

---

* Captain J. W. Morton was in chief command, with R. M. Blakemore as Adjutant. His battery was commanded by the gallant Lieutenant T. S. Sale, assisted by Lieutenants J. M. Mayson and G. T. Brown ; Rice's Battery was commanded by Captain T. W. Rice, with Lieutenants B. F. Haller, H. H. Briggs, and D. C. Jones as subalterns. Lieutenants J. C. Barlow and W. J. D. Winton, of Thrall's Battery, casually present, and acting as volun-

About two miles from the cross-roads, the enemy rallied at length in strong force, and again made stout battle for about half an hour, in the course of which, concentrating, they made a spirited charge upon their eager pursuers, and drove them back upon Rice's Battery ; but that, opening with double charges of canister, and Lyon's Brigade springing forward with loud cheers, hurled them back with so stormful an onset, that the Federal array dissolved before it into a molten mass of fragments and stragglers, and their defeat was consummate. The largest portion of their wagon-train was left on the ground, with many caissons, and the road was so thickly strewn as to be encumbered with the dead, the dying, and the wounded, with cast-away arms, accoutrements, baggage, dead animals, and other wreck and residuum of a routed army. It was now sunset, but the pursuit was maintained, weary and over-spent as the Confederates were, for some five or six miles beyond, and until it became quite too dark to go farther.

In the mean time, Barteau's Regiment, (Second Tennessee, not more than 250 strong,) which, as will be remembered, had been detached from Carrollville to get rearward of the enemy on the Ripley road, effecting the movement, attacked the Federal rear with skill and resolution. This drew to that quarter a large part of their cavalry, while the battle was raging with greatest fury at the cross-roads. Deploying his men as skirmishers, on a line of nearly three quarters of a mile, and with other admirable and daring dispositions of his force,

---

teers with the batteries of Rice and Morton respectively, were conspicuous for their conduct. The spirit that animated the men may be illustrated by the behavior of one—Jimmie Moran, of Morton's Battery — who, when shot through the arm, on being told by his officers to go to the rear, invariably replied, " No, sir, I'll stay with you as long as I can stand up," and continued to drive his gun-team with his arm in a sling through the entire fight. Morton's Battery consisted of four three-inch rifle guns, and Rice's of two twelve-pounder howitzers, and two six-pounder smooth-bore guns.

well calculated to conceal his weakness, Barteau contributed materially to disturb and disorder the enemy, and prevent the escape of their train.

As the negro soldiery broke, after their last stand, they were seen generally to tear something from their uniform and throw it away, which subsequently proved to have been a badge on which was printed " REMEMBER FORT PILLOW," while at the same time their officers (whites) threw off their shoulder-straps or insignia of rank.

II.

As soon as the several commands were reassembled, and the darkness had somewhat diminished, about one o'clock on the morning of the 11th, Forrest gave orders for the immediate resumption of the pursuit. Rucker's Brigade—with the Seventh Tennessee leading—took the advance, and within three miles struck the Federal rear about daylight, at Stubbs's farm. A slight skirmish ensued, when the enemy broke, abandoning the remainder of their wagon-train, nine pieces of artillery, and some twenty-five ambulances, with a number of wounded, at the crossing of a small fork of the Hatchie.*

The enemy, as was apparent, were now greatly scattered through the surrounding country. Forrest, therefore, threw out a regiment on either side of the highway, to sweep for some distance to the right and left, and all the morning the din of firearms was to be heard at the harsh, stern work of war.

Bell's Brigade was now in advance, having, soon after sun-

---

* During the night, Lieutenant Frank Rodgers, of Rucker's staff, with a detachment of ten men, hanging constantly and closely upon the Federal rear, with an ardent daring that never was surpassed, made a series of attacks, and greatly harassed and annoyed the enemy, numbers of whom were thus killed or wounded.

rise, relieved Rucker, whose horses were exhausted. And about four miles eastward of Ripley, the Federals were found rallied and in position for another stand at the crossing of Hatchie creek, where the "bottom" was almost impracticable, except by the road over a causeway for some 300 yards. They had already effected the passage of the stream, and were drawn up on a ridge, some seven hundred yards from its west bank, with a strong line of skirmishers lining a fringe of woods near the water's edge, to dispute the Confederate advance. No artillery being visible, Forrest quickly dismounted two regiments of Bell's Brigade, moved with them, and his escort mounted, up the creek, leftward, and crossed without any resistance, taking the Federals on their right flank. At this moment they again broke, after a very slight skirmish, and the whole Confederate force, crossing the stream, resumed the pursuit.

As the advance of Bell's Brigade—Wilson's Regiment—approached Ripley, about eight P.M., the enemy were found drawn up in two strong battle-lines, just in the outskirts, north-west of the place, stretching across the roads leading to Lagrange and Salem.* Forrest coming up with his escort, immediately dismounted them and Wilson's men, and without waiting for any additional force, advanced with his habitual audacity to the attack ; but sending orders, however, to General Buford to throw Rucker around to gain their rear on the Lagrange road, and to hurry up with the other regiments.

Wilson's Regiment and the escort deployed as a thin line of skirmishers half a mile long, advancing under cover of the houses and fences of Ripley, opened with an effective fire upon the Federal lines, inflicting so sharp a loss that, after a few moments, they broke, leaving upon the field thirty of their

---

* Ripley is twenty-five miles from Brice's Cross-Roads.

dead and sixty wounded, including a colonel of infantry.* At
the same time, Lieutenant-Colonel Jesse Forrest charged
with one company, mounted, of Wilson's Regiment, with such
hardihood and tenacity that, it is understood, the commander
of the Federal cavalry and rear-guard narrowly escaped capture.

Buford, having now brought up the other troops, was directed to pursue with Lyon's and Rucker's Brigades, and hang
closely upon the Federal rear, on the road toward Salem,
through Davenport, while, taking Bell's Brigade, Forrest
would endeavor to reach Salem sooner by a left-hand way,
somewhat more direct, with the hope of thus intercepting the
main body of the retreating enemy at this point. Buford,
however, took up the pursuit with such vigor that this expectation was disappointed. Directed to lead, and charge
without dismounting, Rucker made several spirited onsets
upon the Federal rear-guard.† Sweeping it rapidly ahead of
him, capturing several hundred prisoners, Rucker's horses became finally so jaded that Buford relieved that brigade with
Lyon's. Under this rearrangement a charge of signal gallantry was made by Faulkner's Regiment, under Major Tate,
driving the Fourth Missouri (Federal) cavalry back through
the ranks of their infantry, which had been halted for a
stand, and here several hundred prisoners were captured. By
the time, however, Salem was reached, it was apparent that
no body of the Federal force was retreating on that road, but
only widely dispersed stragglers. Rucker and Johnson were
here turned back to scour the country for Federal stragglers
and property—harness, small-arms, accoutrements, and ammunition with which the road was profusely strewn—while Buford,
turning northward, with Lyon's Brigade and Russell's Regi-

---

* Colonel George M. McCaig, One Hundred and Twentieth Illinois Infantry.
† Captain W. J Tate was killed here. See Appendix for sketch.

ment, resumed the chase. One detachment, under Lieutenant-Colonel Holt, followed the road toward Lamar, and the
other toward Lagrange. These, however, were reduced to
small numbers ; for so exhausted had the horses now become
generally, that few were able to keep up, and reach the
extreme points of pursuit on the 11th, which, on the way to
Lagrange, was Davis's Mill, where Buford halted after dark,
and gave his men and animals several hours' rest.

Meanwhile, Forrest having led Bell's Brigade, as we have
related, by the shorter route, nevertheless, on reaching Salem
found that Buford was in his advance. Thereupon, permitting
Colonel Bell to return to the battle-field, to look after the dead
and wounded, he directed Colonel Wilson to proceed with the
brigade on the route taken by Buford, and sweep the country
for prisoners and arms ; but not long after, dispatched orders
to Buford recalling the pursuit.*

The enemy began their retreat about four P.M. on the 10th,
and by five P.M. on the 11th they had been driven, with heavy
loss, in frequent collisions with the Confederates, quite fifty-
eight miles, with the loss also of nineteen pieces of artillery,†
twenty-one caissons, over two hundred wagons, and thirty
ambulances, with parts of their teams and large quantities of
subsistence, ammunition, and other *materiel* of war. More
than 2000 officers and men, including the wounded, were
taken prisoners ; and 1900 of their dead were left upon the
field or by the wayside, between the battle-field and Ripley.
Seldom, almost never, was an army more completely beaten
and dispersed than that of Sturgis on this occasion ; beaten,

---

* Several miles before reaching Salem, the Confederate General fell from
his horse from sheer exhaustion, and
for more than an hour lay in a state of
stupor by the road-side.

† Seventeen pieces of artillery were
actually captured ; two were buried by
the Federals.

too, as has been seen, by a force of fighting men at no time exceeding 3200 men, that is to say, little over one third of the Federal army.* The Confederate losses were severe, at least 140 officers and men killed. and nearly 500 were wounded.

III.

Having directed the return of his command to the battle-field, General Forrest, still greatly fatigued and exhausted by the extreme mental exertion he had undergone, now set out in the same direction and slept Saturday night, (11th,) with his staff and escort, at the house of a paternal uncle—Orrin Beck—three or four miles from Salem, and almost within sight of the little farm upon which had been passed the years of his youth, for the most part in a hard, resolute struggle for the means of support for a widowed mother and her family of eleven children.

Returning slowly on the next day toward Ripley, the Confederate General tarried at that place on the night of the 12th, and did not reach Brice's Cross-Roads until the morning of the 13th. His first act was to issue an order for the collection of the wounded of both sides, and their early removal to hospitals on the line of the Mobile and Ohio Railroad. And from the same place a general order was issued requiring his division and brigade commanders to make detailed reports to his headquarters of all captured property of every description which had been collected by their several commands. These details attended to, he repaired that afternoon to Guntown Station, on the Mobile and Ohio Railroad, five

---

* And of this number one fourth, or one man out of every four, was detached to hold the horses of their comrades, fighting as infantry, and therefore took no combatant part in the battle, and reducing the fighting men actually to about 2300 men.

miles southward, where, establishing his headquarters, he immediately addressed himself to the reorganization of his command, and its redisposition for future service.

COMMENTARIES.

1. This battle has been described by Federal writers as having been fought at Guntown ; it occurred, however, at Brice's Cross-Roads, in close proximity to Tishomingo creek, on which account the victors have always called it the battle of Tishomingo. The Federal force engaged, says their Official Report, consisted of Warren's and Winslow's Brigades, 3300 cavalry, and Wilkins's and Hoge's (white) and Benton's (negro) Brigades of infantry, 5400 strong.

2. The action was far bloodier than it would have been had not the negroes entered upon the campaign inspired by their officers with the conviction that no quarter would be given them—inspired, too, with the resolution to give no quarter.* Impressed with this notion, animated by the apprehension engendered, they perversely refused to halt and surrender. Wildly persisting in seeking safety in flight, they were necessarily shot down for a time to such a degree that the affair became very like a grand *battue* for wild game.

3. For a week previously the Confederates, be it remembered, had been marching, with scant periods of rest, night

---

* We have seen circumstantial, dramatic accounts in Federal newspapers of the day, detailing the administration of the oath to the negroes to give no quarter. General Washburne, in his letter to General Forrest, printed hereinafter p. 487, confesses such an oath was taken, and that these very negroes were permitted by him to take the field with such purposes ; and yet had written a letter, (also printed *forward*, p. 489,) complaining that they had been unmercifully dealt with in battle. The famous Oxenstiern said, "*Le son du tambour dissipe les pensees.*" Assuredly the drums around the Federal General must have driven thought from his head.

and day—through drenching rains, over muddy roads and bank-full streams, so that they were greatly fatigued. Nevertheless, officers and men were made invincible by a determination to conquer. The courage manifested throughout, rarely equaled in the aggregate on any field, has never been surpassed. General Buford rendered signal aid to his superior in the general conduct of the battle ; the brigade commanders, Colonels Bell, Lyon, and Rucker, were men not only of shining courage, but of strong force of character, and the several regiments engaged were admirably handled by their immediate commanders.

4. In this battle the genuine military capacity of General Forrest would seem to have been demonstrated. It has been thought and asserted by many that his successes were largely due to uncommon good fortune, coupled with audacity ; but it must be apparent that this brilliant victory was won by his prompt comprehension of the situation on the morning of the 10th June, and his recognition of the possibility of taking his adversary at the sore disadvantage of being attacked while his column was extended in a long line, moving over the narrow roads of that densely wooded region. Seeing his advantage at its right value, he planned and executed with equal celerity ; and never did soldiers fight, we repeat, with greater tenacity or intrepidity than those he led that day.

5. In this affair, furthermore, was illustrated the sovereign efficacy in war of the *defensive-active*, with the concentration and speedy employment of one's whole force when the battle moment has come. Forrest brought his entire strength into action, and kept no reserves unemployed. In this he was right ; for a reserve is an unnecessary subtractive from—and emasculative of—a force so small as that which he commanded ; and victory is surest won on such occasions when every man is launched, and every gun available is employed, as strenuously and swiftly as possible.

CHAPTER XIX.

BATTLE OF HARRISBURG.

Rapid March of Chalmers from Monte Vallo—Mabry's Brigade added to Forrest's Cavalry—Correspondence between Generals Forrest and Washburne—Forrest, anticipating a strong Hostile Movement, reported the Facts to his Superior—Approach of Enemy under Major-General A. J. Smith—The Country devastated by the Federal Army—Major-General S. D. Lee in Command of Confederates—Affair at Pinson's Hill, also at Barrow's Shop—Forrest Reconnoitered the Federal Position—Battle of Harrisburg, July 14th—Confederates worsted, but Federals refuse to advance from their Intrenchments—Retreat of General Smith on the 15th of July—Federal Ambuscade at Town Creek—Commentaries.

June 14th to July 16th, 1864.

As will be remembered, Chalmers, under orders from Major-General Lee, had left Monte Vallo with McCulloch's Brigade on the 10th of June, to return by forced marches to Mississippi. Notwithstanding the heavy rains, consequent muddy roads and swollen streams encountered, he was at Columbus, Miss.—one hundred and twenty miles from Monte Vallo—by one P.M. on the 13th June, and there found orders to halt for further instructions.

Mabry's Brigade likewise had come within the limits of Forrest's command, and was posted at Okolona.* It had

---

* Composed of the Fourth Mississippi, Colonel C. C. Wilburne; Sixth Mississippi, Colonel Isham Harrison; Thirty-eighth Mississippi, Major Ro-

been previously on service in the quarter of the Yazoo river, until ordered by General Lee to push forward to assist in repelling the expedition, the fate of which we have just related. Reaching the vicinity too late to take part in the combat or pursuit, it became, however, thenceforward an effective part of FORREST'S CAVALRY.

During the latter part of the month of May, a controversy had grown up between the Federal commander at Helena, Ark., and the Confederate commander on the opposite side of the Mississippi river, who had initiated the correspondence in regard to courses alleged to be in breach of the laws of war. This coming to the notice of General Forrest, he at once, disapproving what had been done by his subordinate, forbade such communications thereafter between his lieutenants and Federal commanders. And almost his first official act on reaching Guntown was to make the Federal commander at Helena acquainted with his own views in the premises. The communication to that end and copies of the correspondence in question were forwarded, by flag of truce, to the Federal commander—Major-General Washburne—at Memphis, on the 14th, for perusal, and the transmission of his own letter to its address. At the same time the Confederate General took occasion to address General Washburne the following :

> "HEADQUARTERS FORREST'S CAVALRY, } IN THE FIELD, June 14, 1864. }

"GENERAL:*   .   .   .   .

"It has been reported to me that all your colored troops stationed in Memphis took, on their knees, in the presence of Major-General Hurlbut and other officers of your army, an oath to avenge Fort Pillow, and that they would show my troops no quarter. Again, I have it from indisputa-

---

bert McKay commanding; and the Fourteenth Confederate, Colonel F. Dumontiel.

* The omitted paragraph relates simply to the inclosures.

ble authority, that the troops under Brigadier-General Sturgis, on their recent march from Memphis, publicly and in many places proclaimed that no quarter would be shown my men. As they were moved into action on the 10th, they were exhorted by their officers to remember Fort Pillow. The prisoners we have captured from that command, or a large majority of them, have voluntarily stated that they expected us to murder them, otherwise they would have surrendered in a body rather than taken to the bushes after being run down and exhausted. The recent battle of Tishomingo creek was far more bloody than it would otherwise have been but for the fact that your men evidently expected to be slaughtered when captured, and both sides acted as though neither felt safe in surrendering, even when further resistance was useless. The prisoners captured by us say they felt condemned by the announcements, etc., of their own commanders, and expected no quarter.

" In all my operations since it began, I have conducted the war on civilized principles, and desire still to do so ; but it is due to my command that they should know the position they occupy and the policy you intend to pursue. I therefore respectfully ask whether my men now in your hands are treated as other Confederate prisoners of war, also the course intended to be pursued in regard to those who may hereafter fall into your hands.

" I have in my possession quite a number of wounded officers and men of General Sturgis's command, all of whom have been treated as well as we were able to treat them, and are mostly in charge of a surgeon left at Ripley by General Sturgis to look after the wounded. Some of them are too severely wounded to be removed at present. I am willing to exchange them for any men of my command you have, and, as soon as able to be removed, will give them safe escort through our lines in charge of the surgeon left with them. I made such an arrangement once with Major-General Hurlbut, and am willing to renew it, provided it is desired, as it would be better than to subject them to the long and fatiguing trip necessary to a regular exchange at City Point, Va.

" I am, General, etc.,

N. B. FORREST,

Major-General."

This communication, dispatched with a flag of truce borne by Lieutenant-Colonel R. W. Pitman, an officer of Forrest's staff, drew an answer as follows :

"HEADQUARTERS DISTRICT OF WEST-TENNESSEE, ¿
MEMPHIS, TENNESSEE, June 19, 1864.

" *Major-General N. B. Forrest, Commanding Confederate Forces :*

"GENERAL : Your communication of the 14th instant is received. The letter to Brigadier-General Buford will be forwarded to him.

"In regard to that part of your letter which relates to colored troops, I beg to say that I have already sent a communication on the same subject to the officers in command of the Confederate forces at Tupelo. Having understood that Major-General S. D. Lee was in command there, I directed my letter to him. A copy of it I inclose.

"You say in your letter that it has been reported to you 'that all the negro troops stationed in Memphis took an oath, on their knees, in the presence of Major-General Hurlbut and other officers of our army, to avenge Fort Pillow, and that they would show your troops no quarter.' I believe it is true that the colored troops did take such an oath, but not in the presence of General Hurlbut. From what I can learn, this act of theirs was not influenced by any white officer, but was the result of their own sense of what was due to themselves and their fellows who had been mercilessly slaughtered.* I have no doubt that they went into the field, as you allege, in the full belief that they would be murdered in case they fell into your hands. The affair of Fort Pillow fully justified that belief. I am not aware as to what they proclaimed on their late march, and it may be, as you say, that they declared that no quarter would be given to any of your men that might fall into their hands.

"Your declaration that you have conducted the war on all occasions on civilized principles can not be accepted ; but I receive with satisfaction the intimation in your letter that the recent slaughter of colored troops at the battle of Tishomingo creek resulted rather from the desperation with which they fought than a predetermined intention to give them no quarter. You must have learned by this time that the attempt to intimidate the colored troops by indiscriminate slaughter has signally failed, and that, instead of a feeling of terror, you have aroused a spirit of courage and desperation that will not down at your bidding.

"I am left in doubt by your letter, as to the course you and the Confederate Government intend to pursue hereafter in regard to colored troops,

---

* Here is a distinct admission that the negro troops with Sturgis had gone into the field with the declared intention to give no quarter.

and I beg you to advise me, with as little delay as possible, as to your intention. If you intend to treat such of them as fall into your hands as prisoners of war, please so state. If you do not so intend, but contemplate either their slaughter or their return to slavery, please state *that*, so that we may have no misunderstanding hereafter. If the former is your intention, I shall receive the announcement with pleasure, and shall explain the fact to the colored troops at once, and desire that they recall the oath that they have taken. If the latter is the case, then let the oath stand, and upon those who have aroused this spirit by their atrocities, and upon the Government and people who sanction it, be the consequences.

"In regard to your inquiry relating to prisoners of your command in our hands, I state that they have always received the treatment which a great and humane government extends to its prisoners. What course will be pursued hereafter toward them must, of course, depend on circumstances that may arise. If your command, hereafter, do nothing which should properly exclude them from being treated as prisoners of war, they will be so treated.

"I thank you for your offer to exchange wounded officers and men in your hands. If you will send them in, I will exchange man for man, so far as I have the ability to do so.

"Before closing this letter, I wish to call your attention to one case of unparalleled outrage and murder, that has been brought to my notice, and in regard to which the evidence is overwhelming.

"Among the prisoners captured at Fort Pillow, was Major Bradford, who had charge of the Fort after the fall of Major Booth. After being taken a prisoner, he was started with other prisoners, in charge of Colonel Duckworth, for Jackson. At Brownsville they rested over night. The following morning, two companies were detailed by Colonel Duckworth to proceed to Jackson with the prisoners. After they had started, and proceeded a very short distance, five soldiers were recalled by Colonel Duckworth, and were conferred with by him. They then rejoined the column, and after proceeding about five miles from Brownsville, the column was halted, and Major Bradford taken about fifty yards from the roadside and deliberately shot by the five men who had been recalled by Colonel Duckworth, and his body left unburied upon the ground where he fell. He now lies buried near the spot, and, if you desire, you can easily satisfy yourself of the truth of what I assert.

"I beg leave to say to you, that this transaction hardly justifies your remark, that your operations have been conducted on civilized principles ;

and until you take some steps to bring the perpetrators of this outrage to justice, the world will not fail to believe that it has your sanction.

"I am, General, respectfully, your obedient servant,

C. C. WASHBURNE,

Major-General."

Besides this communication, so stuffed with harsh epithets, and the unsoldierly discourtesy of the gownsman in controversy, it seems that, while Forrest's letter of the 14th of June was on its way to the Federal headquarters, one touching the same subject had been written by General Washburne, and dispatched on the 17th to Major-General Lee, which we also print as a part of the history of the day :

"HEADQUARTERS DISTRICT OF WEST-TENNESSEE, }
MEMPHIS, TENNESSEE, June 17, 1864. }

"*Major-General S. D. Lee, Commanding Confederate Forces, near Tupelo, Mississippi.*

"GENERAL : When I heard that the forces of Brigadier-General Sturgis had been driven back, and a portion of them probably captured, I felt considerable solicitude for the fate of the two colored regiments that formed a part of the command, until I was informed that the Confederate forces were commanded by you. When I heard that, I became satisfied that no atrocities would be committed upon those troops, but that they would receive the treatment which humanity, as well as their gallant conduct, demanded. I regret to say, that the hope that I entertained has been dispelled by facts which have recently come to my knowledge.

"From statements that have been made to me by colored soldiers, who were eye-witnesses, it would seem that the massacre of Fort Pillow had been reproduced at the late affair at Brice's Cross-Roads. The details of the atrocities there committed I will not trouble you with. If true, and not disavowed, they must lead to consequences, hereafter, fearful to contemplate. It is best that we should now have a fair understanding upon the question of treatment of this class of soldiers.

"If it is contemplated by the Confederate Government to murder all colored troops that may by the chances of war fall into their hands, as was the case at Fort Pillow, it is but fair that it should be truly and openly avowed. Within the last six weeks, I have, on two occasions, sent colored troops into the field from this point. In the expectation that the Confederate Government would disavow the action of their commanding general at the Fort Pillow massacre, I have forborne to issue any instructions to the colored troops as to the course they should pursue toward Confederate soldiers that might fall into their hands ;* but seeing no disavowal on the part of the Confederate Government, but, on the contrary, laudations from the entire Southren press of the perpetrators of the massacre, I may safely presume that indiscriminate slaughter is to be the fate of colored troops that fall into your hands.   But I am not willing to leave a matter of such grave import, and involving consequences so fearful, to inference, and I have, therefore, thought it proper to address you this, believing that you would be able to indicate the policy that the Confederate Government intended to pursue hereafter in this question.   It it is intended to raise the black flag against that unfortunate race, they will cheerfully accept the issue.   Up to this time, no troops have fought more gallantly, and none have conducted themselves with greater propriety. They have fully vindicated their right (so long denied) to be treated as men.   I hope that I have been misinformed in regard to the treatment they have received at the battle of Brice's Cross-Roads, and that the accounts received result rather from the excited imaginations of the fugitives, than from actual facts.

" For the government of the colored troops under my command, I would thank you to inform me, with as little delay as possible, if it is your intention, or the intention of the Confederate Government, to murder colored soldiers that may fall into your hands, or treat them as prisoners of war, and subject to be exchanged as other prisoners.

" I am, General, respectfully, etc.,

C. C. WASHBURNE,

Major-General."

As this communication passed through Forrest's hands, he made an immediate reply, which we reproduce :

" HEADQUARTERS FORREST'S CAVALRY, TUPELO, }
June 23, 1864. }
" *Major-General C. C. Washburne, Commanding U. S. Forces, Memphis :*
" GENERAL : I have the honor to acknowledge the receipt (per flag of

---

* But admits in the letter, *ante,* p. 487, that he knew at the same time those troops had gone into the field breathing vengeance, and sworn to give no quarter to Confederates that might fall into their hands. See Commentaries.

truce) of your letter of the 17th instant, addressed to Major-General S. D. Lee, or officer commanding Confederate forces near Tupelo. I have forwarded it to General Lee, with a copy of this letter.

"I regard your letter as discourteous to the commanding officer of this department, and grossly insulting to myself. You seek, by implied threats, to intimidate him, and assume the privilege of denouncing me as a murderer, and as guilty of the wholesale slaughter of the garrison at Fort Pillow, and found your assertions upon the *ex parte* testimony of (your friends) the enemies of myself and country.

"I shall not enter into the discussion, therefore, of any of the questions involved, nor undertake any refutation of the charges made by you against myself. Nevertheless, as a matter of personal privilege alone, I unhesitatingly say, that they are unfounded, and unwarranted by the facts. But whether these charges are true or false, they, with the question you ask, as to whether negro troops, when captured, will be recognized and treated as prisoners of war, subject to exchange, etc., are matters which the Governments of the United States and the Confederate States are to decide and adjust, not their subordinate officers. I regard captured negroes as I do other captured property, and not as captured soldiers ; but as to how regarded by my Government, and the disposition which has been, and will hereafter be made of them, I respectfully refer you, through the proper channel, to the authorities at Richmond.

"It is not the policy or the interest of the South to destroy the negro ; on the contrary, to preserve and protect him ; and all who have surrendered to us have received kind and humane treatment.

"Since the war began, I have captured many thousand Federal prisoners, and they, including the survivors of the 'Fort Pillow Massacre,' black and white, are living witnesses of the fact, that, with my knowledge or consent, or by my orders, not one of them has ever been insulted or maltreated in any way.

"You speak of your forbearance, in 'not giving to your negro troops instructions and orders, as to the course they should pursue in regard to Confederate soldiers that might fall into (your) their hands,' which clearly conveys to my mind two very distinct impressions. The first is, that, in not giving them instructions and orders, you have left the matter entirely to the discretion of the negroes as to how they should dispose of prisoners ; second, an implied threat, to give such orders as will lead to 'consequences too fearful' for contemplation. In confirmation of the correctness of the first impression, (which your language now fully develops,) I refer you most respectfully to my letter from the battle-field of Tishomingo creek, and forwarded to you, by flag of truce, on the 14th instant. As to the second impression, you seem disposed to take into your own hands the settlement which belongs to, and can only be settled by, your Government. But if you are prepared to take upon yourself the responsibility of inaugurating a system of warfare contrary to civilized usages, the onus, as well as the consequences, will be chargeable to yourself.

"Deprecating, as I should do, such a state of affairs ; determined, as I am, not to be instrumental in bringing it about ; feeling and knowing, as I do, that I have the approval of my Government, my people, and my own conscience, as to the past ; and with the firm belief that I will be sustained by them in my future policy, it is left with you to determine what that policy shall be—whether in accordance with the laws of civilized nations, or in violation of them.   Very respectfully, etc.,

N. B. FORREST,

Major-General."

On the 15th of June, General Forrest, repairing to Tupelo with his staff and escort, established his headquarters at that central position. Meanwhile, his troops, after burying the dead, collecting and removing the wounded, and gleaning the field of all spoils and trophies, had been distributed at points deemed most advantageous for the easy subsistence of men and animals, as well as their rapid concentration in an emergency.* About this time General Roddy, with his entire force, was placed under Forrest, and that officer accordingly was ordered to establish his headquarters at Corinth, taking thither his other—Patterson's—brigade, except three hundred men to be left in North-Alabama.

For the next fortnight, General Forrest, ever diligent, ever looking into all matters of administration with his own eyes, with unremitting energy, pressed forward his preparations to

---

* Chalmers was at Columbus with McCulloch's Brigade and Walton's Battery, and after a few days, Rucker's Brigade was directed to take post at the same place. Buford's headquarters were at Guntown, and his division — Bell's and Lyon's Brigades — was quartered in that neighborhood. Mabry's Brigade was at Okolona. And Johnson was ordered to Corinth.

meet any endeavor of the enemy. Numerous parties from the regular scouting companies of his command were kept far in advance upon all the approaches from any hostile quarter. Forage and subsistence were collected at central points upon all routes of possible operations. And among his measures at this period was the organization into an infantry battalion of all the men of Roddy's, Buford's, and Chalmers's Divisions, who were without serviceable horses. All their horses, and other unserviceable animals of the command, were then collected and sent to favorable points for recuperation. Special efforts were directed likewise to the restoration of the battery teams to the most efficient condition. And nothing, indeed, seems to have been omitted that was practicable for placing his whole force in the most effective fighting condition.

On the 22d, orders were given to Roddy to observe closely on the road westward toward Lagrange, and in the direction of the Tennessee river at Clifton ; also to be in readiness to move at a moment's notice in the best practicable condition for active service. A letter written about this time to his trusty captain of scouts, will show what he exacted of that branch of his command, and the steps taken to secure accurate information :

"Captain," writes one of his Adjutant-Generals, (Captain Anderson,) "I am directed by the Major-General Commanding to say that he is not satisfied with the meagre and unreliable information received from your men. He wishes you to order them to scout well and close up to Memphis and the railroad, and give him reliable information as to enemy's position and movements ; also their numbers. Endeavor, also, to send a scout up toward Randolph, above Memphis, to ascertain whether any troops are moving up the river from Memphis. He also wishes you to have him advised promptly, by telegraph, from Holly Springs, Oxford, or Senatobia, and by courier line from Holly Springs, *via* Ripley, to this place.

"A movement of the enemy in force is anticipated, and he desires that you order your men not only to learn all they can, but see for themselves."*

Sharp and stringent orders were likewise issued to his medical officers, commanding more rapid movement of the wounded from the vicinity of the late battle-field. Detachments were thrown out to glean absentees and deserters, and a field-officer was dispatched to West-Tennessee to declare an amnesty to all deserters who would return to their colors.

By this time, information was received from sources so reliable as to satisfy the Confederate General that a Federal force was preparing to march from Memphis against him, larger than either of the columns which he had discomfited. Informing his superior of the fact, he made new and additional dispositions to keep the impending Federal movement under the closest observation. Among the steps to this end was the detachment of a picked battalion of 200 men, drawn from Buford's Division, on the 23d, advanced to Ripley to hold in observation the many roads converging upon that important strategic position.

On the 25th, he communicated for the information of his superior—Major-General Lee—his views, in writing, of the actual objective of the impending hostile movement, its strength and progress. That communication is so characteristic of the Confederate General that we spread it upon these pages :

" From the information I have, am clearly of the opinion that the force now moving from Memphis meditate the destruction of the Mobile and Ohio Railroad, as far down as possible ; and then turn across to the

* General Forrest, however, acknowledges himself greatly indebted to Captain Thomas Henderson, his officers and men, for their habitual vigilance, courage, and intelligence which enabled them to render incalculable service. In fact, their operations were invaluable.

Central Railroad, destroy it, and return to Memphis. I therefore advise the removal of our surplus stores from Grenada and other points across in the direction of Meridian. I do not believe they design joining Sherman. Most of their force consists of ' one hundred day men ;' at any rate, a large number of that character have arrived, and are arriving, at Memphis. My scouts report that 184 wagons and twenty ambulances passed Forrest Hill, eighteen miles east of Memphis, and that 1200 troops have passed up; but I think that an over-estimate of the number which has thus far left Memphis for up the road. I have no doubt but that they have and will move with 18,000 to 20,000 men, a portion of which will be used to garrison the points already fortified on the Memphis and Charleston road. With a base secured as far east as practicable, they will then attempt the programme previously referred to. I respectfully suggest, therefore, that the Major-General Commanding order up (as far this way as forage will permit) all the available troops of his department. Besides three companies of scouts, I have 200 men at Ripley, and intend sending 200 more under Colonel Forrest, to go as near Lagrange as possible, and ascertain what is going on, and keep me fully posted. Would move a greater force there but for the difficulty in supplying it with forage, not having a sufficiency of mules.

" Have ordered all General Roddy's force to Corinth, except 300 men, to be left in the valley to meet any raids from Decatur. Also, ordered him to send his wagon-train and all his unserviceable and broken-down stock to this place, to be provided for and pastured."

About the same period—June 27th—another letter, addressed to General Roddy, may be cited as showing the scope of his preparations, and the method and attention to details that characterized his instructions to his subordinates :

" I am directed by the Major-General Commanding to say that he desires you to move all your wagons, unserviceable horses, dismounted and unarmed men to this place, reserving and keeping with you only wagons sufficient for your ordnance, and the smallest quantity of cooking utensils that will do your command. Take your best teams for your ordnance and cooking utensils.

" Have one hundred rounds of ammunition to the man, forty in cartridge-boxes, and balance in wagons, together with as much artillery ammunition as you may think sufficient. Keep five days' rations for your command, and be prepared for a move at a moment's notice. You will send your dismounted and unarmed men, wagons, and unserviceable horses down, in charge of a competent officer or officers, and have all your men, with horses, able for duty, armed from those whose horses are unserviceable. Two days' rations of hard bread for all the troops you may keep at Corinth, will be sent you as soon as the number is ascertained and reported. The east side of the railroad from Baldwin is the best road to this place. Direct your wagons to come that route.

" Respectfully, etc.,

CHARLES W. ANDERSON,

A. A. A. General."

Two General Orders—Nos. 56–7—and a circular of this date (27th) are likewise of noteworthy characteristic import. The first is as follows :

" The several commands of the army are now well supplied with wagons, all complete, to wit : Wagon-bows and sheets, feed-boxes, extra tongues, and tongue-props, in good order, being so turned over to them from the recent captures of the enemy.

" Unless quartermasters are vigilant and attentive in the preservation of these things, they will soon be lost or destroyed by the carelessness of teamsters and wagon-masters. It is therefore the intention of the Major-General Commanding, whenever he finds a wagon, in camp or on the march, deficient in any of these needed articles, with all of which it has been supplied, or finds them damaged, or neglected, or missing, to hold the proper party to a most rigid responsibility, and without mercy, inflict the severest punishment known to the regulations, upon the head of that officer in whose department such neglect shall be found."

The other order is in regard to detailed men, a numerous class in Confederate armies, and directed that :

" Hereafter, every detailed man in all the departments will be armed with his gun and necessary accoutrements to go into the fight, and it is expected and will be required of them so to do. One clerk in each department will be excepted from this order. Division, brigade commanders, and heads of departments will be held accountable for the full execution of this order. There will also be exempted one wagon-master with trains."

The circular concerned a vice very common during the war, and was as follows :

" On account of the many incorrect, improper, and contradictory dispatches and articles written by officers and others of this command for publication, in many of which have been developed and made public its positions, movements, numbers, and operations, the Major-General Commanding forbids that dispatches or letters trenching upon any of these points be written and sent from this command unless first submitted to and approved at these headquarters, or by the Major-General Commanding the Department. And that there may be no misunderstanding upon this point, he directs that the order be read at dress-parade, the ensuing week, at least three times."

Forrest now began to concentrate and redispose his troops. Chalmers's Division was brought up from Columbus to Verona ; the outpost at Ripley was increased to 400 men, placed under Lieutenant-Colonel Jesse Forrest, who was instructed to open dispatches from scouts and only to express the important to headquarters, so as to avoid unnecessary work for his couriers and their horses ; and orders were issued for all to be held in readiness for movement at a moment's notice. The absentees, however, from the various regiments were very numerous, despite his constant efforts to reduce the number.*

II.

For the first week in July the work of preparation for the menaced conflict was pressed with unabated activity and attention to detail. The outpost at Ripley was strengthened to 600 men, the command of whom was devolved upon Lieu-

---

* At the end of June, Forrest's Cavalry were disposed as follows : Chalmers's Division—Rucker's and McCulloch's Brigades—at Verona, Buford's—Bell and Lyon—at Tupelo, Mabry's Brigade at Saltillo, and Roddy's Division—Johnson's and Patterson's Brigades—at Corinth, or in North Alabama.

tenant-Colonel S. M. Hyams, First Mississippi Partisans. And on the 8th, Bell's Brigade was thrown forward, from Tupelo, some fifteen miles to the north-westward, to Ellistown, with one of his regiments detached as an outpost in advance of that position. General S. D. Lee came up on the same day, with some eight or nine hundred infantry, from Mobile. Mabrey was also directed to move on the next day fròm Saltillo toward Ellistown. At the same time the whole command was directed to draw and cook their meat-ration for several days, while all tents and superfluous baggage were ordered to be sent by rail to the southward.*

Meanwhile, on the 7th, Lieutenant-Colonel Hyams had had a skirmish with a strong Federal column a few miles in advance of Ripley, and had been forced, by the weight of greatly superior numbers, to fall back, first to Ripley and then to Ellistown, on the 8th. Generals Lee and Forrest visited Verona on the 9th, and examined the ground carefully in that neighborhood, with a view to the selection of a position for a stand against the approaching Federal force. That force was rapidly drawing near, ravaging and wasting the country far and wide through which they passed, and marking their route by a broad belt of smoke and flame at the moment, and later of ashes, charred ruins, and blackened, crumbling chimney-stacks.† At three P.M. on the 9th, the head of the main Federal column had reached a point six miles south of New-Albany, on the road to Pontotoc and Chesterville. McCulloch's Brigade, therefore, was thrown out to Pontotoc, and Rucker to a point four miles west of Tupelo, at the intersection of the road from Pontotoc with the one from Chester-

---

* The Federal column concentrated at Lagrange took the field at least 13,000 strong, under Major-General A. J. Smith, on the 5th of July.

† The Federal column crossed and encamped on the south bank of the Tallahatchie on the 9th.

ville to Okolona. Roddy, likewise, was ordered to hasten, by forced marches night and day, to Okolona ; and Buford to mass his division at Ellistown, at which point Mabry's Brigade was also quartered.

The movements of the enemy now developed, apparently, a line of march toward Okolona. Accordingly, Buford was ordered to move with the force at Ellistown across to Pontotoc, whither, as will be remembered, Chalmers had also been directed to move with his division at daylight on the 10th, and, effecting a junction with Buford, was instructed to assume command of all the Confederate forces in that quarter, with orders to skirmish vigorously, but to avoid being drawn into a general engagement. By a forced march during the night of the 9th, Buford reached the vicinity of Pontotoc early on the morning of the 10th. His orders also were to throw his division across the path and on the flank of the enemy, skirmishing heavily, and to retire slowly in the direction of Okolona if overmatched. The enemy now was moving in the direction of Pontotoc in three columns, each preceded by a force of cavalry.

Generals Lee and Forrest established their headquarters at Okolona, and the former, as senior, took the general direction of affairs. Chalmers's Division had been pushed forward rapidly, on the morning of the 10th July, to the vicinity of Pontotoc, and the Confederate force was further reënforced, the same day at Okolona, by Neely's and Gholson's Brigades, which had been brought up dismounted, the former from Alabama and the latter from South-Mississippi.

In the mean time, Buford and Chalmers kept detachments well in advance of their respective positions, and a constant skirmish was maintained with the advancing enemy, and Buford threw out a detachment of 100 picked men, under Captain Tyler, of Faulkner's Regiment, to gain the Federal rear and cut off his communications. And on the 11th, the dismounted force at Okolona, including Neely's and Gholson's Brigades, were thrown forward to Prairie Mound, to construct a line of intrenchments at that point.

On the morning of the 11th, the enemy, quitting their camp some four miles northward of Pontotoc, at sunrise, pushed Mc-Culloch and Barteau slowly before them, until McCulloch was relieved by Lyon with his brigade at Pinson's Hill, a strong position two miles south of Pontotoc, which General Lyon strengthened by infantry cover of rails and logs. The Federals, however, moving cautiously and slowly, after feeling Lyon's pickets, disappeared from his front about sunset. At this time, or nightfall, the position of the Confederate forces appears to have been as follows : Barteau's Regiment occupied the extreme right, on the Tupelo road, supported by Rucker's Brigade on the left and somewhat in the rear, on a way known as the Cotton-gin road. Mabry supported Lyon on the Okolona road, and McCulloch held the Pontotoc-Houston road, to the leftward of Lyon, with a small force thrown out on the extreme left and south-west of Pontotoc, to watch the road from that place to Oxford, while numerous scouts were to encircle the Federal army. During the night, however, Barteau was withdrawn to his brigade. With his forces thus disposed, Chalmers was now ordered to skirmish obstinately with the enemy, and, if practicable, to detain them from reaching Okolona for two days longer, so that the preparations might be completed for their reception.*

On the morning of the 12th, the enemy, after some preliminary skirmishing, attacked Lyon's position vigorously, but were foiled without difficulty. Seeing, however, that a force

---

* The country was traversed with many roads leading toward various points along or near the Mobile and Ohio Railroad, so that it was a matter of extreme difficulty to ascertain the ultimate line of march of the enemy, first from New-Albany and subsequently from Pontotoc.

was moving so as to gain his rear, Lyon withdrew several hundred yards to another strong position. Simultaneously, Federal columns had moved out respectively on the Tupelo and Houston roads, encountering and being checked by Duff's Regiment on the former, and by Willis's Texas Battalion on the latter. And thus stood affairs at sunset on the 12th.*

During this time, however, General Lee was receiving dispatches from the Confederate commander at Mobile, reporting that he was assuredly threatened with a grave attack by land and water, and urging the return at least of the troops withdrawn from his command. At the same time, he was advised by General Joe Johnston that no reënforcements need be expected from his army. Unwilling to leave •Mobile thus weakened and exposed, after a free consultation with Forrest and other superior officers of his command, General Lee determined to draw the enemy into an immediate engagement. And with that object the Confederate General put all his forces of every sort in motion, on the night of the 12th, for the position occupied by General Chalmers, four miles southeast of Pontotoc, on the Okolona road, whither he repaired in person during the night, accompanied by General Forrest.†

* Several of Forrest's dispatches of this day to his subordinates are noteworthy. To General Chalmers he writes from Okolona that, "If the enemy moves on you this morning, let him come, keeping his flank and rear well watched and guarded, so that you may know promptly of any change of direction. Skirmish slightly with him. A section of artillery has been sent up which you will use occasionally, as though feebly resisting his advance. . . . Should the enemy turn back, you will attack and hold him until the General can move up with the balance of the troops." Somewhat later, writing to the same officer, he says, "You must find where the enemy is and what he is doing. You have force enough to do this, and it must be done."

† The forces thus put in motion were Bell's Brigade, General Roddy's command; Gholson's State Troops, under Colonel Ham; and the infantry and dismounted men, under Lieutenant-Colonel Beltzhoover, with six pieces of artillery.

On the morning of the 13th, pending the coming up of the infantry and Neely's and Gholson's dismounted brigades, the Federals having shown no disposition to advance, General Forrest went forward to reconnoitre the enemy's position, with Mabry's Brigade, Walton's Battery, and his escort. Within two miles of Pontotoc, (on the Okolona road,) a Federal outpost was encountered, which retired, skirmishing pertinaciously, however, at all favorable positions, until finally driven by Mabry through Pontotoc, and to the Tupelo road. It was now Forrest learned that the main Federal force had been in movement toward Tupelo for several hours. Informing General Lee of this fact, and taking the same direction, he followed with his escort and Mabry's Brigade for four miles at a gallop, when, coming up with, he drove their rear-guard rapidly back to the main column, and this brought about some sharp fighting. The enemy, however, continued their movement without halting to make any serious combat, as far as a creek about ten miles eastward of Pontotoc, though closely pressed by Forrest with his small force, with the hope that he might provoke the Federal Commander to turn and grapple with his daring pursuer, and thus give time for General Lee to come upon their flank with the main Confederate force across from the Okolona road. But in this expectation he was balked. The roads upon which Chalmers's and Buford's Divisions had to advance were narrow ways through dense woods, in large part very unfavorable for the rapid movement of cavalry; General Lee, moreover, was unable to throw his forces upon the Federal flank while in movement, as soon as or in the manner that had been anticipated. At the creek in question, however, the enemy drew up, and stood at bay ; but, after a short skirmish, crossed to the east bank, and resumed their march toward Tupelo. In this affair a section of Walton's Battery was used with some effect.

Meanwhile, Chalmers, moving across toward the Tupelo

road, with Rucker's Brigade, struck it about three P.M., at Barrow's shop, twelve miles from Pontotoc. At the time the
enemy were moving along in excellent order, their wagons
and artillery on the road, guarded on either flank with infantry, having flankers thrown out likewise. Selecting a favorable position in the edge of a wood, skirting an open field
through which the road passed about one hundred yards distant, Rucker's men, dismounted, were quietly formed, and
opened a heavy fire of musketry upon the moving column.
But, unfortunately, a small detachment, which had been sent
to reach the road somewhat to the eastward, came in collision
with the Federals before Rucker had succeeded in forming his
line, and the enemy were found also in line fronting and overlapping him, and returned his fire almost simultaneously, with
one of the most destructive character. For an instant, however, some of Rucker's men had driven the Federals from a
portion of their artillery and wagons ; but this was a transient
success, for the devastating fire, instantaneously poured into
Rucker's small brigade from flank and front, could not be
withstood ; and the Confederates were forced to withdraw,
with severe loss, to their horses, where they re-formed, and
stood in admirable spirit, under the circumstances, awaiting
the onset of the enemy.* To which, howbeit, they were not
subjected, for the Federal column was content to resume its
march, burning some of their wagons whose teams had been
lost. We have said the Confederate loss was severe ; it included the mortal wounding of the brave Captain W. G. Middleton, Eighteenth Mississippi ;† the gallant Colonel Duff,

---

* The Federals lost here eight wagons, two ambulances, and one caisson,
the teams of which, having been killed
in Rucker's attack, they were burned
and abandoned. The Federal troops
chiefly engaged at this point appear to
have been the Seventh Minnesota and
Twelfth Iowa regiments, which suffered somewhat.

† This officer had also been severely
wounded at Fort Pillow, while acting
most gallantly.

disabled by a severe wound ;* and Major C. C. Clay, Seventh Tennessee, who was again dangerously wounded.†

A little later, Buford had struck the head of the Federal column with Bell's Brigade and Morton's Battery, about seven miles west of Tupelo. The Federals, however, were not to be taken unaware, but moving thoroughly prepared for an attack, their column well closed up, well shielded by flankers, and their wagon-train fully protected. Buford being ordered by General Lee to attack, Bell's Tennesseeans went into action with their accustomed alacrity and courage. But the odds opposed were too heavy, and after considerable loss Buford was compelled to withdraw from the combat ; doing so just as the Kentucky Brigade, now under Colonel Crossland, reached the scene.‡ The two brigades were then formed in a favorable position to repel any attack.

Forrest, meanwhile, now reënforced by Rucker's Brigade, had been hanging closely upon the Federal rear, and a succession of sharp skirmishes ensued until dark, and up to within about three miles of Tupelo. A thin line of troops was then left, and the rest of the Confederate forces were withdrawn somewhat, and bivouacked ; Chalmers's Division at the intersection of the Pontotoc with the Chesterville-Okolona road ; Buford lay in his front, about one mile west of Harrisburg ; and Roddy and Mabry to his right. The day had been so excessively

---

* Duff's Regiment lost forty-seven killed and wounded, including their Colonel, severely wounded, as we have said above. Captain E. B. Cochran and Lieutenants J. T. Clayton, E. W. Jennings, and William H. Barr, (carrying the colors,) were killed ; while Captain Johnson, acting as major of the regiment, and Lieutenant L. G. Knowles, were wounded.

† Major Clay had been wounded previously, in February, 1864, while in the pursuit of Grierson and Smith, north of Okolona, Miss.

‡ Lyon's Brigade was now under the command of Colonel Edward Crossland, (Seventh Kentucky,) General Lyon having been assigned to the command of a division formed of infantry and dismounted troops.

warm and oppressive, that the dismounted command, moving slowly and with much straggling, were not upon the field by the night of the 13th. By daylight, however, a portion had come up, but greatly exhausted by their long march under the hot sun of the season.*

The position held by the enemy was a cross-road hamlet— called Harrisburg—of a few houses, scattered at wide intervals, over a somewhat commanding ridge. It was well chosen for defense ; and those strong, natural advantages, Major-General A. J. Smith immediately set his troops to improving, as far as practicable, during the night, by breastworks made of rails and logs, and the materials of cabins and outhouses, torn down for that purpose, and covered with earth. This was discovered by General Forrest in a reconnoissance, which, accompanied by Lieutenant Sam Donelson, of his staff, he made about midnight, to within fifty yards of the Federal position, riding along and reconnoitering the lines for nearly a mile.

Directing Colonel Mabry to throw forward skirmishers to within close proximity of the enemy, Forrest repaired to General Lee's headquarters, and reported what he had ascertained. Hoping to be able to draw his adversary into an offensive movement in the morning, General Lee directed the immediate disposition of his force for that contingency, and the erection of temporary infantry cover—of rails and fallen timber—on the line selected as best for receiving an attack. Buford's Division was therefore advanced somewhat, and formed by daylight in line across the Tupelo-Pontotoc road, one mile and a half westward of Harrisburg ; Mabry's Brigade being on the left, and Crossland's (Kentucky) Brigade on the

---

* Cavalrymen, whose horses were unfit for service, and heavy artillery from Mobile. They had been marched in haste a distance of forty-six miles.

right of that highway, with Bell's Brigade as a support or reserve immediately in rear of Mabry. Roddy's Division, at the
same time, had taken post to the right of Buford's front line,
and Chalmers's division of cavalry, and Lyon's of infantry,
(not yet up,) were held as reserves.

III.

BATTLE OF HARRISBURG.

The Confederate force confronting their adversary on the
morning of the 14th of July scarcely exceeded eight thousand
officers and men.* The Federal army consisted of the Sixteenth Army Corps, and fell little short of thirteeen thousand
infantry, three thousand cavalry, and twenty-four pieces of
artillery.† Their position—an eminence of crescent outline,
convex toward the west, naturally strong, as we have observed

---

* Chalmers's Division :
McCulloch's Brigade, . 1400
Rucker's " . . 900—2300
Buford's Division :
Bell's Brigade, . . . 1300
Lyon's " . . 900—2200
Mabry's " . . . 1000
Roddy's Division :
Patterson's Brigade, . 700
Johnston's " . 800—1500
Lyon's Infantry Division :
Beltzhoovers's Battalion, 900
Gholson's (dismounted)
Brigade, ... 600
Neely's (dismounted)
Brigade, ... 600—2100
———
9100
Artillery : Morton's Battery, 4 guns.
Rice's " 4 "

Artillery : Walton's Battery, 4 guns.
Thrall's " 4 "
Ferrell's " 4 "
—
20

The cavalry being fought as infantry,
one fourth were detached as horse-
holders, and took no part.

† Subdivided as follows : First Division of Infantry, under Brigadier-General Mower ; Third Division, under
Colonel Moore ; and a Brigade of Negro Infantry, under Colonel Benton ;
with Grierson's Division (four brigades)
of Cavalry. (Correspondents of New-
York *Times,* and Missouri *Democrat,*
Memphis, July 22d, 1864.) These writers, however, place the strength of the
whole force at only 13,000.

—had been strengthened by breastworks, thrown up during the night and that morning, and commanded all the approaches, especially toward the west and south.* The ground toward the Confederate lines was undulating or broken ; and on the Tupelo road there were woods to within two hundred yards of the Federal intrenchments, when an open field intervened, on the right and left of which extended around, between the Federal and Confederate lines, broad, open fallow fields. That is to say, while in the centre, any attack on the Federal position must necessarily be made for two hundred yards over open ground, up a gentle slope, swept by artillery and mus-ketry ; at all other points the ground of approach was open for almost a mile. And thus, as may be seen, the advantages of position were clearly and formidably with the Federals, who, besides, had a decided numerical superiority.

By seven o'clock A.M., having seen that the Federal Commander gave no evidence of a purpose to come forth from his stronghold and give battle, Major-General Lee felt obliged to take the offensive immediately, even though he were forced to attack him upon ground of his own choosing. The precarious posture of affairs at Mobile, and the urgency of the demand for reënforcements to that important seaport, it is believed were the considerations which swayed him at the moment. Accordingly, acquainting General Forrest with his purpose, General Lee ordered him to prepare the command for battle. Presently, too, skirmishers were thrown forward from Buford's

---

* The Federal lines on the morning of the 14th were somewhat less than two miles from right to left, and rested, the left on the railroad south of Tupelo, and the right extended about half a mile northward of Harrisburg. The strength of the Federal position is forcibly alluded to by the correspondents of the New-York *Times* and Missouri *Democrat,* who say expressly, that the *ground* gave the Federals "a decided advantage." "*It was a magnificent position in which to receive an enemy,*" is the language used by one of these writers. "*The Federals were sheltered by the woods ; the Confederates were exposed.*"

Division, and Morton's Battery began an active fire from a hill half a mile from the Federal lines, and for some moments a fruitless effort was made in this way to provoke the Federal Commander to take the offensive.

Meanwhile, the Confederate order of battle was so modified that it stood as follows: The extreme right was held by Roddy's Division, leftward of which Crossland's Brigade was next in line, with Rice's Battery. Bell's Brigade was formed on the immediate left, or north of the Tupelo road, with Mabry first, and Rucker next, on his left, and Morton's Battery, under Lieutenant Sale, was attached to this flank. McCulloch's Brigade, and Neely's and Gholson's dismounted men, with Thrall's and Ferrell's Batteries, constituted a second line, or reserve, posted behind slight intrenchments of rails and timber across and perpendicular to the Tupelo road.

Finding it impossible to entice the enemy from his cover, or to assume the offensive, the Confederate Commander, about eight o'clock, gave orders for the simultaneous advance of his first line upon the Federal position. At the moment, however, the Confederate order of battle had not been made to conform in outline to that of the enemy, and Buford, moving on the Federal centre, struck it before Roddy had come in collision with the enemy in his quarter of the field.* Consequently, not only was a heavy force of infantry massed to meet Buford's attack with a furious peal—a scorching fire of small-arms, but almost their whole artillery was concentrated upon Bell's Tennesseans, Mabry's Mississippians, and Crossland's Kentuckians. Crossland's Brigade was first engaged, driving the Federal skirmishers rapidly in, and dashing

---

* General Lee's orders really were that his centre should stand still, while the right (Roddy) should have time to swing around into a position as near to the enemy as that held by Buford, but from a misunderstanding, the Kentucky Brigade prematurely began the attack, as we have described.

forward, with loud and hearty cheers, across the open field directly upon the strongest point in the Federal position. The Federals withholding their fire until their daring assailants were half across the field, then opened, as we have observed, with a furious, scathing fusilade, and fast, incessant discharges of canister from many guns. Bell and Mabry quickly following to the onset, nothing could exceed the heat of the fire which they encountered.

As stoutly as ever brave men affronted death, did these brigades face the terrific torrent of fire thus let loose upon their thin, exposed ranks, and no battle-field was ever illustrated by more general and shining courage, than was displayed in this onset. Urged and led by their officers with conspicuous gallantry, the men were pressed up close to the coveted position. Crossland's Brigade, being uncovered on its right, was exposed to an oblique or enfilading fire, under which it staggered, and finally gave way, but not until some of the intrepid Kentuckians had penetrated the Federal intrenchments, where they were either killed or captured. Colonel Faulkner's horse was shot under him, and he twice wounded within sixty paces of the same point, and one third of their numbers, including Lieutenant-Colonel Sherrill, Seventh Kentucky, (killed,) were stricken down, either killed or wounded.[*] Rice's Battery moved forward with the Kentuckians, and, kept well in advance with them, was handled with signal daring and skill. And when the stress of the Federal fire was greatest, Thrall's Battery was thrown forward to close quarters in support of Rice. Served with equal spirit and efficiency, it rendered invaluable aid in covering the withdrawal of the Confederates from under fire.[†]

---

[*] Brigadier-General A. Buford's MS. Official Report. Colonel Crossland, commanding the brigade, and Major Hale, Seventh Kentucky, were among the wounded.

[†] Captain Morton's MS. Notes.

Bell and Mabry's Brigades, having been moved forward with somewhat more deliberation, were halted at short musket-range, and delivered several well-sustained volleys before emerging from the woods into the corn-field which was between them and the enemy. But, advancing, they had not gone more than fifty paces into the field before all were speedily driven back to the cover of the woods, by so deadly a fire that it was not possible to breast it, and from which Mabry's Brigade lost four of its field-officers* killed, and all the colonels of Bell's regiments were wounded in the foremost ranks.† Morton's Battery, commanded by the gallant Sale, had accompanied this movement, and shared in its vicissitudes. Its first position was within five hundred yards of the enemy, but, advancing, it was carried at least one hundred yards nearer under the fire we have mentioned ; and when five out of the seven gunners, and six of the eight horses of one piece were disabled, and its commander, Sergeant Brown, three times wounded. Nevertheless, he remained with his gun until it was carried safely to the rear by hand, by Captain Titus's company of sharp-shooters.‡ Another piece was brought off by Sergeant C. T. Brady, after a wheel had been shot from it.

---

* Colonel Isham Harrison, Sixth Mississippi ; Lieutenant-Colonels John B. Cage, Fourteenth Confederate ; Thomas M. Nelson, Sixth Mississippi Regiment ; and Major Robert C. McKay, Thirty-eighth Mississippi Regiment, were killed.

† Colonels R. M. Russell, C. R. Barteau, A. N. Wilson, and J. F. Newsom, were wounded ; also Lieutenant-Colonel Wisdom and Major Parham, (Sixteenth Tennessee.)

‡ A temporary experimental organization, made up a day or two before the combat, from Confederates in confinement for capital and other grave military offenses. In organizing the company, General Forrest told these men that he would not return them to fight with their companies as yet, but would place them on probation during the impending battle. They were some fifty in number, and acted with conspicuous gallantry throughout the engagement, losing one third of their numbers in killed and wounded. Subsequently, for their good conduct, they were returned to their respective companies.

The remaining pieces, as the troops were forced back, were retired slowly, halting and firing with the utmost resolution and effect. Walton's Battery delivered from its position an effective, long-range fire upon the enemy's artillery, for which its Parrott guns were peculiarly suited; and Ferrell's Battery, the one that was so gallantly and efficiently handled during the pursuit of Colonel Streight, in 1863, was held in reserve.

Chalmers, in the mean time, had been ordered to throw Rucker's Brigade as a support to Mabry, leaving McCulloch to support the centre, and cover the retreat in event of disaster. General Chalmers leading the left and Colonel Rucker the right wing, the brigade advanced, at a double-quick, with a loud shout, and with splendid order entered the open ground between them and the enemy. The heat, that of a sultry July day of the climate, was intense ; without a breath of air, a feverish thirst harassed the men. Nevertheless, and despite an appalling fire of musketry and artillery that swept the ground over which they advanced, Rucker's small brigade struggled onward with resplendent courage for some moments. Twice wounded, Rucker had to leave the field after leading his men to within sixty yards of the Federal trenches ; and many of his bravest officers and men were added to the number of dead and wounded that lay on the field already, belonging to the brigades which had preceded in the onset. At least a third of Rucker's officers and men were stricken down, either by the enemy or by the heat, and the attack was repulsed. So great indeed was the distress from thirst that, for some moments, all organization was at an end, and no authority or orders of officers was heeded until water was found ; and many of the men were so affected by the heat that, scarcely able to walk, with great difficulty they were induced to make the effort to reach a place of safety. However, in a little while, organization being recovered, the brigade was withdrawn in good order, rearward, as far as the position held by McCulloch. Bell's and Mabry's Brigades, having meanwhile exhausted their ammunition, were also withdrawn.

During this time General Forrest had been on the right flank with Roddy's Division, which, when Crossland's Brigade was repulsed, was moved rapidly by the left flank to the position occupied by that brigade at the commencement of the action, and where the division was held to meet any counter or offensive movement of the enemy. Any further attack on the Confederate part upon the enemy's position was clearly imprudent, and it was not attempted. Forrest's staff-officers, however, were actively employed, rallying the brigades on the left ; and his aid and son, Lieutenant Willie Forrest, thrown from his horse by the concussion of a shell, exploded just above him, was carried from the field.

The Confederate attack had now failed at all points, and it was manifest the Federal position and force were impregnable to any offensive operations of the Confederates arrayed against them. General Lee, therefore, ordered his whole force to retire from the field, and occupy the position held at daylight, in rear of McCulloch, and there await the movements of his adversary. But General Smith appears to have been satisfied with being able to foil the attack of his daring assailants, and adventured no offensive movement at all. Therefore, McCulloch's Brigade remained unmolested in its advanced position until about half-past six o'clock P.M., when it was noticed that the enemy were burning Harrisburg. General Chalmers was then directed to reconnoitre as closely as possible with that brigade, the first Mississippi infantry, and a piece of artillery. Some Federal skirmishers, soon encountered, were driven back by McCulloch far enough for him to ascertain that the main Federal force still remained in position at Harrisburg, and the reconnoissance was concluded. Chalmers meanwhile having moved forward with the First Mississippi and artillery to a favorable position, on the left of

McCulloch, before retiring threw some shell among groups of the enemy gathered round the burning houses of the place, and the figures of which, brought into strong relief by the flames at that late hour, afforded fine targets.

About this time, or at sunset, taking Rucker's Brigade, under Colonel Duckworth, General Forrest led it around the Federal left flank, on the road to Verona, some two miles southward of Tupelo, where he soon found himself in the presence of the Federal pickets, who opened a scattering fire. Dismounting the brigade, and taking post across the road, Duckworth threw one tenth of the brigade promptly forward, under Captain John T. Chandler, A. A. A. General, and the Federal skirmishers were brushed back upon their main force. This was presently followed by the advance of the whole brigade, and a sharp skirmish with the enemy, who receded slowly for three fourths of a mile, until about nine P.M., when the Confederates encountered a stormy fire from a heavy force drawn up to receive them. This checked the movement, and in turn the Federals essayed the offensive ; but their onset was speedily brought to a halt by a well-directed fire from Duff's Regiment. Directing a small force to be left well in advance, to watch that road, Forrest withdrew the brigade for the night to a position three miles south of Tupelo, where it bivouacked.

IV.

Apprehensive that the Federal commander, emboldened by the results of yesterday's success, would now attempt to press forward into the prairie country to the southward, to lay waste the growing crops of that fertile region, Major-General Lee resolved to interpose every possible obstacle, and accordingly, before sunrise, the whole Confederate force was concentrated across the anticipated route of march, and drawn up in line of battle, fronting the north, directly across the Tupelo-Verona road, about three miles from the former place. At the same time working parties were dispatched to repair the roads and bridges rearward, for the easy movement of the ordnance trains and artillery, in the event the Confederates were forced back. There being, however, no indications of any offensive movement on the part of the enemy, Buford was thrown forward (dismounted) on the Confederate right, with Crossland's and Bell's Brigades, to feel the Federals in that direction, and coming in contact with their pickets, bore them back for quite a mile upon the left flank of their main force, in some timber, where he halted, and, throwing out skirmishers to cover his own position, stood on the defensive. Meanwhile, so intense was the heat, that as many as eighty officers and men were carried from the field exhausted, some of them insensible, from the effects of the sun.

This was the posture of affairs at eleven A.M., when the authentic and pleasing intelligence was received that the enemy were in full retreat. Chalmers was immediately ordered to move forward rapidly with McCulloch's Brigade (mounted) to ascertain their line of retreat and apparent purposes. Overtaking their rear-guard, some skirmishing ensued for an hour, during which a moving cloud of dust was visible along the Tupelo-Ellistown road, marking manifestly the line of march of a large force.

Meanwhile, General Lee had moved up with his whole command as far as Harrisburg, and Forrest, with his staff and escort, had gone immediately to Tupelo, some of the few houses of which were found in ashes, the others filled with wounded, including 250 Federals, too severely hurt to be removed, and few of whose wounds had been dressed.*

---

* In consequence of this neglect, and the extreme heat of the weather, many of the wounds, both of the Confederates and Federals found in Tupelo, were fly-blown and already in a putrid, maggoted condition, from which the men suffered fearfully.—*Notes of General Forrest.*

While Chalmers was directed to press on with McCulloch's Brigade, and attempt to get on their flank westward of the Ellistown road, Buford, about two P.M., was ordered to goad their rear with his division, now dwindled down, howbeit, to not more than 1000 effectives. Following vigorously, and moving at the head of his column with a section of Rice's guns, just as Buford approached Town creek, four miles beyond Tupelo, a warm volley was suddenly poured into the head of his column from a heavy ambuscade in a corn-field, while his own force was moving along a narrow road through a dense "black jack" thicket. The character of the ground made it extremely difficult to deploy forward any effective body of troops, and Bell's Brigade receiving the first outburst of the ambush, was driven back in confusion. The road was blocked up at the same time with led horses and artillery, and for a short while, had the enemy pressed their advantage with vigor, the situation was critically perilous. Buford, however, assisted by his officers, promptly rallied his men; Bell's and Crossland's Brigades also became engaged with their wonted spirit, and Rice's Battery was effectively brought to bear upon the somewhat rising ground, though it suffered both in horses and men. General Forrest now came up, moreover, and assisted materially, by his presence and words, to sustain the men in their unequal combat ; and McCulloch's Brigade pressing up at a gallop, he ordered it dismounted and thrown into action on the left of Buford's Division. That veteran force making a characteristic charge, pushed the enemy back in its front. This was not done, however, without considerable loss, and Forrest, who rode with it in the onset, was painfully wounded in the right foot, and its intrepid commander, Colonel Bob McCulloch, was struck in the shoulder. Meanwhile, General Chalmers had conducted Kelly's Regiment, (mounted,) of the same brigade, still further to the left, to turn, if possible, the Federal flank. Advancing well into a corn-field in his front, and pressing back his immediate enemy, he discovered, happily in time, that his left flank was overlapped at the moment by a superior force, in the same field, hidden by the high corn, and he was forced to fall back to the edge of the field to avert disaster. In this he succeeded without being followed, while McCulloch's movement saved Buford's horses, and artillery. Forrest's wound was now so painful that he was obliged to quit the ground; the command therefore devolved upon General Chalmers. Riding to Tupelo, to have his wound dressed, he reported the situation to General Lee, who immediately repaired to the front. In the mean while, the enemy finding himself borne back by McCulloch, threw forward fresh infantry, far too strong to be withstood by the small force of Confederates present or available, and who were forced to recede in the face of overpowering odds ; but Chalmers, though hard pressed, retired safely, just about nightfall, beyond the reach of the enemy, who, fortunately, was not disposed to follow up his advantage with any energy. General Lee having come upon the ground, ordered McCulloch's Brigade to bivouac in observation for the night within half a mile of the crossing of Town creek. Buford's Division was assembled not far distant, and the rest of the Confederate force slept for the night in the vicinity of Tupelo—all exhausted by the work of the last three days, and greatly distressed by the weather.

Nor was the condition of the command found to be materially better on the morning of the 16th. The heavy marches of the last sixty or seventy hours, and scanty forage, had broken down very much all the horses, while battle casualties and the fierce tropical rays of the sun had depleted the ranks to such a degree that further pursuit in force, had it been of any material military advantage, was impracticable. Seeing this, General Lee made his arrangements and dispositions accordingly.

Chalmers was directed to pursue with Rucker's and Roddy's Brigades, and a section of artillery. The rest of the cavalry were ordered to retire on the road to points between Tupelo and Okolona, where they could be most readily supplied with forage and subsistence ; the infantry were dispatched by rail to Mobile. Gholson's Brigade (State Troops) was likewise returned to their horses at Jackson's, and the wounded, including the Federal, having been collected as rapidly as possible, were sent by railway to Forrest's hospital at Lauderdale Springs, near Meridian, Mississippi.* These orders being given, General Lee, satisfied from reports of scouts that the Federal army was assuredly in retreat upon Memphis, left on the 17th, to repair elsewhere within the limits of his command, where his presence was required.

Chalmers, taking up the pursuit as swiftly as practicable in the jaded condition of his animals after the march of fourteen miles, seized a hill in full sight of the smoke of the camp-fires of the Federal army, after having driven an outpost from a creek in front of their encampment ; leaving a regiment to hold this position, during the night he moved some two miles to the eastward, to Knight's Mill, with a view of attacking their flank on the next day, at some favorable opportunity. On the morning of the 17th, Roddy was dispatched across the country to seek an opportunity to strike their flank at Kelly's Mill, on the Ripley road, while Chalmers would follow, with Rucker's Brigade and the artillery, to hang upon and harass their rear ; but this position proved untoward, as it was found the enemy, turning leftward at Ellistown, had moved in the direction of New-Albany, and not toward Ripley. The

---

* This hospital, admirably arranged and managed by Surgeon Thompson, of Kentucky, was a credit to the Con- federate service, as well as to the medi- cal officers connected with it.

horses, moreover, for the most part, were now so manifestly unfit for further pursuit, that the Confederate commander rightly determined to abandon it. Detaching some 250 men to follow in observation, Chalmers returned to Tupelo with the rest of his command, while the Federal army was making its way rapidly in the direction of Memphis, by way of Holly Springs.

COMMENTARIES.

1. The Federal Commander assuredly displayed much watchfulness in his movements, but the least possible vigor or enterprise. He appears to have restricted his movements after crossing the Tallahatchie, to the defensive against an antagonist very much his inferior in numbers. Had he pressed the advantage gained on the afternoon of the 14th July with resolution, and with his whole force, as the Confederates fell back repulsed and badly cut up, as he could plainly see, the consequences for the Confederates must have been ruinous. Although he remained in possession of his strong, intrenched position (including that night) for fifteen hours after the close of the battle, and removed his wounded and some of the Confederates to hospitals in Tupelo, yet such was the demoralized condition of his force that the wounds, neither of the Federals nor Confederates in hospital appear to have been dressed. And when he began the retrograde, as is alleged, for want of subsistence and ammunition, it was made with all the celerity and other appearances of a retreat ; for, leaving one division under Brigadier-General Mower to cover his rear by making a stand at the extremely favorable position of Town creek, he pushed his train on toward Memphis, with all haste, escorted by the remainder of his force. Indeed, in view of General Smith's mere military movements, it is difficult to comprehend with what objective the campaign was undertaken.

2. It must be regarded as an error on the part of the Confederate General to deliver battle at Harrisburg upon a field chosen by his adversary, and, as we have seen, peculiarly favorable for that adversary. Furthermore, victory, under all the circumstances, never within the scope of reasonable probabilities for the Confederates, was made even less possible by the adoption of the *parallel* order of battle rather than the *oblique*, and the massing of the Confederates upon either wing,—and subsequently also by throwing the troops into battle by fragments, so that brigades were worsted, sadly cut to pieces in detail.

3. The courage and tenacity with which the Confederates fought on the 14th, in front of Harrisburg, and on the 15th at Town creek, is apparent from the formidable lists of killed and wounded that resulted. Buford's Division, including Mabry's Brigade, lost 22 officers killed and 104 wounded, and 825 enlisted men were killed and wounded. In Chalmers's Division, both brigade commanders were severely wounded.

4. It was a somewhat singular procedure for General Washburne to complain, as he did in his letter to General S. D. Lee, that his negro troops had not received quarter, when he admits, in the subsequent letter to Forrest, that he was aware, when he sent them forth, they had taken an oath not to give Forrest and his men quarter in that very expedition. Since this chapter was in type, we have found in the New-York *Times*, of July 3d, 1864, in a letter written by one Doctor Hunt, from Memphis, to his newspaper, the Buffalo *Express*, a reference to the correspondence, which shows he had been in immediate conference with General Washburne on the subject. This writer says: " The negro regiments of Sturgis' expedition *took a solemn oath before starting that they would neither give nor take quarter if they met Forrest.* They kept their oath—took no prisoners." This was not written in irony, but in exaltation of African courage.

CHAPTER XX.

Correspondence with Department Commander; also Governor of Missis-
sippi—Command distributed for Defensive Purposes—Theatre of
Operations transferred to Oxford, Miss.—Operations of General
Chalmers in that Quarter—Confederates pressed by largely Superior
Force — Federal Devastations — Forrest made Counter-Movement
upon Memphis — Extemporized Bridge — Confederates penetrated
Memphis to the Gayoso House—Success of the Operation—Federal
Forces withdrawn from quarter of Oxford to succor Memphis—Gene-
ral Forrest established his Headquarters at Grenada, Miss.

July 17th to August 25th, 1864.

SUFFERING acutely from his wound, nevertheless General
Forrest remained at Tupelo for twenty-four hours, looking to
the care and removal of the wounded, the burial of the dead,
the collection of small-arms from the late battle-fields, and the
location of the troops. He then went by rail to Okolona,
where he remained until the 22d, though he had turned over
the direct command to Brigadier-General Chalmers.

For the remainder of the month the important movements
of the command were the following : The State Troops, relieved on the 20th from further service with Forrest, were
ordered to report back, at Jackson, to the Governor of Mississippi. Roddy, detached with his division, on the 28th proceeded by rail to Montgomery, to meet a hostile expedition
menacing the interior of Alabama, while his horses and wagon-train were sent across the country to the same point a
week previously ; and Mabry's Brigade, likewise detached on

the same day, repaired (mounted) to Canton, Miss., to assist in repelling a Federal movement from the southward. Meanwhile, the other portions of the command had been distributed with a view to recuperation. Buford's Division, first at Egypt Station and subsequently at Shannon Depot, on the Mobile and Ohio Railroad ; and Neely's and McCulloch's Brigades,* (Chalmers's Division,) in the vicinity of Oakland Church, eight miles west of Egypt Depot, positions at once healthy and convenient to forage and subsistence. Staff-depots, moreover, were established at suitable points for the accumulation of supplies ; while comprehensive measures, including the offer of amnesty, were taken to bring back absentees to the ranks, and to re-horse the command. The scouting service, likewise reorganized, was stimulated to even greater activity in the procurement of prompt and accurate information in regard to all movements of the enemy of a hostile character. And fortifications were put under construction at Prairie Mound, as the most favorable position for protecting the approaches to the prairie country, a measure of vital interest to the planters of that section, who were called upon to supply the labor and tools.

On the first of August, though still suffering from his wound, General Forrest returned to headquarters at Okolona, but did not reassume command for several days. In the mean time scouts had continued to bring in intelligence of the concentration of Federal troops and other indications of early hostile movements from the direction of Memphis ; and active preparations were therefore made in all the departments of Forrest's command to meet it as effectively as practicable. A letter, written by General Chalmers, on the 1st of August,

---

* Chalmers's Battalion (Eighteenth Mississippi) was detached at Abbeville, on the Mississippi Central Road, with scouts thrown forward as far in advance as Senatobia and Holly Springs.

to the department commander, will best show not only what was the actual military situation at the moment, but also the measures and dispositions which General Forrest regarded as best calculated, with his resources, to baffle the hostile purposes of the enemy.   It is as follows :

"HEADQUARTERS FORREST'S CAVALRY,
OKOLONA, MISSISSIPPI, August 1, 1864.

" COLONEL :   Our scouts report that the enemy is making preparations to move from Memphis, Vicksburg, and North-Alabama, at the same time, and, if successful, to concentrate at Selma.

" There are now fourteen thousand infantry and cavalry assembled at Lagrange, and they are reported repairing the Mississippi Central Railroad. Three regiments of infantry and two of cavalry are reported moving from Decatur to Moulton, Alabama.   The communication with Little Rock by White River is open, and the troops from Smith, reported as going up that river, have returned to Memphis.   Some troops, number unknown, have been sent down the river toward Vicksburg. If the enemy moves in three columns, as expected, it will be impossible for us to meet him ; and, after consultation, Major-General Forrest and I have concluded to recommend a consolidation of the troops in this department to meet one column.

" The northern column will be the largest ; if we can defeat it, the others may be easily overtaken, and crushed. We have accumulated supplies at Grenada and Oxford, so that the cavalry from Jackson can be well subsisted, should you think it advisable to move them there. We can subsist our force better upon this line than any other, and it is valuable to the Confederacy, therefore, more important to be defended. The column from Vicksburg could do but little damage before reaching Demopolis ; and if we should defeat the enemy here, could, by means of the railroad, intercept him at Meridian, on that line.

" The force moving from Decatur is, as yet, reported small, and ought to be checked by the reserves and other troops in Alabama. We beg leave, therefore, to suggest, for the consideration of the Major-General commanding the department, that the forces from below be concentrated with this command on this northern line.   But should he disapprove, we still recommend a concentration of our whole force to meet one of the columns. We are preparing fortifications here, which, if manned by the whole force we had here before, may enable us to defeat the enemy.

" Our effective force is 5357, but we are very much crippled in officers.

Both of my brigade commanders are wounded, also a brigade commander of General Buford's Division, and most of the field-officers of the command were either killed or wounded in the late engagement.

" I am, Colonel, very respectfully, etc.,

JAMES R. CHALMERS,
Brigadier-General Commanding.

"*Colonel George Deas, Chief of Staff, Department of Alabama, Mississippi, and Louisiana.*"

Meanwhile, orders had been issued to the proper staff-officers and commanders, to collect and issue, by the 3d of August, ten days' rations to the whole force ; one hundred rounds of ammunition for small-arms, and two hundred of artillery were also prescribed ; all further furloughs were forbidden, and leaves of absence, and officers on special detached service were recalled. And on the 2d, McCulloch's Brigade (Chalmers's Division) was ordered to move at daylight on the next morning through Pontotoc to Oxford.

On the 3d, General Forrest resumed command, and General Chalmers set out with his staff, escort, and Thrall's Battery, to repair with McCulloch's Brigade to Oxford. One of Forrest's first acts was a characteristic letter, addressed through a staff-officer, to Colonel Woodward, then on special service in West-Tennessee or North-West Kentucky. We give it, as illustrating the close attention to details which characterized the Confederate General.

" HEADQUARTERS FORREST'S CAVALRY, }
OKOLONA, MISSISSIPPI, August 2, 1864.

" COLONEL: I am directed by the Major-General Commanding to say that it is entirely out of his power to send the ammunition you want. It is not safe to do so in the first place, and we are without transportation to spare. The movements of the enemy require all we have for a move at a moment's notice

" The General also directs that you will come out with all the men you can get by the 10th September. Absentees, who come out with you from the command or army, will not be molested. . . . We have many companies without officers, and parties who can bring out from twenty to forty men can be placed in the West-Tennessee regiments of this command, and those raising the men can get position. There are also three Kentucky regiments here that need filling up, and your own also, which will give Kentuckians a chance to be with Kentucky troops.

" Say to all, that they must come out ; every man is needed at this time. Those who fail, or refuse to come, you will arrest, dismount, disarm, and if necessary, bring in irons. It is hoped, however, that all will respond ; otherwise, when caught, they will be punished to the full extent of the law.

" You will also call the attention of all parties attempting to raise commands to the fact, that no new organization can be made for service in the Confederate States army. The following paragraph from General Order No. 42, A. and I. General's Office, April 14th, 1862, prohibits it, and revokes any authority given.

" ' X. All authorities heretofore given to raise troops, or to recruit for any particular command, are hereby revoked.'

" They must attach themselves to some regular command, organized prior to April, 1863.

" By authority direct from the President, which authorizes Major-General Forrest alone, can they be received into his command as troops from West-Tennessee, unless they select an organization organized prior to the date above. By bringing out their men, they can join the command, and where competent, and with a fair proportion of men, can get position.

" Respectfully,
CHARLES W. ANDERSON,
A. A. A. General.

" *Colonel T. G. Woodward, West-Tennessee.*"

On the 4th, Neely's Brigade (Chalmers's Division) was also put in motion for Oxford, and General Chalmers was directed to impress negroes, northward of the Tallahatchie river, to the number of five hundred, with axes, spades, and other implements, and employ them in the construction of fortifications at Grenada, Graysport, Abbeville, and such places as he might deem necessary, on the Tallahatchie river ; and also to ob·struct all the fords and roads on that river, except such as he might fortify ; while, in a letter of the same date, Chalmers was further directed to impress negroes around Grenada, to repair the works there; and to take every negro that he could lay his hands on to do the work indicated. He was also authorized to direct Mabry's Brigade to repair to Grenada, and was specially charged to use the utmost energy in the construction of defensive works, and the obstruction of the roads and fords in that region. At the same time, the Governor of Mississippi was addressed, with a full account of the hostile movements apparently impending over his State from various quarters; and it was suggested that the Legislature should adjourn at once, and the members return to their respective districts to rally the people. "It is plain," Forrest wrote, "we are to be invaded from various points, and my reliance for help in the defense of North-Mississippi is alone with the people. They must act, and act promptly, if they would save the country from devastation. Their organization is left with the officers commanding the reserves. All in my power will be done to assist in rendering them effective, and placing them where they can be of most service."

During the 5th, General Chalmers arrived at Oxford with McCulloch's Brigade and Thrall's Battery, and established his headquarters at that place. And on the same day, General Forrest addressed to his superior, Major-General Maury, the Department Commander, a letter which discloses the exact condition of his command at the moment, as may be seen:

"HEADQUARTERS FORREST'S CAVALRY, ⎫
OKOLONA, MISSISSIPPI, August 5, 1864. ⎭

"GENERAL: I have the honor to acknowledge the receipt of your letter of the 2d inst., and in reply, allow me to say that I can well understand and realize the responsibility of your position, and the difficulties under which you labor, in the command of a large department, with forces inadequate for its defense, when assailed, as it now appears to be, from all quarters. I regret very much that recent engagements in North-Mississippi (Tishomingo and Harrisburg) have reduced my command so much in numbers. But especially am I deficient in field-officers and brigade commanders. General Lyon having left the department, Colonels McCulloch and Rucker wounded, leaves me, aside from Colonel Bell, without experienced brigade commanders, and in Bell's Brigade the greater number of field-officers are killed or wounded.

"Nevertheless, all that can shall be done in North-Mississippi to drive the enemy back. At the same time, I have not the force to risk a general engagement, and will resort to all other means in my power to harass, annoy, and force the enemy back. I have ordered the impressment of negroes for the purpose of fortifying positions, blockading roads and fords, and shall strike him in flank and rear, and oppose him in front to the best of my ability, and fight him at all favorable positions along his line of march. I am of opinion that his move will be in this direction ; that the feints against the Mississippi Central Railroad are made to draw my forces west, and give him the start toward the prairies. I have ordered Mabry to Grenada, a brigade to Pontotoc, and General Chalmers, with one of the best brigades I have, has gone to Abbeville, with instructions to blockade fords, fortify positions, and repair the works on Tallahatchie and Yallabusha rivers.

"With Buford's Division I shall await further developments. I have sent a battery of four guns with General Chalmers, another with the brigade to Pontotoc, and have two batteries here yet. My artillery, in all, numbers sixteen pieces, and my effective force as formerly reported, with Mabry added. You may rest assured, General, of my hearty coöperation in all things and at all times. I can take the saddle with one foot in the stirrup, and if I succeed in forcing this column back, will be ready to move to your assistance at short notice, mounted or by rail.

"Will arrange with Governor Clark for a proper disposition of the State forces, and all reserves he may be able to bring to my assistance.

"Will write you or telegraph as often as deemed necessary.

N. B. FORREST,
Major-General.

'*Major-General Maury, Commanding Department.*"

At this time, the Federals, having repaired the Mississippi Central Railroad as far as Waterford—eight miles south of Holly Springs—were running trains to that point, and had advanced from Lagrange with their main force to Lumpkin's Mill, one mile north of Waterford, with outposts and heavy picket force thrown forward to the north bank of the Tallahatchie.* The route or direction of the march of the Federal column being now somewhat developed, General Forrest began to move his forces westward ; and by the 8th had thrown Neely's Brigade (Chalmers's Division) and Buford's Division, and the artillery to Pontotoc, with their trains, with orders to be ready to take the field on the 9th.

Chalmers was instructed to make as stout and prolonged a defense of the line of the Tallahatchie, and his position south of it, as was practicable with his resources ; but if over-matched and forced back, to burn all the railroad bridges and trestles as he retired. At the same time, orders were given for the removal southward of Okolona of all rolling stock of the Mobile and Ohio Railroad, and working parties of negroes. Buford was directed to keep his scouting parties well forward to the Tallahatchie river, and westward along that stream, to gain and report early information of any hostile movement from the direction of Holly Springs toward Pontotoc ; and, further, to keep his command concentrated, so that in an emergency they might operate in their full strength.

Giving information of the military situation in a letter of the 8th of August, to Governor Clark, the Confederate General expressed the opinion that the enemy intended following the line of the Central Railroad, and that, while he should make every effort with his means to impede his antagonist, and strike him on flank or rear, yet so inadequate were his forces that he could not hope to interpose any very effective or successful obstacle ; and hence, " unless Missis-sippians rallied to the defense of their homes, the State must be devastated." On the 9th, having made his arrangements

---

* General A. J. Smith was still in command with a force estimated by scouts and the people of the country at from fifteen to twenty thousand, with a force of three divisions, including 3700 cavalry, and thirty-eight pieces of ar-tillery. He doubtless also had fully 10,000 infantry.

for the supply of his command, General Forrest established his headquarters at Pontotoc, still suffering a good deal from his wounded foot, which he was obliged to wear in a sling.

Meanwhile, the Eighteenth Mississippi Battalion—not over three hundred strong—had been holding the Tallahatchie river in advance of Abbeville, with scouting parties northward of the river, in the immediate presence, and constantly skirmishing with the Federal pickets.* The southern bank of the Tallahatchie, occupied by the Eighteenth Mississippi Battalion, however, was highly unfavorable for defense, being commanded from the opposite side. It was stripped of timber for fully half a mile, while the north bank was well wooded up to the water's edge, giving complete shelter for skirmishers. Taking advantage of this, the enemy drove the Confederate pickets from their posts on the river bank on the morning of the 8th, and immediately threw several small bodies of troops across to the southern side. In the mean time, the Eighteenth Mississippi having been withdrawn to a slight ridge in the edge of the woods, half a mile from the river, had strengthened that position by breastworks of rails and timber ; but as it could be easily turned on either flank, it was only occupied as a post of observation. During the day, Chalmers had moved up his main force to Abbeville ; at night-fall, however, leaving a regiment to hold the position, his whole force was withdrawn to Hurricane creek for forage, but resuming his position in advance early the next morning. As will be remembered, he had only one small brigade and a section of artillery to guard and hold a line of some six or eight miles, from Wyatt's, on the west, across in front of Abbeville, to a point some two or three miles east of that

---

* At the same time the Second Missouri Cavalry were at Wyatt, and the First Mississippi Partisans at Abbeville. The remainder of McCulloch's Brigade was at Hurricane creek, six miles north of Oxford.

place, which made it impracticable for him to hold his position, as the Federal column now began to press forward seriously, and the Confederates were obliged to retire. But this was done with deliberation, in admirable order, with their front constantly toward the enemy, who followed closely, but would make no attack unless it could be done with every advantage of numbers and position. "Like fierce wolves, they circled around the Confederates, gradually drawing nearer and nearer, but not daring to close in, when their desired victim stood at bay."[*]

Destroying all bridges (small structures) and trestle-work along the line of the railroad, Chalmers fell back at four P.M., on the 9th, to Oxford, and formed line of battle in the northern outskirts of that place. The Federals came up immediately, and opening with a fierce cannonade—the shells for the most part flying over and harmlessly beyond the town—they resorted to a flank movement, instead of a direct attack, upon Chalmers's position. Seeing this, the Confederate General withdrawing his force through the town, formed it in a line of battle, on some hills immediately southward of Oxford, as the enemy entered, simultaneously, on the Wyatt, Abbeville, and Pontotoc roads, so close upon the heels of the Confederates that, had they pressed vigorously and rapidly onward, Chalmers's small command must have been reduced to great peril, and its extrication almost impossible. But, apparently content with the achievements of the day, the Federal Commander (General Hatch) did not improve his advantage, nor attempt to pursue, that day, beyond Oxford.[†] Boldly holding his position in line until six o'clock, Chalmers then retired southward, and, leaving the veteran Second Missouri two miles below

---

[*] MS. Notes of Captain W. A. Goodman.

[†] His force consisted, it is believed, of ten or eleven regiments of cavalry and some artillery.

Oxford, to watch the movements of the enemy, led the rest of his command to Taylor's Station, nine miles south of Oxford. Meanwhile, Neely's Brigade and a battery were *en route* since that morning from Pontotoc, to join him.

On the morning of the 10th, finding that the Yocona was much swollen, and there being little or no forage northward of it, Chalmers crossed to the south bank of that stream, and took a position to defend the crossing over it ; and a part of Mabry's Brigade having come up, it was placed in position on the right of McCulloch's Brigade.*

The Second Missourians having been still left in position within two miles of Oxford, they were feebly attacked, about ten A.M., by a Federal force, which retired, however, after a little while, and there was no more fighting during the day. That morning early, General Forrest had left Pontotoc with Bell's Brigade and Morton's Battery, and by a forced march, effecting a junction with Neeley on the way, succeeded in reaching Oxford by eleven o'clock that night.† The place, however, had been evacuated after dusk by the Federal cavalry, whose commander, evidently having no stomach for a rencounter with the redoubtable Confederate cavalry leader, rapidly retired upon the main cavalry force at Abbeville, upon hearing of Forrest's approach, and the Confederate cavalry horses were fed on the forage that had been distributed to those of their adversary. When many of the citizens of Oxford went to sleep that night, the town was full of Federal soldiers ; but to their joy and astonishment, the next morning they found

---

* McCulloch's Brigade was commanded by Colonel William B. Wade, Eighth Confederate Cavalry.

† Buford was left at Pontotoc with the Kentucky Brigade and a battery, to guard against any flank movement in that direction ; and the Seventh Tennessee and Forrest's old regiment of Neely's Brigade, were absent also on detached service at the time.

the pavements and public square covered with their gray-clad countrymen, still holding their jaded horses by the reins, as they slept soundly after their long ride.*

It is said the conduct of the Federal soldiery on this occasion in Oxford was not so generally in flagrant disregard of the laws of war with respect to non-combatants, private property, and the privacy of families of women and children as had characterized their recent operations in Mississippi ; but we have to record one conspicuous exception in the brutality and rapacity of the Federal commander, General Edward Hatch. Having established his headquarters at the house of Mrs. Jacob Thompson, his soldiers were suffered to prowl about the premises, and plunder many articles of considerable value, such as were to be found in the mansion of a lady of her affluence and social station. Appealing to General Hatch for a " SAFEGUARD " from this unsoldierly spoliation, he, wanting in the manners of a gentleman, as of the instincts of a soldier, leaning back in a comfortable arm-chair, superciliously answered that his men could take any thing they might wish, except the chair in which he was then seated. And later, when about to retire, he caused his ambulance to be filled with pictures, china, and glassware, and such other articles from the house as had attracted his fancy.†

Immediately after Forrest had reoccupied Oxford, he dispatched orders to General Chalmers to return with his command ; and this was done early on the 11th. Chalmers's Division was then reconstituted, embracing McCulloch's, Neely's,

---

* MS. Notes Col. T. H. Logwood.

† The testimony on this point, as well as concerning other acts of kindred character on the part of General Hatch, is incontrovertible. Mrs. Thompson is the wife of the Hon. Jacob Thompson, once Secretary of the Interior of the United States, who was absent abroad at the time in the service of the Confederate States.

and Mabry's* Brigades ; and, with Bell's Brigade, were ordered to take post that afternoon at Hurricane creek, five or six
miles southward of Abbeville.

The pickets of the hostile cavalry were soon in collision,
and a number of fruitless rencounters took place for the next
two days ; until three P.M., on the 13th, when a spirited attack
was made upon Mabry's Brigade and Chalmers's (Eighteenth
Mississippi) Battalion, holding the road from Wyatt, and
forming the Confederate left flank.   But for the promptness
with which Lieutenant-Colonel Chalmers brought his battalion into action, and the tenacity with which these brave Mississippians held their position against great odds, until the
remainder of the command could be formed and take part in
the action, the whole command would probably have been
borne back in disorder.   Soon, however, the engagement
became general along the whole line of Hurricane creek ; and,
finally, the Confederates, by the sheer weight of numbers,
were pressed back, after having inflicted some loss upon the
enemy.

Without being pressed, the Confederates took up a position
about half-way between Hurricane creek and Oxford, where
they remained for several days, frequently engaged in warm
skirmishes along the line of this creek, behind which the
Federal force had been cautiously withdrawn.   And on Monday, the 15th of August, General Chalmers, taking a detachment of some two hundred men from Neely's Brigade, moving
out to reconnoitre on the Abbeville road, drove the enemy's
pickets with such ease before him that he dashed into Abbeville.   The place was occupied, at the moment, by two brigades of infantry, which, taken unawares, were thrown into

---

* This brigade was now reduced by   of horses to not more than 600 mount-
battle casualties and the breaking down   ed men, present, fit for duty.

confusion, and retreated in disorder, pursued by the Confederates, until it became prudent to halt.   But this was not done
until General Chalmers could distinctly see a large force of
infantry drawn up in line of battle, doubtless expecting an
onset from the whole of Forrest's force.   Chalmers then
quietly withdrew, and carried his little command safely back
without loss.

Meanwhile, the Federal forces about and northward of
Abbeville had been guilty of the harshest excesses toward the
defenseless inhabitants of that region ; spreading destitution
on all sides, they inflicted manifold outrages, and every species
of humiliation.   General Smith, an educated soldier, claims to
have given special orders for the protection of the people on
the routes traversed by his army ; but with that he appears to
have been satisfied, and surely must have given no thought
whether his orders were obeyed or not.   He can scarcely
have been ignorant that they were grossly disobeyed, and
that the path of his army was marked by conduct utterly
unbecoming the age and any civilized soldiers.*

Buford was now ordered to repair with the rest of his division (Kentucky Brigade) to Oxford.   And, by the morning of
the 18th, from the reports of scouts, it became evident that,
having rebuilt the railroad to Abbeville, collected supplies of
subsistence and forage, and laid a pontoon-bridge across the Tallahatchie, the Federal commander designed to concentrate his
whole force at Abbeville, with the view to serious offensive
movements beyond.   Knowing his inability to contend successfully with the force of his opponent, Forrest rapidly reviewed
the situation, and happily resolved upon a counter-movement.
That is to say, he determined to lead a picked detachment of

---

* In proof of this there is abundant   the correspondence to Northern jour-
testimony, which might be cited from   nals, from that force at the time.

his command, and by a sudden *coup de main* threaten if not capture the city of Memphis, with the effect, as he hoped, of forcing General Smith to return to the relief of that place.

After a free consultation with his second in command— General Chalmers—the necessary orders for the expedition were immediately issued, and detachments of Bell's and Neely's Brigades, and a section of Morton's Artillery, under Lieutenant Sale, were directed to be got ready to move that afternoon.

II.

Short as was the notice, by five P.M. on the 18th of August, the Confederates detailed for the expedition had made their preparations, and were ready to spring into their saddles ; for by this time Forrest had impressed his characteristic qualities upon his whole command.   After their ranks had been carefully culled of those whose horses, on inspection, did not promise ability for the forced marches before them, the detachments selected for the expedition constituted a force of about 1500 officers and men, and four guns.   And this command, a little after five P.M., went forth in the midst of a heavy, pelting rain, which had been falling, without intermission, all day, as indeed, for much of the time during several previous days. The streams, as a matter of course, were all greatly swollen, and Forrest had to take a circuitous route, of some forty miles, to Panola, in the first stage of the expedition, over roads as deep with mud as torrential rains could make them.   But the men who followed met the difficulties of the way with hearty good-will ; and there were no laggards, no croakers, no gloomy, but a long array of eager, hopeful faces.   All night of the 19th the march was continued, through rain and mud, and dense darkness, swimming many streams, and hauling the artillery by hand across and up frequent slippery hills.

When the command reached Panola, it was seven o'clock A.M., by which time the artillery horses were found to be so fagged as to make it imprudent to take more than a section beyond that point. Accordingly, a selection being made of the most serviceable horses, all unfit were sent rearward to Grenada. One hundred men were also left with their horses, which were found unable to endure the fatigues of the expedition. Resuming the march, about ten o'clock A.M., over roads knee-deep with mud and water, by the time the command reached Senatobia, twenty-three miles northward of Panola, Forrest saw that his animals were so distressed, it was prudent to go no further that day.

Before leaving Senatobia, on the morning of the 20th, learning it would be necessary to bridge Hickahala Creek, a deep stream, running sixty feet broad, with full banks, the Confederate General spread detachments over the intermediate country to collect the lumber of cotton-gin-house floors, and carry it on their shoulders to the crossing, about four miles beyond. In this manner, with little delay, the necessary quantity was transported to the proper point. There was also a small, narrow flat-boat, about twenty feet long, but no other means of ferriage whatsoever ; and the construction of a bridge necessarily began.

Out of the abundant, luxuriant grape-vines of the country a strong, twisted cable was made ; this, quickly stretched across the stream, was firmly fastened to a tree on either bank. At the same time, some dry cedar telegraph-poles were cut down, and tied together, with grape-vines also, into large, but comparatively light, fascines, and rolled into the river to serve as pontoons. Floated into position, two of these were attached to the cable, likewise with grape-vines, and the flat-boat was placed and fastened, intermediately, in the same manner as the central pontoon. Telegraph-poles were then laid across as *balks ;* over these the flooring (from the gin-

houses) was spread, and a practicable bridge was thus impro-
vised in little more than sixty minutes.   The command began
the crossing at once, in columns of two, the men leading their
horses, and the artillery, unlimbered, was safely carried over
by hand.

Cold Water river, six or seven miles beyond, was also found
beyond fording, with only a small ferry-boat capable of transporting four horses at a time; and here, again, a bridge was
absolutely requisite, and one, too, double the length of that
at Hickahala. Another grape-vine cable was quickly prepared,
and, happily, some dried cypress logs were found at hand, with
which pontoon rafts were made and disposed, as at the Hickahala; while the ferry-boat constituted the midway pontoon.
Telegraph-poles furnished the necessary material, and neighboring gin-houses the requisite flooring.   In less than three
hours, the second bridge being ready for service, the command began the passage, which, as before, was effected without casualty.   And the Confederates were as far as Hernando, only twenty-five miles from Memphis, before nightfall.

Forrest was here met by some of his scouts, who had left
Memphis that day, with accurate information touching the
position and strength of the enemy's troops in and around the
city, where all was quiet, and without the least expectation of
the foray impending.   Halting at Hernando but a few moments, the command now took the direct road to Memphis;
but so deep was the mud, and so great the fatigue of the animals, that it was quite three o'clock Sunday morning of the
21st before the Confederate advance had arrived in the vicinity of the city. Meanwhile, however, when about ten miles
distant, Forrest was met by several citizens of the place, from
whom he gleaned further information in regard to the numbers and positions of the Federal troops, and the location of

their prominent officers.* And on arriving at Cane creek, only four miles from Memphis, several of Henderson's trusty scouts came up, with exact intelligence of the position of the pickets on that particular road. From these, moreover, the Confederate Commander learned that there were fully five thousand troops, of all arms, in and around the city, for the most part negroes and one hundred days' men.

Directing his force to be closed up, and summoning the commanders of his brigades and detachments to the front, Forrest gave to each definite and comprehensive instructions, as to the part assigned their respective commands in the approaching drama; and, at the same time, the necessary guides were distributed.

To a company commanded by Captain William H. Forrest was given the advance, with the duty of surprising, if possible, the pickets; after which, without being diverted by any other purpose, it was to dash forward into the city, by the most direct route, to the Gayoso House, to capture such Federal officers as might be quartered there.† Colonel Neely was directed to attack, by an impetuous charge, the encampment of the one hundred days' men, across the road in the outskirts of Memphis, with a command composed of the Second Missouri, (Lieutenant-Colonel McCulloch,) Fourteenth Tennessee, (Lieutenant-Colonel White,) and the Eighteenth Mississippi, (Lieutenant-Colonel Chalmers.) Lieutenant-Colonel Logwood was to press rapidly after Captain Forrest to the Gayoso House, with the Twelfth and Fifteenth Tennessee

---

* This information was communicated in the hearing of the field-officers of the command, who were called up by General Forrest for that purpose, so that it might be impressed upon their minds, and they be the better able afterward to execute his subsequent orders with intelligence.

† Major-General Hurlbut was known to lodge at that hotel, with a number of Federal staff-officers.

regiments, placing, however, detachments to hold the junction respectively of Main and Beal, and Shelby and Beal streets, and to establish another detachment at the steamboat landing at the foot of Union street. Lieutenant-Colonel Jesse Forrest was ordered to move rapidly down Desoto to Union, and thence leftward, along that street, to the headquarters of General Washburne, the Federal Commander, whose capture it was his special duty to make.

At the same time, Colonel Bell held in reserve, with Newsom's and Russell's Regiments and the Second Tennessee, under Lieutenant-Colonel Morton, with Sale's section of artillery, was to cover the movement. And upon all commands the most rigid silence was enjoined, until the heart of the town was reached, and the surprise had been secured. These dispositions and orders having been made, the several detachment commanders rejoined their troops, formed them immediately into column of fours, and at about a quarter past three A.M., Captain Forrest began the movement.

It was still very dark ; the night having been sultry and damp, a dense fog had been generated, which enshrouded the whole country to such a degree that neither man nor horse could be distinguished at the distance of thirty paces, as Captain Forrest moved slowly and noiselessly across the bridge at Cane creek. But anxious that no misconception of orders should mar the success of the operation, the Confederate General halted his column, after it had moved about half a mile, and dispatched his aid-de-camp, Captain Anderson, to see that each officer understood precisely and clearly the duty that had been specially intrusted to his execution, and to ascertain, moreover, whether each command was well closed up. That efficient staff-officer, not long absent, making a satisfactory report, General Forrest gave orders for the movement to be resumed at a slow walk.

Captain Forrest preceded his command some sixty paces,

with ten picked men of his company, until about two miles from Court Square. The sharp challenge of the picket, "Who comes there?" was suddenly heard to break the stillness of the morning hour, as also the Confederate Captain's cool and prompt reply:

"A detachment of the Twelfth Missouri Cavalry with rebel prisoners."*

The customary rejoinder quickly followed:

"Advance one."

Captain Forrest rode forward in person, having previously, in a low tone, directed his men to move slowly but closely behind him.

Meanwhile, General Forrest, with his escort, moving with the head of the main column, was but one hundred paces rearward, with not a little anxiety, heard the challenge, as also, some moments later, the sound of a heavy blow, followed soon by the discharge of a single gun. Captain Forrest, it seems, as he rode forward, met the Federal picket, mounted, in the middle of the highway. As soon as he was within reach of the unsuspecting trooper, the Confederate officer felled his adversary to the ground by one blow with his heavy revolver, while, at the same instant, his men sprang forward and captured the picket-post of some ten or twelve men—dismounted at the moment—a few paces rearward, to the left of the highway, without any noise or tumult, except the discharge of the single gun, heard, as we have said, by General Forrest. Sending the prisoners immediately to the rear Captain Forrest pressed on for a quarter of a mile, when he encountered another outpost, which greeted him with a volley. The daring Confederates dashed forward, however,

---

* This particular regiment was designated, because it was known to the Confederates to be one of those then absent from Memphis, in the field, with General Smith.

and scattered the enemy in every direction. But, unhappily, forgetting the strict orders to be as silent as swift in their operations, shouting lustily, and the contagion spreading, the cheer was taken up and resounded rearward through the whole column, now roused to a state of irrepressible eagerness for the fray.

By this time the head of the column was in a few paces of the Federal camp, on the outskirts of the city ; day was breaking, and a long line of tents were visible, stretching across the country to the eastward and westward of the highway for nearly a mile. The alarm having been given, and the orders prescribing silence generally forgotten by his men, General Forrest directed the ever-present GAUS to sound the charge, and all the bugles of the several regiments took up and repeated the inspiriting notes. Another cheer burst forth spontaneously from the whole line, and all broke ardent- ly forward in a swift, impetuous charge.

Two only of Neely's regiments charging into the encamp- ment rightward, or eastward, of the road, the way, for some moments, was obstructed by another of his command, so that Logwood was unable to push on and enter the city as soon as had been expected. Moreover, in making the attempt to break through, his men became intermingled with those of Neely's Regiment, so much confusion resulted, for the great- est exultation now prevailed among the men. Meanwhile, Captain Forrest charging rapidly down the road toward the city, with his little band, (some forty strong,) encountered an artillery encampment eight or nine hundred yards beyond the infantry cantonment. Sweeping down with a shout, and a volley from their pistols, the Confederates drove the Federals from their guns, (six pieces,) after killing or wounding some twenty of the gunners. This effected, they pressed forward into the city, and did not halt until they drew rein before the Gayoso Hotel, into the office of which Captain Forrest and several of his companions entered, without dismounting ; and in a moment, his men spreading through the corridors of that spacious establishment, were busily searching for General Hurlbut, and other Federal officers, to the great consternation of the startled guests of the house. Some of the Federal officers, roused by the tumult, rushing forth from their rooms, misapprehending the gravity of the occasion, offered resistance, and one of their number was killed, and some others captured ; but Major-General Hurlbut was not to be found. Happily for that officer, his convivial or social habits having led him out of his quarters the evening before, they had also held him in thrall and absent from his lodging throughout the night.

Meanwhile, also, Colonel Logwood having broken through the obstructions in his path, with a large portion of his demi-brigade, found a formidable line of Federal infantry drawn up facing the road on his right, or eastward, which opened a warm musketry fire upon the head of the Confederate column. Ordered to push on into the heart of the city without halting to give battle on the wayside, Logwood, placing himself at the head of his men, pressed onward for some distance, running a gauntlet of small-arm volleys, until a turn of the road brought him in the presence of a line of infantry directly across the way, and sweeping it with their fire. There was a fence on the one hand, a broad, deep ditch on the other. Unswerved, on rushed the Confederates with their well-known yell—the men with their rifles poised as so many battle-maces, and their officers, sabre in hand—burst through the opposing ranks. Hastening onward, a battery was seen to the leftward, but commanding a straight reach of the road ahead, and the gunners of which were busily charging the pieces. In view of the danger his command incurred from this battery, Logwood was obliged to charge and disperse those who manned it ; and giving the command to charge, again his men clubbed their rifles, and with a shout, swooped down upon their luckless enemy, a number of whom were knocked down at the pieces, while the rest were driven off before they were able to fire a gun.* Resuming his charge toward the city, Logwood, in a few minutes, entered and galloped down Hernando street to the market-house, and up Beal, across Maine, to the Gayoso Hotel. The men, wild with excitement, now dashed forward at a run, shouting like so many demons, regardless of the fire opened upon them by the Federal militia from windows and fences. The women and children, and some men, were screaming or crying with affright, or shouting and clapping their hands, and waving their handkerchiefs with joy, as they recognized the mud-be-spattered, gray uniforms of the Confederate soldiery in their streets once more. Soon, indeed, the scene was one of memorable excitement. Memphis was the *home* of many of those gray-coated young riders who thus suddenly burst into the heart of their city that August morning ; and the women—young and old—forgetting the costume of the hour, throwing open their window-blinds and doors, welcomed their dear countrymen by voice and smiles, and every possible manifestation of the delight inspired by such an advent. Reaching the Gayoso finally, however, Colonel Logwood completed the search of that hotel for Federal officers, after which, collecting his men in hand as soon as possible, he began to retire by Beal street, about nine o'clock, as it was learned, through scouts, that a strong Federal force was being rapidly concentrated upon that point.

During this time, it will be remembered, Lieutenant-Colonel Forrest, also, had been ordered to penetrate the city.

* This, doubtless, was the same battery encountered and taken previously by Captain Forrest, and re-manned after he had passed.

Speeding with his regiment toward the headquarters of Major-General Washburne, on Union street, he reached that point without serious resistance, to find, however, the Federal commander had already flown ; but several of his staff were captured before they could dress and follow their fleet-footed leader.

Meanwhile, Neely had met serious resistance in the execution of his orders. The infantry—at least a thousand strong —which it was his part to attack, as we have seen, had been formed in line in time to receive his force with a warm fire of small-arms. Seeing this check, General Forrest, who had remained with the reserves under Colonel Bell, led them rapidly by the right flank to reënforce Neely ; but on the way developed a cavalry encampment just eastward of the infantry, from which the Confederates were received by a heavy fire. Being in advance, as usual, Forrest charged promptly with his escort (mounted) over intervening fences and through some gardens, dispersing the dismounted occupants of the encampment, and capturing nearly all their horses, with a number of prisoners. Neely, at the same time making a vigorous onset upon the infantry, succeeded in driving them, with some loss, from their position. Whereupon they and the dispersed, dismounted cavalry took refuge in the extensive brick buildings of the " State Female College," several hundred yards distant, a strong defensive position. Followed by the Confederates, the enemy poured a noisy and annoying fire from behind the cover afforded by the college. At this Forrest ordered up Lieutenant Sale with the artillery, and dismounting some of the troops, made an effort to dislodge the Federals, and an animated skirmish ensued. A number of shells were thrown and exploded in the main building ; but it soon became apparent the position was only to be gained at a loss far greater than was required for the success of the expedition, and the attempt was not made.

Finding that the enemy were rapidly rallying and assembling, Forrest had previously ordered the troops to evacuate the city, and concentrate at the Federal infantry camp which we have mentioned. This order found the Confederates greatly dispersed and widely spread over the city, many with the hope and object of meeting and greeting friends and kindred ; but for the most part, intent upon the discovery and appropriation of horses. Few, indeed, retained their regimental, or in fact, company organizations. As soon, however, as they could be collected, and Lieutenant-Colonels Logwood and Forrest having effected a junction on Desoto street, they moved out together, but encountered a strong body of infantry, formed across the road, near Provine's house, as a support for the battery there—the gunners of which were twice dispersed previously—was found re-manned once more, and commanding the road. A warm collision occurred, in the course of which Captain Peter Williams, Fifteenth Tennessee, charging the battery with his company, (I,) was in turn charged and driven back ; but reënforced by Company H (Lieutenant Witherspoon) of the same regiment, the battery was again charged and taken.* Colonels Logwood and Forrest then hastened to rejoin their commander, as directed ; and as all the Confederates were now withdrawn from the city, except some stragglers and those who had been captured or killed, General Forrest gave orders for the whole force to withdraw. The object of the expedition having been in the main attained by the confusion and consternation into which the garrison had been thrown by his operations of that morning, it only remained, to secure the entire success of Forrest's plans, that General Smith should receive as early intelligence of the occurrence as practicable,

---

* Captain Williams had his arm broken in this affair.

and, therefore, he retired to give General Washburne leisure and opportunity to telegraph the menacing situation at Memphis, and to ask for succor, which it was felt assured he would do.

Meanwhile, some of the Confederates who had lingered in the city, or had lost their way in the general dispersion which occurred, were chased out by a body of several hundred Federal cavalry, a strong detachment of which made a dash at some of Forrest's men still in the infantry camp, and just in the act of mounting. Seeing their jeopardy, Forrest sprang forward with a small detachment of the ever reliable Second Missouri, that happened to be most convenient, and a close, sanguinary collision took place   Among the slain, on this occasion, was a Federal field-officer,* who, while urging his men to the attack, was mortally wounded by the hands of the Confederate leader himself. With this affair the contest terminated, and the Confederates moved back southward on the Hernando road for about a mile, when they were halted, and directed to exchange their jaded horses for those captured in the city, some four hundred in number.

It was now found that some 600 prisoners had been brought away, including some citizens, and many convalescent soldiers, who, when the alarm was given, having fled from their hospitals into the streets, had been captured. Nearly all were bareheaded, and numbers were without shoes or clothing, except that in which they slept. After some delay at this point, the march was resumed about midday, but on reaching Cane creek, it was apparent few of the prisoners were able to walk in their shoeless condition, while the convalescents were utterly unable to make such a march as was impending. The Confederate General, there-

---

* Colonel Starr.

fore, dispatched a flag of truce by Captain Anderson, accompanied by a captured staff-officer, to propose, as an act of humanity, that the prisoners in his possession be exchanged for those of his own command, taken that morning, and that the rest would be turned loose on parole, provided General Washburne would accept the arrangement as binding. But in the event that this proposition were rejected, he would wait at Nonconnah creek for the necessary clothing to be sent out. About a little after two P.M., Captain Anderson returned with General Washburne's reply, to the effect that having no authority to recognize the proposed parole of the prisoners, he could not do so ; but thanking the Confederate General for the proffered privilege of supplying them with clothing, that should be done as speedily as possible.* After some delay, Colonel W. P. Hepburne and Captain H. S. Lee, two officers of the Federal army, appeared with a flag of truce, and clothing for both officers and men, which were promptly and properly distributed. This done, the prisoners were drawn up, and after examination by surgeons, the able-bodied were selected, some 400 in number, and mounted upon the led or supernumerary horses, to accompany the command. The others, that is, the sick or disabled, and all citizens, then marched back across the Nonconnah, were turned adrift, to return to Memphis, but with the promise exacted not to bear arms, or otherwise injure the Confederate cause, until they should be regularly exchanged.

Another difficulty now presented itself, in connection with the remaining prisoners. Exposed since leaving Oxford to the continuous heavy rains, and in the swimming of streams,

* We can not understand General Washburne's assertion that he had no authority to recognize the parole ; for it was in the power of the prisoners themselves to give their parole, in which case General Washburne was bound to recognize them.

the rations of the command, it was found, had been almost all destroyed, and there were consequently none for issue to the prisoners.   In this dilemma, with that readiness which ever served him, General Forrest, before leaving Nonconnah, wrote to General Washburne, and setting forth in emphatic terms this inability to feed his prisoners, suggested, as he would not receive them on parole, that he should, at least, send something that night for them to eat on the road to Hernando, where he would be found.   This communication having been dispatched, Forrest resumed his movement toward Hernando, at which place—seventeen miles distant— he arrived in four hours, and then halted for the night.

About daylight, Colonel Hepburne, Captain Lee, and several Federal officers, overtook the Confederate command, with two wagon-loads of supplies, of the contents of which, after issuing two days' rations to the prisoners, enough was left for the whole command for a day.

Remaining at Hernando, as if intending to retire no further, Forrest gave his men rest until the Federal officers, with the subsistence wagons, had left to return to Memphis, when— about eight A.M.—he rapidly resumed his march to Panola, which place he reached by ten o'clock that night.   Here he remained until the next day, when, with his staff, escort, and the section of Morton's Battery that had been with him on the expedition, he went by rail to, and fixed his headquarters at, Grenada, while the several commands that had accompanied him to Memphis, were distributed to their respective divisions.

III.

Reverting to affairs at Oxford, we find that General Chalmers skillfully disposed and handled his small command (about two thousand effectives) to conceal the absence of his superior with so important a part of the Confederate force.   With this

view, during the 19th of August, he made several sharp attacks
upon the outposts on all the roads occupied by the Federals.
Nevertheless, the enemy pressed forward heavily, to within
four miles of Oxford, and Chalmers had to recede to a position about one mile northward of that place, with a strong
line of pickets maintained, however, in the immediate presence
of the enemy.   Meanwhile, the long-continued rains had materially injured the Confederate ammunition, as had been
shown during the skirmishes of the day, and there was a good
deal of uneasiness and discouragement, as a consequence,
among the troops.* Buford, however, came up with the Kentucky Brigade, and took position in the line in front of Oxford.

The theatre of these operations—between the Tallahatchie
and the Yocona—is a rolling, broken country, but without any
very high hills or ridges.   Much of it had been cleared, and
was extensively cultivated before the war ; the uncleared timber was not lofty, but very dense, with undergrowth. All the
positions were easily turned ; and on both sides of Oxford
were highways from Abbeville, by which an army passing the
place might reach one of the bridges of the Yocona.   That
stream, when swollen by rains, as at this time, could only be
passed by bridges, of which two remained standing, (Oliver's
and Carr's ;) but the roads leading to these through the bottoms, on the northward, traversed quicksands, which made
them almost impracticable.   All the streams and gullies were
now overflowing their banks, and every road in the vicinity of
Oxford was greatly cut up by the constant movement of troops,
artillery, and train.

Reënforced by Buford, Chalmers made a spirited attack on
the enemy during the morning of the 20th, about four miles

---

* So bad was the ammunition in the   the 19th, only thirty-seven guns out of
hands of the men that, in the affair of   five or six hundred would discharge.

in advance of Oxford, on the Abbeville road, but, greatly overmatched, in the end was obliged to retire. At the same time,
in view of the condition of the roads in his rear, and of the
growing difficulties of the passage of the Yocona, he ordered
his train behind that stream in advance of his own retreat—
presently inevitable.

But on the morning of the 21st, still making a show of
offensive purposes, Chalmers was skirmishing with the enemy
in his front at eleven A.M. At that hour, however, he received
intelligence that a strong body of Federal cavalry was making
a detour, by way of College Hill, with the evident object of
getting rearward, and cutting off his retreat across the Yocona.
It was therefore an act of transparent necessity to retreat as
rapidly as practicable behind that stream, which, under the
circumstances we have described, was already a matter of
difficulty. Able to pass the Yocona only by the two bridges
we have mentioned, had the enemy pressed vigorously with
their heavy cavalry force, there must have been grave difficulties in the movement; but happily, it was accomplished without disaster or molestation ; and Chalmers, fixing his headquarters at Springdale, disposed his small command to make
an obstinate contest in the event the enemy advanced. His
men, however, having been on duty continuously for more than
twenty days, they and their horses were greatly jaded, while
little of the ammunition was fit for service.

During this time scouts were held closely around Oxford,
and General Chalmers left one of his staff—Captain L. T.
Lindsey—with a telegraph station within three miles of the
place, to secure constant telegraphic communication touching
hostile movements in that direction. The Federal advance,
however, did not enter Oxford until about eight o'clock on the
morning of the 22d, but a column of infantry soon followed.
The cavalry were speedily and widely scattered through the
town, but the infantry were kept in ranks. Up to noon,

although there were a number of petty acts of spoliation on the part of individual soldiers, yet no general disposition was shown either to license or commit arson and rapine. The railroad depot was burned in the morning, but, as yet, no private buildings were set on fire. Suddenly, about midday, however, this forbearance ceased. Orders were then given by the Federal commander for the burning of the public buildings and unoccupied houses ; and in a little while, to quote the language of a Federal chronicler, " the public square was surrounded by a canopy of flame ; the splendid court-house was among the buildings destroyed, with other edifices of a public character. In fact, where once stood a handsome little country town, now only remained the blackened skeletons of the houses, and the smouldering ruins that marked the track of war."* In this conflagration were consumed all the principal business houses, with one accidental exception, the two brick hotels of the place, and, of course, the flames speedily spread to several dwellings occupied by women and children, and sick persons, happily rescued, however, from destruction by the exertions of the inhabitants of Oxford.

One occupied mansion, howbeit, was burned to the ground under circumstances which make the act noteworthy in these pages. It will be recollected, Mrs. Thompson's house, several days previously, had been despoiled by the Federal cavalry commander and his men. Major-General Smith now sent an officer of his staff with a detachment to burn it. Mrs. Thompson made a dignified, earnest, but vain appeal that her house might be spared her. Only fifteen minutes were

---

* That is, war, as was now made by Federal commanders, revived from the days of Tilly. This destruction of public buildings by Federal commanders is altogether inexplicable, since they made war, as they and their Government maintained, to restore the authority of the United States over the invaded region. These buildings could be of no possible military use.

granted for the removal of any articles which she might specially wish to save ; but these, as fast as they were brought from the house, in the presence of Federal officers, were ruthlessly stolen from her by the soldiery who clustered around, so that scarcely an article, other than the clothing on her person, escaped fire or pillage.*

Up to midday, guards had been set as if to repress pillage; these were withdrawn about that time, and for several hours thereafter Oxford was delivered up to riot and rapacity. Houses on all sides were broken into and despoiled of clothing, bedding, and provisions, which, if not carried off, were maliciously destroyed. Carpets were torn up, curtains cut down, and furniture broken in downright wantonness ; and in a number of instances the torch was set to houses thus rifled, and only the exertions of their terrified occupants saved them from destruction. Some subaltern officers were greatly chagrined, and displayed a disposition to restrain their men from acts so disgraceful to their vaunted flag ; but no officer of rank was heard to interpose his authority for the suppression of disorder in a place which there had been no effort to defend, nor any conflict in its immediate vicinity. The men, thus assured of the countenance of their commander, set all opposition to their licentiousness at defiance, until five P.M., when they were suddenly withdrawn, and the enemy began their retreat northward so rapidly as to reach Holly Springs by ten A.M., on the next day. So completely, however, had they done their work in Oxford, that its non-combatant inha-

---

* " In the suburbs of the place was situated the splendid residence of the Hon. Jake Thompson. To this, General Smith also ordered the torch to be applied ; and it also, with its fine furniture, which could not have cost less than one hundred thousand dollars, was entirely consumed. The Federal soldiers stood by and gazed upon the scene of destruction with feelings better imagined than described. They will not soon forget that visit to Oxford." —*See Correspondent Chicago Times, dated Cairo, September 12th, 1864.*

bitants, mostly women and children, were left absolutely destitute of food until the soldiers' rough rations could be brought
up from the Confederate depots south of the Yocona, and distributed among them.

The news of the Federal retreat was rapidly communicated
by telegraph to General Chalmers, who promptly made his
dispositions to advance upon their trace at daylight on the
23d. This he did in two columns. Buford, with McCulloch
and the Kentucky Brigade, took the road across Oliver's
Bridge, and General Chalmers moved with Mabry over Carr's
Bridge, near the line of the railroad. Notwithstanding repairs, the ways across the Yocona "*bottom*" were still well-
nigh impracticable, and caused delay; nevertheless, McCulloch's Brigade, (Colonel Wade,) being in advance and pressing on through Oxford, overtook the enemy's rear-guard near
Abbeville. The advance of the brigade, (Fifth Mississippi
and the Forrest Regiment,) attacking with vigor, became
entangled and almost surrounded by the superior force assailed, and suffered severely, but were finally withdrawn behind
Hurricane creek, where the whole command was formed in
line of battle in anticipation of an attack, though none was
made. During the 23d, Walton's Battery did handsome execution upon the Federal ranks on several occasions.

On the morning of the 24th, it was apparent the Federal
army was retiring, but not rapidly, in consequence of difficulty
in crossing the Tallahatchie, their bridge over which had been
broken. In the jaded condition of the troops and ineffective
state of the ammunition, it was not practicable for the Confederate commander to harass his adversary materially. Moreover, supplies were now extremely difficult of transportation
over the roads of the country, consequently General Forrest
ordered Chalmers to fall back southward of the Yocona again,
leaving detachments of scouts to keep in close observation of

the movements of the enemy, with three regiments on an out-post several miles south of Oxford, at the point to which the Mississippi Central Railroad was in running condition from the south.

CHAPTER XXI.

Forrest's Cavalry reorganized—McCulloch's Brigade detached—Repair of Mobile and Ohio Railroad to Corinth—Expedition into Middle Tennessee—Happy Ruse and Capture of Strong Works at Athens, Alabama — Successful Attack upon Works at Sulphur Trestle—Destruction of Trestle and Large Railroad Bridges—Federals in Superior Force take the Defensive at Pulaski—Demonstration in Quarter of Tullahoma—Country alive with Federal Corps called forth by Forrest — Forrest divided Forces—His Operations from Spring Hill to Columbia—Failure to Capture Huntsville—Dangerous Rising of the Tennessee River — Difficulties of Ferriage surmounted—Handsome Affair of Colonel Kelly at Eastport—General Forrest planned Expedition for the Destruction of Federal Depots at Johnsonville—Chalmers's Demonstration against Memphis—Commentaries.

August 23d to October 15th, 1864.

ON establishing his headquarters at Grenada, General Forrest found assembled there, as we have mentioned, several battalions of " State Reserves," under Colonel Pettus and Lieutenant-Colonel Davis.* His other troops, for the rest

---

* Composed of men exempt from conscription, but called forth, under the laws of the State of Mississippi, in the exigency. Among them, however, were many of the " exempt classes," who were able-bodied men in all respects, fitted for the most active military service, and this fact excited among the veterans feelings of antagonism, which found expression in the rude but expressive humor of the camp-fire, such as " Tax in kind," the epithet by which

of the month, were mainly distributed with reference to convenience to supplies of forage and subsistence.*

About the end of the month, however, under a requisition from Major-General Maury, Chalmers's Division was detached to proceed to West-Point, on the Mobile and Ohio Railroad, *en route* to assist in the defense of Mobile. Mabry's Brigade had likewise been ordered away to coöperate with General Wirt Adams in the direction of the Yazoo. Moreover, a reorganization was directed of the brigades and divisions, and every other possible preparation was made for early active service.† Meanwhile, also, Brigadier-General Lyon had re-

---

this class were so habitually designated that General Forrest found it necessary to issue a circular calling upon the officers of his command to repress the practice with the utmost vigor.

* Chalmers's Division was quartered for a time ten miles west of Water Valley, a station on the Mississippi Central Railroad, eighteen miles south of Oxford; and subsequently at Oakland, a station half-way between Panola and Grenada, on the Mississippi and Tennessee Railroad. Buford's Division chiefly at Oxford.

† Forrest's Cavalry, as constituted under this order, was as follows: CHALMERS'S DIVISION, McCUL-LOCH'S BRIGADE, *Colonel Robert Mc-Culloch commanding.* Second Missouri Cavalry, Lieutenant-Colonel R. A. Mc-Culloch commanding; Willis's Texas Battalion, Lieutenant-Colonel Leo Willis commanding; Seventh Mississippi Cavalry, (formerly First Mississippi Partisans,) Lieutenant-Colonel Samuel M. Hyams commanding; Fifth Mississippi Cavalry, Major William Gaston

Henderson commanding; Eighth Mississippi Cavalry, Colonel William L. Duff commanding; Eighteenth Mississippi Cavalry, Colonel Alexander H. Chalmers commanding. RUCKER'S BRIGADE, *(formerly Neely's,) Colonel Edward W. Rucker commanding.* Forrest's (old) Regiment, Lieutenant-Colonel D. C. Kelly commanding; Seventh Tennessee, Colonel W. L. Duckworth; Fourteenth Tennessee, Colonel J. J. Neely; Fifteenth Tennessee, Colonel F. M. Stewart; Twelfth Tennessee, Lieutenant-Colonel J. U. Green, commanding. BUFORD'S DIVISION: LYON'S BRIGADE, *Brigadier-General H. B. Lyon commanding.* Third Kentucky Cavalry, Colonel G.A.C.Holt; Seventh Kentucky, Colonel Ed. Crossland; Eighth Kentucky, Lieutenant-Colonel A. R. Shacklett commanding; Twelfth Kentucky, (Faulkner's,) Colonel W. W. Faulkner. BELL'S BRIGADE, *Colonel T. H. Bell commanding.* Second Tennessee, Colonel C. R. Barteau; Nineteenth Tennessee, Colonel J. F. Newsom; Twentieth Tennessee, Colonel

joined Buford's Division, and Colonels McCulloch and Rucker returned sufficiently recovered from their wounds to be put at the head of their respective brigades. And on the 4th of September, Forrest, directing Buford to hold his division in readiness to follow at a moment's notice, left Grenada with his staff and escort to proceed, by way of Jackson and Meridian, to take part in the defense of Mobile.

McCulloch's Brigade—except the Fifth Mississippi*—the advance of Chalmers's Division, having reached West-Point on the 3d, was at once dispatched by rail to Mobile, and remained there, detached from Forrest's Cavalry, for six months ; but just as Rucker's Brigade was about to set out, on the 4th, for the same point, a telegram was received from General Maury, dispensing with further aid from Forrest's command. And that telegram made it unnecessary for General Forrest himself to go beyond Meridian, where he arrived on the 5th. The situation, however, determined him to establish his headquarters for the present at Verona, whither General Buford was ordered with his division. Orders were given at the same time to impress negroes and employ them, guarded by details of dismounted men, to repair the Mobile and Ohio Railroad as speedily as possible to Corinth, as General Forrest had now conceived the plan of throwing his force, with that of Roddy, across the Tennessee river upon the line of Sherman's communications in Middle Tennessee, and cutting him off from his base of supplies. For the next fortnight all the preparations for this important operation were .pursued under the sanction of the Department Commander with characteristic extent and vigor. General Chalmers was directed to take post at Grenada, in command of all the troops not to

---

R. M. Russell ; Twenty-first Tennessee, (formerly Sixteenth,) Colonel A. N. Wilson.

* This regiment was absent at the time on detached service.

be carried upon the expedition impending.* And General Roddy was instructed to repair, with his command in North-Alabama, the bridges and breaches in the Memphis and Charleston Railroad to the eastward of Corinth, as well as to prepare boats for the ferriage of the Tennessee river in the vicinity of Cherokee Station. Moreover, by the 15th, Bell's, Lyon's, and Rucker's Brigades, with the artillery, were concentrated at Verona, previous to which, on the 13th September, a general order—No. 75—had been issued in these terms :

" I. This entire command will be in readiness to move on the morning of the 16th instant, with four days' cooked rations. They will leave all baggage except one blanket and one change of clothing. All ordnance stores will be shipped by railroad, and the ordnance-trains of the command will assist in transporting forage, forage and ordnance-trains moving together. Three days' rations of corn for the command will be carried in the ordnance and forage-trains.

" II. The command will be supplied with one hundred rounds of ammunition to the man, forty of which will be taken in the cartridge-boxes, the balance to be shipped by railroad.

" III. Adjutants will not be allowed to take any more papers than will be necessary for active field-service. No desks will be taken, or other boxes or baggage allowed to be carried.

" IV. All extra wagons, disabled horses, and baggage will be sent back to Suquatoncha creek, near West-Point. One officer from each brigade and one man to every ten horses will be sent back with the extra wagons, baggage, and unserviceable horses.

" V. All dismounted men will be ordered to report to Lieutenant-Colonel Barnett, for the purpose of being organized into a battalion.

" VI. Lieutenant-Colonel Barnett will organize all dismounted men into a battalion, and be in readiness to move on the morning of the 16th instant with rations and ammunition as above.

" VII. A full and complete field report of arms, ammunition, horses and their condition will be sent to these headquarters by the morning of the 15th instant."

* Mabry's Brigade, brought up from Lexington — the Fifth Mississippi of McCulloch's Brigade—and the "State Reserves" or militia.

Other judicious and comprehensive orders were issued, regulating the movement and the general conduct of the troops,
especially one, stringently forbidding and guarding against
depredations upon the property and premises of their countrymen.

On the morning of the 16th, as directed, Buford's Division
and Rucker's Brigade, (under Colonel Kelly,) with the horses
of Morton's and Walton's Batteries, marched, with the view
of striking the Memphis and Charleston Railroad at Cherokee Station, eastward of Iuka, near which it was expected to
pass across the Tennessee river, and this march was accomplished by sunset on the 19th.* General Forrest, accompanied by his Adjutant-General, Major Strange, also left Verona
on the morning of the 16th, with a battalion, 450 strong, of
dismounted men, under Lieutenant-Colonel Barnett, and the
guns and caissons of his batteries, to proceed by the Mobile
and Ohio Railroad for the same destination by way of Corinth.
Four trains followed freighted with subsistence, ordnance,
and quartermasters' stores for his command. Obliged to repair a number of the bridges and trestles on the railroad, he
did not reach Corinth until the evening of the 17th. Transferring his trains to the Memphis and Charleston Railroad,
the Confederate General, early on the 18th, resumed the
movement with his wonted determination and disregard of
obstacles. All the wood used by the locomotives had to be
cut by the wayside by his troops, who likewise, in the absence
of tanks, kept the boilers filled with water brought in buckets
from the streams that bordered or intersected the road   Many
parts of the roadway had to be patched, and long "cuttings"
cleared of earth and rubbish, frequently several feet deep,

---

* General Forrest's staff and the principal part of his escort accompanied this
column.

which had accumulated upon the track. Nevertheless, by the evening of the 19th every hinderance had been overcome, and Forrest reaching Cherokee Station with his trains, his whole forces and resources were thus auspiciously collected at that point.

Roddy's Division was reported to be in readiness for the field, but during the 20th, the whole command remained at Cherokee Station, actively occupied in cooking their rations, or other preparations, especially the shoeing of their horses. Exclusive of Roddy's men, Forrest's force now numbered three thousand, rank and file, including the battalion of dismounted men, and with this command the movement was inaugurated on the morning of the 21st—scouts previously dispatched by General Roddy having communicated the satisfactory intelligence that there was no hostile force at hand to dispute the passage of the Tennessee river. General Roddy had collected the requisite means of ferriage for the

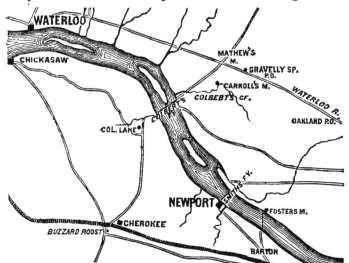

artillery at Colbert's Ferry, just above the head of Colbert's shoals, about seven miles from Cherokee Station, and to that

point Barnett's Battalion and the batteries repaired, while
the cavalry moved to the ford at the lower extremity of the
shoals.

The river, at this point, was about 2000 yards broad, in a
straight line ; but the ford, extremely tortuous, and winding
along the shallows on the ledges of the shoals, was quite two
miles in length. The whole stream was filled with ledges of
rock, some of which jutted high above the water, while over
others the swift surging current broke heavily and boiled in
frothy tumult ; and profound crevices, or holes, marked the
spaces between, by the comparative smoothness of the deep
water that flowed over them. Placing a guide at the head of
the column, Forrest directed it to make the crossing in a
column formed by twos, and kept well closed up, so as not to
lose the devious and obscure pathway through the breakers.
Thus disposed, the Confederate cavalry venturing into the
river, boldly dared the perils of a ford, to stray from which a
few feet, either to the right or left, were almost certain destruction ; for falling into some pit, the luckless trooper would
have been drawn irretrievably down-stream by the current,
and dashed against the jagged rocks which crowded the
rapids on all sides, with almost certain hazard of being disabled and drowned. At one time the whole ford, from side
to side, was filled with horsemen, presenting the appearance
of a huge, sinuous, tawny serpent, stretched across the river
among the breakers.

This serious operation having been happily accomplished,
the Confederate forces were pressed on with Forrest's habitual diligence and celerity, to within two miles of Florence,
and bivouacked for the night. In motion seasonably on the
22d, Roddy's command, which had been crossed the day before at Bainbridge, and in that vicinity, effected a junction at
Shoal creek with the troops from Mississippi, and Forrest's
whole force was now assembled, about 4500 strong, of all

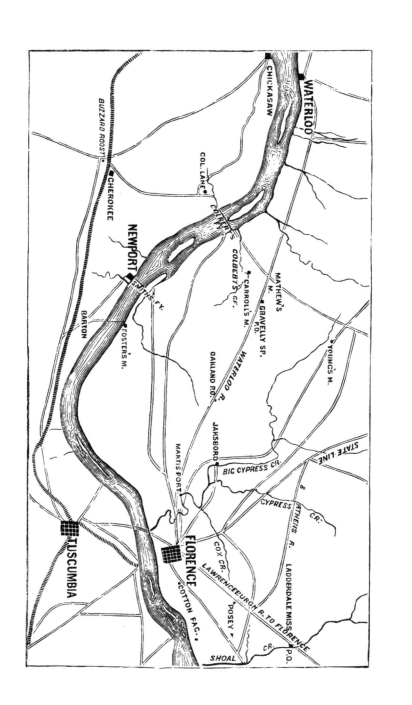

WATERLOO

CHICKASAW

BUZZARD ROOST

CHEROKEE

COL. LANE

COLBERT'S

NEWPORT

SMITHS F'Y.

BARTON

FOSTERS M.

CARROLL'S G.F.

COLBERT'S G.F.

CARROLL'S M.

GRAVELLY SP. P.O.

MATHEW'S M.

WATERLOO R.

OAKLAND P.O.

YOUNG'S M.

JAKSBORO

MARTIS PORT

BIG CYPRESS CR.

STATE LINE

CYPRESS CR.

ATHENS R.

LAUDERDALE MISS

TUSCUMBIA

FLORENCE

COTTON FAC.

COX CR.

LAWRENCEBURGH R. TO FLORENCE P.O.

POSEY

SHOAL CR.

arms.* The line of march taken led by Athens, Alabama, an important point on the Nashville and Decatur Railroad, known to be occupied in force by the enemy, and in that immediate vicinity the Confederate column arrived about sunset on the 23d of September.

A considerable Federal encampment was visible in the north-eastern suburbs of the place. The Confederate leader pressing forward his command, mounted, at once upon the cantonment. So sudden, so unexpected was his appearance and the onset which followed, that its occupants were forced to take refuge in a fort about three quarters of a mile distant, southward of Athens, leaving the horses and equipments of their cavalry in the hands of their ever enterprising enemy. Losing no time in preliminaries, or in the weighing of plans, Forrest deployed his force so as to encompass the town, (with possession of the Federal encampments,) and three sides of the fort, and thus awaited daylight, before undertaking further operations. A heavy rain fell during the whole night in which the men, for the most part, were forced to bivouac without shelter, and much of their ammunition was injured.

Fully three hours of the morning of the 24th were necessarily occupied in this position in preparation for the attack. The dismounted men were established meanwhile as supports to the artillery, which occupied four commanding positions around the redoubt, and about eight hundred yards distant from it. Bell's Brigade was placed in line about the same distance east and south-east of the work ; Lyon about six hundred yards immediately southward ; and Kelly, with Rucker's Brigade, as far from the Federal position, to the

---

* Roddy's forces, about 1500 strong, were under the command of Colonel William A. Johnson, Roddy having remained at Tuscumbia, being too sick to accompany his command, and thus General Forrest was deprived of the services of this valuable officer.

westward of it, while Johnson occupied the town with Roddy's men, so extended in three lines through the streets as to make it impossible for the enemy to estimate their actual strength.   Detachments from each brigade were held, mounted, and thrown out to cover all the approaches, and the rest, or greater part of the command, were dismounted, with the usual horse-holders, who were concentrated in one body. Thus, by half-past ten A.M., the Federal position was thoroughly invested with a double line of riflemen, the foremost circle (skirmishers) being within one hundred and fifty yards of the Federal trenches.   Being now ready for the attack, the Confederate Commander determined to test the efficacy of a flag of truce, and accordingly ordered the signal for a parley to be sounded.

A few moments later, a Confederate staff-officer—Major Strange, accompanied by Captain Pointer—bearing the usual flag of truce, presented a formal demand for the unconditional surrender of his position.   The answer, an absolute refusal to capitulate, was not long delayed.   Not at all disconcerted, however, General Forrest immediately sent forward another communication requesting a personal interview with his adversary, which soon took place.

The Confederate General, at once approaching the business of the interview, earnestly expressed his desire to avoid the unnecessary shedding of blood ; declared that his means, including artillery, were so ample that he could carry the position by storm, without any hazard of failure ; and so assured did he feel—he observed—of this fact, that he was quite willing to exhibit his forces to the Federal Commander, who would find it to be fully 8000 strong, of all arms.   In reply, Colonel Campbell, the Federal Commander, remarked that, of course, if he could be satisfied such a force actually surrounded him, he would not feel authorized to maintain so useless a defense.   Forrest's dispositions being favorable for his purpose, with characteristic adroitness and audacity, he proposed that his adversary should at once review his lines, and they rode together for that purpose.

The first troops displayed were the dismounted cavalry, who, armed with Enfield rifles, were deployed as infantry, which they were represented to be. Some six hundred yards rearward the horse-holders were drawn up, mounted, the horses in their charge so disposed as to be mistaken for a body of at least 4000 cavalry, the number indicated by the wily Confederate. The batteries were exhibited in turn, and adroitly shifted from position to position, so as to do double duty in the display. By the time the inspection was concluded, Colonel Campbell declared that what he saw far exceeded his conception of the force that confronted him, a force which, he added, appeared indeed to be fully 10,000 strong, and made defense on his part fruitless and unwarranted. He therefore proposed to capitulate, asking only that his officers might be allowed to retain their private property and side-arms. Of course, this proposition was accepted without discussion ; and Major Strange and Captain Anderson, of the Confederate staff, returned with him, in order that the surrender should take place as speedily as practicable. Accordingly, the garrison was soon marched forth without arms, some 1400, rank and file—in great part new troops —and the capitulation was effected by one P.M.*

Previously, howbeit, just as Rucker's Brigade (Kelly) had taken its position in the line of investment, a train came up from the direction of Decatur, filled with Federal infantry, who disembarked, over 400 strong, near a block-house, about

---

* The work thus surrendered was a strong, square redoubt, built upon a high hill, with parapets from eight to ten feet high, encompassed by a ditch ten feet deep and fifteen feet broad, also with a line of *abatis ;* and the ditch was lined with sharpened palisades.

one mile from the work, and were moved forward with the evident purpose of forcing their way to a junction with the invested garrison. The Seventh Tennessee, having been already posted in observation in that quarter, became immediately engaged in a lively skirmish with these troops, as, soon after, did a detachment of Wilson and Russell's Regiments, under Lieutenant-Colonel Jesse Forrest, detached for that purpose by Colonel Bell from his brigade. About 150 of the Fifteenth Tennessee, under Lieutenant-Colonel Logwood, also fell upon their left flank. The enemy fought, and were handled with decided courage and resolution ; many of their number were killed and wounded. Pressed, however, on all sides, finally, after a struggle of nearly an hour, and under the stress of a fire in front and flank, throwing down their arms, they surrendered to the number of 400, after having inflicted upon the Confederates the loss of some of their best officers and men.*

Two block-houses still remained in the vicinage to be reduced ; one half a mile and the other one mile and a half distant from Athens, on the line of the railroad to Decatur. Both were immediately and simultaneously summoned to capitulate. The one most remote succumbed at once, and the garrison laid down their arms on the like terms to those granted Colonel Campbell.† But a stouter soldier, apparently, held the other fortalice ; for, when called upon to surrender, he haughtily answered, that, having been placed in command by his government, he would forfeit his life rather than yield.

During the parley, Captain Morton, Chief of Artillery, having casually but closely observed the block-house, formed and expressed to General Forrest the opinion that, notwithstand-

---

* Lieutenant-Colonel Jesse Forrest was severely wounded through the thigh.   † This garrison consisted of eighty-five, officers and men.

ıng the great thickness of its walls, of hewn oak timber, by firing at the joints—somewhat wide from shrinkage—he might penetrate within the work with his projectiles. Thereupon Morton was ordered to turn four of his three-inch rifled pieces upon it. This done at a range of not exceeding three hundred yards, the first shot—from one of Mayson's section—striking the roof, scattered earth and plank in every direction, while two other shells, penetrating, exploded, and killed six and wounded three of the garrison. The effect was instantaneous; the wicket was thrown hurriedly open, and an officer, rushing forth with a white flag, exclaimed in accents of great excitement, as General Forrest rode forward in person to meet him : "You have killed and wounded nearly all my men ; your shells, sir, bore through my block-house like an auger !" This garrison numbered thirty-five, officers and men, making the aggregate of prisoners now taken around Athens 1900.

General Buford and Colonel Johnson were now actively occupied supplying their respective commands from the Federal cantonments and depots with such articles and equipments as their men most needed. The former was able to improve materially the armament of his division, and to provide about 200 of his dismounted men with excellent mounts. Some twenty wagons and teams were among the spoils, and these were promptly loaded with such supplies, medical stores and instruments, and ammunition, as were selected by the proper staff-officers. Colonel Wheeler, of the First Tennessee Cavalry, having come up about this time with some two hundred men belonging to General Wheeler's Cavalry, left in the country during that officer's recent expedition, his men too were furnished with arms and equipments. The rest of the stores, to a considerable amount, were then set on fire and consumed, together with the two block-houses, the adjacent trestle-work of the railroad, which they commanded, and all the buildings in and around the redoubt that had been used by the enemy. Meanwhile the dead were buried, and the wounded of both sides collected and properly disposed of in Athens for treatment. The other results of the day not already enumerated were the capture of four pieces of artillery and five or six ambulances, while some forty of the enemy were killed and about one hundred wounded. The Confederate loss was not over twenty killed and sixty wounded, casualties which preceded the capitulation of the redoubt, and mainly in the skirmish with the infantry exterior to it.

The block-house buildings, bridges, and trestle-work having been burned to the ground, the prisoners, captured artillery, and wagon-train, properly guarded, about five P.M., were dispatched rearward in the direction of Florence. And at the same hour Forrest put his main command in motion again, along the line of the Tennessee and Alabama Railroad, to the northward, for what is known as the " Sulphur Trestle," in which direction he moved that evening, eight miles, before bivouacking. On the way, two other block-houses were encountered and captured with their garrisons, after short negotiations, in which the Federal officer whose block-house Morton's projectiles had so readily perforated related that incident with quite enough of warmth of color in his description to produce the effect for which he had been carried along. Both these block-houses and the bridges which they guarded were destroyed, and, with seventy officers and men, captured without firing a gun, were the closing results of the day.*

III.

Early in the morning of the 25th, Forrest was in front of Sulphur Trestle, after a march of only three miles from his

---

* This was effected by a detachment from Roddy's Division, under Lieutenant-Colonel F. M. Windes.

bivouac. The position was known to be defended by a strong redoubt, garnished with artillery and heavily garrisóned, as well as by several block-houses. The trestle was a costly structure which spanned a deep ravine, with precipitous sides, some four hundred feet broad. It was sixty feet high, and, as may be seen, formed a most vulnerable link in the chain of communication and supply between the Federal forces in North-Alabama and their base at Nashville. Hence, its protection was a matter of vital military importance to the former, and accordingly the position had been fortified. A square redoubt, with faces of about three hundred feet in length, had been thrown up on an eminence to the southward, so as to command the trestle and all approaches. This was furnished with two twelve-pounder howitzers, skillfully arranged, to be fired through embrasures, sweeping all possible avenues to the trestle ; while, some two hundred yards in advance, on three sides, it was surrounded by a line of rifle-pits. And two formidable block-houses were built in the ravine, at each extremity, so as to command the ravine and prevent hostile approach to the trestle by that way. These block-houses and the redoubt were garrisoned by about one thousand men.*

His brigade being in advance, Colonel Kelly, supported by Roddy's command, was ordered to drive the Federal pickets and skirmishers within the redoubt. Leading this gallant brigade, with their characteristic promptness, across an open field, Kelly charged the rifle-pits, and made the enemy seek shelter, after a short skirmish, in the fort, but not without the loss of several valuable men, while his own horse was wounded under him, and those of several of his field-officers were killed. Making a close reconnoissance, Forrest saw that the works

---

* Third Tennessee (Federal) cavalry, 400 strong, and about 600 negro infantry.

made the position almost inexpugnable to his resources, especially since the block-houses were sheltered from his artillery.
Nothing daunted, however, relying on himself, and ever fertile
in resources, he spent several hours in unimportant light skirmishes, in the course of which he succeeded, with slight loss,
in establishing a considerable portion of his force within one
hundred yards of the breastworks of the redoubt, under cover
of the acclivity of the ridge upon which it was built, and some
ravines which seamed it. In the mean time, also, Captain
Morton had found, and reported four positions for his artillery
severally within eight hundred yards of, and commanding
the works, from which he might easily explode his shells in it.
At this stage of operations Forrest determined to resort again
to the artifice of demanding a surrender, and, accordingly,
Major Strange was sent forward, under a flag of truce, with
the summons. Fully an hour elapsed before he returned with
the answer—a positive refusal.

Captain Morton was now ordered to establish his batteries
in the positions we have mentioned, and to open with them
without delay ; meanwhile, a lively skirmish was commenced,
and kept up by the Confederate riflemen—a fire, however,
more noisy and ostentatious than effective, for they were directed to be kept under cover, and to avoid loss. Walton's
guns were soon in position at two points, from which he enfiladed a large portion of the southern and western faces of
the work, while Morton's own battery, to an equal extent,
raked its other two faces, and Ferrell's guns were brought to
bear from a somewhat more exposed position in a corn-field,
within short range of the fort. From these hurtful positions
the Confederate artillery was speedily plying with perceptible
effect. For a time, the enemy responded vigorously with two
twelve-pounder howitzers ; but a shell from Lieutenant Sale's
section of Morton's Battery, striking the lower lip of one of
them, glanced, and striking the axle, exploded, killing, it is

said, five men, while overturning the piece ; and soon the other was dismounted by a shot planted squarely in its mouth by Lieutenant Brown of the same battery. The Confederate practice was excellent ; every shell fell and exploded within the Federal work, whose faces, swept in great part by an enfilading fire, gave little or no shelter to the garrison, who were to be seen fleeing alternately from side to side, vainly seeking cover. Many found it, as they hoped, within some wooden buildings in the redoubt, but shot and shell crushing and tearing through these feeble barriers, either set them on fire or leveled them to the ground, killing and wounding their inmates, and adding to the wild helplessness and confusion of the enemy, who, though making, meanwhile, no proffer to surrender, had, nevertheless, become utterly impotent for defense. Seeing their situation, and desiring to put a stop to the slaughter, Forrest, ordering a cessation of hostilities, again demanded a capitulation. This time, the demand was promptly acceded to, and the capitulation of the block-houses, as well as the redoubt, was speedily accomplished through the proper staff-officers.

The interior of the work presented a sanguinary, sickening spectacle, another shocking illustration of the little capacity for command, scant soldierly aptitudes, and deficiency of military knowledge of those appointed by the Federal Government over their negro troops, rather than an example of a stout, loyal maintenance of a soldier's post on the part of the garrison. As we have said, all the buildings within the parapets had either been razed or burned to the ground. Eight hundred rounds of ammunition had been expended by the Confederate artillery in this affair, and at least two hundred Federal officers and men lay slain within the narrow area of that redoubt, giving it the aspect of a slaughter-pen. Among the dead were Colonel Lathrop, the commander, and a number of officers ; comparatively few of the garrison had been wounded. The bursting shells had done their work effectively upon this poor, mis-officered force, whose defense, manifestly, from its feebleness, had been thus prolonged, because the officers, paralyzed under the tempest of iron showered upon them, knew not what to do in the exigency.* Eight hundred and twenty officers and men capitulated ; the other results were two pieces of artillery, twenty wagons and teams, about three hundred and fifty cavalry horses, with their equipments, complete, and a large quantity of ordnance and commissary stores.†

During this operation, intelligence was received that the enemy, hearing of the movement, were evacuating their block-houses and fort at the bridge over Elk river, some six or seven miles to the northward. Buford, therefore, was detached, with Lyon's Brigade, to push forward and destroy the bridge and its defenses. Having already expended so large a portion of his artillery ammunition, Forrest now determined to send back to Florence, and across the Tennessee, four pieces of his own artillery, the captured guns and wagon-train, and prisoners, with a suitable escort, commanded by Lieutenant-Colonel Logwood. The other troops were set to burying the dead, collecting and providing for the wounded of both sides, and employed in the destruction of the trestle and block-houses. The trestle had first to be cut down—not a light work—and was then set on fire. Through the night the Confederates were thus occupied, so that by six A.M. on the 26th, there remained of that huge work naught except a heap of ashes, and coals, and charred beams.

---

* The Federal wounded scarcely exceeded thirty.

† This was not achieved, however, without some loss on the Confederate side. Captain James J. Kirkman, (of Florence, Alabama,) in command of Colonel Johnson's escort, was among the killed. Major John H. Doan and Captain Carter, of the same command, (Roddy's,) were severely wounded.— *MS. Notes of Captain J. J. Scanlan.*

Bell's Brigade was now dispatched to catch up with and rejoin Buford at Elk river, as General Forrest set out with Kelly and Johnson, by other roads, toward Pulaski, the latter marching through Upper Elkton, while Forrest, with Kelly, moved by a way nearer the line of the railroad, so as to be within supporting distance of Buford, who was ordered to advance along that line as far as Richland creek, seven miles south of Pulaski; and there Johnson, also, was instructed to join him.

Buford, moving along the railroad, after he had destroyed the large railroad bridge and block-houses at Elk river, destroyed another deserted block-house, and about 10,000 cords of wood, collected for the operations of the road, in the burning of which he likewise effectually impaired at least a mile of the track. The command was then concentrated, and moved on to Richland creek, over which there was a truss railroad bridge, 200 feet long, defended by a heavy block-house, the garrison of which capitulated after a few shells had been burst against it.* The bridge and block-house were then consigned to the torch, and the command bivouacked for the night.

Early on the 27th, Forrest was again in motion toward Pulaski, Buford moving still by the railroad, Johnson to the right of it, deployed across the turnpike, followed by Kelly. In this order the Federal pickets were encountered a mile beyond Richland creek, and were borne back for another mile, when a heavy Federal force was developed in line of battle, stretched across the turnpike and railroad—here about 400 yards apart—and on a range of hills affording an excellent position. It was a mixed force of cavalry, artillery, and infantry, apparently not less than 6000 strong; while the

---

* Forty-five officers and men were taken here.

Confederates present did not number over 3300 men and four guns. Nevertheless, their leader, resolved on the offensive, dismounting them, deployed Buford's and Johnson's small divisions across the roads, as Kelly, still mounted, was boldly launched to make a detour to the eastward and gain the Federal rear.

Deploying his escort, some sixty rifles, on foot, as skirmishers, in front of Johnson and to the rightward of the turnpike, Forrest threw forward that indomitable band of combatants. Charging, with characteristic intrepidity, up a hill held by the enemy in that part of the field, they brought on the engagement and gained the position, with a loss of seven or eight of their number killed or wounded.   Meanwhile, Buford and Johnson pressed up with vigor, and an animated musketry and artillery affair ensued.*   The enemy, however, did not stand their ground, and soon were observed retiring toward Pulaski.   At this, directing his escort to remount, Forrest made a dash with them and his staff at the Federal rear, and a running skirmish was kept up for five or six miles in the course of which, the enemy halting frequently, turned and made battle at every favorable position, until Forrest, concentrating his forces, deployed, and threw his men forward with his wonted aggressive tactics.†   Then, in each instance, the enemy withdrew, till finally, about three P.M., they filed into position behind their works at Pulaski.   These consisted of a chain of detached redoubts of commanding positions, interlinked by rifle-pits, the whole furnished with artillery, and bristling with *abatis.*

---

* Here Colonel Johnson was dangerously wounded by a rifle-ball in the leg, below the knee, and the command of Roddy's force devolved, for the rest of the expedition, upon Colonel J. R. B. Burtwell. Lieutenant John Moore, Fourth Alabama, was slain.—*MS. Notes of Captain J. J. Scanlan.*

† Gaus, Forrest's favorite orderly bugler, ever by the side of his leader, had his bugle disabled by three balls in this ride.

Manifestly, nothing was to be achieved by the sword-in-hand process here, and it had been a folly to have attempted the offensive even, had not the force in occupancy been greatly superior to that under Forrest. However, he made a menace of an attack upon the southern and eastern faces ; pushing forward a strong skirmish line, he pressed it slowly but steadily up to within 400 yards of the Federal intrenchments by nightfall in that quarter.* And after dark, a broad, long belt of camp-fires, by his orders, blazed on a ridge about a mile and a half from the threatened part of the Federal works. Maintaining his pickets close up to the enemy, and renewing the camp-fires about nine o'clock, the Confederates were quietly formed, and at ten o'clock, drew off by the road to the eastward, in the direction of Fayetteville, with the purpose of striking the Nashville and Chattanooga Railroad at, and in the vicinity of, Tullahoma.† That railroad was the main channel of supply and recruitment for Sherman's army, then at Atlanta, Georgia, and Forrest's object was to destroy as much of the track and as many of the bridges upon it as possible. The rain, however, began to pour down, and the night became soon so dark that the ordnance train could not be forced along over the miry, rugged roads of the country, and the command was halted for the night, after a short march of six or seven miles.

But at daybreak, on the 28th, the movement was resumed,

---

* In this affair Forrest's Cavalry had the misfortune to lose Captain Edmund Daley, who fell at the head of the Twelfth Tennessee Cavalry, the command of which had devolved upon him. During the first twelve months of the war he had served in an infantry regiment, after which, raising a company of cavalry, he became attached to the Twelfth Tennessee. He was an officer of zeal, courage, and intelligence, and his death made a chasm in his regiment.

† Forrest also sent back to Florence from in fron of Pulaski all supernumerary wagons and teams, some 200 prisoners, and 40 wounded men, under a suitable escort.

and though the route was by narrow cross-ways, through a broken, extremely rough country, made boggy by recent hard rains, nevertheless the command, much of the time at a sharp trot, marched forty miles, and bivouacked at dark, five miles beyond and northward of Fayetteville.* Still pressing on, the next day, toward Tullahoma, till within fifteen miles of that place, Forrest there was met by scouts, with the tidings that a heavy column of Federal infantry was advancing from Chattanooga to meet him ; and that the forces which he had left in the lurch, intrenched at Pulaski, were now on the way, by rail, through Nashville, to confront him at Tullahoma. Thus anticipated, the Confederate Commander found it expedient to make a radical change in his plan of operations.

His horses, now in great part unshod, were foot-sore, as well as greatly fatigued by excessive, prolonged hard service. It was still raining, moreover, and the Tennessee river was rising rapidly, while there were no means of ferriage available, except a few old flats at or near Florence. And besides, the enemy in the country were greatly his superior in numbers, even in cavalry. The situation was extremely precarious, and one indeed that required a large measure of coolness and judgment for extrication. Forrest, therefore, resolved to subdivide his command. One detachment, of 1500 men and the artillery and wagon-train, he placed under General Buford, with orders to move swiftly upon Huntsville, seize that place if practicable, and afterward, destroying as much of the railroad thence to Decatur as he could, throw his command south of the Tennessee at that point, if the means were found there. Putting himself at the head of the other detachment, likewise about 1500 strong, he proposed to move rapidly across the country to Spring Hill, strike the railroad there, and break it

---

* MS. Notes Lieutenant Robert J. Black, Seventh Tennessee Cavalry.

up between that point and Columbia, and at the same time drawing after him hostile forces that otherwise would be sure to follow Buford, and prevent, most probably, the escape of the Confederate wagon-train and artillery across the Tennessee river. He had also received information, through citizens, that a vast amount of army-stores had been collected at Johnsonville, on the Tennessee river, the terminus of the Nashville and North-Western Railroad, destined and essential for the Federal forces at Chattanooga and Atlanta. This depot, and the bridges on the railroad leading to it, it was likewise his purpose to destroy, if the condition of his horses, on reaching Spring Hill, would warrant him in undertaking it.*

Both subdivisions were in motion on the evening of the 29th. Forrest, taking the road through Lewisburg, in Marshall county, encamped at a hamlet called Petersburg, where he learned, through scouts, that a strong Federal cavalry force, on the march from Pulaski to Tullahoma, was only eight miles distant, to the north, at the time. Nevertheless, as his weary animals required rest, he remained encamped until daylight on the 30th. Then resuming his march across the country, passing through Lewisburg, and crossing Duck river at Hardison's ford, to the eastward of Columbia, Forrest reached Spring Hill about meridian on the 1st of October.

Here, seizing the telegraph-office by surprise, he found the line in operation from Pulaski to Nashville, and most opportunely intercepted several official dispatches, which gave precise information with regard to the location at the time of the principal bodies of troops which were afield in pursuit of him. From one of these he was particularly annoyed to learn that General Steedman was marching with a heavy column toward Huntsville, with the evident object of cutting off his retreat to

---

* Forrest's immediate command now consisted of parts of seven regiments, of Lyon's, Bell's, and Rucker's Brigades, choice fighting material.

the south bank of the Tennessee river. Having thus acquired as much information as possible touching the movements of the enemy, he now sent several misleading, spurious dispatches to General Rousseau, in regard to Confederate movements, especially one, reporting that " Forrest" was still destroying the Nashville and Decatur Railroad, and the block-houses in that direction. These messages being dispatched, he broke up the telegraph-line around Spring Hill, and at two P.M., turned the head of his column toward Columbia, having previously detached a force to destroy the small trestles on the railroad as far northward as Franklin.

The roadside was found strewn with large piles of wood, collected for the locomotives. These were burned, as also an extensive Government saw-mill and a large quantity of public lumber, about three miles southward of Spring Hill ; and here were captured thirty fat oxen, six wagons, and some forty mules.* Near by were several strong block-houses, but being now without artillery, Forrest was perplexed as to the speediest method for their reduction. Howbeit, promptly displaying his force so as to make a formidable show, the oft-tried device of a peremptory demand for a surrender was again adventured. Meeting with an equally prompt refusal, he next requested a personal interview with the Federal Commander, which being assented to, they met. The Confederate General expressing his earnest desire to avoid unnecessary bloodshed, urged that the defense of an untenable place should not be attempted, for he could not be responsible for the consequences if forced to carry the position by storm. Then proposing to show to

---

* This wood was piled and burned upon the railroad, by Colonel Bell, who had previously and ingeniously caused the rails to be firmly fastened at each extremity by spikes. In this way, longitudinal expansion, under the heat of fire, being prevented, the rails were warped into short curves, which rendered them useless for three miles of the road.

his adversary the forces at his disposition, so that it might be seen there was no deception on the Confederate side, and furnishing a horse to the Federal commander, they actually made together a rapid survey of the investing force, in the course of which some of the Confederate officers, taking the hint, were heard to speak impatiently to each other of the delayed approach of several rifled batteries.   Moreover, Forrest assuring his antagonist, as he was approaching his ambulance, that he had the means to destroy the block-houses without artillery, called upon the driver of that vehicle to bring him a vial of "Greek fire."   This being done, it was thrown and broken against a fresh oak stump, and the fluid spreading, the blaze immediately covered the still green bark. The men cheering lustily at this, for the "Greek fire," Forrest, taking advantage of the tumult, remarked that as his men were growing excited, it were best for them.to retire toward the block-house, whither they galloped immediately, before the officer was able to scan the positive effects of the Greek fire.   The Federal officer now expressing himself satisfied as to the hopelessness of any defense, under the circumstances, capitulated both block-houses at five P.M., with sixty-five officers and men.   Both structures and the truss bridge—150 feet long—which they guarded, were now thoroughly fired and destroyed.   Major Strange was next dispatched, with a flag of truce, to demand the surrender of another block-house, half a mile distant.   The commander was a German, who, greatly excited by the demand, refused not only to yield but to hold any conference, swearing roundly that he had heard of Forrest before ; that he was a d—d rebel, with whom he would have nothing to do.   The man even went so far as to threaten to fire on the flag.   Hearing this, Forrest set men to collecting and filling sacks with dry chips and other light combustibles, which were then saturated with turpentine and oil, carried for the contingency.

It was now nine o'clock, and very dark. Dismounted men were at once pressed close up to the work, under cover of the railroad embankment, and opened a noisy fire upon the block-house, during which others—picked men, provided with bags of combustibles — crept to the bridge, and placing these under its braces, at the signal ignited them with the Greek fire, a small vial of which each man carried also. In a moment the bridge was effectually in flames, and the men who had applied the fire rejoined their companies without hurt.* The Confederates, now cheering heartily, bantered their adversary, while the Dutchman swore profusely as, remounting, the Confederates rode away.

While this was going on, Colonel Wheeler, whose command was now increased to five hundred men, had been detached, and directed to menace Columbia.† Meeting the stage with several Federal officers, these were captured and the horses appropriated. Coming presently, however, across a force of three hundred Federal cavalry, moving after the stage, a sharp collision occurred, in which the Confederates were worsted to the verge of disaster. But, happily, a detachment of the old Forrest Regiment, under Captain Forrest, came up opportunely, and Wheeler, thus reënforced, charged in turn, and drove the enemy rapidly back into Columbia, capturing some twenty-five prisoners and fifty horses. Moving then down to the north bank of Duck river, he remained for several hours menacing the passage of the stream and an attack upon Columbia; but after eight o'clock, quietly withdrawing, rejoined his command, two hours later, on the road leading down Duck river, toward Williamsport.

---

* This bridge was burned by Colonel Russell and his regiment of Tennesseeans.

† As will be remembered, these men belonged to the different regiments of General Wheeler's command, and had been left in Middle Tennessee on the occasion of his recent expedition.

Four block-houses and as many large truss railroad bridges had been burned, and so effectually was the railroad impaired that it would be useless to the enemy for weeks. At the same time scouts reported the rapid rising of the Tennessee river ; that Buford, unable to capture Huntsville, had likewise failed to destroy the Memphis and Charleston Railroad ; that General Steedman was moving with a column of infantry, reported to be 8000 strong, with the evident object of intercepting the Confederates, in their retreat at Decatur ; that a heavy cavalry force was pressing across from Tullahoma toward Florence, and a column of infantry and cavalry under Rousseau, from the direction of Nashville. Thus fully 15,000 Federal troops had been drawn into the field, and Forrest determined to effect a junction with Buford without delay, for in that event he would be able, he hoped, to beat off any cavalry force that he might meet, and by manœuvre he would elude any infantry column, if unable to effect the passage to the south bank of the river.

By sunrise on the 2d of October, scouts reported that Rousseau was in motion.* Hearing from Buford that he was moving toward Florence, Forrest immediately threw his command to the south bank of Duck river. Spreading details over the country to collect beef cattle and bread-rations, he meanwhile halted his main force about six miles from Columbia, which he next proceeded to threaten with an attack, by a detachment of cavalry under his own immediate command. The pickets were soon driven in, but the position was found to be well fortified ; nevertheless, remaining on the outskirts of the town until late that evening, he harassed the garrison and burned some short trestles in the direction of Pulaski. Meanwhile, his main force, after his commissary details had dis-

---

* Rousseau's infantry mainly moved in wagons, to secure rapid transportation.

charged their duties, had moved across to Mount Pleasant and bivouacked, and there he joined them that night.*

On the 3d, the movement began definitely for there passage of the river and the evacuation of Middle Tennessee. Moving across the country toward Florence, through Lawrenceburg, Forrest encamped on the night of the 5th within seven miles of the former place, whither Buford had preceded him, and was already ferrying the train and artillery at the mouth of Cypress creek and Newport.

Detaching Company B of the Seventh Tennessee to push on with the beef cattle by the direct road to Colbert's Ferry, at the head of Colbert Shoals, General Forrest led the rest of his command, before daylight, to Florence. The rapid approach both of Steedman and Rousseau made the situation urgent; and the Confederate General now gave his special attention to every possible means for increasing the facilities for ferriage, by distributing his command at all practicable points of crossing, from the mouth of Cypress creek to Colbert Shoals. The river, already very high, was still rising, and so full of driftwood as to be extremely dangerous to the swimming horses; while three small flat-boats and not more than half a score of skiffs were the means of ferriage at the disposition of the Confederates. Nevertheless, by midday on the 7th, all the artillery, the wagon-train, and a portion of the troops, had been safely landed on the south bank of the Tennessee, as well as a large number of horses.

But the river, nearly a mile wide, had now become much agitated by high winds, so that the waves breaking constantly over the skiffs, they could only be kept from swamping by being bailed incessantly by the men with their hats; and the flats, blown by the wind and drifted by the current, lost fully

---

* Among the supplies now collected were over 150 head of beef cattle.

half a mile down-stream at each crossing. During this time, also, both Steedman and Rousseau were drawing so dangerously near that a counter-movement became necessary for their delay. Accordingly, the Second, Sixteenth, and a part of the Seventh Tennessee were detached to move back on the State line and Athens roads, toward Shoal creek, to meet and skirmish with the approaching foe, while Lieutenant-Colonel Windes was directed to make a detour with his regiment to the north and rear of the hostile column, on the Lawrenceburg road, which he was to strike from that quarter.* This service Colonel Windes performed with notable judgment and daring ; in fact, so effectively that he checked and retarded the Federals from reaching Florence until late on the morning of the 8th. And, a little later, the Second, Seventh and Sixteenth Tennessee regiments handsomely disputed the crossing of Cypress creek, west of Florence, repulsing several efforts of the enemy to pass that stream, until General Steedman, finding himself unable to force the position, had sent a brigade of his cavalry around, by a crossing three miles above. About to be taken in reverse, the Confederates were now obliged to retire by the Newport Ferry road, doing so doggedly, however, and standing at bay to gain time at several favorable positions.

Quite as many as 12,000 of the enemy were now within a few miles of one of the Confederate ferries ; and at least 1000 of Forrest's men, with their horses, were still on the north bank of the river, besides those confronting and engaged with Steedman and Rousseau, whose advance-guard was at length in such menacing neighborhood that, in the skirmish which ensued, their rifle-balls plashed in the water among the Confederate men and horses. Abandoning that ferry, Forrest

---

* Fourth Alabama Regiment, 300 strong.

directed Windes to fall back on the Waterloo road, with the hope of attracting the enemy in that direction. The Federals pursuing, Windes, coöperating with Wilson (Sixteenth Tennessee) and a squadron of the Seventh Tennessee, falling back slowly, kept them actively engaged and engrossed in a series of skirmishes all day during the 9th, giving the Confederate General the opportunity to complete the ferriage of his cattle from an island at the head of Colbert Shoals, and to throw the rest of his horses and men to the south bank, except those under Windes and Wilson, whom he directed to scatter to the rear of the enemy that night, and recross the river at such times and places as they might find practicable. The highest credit is due to Colonel Windes, and the officers and men of his own and of the Second, Seventh, and Sixteenth Tennessee regiments, for their heroic conduct during this day.*

Under the difficulties and obstacles we have enumerated, Forrest, by sunset on the 9th, had transported to the south bank of the Tennessee 2500 men and their horses, as many as 100 cattle, about fifty wagons and teams, and eight pieces of artillery ; a military feat which illustrates the energy, the decision, and the fertility in resources which characterized his operations, and were habitually at his command. His loss on this occasion was that of two men and about twenty horses drowned. Windes and Wilson subsequently, about the 13th, effected the re-passage of the river at Newport ferry, bringing off fifty prisoners.

Roddy's troops were at once detached, to report again to their commander at Tuscumbia, and on the evening of the

---

* Lieutenant-Colonel G. H. Morton, commanding the Second ; Lieutenant-Colonel William F. Taylor, the Seventh ; and Colonel A. N. Wilson, the Sixteenth Tennessee Regiments.

10th the rest of the command was again concentrated at Cherokee Station, and to the west of it.* The Federal General, having found no opponent in his presence or within reach that morning, after several hours of fruitless search, had countermarched to Florence.

During the ferriage of the Tennessee, General Forrest, with his usual close attention to all the details effecting his operations, crossed and recrossed repeatedly from one side of the river to the other; and believing that the enemy might send gunboats and a strong force up the river to intercept his re-passage of it, he detached, as early as the 8th, a squadron of the Seventh Tennessee, which had crossed the day before, to make ·a reconnoissance along the bank of the river in the vicinity of Chickasaw, and keep him advised of any hostile movement in that quarter.†

On the morning of the 11th, Buford's Division was put in motion for Corinth, and breaking up his depot at Cherokee Station, General Forrest repaired by rail, with his staff and escort, to the same point, where Buford arrived on the morning of the 12th. Meanwhile, scouts had reported the presence of detachments of the enemy at several points on the north bank of the Tennessee, between Waterloo and Clifton, apparently with the object of crossing the stream. Buford, therefore, was immediately directed to repair, with his division, to Pittsburg Landing, where it was anticipated General Washburne would attempt to recross from Middle Tennessee with a brigade of infantry and his cavalry, with which he had gone from Memphis to coöperate with the Federal movements against Forrest. And Rucker's (Kelly's) Brigade was likewise ordered in the same direction, to

---

* Rucker's Brigade, under Kelly, was at Corinth.

† Companies B and C, under the command of Captain James P. Russell.

coöperate with Buford. Henderson's scouts were established between Bear creek and Pittsburg Landing, others were spread along the river to the northward, to keep watch upon gunboats and transports, and every practicable measure was taken to secure early intelligence of hostile movements.

IV.

In the dispositions made to meet any attempt to throw a force against Forrest by the river, Colonel Kelly was dispatched to Eastport, where he arrived with less than 300 men, and Walton, with a section of his battery,* just as a fleet of three Federal transports, heavily laden with infantry and artillery, and convoyed by two gunboats, came in sight.† Fortunately, his presence was unobserved, and dismounting his troopers, he threw all, except the necessary horse-holders, to within six hundred yards of the river, behind the crest of a ridge near the landing, while Walton's guns were established, without being seen, in some old fortifications on a hill about 800 yards from, and commanding the point of debarkation, at which the transports were already making fast. Before these dispositions were completed, however, the enemy, throwing out their staging-planks, began to disembark rapidly, while the gunboats came to anchor opposite, in the stream, about 150 yards from the shore. Fully 1200 officers and men, three six-pounder rifle-guns, and about sixty horses were ashore, and the infantry formed in line toward the northward, along the river bank, before Kelly suffered his riflemen and artillery to open upon them, at a moment when the staging was still filled with troops.

---

* This command consisted of detachments of the Twelfth Tennessee, Captain Bell, and of Forrest's old regiment, Captain Barbour commanding.

† The approach of this fleet and expedition had been ascertained and duly reported by Keizer's scouts.

The Confederate artillery was admirably handled by Walton, who opened the action by one shell thrown and raking the troops, while another, aimed at a transport, tearing through it, was seen to explode in one of the gunboats. At the same moment, the riflemen poured a warm, well-sustained fire into the infantry ashore, creating the wildest disorder. Breaking ranks beyond the control of their officers, they rushed *en masse* toward the transport. Shell after shell was sent plowing through the flying throng, others crashed and splintered through the sides of the transports, and at least one was again exploded in a gunboat. At this juncture, the cables of the transports being cut loose, drifting off from the bank, their stagings were dropped into the water when crowded with men, who were plunged headlong into the stream, as well as another gun and caisson.

The Confederate artillery continued to play rapidly on the transports and gunboats, while Kelly's riflemen kept up a scathing fire upon the infantry left upon the bank. Many of these, in their panic, springing into the river, attempted to swim to and clamber upon the steamers. Meanwhile, the commotion in the water caused by the wheels of the steamers, washing over, submerged and strangled many of the swimmers, who, in their death-throes, grappled with each other, and it is probable that at least 200 were drowned. The cooler-headed of those ashore, recognizing the situation, ran down the river-bank, except some fifty, who, throwing down their arms, surrendered. The transports, making no effort to save those of their people who were in the water, were soon under headway down-stream, intent upon getting from under fire of the Confederate artillery, whose shells ricochetting along the water, repeatedly struck them, until they escaped out of range. Meanwhile, the Federals ashore, abandoning their guns, knapsacks, blankets, and haversacks, had reached a part of the river-bank so rough and precipitous that it was difficult to pursue them with the cavalry, and some four or five hundred of the fugitives effected their embarkation about half a mile below, upon one of the steamers which ventured to touch the bank for that purpose, but some stragglers were picked up in the woods. The results of this brilliant little affair were the capture of seventy-five officers and men, three pieces of rifled field artillery, and sixty horses, one gun and two caissons sunk in the river, and the drowning and killing of at least 250 Federal officers and men, including those hurt on the transports and gunboats. Meeting with such a summary hostile reception, the Federal fleet left that portion of the river as rapidly as possible, reporting, it is said, that they had been attacked and beaten off by all of Forrest's Cavalry.

About this time, the cavalry belonging to General Wheeler's command, which had been brought out under Colonel Wheeler, of the First Tennessee Cavalry, were detached, with orders to repair to Gadsden, Alabama, and rejoin their division. And on the 14th, Buford was instructed, after leaving several·regiments in observation upon the banks of the Tennessee river, to return to Corinth with the rest of his command, including Rucker's (Kelly's) Brigade, for the purpose of reshoeing and refitting for the field.

Ever on the outlook for new theatres of operation, as soon as he had safely effected the re-passage of his forces from Middle Tennessee, Forrest reporting to Lieutenant-General Taylor, his superior, from Cherokee Station, the results of his expedition, asked that General Chalmers, who had been detached from his command during his absence, should be restored to it, to enable him to make another expedition into the northern part of West-Tennessee, with a special view toward the de-struction of the Federal depot at Johnsonville. This depot, as he explained, had been established in consequence of the dangers incurred from guerrillas, and other difficulties in the navigation of the Cumberland, and the greater part of the supplies for Sherman's forces and those serving in Middle and East-Tennessee were accumulated here in large quantities for transportation thence, by rail, by way of Nashville. General Taylor promptly approving the projected operation, Chalmers was directed to report at Jackson, Tennessee, with such forces as he might be able to assemble there ; and orders were given to the rest of Forrest's Cavalry to secure their efficiency and early readiness for the expedition.

While Forrest, as we have related, was operating so successfully in Middle Tennessee, the troops, which had been left meanwhile in Mississippi, under Chalmers, had not been inactive. But nothing fruitful was the result, however, of all their continuous exposure, hard riding, and several daring scouts, except that, having been ordered by General Taylor to make a demonstration in the immediate neighborhood of Memphis, to create a diversion in favor of Forrest, at the time he was repassing to the south bank of the Tennessee, Chalmers presented himself, with about 1000 of his veterans and a few State troops, in the vicinity of that place on the morning of the 8th of October. At the moment, a force of nearly 7000 infantry and cavalry were concentrated in the place, apparently on the eve of an expedition ; and the approach of Chalmers producing the liveliest apprehension, stimulated the Federal commander to the most active preparations for the defense of his position. Taking the defensive, the enemy placed strong guards upon all the approaches to Memphis ; these threw up breastworks across all the roads, while barricades of cotton were erected at various points in the city itself, especially at the several crossings of Gayoso bayou, the bridge-floorings over which were torn up. The militia were called out ; outlying regiments and depots were withdrawn ; the forts were strongly manned, and the streets were heavily patroled. Manifestly, so grave and serious did the Federal General re-

gard the situation, that he must have felt unwarranted in detaching any force of sufficient strength, at that juncture, to
attempt to obstruct or harass Forrest's movements, if he had
previously entertained such a design. It was on returning
from this expedition that Chalmers received the order which
we have mentioned, to meet Forrest at Jackson, Tennessee.
The horses, however, of Mabry's Brigade, to a large extent,
had become unserviceable, so that Chalmers was unable to
march with more than 750 men.

COMMENTARIES.

In the course of the expedition into Middle Tennessee,
General Forrest placed *hors de combat* fully 3500 Federal officers and men, including those taken prisoners. He also captured 8 pieces of artillery, with their caissons and ammunition, 900 head of horses and mules, more than 100 head of beef
cattle, about 100 wagons, the most of which were destroyed,
3000 stand of arms and accoutrements, with large stores of
commissary, ordnance, and medical supplies. He destroyed 6
large truss railroad bridges, nearly 100 miles of railroad, 2
locomotives, and some 50 freight cars, several thousand feet
of heavy railroad trestling, a Government saw-mill, with a
large amount of lumber, at least 5000 cords of wood, and,
finally, captured and destroyed 10 of their best block-houses,
which, with one exception, be it noted, were actually impregnable to ordinary light field-artillery. He also brought out of
Middle Tennessee a thousand men added to his own immediate command, as well as 600 or 800 who had straggled from
Major-General Wheeler in the course of his recent expedition
in that region. All this was achieved at the expenditure of
about 300 officers and men killed and wounded, but, unfortunately, among the killed and disabled were several of his best
officers. It was accomplished, moreover, in twenty-three days,
in the course of which, from Corinth back to Cherokee Station,
the Confederate troops marched over five hundred miles.

BRIGADIER-GENERAL H. B. LYON.

CHAPTER XXII.

Campaign to Kentucky Border—Buford's Successful Operations against Federal Gunboats and Transports—Capture of United States Steam Gunboat Undine and Transports Venus, Mazeppa, and Cheeseman— Operations of Forrest's Cavalry Afloat — Successful Operations against Federal Depot at Johnsonville—Destruction of Warehouses, Gunboats, and Transports—Description of Scene—Summary of Results—Forrest ordered to join General Hood in Middle Tennessee— Abortive Effort to pass the Tennessee at Perryville—Wretched Condition of the Roads—Forrest's Cavalry assembled at Florence, Alabama—Hood's Army concentrated there.

October 17th to November 17th, 1864.

EARLY on the 17th, Buford's Division was set in motion with two batteries, (Morton and Walton,) for the vicinity of Jack's creek, and on the next day General Forrest followed with his escort and Rucker's Brigade, still under Kelly, *en route* for Jackson, by way of Purdy and Henderson Station, effecting a junction at the latter place with Chalmers on the morning of the 20th. Meanwhile, scouts and detachments of cavalry, under intelligent and trusty officers, were thrown out to watch all the crossings of the Tennessee river from Hamburg to Clifton, where the enemy appeared to be concentrating, as if designing to cross. On the morning of the 20th, Buford was directed to take position at Lexington, about twenty-five miles eastward of Jackson, and a central position for observation. The next day Forrest established his headquarters at Jackson, where Colonel Rucker, having reported for duty, was reassigned to the command of his brigade, which thereupon was reported again to General Chalmers, as Divisional Commander.*

Remaining at Jackson until the 28th, seeing, meanwhile, that the enemy was indisposed to venture into West-Tennessee, on the 24th Forrest ordered Buford to move northward, and establish his division at Huntingdon. Chalmers was directed to occupy the vicinity of McLemorcsville, and active staff-officers were sent forward to ascertain the forage and subsistence resources of that region, while reliable scouts were dispatched to Union City and Paducah to glean information from that quarter. At the same time the commanders of all outlying detachments were specifically instructed to interpose no obstacle whatsoever, if the enemy attempted to pass to the west bank of the Tennessee; and all were further directed to give special attention to the collection of absentees in their respective neighborhoods. Bell's Brigade, being in the vicinity in which it was raised, the men, in succession, were permitted to visit their homes to refit, both their clothing and mounts, until the 26th. General Roddy was also requested to move to the neighborhood of Corinth as many of his division as could be prudently spared from North-Alabama, and thus be in position to oppose any effort of the enemy to strike in that direction, and Lieutenant-General Taylor was also urged to send a force temporarily to the same important position.†

---

* As reconstituted, this division included Rucker's and Mabry's Brigades, and a battery and section of artillery.

† Letter to Lieutenant-General Taylor, October 24th, 1864. We cite from that letter the following passages, as shedding light upon the views of General Forrest at the time: "I shall do the best that can be done, and in every way do all in my power to create a diversion in favor of General Hood. I left a regiment at Corinth, and feel some solicitude for its protection, as the preservation of the Mobile and Ohio road

Buford's Division having been reassembled, he was then ordered to repair with it, by way of Paris, to the mouth of the "Big Sandy" river, or in that vicinity, and "blockade the river" at the most effective point for that purpose, throwing out scouts as far northward as old Fort Henry, and a section of twenty-pounder "Parrott" guns, brought up from Mobile, were sent to him for that purpose. Chalmers, a day later, was also directed to take position with his division at Paris, in supporting distance of Buford, in the event that officer should require aid. Buford, moving on the afternoon of the 26th, with Bell's and the Kentucky Brigade, two twenty-pounder "Parrotts," and Morton's Battery of three-inch rifles, arrived at Paris the next day, though his horses were in wretched condition, especially those of the artillery. Reaching the river at the "mouth of Sandy" on the 28th, Buford, after a careful reconnoissance, selected the old Confederate "Fort Heiman" and "Paris Land-

---

may prove to be of great importance, especially so should it, in any event, be necessary in transporting supplies to the 'Army of Tennessee.' I respectfully suggest, therefore, that, if possible, you send a force up to Corinth, as the enemy at Clifton may cross above and move on the line of the Memphis and Charleston road, looking to a junction with the forces now at Memphis. Should they do so, there is nothing to prevent them from occupying Corinth and destroying the road southward. There are about seven hundred of Mabry's Brigade, with disabled and unserviceable horses, at or near Grenada, and a section of artillery also at that place ; and I submit for your consideration and action the propriety of sending these men across to West-Point or Tibbee Station, on the Mobile and Ohio Railroad, where they can be placed upon cars, and sent up to Corinth, as also the section of artillery; while their horses could be left meanwhile in the prairies, to be recruited. . . . . . These suggestions are simply for your consideration, believing, as I do, that all the forces not necessary for the protection of points exposed or threatened should be placed at once in position to protect the Mobile and Ohio Railroad; as its occupation and preservation may be of vital importance to General Hood, as well as protection to myself, it being the base of supplies for my own and General Roddy's commands."

ing," some five miles apart, as most favorable for the location of his batteries. From those points he could command the river, both up and down from two to three miles, and accordingly established Bell's Brigade, with a section of Morton's Battery, at the latter.* Lyon was put in position with his brigade at Fort Heiman, the twenty-pounder Parrotts at the old works, and Brown's section of artillery four or five hundred yards below in position, with orders not to disturb any transports or gunboats until the batteries were thoroughly prepared for action, nor then to fire until such steamer or steamers should have passed into the reach of the river between the batteries. In the mean time, Colonel Wilson, (Sixteenth Tennessee,) and Lieutenant-Colonels Wisdom (Newsom's) and White, (Fourteenth Tennessee,) were actively engaged in watching the movements of the enemy at various points on the Tennessee river, southward of Clifton, while Keizer's scouts were in close observation upon Memphis ; and on the 28th, For‑ rest, with his staff and escort, setting out for Paris, reached that place on the evening of the 29th.

By daylight on the 29th, Buford's Batteries, well masked, were in effective condition, as well as judiciously disposed, and at nine A.M., the transport steamer Mazeppa, heavily laden—with a barge in tow—unaware of the lurking danger, passed the lower battery at Fort Heiman. A section of Morton's guns, 600 yards north of the old works, was immediately opened upon her, followed promptly by the heavy Parrotts, and with such effect that, her machinery being speedily disabled, she became unmanageable, and drifting to the opposite shore, was deserted by her crew.† An officer

---

* Commanded by Sergeant Lemuel Zarring.

† Morton's section was commanded by Lieutenant J. W. Brown, and the section of twenty-pounder Parrotts by Lieutenant W. O. Hunter. — *Notes of Captains Morton and Walton.*

of the Third Kentucky, Captain Gracy, voluntarily swam to her with the aid of a log, and brought back a yawl, in which General Buford, with a party of men, at once repaired to the Mazeppa, and taking possession, she was quickly warped by a hawser across to the west bank of the river. She proved to be heavily freighted with hard bread, blankets, shoes, clothing, axes, and other military stores, and by five P.M., the greater part of these were safely discharged upon the bank of the river.

At this juncture, however, three Federal gunboats came upon the scene, and taking position out of range of the Confederate guns, shelled the landing and the Mazeppa with such vigor and precision that Buford found it expedient to burn the steamer, and address himself at once to the security and removal of the stores already landed. Setting the Mazeppa on fire, she was soon consumed, and shortly after sundown the gunboats withdrew down the Tennessee. Thus left in possession of the field, the Confederates worked all that night, and during the 30th, in hauling the captured supplies to a place of security, with wagons and teams mainly impressed for the service from the neighborhood. On the morning of the 30th, another transport, the Anna, from above-stream, passing Colonel Bell unaware of the snare in her path, drew the fire of the section of three-inch rifles there ; the heavy Parrotts next opened ; but Buford, anxious to capture the boat uninjured, if possible, galloping to the bank, ordered her to come to. Promptly replying that he would do so, the pilot ringing his signal-bell to that effect, Buford directed the firing to cease. The pilot then cried out that he would round to at the lower landing, but really kept on his course. Speedily apprehending perfidy, the Confederate General ordered the batteries to reopen ; nevertheless, the Anna made good her escape from under fire, though well riddled and badly damaged.

Several hours later, the gunboat Undine came in sight, also from above, convoying the transport Venus, with two barges attached. Permitted to pass by a short distance, the upper battery was turned upon the gunboat, which then engaged the Confederates with spirit for nearly an hour, during which Bell's sharp-shooters were so actively employed that, under the effect of the three-inch artillery and the Confederate riflemen, it presently dropped down the river in contact with the battery at Fort Heiman, which was speedily found too formidable to attempt to pass, however. The Undine withdrew with the Venus, above and behind the bend of the river, from which position it began a noisy shelling of the battery, at the same time repairing damages in the hull and steampipe. During this time, or about midday, another transport, the J. W. Cheeseman, coming down-stream, was speedily brought to, disabled in her machinery by the artillery at the Paris Landing.

Meanwhile, on the afternoon of the 29th, General Chalmers had reached Paris with his division ; and soon after, General Forrest arrived with his staff and escort at the same place, where he received, that night, Buford's dispatch announcing the capture of the Mazeppa, with her cargo, as well as her subsequent destruction. Chalmers was then ordered to repair to Paris Landing, with Rucker's Brigade and four pieces of artillery, early on the morrow.* Leaving Mabry's Brigade and Thrall's Battery at Paris, and moving at daylight, he reached Paris Landing, after a march of twenty miles, about midday.

Just before the arrival of General Chalmers, Captain Morton had come up with orders from General Buford to transfer the

---

* This artillery consisted of a section of Rice's Battery, Lieutenant Briggs commanding, and a section of Walton's Battery, Sergeant Crozier commanding.

section of his battery there to the immediate vicinity of the gunboat, and recommence the attack. Informed of this fact, and the situation of affairs, Chalmers, after consultation with Colonel Bell, directed that officer to move his artillery as near as possible to the Undine and Venus, and drive them from their shelter. Some serious difficulties, however, being re- ported to be in the way of transporting the artillery to the proper point, Colonel Rucker made a personal reconnoissance, and finding the movement to be practicable, was then ordered to take the section of Walton's Battery, (two ten-pounder Parrott guns,) supported by the old Forrest Regiment (Kelly) and the Fifteenth Tennessee Cavalry, (Logwood) and at- tack as quickly as possible. Dismounting, and taking a position under cover of the bushes, below the gunboat, Colo- nel Kelly, opening a rapid fire both upon the Venus and at the port-holes of the Undine with his rifles, attracted the attention of the enemy, while the artillery, under Sergeant Crozier, was moved up by hand into a favorable position, from which a vigorous fire was promptly opened, and main- tained with such precision that the enemy, unable to make head with their armament—eight twenty-four pounder howit- zers—after a vain but spirited endeavor to do so, was driven to the opposite shore. One shot striking the bow, passed through from stem to stern, and she had been forced to close her port-holes from the effects of sharp-shooters. Her officers and men not killed or wounded then escaped ashore. Mean- while, the Venus had been surrendered to Colonel Kelly, who, going on board with two companies, took possession of the Undine, raised steam, and carried both gunboat and transport to Paris Landing.

During this time another gunboat, descending the stream at the sound of the conflict, came to anchor about a mile and a half above the section of Rice's Battery, (Lieutenant Briggs,) which Chalmers had established several hundred yards southward of the position that Morton's guns had held, and began a vigorous shelling of the Confederate position. Briggs's pieces being too far from the gunboat for execution, Chalmers directed them to be moved up to shorter range, supported by his escort and a company of Alabama Cadets* as sharp-shooters. Securing a good position, the Confederate artillery, after a brief, spirited engagement, forced their adversary to weigh anchor, and withdraw up the river.

Both the Undine and Venus proved a good deal shattered, but not injured materially, either in hull or machinery; whereupon mechanics, gleaned from the command, as well as those on the Venus, were set to work to place them in serviceable condition, which was effected by the afternoon of the 31st. A detachment of infantry had been on the Venus, ten of whom were killed or wounded, and an officer and ten men were captured. The barges, being empty, were destroyed. The Cheeseman, on inspection, was found to be irreparably injured, with the resources and time at the disposition of the Confederates; she had, however, a small freight of commissary stores, including coffee, candies, and nuts, and a quantity of furniture. The former articles, appropriated by the troops, were greatly enjoyed, long unaccustomed as they were to any but the roughest army rations. The boat was burned by order of the Confederate General.†

The Undine, one of the largest of the class of gunboats designated as " tin-clads," from the lightness of their sheet-iron plating, carried, as we have said, an armament of eight twenty-four pounder brass howitzers, which, with her equip-

---

* Belonging to the Seventh Alabama Cavalry, detached as escort to Colonel Rucker.

† The furniture, together with such supplies as could not be carried away was distributed among the citizens of the vicinage.

ments, were speedily made serviceable, though an attempt had been made to spike two of the guns, and disable another by a shell jammed in its muzzle.

General Forrest, coming upon the ground on the morning of the 31st, with his habitual energy urged forward the preparations for moving upon Johnsonville. Crews and officers were detailed from the command for the Undine and Venus, upon both of which the Confederate flag was now floating, to the great delight of the men, none of whom had seen that flag upon an armed vessel since the Confederate gunboats went down at Memphis in 1862. Captain Gracy, of the Third Kentucky, commanded the Undine ; and Lieutenant-Colonel W. A. Dawson the Venus, while upon the latter the two twenty-pounder Parrotts were placed as armament ; and that afternoon the Confederate General made a " trial-trip " with his fleet as far as Fort Heiman, to see that all was in efficient service. As they rounded out into the stream, the troops, drawn up in line, made the air ring with cheer upon cheer for Forrest and his cavalry upon their novel element. At Fort Heiman, stopping long enough to take on board the Venus a quantity of shoes, blankets, and hard bread, which had been secured from the Mazeppa, he moved back to the Paris Landing, satisfied that both boats were in serviceable condition, and orders were given for a general movement on the following morning. Lieutenant-Colonel Dawson, placed in command of the fleet, was instructed to move slowly up the river, as soon as the cavalry and artillery had taken up their line of march along the bank, so that he might keep his steamers under cover of the batteries. Chalmers's Division, being in advance, was to be kept as close to the river as possible, to shield the steamers from any attack from the southward, while Buford, following Chalmers, was to cover them from any gunboats which might come from the direction of Paducah.

At noon on the 1st November, all were in motion, as directed, but a steady rain began to fall, and the roads, naturally rough and through a rugged country, became slippery and difficult. That night the Confederate column encamped just south of the ruins of the railroad bridge over the Tennessee river, and the steamers were anchored under the shelter of the field-batteries ashore. A hard rain through the night, making the roads worse even than before, the troops moved slowly ; and the fleet, unfortunately, steamed ahead of the supporting land-batteries, until at a sudden bend in the river, above Davidson's Ferry, they were brought into the immediate presence of three Federal gunboats, when an immediate animated collision ensued. The Venus, soon receiving a shot among her machinery and her tiller-rope being cut, became unmanageable, so that Colonel Dawson was obliged to run her ashore ; and as the Undine, overmatched, fell back, he, with his crew, abandoned the Venus under a hot fire. She was then recaptured by the enemy with her armament and the stores that had been taken from the Mazeppa.* In the mean time Chalmers put his artillery in battery at Davidson's Ferry in time to make an effective diversion in favor of the Undine, and the enemy, forced to forego their prey, bore off, taking the Venus in tow. After this untoward affair, resuming the march, the head of the Confederate column encamped that evening a mile below Reynoldsburg, General Forrest sleeping some four miles to the southward.

Meanwhile, Mabry had been directed, several days previously, to establish himself, with Thrall's Battery and his brigade, on the river above Johnsonville, and accordingly he had taken a position—as he reported at Chalmers's headquarters, three

---

* The tiller-rope of the Venus, doubtless, was cut by her old engineer, who had been retained on duty with her engines.

miles south of the destined point of attack, where he had been joined by the Seventh Tennessee, (Lieutenant-Colonel Taylor,) from the southward.

Mabry was now directed to establish his command as nearly opposite to Johnsonville as possible the next morning, keeping carefully out of sight of the enemy ; and during the day the rest of the Confederate forces were concentrated in the same direction from below. But meanwhile, some light skirmishing occurred with several gunboats that were now hemmed in between Mabry, on the south, and Buford, on the north, though without substantial results, and thus stood affairs on the morning of the third, when five heavily-armed gunboats appearing from below, engaged in a sharp skirmish with the Confederate batteries, in the course of which shells were thrown quite three miles, from thirty-two-pounders,· among the Confederates and their horses, with great din and uproar, as they crashed through the dense, lofty, forest trees of the country, But happily without harm. For a time the Undine took part in the conflict, and also two of the gunboats from Johnsonville ; but the former having been struck as many as three times, and being within close range of the gunboats, both from above and below, her crew, far better accustomed to the headlong charge and unhampered warfare of the trooper or dismounted rifleman, than to be cooped up in the narrow gun-room of a ship-of-war, became demoralized, and turning the bow of their vessel hurriedly to the bank, set her on fire, and made off for their horses as fast as they could scamper, fonder of the trooper's saddle than ever before. And thus terminated the short-lived operations of Forrest's Cavalry afloat.

During this time, though a cold rain had been falling incessantly, never postponing any thing for to-morrow which he might possibly do at the moment, the Confederate General had made a close reconnoissance of Johnsonville.

The river here was about eight hundred yards broad. Johnsonville itself, independent of the depot buildings, was a small hamlet at the mouth of, and just southward of, a creek, and was built upon the slope of the river-bank, which, rising gently from the water's edge, in the distance of three hundred yards attained an elevation of only about forty feet, and terminated in a bench or plateau, the upper or northward verge of which, nearest the creek, was surmounted by a hill about one hundred feet above the level of the water. Upon this eminence an extensive redoubt had been built, that overlooking commanded the western bank with the heavy ordnance with which it was armed ; and a long line of rifle-pits enveloped the depot near the water's edge and to the south. The western bank, from which the Confederate leader expected to operate, is abrupt near the river, about twenty feet above the level of the water, and descends, as it recedes, toward the west. It was thickly covered with heavy timber, except immediately in front of the depot, where the trees had been felled for some distance rearward to give range for their guns, and prevent any hostile approach under their cover. But, notwithstanding the defensive advantages of the position, and the preparations made for the event of an attack, Forrest saw, or was satisfied, after his reconnoissance, that if he could get his guns in certain positions which he selected, he might readily destroy, not only the depot and vast accumulation of supplies there collected, but the gunboats and transports then at the landing.

In the mean time, Brigadier-General Lyon, who had been detached from Middle Tennessee, on an expedition into Kentucky, had reported, with some 400 men. Lyon had been an artillery officer of the regular service before the war, and stood high with Forrest, for his professional skill as well as energy ; he was, therefore, ordered to take Thrall's Battery, (twelve-pounder howitzers,) then near at hand, and establish it as close to the river-bank as practicable, immediately opposite the upper or southern part of the landing. Losing no time, moving Thrall's guns as near to the desired point, with horses, as he might, without risk of discovery, Lyon then pushed his pieces some three hundred yards nearer the river, by hand, and to within easy range of the steamers and gunboats. At the point thus secured, the river-bank fell off rapidly westward, and formed a natural rampart, behind which Lyon sunk chambers for his guns, and cut embrasures through the solid, natural parapet in his front. The men worked all night, and with such alacrity, that the battery was ready by eight A.M. on the 4th, completely shielded from the gunboats, but to some extent open to a plunging fire from the redoubt.

Colonel Rucker, who also had much experience as an artillery officer, at Madrid Bend, in the early days of the war, was likewise directed to establish another battery (Morton's) just opposite to Johnsonville, and to place four more pieces, a section (Briggs's) in position four hundred yards to the northward, and the other one mile and a half below, to protect the crossing of a shallow bar. Morton's guns were sunk, like Thrall's ; but the other sections were not, so that they might be able to give chase to any steamer which should attempt to pass below or get by. Rucker, who had met with great difficulty in getting his pieces into position, after hauling Morton's guns through a cypress swamp for half a mile, had been obliged to lift and carry them over the fallen timber for some distance, before placing them in their assigned positions. Seeing that daylight would be upon them before their work could be completed, Lyon and Rucker had contrived artificial screens of beech bushes, which, skillfully intermingled with those already growing along the river-bank, effectually masked their working parties. Meanwhile, Buford on the left, or northward, and Chalmers on the right, held their men carefully concealed in the timber or behind logs, and in the ravines, in supporting distance of the batteries.

By twelve M., all was ready on the Confederate side. Forrest then, having the watches of his several subordinate commanders compared and set uniformly, ordered that his batteries should open fire simultaneously and precisely at two P.M.

In the interval, the gunboats from below had withdrawn out of sight ; the three at Johnsonville were quietly moored at the landing, but with steam up, and their upper decks covered with their officers and crew, the latter either busy scrubbing, or washing their clothes.   Straggling troops were sauntering about over the hill-side or pacing the parapet of the redoubt ; laborers were at work landing stores from transports and barges ; passengers lounged upon the decks of the transports and steamers, smoking or chatting ; and some ladies were to be seen coming down the bank, evidently in anticipation of an early departure on some one of the steamers, several of which were getting up steam.   It was apparent there was not the least suspicion of the impending tempest, and that the Federals must imagine the Confederates had withdrawn from their neighborhood without the ability of doing them any harm. Meantime, General Forrest anxiously surveyed the scene with his glasses until the moment for action had come.   Then aiming with his own eye and hand a piece in Morton's Battery, at the appointed instant, ten pieces, carefully trained upon the gunboats at the landing, were discharged with such harmony, that it could not be discerned there was more than one report —one heavy gun.   At the moment, several gunboats were just beginning to swing out into the stream, as if for a cruise. Immediately, steam and smoke poured forth from the boats and at every aperture from one of them, while her crew were seen jumping into the river nearest the shore and swimming for the landing, showing that her steam apparatus was mortally hurt.   Another of the gunboats turned toward the landing ; and the ladies just approaching the transports rushed wildly up the hillside toward the fort.   Only one of the gunboats returned the fire, but the redoubt burst forth with a storm of shells, thrown with much precision. At the third discharge, however, of the Confederates' battery, the boiler of one of the gunboats—not in action—was evidently perforated, for the agonizing screams of the wounded and scalded were plainly heard across the broad river; but the Confederates plied their artillery with unabated energy, and the sharp-shooters joining in, their unerring rifles kept up a fierce deadly fire at the ports of the gunboats, especially the one that gave battle. The conflict had now been maintained for an hour, and the guns of the redoubt, soon getting the range, threw their shells so accurately, that several were dropped into the sunken gun-chambers, but without further harm than breaking the rammers in the hands of the gunners in two instances, for they sunk so deep before they exploded that they did no injury. The two disabled gunboats were now wrapped in flames, and the commander of the third, after a stout contest, unable to endure it any longer, ran her ashore, when she was immediately deserted by her crew, as the other two had been.

Orders were now given to turn Morton's guns upon the redoubt, and right speedily they were exploding their shells within its precincts, though a mile distant, and elevated at least eighty feet above their level. By this time, the burning gunboats having drifted against some loaded barges, these were quickly in flames. And Thrall's guns, being turned upon two transports and some barges lying somewhat above the landing, soon succeeded in setting them ablaze; then their cables burning, they went adrift and were carried by the current down-stream, in contact with another transport to which the fire was communicated, and thence spread in a little while under the influence of a brisk down-stream breeze to the other transports and barges at the landing. It was now four P.M., and every gunboat, transport, and barge was on fire.

Thus far, as successful as could be hoped, Forrest directed

his batteries to the main work in hand, the destruction of the warehouses and supplies ashore. Discovering a large pile of hay, a few deftly-exploded shells kindled it into a consuming fire that soon spread to vast heaps of corn and bacon adjoining. And descrying higher up the slope a large pile of barrels under tarpaulins, suspecting that they contained spirits, Briggs's section, armed with James's rifles, was directed to be brought to bear upon them, using percussion primers.* A few well-aimed shell were thrown with the happiest effect, for a blue blaze, unmistakably alcoholic, was quickly seen to dart from under the tarpaulins. At this, a loud shout burst from the Confederates, though many, doubtless, were athirst for that which they saw swallowed up by the ravening fire. Soon the barrels began to burst with loud explosion, and the burning liquor ran in torrents of livid flame down the hillside ; spreading a flame in its course toward the river, and filling the air with the blended yet distinct fumes of burning spirits, sugar, coffee, and meat.† Meanwhile, all the warehouses and buildings were ignited, and the work of destruction effectually accomplished ; therefore, stopping the fire of his artillery, Forrest directed the main part of the cavalry to move rearward several miles, to where his train was established, and feed their horses. And after dark, all the artillery except Briggs's section were likewise withdrawn to the same point—Rucker's Brigade being left as a support to the artillery section and to picket the river. As the Confederates retired, the air was still redolent with the savory odors of that enormous roast of subsistence in which they had been engaged, and the night was made almost as luminous by the conflagration as the day.

---

* Captured from the Federals at Tishomingo creek.

† The Confederates had been on short rations all day, yet some of them declared at night that the effect of the fumes we have mentioned was to make them feel as if they had been eating heartily.

Riding back to the river early on the morning of the 5th, the Confederate General had the satisfaction to see that naught remained opposite of the opulent depot of yesterday but the isolated redoubt, gloomily surmounting and guarding with its wide-mouthed guns broad heaps of ashes and charred, smoking *débris*. Nothing was left unconsumed ; neither gunboats, transport, or barge had escaped ; the railroad depot, filled with supplies, and the warehouses and other buildings of the depot had ceased to be, as well as the large piles of stores that, on noon of the day before, had covered several acres of the surrounding slope.

Briggs's guns were now ordered to be withdrawn ; but as this was being done, a regiment of negroes, emerging from their covert, displayed themselves upon the opposite bank in amusing, irate antics. Throwing off their coats, and shaking their clenched fists at the hated Confederates who had wrought the desolation around them, they hurled across the stream upon the morning air their whole arsenal of explosive, offensive epithets, oaths, and maledictions. Thereupon the section was halted and turned upon the absurdly frantic negroes, while Rucker's veterans, bringing their far-reaching rifles down upon them, one volley and a salvo speedily dispersed the howling, capering crowd, who scampered away in the wildest confusion ; but a number were left dead or wounded upon the river-bank. This drew a few shell from the redoubt, but the Confederates moving off unharmed, rejoined their comrades.

As results of this happily-conceived and well-executed operation, it remains to recount the destruction at Johnsonville of three gunboats, eleven transports, and some eighteen barges ; and of buildings, quartermasters' and commissary's supplies, according to the Federal estimate, to the value of over eight millions of dollars. Previously, the gunboat Undine had been captured, and also destroyed, as well as the transports Cheeseman and Mazeppa, and three barges, from which last a large amount of subsistence, blankets, and shoes, as already stated, had been secured. This had been accomplished with the loss of the two twenty-pounder Parrotts, which fell into the hands of the enemy with the transport Venus, upon her recapture, and two men were killed and four wounded.

The Confederates, as may be supposed, were highly elated and gratified by the results we have just enumerated, a brilliant close indeed to their operations in West-Tennessee; so that though put in motion, under a hard, chilly rain, toward the south, yet all marched off cheerfully. Their commander had just received orders from General Beauregard, directing him to repair, with his entire command, to Middle Tennessee, and form a junction with General Hood, between Florence and Columbia; and with that object he now took the field—marching twenty miles that afternoon, in the direction of Perryville, where he hoped to effect the passage of the Tennessee river.

The roads were extremely deep with mud, as in fact they had been ever since leaving Jackson, on the way to Fort Heiman, and up to Johnsonville. The horses, moreover, had been much of the time on scanty rations, and began, especially those of the artillery, to show fatigue perceptibly. Nevertheless, the Confederate force reached Perryville by the afternoon of the 6th.

Forrest had preceded his command with his staff and escort, and went to work at once to build a raft with planks and timber taken from an adjacent building; and Chalmers and his staff coming up, went to work to build another; but upon trial, neither would answer any useful purpose. Meanwhile, two yawls were brought up on wagons from the Undine, and with these the crossing began that night. By daylight, the Fifteenth Tennessee had been thrown across, with its horses, which had been made to swim. The rain fell without intermission, and the stream rising at the rate of two feet in twenty-four hours, was filled with driftwood. Howbeit the crossing continued during the 7th, until the Seventh Tennessee and Forrest's old regiment (Kelly's) — or about 400 of Rucker's Brigade—had been crossed with the yawls. Meanwhile, some pontoons came up, and an effort was made to construct a raft with them that would carry the wagons; a small, frail flat also had been built; but this and the raft proved to be unable to stand the driftwood with which the rapid current of the stream was flooded. Therefore, directing Rucker to move forward to Mount Pleasant, to effect a junction with General Hood, Forrest, on the morning of the 8th, determined to abandon the effort to cross the river at Perryville, and push forward to Florence. Chalmers was directed to move directly upon Iuka by the river roads in that direction, which were found as bad as possible. Buford marched with his division by way of Corinth. Artillery moved with both divisions, and both commanders were instructed to send out detachments through the country to exchange their fagged animals with the people for others fit for service, and thus effectively rehorse their artillery at least. But failing peradventure in this, oxen were to be resorted to.

The rain still poured down in torrents as the Confederates pressed on over the red clay hills of the country, and through the deep mud and mire, all weary and constantly wet to the skin; and one day so nearly impassable were the roads that, working from sunrise until after night, Morton's Battery was only transported two miles and a half. Unable to get fresh horses, the artillery teams were increased from twelve to sixteen horses to a gun, and oxen being impressed, eight of them were attached to a piece, after which, there was less difficulty. Chalmers finally reached Iuka, with a part of Rucker's Brigade and the Fifth Mississippi, on the 13th; Mabry's Brigade having been detached, under order from General Forrest, the day before, to garrison the depot at Corinth. Meanwhile, Buford, moving by roads further westward, reached Iuka, with his division, on the 16th, and passed on to Cherokee Station, the terminus of railway transportation.* Chalmers, in the interim, was engaged in having his horses shod and with other necessary preparations for the field. All extra baggage and artillery, except eight pieces and the disabled horses of both divisions, were ordered to Vernon, Mississippi; and on the 16th, both divisions were ordered to move up to Florence, where Chalmers arrived on the afternoon of the 7th, having crossed the Tennessee on a pontoon-bridge, constructed for General Hood's army; and his command, moving out, encamped two miles to the northward of the town. Buford did not cross until the morning of the 18th.†

The army of the Tennessee was found encamped on both sides of the river, and had thrown up a strong *tête-de-pont*, with other fortifications, to protect the pontoon-bridge by which Chalmers and Buford crossed. Florence was filled at the time with general officers and their staff, soldiers, baggage-wagons, ambulances, and ordnance-trains, and all betokened an early march. The troops appeared to be in fine spirits, but the ranks of every regiment were attenuated to an unpromising degree. Besides, the wretched roads and gloom of the weather were inauspicious. All the supplies were drawn by railway to Cherokee Station, and thence sixteen miles by wagons, over roads by constant use almost impassable, and now thick-strewn with wagons broken down or ruined, and mules which had literally " died in harness," " and in the last ditch." Alto-

---

* General Forrest having reached Corinth on the 12th, repaired by rail to Cherokee Station, and thence to Tuscumbia on the 13th, and had an interview with General Beauregard.

† Such was the condition of Buford's artillery horses, that he was ordered to use the led horses of his officers and dismount their negro servants, and if that did not supply the requisite number, to make up the deficiency by dismounting some of the men from each regiment.

GEN W. H. JACKSON

gether, indeed, the movement "looked like the desperate venture of a desperate man," says a staff-officer. "But among all the troops whom we saw—officers and men—there was no faint-heartedness, but, on the contrary, an evident desire to go forward and fight it out."

CHAPTER XXIII.

THE HOOD CAMPAIGN.

Sketch of General Hood's Plans and Movements—General Forrest ordered to him—Confederate Forces—The Campaign Opened—Operations antecedent to Franklin—Battle of Franklin—Advance upon Nashville—Detached Operations of Forrest around Murfreesboro—Battle of Nashville—Retreat of Confederate Forces—Forrest in Command of Rear-Guard—Brilliant Character of his Operations—Safe Repassage of the Tennessee River—Commentaries.

November 15th to December 31st, 1864.

IT is sufficient for the scope of this work to say that Lieutenant-General Hood, with the sanction of his Government, having left his adversary, General Sherman, in possession of Atlanta—about the 1st of October—had moved rapidly northward with the whole Confederate force at his disposition. First, striking Sherman's communications at Big Shanty, just north of Marietta, the Confederate General had destroyed the railroad at intervals thence to Dalton ; and then, after some manœuvres and demonstrations in that quarter, moving by way of Gadsden, had pressed on with the purpose of throwing himself into Middle Tennessee, near Gunter's Ferry, the southernmost point on the Tennessee river. His object was to fall on Sherman's communications, and thus oblige him to withdraw and give up Atlanta and North-Georgia ; not only to reestablish those communications, but as a necessity to avoid the starvation of his army. This was the original plan of operations ; and finding it well on foot when assigned to the chief command of all Confederate forces in the State of Tennessee, Georgia, Alabama, and Mississippi, General Beauregard, in order to give it all possible aid within his power, ordered General Forrest to coöperate with his cavalry, by an early junction with General Hood in Middle Tennessee.

From some causes, as yet unexplained, instead of moving directly to Guntersville, only forty miles distant from Gadsden, where General Hood had concentrated his army as early as the 21st day of October, that General turned the head of his command to Decatur. There, howbeit, he found so strong a hostile force ready to dispute his passage of the Tennessee, that he felt constrained not to attempt the operation at that point, and after a delay of three weeks, he began to throw his army across the river at Florence, Alabama.

The forces under General Hood were divided into three corps, consisting of

An effective total of infantry, ...	25,000
An effective total of artillery, ...	2,000
And Jackson's Division of cavalry, ...	2,000*
Total, ...	29,000

To this force was now added Forrest's Cavalry, about 3000 effectives,† swelling the Confederate army about to take the field in Middle Tennessee to 32,000 men, of which 5000 were cavalry ; and over these General Forrest was placed in chief

---

* Armstrong's Brigade numbered about 1300 men. Ross's Brigade, 686. Total, 1986.

† Buford's Division was reduced to about 1200 men, all but about 750 of Bell's Brigade being on furlough to procure remounts at the moment the order to join Hood was received, and had not had time to reassemble ; and all but 450 of the Kentucky Brigade were absent on detached service.

command, on reporting to the commander of the forces, as early as the 17th.

On that day, in a "circular" assuming command, he expressed, in a few hearty words, his sense of the responsibility of his position, his reliance upon the cordial coöperation of all subordinates as well as upon the "patient endurance and unflinching bravery" of the troops placed under him. Other orders directed immediate preparations for the field, and forward movement on the 21st. Meanwhile, Jackson's Division was in advance on the Lawrenceburg road, ten or fifteen miles from Florence, and both Chalmers and Buford had been also thrown out as early as the 19th in the same direction, as far as Prewett's Mill, to secure forage for their horses, with special instruction, likewise, to give daily notification at Forrest's headquarters of the precise location of each division. They were also to glean the country of cattle, and set the mills of the neighborhood to grinding all the meal possible ; and, further, were to keep scouts well out in advance toward Pulaski, and on the right flank, to gain definite information touching movements, positions, and numbers of the enemy. And at the same time Captain Keizer had been thrown forward with scouts to Waynesboro, and to spread them over the country from Johnsonville to Columbia. A demi-brigade under Colonel Biffle was also pushed forward to Waynesboro about the 21st.*

On reaching Butler's creek, on the 19th, Buford found that a brigade of Federal foragers was also in that vicinity. Throwing out the Kentucky Brigade with Huey's Battalion,† he soon came in collision with the enemy, who made a spirited

---

* Some 500 strong, detached from Dibrell's Brigade, and during the campaign were transferred from Jackson's Division to serve with Chalmers's.

† About 150 men, recently recruited in Kentucky.

contest ; but it so happened that General Armstrong, of Jackson's Division, being in the immediate neighborhood—in the same field, in fact—in quest of forage likewise, heard the firing, and making for the scene, suddenly fell upon the Federal right flank. Thus brought between two fires, the enemy fled precipitately across Shoal creek, but the gallant Colonel Crossland was once more severely wounded.

The general advance having commenced, Buford and Jackson, moving by the highway through Lawrenceburg, were in that vicinity on the morning of the 22d. Driving in the enemy's skirmishers and opening communications, both Jackson and Buford arranged for an immediate attack upon the place, though it was understood from the scouts (Henderson's) that it was occupied by quite as large a force as 4000 Federal cavalry.

II.

Disposing Wilson's and Newsom's Regiments on the northward, and Nixon's (all of Bell's Brigade) on the south-west of Lawrenceburg, with the Kentuckians under Faulkner to the west of the town, while Jackson encompassed the southward, an animated skirmishing began with the enemy, found in line of battle on the road to Pulaski. Jackson, bringing his artillery into active play from a favorable position, and pushing forward Armstrong's Brigade upon the position, the Federals rapidly withdrew toward Pulaski, leaving their forage in the hands of the Confederates.* Meanwhile, Chalmers, moving that morning with Rucker's Brigade on what is known as the Middle or Henryville road, encamped near the hamlet of West-Point on the night of the 21st, and during the 22d

---

* In this little affair Lieutenant William Hunt, Twenty-eighth Mississippi, was particularly distinguished while commanding the leading squadron.

was engaged in having his horses shod. And here, during that day, the advance of the infantry, pursuing that road, came up. Moving on the 23d toward Henryville, up the valleys of several meandering streams, Rucker struck a Federal cavalry force, about three P.M., soon after his road intersected the turnpike from Waynesboro to Mount Pleasant. It was the Fourteenth Tennessee (Lieutenant-Colonel White) that first became engaged, having been fired upon by an outpost, which, being put to flight, retreated upon a Federal brigade of cavalry, encamped to their rear about six miles beyond Perryville, and where they were drawn up in line of battle quite 1500 strong.

Rucker's Brigade did not now exceed 800 troopers ; as will be recollected, Biffle was at Waynesboro, and the rest of the Confederate cavalry *en route* toward Pulaski, while the infantry were some ten miles southward ; but General Forrest, coming upon the scene, ordered Chalmers to advance and engage the enemy, sending Kelly with the old Forrest Regiment around by the left, to gain the Federal rear, if possible. At the same time, the Confederate General, leading his escort, some eighty strong, rapidly around the Federal right flank, attempted to form a junction with Kelly. Having, however, an unobstructed road, he struck the enemy's rear three miles from where Chalmers was fighting, and a running fight ensued for two miles in the direction of Mount Pleasant. The escort being well mounted, some of the enemy were overtaken and captured, including an officer, from whom General Forrest learned that only one regiment was engaged skirmishing with Chalmers, and that the rest of the brigade had gone into camp, a mile still nearer Mount Pleasant. Continuing the pursuit, however, the General and his escort were soon in the very midst of that encampment, whose occupants at the instant were dismounted feeding their horses. The escort all wore rubber overcoats and leggings, captured at different

times from the enemy, and this caused them, as they dashed
into the camp, to be mistaken by the Federals for their own
troops ; but as the Confederates fired their pistols in rapid
play into the thronging encampment, recognizing at last their
mistake, the enemy broke and scattered in great confusion,
only one regiment having been rallied. This forming, presently poured a volley into the escort, killing three and
wounding five of their number, but after that, retreated likewise, leaving General Forrest and his escort in possession of
the encampment, after having killed and wounded in the chase
and onset about thirty men, and capturing sixty prisoners,
with as many horses. Hearing the firing, the Federal pickets
fell back into camp, and were also captured, some eight or
ten in number. It was now dark, and knowing that a portion
of the hostile brigade was still between his force and Chalmers, Forrest, as a matter of prudence, turned in that direction ; but leaving the highway finally, for a distance of two
hundred yards, he concealed his prisoners under charge of
some forty of his men, and returned with the other portion of
his escort to the road to await the approach of the enemy,
whom he heard engaged with Chalmers about a mile distant.
They were evidently yielding slowly to the Confederates, giving back toward Mount Pleasant, and soon a detachment was
to be heard approaching at a walk. Forrest at once dis
mounting his escort, posted them in the edge of an opportune
thicket, where they rigidly awaited the approach of the foe to
within ten feet. Then pouring forth a volley, many men and
horses went to the ground, and the rest of the surprised detachment scattered in wild confusion. But meanwhile another, following the same road, coming up at a trot, speedily
met the same warm reception. The rest of the Federal command, finding they were ambuscaded, while the woods were
too dense for them as a body to find a way through in the
dark, now made a right gallant charge down the road. The

escort stood their ground, however, with characteristic fear-lessness, and another volley from their deadly Spencer rifles*
again emptied many saddles, and more than one horse was
added to the number which already blocked up the narrow
road. Meanwhile, Rucker's men, hearing the uproar, charged
likewise at full speed, and with loud shouts, in the same direc-tion. Mistaking this for a hostile approach of a fresh and
still larger force, the escort at length fell back to remount ;
but, fortunately believing that he recognized the cheers of his
own men, Forrest, springing forward, cried out, " Rucker !"
That officer, after his wonted fashion, was at the head of his
column, and answered the hail of his commander. The escort
was at once remounted, and ·the whole force moved back about
half a mile to the Federal encampment previously mentioned.
There was found an abundance of forage and subsistence
abandoned by the enemy, and the Confederates found it like-wise an opportune bivouac. In the engagements of this day,
Rucker's losses and those of the escort counted up as many as
five killed and thirty wounded ; that of their enemy quite
four times that number, exclusive of some sixty prisoners.

During this time Buford and Jackson had been moving
swiftly across the country in the direction of Linnville, on the
Tennessee and Alabama Central Railroad, northward of Pu-laski, so as to cut the Federal communications with Columbia,
as it was understood the enemy were assembling for a stand
at Pulaski. They did not reach Linnville, however, that day,
and had no hostile encounters.

About two o'clock A.M. on the 24th, Rucker was again in
the saddle with his brigade, and, moving rapidly by way of
Mount Pleasant, about daylight he overtook the Federal rear
near the house of General Lucius Polk, in the neighborhood

---

* Repeaters, which had been captured from the Federals.

of Columbia. Without making a stout stand, they were presently borne back upon their fortifications and a large infantry force. This pursuit closed, however, with a gallant charge upon the infantry pickets that cost the life of the gallant Lieutenant-Colonel W. A. Dawson. Leading the men across a small bridge near the town, he fell mortally hurt as he was wrenching a Federal standard from the tenacious hands of its bearer.* Meantime, Forrest and Chalmers came up, and Rucker, boldly deploying his men dismounted as riflemen, maintained a lively skirmish with the pickets all the afternoon.

In the mean time, Jackson and Buford continuing the pursuit toward Pulaski by separate roads, the former, at night on the 23d, on coming within eight miles of that place, ascertained that the enemy were rapidly evacuating the country. He therefore, next day, as well as Buford, moved by roads more directly northward until, on reaching Campbellville, about noon, he found in his front more than a Federal division,† under Hatch. Promptly making his dispositions for an attack, a part of Ross's Brigade was thrown forward, while Armstrong's Brigade, making a detour, fell upon the Federal right flank and rear, and Young's Battery was opened with great fury and effect from a favorable position.

At the same moment, Buford's guns were also heard in action about a mile distant. Coming up with the enemy on his line of pursuit, Buford had previously attacked them with Bell's Brigade and Huey's Kentuckians, or less than 1000

---

* This is the same officer who, as related in Chapter XXII., was placed in command of the gunboat Undine when the attempt was made to use her in the operations against Johnsonville. Evidently Colonel Dawson was one of those ever-ready, valuable officers whom General Forrest so liked to have around him, and was apt to work hard and in manifold ways.

† The Federal forces fought were at least 4000 strong. (Reports of Generals Jackson and Buford.) We infer from Swinton that Croxton was also there.

men, and maintained a vigorous combat until Jackson came up, when both divisions, with a common aim though a separate impulsion, were thrown upon their enemy. The effect was the complete rout of their adversary. In Buford's quarter of the field Newsom, charging with the Nineteenth Tennessee, dispersed several regiments and captured more than 100 prisoners; and Jackson's troops, pressing the advantage vehemently, captured as many more, with their horses and equipments, four stands of colors, and sixty-five head of beef cattle.

It was now late, and Buford and Jackson bivouacked, Armstrong at Linnville and the other brigade somewhat short of that place. Moving early the next day, they also took position in the vicinity of Columbia, Buford's right resting upon Duck river, his left upon the Pulaski turnpike, and Jackson upon the Chapel Hill turnpike.

At the moment, Columbia was occupied with the Fourth and Twenty-third Federal Army Corps and Wilson's Cavalry* with heavy bodies of skirmishers in position behind a line of rifle-pits stretching around the town, about one mile and a half from it. From an elevated position, in rear of Chalmers, the main body of the enemy were to be plainly seen, drawn up in three lines of battle. Nevertheless, though Buford and Jackson pressed their skirmishers back at several points on numerous occasions, and had seized and held portions of their advanced line, from which they had been expelled, yet was no disposition manifested by the enemy to come to any serious engage-

---

* The Federal force appears to have been (*vide* Swinton's *Decisive Battles of the War*, p. 441) Fourth Corps, 12,000 men, Twenty-third Corps, 10,000, and 7700 cavalry—that is, Hatch's Division, 4000, Croxton's Brigade, (?) 2500, and Capron's, 1200. Hence, Swinton is in error in his assertion (p. 442) that even at that stage of the campaign Hood "far outnumbered, above all, outnumbered in cavalry," his adversary. In cavalry it was Hood who was "outnumbered."

ment. And Chalmers's artillery, from an enfilading position, by a few well-aimed shells drove a considerable infantry force from the shelter of their rail breastworks in rapid flight.

That evening, Lee's (S. D.) Corps of infantry came upon the ground, and bivouacked in the vicinity of Chalmers, to whom Biffle also reported with his demi-brigade.

During the 26th and 27th, a good deal of unprofitable skirmishing was kept up between the enemy and Forrest's command—dismounted and acting as riflemen—while the Confederate artillery was employed on the 26th with execution so decided that the Federals were forced to quit their outer line of cover. Meanwhile, all of General Hood's infantry having come up, they replaced Forrest's Division, which then was re-disposed, Chalmers at Webster's Mills, about ten miles southwest of Columbia, Buford in the neighborhood of Berlin, on the Lewisburg turnpike ; and Jackson at Fountain's creek, on the Shelbyville turnpike.

On the night of the 27th, General Forrest was called to General Hood's headquarters. A full conversation was then had concerning the roads, nature and condition of the country, and he was ordered to attempt to throw the cavalry to the north side of Duck river early the next morning, to cover the construction of the pontoon-bridge for the passage of the infantry. Accordingly, Buford was instructed to pass the stream on the Lewisburg turnpike, Chalmers about Holland's Ford, some seven miles eastward of Columbia, and Jackson two miles still farther eastward, at Hall's Mill, while Forrest, with his escort and Biffle's force, was to attempt a ford two miles westward of Chalmers.

The enemy, however, had evacuated Columbia during the night, and taken up a strong fortified position on the north bank of Duck river, from which, during the 28th, they threw an occasional shell at the Confederate infantry, as they were exposed in their movements in the vicinity of the place ; but at the same time they had commenced to retire toward Nash-ville.

The weather was cold and disagreeably wet. The fords of Duck river all greatly swollen and swift, their passage was not only tedious but hazardous, for only the tallest horses could effect it without swimming. Jackson—Armstrong's Brigade in advance—had also to force his way across, under a sharp fire ; but both he and Chalmers, late that afternoon, stood upon the north bank of the stream with their divisions. Buford, however, was resisted by a strong force, in face of which it was impracticable to pass. Late as it was, the Con-federates northward of Duck river were pressed ahead. While Armstrong pressed after the enemy northward, Jackson had led Ross's Brigade, about sunset, over upon the Lewisburg-Franklin turnpike, where Buford's passage of the stream was being disputed, and making a vigorous attack, after a severe conflict, he drove off the enemy from the contested ground, and captured their field-train, including ordnance-wagons, a stand of regimental colors, several guidons, and about eighty men with their horses.

Meanwhile, Chalmers, having moved toward the north-east for some hours, after dark, over roads extremely rugged and difficult, was directed by General Forrest to halt and bivouac about four miles from the river.

Buford, having been prevented from crossing, as we have recounted, threw his force across, however, by daylight on the 29th. In the mean while, Forrest, not able during the night to ascertain Buford's movements, had sent orders to Chal-mers and Jackson to resume the pressure upon the Fede-ral cavalry toward Hurt's Cross-Roads, before dawn on the 29th, the first by a narrow country road, through the cedar thickets of that region, and the latter by the turnpike from the Lewisburg-Franklin road. Jackson, coming up with their rear near Rally Hill, engaged with animation, and drove the enemy steadily back in a series of well-contested combats. At the same time Chalmers had been engaged in some sharp brushes with the Federals in his path. Fighting for the most part dismounted, he had several times during the day charged in the saddle, and his escort bugler was shot by his side. Meanwhile, Buford had also came up, and the whole Confederate cavalry were now assembled near Hurt's Cross-Roads, in the immediate presence of a superior hostile force.

An immediate attack was then ordered, and a sharp encounter resulted, in which the enemy were borne steadily but doggedly rearward, as far as Mount Carmel, on the Lewisburg-Franklin road. The country, rocky and rugged, was thickly clad with cedars, and difficult, of course, for cavalry movements, so that, for the most part, the fighting was on foot, which, however, was now Forrest's habitual tactics. Armstrong's Brigade, all fighting admirably, and ever well led, here had an obstinate combat, in which the Twenty-eighth Mississippi was especially distinguished, and Buford's men were thrown into action with their accustomed vigor. Pressed back by their eager, indomitable enemy, now mounted, the Federal cavalry turned and stood at bay at several favoring positions, from which they were driven only after most obstinate contests up to within five or six miles of Franklin. Here leaving several regiments in observation, Forrest turned off abruptly, and moved swiftly across the country toward Spring Hill with the rest of his force.

Meeting a small cavalry force, it was at once brushed back upon a large infantry command found in occupation of a long line of breastworks extending around east and south of the place, while another infantry column was known to be *en route* between Spring Hill and Columbia on the turnpike. Every disposition was now made to attack and check the infantry in movement, and some sharp skirmishing had taken place, when General Forrest received a dispatch from General Hood, directing him to attempt to hold the enemy in check at that point until Cheatham's and Stewart's Corps, then *en route*, should come up. The skirmishing, therefore, was continued with such effect, that the enemy withdrew all their pickets and outposts behind their fortifications, and about four o'clock, Forrest, dismounting his whole force, disposed it as if in menace of a general attack.*

At length Cheatham's Corps of infantry came up, and Cleburne's Division being advanced and formed in line on the left of Chalmers and Buford, it was arranged that a serious, joint attack should be made upon the Federal position. Chalmers and Buford, however, were nearly out of ammunition, and the plan of attack was, that after the onset Cleburne should hold the ground gained until the rest of the troops should come up. The attack was handsomely and successfully made ; for, after a short though stubborn stand, the enemy yielded the position and fell back upon a second line, which, however, was not a strong one. It was now dark ; Forrest's men, engaged in action since sunrise, had exhausted their ammunition and were worn down from hard work— without intermission for the past week ; therefore they were withdrawn to feed their horses and bivouac out of immediate contact with the enemy's pickets, the infantry being left to hold the ground acquired.

About nine that night, General Stewart's Corps came up to the immediate vicinity of General Forrest's headquarters, and these two officers meeting, after a short conversation, found that their orders appeared to conflict. Accordingly, they rode together to General Hood's headquarters, a mile distant.† On the way thither, however, Forrest was surprised

---

* Since writing the foregoing, we find from Swinton's *Decisive Battles of the War*, p. 444, that the Federal force at this point consisted only of Stanley's, Fourth Corps, and Ruger's Division of the Twenty-third.

† At the mansion of Mr. Thompson.

to find that Cleburne's Division had been withdrawn from the position in which he had supposed it was to remain through the night, and had gone into bivouac somewhat remote from it, where the men were engaged cooking their rations, leaving no Confederate soldiers interposed across the highway south of Spring Hill, and therefore throwing that road open to the rear divisions of the Federal army. At the same time, also, a dispatch overtook him from Jackson, who had been thrown round with his division across the turnpike northward of Spring Hill, reporting that, being overmatched, and pressed back from the road, he stood in need of immediate aid. Buford and Chalmers, having already expended sixty rounds of ammunition during the day, were without a cartridge.* Forrest, therefore, hurried on to report the situation to the General-in-Chief. General Hood seemed surprised that Cheatham's Corps had not been held in position across the turnpike, declaring that he had so ordered it expressly. Turning, then, to General Stewart, he inquired whether he could not establish his corps in that position. There was some immediate obstacle, and the Confederate General now asked Forrest if he could not throw his cavalry upon the turnpike in time to check the Federal retreat? The cavalry General replied : " That, as Chalmers and Buford were without ammunition, their commands would be inefficient, leaving him only Jackson's Division for the service. That, luckily, had captured enough ammunition in its operations of the day for present purposes. But he would do the best he could in the emergency." General Hood then remarked that he would order his corps commanders to furnish the requisite ammunition. Forrest, unaccustomed to delay in the execution of his orders,

---

* Their ordnance-train had been left behind at Columbia with that of the whole army, and by mischance was placed at the extreme rear of that train, so that it did not come up until the Confederates confronted Nashville.

thereupon hurried off to make application for ammunition ; but neither Cheatham nor Stewart were able to supply it, their ammunition-trains, also, having failed to come up. Returning to his own headquarters, he found General Jackson awaiting him. Explaining the situation of affairs as well as General Hood's expectations, Jackson, engaging to establish his division upon the road at Thompson's Station and endeavor to hold the rearward column of the enemy in check at that point, left at once with that object.*

Having thus done all in his power to interpose a barrier between the divided portions of the Federal army, Forrest reported, through a staff-officer, to his superior, his inability to obtain ammunition, and what he had done in the exigency. By midnight, Jackson's guns began to be heard in an animated engagement in the north, and a continuous uproar of musketry resounded from that direction throughout the night ; and never did so small a force fight more tenaciously or stoutly than Jackson's little division on this occasion. The highest credit is the just meed of officers and men alike. The force encountered, a heavy column of infantry pressing on toward Franklin, was too powerful, however, for Jackson's slender force. He was unable to do more than harass the masses that forced their way by him during the night, and to oblige them to abandon a number of wagons, which he burned, while a considerable number of the enemy were killed and captured ; and one of his brigades (Ross's) came upon and destroyed a train of cars near Thompson's Station.

On the morning of the 30th, procuring ammunition from Walthall's Division for Buford and Chalmers, the latter was at once detached across west of Spring Hill to the Carter's Creek turnpike, to cover the left flank of the Confederate

---

* Jackson's Division, as will be remembered, took the field only 2000 strong.

army ; while the Kentucky brigade of Buford's Division was likewise detached to move with a similar object, in connection with Hood's right flank, on the Lewisburg pike. At the same time, Forrest, with his escort and Bell's Brigade, moved forward upon the Franklin turnpike in advance of the infantry. About six miles in advance of Spring Hill he came up with Jackson, still hanging closely upon and harassing the Federal rear-guard. Bell was then thrown forward to take part, and a continuous skirmish resulted for some four miles, until the enemy had withdrawn behind their lines in front or south of Franklin.

These lines and the position Forrest at once proceeded to reconnoitre with his habitual boldness and thoroughness, after which he returned to meet General Hood, whom he found at the head of his army three miles south of Franklin, about one P.M. The whole army was halted, and no movement occurred for at least one hour.

III.

Franklin lies in a bend, and on the south bank of the Harpeth river, on a gentle plateau. A commanding eminence, known as Figuer's Hill, which rises abruptly just across the stream eastward of the town, commands the place and all the approaches for miles to the southward.* Immediately in front, or southward, of the town, a line of breastworks, with a narrow ditch, extended for fully three fourths of a mile from the river, on the west, across the throat of the horse-shoe shaped bend in which Franklin is built. This breastwork, made quite strong when occupied formerly by the Federal forces, had been further strengthened for the present emergency, and it was heavily garnished with field-batteries.

---

* On it was an observatory, erected in a tree, from which a complete view was commanded of the whole scope of country.

General Hood, however, was of the belief that the main
Federal force was already in rapid retreat, and that the apparent defensive preparations were merely counterfeit, with
the view of gaining time to secure that retreat. This conviction he expressed to General Forrest, when that officer reported the formidable military resources with which the position bristled. His determination, therefore, was to defeat it,
by immediately storming the place, rather than to turn it.*
Accordingly, by four P.M., the preparations for that ill-starred
operation were completed. As ordered, Forrest had formed
Jackson's and Buford's Divisions immediately on the right of
Stewart's Corps of infantry ; Buford's men, dismounted, filling
the space between the Lewisburg turnpike and the Harpeth
river ; and Jackson's having been thrown to the south bank
of the stream, to engage and occupy the cavalry, and also the
force which held and was firing from a redoubt in that quarter.
At the same time, Chalmers's Division—including Biffle's
demi-brigade—was on the extreme Confederate left.

At half-past four P.M., the onset began. The Federal forces
were commanded by Major-General Schofield, and consisted
of the Fourth and Twenty-third Corps, (22,000 infantry,)
formed in a semi-circular line, curved toward the south, filling
their whole line of intrenchments, while the cavalry, under
General Wilson, were mainly disposed northward of the Harpeth, to cover their rear and flanks from that direction. Moving in line with the infantry, Buford soon came, however, in
collision with a heavy cavalry force, but advancing steadily,
after an engagement of more than half an hour, in which his
men fought with their wonted steadiness, their immediate

---

* At this day it is scarcely necessary
to point out how General Hood could
have manifestly gained his purpose better, than by storming the position, by a
very short detour.

adversary withdrew across the Harpeth. Meantime, Chalmers on the other flank drove in the skirmishers in his front, and charging, forced a detachment to give up a stone wall in advance, and retire behind the breastworks. Pressing them hotly to within sixty yards of their lines, he was not strong enough to attempt to storm their present cover; he there-fore established his own men under convenient shelter, from which he maintained an incessant skirmish in that part of the field.

By this time, the Confederate infantry—Stewart's and Cheat-ham's Corps—Lee in reserve—had moved directly upon the breastworks, and were fiercely engaged at all points. Stewart's and Cheatham's men, charging with their superb spirit upon an extensive line of intrenchments held by a Federal division, carried it, capturing some six hundred prisoners.* The ground of approach to the main position was open, with very slight shelter ; but on pressed the Confederates, with little halt, after their first success, though now fully aware of the appalling gravity of the work in hand. They were presently met by a broad, desolating tide of musketry, while shot and canister, both from the intrenchments in front and the redoubts on Figuer's Hill, smote down their gallant ranks from flank to flank. The slaughter, indeed, was now deplorable. The enemy, ensconced behind stout breastworks, with almost a single salvo of their numerous artillery swept away entire Confederate regiments, and thinned all the others to a heart-rending degree. But with characteristic, unconquerable reso-lution the survivors—staggered for a moment—still moved forward, and many reached the intrenchments, and in attempt-ing to surmount them were slain. War ever devours the best,

---

* We see Swinton says this position was occupied by only two brigades of Wagner's Division, Fourth Corps.

and here perished, unhappily and without profit, some of the choicest officers of the Confederate service. Notable of the number was Major-General Cleburne, without superior as a division commander. After having filled, with confessed distinction, every grade and command to which he had attained, he was killed while attempting to leap his horse over the enemy's works. Though his precious life was thus wasted, his superb conduct, " honored in death, shall glory gain out of the lips of foes." In a like endeavor, about the same time with Cleburne, fell the accomplished soldier, Brigadier-General John Adams, just as his genuine worth was beginning to be appreciated in the service to which he gave his life.

In this fearful onset the first line of the Confederates had been almost annihilated. A second and indeed a third line were, nevertheless, brought up, and thrown forward with kindred hardihood to meet, as might be expected, the same sanguinary reception, the same repulse with gaping ranks ravaged of their best officers and men. For in vain, under the circumstances, were all their efforts to carry the position and this general display of as superb valor in officers and men alike as ever signalized a battle-field.* By this time it was dark, and affairs were past any remedy for that night ; nevertheless, small detachments of the Confederates, that had gained lodgments at different points in the ditch, held their ground, and kept up across the *épaulement* an animated skirmish with the enemy until midnight, when Schofield withdrew, and resumed his retreat upon Nashville, leaving his dead and the greater part of his wounded in the hands of the Confederates, as well as some subsistence and other supplies.

---

* It has not come within the scope of this work to enter into an elaborate sketch of the details of this battle. It is proper to say, however, that the Confederate infantry assailing the position did not reach 25,000, while, as we have seen, the force assailed in their strong intrenchments numbered 22,000, backed by at least 7700 cavalry.

The loss of Forrest's Cavalry in this mortal battle was comparatively light compared with that of the infantry, which, including some 700 prisoners, was over 6000, embracing six general officers killed and six wounded.* The enemy, fighting, as we have said, from behind excellent cover, suffered lightly —according to their reports having lost not more than 2336, of which 1104 were prisoners.†

It having been discovered that the enemy had evacuated the position, the cavalry were at once ordered to move in vigorous pursuit. Accordingly, Chalmers, still holding the left flank, was directed to bear leftward to the Hillsboro-Nashville turnpike, and follow it to the latter place ; Buford, thrown across the Harpeth rightward of Franklin, in conjunction with Jackson, at the same time hung close upon the Federal cavalry on that flank, eastward of the Franklin highway. Forrest himself had his headquarters with this force. Coming up with their adversary within four or five miles, several sharp bits of fighting resulted, as the hostile cavalry was forced back toward Brentwood ; and in that vicinity Buford and Jackson, coöperating, made several dashing charges. These threw the Federal column into a good deal of disorder, while as many as three stands of colors and a hundred prisoners, with their horses, were won on these occasions. On Chalmers's flank slight or no impediment was encountered. When within six miles of Nashville, however, the cavalry divisions were halted and thrown into position for the night, directly in advance of the infantry, on a line stretching from the Nolansville turnpike on the right across, a distance of six miles, to the Granny White turnpike.

---

* We can not give the exact losses of Forrest's Divisions at Franklin. Chalmers's Division, however, had lost (killed and wounded) 116 officers and men ; and Buford's 91, in the several affairs in which they had been engaged in the past week.

† We take these numbers from Swinton, habitually well informed of what he writes.

On the next morning, Chalmers, with Biffle's demi-brigade on his left, was moved up early to the immediate vicinity of Nashville, on the Hillsboro and Harding turnpikes, while Forrest advanced with Buford and Jackson, by the Nolansville road, to within three miles, but in full view of the State House. But presently, the infantry having followed and relieved the cavalry without loss of time, about midday, Forrest began a series of characteristic operations for the destruction of the railroads and telegraph lines communicating with Murfreesboro and Chattanooga, and the block-houses which guarded them.

IV.

Buford's Division was now reduced by the casualties of the campaign to 1000 effectives ; with that force he was directed to destroy the stockades on the Nashville-Chattanooga Railroad, while maintaining a chain of pickets on the right of the Confederate army across to the Lebanon turnpike. Intrusting this service to Bell's Brigade, Buford moved promptly with his Kentuckians to attack the block-houses. First investing the one known as No. 1, it proved to be capable of a prolonged, formidable defense. Cruciform in figure, its walls were built of unseasoned oak timber, at least three feet thick, upon which field-artillery made little impression ; as upon the roof of the structure also, which, being well covered with earth, was, moreover, not easily combustible. Bell was now sent for likewise. But so dangerous, if not impracticable, were the operation manifestly that the men of neither brigade were in the humor to undertake to storm the fortalice. Morton's Battery, however, was set to work to pound it, and, it seems, with the effect of killing ten and wounding twenty of the garrison. Meanwhile, a train came up from the direction of Murfreesboro, with some negro troops, who escaped for the most part, though the train was captured and destroyed. Thus invested and battered by Morton's guns, on the morning of the 3d December the garrison capitulated—some eighty officers and men.

This happily achieved, No. 3 was next essayed, as also No. 2—the block-house on Mill creek—and both succumbed after some delay and parley, on the morning of the 4th. All three were destroyed. The other results were 250 officers and men captured, including those taken with the train on the 3d. Leaving a detachment of 250 men, under Colonel Nixon, to guard and picket from the Murfreesboro road to the Cumberland river, Forrest set out on the morning of the 5th, with Jackson and Buford, for Murfreesboro. At Lavergne, Jackson was ordered to move around to the right, and reduce a redoubt in that quarter, while Forrest himself, with Buford, beset the block-house (No. 4) near by. At the usual formal demand to surrender, with which the Confederate leader habitually initiated his operations of this character, the work was yielded, with 40 officers and men ; and in the same way the redoubt surrendered to Jackson, with 80 officers and men, two pieces of artillery, several wagons and teams, and a considerable store of military supplies.*

The block-house and a number of barrack buildings having been burned, the expedition was resumed ; but the force was strengthened by Bate's Division, ordered to coöperate.† That evening the cavalry approached within four miles of Murfreesboro ; but the infantry was unable to reach the scene until the next morning. Meanwhile, a cavalry detachment thrown out at Lavergne had captured and destroyed another block-house, (at Smyrna Station,) and added 35 prisoners to those already taken that day.

---

* This block-house guarded a trestle-bridge over the creek, and the redoubt on a hill south-east of Lavergne, guarded the railroad for some distance in that direction.

† Bate's Division had been previously detached to operate against Murfreesboro, but was met by a force four miles in advance of the place, and forced to fall back.

Soon after the infantry came up in front of Murfreesboro, it was formed in line, and, promptly throwing forward skirmishers, offered battle, which, after some feeble skirmishing for two hours, the enemy refused unless attacked in position, and accordingly suspended firing. Meanwhile, Forrest, taking about 150 of Pinson's Mississippi Regiment, made a careful close reconnoissance; and driving back some pickets behind their intrenchments, captured a few prisoners. Afterward, he likewise made a complete circuit from the right around to the Murfreesboro turnpike, with the result of ascertaining from close inspection that the works were really impregnable to the force at his disposition, occupied as they were known to be with full 8000 men, under General Rousseau. On the evening of the 6th, Forrest was slightly reënforced by two small infantry brigades, (Sears's and Palmer's,) about 1600 men, making his force now about 6500 strong, of all arms. It was late, however, and no further operations were attempted that afternoon.

Taking post early on the morning of the 7th with Palmer's Brigade (infantry) on a hill southward of the Wilkerson turnpike, two miles from Murfreesboro, General Forrest presently observed a heavy hostile column swiftly emerging from Murfreesboro by the Salem road. At the moment the Confederates were spread over a crescent reaching from the Woodbury turnpike, on the eastward, to Palmer's position. A new disposition was necessary to meet the menaced attack. Retiring Palmer rapidly to the north side of the Wilkerson road, Forrest threw forward a line of battle extending from Overall's creek in the direction of Murfreesboro. It was formed of Bate's Division and Sears's and Palmer's Brigades, with Jackson's Division of cavalry, a brigade disposed on each flank of the infantry.

Meanwhile, the enemy moving handsomely forward, drove in the Confederate pickets and pressed vigorously forward to grapple with the main line. From some inexplicable cause the

Confederate infantry, except Smith's Brigade, fell into disorder, and did not stand to meet the oncoming charge, so that two pieces of artillery were captured almost without a struggle. Seizing the colors of one of the broken regiments, Forrest, throwing himself prominently in front, sought to rally his demoralized lines. Major-General Bate, and other officers, coöperated strenuously in a like endeavor; but all in vain. No appeal or personal example could restore the spirits of these troops, veterans though they were of every hard-fought field in the West, and the peers in repute for shining conduct on all previous occasions of any of that army.* In this exigency, Forrest dispatched Major Strange to General Jackson, to acquaint him with the critical situation, and to say that all depended upon the staunchness and gallantry of his division. With admirable spirit was the responsibility accepted. Ross's Brigade was instantly thrown forward in front, while Armstrong attacked vigorously on the right flank and rear, and such was the resolution and vehemence of these charges that, first checking, they presently forced the enemy to give back and yield the field. This happily accomplished, the infantry were withdrawn to Stewart's creek, eight miles northward from Murfreesboro, but the cavalry bivouacked in their former position before Murfreesboro.

While this was going on, Buford on the left, about midday, moving down the Woodbury road with some 500 men and Morton's Battery, had met and fought a strong Federal force at the college, in the eastern verge of the town. With men

---

* Forrest, on this occasion, rode his favorite gray horse King Philip, of whose bellicose traits we have made previous mention. Catching sight of the offensive blue uniform, King Philip was only restrained with great difficulty from rushing down upon the enemy for an individual battle. Gaus, his favorite bugler, was also by his side as usual, blowing the charge with habitual intrepidity. This drew the fire of a regiment scarcely a hundred yards distant, without any other harm than the spoiling of another bugle for Gaus, the one he was blowing being actually riddled, as once before, with rifle-balls.

dismounted, and operating as riflemen, and using his artillery with free hand, he steadily drove them into the place, and followed as far as the court-house, which he forced the enemy to vacate, under the pressure of two of Morton's ever well-handled guns.   But soon reënforced with infantry, the Federals rallied, and Morton became engaged in the heart of the town until two P.M., losing nearly every horse of one of his pieces, which was only saved by being carried off by hand. At that hour, Buford was ordered by General Forrest to establish his command upon the left flank of the Confederate line, then engaged as we have mentioned.   As he attempted to execute this order, the enemy pressed after with a heavy force, for a time with menacing vigor, and he was not able to reach the scene until after Jackson's Division had so handsomely repulsed Milroy and brought his daring sortie to a baffled close.

For several days following, the cavalry remained in position before Murfreesboro, but without noteworthy collision with the enemy.   In the mean time Bate's Division was recalled to its corps at Nashville, and a small brigade under Colonel Olmstead instead was substituted.*   But on the 10th, Buford was detached, with his Kentuckians, to take post at the Hermitage, and establish pickets along the Cumberland, between Huntsville and the mouth of Stone river, so as to obstruct the navigation of the former stream above Nashville. Another purpose was to drain the country of persons liable to military service, animals suitable for army purposes, and subsistence supplies.   This delicate, arduous, and at the moment, perilous service, General Buford discharged with notable efficiency, though his force at no time exceeded 300 men.

In the interval, the infantry brigades were engaged tearing up and destroying the railway between Lavergne and Mur-

---

* Leaving General Forrest three small brigades of infantry.

freesboro ; and Jackson having been thrown with his division to the southward, Ross's Brigade, on the 15th, surprised and captured a train of cars *en route* from Stephenson, freighted with subsistence for the garrison at Murfreesboro. It was gallantly defended by the Sixty-first Illinois Infantry for a time ; but overcome, 150 of their number were captured, while the rest secured refuge in a strong block-house near by. Some 200,000 rations fell into the hands of the Confederates, who had, however, to destroy the greater part, as well as seventeen cars and the locomotive. The day before moving out east-ward of Stone river, with two of his infantry brigades, to intercept a Federal foraging-train reported in that quarter, General Forrest, on the evening of the 15th, received an order from General Hood to hold his force in hand ready for the emergencies of a general engagement which had then com-menced at Nashville. Thereupon the immediate concentra-tion of his command was directed to take place at Wilkerson's Cross-Roads, six miles distant, and that was effected, with the exception of the Kentuckians absent with Buford, during the next day. And happily so, for that night a staff-officer brought intelligence of the disastrous issue of the battle for the Confederates, and orders for Forrest to fall back by way of Shelbyville and Pulaski.

Buford was now ordered to retire through Lavergne, and cover Forrest's rear until the artillery and wagon-train were well in motion. But as his sick and baggage-train were at Triune, Forrest fortunately did take up his line of retreat through Shelbyville, but by way of Lillard's Mills, on Duck river, while Armstrong's Brigade was detached to push across at once to get in the rear and cover Hood's beaten corps.

The infantry with Forrest were barefooted. The country to be traversed, naturally rugged and obstructed by cedar thickets, was rendered almost impracticable by the deep mire wrought by recent heavy rains. It was late in December ; he was encumbered with prisoners, several hundred head of hogs and beef cattle, and few marches have been more toil-some or involved more suffering. But Forrest led it in per-son, and with his officers did all that could be done to cheer and urge his men forward, and to repress straggling. Reach-ing Lillard's Mills, Duck river was found to be rising rapidly. Pressing the passage at once and vehemently, after the pri-soners,* cattle, and about half the wagons had been thrown over, the stream became unfordable, and Forrest was obliged to move westward to Columbia to secure a crossing for his other baggage and ordnance-trains and artillery.

V.

While these detached operations, which we have recounted, were taking place under the immediate direction of General 'Forrest, Chalmers had remained, with his division distributed upon the right and left flanks of the Confederate army, in front of Nashville, his headquarters on the Harding turnpike, about four miles from the city.† As early as the 3d of De-cember, Lieutenant-Colonel Kelly was detached, with some 300 men of Rucker's Brigade and Briggs's section of artillery, to take post and blockade the Cumberland twelve miles below Nashville. On reaching the scene, he was so fortunate as to capture two transports laden with army horses and mules *en route* down-stream. However, four gunboats quickly ap-peared, and Kelly's artillery ammunition being, unhappily, exhausted, the transports were wrested from his hands despite his efforts to burn them ; but he secured 56 prisoners and 197 horses and mules.

---

* 400 prisoners, 100 head of cattle, and 400 hogs.

† Biffle was upon the right flank, ex-tending to the river above, and Rucker on the left, his pickets reaching to the river below Nashville.

A day or two later, Ector's Brigade of infantry having been sent to relieve Rucker on the Harding turnpike, the cavalry were redisposed.* The Seventh Alabama being left in position on the right of Ector, leftward of the road, the rest of the brigade, about 900 men, were stretched on the left of Ector, across the Charlotte turnpike, to and along the river for four miles, in support of two of Briggs's Parrotts and two sent from an infantry division, which were successfully employed in hindering the navigation even by iron-plated gunboats. Meanwhile, the weather had become very cold ; there had been a heavy snow-fall, upon which a sleet supervened, and the ground was heavily coated with ice for several days. But this did not deter the enemy, as could be seen, from the greatest activity in the trenches, in which there had been employed, we learn, 5000 quartermasters' laborers, as well as many citizens of Nashville, under a general officer of the Regular Engineer Corps of the United States Army, until the place stood girded with a double belt of earthworks — detached forts connected with strong curtains and infantry intrenchments. And behind these had been gathered more than 30,000 men,† besides the two corps of Schofield that had been suffered to escape through the clutches of their adversary, first at Columbia and next at Franklin. Or in all, the Federal force now invested at Nashville mustered 50,000 fighting men, behind intrenchments of the strongest, most scientific character, amply furnished with all the resources and appliances of efficient war. The investing force, on the

---

* Whole brigade was not more than 1200 strong.

† That is, the corps of A. J. Smith, 11,000 strong, brought from St. Louis ; the forces under Steedman, from Chattanooga, some negro troops, and twenty new regiments of twelve-months' men, and 12,000 Wilson's Cavalry.—*Vide* Swinton's *Decisive Battles of the War*, pp. 451-2-5.

other hand, was absurdly small : three small corps of infantry, the wreck that survived the shambles at Franklin and the excessive exposure to the harsh December weather of the climate, and not exceeding 1700 cavalry,* or, at most, a force in hand of but 22,000 of all arms. We know of no parallel to this in war annals ; no instance in which an army so superior as that which Major-General Thomas commanded permitted itself to be so long beleaguered by one so inferior in all but a supreme courage, a blenchless devotion to a cause, as was arrayed under the tattered Confederate battle-crosses upon the ice-clad hills that encircled Nashville.   It is said the Federal leader waited to complete the organization of his cavalry, in order that, after having routed his adversary, he might insure his destruction by having some 9000 cavalry† to launch upon his broken, demoralized ranks.   That being so, it becomes singular that there was not a more vigorous effort made to that end, a more vehement, damaging employment of that powerful element of his strength.

However, as early as the 13th there were portents in the air of the storm about to burst upon the Confederates.   Indications were manifest of an early offensive movement on the part of the enemy, especially in the transfer to the south bank of the Cumberland of a very large cavalry force.   At the same time the Confederates had thrown up rifle-pits and had commenced to construct some detached earthworks.   But exterior to the enemy, their line was necessarily of much greater length, and really, as has been aptly said of it,‡ "it presented

---

* Jackson and Buford being with Forrest at Murfreesboro, as also three brigades of infantry.

† We learn from Swinton that it numbered full 12,000 men, about 1500 of whom were badly and 7500 finely mounted.—*Decisive Battles*, p. 455.

‡ MS. Notes of Captain Walter A. Goodman, ever reliable, very full, and acute and sound in their observations.

the, appearance of the skirmish-line of an investing army rather than of that army itself." And we repeat, never in military operations have two belligerent forces occupied toward each other an attitude so anomalous as that maintained by the Federal and Confederate forces at Nashville on the eve of the 14th of December, 1864.

It does not come within the purview of this work to describe in detail the disastrous results that befell the Confederate army in that quarter on the 15th and 16th December. We shall therefore confine our recital mainly to the part taken by the cavalry or by the troops with whom Chalmers coöperated.

It must be observed, however, the enemy, making a feint of an attack on the Confederate right, hurled the mass of his forces upon Hood's left flank. As will be recollected, Rucker was in that quarter with his brigade of about 1200 cavalry. The gunboats opened, soon after daylight, upon his left with a boisterous cannonade, and speedily a heavy division of cavalry, closely supported by infantry, advanced along the Charlotte road simultaneously with another of like character along the Harding way. The country was broken and wooded, and a heavy fog, hanging low over the scene, so enshrouded these movements, that they passed without observation, until almost ready to burst in full force upon the lean Confederate lines. Ector's Brigade, on the Harding turnpike, was struck by the mass, and forced to swing eastward for support upon the infantry, leaving the Seventh Alabama Cavalry to seek a junction with the rest of Rucker's Brigade westward of the road. And thus the Harding turnpike was now left in possession of the enemy, while a part of Chalmers's wagon-train, which had been left for security in rear of Ector's Brigade, was captured. Meanwhile, Chalmers with Rucker had maintained an obstinate unequal combat on the Charlotte turnpike; but Chalmers held his ground until what had happened rightward was reported, and it was manifest he was now isolated from the

Confederate army. He therefore retired by a cross-road to a point on the Harding turnpike, being without orders in the exigency, and unable to communicate with General Hood. Advancing up the road in the direction of his enemy, with his escort and a small detachment, after a spirited skirmish, in which the enemy encountered were repulsed, Chalmers ascertained. about dark, by a personal reconnoissance and from scouts, that the Confederate left wing was still in position in the main lines eastward of the Harding turnpike, on the Hillsboro road. Rucker was then directed to take position for the protection of its left flank, which he effected just before dawn at the point where the cross-road from Brentwood strikes the Hillsboro turnpike. Here he was speedily assailed by a strong cavalry column, apparently bent on turning the Confederate left flank. Made aware of the emergency, Chalmers presently moved across with his escort and Kelly's Regiment (the old *Forresters*) to the Granny White turnpike, just in time to meet there a hostile cavalry force. Securing a strong position, he held his enemy at bay, and Cheatham's ambulance-train, meanwhile, was enabled to escape capture. In the mean time, Rucker, with a part of his brigade,* was hotly beset, by forces equally strong, on his front and left flank. Sorely pressed, Chalmers ordered the concentration of his cavalry immediately in front—northward—of Brentwood, and about half-past four P.M., went to seek orders from General Hood. Very soon, between sundown and dark, a dispatch from General Hood to General Chalmers was received, and handed to Colonel Rucker, in the absence of his superior. It was the announcement of defeat and his retreat, with orders that the

---

* The Seventh Tennessee had been sent off on escort service that morning to Franklin.

cavalry should resist at all hazard the pursuit of the Federal cavalry by the Granny White turnpike.

Rucker—formed by nature, except perchance in stature, for a cavalry leader—swiftly drew up his dauntless veterans in line across the designated road, and placing Colonel Kelly in command, went rearward with his escort a half-mile, there to build some breastworks of rails at the intersection of the road from Brentwood with the Granny White turnpike, and across the latter. But before this could be done, a largely overwhelming force was upon Kelly, who maintained desperate but unavailing battle as long as possible against the odds accumulating upon him. Rucker, meanwhile, working at his breastworks—as Rucker can—was then joined by the Seventh Alabama, which as yet had been rearward; but while throwing it into position well to the leftward, the Twelfth Tennessee fell back with the ill-tidings that Kelly had been driven from his ground. Colonel White, its commander, was directed to form behind the breastworks, just leftward of the turnpike, and Rucker then repaired in person farther to the left, to dispose the Seventh Alabama precisely as he wished. Returning presently to the point he had indicated for the Twelfth Tennessee, he found himself in the midst of a mounted regiment; inquiring for the commanding officer, he was immediately approached by an officer so closely that both saw, from their uniforms, they were enemies. Both drawing their sabres, sprang to the conflict with the like spirit. The weather was, however, so cold that the combatants could not manage their horses, and Rucker's sabre, as he struck with all his power, missing its aim, fell from his hand. In immediate contact with his foe at the moment, he grappled and wrenched his sword from the Federal officer. Seeing that he was in the midst of at least a Federal regiment, the Confederate officer rapidly glanced around for an avenue of escape. In his front were breastworks of rails, in his rear a hostile regiment. Turning his horse, he boldly dashed toward the right, with the purpose of threading, in the darkness, his way between the line of breastworks and the enemy; but the latter shouting, "Shoot the man on the white horse!" in an instant hundreds of weapons were leveled and fired at him. One ball, taking effect, shattered his left arm above the elbow,[*] just as the dauntless Rucker struck an adversary who was trying to cut off his escape. But his own horse falling at the instant, he was thrown violently to the ground against some rails, and rendered speechless from the concussion, though conscious of what was happening around. For a moment, there was a rush upon the prone Confederate, as of so many hounds upon the dead quarry of their long pursuit. After some moments of wild, fierce clamor and rough handling, Rucker, replaced on his horse, was carried to General Hatch, a short distance off, and questioned, with the result that the Federal Commander was probably satisfied that Forrest (previously supposed to be at Murfreesboro) had come up and was covering Hood's retreat.

As Rucker was being carried, however, to General Hatch, some one shouting for the Federal Commander, the Seventh Alabama was made aware of the proximity of the enemy. Major Randolph immediately moved on in the indicated direction, and so intently were all interested in the examination of the Confederate, that a sudden volley from the Seventh Alabama, killing and wounding a good many of Hatch's escort, was their first admonition of the danger. The Federals scattered, but carried their prisoner away, though vigorously pressed by Randolph for a mile.

Kelly had previously fought manfully for the position assigned, but such were the odds assailing him that he was forced from it, as we have said, and a general *mêlée* occurred in the dark.

---

[*] Amputation was subsequently performed in the hospital at Nashville.

The Seventh Alabama, were able, however to check the further progress of the Federal cavalry down the turnpike ; and notable in their ranks for splendid courage on the occasion, as through the day, were a company of cadets from the Alabama University—mere youths—commanded by one of their number. The unconquerable tenacity, the brilliant valor of these boys, who faced and fought all odds, until their ranks were cut to pieces, excited general notice and praise.

In the main, the darkness which shrouded the field was decidedly propitious for the vanquished, for it concealed their fearful weakness — their shattered, disorganized condition. Some regiments, however, preserved a nucleus embodied, and bivouacked within near sight of the Federal camp-fires. Meantime, until eleven, the roads toward Franklin had been swarming with infantry, preserving little or no organization. Then, worn down and overcome by fatigue, they fell by the wayside, and rested for the night as they could.

Fortunately, the Federal cavalry were not handled with resolution, and bivouacked after the rencounter with the Seventh Alabama. Had they been pressed forward, with all their redoubtable numbers, (nine thousand,) they must have inflicted irremediable damage that night upon General Hood's army. Doubtless the impression adroitly given by Rucker of Forrest's presence had a material effect in staying the movement ; for Forrest was not a soldier whom they were willing to meet in the dark or with unlaced harness.

It was not a juncture for sluggards. The infantry were early afoot again, some by the Franklin and others the Lewisburg turnpikes ; and by three o'clock A.M., Chalmers's Cavalry were in their saddles, following and covering the rear on both roads, but crossing the Harpeth near Franklin immediately after Lee's Corps. That corps, though greatly reduced, had preserved its organization, and was placed as the rear-guard of the army. Here, too, Buford joined with the Kentuckians and a part of Bell's Brigade, and Chalmers, assuming general command of the cavalry, was directed to receive his orders from General Lee, who was presently wounded, however, in a reconnoissance, so that the command was devolved upon Major-General Carter L. Stevenson.

Meanwhile, the enemy, though not following with that vigor which their superiority and long preparations portended, yet were getting troublesome. But a favorable position intervening, about six miles southward of Franklin, the Confederate cavalry were halted, formed astride the highway, and awaited the onset. Right speedily this ensued, and a succession of weighty charges were beaten back. But the Federals persisted, and gathering volume, poured down with such a tide that the Confederates were swept back about dark to a second position, where they happily gained another foothold—one, moreover, of great strength, which was held. In this affair there were numerous hand-to-hand conflicts between officers and men. General Chalmers himself shot one Federal and captured another; and General Buford and Chalmers's accomplished Adjutant-General, Captain Goodman, becoming entangled in the *mêlée* with the enemy, narrowly escaped. The weather, still wet, was very cold, the roads desperately muddy, horses and men so hungry and jaded that despondency was now stamped upon the sombre features of the hardiest.

That night, (17th,) the infantry rear-guard bivouacked about Thompson's Station, while the cavalry rested southward, at Spring Hill, and were there reënforced by Armstrong's Brigade. The infantry passing southward, the cavalry were again disposed to cover their retreat; and Cheatham's Corps relieved Lee's as the infantry rear-guard. Thereupon, Cheatham, to secure the passage of the trains across Rutherford's creek, then greatly swollen by the rain-fall, halted his corps two miles southward of Spring Hill, and intrenched. He was thus able to hold the enemy at bay, while the train was safely thrown southward of the dangerous stream. Then, late that afternoon, he withdrew slowly across it, his rear and flanks covered by cavalry ; but as the Federal cavalry continued to be handled with singular languor, there was no collision. By this time, the main Confederate forces were passing Duck river, six miles rearward, and Cheatham and the cavalry held the line of Rutherford's creek the night of the 18th. It was then, during the night, the redoubtable battle-flag of Major-General Forrest reappeared among his men, with the rear-guard. As Cheatham's available force of infantry did not now exceed 1500 men, Forrest offered to relieve him with his men, and this was sanctioned.

VI.

On the morning of the 19th, the enemy's cavalry were early afield and, in formidable numbers, displayed a resolute purpose to force the passage of Rutherford's creek, while a considerable column was observed in movement, as if aiming to cross Duck river, below the junction of the creek with it. But up to three P.M., they were unable to break the barrier of the creek. And meanwhile, the Confederate train and main force were safely behind Duck river. Then the rear-guard likewise was withdrawn southward of that stream without hinderance, and bivouacked the night of the 19th at Columbia.

There, on the morning of the 20th, Walthall's Division, Stewart's Corps, reënforced by five other fragments of brigades —in all only 1900 bayonets—was placed under the orders of General Forrest as commander of the rear-guard ; and he was directed to hold the position to the last possible moment, retiring, when forced to do so, upon Florence, by way of Pulaski, doing what were possible meanwhile to gain time for the safety of the remains of the Confederate army.*

---

* These orders and dispositions re- the 19th, between Generals Hood and
sulted from an interview the night of Forrest, in which the former expressed

Of Walthall's force, at least 300 were shoeless, and so foot-sore as to be unable to march and bear arms, and were there-fore detached on the wagon-train. For some reason the enemy did not appear in force until late that afternoon, when, although Columbia was manifestly unoccupied by any part of the Confederate army, they opened upon it a furious cannon-ade of shot and shell. Hoisting a flag of truce, Forrest had an interview—the stream between them—with General Hatch, whom he formally assured that Columbia was only occupied by non-combatants and the wounded of both armies. He also proposed the exchange of some 2000 prisoners, the fruits of the campaign, who were, as he acquainted him, without blankets or proper clothing for the inclement season, and must therefore perish, in many cases, from cold, if not ex-changed.* After a delay of two hours, the answer—in the name of General Thomas—was a refusal either to exchange prisoners or to receive those Forrest had on parole, with the understanding that a like number should subsequently be re-turned. The shelling, however, was discontinued.

Forrest, after a careful examination into his resources, found that he had only 3000 officers and effectively mounted men, with 1600 infantry and eight pieces of artillery. With this force he was expected to confront and keep off a hostile army

---

the belief that he could not escape in such weather, with unfavorable roads and broken-down teams. Forrest re-plied, that to remain there would cer-tainly result in the capture of the whole force, but that, if reënforced with 4000 infantry, he would undertake to secure time and opportunity for the escape of all across the Tennessee. General Hood rejoined that he should have the in-fantry.

* The cold of the night of the 19th

and morning of the 20th was of unusual severity—indeed, beyond the experience of any one with Hood's army. We learn, besides, from General F., that as many as a fourth of these prisoners must have perished from exposure, and many more were disabled on the re-treat. He did what he could to allevi-ate their wretched condition, as well be-fore as after the strange, unjustifiable refusal to receive them, even on parole, for subsequent exchange.

of 10,000 cavalry, and possibly 30,000 infantry. Seldom or never has a soldier been placed in a graver situation, or one from which extrication seemed so little probable. We are assured, however, " that at no time in his whole career was the fortitude of General Forrest in adversity, and his power of infusing his own cheerfulness into those under his command, more strikingly exhibited than at this crisis. Defeated and broken as we were, there were not wanting many others as determined as he to do their duty to the last, and who stood out faithfully to the end ; but their conversation was that of men who, though determined, were without hope, and who felt that they must gather strength even from despair ; but he alone, whatever he may have felt, (and he was not blind to the dangers of our position,) spoke in his usual cheerful and defiant tone, and talked of meeting the enemy with as much assurance of success as he did when driving them before him a month before. Such a spirit is sympathetic, and not a man was brought in contact with him who did not feel strengthened and invigorated, as if he had heard of a reënforcement coming to our relief."[*]

During the night of the 21st, the enemy effected the passage of Duck river, above the town, with their cavalry, and by morning their infantry began to cross ; whereupon Forrest put his forces in retreat, the infantry moving by the Pulaski road. Jackson's and Buford's Divisions covered the rear, and Chalmers's the right flank, moving by the road through Bigbyville,[†] while the left was carefully guarded by detachments of scouts. Pressing closely after, the enemy came up with and opened warmly with artillery upon Forrest's rear-

---

[*] Notes of Captain Walter A. Goodman.

[†] The remains of Chalmers's Division he had organized at Columbia as a brigade—about 500 men—which he commanded in person.

guard, about three miles southward of Columbia, and under this stress the Confederates continued their retreat until a strong defensive position was found in a gorge between two high ridges, three miles further on.   Here a stout stand was made until the 23d, and the Federals were held in check by the cavalry.   Resuming the retreat then, to gain time for the movement of the stock and wagon-train, another stand was made on the 24th south of Lynnville, and Walthall's infantry being brought into action, a severe engagement ensued for several hours, after which the Confederates fell back in good order two miles, to a favorable position just in advance of Richland creek, where dispositions were made for another combat.   Armstrong's Brigade was here placed in support of six pieces of artillery, established upon and sweeping the turnpike ; the infantry held the crossing of the creek ; Chalmers and Buford were drawn up in line with and to the left of the artillery, while Ross's Brigade was on the right.   A vigorous artillery conflict then resulted, in the course of which two Federal guns were dismounted.   Meanwhile the enemy pressing Chalmers and Buford heavily with superior masses of cavalry, forced the creek to the Confederate right.   But Jackson's Division was sent to meet them, and for several hours a warm conflict was maintained—in which the enemy lost heavily and the Confederates lightly, but among the wounded was General Buford, whose division was then temporarily consolidated with Chalmers's forces.   The Federals, however, being now reënforced, Forrest withdrew toward Pulaski without further molestation that day.   During the past thirty-six hours, however, the fighting had been with little intermission.   The Federal cavalry had been constantly making strenuous efforts to flank Forrest's force, while their infantry had pressed vigorously onward by the highway ; but each Confederate officer and man appeared to act and fight as if the fate of the army depended on his individual conduct.   And never were there manifested

higher soldierly virtues than by Forrest's heroic band—
including the infantry—the virtues of fortitude, unblench-
ing valor, and an unconquerable cheerfulness and alacrity
under orders.

The roads now, grown even worse than before, were nearly
impracticable for wheels, hence it became necessary to destroy,
at Pulaski, a quantity of the ammunition of the army, which
could not be carried off, also several locomotives and two
trains of cars. Jackson was then left there with orders to
make an obstinate stand, while the other divisions of the rear-
guard retired ; and well did that division—Armstrong's and
Ross's veterans—discharge that service, retiring only when
about to be overwhelmed.

No further stand was now attempted until the Confederates
reached and took post upon Anthony's Hill, seven miles beyond Pulaski. It was now only forty-two miles to Bainbridge,
the point on the Tennessee river where Hood's army was to
cross, but as yet many of his infantry had not reached the
river-bank ; the main part of the ordnance-train had been
abandoned, and the horses necessarily taken to transport the
pontoons, many of which also were known to be still some
distance from the river. At the same time the enemy were
reported to be in portentous numbers and proximity. General Wilson had already passed Pulaski with 10,000 cavalry,
and Thomas had reached that point with a large force of infantry, and both were pressing onward in hot pursuit. To prevent the annihilation of Hood's army, it was necessary to
make a yet more obstinate effort to delay the approaching
enemy as long as possible, and fortunately the ground was
highly favorable to that end. The approach to Anthony's
Hill, for two miles, was through a defile formed by two steep,
high ridges, which, uniting at their southern extremity, formed the hill, the ascent of which was sudden, and both the
ridges and hill were thickly wooded.

Morton's Battery was established upon the immediate summit of the hill, so as to sweep the hollow below and the road through it. Along the crest of the hill and around on the ridges, were grouped Featherston's and Palmer's Brigades of Walthall's Division, reënforced by 400 of Ross's Texans and as many of Armstrong's Mississippians, dismounted. The rest of Jackson's Division were disposed as cavalry on either flank, with Reynolds's and Field's Brigades of infantry formed in a second line as a reserve. The infantry had further strengthened their position by breastworks of rails and timber, and a line of skirmishers were posted under cover on the hill-side. At the same time Chalmers was halted about a mile and a half to the rightward, on the road by which he was moving, to guard that flank from being turned. So broken and densely timbered was the ground that the concealment of the Confederate forces was complete.

Scarcely, however, were these dispositions made when, about one P.M., the Federal cavalry, driving the Confederate rear-guard into the mouth of the glen, followed hotly. But the place at length began to look so dangerous, that their commander apparently thought it requisite to dismount several of his regiments before undertaking the ascent of the hill. These he pushed forward on foot with a piece of artillery. The Confederates, meanwhile, had ridden rapidly through the hollow, and up and over the hill, as if left unsupported, as the enemy was suffered to ascend within fifty paces of the skirmishers without hinderance. Then Morton breaking the grim silence with canister, the skirmishers enveloped them with a hot, galling fire of musketry from front and flank, followed quickly by a heavier fire from the main line of infantry. The enemy, thoroughly surprised, returning but a scattering, feeble fire, gave way in disorder, as the Confederates sprang forward with a shout, and charged down the hill after them, through the horses of the dismounted men, only halting once to deliver another fire. Thus the enemy were driven back in great confusion out of the defile, when Forrest recalled his men from their eager pursuit, to avoid becoming entangled with the Federal infantry, the advance of which, he apprehended, was near at hand. The enemy left behind one hundred and fifty, killed and wounded, some fifty prisoners, about three hundred cavalry horses, as many overcoats, and a twelve-pounder Napoleon gun, with its team of eight horses intact. The Confederate losses did not exceed fifteen killed and forty wounded.*

It was now nearly four P.M., and heavy Federal cavalry columns having made the detour both to the right and left of the road through the ravine, were beginning to press both Ross's and Armstrong's mounted men, and Chalmers reported the near approach, in his quarter, of a heavy force. All the advantages of the situation had been exhausted, its further defense was therefore inexpedient, and Forrest at once gave orders to retire, which was done in good order, carrying off his prisoners and captured gun. The roads were now as bad as ever an army encountered, and the horses had to be pushed through mud and slush every step of the way, often belly-deep, and never less than up to their knees. The men marched, barefooted in many cases, often waist-deep in ice-cold water, while sleet beat upon their heads and shoulders ; nevertheless, by one o'clock that night, they had reached Sugar creek, fourteen miles from Anthony's Hill. There the stream was clear, with the pebbly bottom ; and the men were brought to a halt, in order to wash the mire from their ragged clothing, and, building fires, were suffered to remain at rest until daylight.

But at dawn the Federal cavalry was up again, and, in heavy mass, attacked Ross's Brigade, now manifestly bent on a vigo_

---

* It was here Forage-Master William M. Strickland was killed, of whom we have made note *ante* page 461.

rous attempt to press forward over all obstacles, so as to strike
Hood's force before it might escape across the Tennessee.
The road to the river was now filled with the *débris* of Hood's
army.   His ordnance-train was still at Sugar creek, while the
mules had been used to assist in drawing the pontoon-train
to the river; but having been returned, the ordnance-train
was just on the point of moving.   It was, therefore, necessary
to make another resolute stand to secure that movement.
Accordingly, about sunrise, Reynolds's and Field's Brigades,
of Walthall's Division, were put in position some two hundred
yards southward of the ford, across a narrow ravine, and
upon a high ridge to the north of the creek and ravine, where
they threw up cover with rails and other material at hand,
while two other brigades (Featherston's and Palmer's) were
established in a strong position, half a mile further to the
rear, which was also strengthened by logs, rails, and some old
out-houses.   Jackson's brigades were grouped, Ross on the
right and Armstrong on the left of the first line of infantry,
and Chalmers was halted in a strong position, where the
parallel road which he pursued crossed Sugar creek.   Fortunately, a dense fog enveloped the position, and enabled the
Confederates to remain concealed.

About half-past eight A.M., the enemy's cavalry were to be
heard fording the creek, scarcely one hundred yards in front
of the Confederate infantry, until several regiments had been
crossed over and formed in line.   The fog vailed their movements, but it was apparent that, apprehensive of a lurking
danger, the enemy had dismounted and were advancing, with
a part of their force, on foot, in front of the cavalry.   Thus
disposed, the Federals came within thirty paces of the breastworks across their path, when, from behind it, a broad stream
of rifle-balls, cleaving through the thick fog, spread confusion instantly through the Federal ranks, and, springing forward, the infantry pressed their advantage with such vigor
that the enemy, unable to recover and rally, were driven back

through their horse-holders and among their cavalry, thus increasing the disorder. The creek was about saddle-skirt deep, and through it the Federal cavalry dashed rearward, without regard to any ford, and after them followed Walthall's dauntless men, charging waist-deep through the icy water. Ross, charging at the same time up the east bank of the stream with about eighty men, rode over at least a regiment of the disordered enemy, capturing a number of men and horses. At the same time, Colonel Dillon, making a circuit with the Second Mississippi, of Armstrong's Brigade, cross- ed the creek above, struck the enemy on the other flank, driving them pell-mell up the defile for a mile, and killing and wounding many. Pursuit was now recalled, as at An- thony's Hill, for fear of collision with the Federal infantry, but the position was held by the Confederate infantry until twelve o'clock, up to which, the enemy having made no demonstration upon the position, they were again put in movement for the river. The substantial results of this handsome affair were the capture of at least 150 horses and many overcoats, of great value to the men in weather so inclement. As many as one hundred officers and men were taken prisoners, and at least four hundred of the enemy and their horses were placed *hors de combat*. But the most valua- ble effect was, that it checked further close pressure upon the rear of Hood's army by the Federal cavalry, who had now been punished so severely in men and horses, here and at Anthony's Hill, as to be altogether unwilling to venture an- other collision with their formidable adversary. In the mean time Chalmers, having been attacked in his position, repulsed his enemy handsomely, and charging in turn, captured some prisoners, thus checking the hostile movements in that direc- tion also.

At one P.M., Forrest's Cavalry was next withdrawn ; and that night Walthall's Division bivouacked within sixteen miles of the Tennessee river, and on the following day returned under the command of Lieutenant-General Stewart. And on the afternoon of the 27th, a corps of infantry being left to hold the north bank of the Tennessee, the cavalry, relieved from further rear-guard duty, were ordered to cross to the south bank of that stream on the pontoon-bridge. Chalmers's command brought up the rear after night, and there was not a man of all that battle and weather-tempered band who did not feel a sense of supreme relief at the moment.

COMMENTARIES.

1. General Forrest completed his passage to the north bank of the Tennessee, on the 18th day of November, with not more than 3000 men, and was then placed in chief command of the Confederate cavalry with Hood's army, which, with Jackson's Division, numbered 5500 effectives, officers and men. The campaign, with its eventful disasters, lasted 35 days, during which Forrest's Cavalry were incessantly in sharp conflict with the enemy, at a season of singular inclemency. With this force he captured and destroyed 16 block-houses, 20 considerable railroad bridges, more than 30 miles of railroad, of immediate vital importance to the communications of the enemy, 4 locomotives, at least 100 cars, and 100 wagons. He captured as many as 1800 of the enemy, 100,000 rounds of ammunition, 200,000 rations, and 9 pieces of artillery ; and brought away 3 pieces of artillery and 10 wagons and teams more than he had carried in, besides many horses, while the aggregate of the killed and wounded of the enemy may be set down at 2000. At the same time, nothing in the annals of war exceeds in soldierly excellence the conduct of the Confederate rear-guard from Columbia to Shoal creek ; and the results signally illustrated how true it is in war, as the Latin poet says :

"They can, because they think they can."*

---

* Possunt quia posse videntur.

VIRGIL.

BRIGADIER-GENERAL ALEXANDER W. CAMPBELL.

CHAPTER XXIV.

FINALE.

Headquarters at Corinth—Rucker's and Bell's Brigades furloughed, others sent to Okolona—Headquarters at Verona—General Forrest assigned to Command of Cavalry of the Department—Reorganized Divisions under Generals Chalmers, Jackson, and Buford—Made a Lieutenant-General—Formidable Preparations for a Federal Raid— Major-General Wilson's Movement against Monte Vallo—Conflicts in that Quarter—Forrest in Collision with the Enemy—Affairs at Bogler's Creek and Dixie Station—Stirring Personal Combats—Forced into Selma—Dispositions for Defense—Selma stormed by Wilson, and Confederates dispersed—Adventures of General Forrest and Escort—Headquarters at Gainesville—Forrest's Cavalry lay down their Arms under Parole—Concluding Observations.

January 1st to May, 1865.

GENERAL HOOD having established his headquarters at Tuscumbia, General Forrest, repairing thither, reported the broken-down condition of his horses and his inability to forage them in that region. He was, therefore, permitted to put his whole corps in movement, on the 29th of December, for Corinth, leaving to General Roddy's small cavalry force the duty of covering Hood's rear. This soon brought Roddy in sharp collision with a largely superior Federal force that had been thrown southward of the Tennessee at Decatur, and which pressed him actively back toward Tuscumbia. Armstrong's Brigade was therefore recalled and directed to remain rearward of Hood's infantry until they had passed westward of Cherokee Station. On the 30th of December, Forrest, reaching Corinth, furloughed the West-Tennesseeans of Bell's Brigade, to proceed to their homes for fresh horses and clothing. And a few days later, the like privilege was granted to Rucker's Brigade, and, indeed, to all the cavalry whose homes were not either too remote—as Ross's Texans—or beyond the Confederate lines.

On New-Year's day, 1865, Hood's infantry, beginning to arrive, were dispatched, as rapidly as practicable, by rail to Tupelo. At the same time, all the cavalry not on furlough were ordered to Okolona, to recuperate in that country, so rich in forage.

One of General Forrest's first acts at Corinth was, on the 2d of January, to indite a letter to Lieutenant-General Taylor—to whose command he had been now returned—exhibiting the situation, with a close grasp of details, a broad reach of military views. Remaining there until the 9th or 10th, he dispatched picked, trusty scouts into Middle Tennessee, to ascertain the exact situation of the main body of the enemy, and reliable *indicia* of probable offensive movements. General Bell was likewise recalled by the 25th, with orders, as he returned, to glean West-Tennessee for absentees from military service. And at the same time, measures were taken to secure timely information of any offensive movement from the quarter of Memphis, or up the Tennessee river. Then, leaving Ross's Brigade to garrison Corinth, about the 12th of January, Forrest established his headquarters at Verona, some fifty-five miles southward of Corinth. Here, occupied assiduously with measures looking to the recruitment of his gaunt ranks, the re-horsing of cavalry and artillery, and to the close, stringent search of the country for absentees from his regiments, Forrest remained until about the 1st of March. For some time aware that he was to be assigned to the command of the cavalry of the Department of Alabama, Mississippi, and East-Louisiana, the order to that effect reached him about the 24th of February, when he assumed the command assigned him. It embraced about 10,000 men, widely dispersed over three States, and to combine these as speedily as possible for the most part into one coherent, effective body became his immediate aim.

One of his early measures was to group the troops of the several States into State divisional organizations, as far as practicable. Brigadier-General Chalmers was placed over the division embracing the brigades made up of Mississippians; Brigadier-General Buford, one constituted of the Alabama cavalry and the gallant remains of his old Kentucky brigade, with orders to proceed to Monte Vallo, Ala., and there organize his new division. The Tennessee troops, with Ross's Texans, were assigned to the command of General Jackson. And, as under this arrangement Colonel McCulloch necessarily lost the command of a brigade after having exercised it so long with distinguished efficiency,* his regiment, the famous Second Missouri Cavalry, was excluded from either brigade or divisional association and constituted a special scouting force, receiving orders direct from Forrest's headquarters. These and other orders, devised for the thorough organization of his resources—including the Mississippi Militia†—upon the most effective footing possible, were promptly matured and issued. Indeed, nothing calculated to that end appears to have been overlooked. But meanwhile, he had been promoted to the grade of Lieutenant-General.‡

Before the middle of March, Chalmers's Division was organized with an effective aggregate of 4500,§ divided into three

---

* He had been many times recommended for promotion since early in 1862—that is, by all his commanders. Colonel Bell was promoted about this time, and Brigadier-Generals Starke and Campbell having joined, there was no longer a brigade command vacant.

† Composed of classes of citizens not subject to military duty under the conscription laws of the Confederate States.

‡ Commission dated 28th of February, 1865.

§ Up to the 17th of March, Chalmers was at Columbus, Miss., and Buford at Monte Vallo, Ala.

brigades, commanded respectively by Brigadier-Generals F. C. Armstrong, Wirt Adams, and Peter B. Starke. Jackson also had his division in shape, about 3800 strong, the Tennessee brigades of Generals T. H. Bell and Alexander W. Campbell being increased to 3200 rank and file. As yet, Buford had not been able to organize his division. Roddy's force, which was to constitute an important part of it, was necessarily detached, and actively on duty in North-Alabama, watching the movements of a heavy Federal cavalry force, accumulated just across the Tennessee river, at Gravelly Springs. The other two brigades, (Alabamians,) Clanton's and Armstead's, constituting his command, were likewise detached, guarding one of the then threatened flanks or approaches to Mobile.

During this period, thus mainly occupied—from the first of January to the middle of March—with the cares of reorganization, numerous hostile demonstrations had taken place upon the outskirts of the territory intrusted to General Forrest, and as many counter movements on his side were made ; but in each instance the enemy recoiled without a collision. Meanwhile, also remaining at Verona until the 1st of March, he had then transferred his headquarters to West-Point, forty-two miles southward, on the line of the Mobile and Ohio Railroad.

In the interval the Federal authorities had not been inactive. The cavalry in Middle Tennessee, to the number of 22,000, had been collected in cantonments about Gravelly Springs and Waterloo, just northward, as we have indicated, of the Tennessee river, near favorable points for the passage of that stream, for piercing either the heart of Alabama or Mississippi. Formed into five divisions, Major-General James Wilson was in command of this formidable force. A distinguished graduate of the West-Point Military Academy, and standing very high as a cavalry officer with his superiors, Wilson had devoted himself to the drill, organization, and discipline of his corps. Instituting "a thorough system of instruction," he used every effort to bring this splendid body of horse into the highest possible state of efficiency and mobility.* His men all in hand, the vast resources of the arsenals and supply depots of the United States were at his easy disposition, and so he was left free to give his thoughts and care exclusively to the military mould-ing of his force. His adversary, on the other hand, had his means, as we have seen, scattered over at least two great States, Alabama and Mississippi. He had to recruit his regiments, to disperse his men to procure remounts, and secure cloth-ing, to glean the lean Confederate arsenals and armories for weapons and ammunition, to watch a long frontier bristling with foes ; in sooth, not only to mould resources into effective form, but in great part to create them.

In February, however, one of Wilson's Divisions was de-tached for service elsewhere, but he was left with 17,000 men, 5000 of whom, it appears, were without horses.† Those mounted, about twelve thousand strong, constituted three divisions, under Generals McCook, Long, and Upton. Mean-while, Canby had commenced his operations for the reduction of Mobile. And on the 18th of March, General Wilson threw his three mounted divisions, with about 1500 dismounted men, to the south side of the Tennessee at Chickasaw Station, on the Memphis and Charleston Railroad, with the immediate object of making a diversion in behalf of the operations against Mobile, by penetrating deep into Ala-bama. Four days later, accordingly, he set out from Chicka-saw upon his expedition, invested by General Grant with the widest range of discretion in his operations. His equipage included a pontoon-train of fifty wagons ; otherwise, he moved

---

* *Vide* Andrews's History of the Campaign of Mobile, p. 243.
† *Vide* Andrews.

with not more than 250 supply and baggage-wagons. But each man carried five days' "light rations" in his haversack, and on his horse twenty-four pounds of grain, 100 rounds of ammunition, and a pair of extra horse-shoes. Five days' rations of hard bread and ten severally of sugar, coffee, and salt were carried, moreover, on pack animals.

As we have said, Roddy had been in watchful observation of this force for some time, and so wary a soldier as Forrest had not failed to hold it under constant surveillance. He was therefore promptly informed of Wilson's movement upon Chickasaw, and of his departure for that point.

In anticipation of it, however, Chalmers, as early as the 17th of March, had been ordered to establish himself with Armstrong's and Starke's Brigades (3200 strong) at Pickersville, Alabama, the other brigade of the division (Wirt Adams's) at the moment being on the march to Columbus, from Jackson, Mississippi. Bell's and Campbell's Brigades—some 3200 men —were at West-Point.* Therefore, 6400 men, with such force as Buford might assemble, were all that Forrest could rely on to confront his adversary, as it was thought essential to leave Adams's Brigade to guard the line of the Mobile and Ohio Railroad. Having duly communicated to General Taylor tidings of the dangerous expedition afield in his department, that officer, on the 24th, telegraphed orders to Forrest to concentrate his available forces upon Selma, the supposed objective of the enemy.

Meanwhile, both Chalmers and Jackson had for some days been held in readiness to move at "*six hours' notice*," and on the 25th Armstrong's Brigade and a battery were put in motion for Selma. The next day Chalmers's other brigade, (Starke's,) and Bell's and Campbell's Brigades, of Jackson's Division, were likewise ordered to march in the same di-

---

* Ross's Brigade was still at Corinth.

rection—Jackson's command moving first upon Monte Vallo, about fifty miles from Selma, and forty eastward of Tuscaloosa, important as the centre of a number of iron mines and foundries, worked for the Confederate Ordnance Department. On the 27th, Forrest also set out for the theatre of impending operations. At Columbus he learned, through scouts, that it was manifest the Federal column was aiming for Monte Vallo. This he at once reported to his superior, General Taylor, by telegraph, and urged the concentration of all possible resources for the defense of Selma. Directing Jackson now to press forward to Tuscaloosa with the utmost celerity, Forrest set out for the same point on the morning of the 28th, and reached there in a ride of thirty hours. There he learned definitely of the movement toward Monte Vallo. Again communicating with General Taylor, he reported his movements and dispositions.

In the mean while, the enemy, with 13,000 horse, 1500 infantry, and three batteries, had taken two lines of march ; Upton's Division the most eastern, through Russellville to Saunders's Ferry on the west fork of the Black Warrior river ; the other two—long in advance with the pontoon-train—following the road toward Tuscaloosa. General Wilson, on the 27th, was at Jasper, and there hearing of Chalmers's movement, apprehending that it portended a concentration of Forrest's Cavalry to meet him, he at once stripped to his pack-train and artillery, and ordered his three divisions to move in light order, with all haste, by way of Elyton, to Monte Vallo, leaving the wagon-trains to follow. He was at that place on the 30th, and there detached Croxton's Brigade—McCook's Division—to hasten to Tuscaloosa to burn the University,* and the military stores accumulated there.

---

* A military organization had been given to this University, but that assuredly did not warrant the order to burn the buildings, and it was a savage act, unworthy of civilized war. See Andrews, p. 246.

It was Upton's Division that, flooring the railroad bridge near Hillsboro, crossed the stream then, and pushing on, approached Monte Vallo, late on the evening of the 30th, when he encountered Generals Dan Adams and Roddy.   Several days previously, General Roddy, having been ordered by General Taylor to hasten southward with his command to meet a hostile force moving northward from Pensacola against Montgomery, had already been thrown across the Alabama river at Selma, when the order was countermanded, and his destination changed to Monte Vallo, to report to General Adams.   Recrossing the river, and making a forced march of fifty miles, he reached the scene just in time to meet Upton's Division, with his petty force, a little northward of Monte Vallo. Overborne by numbers, after a sharp rencounter, Adams and Roddy were driven back through the place, and the Federal Commander was enabled to execute the purpose which had led him thither—the destruction of four iron-furnaces, a rolling-mill, and five collieries in the neighborhood. On the 31st, the other two Federal divisions arrived, and also General Wilson, in person.

The Confederates, meanwhile, having rallied, had reappeared before the place as the Federal Commander reached the scene. Upton's Division was at once thrown out to engage them, and a keen collision ensued.   Greatly inferior in numbers, the Confederates were soon worsted, and driven southward, toward Randolph, to the " Six Mile Creek," where Roddy, being reënforced by Crossland's small brigade of Kentuckians, and the ground being rather favorable, a stand was made. As Crossland came up, he threw his little force gallantly across the road down which the Federals were pressing strenuously, and presently, taking the offensive, he charged, in turn, half a mile, thus gaining a good position at a bridge, which he was able to hold against several vigorous attempts to dislodge him, and until at length he was about to be turned on both flanks.   Then, sending his horses rearward, Crossland fell

back slowly on foot, as the enemy pressed hotly after, receiving, however, at least one galling fire from Crossland's deadly
rifles. The situation was one of extreme peril, but as the
ground—a thick pine wood—was favorable, he, with equal
skill and resolution, kept a steady front to the enemy of half
his men at a time for several miles, while the other half would
fall back, re-form, and await the enemy in its turn. The Federals charged, by regiments, with much spirit and vigor, but
were met with a courage and tenacity that has never been
exceeded. Crossland, originally reduced to about 600 rank
and file, now finding that he was rapidly dwindling away by
the casualties of the conflict, attempted to remount ; this being observed, the enemy charged upon the Kentuckians while
thus engaged, and some captures resulted, making his losses
in killed, wounded, and prisoners, a little over 100 men. The
rest of his command he was able to lead safely away from the
field. Meanwhile, General Roddy had rallied or massed the
greater part of his brigade a short distance northward of Randolph, and there Crossland joined him.

During this time, Forrest was rapidly riding across the
country from Centreville toward Monte Vallo, with his staff and
escort, some seventy-five in number, and it so happened he
came within sight of this road, just where the conflict we have
related had been fought, and he observed that it was filled
with Federal cavalry, at a rapid trot moving southward. Ever
swift and daring in his measures, he determined to avail himself of a favorable conformation of the ground to make a dash
at the hostile column, great as was the disparity. Accordingly,
forming his little following—upon each man of whom he could
rely—into a column of fours, when within fifty yards of the
road he charged boldly from his covert into the moving mass,
and broke through. Turning, he now dashed upon the fragment northward of him, and drove it rearward for half a mile.
But there his adversary stood drawn up in a heavy line of
battle to receive him. Changing his direction at once to the

southward at a charging pace, he now found the road strewn with signs of a recent battle, including some fifteen or twenty dead Federals and some ten or twelve of Crossland's Kentuckians ; moreover, having also captured several prisoners, he learned that there had been a good deal of fighting in that quarter, and that General Wilson was already southward of him, pressing Roddy and Crossland back toward Selma.   In his own little affair he had lost three men, and being in the very midst of the whole Federal force with now less than 75 men, it was incumbent upon him to withdraw, and find his way speedily to the main body of his force southward.   Making a slight detour from the line of the road, after a rapid ride of six or eight miles, he succeeded in finding Roddy and Crossland, about ten o'clock at night, confronting the enemy near Randolph.

Informed of the situation and of the occurrences of the day, he dispatched an order to Jackson—supposed to be at Scottsville—to move swiftly across to Centreville, and, throwing his division upon Wilson's right flank, harass him as much as possible, after which to effect a junction before they were forced back into Selma.   Again reporting the situation to General Taylor at Selma, Forrest repeated his recommendation of a general concentration for the defense of Selma, and inquired the present locality of Chalmers's Division.   The answer being that Chalmers was then at Plantersville, about twenty miles southward of Randolph, Forrest requested—by telegraph—that the division should at once be dispatched to his aid in the direction of Randolph, so that he might delay the enemy as long as possible, and secure time, both for the concentration of troops for the final defense of Selma, and the removal of stores from that depot.

During the night of the 31st, the enemy remained quietly in front of Randolph ; but they had intercepted dispatches both from Jackson and Captain Anderson, of Forrest's staff, which divulged to General Wilson the plans of his adversary, the scattered disposition, at the moment, of the Confederate forces, and the weakness of Forrest's command, then immediately in his front. Jackson, as he ascertained from these dispatches, was still westward of the Cahawba, moving toward Centreville. Already he had come in collision with Croxton, and was expecting another conflict. Wilson, therefore, cognizant of the small available force in his path, detached McCook with another brigade to seek to form a junction with Croxton and occupy Jackson, while he would press directly for Selma with his other divisions, still at least 9000 strong.

To meet this force, Forrest had now little over 1500 men, portions of Roddy's and Crossland's Brigades, and some raw militia that had been in garrison at Monte Vallo under General Dan Adams.

At sunrise, on the 1st of April, the enemy were promptly in their saddles, Wilson now, as we have said, fully conscious of the extreme weakness of any enemy he could possibly encounter. The Confederates, of course, retired, but in the course of the next eight or ten miles there was some spirited skirmishing with the Federal advance, which several times was checked by Forrest and his escort, and portions of Roddy's and Crossland's commands. Giving General Taylor telegraphic intelligence of his inability to make substantial head against Wilson with his present force, about twelve M., Forrest learned, to his chagrin, from Captain Goodman, of Chalmers's staff, near Maplesville Station, that that officer was not southward, on the Plantersville road, as had been reported, but was really northward, moving by another road to the left hand. Couriers were accordingly dispatched hurriedly in all probable directions, to find Chalmers, and guide him to a junction in front of Selma, at the expense, if needful, of his train and artillery. Several hours later, a dispatch from General Chalmers himself, announced his exertions to reach a point southward (Dixie Station) as soon as his horses would enable him. Having learned, meanwhile, from General Adams, that there was a strong defensive position some four miles southward, that officer was directed to fall back and occupy it with the artillery and the main body of Roddy's, Crossland's, and his own men. Forrest then threw himself across the path of the enemy with his escort and 100 of the Kentuckians, resolved to dispute every inch of the ground, to gain time for Adams to get into position and arrange for its defense. For several miles did he boldly grapple with the Federal advance, constantly checking it by a series of charges of characteristic audacity, and only falling back when the numbers brought up were overpowering. But by four P.M., he had been forced to fall back upon Adams, where he hoped for a junction also with Chalmers.

The position was, in fact, very favorable for defense. Bogler's creek, with rugged banks, intersected the railroad and highway, forming a narrow valley rightward of the former, with steep, wooded hills commanding the several approaches from Randolph and Maplesville. On these ridges the Confederates were drawn up — Roddy's Brigade immediately astride the highway, supporting the artillery, which swept both the road from Randolph and the one from Maplesville ; on his left lay Crossland, and on his right Adams with the remains of the State troops, and a small infantry battalion from Selma, resting rightward on Mulberry creek. They did not exceed in all 1350 men, and to these now Forrest added about 150 officers and men, making a force of scarcely 1500 men, and six guns.

About four P.M., the enemy—Long's Division—came up, and promptly and resolutely assailed the right of Roddy's position with a mounted battalion, (Seventeenth Indiana,) with drawn sabres. It was handsomely done, and the Confederates were thrown into a good deal of confusion, giving way in disorder. Forrest, observing the disaster, dashed upon the scene with his staff, and, assisting Generals Roddy and Adams, succeeded in reëstablishing their lines, while a number of the enemy were left on the ground either killed or wounded. Having thus restored the integrity of his lines in that quarter, Forrest returned to where his artillery was posted.

During this time the other Federal division—Upton's—guided by the sounds of battle, had been rapidly approaching by the Maplesville road. Previously, Forrest had thrown forward that indomitable, hard fighter, Lieutenant Nathan Boon, of his escort, with ten men, to reconnoitre, and presently the shrill clangor of a bugle was heard beyond an old field in front of the Confederate position, and, soon after, Boon and his little band dashed into sight, closely pressed by the enemy, who charged across the field in right gallant fashion in line. The Confederates now opened upon them with a destructive fire, both of canister and rifles, emptying a number of saddles. In the mean time, Upton, having come upon the scene rightward, dismounted his division, and pressed up to the attack upon the Confederate right. There were the militia, and they could not be made to stand, but fell back in confusion. The left had held their position successfully, but there was now imminent risk of being turned and cut off from the ford of Dixie creek; Forrest therefore ordered his line withdrawn to secure that crossing. This being observed, doubtless, by the enemy, a vigorous charge by platoons was made, to meet which Forrest had at the moment available only his famous escort and staff and the section of Adams's artillery. From the latter, one discharge was secured, but, seeing that the infantry support had gone, the artillerists abandoned their guns in position, and retreated abruptly. On came the Federal cavalry, with their sabres drawn, when Forrest sprang to meet them with his escort; but he was swept back into the woods about fifty yards by the overwhelming stress of numbers; and such was the momentum of the Federal charge, that one of their horses, striking squarely against the wheel of a piece, broke every spoke, and split his own breast open. A single artillerist had remained staunchly at that piece; gathering a handspike from the trail, with one blow he dashed out the brains of the overthrown trooper, and knocked another from his seat, after which feat, shouldering his handspike, he deliberately made his way rearward.

By this time, five P.M., General Forrest, his staff, and escort were engaged in a hand-to-hand *mêlée* with the enemy, and the General became involved in one of those personal rencounters that have marked his life, and his escapes from which appear incredible. He was set upon by four troopers in the road at one moment. Shooting one, the others dashed down upon him with uplifted sabres, which he attempted to parry with his revolver, but received several slight wounds and bruises, both on his head and arm. Three others came up, meanwhile, and took part, so that actually as many as six troopers were either attempting to sabre or shoot him. By this time the hammer of his pistol had been hacked away, so that the weapon was useless, while his right arm was sorely weakened by the many blows which had fallen upon it. His staff and escort could not help him ; for all, at the moment, were strenuously engaged in the like personal combats. On either hand the roadway was hedged by a dense, impenetrable thicket, and rearward was choked by a two-horse wagon, which barred his escape in that direction, while his enemies filled the road frontward, fiercely cutting and shooting at him. Escape, indeed, seemed hopeless ; for, as if to render it utterly so, his horse was now severely wounded by a pistol-ball in the thigh. But it was not the habit of the man to look upon aught as hopeless. Wheeling his horse toward the wagon, giving him the spur fiercely, and lifting him with the bridle, the brave animal rose into the air, and surmounted the obstacle at the bound, going some thirty steps before he was halted, and Forrest turned to survey the field. Scarcely had he done so, when he was charged by a Federal officer, who lunged at him with his sabre ; but Forrest parried the thrust with his other pistol, which he had been able to draw, and, firing, killed his resolute adversary.* By this time, however, those whom he had eluded by his desperate leap over the wagon had contrived to pass it, and were again upon him ; but Colonel M. C. Galloway (of Memphis) and Dr. Jones, of his staff, by this time had come to the aid of their imperiled chief, and, firing, had each put an adversary *hors de combat.* Forrest killed yet another, and Galloway, wounding still another, took him prisoner. Meanwhile, the escort, fighting with their usual fearless prowess, had first checked and then driven their enemy back, which discovered by the few who survived, they retreated precipitately, leaving him and his intrepid party masters of the field. The enemy had used the sabre almost exclusively. Forrest and his staff were armed, each with two navy revolvers, and the men with Spencer rifles as well as pistols. It was a contest of sabres with firearms, in a thick wood, with the odds of four to one against the Confederates. Forrest, Lieutenant Boon, and five of his men only were wounded, while some thirty of the enemy were killed and as many as sixty were left in hospital, near by, badly wounded.

The caissons had been carried off, but it was necessary to abandon the section of artillery to the enemy, as Forrest fell back across the creek. Previously, likewise, some 200 of the State troops and infantry had also fallen into their possession.

This stand and combat which we have related, would not have been undertaken but for the supposition that General Chalmers, from his reported short distance from the ground, would be able to bring his division up in time to enable Forrest to profit by the favorable character of the position to make a prolonged, effective resistance there. But Chalmers, untowardly diverted and retarded by conflicting orders, and bad roads and swamps across his route, had really gone toward Marion with Starke's Brigade.

---

* Captain Taylor. *Vide* Andrews, p. 250.

Adams's men were now utterly demoralized, and many too, of Roddy's were dashing rearward toward Selma, with little or no organization ; meanwhile, the enemy were persistently pressing after.   But Forrest still interposed his staff and escort across their path, and again a squadron, apparently, was launched upon him ; but standing at bay, they were repelled and driven back across a creek.   Roddy, meanwhile, having gathered some three or four hundred of his best men, was ordered to cover the rear as long as practicable.   By this time, Forrest's wounds had become very painful, and he rode with his staff and escort rapidly to Plantersville.   General Adams was there, and had succeeded in again embodying the mass of the Confederates.   But, unluckily, Chalmers was not there. Scarcely had General Forrest had time to telegraph General Taylor the present state of affairs, before the eager enemy appeared, and, without halting, dashed down upon the Confederates, who at the instant, for the most part, were occupied drawing forage and subsistence from the stores accumulated there.   Straightway the panic was general, there was mounting in hot haste, and the larger portion made off, as fast as their horses could carry them, to Selma.   But around Forrest rallied his matchless escort, each one as doughty as any Paladin of story, and with them he quickly sallied forward.   Presently, a short but most spirited engagement took place, which, thanks to the virtue of the Spencer (repeater) rifle in the sure, steady hands of that sturdy band, resulted in forcing the Federals to retire upon their main force about sunset.

Apprehensive that Roddy and the rear-guard had been captured, after a brief conference with Adams, Forrest directed that officer to fall back, that night, to Selma, with such forces as could be collected, while he would go in quest of Chalmers with his escort, now reduced to not more than forty men, by courier and other detached service, and casualties.

Taking the road toward Marion, some five miles from Plantersville, Forrest was relieved somewhat by coming upon Roddy and his detachment, seeking their way toward Selma, after having been pressed off the road by the enemy. Later, about eleven P.M., he also met Armstrong, with his brigade at a halt, awaiting Chalmers, who, he reported, was still six or eight miles distant, impeded by a swamp and some bad streams across his road. Armstrong was now ordered to hasten to Selma, and Colonel Thomas W. White was dispatched to find Chalmers, with orders to press in the same direction with Starke's Brigade, even though he had to leave his artillery behind. These measures having been taken, at two P.M., the 2d of April, the Confederate General, suffering acutely from his hurts, and worn down with fatigue, halted, and gave his escort opportunity for several hours of rest, and to feed their hungry horses.

We must now turn to the movements, meanwhile, of the divisions of Chalmers and Jackson, so far at least as may shed light upon the causes which hindered a timely concentration of all Confederate defensive resources across the path of Wilson. Armstrong's Brigade, as will be recollected, moved on the 26th day of March, two days ahead of the other brigade (Starke's) of Chalmers's Division ; but he was overtaken by General Chalmers and staff at Greensboro on the 28th, having been detained in the passage of the Black Warrior. At Marion, in consequence of an order from General Forrest prescribing concentration, Armstrong was halted, and Starke's Brigade was ordered thither. The country is one of great fertility, abounding, at the time, in large, highly improved plantations, handsome houses, with pretty villages, and had never been visited or seared by any of the material ills of the war. Little accustomed to see soldiers, the people received Forrest's Cavalry with a boundless hospitality, and made their reception and stay very pleasant ; an unwonted holiday and relaxation from the toils which were their usual lot. Meanwhile, the country was full of rumors of the movements of the enemy. Starke's Brigade came up on the afternoon of the 30th, and that night an order was received from General Taylor, at eleven o'clock, to move upon Plantersville. The Cahawba, after some unavoidable delay in the construction of the pontoon-bridge, was crossed late in the afternoon of the 31st. But swamps and wretched roads made General Chalmers diverge from his projected line of march toward Randolph, and seek practicable roads for his artillery and trains, escorted by Starke's Brigade, Armstrong's Brigade having become detached on the 1st of April.

Jackson's Division, moving on the route assigned it, had encountered Croxton, eight miles north of Scottsville, and, after a sharp fight, dispersed that brigade, capturing a number of prisoners, several stands of colors, one hundred and fifty horses, and Croxton's papers ; but, as the bridge over the Cahawba, near Centreville, was burned by the enemy under McCook, with whom he also had a skirmish, he was unable to pass that stream in time to throw the weight of his splendid division into the unequal scales. Thus, with three of his choicest, largest brigades absent or beyond his control, the morning of the 2d of April dawned upon General Forrest. But, meanwhile, he was riding swiftly, with his faithful escort, toward Selma, where he arrived at ten A.M. He found the place in wild confusion, not unnatural, perhaps, in view of the serious dangers impending. Long trains of cars, freighted with stores and prisoners, were being dispatched toward Demopolis. Steamers at the landing were being loaded with other stores and freight of all descriptions, to be sent up the river to Montgomery ; the streets were thronged with wagons and drays, laden with boxes, barrels, and parts of machinery, and rapidly driven in different directions. Troopers, too, rode hither and thither, seeking their commands and officers. General Taylor, the Department Commander, was still there, but on the eve of departure, by rail, with a train of ordnance and subsistence supplies, for Demopolis.

Selma is upon the west bank of the Alabama river, and

stands upon a bluff nearly one hundred feet above high-water level. There were established one of the chief arsenals of construction and depots of the Confederate States, embracing ordnance foundries for the army and navy. Therefore, the place was extensively fortified by a double line of works, the exterior of which was upon a trace of nearly four miles, which enveloped the town upon all sides save the river-front. These works were of strong profile, and well arranged with bastions, proper ditches, and strongly palisaded at many points ; but they required for their proper defense a very large garrison, one far larger than was now available, as Forrest was satisfied, after taking a careful survey, and the resources at hand for holding them. Nevertheless, as the chief command devolved upon him by the departure of General Taylor at two P.M., he made his dispositions for the attempt, hopeless as it seemed. Armstrong's Brigade, about 1400 strong, was stationed to hold the lines on the left and west, his men being deployed at intervals of ten feet, in order to cover the whole ground assigned the brigade. Roddy's men, and such other forces as were in the place, in all some 1700, rank and file, were disposed in the same extended manner to the right of Armstrong, filling the centre and eastern portion of the line.

The enemy had bivouacked nineteen miles distant, at Plantersville. Taking the field at daylight' that morning, they began to skirmish with the Confederates as early as two P.M., and kept it up until four, when they had completely invested the position, making it impracticable for Jackson and Chalmers now to enter the place. Meanwhile, Forrest had ascertained not only the weakness of his garrison, but likewise that the artillery had been left with a small supply of ammunition, and not one charge of either grape or canister.* Hav-

---

* For example, two of the principal *of General Forrest and Captain Good-* batter es, with twenty rounds of am- *man.* munition and mainly solid shot.—*Notes.*

ing also opened telegraphic communication with General Buford, he found that that officer had not been ordered thither with his disposable forces, and therefore gave the order.

In the interval, under cover of the light skirmishing kept up, as we have mentioned, since two P.M., General Wilson had made his dispositions with decision and celerity. Confident of success, and appreciating the value of the prize almost within his grasp, his approaches were yet made with special care, to avoid the exposure of his men to any profitless, needless loss. An extensive wood in front of Armstrong's position was favorable for this end.

About five P.M., a piece of artillery on the extreme (Armstrong's) left opened upon the Federals, who were forming for an assault in that quarter. Soon, too, all of Armstrong's artillery opened upon similar forces in their front ; and presently the enemy, bringing up a battery to a favorable ridge, replied with spirit, but their projectiles, flying high, did no harm. For a while they appeared little disposed to come to close quarters ; but at half-past five, three strong lines of battle were pushed forward to the assault, not only of Armstrong's position, but of the Confederates on his right. As we have mentioned, the Confederate artillery was not provided with proper ammunition, and despite all the fire that was opened upon the advancing Federal lines, they moved up steadily and handsomely to their work. They were armed with Spencer rifles, repeaters, and breech-loaders ;* and from their massive lines poured out an unceasing stream of leaden hail, to which the return fire of the attenuated Confederate line was as that of a skirmish detachment to the uproar of a battle at its climax.

Forrest had rapidly repaired to the scene where the assault

---

* The Spencer rifle discharges seven loads in quick succession, and is then reloaded in less time than an ordinary rifle.

was most strenuous. Meanwhile, the militia began to falter and gradually quit their places behind the breastworks, leav﹋ ing broad gaps, and Armstrong's right exposed. Roddy was therefore directed to move over and fill the breach; but before it could be effected, the enemy had reached the exposed, de· serted section of the lines, and surmounted it, cutting Roddy and Armstrong in sunder. Turning leftward, they opened an enfilading fire upon Armstrong, who had repulsed three at- tacks upon his front, with severe loss to his immediate assailants. At this, however, Armstrong was forced to withdraw his bri- gade, which having to do under a heavy fire, his loss was very heavy. The last to leave their position were the First Mis- sissippi (Pinson's) Cavalry. Standing stoutly their ground, the enemy were in their rear before they fell back, and their gallant Colonel and a large part of his regiment were taken prisoners. In the mean time, the militia had thrown away their arms, and were swiftly seeking their horses, and divest- ing themselves, as they fled, of all that would betray their late connection with the defense of Selma. The scene generally was one of the wildest confusion. The Confederates, beaten from the breastworks, were rushing toward their horses; in the town the streets were choked with horses, with soldiers and citizens hurrying wildly to and fro. Clouds of dust rose and so filled the air, that it was difficult to distinguish friend from foe. From the houses came the wails and lamentations of terrified women and children, about to be left to the mercies of a storming enemy. The Federals were still firing upon their routed, fleeing adversary.

Further resistance upon a field so utterly lost, indeed as soon as the enemy appeared in such overpowering force before it, was now worse than useless. But what avenue of escape was there left open? For the broad Alabama river as effectu- ally closed the way in that quarter, as the enemy did appa- rently on all other sides. While Armstrong, who throughout the fight had led his men with the most signal gallantry, gathered some of Ashcraft's Regiment around him, and continued to skirmish with the enemy as he fell back into the town, Forrest, assembling his staff and escort, sallied forth from Selma, by the Montgomery road, upon which, happily as yet, there was no hostile force to bar his egress. Armstrong soon followed, with a like sturdy band around him, but mistaking the road, became enveloped in a bend of the river, where, having been closely pursued, he effected his escape by cutting his way out with forty or fifty followers.

Thus Selma fell, and with it the last important arsenal of construction belonging to the Southern people remained in the possession of General Wilson, and the main purpose for which that General had taken the field was accomplished,—just as the illustrious, the "incomparable" army of North-Virginia was forced to abandon its long-held lines at Petersburg, and enter upon a dogged, hopeless, fatal retreat along the valley of the Appomattox, to that field whereon, seven days later, it finally stacked the arms so long borne with such affluence of glory, furled the colors that it had made all-famous, and, quenching its camp-fires forever, practically brought to a close the manful, heroic struggle of the Southern people for a separate national existence and political institutions of their own choice.

Forrest, as we have said, taking the road along the west bank of the Alabama river, some three miles from Selma, across the highway by which the Federal force had approached, suddenly heard in the stillness of the night, the cries of women in distress. Guided by the sound, he and some of his men dashed thither to find a neighboring house in the possession of four Federal "bummers," who, after having rifled it of all jewelry and other portable valuables, were engaged in the effort to outrage the women who lived there. Summary was the fate of these wretches. The escort were now greatly excited and provoked by the incident, and those in the advance-guard, meeting a number of these fellows, loaded down with plunder, did not hesitate to slay them on the spot.

Hearing the sounds of what was happening ahead, Forrest, to check it, took the conduct of the advance himself. Presently capturing a picket-party, he learned that it belonged to a small squadron of the Fourth Regulars, encamped near by, rearward, which he determined to surprise and capture also, small as was his own force. Meanwhile, learning from the picket, also, that there was a scouting party in the neighborhood detached from the same squadron, he dispatched a part of the escort in their quest, with speedy success; for they were soon found, a little distance from the road, and taken without resistance, burdened with articles of jewelry, plate, and the like, from the neighboring houses. Encumbered with prisoners who had to be guarded, he had only about thirty men left disposable for the surprise of the squadron we have mentioned, reported over fifty strong. Nevertheless, he was not diverted from his purpose; but as they approached its immediate vicinity, Captain Jackson, the commander of his escort, stated to him that he was requested on the part of the men to say, they would not attack the enemy if their General led them; for in a night attack he would be exposed to danger which they were altogether unwilling he should incur at that time; that if he would remain where he was, they would cheerfully execute his orders. To this wish of men who had served him so long with superb devotion and valor, Forrest properly acceded, and, halting by the wayside, directed Captain Jackson to do the work in hand, their prey being less than a quarter of a mile distant. Presently Jackson was close upon his adversary without being observed, but then a Federal soldier, springing up, fired his pistol. The escort rushed upon the enemy, as, startled by their comrade, they rose from their blankets and caught up their arms. An animated fight resulted, which was brought to a close in a few minutes, however, by the complete success of the Confederates, thirty-five of the enemy being either killed or wounded, and five captured, with the loss on the other side of only one man wounded,

Rapidly resuming his march, in the course of the next eight miles, they met and captured some more of the plundering "bummers," so that the fruits of the night's operations were at least sixty, either killed, wounded, or captured.

Reaching Plantersville early on the next morning, Forrest here found in a hospital one hundred Federals who had been brought thither by the enemy after their affair with him at Dixie Station, on the 1st of April. Here, too, he halted until three o'clock in the afternoon, to give his jaded men and animals food and rest. Then, retaking his line of retreat toward Marion, scarcely had he gone a mile when he came in collision with the advance of the Federal brigade which had been detached some days previously under General McCook. After their old fashion, the escort promptly charged upon the adversary in their road, and killed, wounded, and captured at least twenty; but further combat was altogether too unequal to be adventured, and Forrest swiftly withdrew by the left flank through the woods. It was now four P.M., and, pushing on all night—crossing the Cahawba river—he reached Marion at ten A.M. on the 4th. Forrest and his band had now been in their saddles, with little intermission, for seven days and nights, with the scantiest fare for men or horses; and all were so greatly worn down that rest and sleep were essential. Here, too, he found Jackson's Division, Chalmers with Starke's Brigade, and the entire train and artillery intact that he had brought from Mississippi.

For the week following, Forrest remained with this force in that vicinity, reassembling so many of his command as had escaped from Selma; and, notwithstanding the inauspicious aspect of affairs, he set to work with characteristic activity to place his own command in condition for service by recruiting, and exchanging his horses and mules, while at the same time closely guarding the line of the Cahawba from Marion to its mouth. Then, on the 15th, establishing his headquarters at Gainesville, he withdrew his force to that quarter. It was here that Northern newspapers began to give the particulars of the surrender of General Lee's army at Appomattox Court-House ; and, presently, the fall of Mobile, followed soon by telegraphical intelligence — about the 25th — that General Johnston had opened negotiations with General Sherman for the final cessation of hostilities. All had now to see that the end was near at hand ; the end of toilsome marches ; the end of night-watches ; the end of fierce battles with an enemy always superior in numbers ; the end of years of hardship and peril ; but alas! the end also of all the proud hopes, which had inspired them throughout, of political independence. So soon as this was comprehended, the deepest anxiety seized upon the men to get home once more, and numbers did not await the last moment, but went off of their own accord. Thus stood affairs on the 9th of May.* General Taylor having previously completed negotiations with General Canby for the cessation of hostilities by the Confederate forces of his department on the same terms as had been stipulated between Generals Johnston and Sherman, on that day Brigadier-General E. S. Dennis reached Gainesville as the Federal Commissioner to execute the proper paroles. General Jackson was appointed a Commissioner on the part of the Confederates to authenticate muster-rolls and other necessary papers, and the work of paroling began ; and in this manner : muster-rolls, in duplicates, of each general and his staff; of each regimental staff; of each quartermaster and commis-

---

* General Croxton, after having destroyed the factories at Tuscaloosa, moving westward, sought to strike and break up the Mobile and Ohio Railroad from Columbus to Meridian. But General Wirt Adams, left at West-Point by Forrest to guard that road, threw himself with about the same force across Croxton's path, near Sipsey river, and, after a warm combat of about one hour, the Federals were beaten back, with the loss of about one hundred killed, wounded, and captured. Adams pursued for some thirty or forty miles, but without securing any other material advantage. *This was the last engagement of the war east of the Mississippi.*

sary, and their employés ; and of each company, were made, and a copy furnished each Commissioner.   To each non-commissioned officer and private was then issued a certificate of parole, bearing the number opposite their names, respectively, upon the muster-rolls, and signed by the two Commissioners.

The officers, however, were required to sign duplicate obligations, as follows :

" I, the undersigned, prisoner of war, belonging to the Army of the Department of Alabama, Mississippi, and East-Louisiana, having been surrendered by Lieutenant-General R. Taylor, Confederate States Army, commanding said department, to Major-General E. R. S. Canby, United States Army, commanding Army and Division of West-Mississippi, do hereby give my solemn *parole of honor* that I will not hereafter serve in the armies of the Confederate States, or in any military capacity whatever against the United States of America, or render aid to the enemies of the latter, until properly exchanged in such manner as shall be mutually approved by the respective authorities."

This was then approved by both Commissioners, and General Dennis added his indorsement, that the officer in question would " not be disturbed by the United States authorities as *long as he observed his parole and the laws in force where he resides*."

On the same day of the arrival of General Dennis at his headquarters, General Forrest issued his address to his troops in the following language :

"HEADQUARTERS FORREST'S CAVALRY CORPS, }
GAINESVILLE, ALABAMA, May 9, 1865. }

"*Soldiers :* By an agreement made between Lieutenant-General Taylor, commanding the Department of Alabama, Mississippi, and East-Louisiana, and Major-General Canby, commanding United States forces, the troops of this Department have been surrendered.

" I do not think it proper or necessary, at this time, to refer to the causes which have reduced us to this extremity ; nor is it now a matter of material consequence to us how such results were brought about. That we are BEATEN, is a self-evident fact, and any further resistance on our part would be justly regarded as the very height of folly and rashness.

" The armies of Generals Lee and Johnston having surrendered, you are the last of all the troops of the Confederate States Army, east of the Mississippi river, to lay down your arms.

" The cause for which you have so long and so manfully struggled, and for which you have braved dangers, endured privations and sufferings, and made so many sacrifices, is to-day hopeless. The Government which we sought to establish and perpetuate is at an end. Reason dictates and humanity demands that no more blood be shed. Fully realizing and feeling that such is the case, it is your duty and mine to lay down our arms— submit to the 'powers that be'—and to aid in restoring peace and establishing law and order throughout the land.

" The terms upon which you were surrendered are favorable, and should be satisfactory and acceptable to all. They manifest a spirit of magnanimity and liberality on the part of the Federal authorities, which should be met, on our part, by a faithful compliance with all the stipulations and conditions therein expressed. As your Commander, I sincerely hope that every officer and soldier of my command will cheerfully obey the orders given, and carry out in good faith all the terms of the cartel.

" Those who neglect the terms, and refuse to be paroled, may assuredly expect, when arrested, to be sent North and imprisoned.

" Let those who are absent from their commands, from whatever cause, report at once to this place, or to Jackson, Mississippi ; or, if too remote from either, to the nearest United States post or garrison, for parole.

" Civil war, such as you have just passed through, naturally engenders feelings of animosity, hatred, and revenge. It is our duty to divest ourselves of all such feelings ; and, as far as in our power to do so, to cultivate friendly feelings toward those with whom we have so long contended, and heretofore so widely, but honestly, differed. Neighborhood feuds, personal animosities, and private differences should be blotted out ; and, when you return home, a manly, straightforward course of conduct will secure the respect even of your enemies. Whatever your responsibilities may be to government, to society, or to individuals, méet them like men.

" The attempt made to establish a separate and independent Confederation has failed ; but the consciousness of having done your duty faithfully, and to the end, will, in some measure, repay for the hardships you have undergone.

" In bidding you farewell, rest assured that you carry with you my best wishes for your future welfare and happiness. Without, in any way, referring to the merits of the cause in which we have been engaged, your courage and determination, as exhibited on many hard-fought fields, have elicited the respect and admiration of friend and foe. And I now, cheerfully and gratefully, acknowledge my indebtedness to the officers and men of my command, whose zeal, fidelity, and unflinching bravery have been the great source of my past success in arms.

" I have never, on the field of battle, sent you where I was unwilling to go myself; nor would I now advise you to a course which I felt myself unwilling to pursue. You *have been* good soldiers ; you *can be* good citizens. Obey the laws, preserve your honor, and the Government to which you have surrendered can afford to be, and will be, magnanimous.
                    " N. B. FORREST, Lieutenant-General."

The utmost eagerness now pervaded the command to procure their paroles. General Dennis, found to be a courteous gentleman, did all in his power to accelerate the work assigned, and in a manner most acceptable to his late adversaries. And by the 16th of May, about 8000 officers and men had been paroled, and allowed to return to their homes.* To that extent at least

> " For them the blooming life is sweet ;
>   Return is not for all."

Ah ! no. Thousands of their comrades, as valiant and strong of soul as ever died on the battle-field in defense of their *birthright*, after having established the proud records of their corps at Fort Donelson, Red Mound, Murfreesboro, Thompson's Station, Prairie Mound, Fort Pillow, Tishomingo, Harrisburg, and in that fearful winter retreat from Nashville, were in their graves on that day when FORREST'S CAVALRY ceased to exist.

CONCLUDING COMMENTARIES.

If by this time our readers have not been able to form a fair and just conception of the distinctive traits of General Forrest, both as a man and a cavalry commander, we have materially failed in the work we undertook, and it were needless now to attempt to make amends by a wordy summary of what

---

* Including about 600 of Scott's Louisiana Cavalry, paroled at Gainesville.

we regard those traits to be. It may not, however, be amiss to say, that one of the lessons of his operations will be in the demonstration of the great utility in war of horses in the rapid transportation of a body of men to the field of battle or operations, there to be employed as riflemen, fighting on foot. The current of belief has been, that any advantage thus secured was more than counterbalanced by the necessary absence, during battle, of the horse-holders—about one fourth. But as Forrest handled his men, we believe it to be apparent he made his corps so effective, by the celerity and uncertainty—to the enemy—of his movements, as to add immensely to the value of mounted operations in war.

Examined closely, his operations will be found based on the soundest principles of the art of war. His tactics, intuitively, and without knowledge of what other men had done before him, were those of the great masters of that art—that is, to rush down swiftly, thunderously upon his enemy with his whole collective strength. He had the happy gift, of knowing how to confirm the courage of his men, how to excite their confidence and enthusiasm, how to bend them, the most reckless, to his iron will. In his composition there is apparent as much sagacity as audacity. Fortitude, animal courage, and vitality of body gave him energy and celerity in action, while all was guided by a judgment and circumspection rarely at fault. At critical instants he was ever quick to see, clear in his previsions, swift to decide, and swift to strike—the very embodiment assuredly of warlike vigor. With every expedition he seems to have been able to increase the influence of his resolute character upon his men, and infuse them with the like spirit.

His combats appear to have been habitually delivered or accepted at the right juncture. Exigencies were encountered with a wise audacity, and without loss of time in weighing probabilities after his preparations were made. When left to himself and to his own resources, General Forrest always prospered.

It may be justly said that no other soldier of either side, during the war—Stonewall Jackson excepted—carried the genuine, distinctive traits of the American character into their operations as did General Forrest. Ever attracted to take the shortest line toward his object, he always knew how to grasp opportunity, and was never at a loss for resources in the most sudden emergencies. Endowed by nature with as stormful, fiery a soul as ever blazed to heat and flame in any soldier, yet surely he accomplished as much by address as by swift, hard-smiting blows. A strong man of action, of sleepless temper, strenuous, aggressive, and to whom war was a killing manner of thing, nevertheless General Forrest was not the less adroit, and wary, and watchful than swift, and resolute, and indomitable in his operations. Essentially as daring a cavalry leader as ever gained distinction, it may, in fine, be said of him, in the words of Napier, that his daring was "*not a wild cast of the net for fortune*," for it was always supported by a penetration and activity that suffered no opportunity to escape.

APPENDIX.

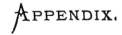

(A.)

STAFF AND REGIMENTAL ROSTERS.

THE STAFF OF GENERAL N. B. FORREST *in his several Grades and Commands.*

NAME.	Grade.	Function.	Date of Appointment.	Remarks.
*John P. Strange......	Major.....	Assist. Adjt.-Gen....	July 21, 1862...	Remained as Adjutant-General through all Gen. Forrest's promotions. Was wounded at Fort Donelson in February, 1862, near Nashville, December, 1862, and at Bolivar, Tenn., May 2d, 1864.
*Chas. W. Anderson...	1st Lieut..	Aid-de-Camp	....	Acting Assistant Adjutant and Inspector-General — acted as an effective inspector through all General Forrest's commands.
*Wm. M. Forrest.....	1st Lieut..	Aid-de-Camp........	July 21, 1862..	Was an Aid-de-Camp through all General Forrest's grades.
*Samuel Donelson	1st Lieut..	Aid-de-Camp........	Jan. 10, 1862..	Was attached to staff when General Forrest became Major-General.
C. S. Severson.........	Major.....	Chief Quartermaster.	Nov. 20, 1861.	Served on General Forrest's staff until late in 1864, when he was relieved by Major Mason.
*R. M. Mason........	Major	Chief Quartermaster.	May 17, 1861.	
*G. V. Rambaut......	Major.....	Chief Commissary...	July 21, 1862..	Remained on Gen. Forrest's staff through all his promotions.
*George Dashiell.....	Captain...	Chief Paymaster....	....	Joined staff of Major-General Forrest.
*J. B. Cowan.........	Surgeon...	Chief Surgeon......	Nov. 1, 1862..	Remained as Chief Surgeon through all General Forrest's promotions.
*Charles S. Hill......	Captain...	Chief Ordnance.		
*John G. Mann.......	Captain...	Chief Engineer......	....	Joined staff in North-Mississippi in 1863.

NOTE.—The organization of the staff marked with * was formed on General Forrest's promotion to grade of Lieutenant-General, and, remaining unchanged up to the time of the surrender, was so paroled.

General Forrest was commissioned Brigadier-General July 21st, 1862, Major-General December 4th, 1863, and Lieutenant-General March 2d, 1865.

Other officers whose names are mentioned in the foregoing work served from time to time transiently but effectively on the staff of General Forrest.

STAFF OF BRIGADIER-GENERAL JAMES R. CHALMERS,* *Commanding First Division, as organized at Como, Miss., January,* 1864.

NAME.	Grade.	Function.	Date of Appointment.	Remarks.
Walter A. Goodman...	Captain...	Asst. Adjt.-Gen.....	July 31, 1862.	
L. Tunny Lindsey.....	Captain...	Act. Asst. Adjt.-Gen.	Oct. 5, 1863.	
Andrew G. Mills......	Captain...	Act. Asst. Insp.-Gen.	May —, 1863..	Relieved Febru'y 27th, 1865, by Colonel Thomas W. White, Eighth Mississippi Cavalry, and afterward (March 16th, 1865) assigned to duty as Captain of Company D, Eighteenth Mississippi (consolidated) Regiment.
George T. Banks......	1st Lieut..	Aid-de-Camp........	Feb. 13, 1862.	
Samuel O'Neill........	Captain...	Chief Quartermaster.	May 28, 1862..	Relieved September, 1864, by Major Wm. Barnewall. Barnewall was succeeded February 1st, 1865, by Major J. P. Horbach. Both assignments made by order of Secretary of War.
William F. Avent.....	Captain...	A.Q.M. and Paym'r..	May —, 1861..	Relieved February 3d, 1864, and assigned to duty at Oxford, Miss., by orders from De-'partment Headquarters. Captain Samuel O'Neill (formerly Chief Quartermaster) was assigned Chief Paymaster of Division February 1st, 1865.
John T. Buck.........	1st Lieut..	Chief Ordnance.	June 2, 1862.	
Brodie S. Crump......	Major.....	Chief Commissary ..	April 24, 1862.	
James R. Barnett......	Surgeon...	Chief Surgeon......	Sept. 25, 1861..	Relieved by orders from Department Headquarters (at his own request) November, 1864, Surgeon G. W. Henderson, Fifth Mississippi Cavalry, appointed Chief Surgeon. His health failing, Surgeon L. M. Hall succeeded February 27th, 1865.

* From MS. Notes of Captain Walter A. Goodman.
NOTE.—General Chalmers's commission bears date February 13th, 1862.

STAFF OF BRIGADIER-GENERAL A. BUFORD, *Commanding Second Division, as organized near Columbus, Miss., March,* 1864.

NAME.	Grade.	Function.	Date of Appointment.	Remarks.
Hunter Nicholson.....	Major. ...	Act. Asst. Adjt.-Gen.	Oct. 31, 1862.	
Thomas M. Crowder..	Captain...	Asst. Adjt.-Gen.	Dec. 4, 1862.	
D. A. Given..........	1st Lieut..	Act. Aid-de-Camp...		
D. E. Myers.........	1st Lieut..	Aid-de-Camp and Act. Asst. Insp.-Gen.	Aug. 1, 1863 ..	Lieutenant Myers was formerly Captain of Company E, Ninth Kentucky Cavalry, and was severely wounded in the battle of Murfreesboro, December 31st, 1862. Having to be retired in consequence, he received the appointment of Aid-de-Camp to General Buford in August, 1863.
James L. Lea........	Captain...	Chief Quartermaster.	Sept. 27, 1861..	Captain Lea was transferred to the staff of General T. H. Bell at the reorganization of Forrest's Cavalry in February, 1865.
J. R. Finch..........	Major.....	Chief Commissary.		
John D. Gardner......	1st Lieut..	Chief Ordnance.....	May 20, 1862..	Assigned from Seventh Kentucky.
Thomas F. Clardy.....	Surgeon...	Chief Surgeon.......	....	Assigned from Seventh Kentucky.
W. M. Cargill........	Major. ...	Quartermaster and Division Paym'r.		

STAFF OF BRIGADIER-GENERAL WILLIAM H. JACKSON, *Commanding Tennessee Division, as organized November,* 1864.

NAME.	Grade.	Function.	Date of Appointment.	Remarks.
E. T. Sykes..........	Captain...	Asst. Adjt.-Gen.		
James C. Jones........	1st Lieut..	Act. Asst. Adjt.-Gen.		
T. B. Sykes..........	Captain...	Asst. Insp.-Gen.		
J. Henry Martin......	1st Lieut..	Aid-de-Camp.		
W. P. Paul.	Major.....	Chief Quartermaster.		
A. P. Slover.........	Major.....	Chief Commissary.		
Arthur Bragden.......	Surgeon ..	Chief Surgeon.		
G. A. Hogg..........	Surgeon...	Asst. Chief Surgeon.		
Lewis Bond..........	Captain...	Chief Ordnance.		
John Waties..........	Captain...	Chief Artillery.		
William Ewing,.......	Lieut	Drill-Master.		

STAFF OF BRIGADIER-GENERAL TYREE H. BELL, *Commanding Bell's Brigade,* Buford's Division, Forrest's Cavalry.*

NAME.	Grade.	Function.	Date of Appointment.	Remarks.
Reuben D. Clark.	Captain...	Act. Asst. Adjt.-Gen.	Dec. 1, 1863...	Mortally wounded at Murfreesboro — December, 1864.
T. E. Richardson......	1st Lieut. and Adjt.	Act. Asst. Adjt.-Gen.	....	Was assigned to duty left vacant by death of Captain Clark, Dec. 1st, 1864.
J. L. Bell........	1st Lieut. and Adjt.	Act. Asst. Insp.-Gen.	May 8, 1864...	Mortally wounded at Tishomingo Creek, June 10th, 1864.
Pleasant A. Smith.....	1st Lieut. and Adjt.	Act. Asst. Insp.-Gen.	May 17, 1862..	On staff from Feb. 15th, 1865.
Isaac T. Bell..........	1st Lieut..	Act. Aid-de-Camp...	Feb. 15, 1864..	Severely wounded at Tishomingo creek, June 10th, 1864.
T. P. Allison..........	Major....	Act. Brigade Q. M ..	Feb. 15, 1864.	
J. L. Lea.............	Captain...	Brigade Quarterm'r..	Sept. 27, 1861.	Became Brigade Quartermaster Feb. 15th, 1865, by transfer from Gen. Buford's staff.
A. G. Harris..........	1st Lieut..	Act. Brigade Com. ..	Sept. 27, 1861..	Subsequently, from Feb. 15th, 1864, served on same staff in Adjt.-General's Department.
D. M. Wormack......	Captain...	Brigade Commissary.	Sept. 16, 1864.	
C. C. Harris..........	1st Lieut..	Ordnance Officer....	Nov. 1, 1863 ..	Apparently Brigade Commissary since Feb. 11th, 1865.

* This brigade was transferred to the division of General W. H. Jackson upon reorganizing the troops in February, 1865. *Vide* " Roster of Bell's Brigade, Jackson's Division. It was first organized March, 1864.

STAFF OF COLONEL ED. CROSSLAND, *Commanding Kentucky Brigade,* Buford's Division, Forrest's Cavalry, as organized May,* 1864.

NAME.	Grade.	Function.	Date of Appointment.	Remarks.
C. L. Randle..........	Captain...	Act. Asst. Adjt.-Gen.	Nov. 1, 1861..	Assigned from Seventh Kentucky. Wounded at Tishomingo Creek.
J. P. Matthewson.	1st Lieut..	Act. Asst. Insp.-Gen.	July 1, 1861.	
William Lindsey......	Captain...	Brigade Quarterm'r..	July 1, 1862.	Assigned from Seventh Kentucky Regiment.
J. R. Smith..........	Major.....	Brigade Commissary.	July 22, 1863.	
Robert A. Galbraith...	Captain...	Act. Aid-de-Camp...	May 30, 1861.	
F. G. Terry..........	Captain...	Act. Ord. Officer....	Sept. 22, 1861..	Assigned from Eighth Kentucky Regiment.

* This brigade was formerly commanded by the lamented Colonel A. P. Thompson, who fell in the attack on Paducah, March 25th, 1864 ; subsequently by General H. B. Lyon. General Lyon having received orders assigning him to another command in East-Tennessee or Western Virginia, Colonel Crossland succeeded to the command of the brigade.

STAFF OF COLONEL ROBERT MCCULLOCH, *Commanding First Brigade, Chalmers's Division, Forrest's Cavalry, as organized January,* 1864.

NAME.	Grade.	Function.	From what Command Assigned.	Remarks.
John T. Chandler.	Captain...	Act. Asst. Adjt.-Gen.	2d Mo. Cavalry ...	Transferred to the staff of Colonel E. W. Rucker, and Lieutenant L. L. Maughs, Bledsoe's Missouri Battery, Army of Tennessee, on detached duty with the brigade, succeeded him. Lieutenant Maughs was wounded in the engagement near West - Point, Mississippi, February, 1864.
W. J. Vankirk....	Captain...	Brigade Quarterm'r.		
J. M. Tyler.......	1st Lieut..	Act. Asst. Insp.-Gen.	Missouri Infantry..	Relieved 1864, and Lieutenant F. R. Wolffe, First Mississippi Partisans, assigned.
J. J. Guyton......	Captain...	Brigade Commissary.	1st Miss. Partisans.	
T. M. Turner.....	1st Lieut..	Act. Aid de Camp...	2d Mo. Cavalry ...	Severely wounded at Town Creek, Miss., July 14th, 1864.
J. J. Hay.........	2d Lieut..	Ordnance Officer....	Prov. Army C. S.	
F. R. Durrett.....	Surgeon...	Senior Surgeon......	2d Mo. Cavalry.	

STAFF OF COLONEL E. W. RUCKER, *Commanding Rucker's Brigade, Chalmers's Division, Forrest's Cavalry, organized September,* 1864.*

NAME.	Grade.	Function.	From whence Assigned.	Remarks.
John T. Chandler..	Captain...	Act. Asst. Adjt.-Gen.	2d Mo. Cavalry ...	Wounded at Athens, Alabama, September, 1864.
Ferdinand Stith...	Captain...	Act. Asst. Adjt.-Gen.		
John Overton, Jr..	Captain...	Act. Asst. Insp.-Gen.	McDonald's Bat'n.	
Frank B. Rodgers.	1st Lieut..	Act. Aid de Camp...	McDonald's Bat'n.	
William O. Key...	Major.....	Brigade Quarterm'r..	Prov. Army C. S.	
R. M. Ligon.......	Captain...	Brigade Commissary.		
C. K. Caruthers...	Surgeon...	Senior Surgeon......	7th Tenn. Cavalry.	
C. N. Featherston.	2d Lieut..	Ordnance Officer....	Prov. Army C. S.	

* This organization existed until the return of General Forrest's command from Middle Tennessee on the "Hood Campaign" and the reorganization of the troops early in 1865. Colonel Rucker having been wounded and captured at Nashville, and the troops reorganized into brigades with reference to States, the larger part, if not the entire command formerly constituting his brigade, were arranged under command of General Alexander W. Campbell, and placed in Jackson's (Tennessee) Division, the officers of the *personal* staff reporting to General Campbell under this arrangement.

STAFF OF COLONEL J. J. NEELY, *Commanding Neely's Brigade, Chalmers's Division, Forrest's Cavalry, as organized May, 1864.*

NAME.	Grade.	Function.	From whence Assigned.	Remarks.
V. B. Waddell....	1st Lieut..	Act. Asst. Adjt.-Gen.	12th Tenn. Cav'ry.	
Ed. Renaue.......	2d Lieut..	Act. Asst. Insp.-Gen.	12th Tenn. Cav'ry.	
M. K. Mister.....	2d Lieut..	Act. Aid de Camp.	15th Tenn. Cav'ry.	
William O. Key...	Major. ...	Brigade Quarterm'r.	Prov. Army C. S.	
S. J. Alexander...	Major. ...	Brigade Commissary.	Prov. Army C. S.	
C. K. Caruthers...	Surgeon...	Senior Surgeon.	7th Tenn. Cavalry.	

STAFF OF BRIGADIER-GENERAL ALEXANDER W. CAMPBELL, *Commanding Campbell's Brigade, Jackson's (Tennessee) Division, Forrest's Cavalry, organized March, 1864. Commissioned Brigadier-General March 1, 1865.*

NAME.	Grade.	Function.	Date of Appointment.	Remarks.
Ferdinand Stith.......	Captain...	Act. Asst. Adjt.-Gen.	Sept. 11, 1864..	Transferred from Rucker's staff.
John Overton, Jr......	Captain...	Act. Asst. Insp.-Gen.	Sept. 11, 1864..	Transferred from Rucker's staff.
William R. Harris.....	1st Lieut..	Act. Aid de Camp...	M'ch 29, 1865..	Transferred from Seventh Tennessee.
A. Warren............	Major. ...	Brigade Quarterm'r..	Dec. 23, 1863.	
W. J. Sykes..........	Major. ...	Brigade Commissary.	Oct. 1, 1862.	
C. N. Featherston.....	2d Lieut..	Ordnance Officer....	April 2, 1863 ..	Transferred from Rucker's staff.

FORREST'S ARTILLERY BATTALION,
AS ORGANIZED MAY 13TH, 1864.

NAME.	Rank.	Date of Election or Appointment.	Remarks.
Morton's Battery.			
John W. Morton......	Captain...	Dec. 23, 1862.	Acting Chief of Artillery, with R. M. Blakemore as Adjutant, and S. K. Watkins Assistant Quartermaster.
T. Saunders Sale......	1st Lieut..	Dec. 23, 1862.	Commanding Battery.
G. Tully Brown......	1st Lieut..	Aug. 28, 1862.	Relieved Sept. 13, 1864.
Joseph M. Mayson....	2d Lieut..	Nov. 26, 1863.	Wounded at Harrisburg, July 14, 1864.
James P. Hanner.....	Surgeon ..	July 14, 1863.	
Rice's Battery.			
T. W. Rice..........	Captain...	Aug. 15, 1861.	
B. F. Haller.........	1st Lieut..	Aug. 15, 1861.	Transferred with one section to Morton's Battery in January, 1865. Surrendered in that battery.
H. H. Briggs.........	2d Lieut..	Jan. 1, 1862.	
Daniel C. Jones.......	2d Lieut..	April 1, 1862.	
Jacob Huggins, Jr....	Surgeon ..	March 26, 1863	
Hudson's Battery.			This battery is spoken of generally in this work as "Walton's Battery."
Edwin S. Walton.....	Captain...	March 7, 1863.	Severely wounded during siege of Vicksburg, in spring of 1863.
Milton H. Trantham..	1st Lieut..	April 12, 1862.	
Green C Wright......	2d Lieut..	Oct. 3, 1863.	
Willis O. Hunter......	2d Lieut..	Oct. 3, 1863.	
R. P. Weaver........	Surgeon ..	July 9, 1863.	
Thrall's Battery.			
J. C. Thrall..........	Captain...	May 12, 1862..	Wounded at Yazoo City, Miss., Mch. 5, 1864.
R. S. Anderson.......	1st Lieut..	May 12, 1862..	Wounded at Shiloh, April 6, 1862.
J. C. Barlow.........	2d Lieut..	May 14, 1862	
W. J. D. Winton......	2d Lieut..	May 12, 1862.	
J. L. Grace..........	Surgeon ..	July 1, 1862.	

SECOND TENNESSEE CAVALRY.

FIELD AND STAFF-OFFICERS.

C. R. Barteau, Colonel.
G. H. Morton, Lt.-Colonel.
William Parrish, Major.

J. M. Hughes, Surgeon.
J. W. Harrison, Asst. Surgeon.
E. O. Elliott, Acting Q. M.

P. A. Smith, Lt. and Adjutant.
S. C. Talley, Chaplain.

CAPTAINS.

T. B. Underwood (B)
M. W. McKnight (C)
William T. Rickman (D)

W. A. De Bow (E)
John A. Brinkley (F)
J. M. Eustis (G)

B. Edwards (H)
S. W. Reeves (I)
O. B. Farriss (K)

FIRST LIEUTENANTS.

T. C. Atkinson (A)
G. W. Smithson (B)
H. L. W. Turney (C)
George Love (D)

George E. Seay (E)
James F. Austin (F)
B. H. Moore (G)

J. Bedford (H)
William Lattimer (I)
J. H. Neal (K)

SECOND LIEUTENANTS.

A. H. French (A)
S. B. Wall (B)
J. D. Core (B)
Samuel Dennis (C)
J. S. Harrison (C)
F. W. Youree (D)
Ed. Bullock (D)

R. B. Dobbins (E)
F. J. Carman (E)
John E. Deming (F)
Newsom Pennell (F)
A. W. Lipscomb (G)
J. J. Lawrance (G)

E. Lassiter (H)
T. L. Stubblefield (H)
J. H. Bettick (I)
W. C. Roberts (I)
F. M. McRae (K)
H. Pryor (K)

FOURTH TENNESSEE CAVALRY.

FIELD AND STAFF-OFFICERS.

James H. Starnes, Colonel.
Perril C. Haynes, Lt.-Colonel.
Peter T. Rankin, Major.

Wm. H. Davis, Lt. and Adjt.
Edward Swanson, Surgeon.
Allen E. Gooch, Asst. Surgeon.

Joseph B. Briggs, A. Q. M.
Moses H. Clift, A. C. S.
Wm. H. Whitsitt, Chaplain.

CAPTAINS.

Aaron Thompson (A)
J. B. Britton (B)
E. L. Lindsey (C)
A. A. Dysart (D)

G. W. Robinson (E)
W. S. McLemore (F)
Andrew McGregor (G)

J. E. Teague (H)
J. M. McBride (I)
Francisco Rice (K)

FIRST LIEUTENANTS.

James C. Candiff (A)
C. C. Rutherford (B)
W. E. Donnel (C)
W. M. Robinson (D)

W. F. White (E)
J. T. Pierce (F)
A. J. Duffey (G)

J. W. Johnson (H)
J. A. Smitherman (I)
J. B. Poston (K)

SECOND LIEUTENANTS.

Benjamin F. Boyd (A)
Silas S. Short (A)
E. L. Collier (B)
S. T. Bass (B)
C. C. Hancock (C)
D. W. Granstaff (C)
F. M. Webb (D)

John Carpenter (D)
W. A. Hubbard (E)
J. W. Norton (E)
S. S. Hughes (F)
S. C. Tulloss (F)
John H. Dice (G)
E. W. Burwell (G)

C. G. Pryor (H)
J. M. Ragen (H)
G. L. Freeman (I)
T. W. Lewis (I)
W. E. Baker (K)
W. A. Young (K)

SEVENTH TENNESSEE CAVALRY.

FIELD AND STAFF-OFFICERS.

Wm. L. Duckworth, Colonel.
Wm. F. Taylor, Lt.-Colonel.
C. C. Clay, Major.

Wm. S. Pope, Lt. and Adjt.
Kenneth Garrett, A. Q. M.

J. C. Word, Surgeon.
W. L. Rosser, Chaplain.

CAPTAINS.

J. W. Sneed (A)
J. P. Russell (B)
John T. Lawler (C)
L. W. Taliaferro (D)

W. J. Tate (E)
C. H. Jones (F)*
F. F. Aden (G)
H. C. McCutchen (H)

J. R. Alexander (I)
J. A. Anderson (K)
Alexander Duckworth (L)
Benjamin T. Davis (M)

FIRST LIEUTENANTS.

H. W. Watkins (A)
H. T. Sale (B)
W. B. Winston (C)
Henry J. Livingston (D)

J. P. Statler (E)
J. J. Blake (G)
J. A. Jenkins (H)

W. P. Malone (I)
J. S. Hille (K)
William Moorer (M)

* Companies E and F became so reduced in officers and men, that they were consolidated.

SECOND LIEUTENANTS.

W. L. Certain (A)
J. D. Mitchell (A)
J. N. Stinson (B)
Robert J. Black (B)
Samuel B. Higgins (C)
A. L. Winston (C)
T. J. Mann (D)

A. A. Johnson (D)
H. Harris (E)
W. C. Mashburne (E)
W. N. Griffin (G)
James T. Haynes (G)
P. A. Fisher (I)
E. M. Downing (I)

John Trout (K)
E. R. Scruggs (K)
Frank Pugh (L)
William Witherspoon (L)
Charles Rice (M)
J. L. Livingston (M)

EIGHTH TENNESSEE CAVALRY.

FIELD AND STAFF-OFFICERS.

George G. Dibrell, Colonel.
F. H. Dougherty, Lt.-Colonel.
Jeffrey E. Forrest, Major.

M. D. Smallman, Lt. and Adjt.
A. C. Dale, A. Q. M.
Jasper N. Bailey, A. C. S.

Wm. H. McCord, Surgeon.
J. Luke Ridley, Asst. Surgeon.

CAPTAINS.

W. W. Windle (A)
Hamilton McGuinness (B)
Isaac G. Woolsey (C)

Jefferson Leftwich (D)
Josiah Bilbrey (F)
Mounce L. Gore (G)

James M. Barnes (H)
James W. McReynolds (I)
Bryan M. Swearongin (K)

FIRST LIEUTENANTS.

Thomas C. Webb (B)
William C. Wood (C)
James W. Revis (D)

William P. Chapin (E)
Jefferson Bilbrey (F)
William Z. Beck (G)

John Hill (H)
Jesse Beck (K)

SECOND LIEUTENANTS.

A. L. Windle (A)
Allen G. Parker (B)
Levi W. Maynard (B)
J. W. Pendergrass (C)
Jackson Davis (C)
William R. Hill (D)

Waman L. Dibbrell (D)
Lloyd W. Chapin (E)
Jesse Allen (E)
Thomas H. Webb (F)
—— Herner (F)
Newton C. Byber (G)

John S. Rhea (H)
Joseph D. Bartlett (H)
James Walker (I)
Simon D. Wallace (I)
Elijah W. Terry (K)

NINTH TENNESSEE CAVALRY.

FIELD AND STAFF-OFFICERS.

J. B. Biffle, Colonel.
A. G. Cooper, Lt.-Colonel.

Roderick Perry, Lt. & Adjt.
Wm. M. Irwin, A. Q. M.

W. S. Johnston, A. C. S.
Henry Long, Surgeon.

CAPTAINS.

J. J. Biffle (A)
James Reynolds (B)
C. F. Barnes (C)
Lewis M. Kirk (D)

Gideon J. Adkisson (E)
J. W. Johnson (F)
John S. Groves (G)
Thomas H. Beatty (H)

Frank Smith (I)
R. L. Ford (K)
Robert Sharp (L)

FIRST LIEUTENANTS.

John W. Hill (A)
—— Littleton (B)
Thomas Helmick (C)
—— May (D)

James Leftwich (E)
J. P. Montague (F)
D. B. Cooper (G)
Dent Pennington (H)

B. F. Burkitt (I)
Thomas Hargroves (K)
Ed. Cannon (L)

SECOND LIEUTENANTS.

Gip Wells (A)
P. Brownlaw (C)
J. Pigg (E)
Pap Nichols (E)

B. S. Hardin (F)
John Johnson (F)
Robert Harris (G)
Jacob Armstrong (G)

J. Davis (H)
Mat. D. Cooper (H)
John Hicks (K)
Robert Clarke (L)

TENTH TENNESSEE CAVALRY.

FIELD AND STAFF-OFFICERS.

N. N. Cox, Colonel.
E. B. Trezevant, Lt.-Colonel.
Wm. E. De Moss, Major.

E. A. Spottswood, Lt. and Adjt.
D. H. White, Q. M.

J. N. Rickman, Commissary.
Julius Johnston, Surgeon.

CAPTAINS.

W. J. Hall (A)
W. H. Lewis (B)
W. H. Whitwell (C)
W. J. Robinson (D)

John Minor (E)
W. W. Hobbs (F)
T. S. Easely (G)

B. G. Rickman (H)
Thomas Fletcher (I)
Thomas M. Hutchinson (K)

FIRST LIEUTENANTS.

John Pace (A)
William Fisher (B)
A. D. Craig (C)
W. P. Edds (D)

Andrew Nesbitt (E)
M. M. Box (F)
J. A. Macauley (G)

W. H. Coode (H)
Clinton Aden (I).
J. Utley (K)

SECOND LIEUTENANTS.

J. W. Townsend (A)
J. M. Randall (B)
Thomas Whitwell (B)
John Horner (C)
Thomas F. Lewis (C)
W. N. Phipps (D)
W. A. Wray (D)

Joseph B. Williams (E)
—— Nesbitt (E)
Jessee T. Hobbs (F)
Charles S. Summers (F)
J. M. Hall (G)
W. J. Frazier (G)

E. H. Shepherd (H)
J. D. Land (H)
B. E. Summers (I)
—— Dodson (I)
W. O. Chapman (K)
J. O. Pinick (K)

ELEVENTH TENNESSEE CAVALRY.

FIELD AND STAFF-OFFICERS.

James H. Edmonson, Colonel.
D. W. Holman, Lt.-Colonel.
Jacob T. Martin, Major.

W. R. Garrett, Lt. and Adjt.
Jesse D. Core, Surgeon.
Wm. H. Anderson, Asst. Surg.

O. G. Gurley, A. Q. M.
J. D. Allen, A. C. S.

CAPTAINS.

Co. A was commanded by Captain Charles McDonald, subsequently of McDonald's Battalion, to which it was transferred in May, 1863.
T. C. H. Miller (C)

John Lytle (D)
A. R. Gordon (E)
Co. F was commanded by Captain Phil. T. Allin, and in May, 1863, transferred to McDonald's Battalion.

Chatham Coffee (H)
Thomas F. Perkins (I)
James Rivers (K)
John M. Rust (L)

FIRST LIEUTENANTS.

John M. Nevils (B)
W. W. Braden (C)
John L. Carney (D)

J. M. Edmondson (E)
Thomas Banks (G)

John C. Bostick (I)
Wm. H. Baugh (K)

SECOND LIEUTENANTS.

E. G. Hamilton (C)
E. F. Rainey (C)
J. H. Butler (D)
N. P. Marable (D)
Robert Gordon (E)

George Rothrock (E)
David S. Chaney (G)
A. S. Chapman (G)
Robert Bruce (H)
William Durley (H)

Malachi Kirby (I)
Sol. Rozelle (I)
Robert McNairy (K)
James Ward (L)

TWELFTH TENNESSEE CAVALRY.

FIELD AND STAFF-OFFICERS.

J. U. Green, Colonel.
G. W. Bennett, Major.
R. B. Bone, Lt. and Adjt.

A. Beaty, Surgeon.
E. H. Sholl, Asst. Surgeon.

S. F. Cocke, A. Q. M.
A. G. Burrow, Chaplain.

CAPTAINS.

Edward Daly (A)
W. T. Carmack (B)
J. L. Payne (C)
J. G. McCauley (D)

C. S. McStusack (E)
William Bell (F)
John Massey (G)

W. M. Craddock (H)
J. B. Scarborough (I)
R. J. McSpadden (K)

FIRST LIEUTENANTS.

W. H. Crite (A)
W. D. Wilder (B)
William Bell (C)
J. Appleberry (D)

J. S. Grandberry (E)
John Matthews (F)
W. W. Freeman (G)

J. C. Haines (H)
R. Johnson (I)
E. H. Cobbs (K)

SECOND LIEUTENANTS.

R. H. Strickland (A)
H. Le Massey (A)
F. E. Brown (B)
J. E. Yancey (B)
R. C. Simonton (C)
C. L. Sullivan (C)

W. M. Parker (D)
J. S. Stewart (E)
James Brooks (F)
Hiram Prewitt (F)
Ambrose House (G)
O. H. Wade (G)

W. J. Overall (H)
L. L. Cherry (H)
William Stewart (I)
William McKirskill (I)
J. T. Briggs (K)
R. A. Williford (K)

FOURTEENTH TENNESSEE CAVALRY.

FIELD AND STAFF-OFFICERS.

J. J. Neely, Colonel.
R. R. White, Lt.-Colonel.
Gwynn Thurmond, Major.

E. S. Hammond, Lt. and Adjt.
M. H. Pirtle, A. Q. M.

T. H. Turner, Surgeon.
R. P. Watson, Asst. Surgeon

CAPTAINS.

S. J. Cox (A)
J. H. Deberry (B)
Z. Voss (C)
L. A. Thomas (D)

E. M. Jacobs (E)
W. J. Hall (F)
A. C. Reid (G)

James Gwynn (H)
E. S. Elliott (I)
C. C. Conner (K)

FIRST LIEUTENANTS.

N. A. Senter (B)
R. J. Strayhorne (C)
J. W. Ricks (D)

A. R. Emmerson (E)
J. M. Moore (F)
W. F. Dillard (G)

B. F. Tatum (H)
A. W. Fleming (K)

SECOND LIEUTENANTS.

M. P. Harbin (A)
J. B. Harris (A)
G. Hicks (B)
John B. Holt (B)
W. H. Swink (C)

James Drake (D)
W. G. Pirtle (E)
M. G. Hall (F)
J. Robertson (G)
J. Reid (G)

D. L. Hill (H)
H. J. Brewster (H)
James Laird (I)
John Langley (I)
W. J. Campbell (K)

FIFTEENTH TENNESSEE CAVALRY.

FIELD AND STAFF-OFFICERS.

F. M. Stewart, Colonel.
T. H. Logwood, Lt.-Colonel.
Sol. G. Street, Major.

John Skeffington, A. Q. M.
A. B. Tapscott, Surgeon.

A. Bruce, Asst. Surgeon.
J. L. Barksdale, Lt. and Adjt.

CAPTAINS.

P. W. Moore (A)
J. L. Garrison (B)
H. T. Hanks (C)

T. Nutt (D)
E. L. Hussey (E)
T. C. Buchannon (F)

R. B. Sanders (G) ⎱
P. M. Williams (I)
J. A. Williamson (K)

FIRST LIEUTENANTS.

W. R. Griffith (A)
John F. Garrison (B)
A. B. Henry (C)

G. W. Yapp (E)
J. P. Thurman (F)
J. M. McCaleb (G)

J. M. Witherspoon (H)
T. W. Allen (I)

SECOND LIEUTENANTS.

R. S. Van Dyke (A)
Richard T. Gardner (A)
W. B. Nolley (B)
W. D. Brown (B)
J. Ray (C)

G. T. Baker (C)
L. C. Street (D)
F. G. Ferguson (F)
E. S. Thurman (F)
P. H. Sutton (G)

R. Y. Anderson (I)
J. L. Seward (I)
R. Stone (K)
V. H. Swift (K)

SIXTEENTH TENNESSEE REGIMENT.

FIELD AND STAFF-OFFICERS.

A. N. Wilson, Colonel.
Jesse A. Forrest, Lt.-Colonel.
W. T. Parham, Major.

F. M. Bell, Lt. and Adjt.
B. M. Bray, A. Q. M.

S. H. Caldwell, Surgeon.
M. D. L. Jordan, Asst. Surgeon.

CAPTAINS.

J. A. Russell (A)
E. D. Polk (B)
J. J. Rice (C)
W. H. Bray (D)

W. H. Simmons (E)
James Stennett (F)
J. W. Fussell (G)

J. W. Carroll (H)
J. C. Gooche (I)
R. E. Dudley (K)

FIRST LIEUTENANTS.

W. A. McCandless (A)
J. C. Shipp (B)
I. J. Galbreath (C)

J. R. Arnold (D)
J. P. Revely (E)
James Tomlinson (G)

M. L. Cherry (H)
H. Lassitter (I)
J. F. Loony (K)

SECOND LIEUTENANTS.

John Coberne (A)
T. F. Wilson (A)
W. B. Malone (B)
J. R. Glover (B)
J. F. Collins (C)
J. D. Walker (C)

J. C. Dodds (D)
J. M. Bray (D)
A. J. Baxter (E)
S. J. Crowder (F)
Thomas R. Mangrum (G)
T. A. Haynes (G)

S. C. Kennedy (H)
M. H. Goodloe (I)
J. B. Northern (I)
W. E. Scales (K)
A. F. Brooks (K)

NINETEENTH (NEWSOM'S) REGIMENT TENNESSEE CAVALRY.

FIELD AND STAFF-OFFICERS.

John F. Newsom, Colonel.
D. M. Wisdom, Lt.-Colonel.
W. Y. Baker, Major.

H. T. Johnson, Lt. and Adjt.
A. B. Crook, A. Q. M.

—— Lockhart, Surgeon.
John Randolph, Chaplain.

CAPTAINS.

W. N. Barnhill (A)
R. M. May (B)
William Wilson (C)
T. H. Taylor (D)

J. B. Michin (E)
J. R. Damron (F)
J. J. Sharp (G)
J. G. Sharp (H)

S. C. McClerkin (I)
W. D. Stratton (K)
Thomas R. Dick (L)

FIRST LIEUTENANTS.

J. T. Settle (A)
Middleton Hayes (B)
William Lee (C)
M. B. Ormsby (D)

R. M. Wharton (E)
A. P. Meeks (F)
M. T. Shelby (G)
J. D. Springer (H)

J. J. Betts (I)
J. C. Miller (K)
William Hollis (L)

SECOND LIEUTENANTS.

J. C. O'Neill (A)
H. Klyce (A)
N. T. Buckley (B)
J. O. Ray (B)
John McBarrett (C)
Thomas Barrett (C)
D. J. Bowdin (D)
W. P. Walker (D)

E. R. Turner (E)
J. R. Adams (E)
A. L. Winningham (F)
W. R. Ledbetter (F)
Absalom Brashear (G)
Robert T. Simmons (G)
J. M. Wardlow (H)

Nathaniel Busby (H)
S. M. Ozier (I)
J. M. Bumpass (I)
J. J. Lane (K)
E. W. D. Dunn (K)
James Stuart (L)
—— Lockman (L)

TWENTIETH (RUSSELL'S) TENNESSEE REGIMENT.

FIELD AND STAFF-OFFICERS.

R. M. Russell, Colonel.
H. C. Grier, Lt.-Colonel.
H. F. Bowman, Major.

S. J. Ray, A. Q. M.
T. C. McNeille, Surgeon.

J. R. Westbrook, Asst. Surgeon.
A. G. Hawkins, Lt. and Adjt.

CAPTAINS.

William Gay (A)
William H. Hawkins (B)
J. T. Mathis (C)

J. A. Shane (D)
W. D. Hallam (E)
J. C. Wilson (F)

J. R. Hibbitts (G)
J. R. Gardner (H)

FIRST LIEUTENANTS.

J. H. Blakemore (A)
N. W. McNeille (B)
J. P. Armstrong (C)

J. R. Dance (D)
J. A. Caster (E)
J. A. Crutchfield (F)

A. C. Miller (H)
W. H. Lawler (I)
M. H. Freeman (K)

SECOND LIEUTENANTS.

J. N. Gay (A)
R. H. Goodman (A)
William H. Courts (B)
M. B. Dinwiddie (B)

U. S. Halliburton (C)
J. W. Herrin (D)
G. F. Nelson (D)
R. C. McLesky (H)

George Cathy (H)
A. J. Killibrew (K)
T. J. Burton (K)

SIXTEENTH BATTALION TENNESSEE CAVALRY.

FIELD AND STAFF-OFFICERS.

J. R. Neal, Lt.-Colonel.
Joseph Paine, Major.

W. B. L. Reagan, Lt. and Adjt. H. W. McElwee, A. Q. M.

CAPTAINS.

James Rodgers (A)
R. F. Mastin (B)

W. P. Darwin (C)
F. M. Murray (D)

Thomas S. Rambaugh (E)
Mike Stoley (F)

FIRST LIEUTENANTS.

Frederick A. Lenoir (A)
W. N. King (B)

H. C. Collins (C)
Thomas H. Mastin (D)

Thomas Williams (E)
E. Eitson (F)

SECOND LIEUTENANTS.

G. A. Montgomery (A)
W. C. Pride (A)
J. T. Vaughn (B)
J. M. King (B)

—— Armour (C)
—— Thommasson (C)
—— Campbell (D)
James Baine (D)

William Williams (E)
W. P. Reed (E)
—— Monegham (F)
Moses Anderson (F)

FORREST'S (OLD) REGIMENT,*

AS ORGANIZED MARCH, 1865.

FIELD AND STAFF-OFFICERS.

D. C. Kelly, Lt.-Colonel.
P. T. Allin, Major.

E. A. Spottswood, Lt. and Adjt. G. A. Cochran, A. Q. M.

CAPTAINS.

T. F. Pattison (A)
James G. Barbour (B)
J. C. Blanton (C)
W. H. Forrest (D)

N. E. Wood (E)
J. F. Rodgers (F)
W. J. Shaw (G)

J. L. Morphis (H)
T. R. Bearfoot (I)
Wiley Higgs (K)

FIRST LIEUTENANTS.

W. J. P. Doyle (A)
C. D. Steinkuhl (B)
Charles Balch (C)

T. H. Magee (D)
D. A. Autrey (G)
M. Nelms (H)

J. M. Duncan (I)
J. P. Johnson (K)

* Mentioned prominently in this work, in different places, as "McDonald's Battalion."

SECOND LIEUTENANTS.

J. A. Powell (A)
James Southerland (A)
R. L. Ivey (B)
J. W. Alexander (B)
Samuel Powell (C)
G. Glenn (C)

S. B. Soliman (D)
Joseph Luxton (D)
W. J. Redd (E)
B. A. Powell (E)
C. A. Douglass (F)
J. S. Nichols (F)

J. H. Jones (H)
W. J. Morphis (H)
E. Wooten (I)
J. C. Savage (K)
John Ramsay (K)

NIXON'S CONSOLIDATED REGIMENT,*

COMPOSED OF NIXON'S AND CARTER'S FOURTEENTH AND FIFTEENTH TENNESSEE REGIMENTS.

FIELD AND STAFF-OFFICERS.

G. H. Nixon, Colonel.
T. H. Logwood, Lt.-Colonel.
J. M. Crews, Major.

W. W. Bayless Lt. and Adjt.
T. H. Turuer, Surgeon.

A. L. Hamilton, Asst. Surgeon
H. R. Shacklett, A. Q. M.

CAPTAINS.

Peter W. Moore (A)
Z. Voss (B)
C. A. S. Shaw (Ç)
A. C. Reid (D)

Calvin Gilbert (E)
J. H. George (F)
J. R. Voss (G)

J. B. Van Houton (H)
N. J. Vaughn (I)
R. H. Dudley (K)

FIRST LIEUTENANTS.

J. L. B. Barksdale (A)
W. H. Wharton (B)
H. J. Brewster (C)
C. C. Conner (D)

J. T. Scott (E)
J. F. Byers (F)
A. C. Harwell (G)

J. L. Herrin (H)
L. Burnett (I)
E. J. Neil (K)

SECOND LIEUTENANTS.

W. R. Griffith (A)
W. M. Weatherly (B)
H. D. Nealson (C)
W. H. Reid (D)
Alonzo Gilbert (E)

B. G. Pierson (E)
P. W. Halbert (F)
J. M. Jackson (G)
George W. Prior (G)

Eugene Allen (H)
G. W. Heath (H)
T. R. Hollowell (I)
J. L. Dismukes (K)

SECOND MISSOURI CAVALRY.

FIELD AND STAFF-OFFICERS.

Robert McCulloch, Colonel.
Robert A. McCulloch, Lt.-Col.
W. H. Couzzens, Major.

N. S. Adams, Acting Q. M.
Lucius J. Gaines, Lt. and Adjt.
F. R. Durrett, Surgeon.

R. E. Howlett, Asst. Surgeon.
J. B. Link, Chaplain.

CAPTAINS.

A. L. Zollinger (A)
Jno. S. Thompson (B)
P. M. Savery (C)

Geo. W. Lyndamoor (D)
F. J. Smith (E)
R. F. Lanning (F)

G. B. Harper (G)
Josiah Tippatt (H)
—— Collins (I)

FIRST LIEUTENANTS.

J. J. Eubanks (A)
Felix Murray (B)
Ed. Aldrich (C)

T. J. Chandler (D)
A. H. Chadwell (E)
C. M. Sutherlin (G)

W. G. Blakey (H)
—— Christian (I)

SECOND LIEUTENANTS.

G. M. Buchanan (A)
W. O. Hall (A)
Thomas A. Bottom (B)
J. R. Chambers (B)
Charles Hayes (C)

J. J. Peck (C)
R. H. Douglass (D)
Z. D. Jennings (E)
W. N. Hinds (E)

John S. Ford (G)
W. A. Thornton (G)
Asa Pittman (H)
—— Quarles (I)

THIRD MISSISSIPPI CAVALRY,

AS ORGANIZED UPON TRANSFER FROM STATE TO CONFEDERATE SERVICE IN MAY, 1864.

FIELD AND STAFF-OFFICERS.

John McGuirk, Colonel.
H. H. Barksdale, Lt.-Colonel.
Thomas W. Webb, Major.

W. Joe Walker, Lt. and Adjt.
T. M. Griffin, Act. Q. M.
J. F. Butler, Surgeon.

A. F. Clayton, Asst. Surgeon.
W. F. Baker, A. C. S.

CAPTAINS.

T. J. Kyle (A)
F. M. Griffin (B)
John W. Logan (C)
Wm. Gwartney (D)

E. L. Richmond (E)
J. G. Kennedy (F)
S. T. Daniel (G)

J. L. Brannon (H)
C. W. Orr (I)
R. H. Turner (K)

FIRST LIEUTENANTS.

E. M. Fewell (A)
J. F. Peeler (B)
S. H. White (C)
Samuel Downing (D)

W. O. Cochran (E)
W. H. Thornton (F)
J. L. Hamer (G)

E. J. Harden (H)
C. M. Richards (I)
James T. Dubard (K)

* These regiments, thus consolidated, mustered an "aggregate present" of 437.

SECOND LIEUTENANTS.

Jos. Fox (A)
L. P. Pipkin (A)
T. J. Grafton (B)
A. Price (B)
Jno. Miller (C)
J. S. Ford (C)
S. H. Bogard (D)

R. A. Butler (D)
C. G. Yarborough (E)
E. Q. Withers (E)
B. F. Bibb (F)
G. W. Sadler (F)
J. G. Hamer (G)
C. C. Wilkins (G)

W. L. Brannon (H)
H. P. Bridgers (H)
R. F. Dickens (I)
R. B. Sheegog (I)
J. H. Carr (K)
J. W. Griffis (K)

FOURTH MISSISSIPPI CAVALRY,

AS ORGANIZED WHILE REPORTING TO GENERAL FORREST IN 186

FIELD AND STAFF-OFFICERS.

C. C. Wilbourne, Colonel.
T. R. Stockdale, Lt.-Colonel.
J. M. Norman, Major.

B. H. Morehead, Lt. and Adjt.
W. C. McCaleb, Surgeon.

V. T. Chew, Asst. Surgeon.
W. W. Vaught, A. Q. M.

CAPTAINS.

D. McCullum (A)
V. L. Terrell (B)
Wm. Martin (C)
G. P. McLean (D)

S. D. Ramsey (E)
Luther Blue (F)
A. C. McKissack (G)

J. J. Whitney (H)
C. Hoover (I)
John B. McEwen (K)

FIRST LIEUTENANTS.

S. R. Allen (A)
John Pope (B)
C. E. Buck (C)
B. B. Thomas (D)

A. J. Short (E)
S. B. McCown (F)
T H. Arnold (G)

W. S. Crawford (H)
D. Williams (I)
W. J. Webb (K)

SECOND LIEUTENANTS.

R. Q. Allen (A)
R. J. Magee (B)
C. Lott (B)
D. B. Humphreys (C)
J. P. Parker (C)
B. F. Atkins (D)
John B. Harring (D)

John T. Hardie (E)
W. H. Bondurant (E)
L. B. McLaurin (F)
Tom Robinson (F)
John Armistead (G)
W. C. Dunn (G)

H. C. Snodgrass (H)
David Kinnison (H)
D. N. Walker (I)
B. C. Quinn (I)
W. J. Driver (K)
E. G. Burney (K)

FIFTH MISSISSIPPI CAVALRY.

FIELD AND STAFF-OFFICERS.

J. Z. George, Colonel.
J. A. Barksdale, Lt.-Colonel.
W. G. Henderson, Major.

J. Moore, A. Q. M.
G. W. Henderson, Surgeon.

John Gerdine, Asst. Surgeon.
R. L. Watson, Lt. and Adjt.

CAPTAINS.

W. B. Peery (A)
J. P. Trotter (B)
W. H. Curtis (C)
W. N. Scales (D)

D. Love (E)
J. P. Povall (F)
J. R. Allen (G)

R. Hill (H)
G. P. M. Turner (I)
A. G. Ward (K)

FIRST LIEUTENANTS.

R. B. Burton (A)
C. Lindsay (B)
Ed. Crippin (C)
W. H. Goff (D)

W. Kelly (E)
R. M. Bridgeforth (F)
H. H. Hightower (G)

J. C. Conner (H)
L. M. Nash (I)
T. M. Blassingame (K)

SECOND LIEUTENANTS.

C. E. Maguire (A)
R. J. Fredric (B)
H. D. Stone (B)
James Flowers (C)
J. C. Ferguson (C)
R. M. Coyle (D)

W. H. Nichols (D)
R. D. McCree (E)
H. F. Moore (E)
R. C. Harrington (F)
W. C. Cole (F)
J. H. Parker (G)

J. R. Hope (H)
M. Park (H)
J. M. Brown (I)
J. F. Rook (I)
E. A. Lampkin (K)
T. E. Neely (K)

SIXTH MISSISSIPPI CAVALRY.

FIELD AND STAFF-OFFICERS.

Isham Harrison, Colonel.
T. C. Lipscomb, Lt.-Colonel.
R. Y. Brown, Major.

John Oliver, Lt. and Adjt.
W. Russell, Surgeon.

M. K. Harrison, Asst. Surgeon.
M. Clay, A. C. S.

CAPTAINS.

S. Harper (A)
H. B. Brown (B)
W. P. Pardue (C)

C. H. Carter (D)
J. E. Hunt (E)
W. S. Harrington (F)

E. J. Runnels (G)
J. H. Richards (H)
C. A. Johnston (I)

FIRST LIEUTENANTS.

Thomas N. Cockrell (A)
M. J. Priddy (B)
J. T. McDougal (C)
Wm. Gilmer (D)

D. J. Ward (E)
B. G. Underwood (F)
John Lampkin (G)

W. D. Carrington (H)
W. M. Bell (I)
W. E. Pope (K)

SECOND LIEUTENANTS.

C. S. Atterbury (A)
J. A. Grant (A)
J. F. Clifton (B)
Wm. Dulaney (B)
W. L. Moody (C)
A. D. Clifton (C)
W. H. Bearden (D)

C. G. Barton (D)
J. Bankston (E)
J. D. Turner (E)
J. Kennedy (F)
J. H. Byers (F)
O. F. Buland (G)
T. S. Pigford (G)

W. W. Whitfield (H)
T. C. Billups (H)
J. M. Arnold (I)
G. W. Betts (I)
T. G. Fields (K)
W. J. Witherspoon (K)

SEVENTH MISSISSIPPI REGIMENT,

AS ORGANIZED MAY 1864.

FIELD AND STAFF-OFFICERS.

Samuel M. Hyams, Lt.-Colonel.
J. M. Park, Major.

W. W. Bailey, Lt. and Adjt.
J. E. Rogers, A. Q. M.

W. D. Carter, Surgeon.
E. A. Cox, Asst. Surgeon.

CAPTAINS.

Thomas Ford (A)
H. T. Counseille 'B)
M. Manney (C)
A. White (D)

W. N. Stansell (E)
H. L. Duncan (F)
John Garrett (G)

C. N. Wheeler (H)
Wm. Young (I)
W. C. Gambill (K)

FIRST LIEUTENANTS.

W. A. Morgan (A)
J. W. Parr (B)
Francis A. Wolffe (C)
J. B. Butler (D)]

John K. Guyton (E)
D. L. S. Mosby (F)
W. A. Crook (G)

H. J. Raglin (H)
W. E. Donaldson (I)
L. C. Meek (K)

SECOND LIEUTENANTS.

W. T. Malory (A)
D. M. Patton (A)
J. J. Reedy (B)
R. F. Dixon (B)
Thomas White (D)]

C. C. McGill (D)
John Golston (E)
W. M. Thomas (E)
W. A. Barkley (F)
James Haddox (F)

V. A. Grace (G)
Jerome Patton (G)
H. Collom (H)
W. B. Swonson (H)
P. S. Souge (I)

EIGHTH OR DUFF'S MISSISSIPPI REGIMENT,

AS ORGANIZED FEBRUARY, 1864.

FIELD AND STAFF-OFFICERS.

W. L. Duff, Colonel.
W. L. Walker, Lt.-Colonel.

T. A. Mitchell, Major.
J. S. Caruthers, Lt. and Adjt.

H. T. Roane, A. Q. M.
B. F. Eads, Surgeon.

CAPTAINS.

Thomas J. Williams (A)
W. T. Therrell (B)
C. W. Johnston (C)
E. B. Cochran (D)

J. M. Brownlee (E)
H. H. Shackleford (F)
Thomas L. Duke (G)

Thomas J. Morris (H)
W. W. Robinson (I)
Wm. E. Cox (K)

FIRST LIEUTENANTS.

Absalom Swaim (A)
E. W. Jennings (B)
Thomas J. Bell (C)
W. F. Irving (D)

S. J. Bailey (E)
R. G. Steele (F)
W. L. Mitchell (G)

E. B. Kilpatrick (H)
Ezekiel Bardwell (I)
W. W. Goin (K)

SECOND LIEUTENANTS.

Thomas J. Kennedy (A)
W. N. Cox (A)
W. F. Young (B)
T. J. Dowdy (B)
W. D. Thornton (C)
T. B. Turner (C)

R. Thompson (D)
T. W. Atkinson (E)
Joseph Woodall (E)
R. L. Bean (F)
T. J. Middlebrook (F)
W. W. Stone (G)

L. G. Knowles (G)
J. T. Morris (H)
C. C. Garrett (H)
R. V. H. Black (I)
E. R. Yerger (I)
J. W. Clarke (K)

EIGHTEENTH MISSISSIPPI REGIMENT,

ORGANIZED MAY, 1864.

FIELD AND STAFF-OFFICERS.

Alex. H. Chalmers, Colonel.
J. Waverly Smith, Lt.-Colonel.

Samuel F. Green, Lt. and Adjt.
R. F. Cock, A. Q. M.

J. T. Chandler, Surgeon.
E. M. Thompson, Asst. Surgeon.

CAPTAINS.

Mills W. Brittnum (A)
E. D. Porter (B)
Wm. H. Carroll (C)

W. G. Middleton (E)
J. H. McCain (F)
J. R. Perry (G)

W. J. Floyd (H)
A. T. Wimberly (I)
W. A. Raines (K)

FIRST LIEUTENANTS.

Hugh A. Reynolds (A)
J. P. Morton (B)
Cal. T. Smith (C)
J. Z. King (D)

John L. Knox (E)
D. M. Slocumb (F)
O. F. West (G)

—— Hubbard (H)
A. T. Farriss (I)
Elbert Oliver (K)

SECOND LIEUTENANTS.

Fred Chick (A)
George Wall (A)
H. H. Hopson (B)
J. Johnson (B)
Clayton R. Jones (C)
W. J. Hughes (C)

Ed. Smith (D)
J. T. Davis (E)
J. L. Harris (E)
E. L. Dooley (F)
—— Dickens (F)
—— Wallace (G)

B. F. Thompson (G)
David Wright (H)
Robert Brown (H)
Americus H. Payne (K)
Joseph P. Goodman (K)

THIRTY-EIGHTH MISSISSIPPI (MOUNTED) INFANTRY.

FIELD AND STAFF-OFFICERS.

P. Brent, Colonel.
W. L. Ware, Lt. and Adjt.

E. Hoskins, A. Q. M.

J. J. Wade, Surgeon.

CAPTAINS.

J. S. Hoskins (A)
W. L. Faulk (B)
J. L. Hart (C)
J. H. Jones (D)

J. A. Bass (E)
J. J. Green (F)
B. M. Black (G)

W. M. Estelle (H)
A. E. Foxworth (I)
J. C. Williams (K)

FIRST LIEUTENANTS.

P. E. Dyson (A)
E. T. Harrington (B)

L. L. Charles (C)
W. B. Graves (F)

M. H. Cuny (H)
John Applewhite (I)

SECOND LIEUTENANTS.

S. D. Gwin (A)
E. S. Leonard (A)
S. F. Smith (B)
J. W. Willoughby (C)

W. L. Jenkins (D)
W. D. Carmichael (F)
John E. Tarpley (H)

Tom Ball (H)
W. Ball (I)
N. L. Ball (I)

CHALMERS'S CONSOLIDATED (MISSISSIPPI) REGIMENT,

FORMED BY CONSOLIDATION OF EIGHTEENTH AND A PORTION OF FIFTH MISSISSIPPI REGI-MENTS, MARCH 16, 1865.

FIELD AND STAFF-OFFICERS.

A. H. Chalmers, Colonel.
J. Waverly Smith, Lt.-Colonel.

W. J. Floyd, Major.
R. F. Cook, A. Q. M.

J. T. Chandler, Surgeon.

CAPTAINS.

A. T. Wimberly (A)
B. F. Saunders (B)
C. T. Smith (C)
A. G. Mills (D)

J. L. Knox (E)
Wm. A. Raines (F)
O. F. West (G)

David Wright (H)
R. L. Watson (I)
R. Hill (K)

FIRST LIEUTENANTS.

Hugh Reynolds (A)
J. P. Morton (B)
James Dinkins (C)
R. E. Smith (D)

George E. Harris (E)
D. M. Slocumb (F)
—— Moore (G)

Robert Brown (H)
R. F. Moore (I)
J. C. Conner (K)

SECOND LIEUTENANT.

Fred Chick (A)
H. H. Hopson (B)
Thomas M. Jones (C)
John G. Burton (C)

I. Z. King (D)
J. Wright (E)
S. F. Green (F)
R. M. Banks (F)

R. T. Bowen (G)
S. H. Hyatt (H)
R. J. Hoke (K)
M. Park (K)

CONSOLIDATION OF ASHCRAFT'S, HAM'S, AND LOWRY'S MISSISSIPPI REGIMENTS,

AT THE REORGANIZATION OF FORREST'S CAVALRY, MARCH, 1865.

FIELD AND STAFF-OFFICERS.

T. C. Ashcraft, Colonel.

W. P. Curlee, Lt.-Colonel.

L. L. Marshall, Major.

CAPTAINS.

T. Brownrigg (A)
George W. Bynum (B)
J. R. Wallace (C)

J. E. Lowry (D)
A. B. Cole (E)
J. C. Fears (F)

S. H. Wood (G)
M. H. Howard (H)
T. J. Rye (I)

FIRST LIEUTENANTS.

W. H. Hill (A)
W. A. Parish (B)
T. R. Strickland (C)
G. W. Frazier (D)

J. E. Davis (E)
C. L. Martin (F)
W. D. Graves (G)

L. M. Coburn (H)
F. J. Thomas (I)
J. K. Gilleylin (K)

SECOND LIEUTENANTS.

George Owen (A)
K. M. Harrison (B)
L. B. Brown (C)
T. G. Stocks (D)
John Coffeewood (D)

Lafayette Weatherell (E)
Lucius Herndon (E)
W. H. Keyes (F)
L. P. McCord (G)
Scott Turner (G)

A. C. Tatum (H)
Wm. Hinds (H)
W. E. Thomas (I)
L. T. Taylor (I)
J. L. Laughridge (K)

THIRD KENTUCKY REGIMENT.

FIELD AND STAFF-OFFICERS.

A. P. Thompson, Colonel.
G. A. C. Holt, Lt.-Colonel.

T. T. Barnett, Major.
C. A. Duncan, A. Q. M.

J. C. Small, Lt. and Adjt.
J. B. Saunders, Surgeon.

CAPTAINS.

H. Blackwell (A)
C. H. Mishew (B)
A. C. McGoodwin (C)
M. Kincade (D)

S. P. Ridgeway (E)
W. L. Stevenson (F)
T. C. Edwards (G)
T. A. Miller (H)

William Sheppard (I)
T. J. Barnett (K)
J. E. Morris (L)
J. Clay Horne (M)

FIRST LIEUTENANTS.

J. L. Noe (A)
G. W. Timberlake (B)
G. W. Rucker (C)
J. A. Turk (D)

G. W. Thomas (E)
Jno. Ashbrook (F)
J. E. Morgan (G)
J. P. Witherspoon (H)

E. B. Rose (K)
W. H. Burruss (L)
William Cheeres (M)

SECOND LIEUTENANTS.

J. P. Brian (A)
W. C. Clements (A)
J. A. Fuller (B)
W. G. Ashbrook (B)
J. S. Wheeler (C)
W. H. Carter (C)
J. H. Jarnutt (D)
J. H. Kilon (D)

S. B. Edwards (E)
J. F. Cacey (E)
J. M. Minhar (F)
J. F. O. Donnelly (F)
W. R. Owens (G)
T. H. Hall (G)
A. H. Duncan (H)
J. M. J. Manning (H)

A. E. Davis (I)
W. J. Charles (K)
R. B. Barnes (K)
W. J. Bushard (L)
S. W. McMurry (L)
T. J. Haile (M)
T. W. Dumas (M)

SEVENTH KENTUCKY CAVALRY.

FIELD AND STAFF-OFFICERS.

Ed. Crossland, Colonel.
L. G. Sherrill, Lt.-Colonel.
H. S. Hale, Major.

T. F. Clardy, Surgeon.
W. Lindsey, A. Q. M.

C. H. Roulhac, Lt. and Adjt.
J. B. McCutchen, Chaplain.

CAPTAINS.

James Lynch (A)
H. C. Watson (B)
Jesse Hinkle (C)
D. P. Walston (D)

J. T. Cochrane (E)
J. W. Logan (F)
D. L. Nowlan (G)

C. W. Jetton (H)
D. S. Campbell (I)
D. H. Grubbs (K)

FIRST LIEUTENANTS.

J. A. McFall (A)
R. M. Seay (B)
J. T. Davis (C)
J. D. Gardner (D)

E. W. Anderson (E)
T. J. Garrett (F)
J. K. P. Wills (G)

J. D. A. Hall (H)
Allen Campbell (I)
Charles La Pice (K)

SECOND LIEUTENANTS.

W. G. Pirtle (A)
B. P. Willingham (A)
W. H. Seay (B)
S. M. Renwick (B)
Baker Boyd (C)
Jno. Heady (C)

R. D. Crest (D)
W. Cochrane (E)
J. B. Adair (E)
T. F. Roberts (F)
D. S. Frazer (F)

W. W. Easely (G)
F. E. Dodd (H)
J. C. Wilson (I)
J. C. Penn (K)
James Frazer (K)

EIGHTH KENTUCKY REGIMENT.

FIELD AND STAFF-OFFICERS.

H. B. Lyon, Colonel.
A. R. Shacklett, Lt.-Colonel.

Jabez Bingham, Major.
J. W. Smith, Asst. Surgeon.

J. H. Beniss, Lt. and Adjt.

CAPTAINS.

J. W. Brown (B)
R. H. Fristoe (C)

J. H. Goodloe (D)
James Powell (F)

F. G. Terry (G)
W. D. McKay (K)

FIRST LIEUTENANTS.

T. B. Jones (A)
J. E. Burchard (C)
John T. Dennis (D)

J. M. Couch (F)
Logan Field (H)

J. T. Redford (I)
J. G. Duncan (K)

SECOND LIEUTENANTS.

J. W. Hamilton (A)
William L. Dunning (B)
J. R. Gilfay (B)
R. T. Albritton (C)

T. B. Dane (D)
B. D. Morton (F)
Lee Turner (G)

A. D. Leadrum (H)
H. T. Rowland (H)
J. A. Duncan (K)

FAULKNER'S KENTUCKY REGIMENT.

FIELD AND STAFF-OFFICERS.

W. W. Faulkner, Colonel.
W. D. Lannum, Lt.-Colonel.

J. M. Malone, Major.
W. A. Thompson, Asst. Surg.

E. A. Manning, Lt. and Adjt.

CAPTAINS.

H. A. Tyler (A)
E. R. Dent (B)
G. W. Clanton (C)
J. J. Wilson (D)

J. Z. Linn (E)
R. P. Cole (F)
J. F. Milton (G)

J. J. Kelleher (H)
N. F. Davis (I)
W. D. Merriwether (K)

FIRST LIEUTENANTS.

G. W. Maraman (A)
E. P. Nailing (B)
W. R. Boaz (C)
R. Thomas (D)

B. W. McClure (E)
L. C. Baker (F)
W. J. Matthews (G)

J. L. Card (H)
G. J. Freeman (I)
L. Donelson (K)

SECOND LIEUTENANTS.

B. H. Welch (A)
P. B. Stoner (A)
G. G. Tyson (B)
John C. Dent (B)
J. A. Berryman (C)
N. B. Morris (C)
H. C. Lawhorne (D)

J. J. Birdsong (D)
O. P. O'Brien (E)
D. McMorgan (E)
J. W. Goodloe (F)
H. L. Raines (F)
J. D. Wilson (G)
R. E. Beckham (G)

J. M. Ezzell (H)
M. B. Beardon (H)
H. D. Wilson (I)
A. J. Bennett (I)
W. H. Anderson (K)
Thomas Stone (K)

FOURTEENTH CONFEDERATE CAVALRY.

FIELD AND STAFF-OFFICERS.

F. Dumontiel, Colonel.
P. C. Harrington, Major.
Ern. Forstall, Lieut. and Adjt.

James Miltenberger, A. Q. M.
Ernest Bourges, A. C. S.

C. P. Henderson, Surgeon.
S. G. Luckett, Asst. Surgeon.

CAPTAINS.

W. O. Weathersby (B)
M. T. Deuson (C)
J. Gonzales (D)

N. G. Rhodes (F)
G. C. Mills (G)
L. S. Greenlee (H)

W. M. Porter (I)
S. F. Williams (K)

FIRST LIEUTENANTS.

Robert Bacot (A)
George P. Harrison (B)
Zeb Williams (C)

R. T. Fridge (D)
W. S. Wrea (F)
Edward Young (G)

P. Boyac (H)
T. P. Kell (I)
E. Applewhite (K)

SECOND LIEUTENANTS.

J. M. Hart (A)
B. O. Callahan (A)
J. M. Cloy (B)
S. T. Kennedy (B)
Z. B. Gatlin (C)
Sam Marshall (C)

J. A. Gonzales (D)
V. A. Ganthram (D)
R. B. Easely (F)
W. B. Lenoir (F)
G. W. Cage (G)
Thomas J. Fuqua (G)

P. M. Watson (H)
James Bosby (H)
L. M. Baldwin (I)
B. T. Temple (I)
W. L. Williams (K)
T. W. Furlow (K)

FIRST TEXAS LEGION.*

AS ORGANIZED MAY 10TH, 1864.

FIELD AND STAFF-OFFICERS.

E. R. Hawkins, Colonel.
J. H. Brooks, Lieut.-Colonel.
J. T. Whitfield, Major.

B. T. Spindle, Lieut. and Adjt.
R. J. Lee, A. Q. M.

T. J. Scurlock, Surgeon.
J. Y. Bradfield, Asst. Surgeon.

CAPTAINS.

J. N. Zachary (A)
J. M. Ingram (C)
David Snodgrass (D)
B. H. Norworthy (E)

Benjamin Griffin (F)
Edward O. Williams (G)
F. M. Smith (H)
Jesse M. Cook (I)

J. J. Welbourne (K)
R. W. Billups (L)
O. P. Preston (M)

FIRST LIEUTENANTS.

B. M. Irwin (A)
J. F. Pleasant (C)
R. L. Elkin (D)
R. J. Bradford (E)

L. R. Williams (G)
W. G. Wellbourne (H)
Thompson Morris (I)

J. W. Middlebrooks (K)
J. H. Barcley (L)
J. B. McKennon (M)

SECOND LIEUTENANTS.

W. T. Rogers (A)
J. W. Urquahart (A)
S. H. Horton (C)
J. W. Gale (C)
J. L. Nance (D)
Adam Adams (E)
J. E. Sharp (E)

W. J. Swain (F)
T. M. Bagley (F)
J. S. Moore (G)
W. L. Snell (G)
H. McAllister (H)
J. A. Welch (I)
W. Bridges (I)

J. M. Taylor (K)
J. V. Logsden (L)
John Williams (M)
H. Murray (M)
D. Griffin (N)
Joel Parks (N)

NINTH TEXAS CAVALRY,

AS ORGANIZED MAY 10TH, 1864.

FIELD AND STAFF-OFFICERS.

D. W. Jones, Colonel.
T. G. Berry, Lieut.-Colonel.
J. C. Bates, Major.

G. L. Griscom, Lieut. and Adjt.
R. C. Simms, A. Q. M.
J. E. Robertson, Surgeon.

J. F. March, Assistant Surgeon.
R. C. Armstrong, Chaplain.

CAPTAINS.

Thomas Purcell (A)
E. M. Wright (B)
J. W. Beckett (C)

M. A. McLemore (D)
David Whiteman (E)
W. E. Alderson (F)

A. R. Wells (G)
Perry Evans (I)
H. C. Dial (K)

FIRST LIEUTENANTS.

F. O. Clare (A)
J. T. R. Jewett (B)
R. W. Gallagher (C)
J. H. Smith (D)

M. N. Scoggins (E)
D. W. Odell (F)
T. C. Hensley (G)

S. A. Griffith (H)
H. G. Haynes (I)
J. C. Garrett (K)

SECOND LIEUTENANTS.

J. E. Moore (A)
F. M. Dyer (A)
W. A. Wingo (B)
C. Duncan (C)
D. C. Robinson (C)

J. S. Wright (D)
Thomas Cox (E)
W. E. Orr (F)
A. B. Claringer (F)
M. Russell (G)

J. W. Smith (H)
J. W. Moore (I)
W. J. Chambers (I)
H. F. Young (K)
W. T. McClatchy (K)

SIXTH TEXAS CAVALRY,

AS ORGANIZED MAY 10TH, 1864.

FIELD AND STAFF-OFFICERS.

Jack Wharton, Colonel.
Peter F. Ross, Lieut.-Colonel.
S. B. Wilson, Major.

Edward Myers, Lieut. and Adjt.
J. J. Baker, A Q. M.

J. H. Hill, Surgeon.
R. B. Sadler, Assistant Surgeon.

CAPTAINS.

J. S. Porter (A)
H. W. Wade (B)
George B. Brown (C)
G. S. Rosamond (D)

Reuben Simpson (E)
R. A. Rawlings (F)
J. McWilson (G)

W. B. Whittington (H)
H. M. Morrison (I)
A. G. Graves (K)

FIRST LIEUTENANTS.

H. T. Moore (A)
A. Richardson (B)
John R. West (C)
G. S. Milan (D)

Josiah Bradley (E)
James Green (F)
W. T. McCann (G)

R. H. Baker (H)
M. M. Guerin (I)
L. H. Graves (K)

* There was no Company B to this command.

SECOND LIEUTENANTS.

C. H. Walworth (A)
J. C. Caruthers (A)
A. P. Thomas (B)
W. H. Thomas (C)
W. P. Wright (E)

T. S. Woods (E)
A. J. Gray (F)
P. S. Taylor (F)
U. Chick (G)
W. H. Riggs (H)

E. R. Collard (H)
W. C. Scott (I)
R. H. Royal (I)
R. C. White (K)

WILLIS'S TEXAS BATTALION.

FIELD AND STAFF-OFFICERS.

Leo Willis, Lieutenant-Colonel.
H. S. Parker, Lieut. and Adjt.

A. G. Evans, A. Q. M.

John Wyatt, Surgeon.

CAPTAINS.

J. T. Leon (C)
W. D. M. Peck (D)

W. R. Sullivan (E)
F. M. Harwood (F)

W. R. Roff (G)

FIRST LIEUTENANTS.

A. Persons (A)
W. F. Miller (C)

F. J. Nally (D)
T. J. Cleveland (F)

—— Sterritt (G)
G. M. Blackshear (H)

SECOND LIEUTENANTS.

W. H. Ridgeway (A)
J. B. Thomas (A)
E. F. Matthews (B)
W. M. Redding (B)
R. J. Johnson (C)

T. W. Hodges (C)
A. S. Gregory (D)
H. McKay (D)
W. H. Logsden (E)
T. T. Hopkins (E)

S. T. Walters (F)
L. E. Kelley (F)
G. W. McKinzie (G)
H. S. Palmer (G)

THIRD TEXAS CAVALRY,

AS ORGANIZED MAY 10TH, 1864.

FIELD AND STAFF-OFFICERS.

H. P. Mabry, Colonel.
J. S. Boggess, Lieut.-Colonel.
A. B. Stone, Major.

W. H. Gee, Lieut. and Adjt.
E. P. Hill, A. Q. M.
Daniel Shaw, Surgeon.

E. B. Blocker, Asst. Surgeon.
N. A. Duckett, Chaplain.

CAPTAINS.

R. B. Gause (A)
J. W. Wynne (B)
John Germany (C)
R. S. Dabney (D)

P. B. Word (E)
R. F. Dunn (F)
S. E. Noble (G)

J. W. Lee (H)
G. A. Connally (I)
S. S. Johnson (K)

FIRST LIEUTENANTS.

J. P. Alexander (A)
A. C. Rorison (B)
W. H. Carr (C)
John E. Yeager (D)

T. M. Soap (E)
S. O. Terrill (F)
D. N. Alley (G)

A. H. Hargrove (H)
A. G. W. Hunt (I)
A. C. Erwin (K)

SECOND LIEUTENANTS.

W. J. Cavin (A)
M. B. Harwell (A)
Taylor Brown (B)
Thomas S. Stephens (B)
R. L. Hood (C)
S. B. Barren (C)
B. P. Nance (D)

A. J. Chambers (D)
W. S. Holman (E)
D. T. Roberts (E)
H. P. Teague (F)
W. C. Cresswell (F)
T. J. Towles (G)
H. L. Taylor (G)

F. M. Henderson (H)
M. W. Moon (H)
W. H. Rutland (I)
J. D. Jackson (I)
F. M. Noble (K)
John Jeffries (K)

Joint resolution of thanks of the Confederate States to Major-General N. B. Forrest, and the officers and men of his command, for their campaign in Mississippi, West-Tennessee, and Kentucky :

Resolved, by the Congress of the Confederate States of America, That the thanks of Congress are eminently, and are hereby cordially tendered to Major-General N. B. Forrest, and the officers and men of his command, for their late brilliant and successful campaign in Mississippi, West-Tennessee, and Kentucky—a campaign which has conferred upon its authors fame as enduring as the records of the struggle which they have so brilliantly illustrated.

Approved May 23d, 1864.

(B.)

LIST OF PRISONERS CAPTURED AT FORT PILLOW.

THIRTEENTH TENNESSEE BATTALION.—*Co. A*—Sergeant R. C. Gunter; Privates J. Childress, A. J. Knight, J. E. Lemon, J. L. Howell, G. W. Kirk, T. F. Burton, J. B. Phipps, J. Clarke, J. Long, C. Swinny, D. Burton, J. Minyard, J. Berry, J. Halford, W. T. Lovett, M. Mitchell, E. Haynes, E. Anthony, V. V. Matthemy, J. Moore. *Co. B*—Privates A. J. Pankey, B. R. McKie, J. H. Scoby, J. Green, A. McKie, W. G. Bowles, E. Jones, A. J. Crawford, S. Hubbs, G. W. Bowles, T. L. Perry, J. W. Stewart, D. Floyd, W. P. Flowers, J. A. Baker, J. C. Steward, W. C. Asprey, J. H. Cover, J. Eason, J. Ellington, Z. Ellington, W. Etheridge, T. M. Paulk, C. F. Bowles, W. T. Hooser, J. Jones, W. Morrow, C. R. Allen, H. Bailey, J. A. Beatty, D. B. Burress, W. J. Mifflin, J. Burruss, W. Woodward, A. H. Barom. *Co. C*—First Lieutenant N. D. Logan; Privates H. Corning, W. L. Tate, N. G. Henderson, T. Wheeless, E. Scarborough, J. Bynum, S. Read, J. Clarke, D. Myers, W. Stafford, A. McGhee, F. E. Neeham, J. A. Smith, J. Ham, J. Pressley, M. Day, D. F. Hood, F. M. Gammon, J. Jones, L. Hohoer, G. L. Ellis, J. H. Webb, H. C. Moore, W. H. Bolls, A. J. Rice, Wm. Ryder, J. Norman, J. Southerland, A. Midîleton, H. S. Morris, J. M. Tidwell, J. M. Knuckles, C. Oxford. *Co. D*—Privates D. Z. Alexander, S. E. Kirk, B. J. Kirk, F. D. Tidwell, Wm. Hancock, John Taylor, J. W. Brown, T. Woods, B. Johnson, J. Wilson, W. R. Johnson, J. Moer, M. Harper, E. D. Stewart, B. F. Ellison, T. P. Pascal, J. M. Wilson, J. W. Gibson, P. S. Alexander, B. W. King, J. Rumage, J. C. Green. *Co. E*—Captain J. L. Poston; Privates J. T. Cochran, A. J. Hall, E. Childress, J. A. Brown, W. G. Poston, J. Smith, O. B. Goodman, S. N. Scarberry, N. C. Kleek, J. Cozort, W. Hines, J. W. Antwine, C. Ellis, A. J. Madlin, A. Carr, J. F. Stamps, R. Richardson, J. A. Haynes, J. M. Smith, T. J. McMurry, J. F. Rolf, J. Shoemate, Henry Clay, J. Arnold, R. Williams, A. J. Sutton, A. Lewis, J. H. Scarboro, T. A. Lunsford, W. J. Scarberry, J. Hodge, H. Jones, W. M. Henley, H. L. Brogden, M. E. Beard; F. Dowling, Quartermaster's Clerk. *Co. (known as Johnson's Escort Co.)*—First Lieutenant P. H. McBride; Private M. H. Blanton.[*] SECOND UNITED STATES LIGHT ARTILLERY.—*Co. D*—First Lieutenant A. M. Hunter; Private J. D. Fox. TWENTY-FOURTH MISSOURI INFANTRY.—*Co.A*—Captain J. F. Young. STIGALL'S HOME-GUARDS.—Privates W. H. Gibson, S. T. Gibson, J. W. Autrey, Wm. Boyer, R. C. Price, S. M. Price. SECOND IOWA CAVALRY.—*Co. L*—Private R. B. Springer. FIRST UNITED STATES REGULAR ARTILLERY.—*Co. A*—Private C. E. Pratt. SECOND ILLINOIS CAVALRY.—*Co. B*—Private H. W. Holloway. FIFTY-SECOND INDIANA INFANTRY.—*Co. G*—Private A. Baker. SEVENTH TENNESSEE CAVALRY.—*Co. A*—Private R. Mullins. *Co. C*—Private R. H. Stewart. *Co. D*—Private W. M. Crews. *Co. M*—Private W. H. Snow. SIXTH TENNESSEE CAVALRY.—*Co. E*—Private J. K. Taylor. SEVENTH KANSAS CAVALRY.—Private T. C. George, (Hospital Steward.) SIXTH UNITED STATES (COLORED) ARTILLERY, (HEAVY.)—*Co. A*—Captain C. J. Eppeneiter; First Lieutenant P. Bishop; Sergeant J. Hennissey; Privates A. J. Hatfield, J. Thompson, Frank Hopper, Tom Norris, Anthony Flowers, Bill Smith, Oliver Jones, Henry Smith, Jenkins Rice, Bill Ward, Monk Moores, Cog Horton, Edmund Trice, Peter Williams, Charlie Williams, Dave Manley, Ray McGhee, Broxton Kirkman, Wilson Johnson, Bill Oates, Solomon Patrick, Henderson Johnson, John Gentry, Sandy Worsham, Wilson Crenshaw, Jim McCauley, Albert Ingram, Jefferson Dobbs, Spott Clayton, Harry Hill, Wm. Gray, Jim Danbridge, Dan Newbern, Dave Oats, Frank Browder, Tom Palmer, Aaron Bradley, David Oats, Henry Smith, Wilson Peyton, David Johnson, Jacob Lumpkin, Moses Wiseman, Lewis Van Eagle, John McHainey, Jim Murrell, Jim Flowers, Sam Baugh, Dick Sallee, Hiram Lumpkin, Jim Pride, John Henry Harper, Dave Flowers.

RECAPITULATION.

	Officers.	Enlisted Men.	Total.
Sixth United States Heavy Artillery, (Colored)	2	54	56
Second Iowa Cavalry	..	1	1
Thirteenth Tennessee Battalion	3	148	151
Second United States Light Artillery	1	1	2
First United States Regular Artillery	..	1	1
Twenty-fourth Missouri Infantry	1	..	1
Stigall's Home-Guards	..	6	6
Second Illinois Cavalry	..	1	1
Fifty-second Indiana Infantry	..	1	1
Seventh Tennessee Cavalry	..	4	4
Sixth Tennessee Cavalry	..	1	1
Seventh Kansas Cavalry	..	1	1
Total	7	219	226

[*] In the recapitulation, Lieutenant McBride is enumerated with the Thirteenth Tennessee.

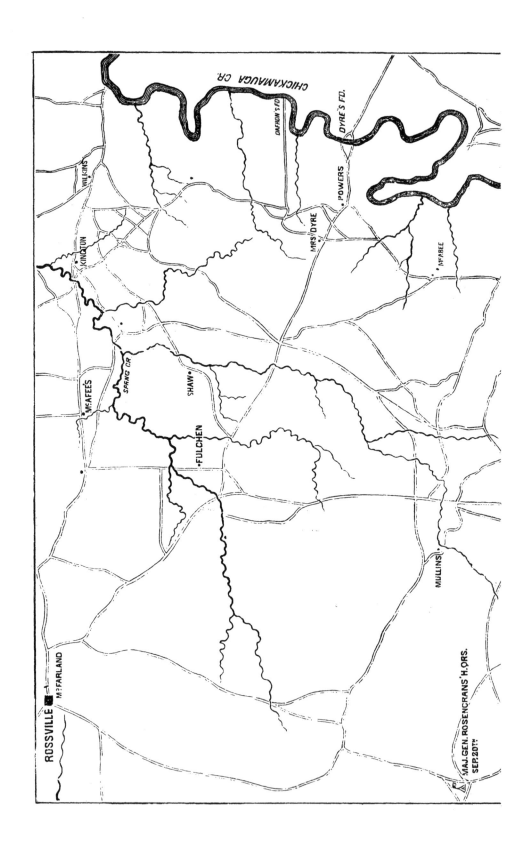

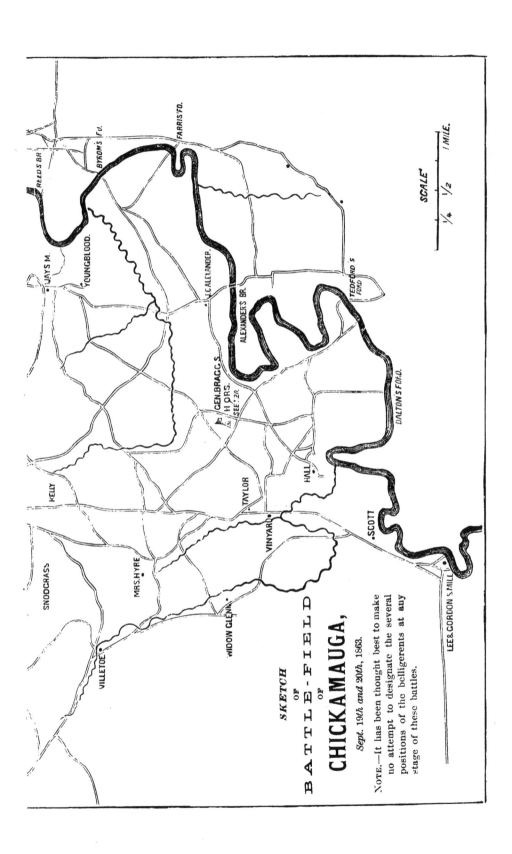

SKETCH
OF
BATTLE-FIELD
OF
CHICKAMAUGA,
Sept. 19th and 20th, 1863.

NOTE.—It has been thought best to make
no attempt to designate the several
positions of the belligerents at any
stage of these battles.

SCALE

¼   ½   1 MILE.

Other titles of interest

ABRAHAM LINCOLN
His Speeches and Writings
Edited by Roy P. Basler
Preface by Carl Sandburg
888 pp., 6 illus.
80404-2 $19.95

THE ABRAHAM LINCOLN
ENCYCLOPEDIA
Mark E. Neely, Jr.
368 pp., more than 300 illus.
80209-0 $18.95

ADVANCE AND RETREAT
General John Bell Hood
New introd. by Richard M. McMurry
376 pp., 6 illus.
80534-0 $14.95

THE ANNALS OF THE
CIVIL WAR
Written by Leading Participants
North and South
New introd.by Gary W. Gallagher
808 pp., 56 illus.
80606-1 $19.95

THE ANTIETAM AND
FREDERICKSBURG
General Francis W. Palfrey
New introd. by Stephen W. Sears
244 pp., 4 maps
80691-6 $13.95

BATTLE-PIECES AND
ASPECTS OF THE WAR
Herman Melville
New introd. by Lee Rust Brown
282 pp.
80655-X $13.95

THE BLACK PHALANX
African American Soldiers in the
War of Independence, the War
of 1812, and the Civil War
Joseph T. Wilson
New introd. by Dudley Taylor Cornish
534 pp., 64 illus.
80550-2 $16.95

A BRAVE BLACK REGIMENT
The History of the 54th
Massachusetts, 1863-1865
Captain Luis F. Emilio
New introd. by Gregory J. W. Urwin
532 pp., 89 photos, 9 maps
80623-1 $15.95

BY SEA AND BY RIVER
A Naval History of the
Civil War
Bern Anderson
344 pp., 20 illus.
80367-4 $13.95

CAMPAIGNING WITH GRANT
General Horace Porter
New introduction by
William S. McFeely
632 pp., 32 illus.
80277-5 $12.95

CHANCELLORSVILLE AND
GETTYSBURG
General Abner Doubleday
New introduction by
Gary W. Gallagher
269 pp., 13 maps
80549-5 $12.95

CHARLES SUMNER
David Herbert Donald
New introduction by the author
1152 pp., 49 illus.
80720-3 $24.95

THE CIVIL WAR
In the Writings of
Col. G.F.R. Henderson
Edited by Jay Luvaas
336 pp.
9 maps and sketches,
1 illus.
80718-1 $14.95

THE CIVIL WAR DAY BY DAY
An Almanac 1861-1865
E. B. Long with Barbara Long
1,135 pp., 8 pages of maps
80255-4 $19.95

SHERMAN'S MARCH TO THE SEA,
Hood's Tennessee Campaign &
the Carolina Campaigns of 1865
General Jacob D. Cox
New introduction by
Brooks D. Simpson
289 pp., 10 maps
80587-1 $12.95

SLAVERY
A World History
Updated Edition
Milton Meltzer
584 pp., 251 illus. 3 maps
80536-7 $22.50

STONEWALL JACKSON AND
THE AMERICAN CIVIL WAR
G.F.R. Henderson
New introduction by
Thomas L. Connelly
740 pp.
80318-6 $16.95

STONEWALL JACKSON, ROBERT
E. LEE, AND THE ARMY OF
NORTHERN VIRGINIA, 1862
William Allan
New introduction by
Robert K. Krick
755 pp., 16 maps, 1 photo
80656-8 $19.95

THE STORY OF THE
CONFEDERACY
Robert Selph Henry
Foreword by
Douglas Southall Freeman
526 pp.
80370-4 $14.95

THOMAS MORRIS CHESTER,
BLACK CIVIL WAR
CORRESPONDENT: His
Dispatches from the Virginia Front
Edited by R.J.M. Blackett
375 pp., 3 photos, 1 map
80453-0 $13.95

THUNDER AT
HAMPTON ROADS
A. A. Hoehling
268 pp., 20 illus.
80523-5 $13.95

TRAGIC YEARS 1860-1865
A Documentary History of the
American Civil War
Paul M. Angle and
Earl Schenck Miers
1108 pp.
80462-X $23.95

THE TROUBLE THEY SEEN
The Story of Reconstruction in the
Words of African Americans
Edited by Dorothy Sterling
512 pp., 152 illus.
80548-0 $15.95

THE VIRGINIA CAMPAIGN, 1864
and 1865
General Andrew A. Humphreys
New introduction by
Brooks D. Simpson
510 pp., 10 maps
80625-8 $15.95

Available at your bookstore

OR ORDER DIRECTLY FROM 1-800-386-5656

VISIT OUR WEBSITE AT WWW.PERSEUSBOOKSGROUP.COM

www.ingramcontent.com/pod-product-compliance
Ingram Content Group UK Ltd.
Pitfield, Milton Keynes, MK11 3LW, UK
UKHW022355170625
459797UK00006B/116